T0228886

GRID COMPUTING
The New Frontier of High Performance Computing

ADVANCES IN PARALLEL COMPUTING

VOLUME 14

Series Editor:

Gerhard R. Joubert
Managing Editor
(Technical University of Clausthal)
Aquariuslaan 60
5632 BD Eindhoven, The Netherlands

2005

ELSEVIER

Amsterdam – Boston – Heidelberg – London – New York – Oxford
Paris – San Diego – San Francisco – Singapore – Sydney – Tokyo

GRID COMPUTING
The New Frontier of High Performance Computing

Edited by

Lucio Grandinetti

Center of Excellence on
High Performance Computing
University of Calabria
Italy

2005

ELSEVIER

Amsterdam – Boston – Heidelberg – London – New York – Oxford
Paris – San Diego – San Francisco – Singapore – Sydney – Tokyo

ELSEVIER B.V.
Radarweg 29
P.O. Box 211, 1000 AE
Amsterdam, The Netherlands

ELSEVIER Inc.
525 B Street
Suite 1900, San Diego
CA 92101-4495, USA

ELSEVIER Ltd.
The Boulevard
Langford Lane, Kidlington,
Oxford OX5 1GB, UK

ELSEVIER Ltd.
84 Theobalds Road
London WC1X 8RR
UK

© 2005 Elsevier B.V. All rights reserved.

This work is protected under copyright by Elsevier B.V., and the following terms and conditions apply to its use:

Photocopying
Single photocopies of single chapters may be made for personal use as allowed by national copyright laws. Permission of the Publisher and payment of a fee is required for all other photocopying, including multiple or systematic copying, copying for advertising or promotional purposes, resale, and all forms of document delivery. Special rates are available for educational institutions that wish to make photocopies for non-profit educational classroom use.

Permissions may be sought directly from Elsevier's Rights Department in Oxford, UK: phone (+44) 1865 843830, fax (+44) 1865 853333, e-mail: permissions@elsevier.com. Requests may also be completed on-line via the Elsevier homepage (http://www. elsevier.com/locate/permissions).

In the USA, users may clear permissions and make payments through the Copyright Clearance Center, Inc., 222 Rosewood Drive, Danvers, MA 01923, USA; phone: (+1) (978) 7508400, fax: (+1) (978) 7504744, and in the UK through the Copyright Licensing Agency Rapid Clearance Service (CLARCS), 90 Tottenham Court Road, London W1P 0LP, UK; phone: (+44) 20 7631 5555; fax: (+44) 20 7631 5500. Other countries may have a local reprographic rights agency for payments.

Derivative Works
Tables of contents may be reproduced for internal circulation, but permission of the Publisher is required for external resale or distribution of such material. Permission of the Publisher is required for all other derivative works, including compilations and translations.

Electronic Storage or Usage
Permission of the Publisher is required to store or use electronically any material contained in this work, including any chapter or part of a chapter.

Except as outlined above, no part of this work may be reproduced, stored in a retrieval system or transmitted in any form or by any means, electronic, mechanical, photocopying, recording or otherwise, without prior written permission of the Publisher. Address permissions requests to: Elsevier's Rights Department, at the fax and e-mail addresses noted above.

Notice
No responsibility is assumed by the Publisher for any injury and/or damage to persons or property as a matter of products liability, negligence or otherwise, or from any use or operation of any methods, products, instructions or ideas contained in the material herein. Because of rapid advances in the medical sciences, in particular, independent verification of diagnoses and drug dosages should be made.

First edition 2005

Library of Congress Cataloging in Publication Data
A catalog record is available from the Library of Congress.

British Library Cataloguing in Publication Data
A catalogue record is available from the British Library.

ISBN-13:   978-0-444-51999-3
ISBN-10:   0-444-51999-8
ISSN: 0927-5452

⊚ The paper used in this publication meets the requirements of ANSI/NISO Z39.48-1992 (Permanence of Paper).

Transferred to digital printing 2006

Printed and bound by CPI Antony Rowe, Eastbourne

EDITOR PREFACE

The main purpose of this book is making available to IT professionals a selection of papers presented at the 2004 International Advanced Research Workshop on High Performance Computing in Cetraro, Italy. The book is intended to be of interest and useful to a number of persons: graduate students of computer science, researchers in the field of grid computing, educators and IT managers who want to understand the key grid computing technical issues and economic benefits.

The book structure will help the reader in accomplishing the objectives mentioned above. Parts 1, 2 and 3 contain papers that discuss the crucial categories of problems in this new technology. Several papers in Part 1 are surveying different aspect of grid computing and will be appreciated by newcomers to the field. The issues of **Performance** have been always the prime driving force in computer technology. Part 2 presents some of them. Part 3 deals with **Applications** that in general are an indispensable motivation for researching and developing new fields of science and related technologies.

It is my pleasure thanking and acknowledging the help of many individuals that have made this book possible.

Janusz Kowalik for contributing to the book structure and style, writing Foreword and helping in the reviewing process. Gerhard Joubert, the Editor of the book series "Advances in Parallel Computing" which now includes this volume, for his support, encouragement and advice on editorial issues.

Jack Dongarra, Miron Livny, Geoffrey Fox and Paul Messina, among others, for advising on scientific issues, before, during or after the Workshop Organization.

My collaborators from the Center of Excellence on High Performance Computing at University of Calabria, Italy, are thanked for their constructive support.

Finally, I feel indebted to Maria Teresa Gauglianone, for her dedication in handling the book's material and for keeping, nicely and effectively, relationships with the contributing authors and the Publisher.

Lucio Grandinetti
Professor and Director
Center of Excellence on High Performance Computing
University of Calabria, Italy

FOREWORD

This volume contains a collection of papers written by persons from scientific and engineering fields, many of whom attended several Advanced Research Workshops in Cetraro, Italy. The Cetraro International Workshops, organized by the University of Calabria began in 1992 when the NATO Scientific Division in Brussels sponsored an Advanced Research Workshop on Software for Parallel Computation.

Since this pioneering meeting there were several biennial workshops in Cetraro focused on quickly developing science and technology of high performance computing.

The idea of the workshops was to invite a relatively small number of world experts who would assess the state of the art, present and discuss the most challenging technical issues and suggest potential solutions.

The Workshops have helped to define and evaluate most pressing research problems in high end scientific computing. This in turn has resulted in many technical books and papers offering solutions and pointing paths to the future.

The Workshop in 2004 was focused on grid computing which appears to be a very promising new technology for the future. Grid computing is a natural development of distributed computing given the recent progress in the networking technology including the Internet. Initially grid computing was tested on large scientific applications and involved the most progressive and technically advanced laboratories, universities and commercial companies. Currently it is expected that the grid technology will spread to commercial and business high end computing and will be used widely as the most advanced and economic computing resource method.

This book is a partial documentation for the 2004 Workshop and devoted almost exclusively to the subject of grid computing. There are two exceptions. The paper on Micro-grids has more general scope and presents ideas related to a general model for instruction-level distributed computing. The second paper, dealing with computer architecture is written by Sterling and Brodowicz. They describe an advanced parallel computer architecture for high performance computing. Although not directly related to grid computing it is likely that the presented PIM architecture could be supporting grid computing in the future.

As a person who has followed the development of grid computing from the very beginning and watched its first commercial applications in The Boeing Company I can say that this book contains very original and technically inspiring papers that could be spring boards to further research and development in this emerging area of computing.

Since grid computation is in the state of rapid development it was appropriate to invite authors representing a wide spectrum of views and ideas. It is also important to point out that the book coauthors come from different segments of information technology and represent academic research, industrial R&D and government organizations.

The book is divided into three major sections: General Issues, Performance and Applications. Several papers discuss problems that are not limited to only one section.

In fact the best contributions touch on several problems and discuss their relationships.

In Part 1 the reader will find papers on Grid Services for Resource Discovery, Data Placements and Management, Advanced Networks, Scientific Computing Environments, Resource Management and Scheduling.

Part 2 represents the subject of performance and efficiency. For example: Job Migration, Risk Management, Framework for Dynamic Reconfiguration and an Advanced Computer Architecture for High Performance Computing.

Part 3 is on Applications, Messaging in Web Service Grid, Transition from Research to Production, Storage and Processing Large Scale Biomedical Image Data.

This volume belongs to a well established book series "Advances in Parallel Computing" which pioneered in promoting parallel computing and currently continues contributing to new paradigms such as grid computation.

Janusz Kowalik
Gdansk University, Poland
Formerly The Boeing Company and University of Washington,
Seattle, USA

LIST OF CONTRIBUTORS

Sudesh Agrawal
Computer Science Department
University of Tennessee
Knoxville, TN 37919
United States

Marco Aldinucci
Italian National Research Council (ISTI-CNR)
Via Moruzzi 1, Pisa
Italy

Giovanni Aloisio
Department of Innovation Engineering
University of Lecce
Italy

Andrea Attanasio
Center of Excellence on High-Performance
Computing
and Dipartimento di Elettronica,
Informatica e Sistemistica
Università della Calabria
Via P. Bucci 41C
Rende (CS) 87030
Italy

Galip Aydin
Community Grids Lab
Indiana University
501 North Morton Street
Bloomington, Indiana
United States

L. Berman
IBM T.J. Watson Research Center
1101 Kitchawan Road
Yorktown Heights NY 10598
United States

Mark Brittan
Mathematics and Computing Technology

Boeing Phantom Works
P.O. Box 3707, MS 7L-20
Seattle WA 98124

Maciej Brodowicz
Center for Advanced Computing Research
California Institute of Technology 1200
E.California Blvd., MC158-79
Pasadena, CA
United States

Massimo Cafaro
Department of Innovation Engineering
University of Lecce
Italy

Umit Catalyurek
Dept. of Biomedical Informatics
The Ohio State University
Columbus, OH, 43210
United States

R. Chang
IBM T.J. Watson Research Center
19 Skyline Drive
Hawthorne, NY 10532
United States

Marco Danelutto
Dept. of Computer Science
University of Pisa
Largo B. Pontecorvo 3
Pisa
Italy

Travis Desell
Department of Computer Science
Rensselaer Polytechnic Institute
110 8th Street
Troy, NY 12180-3590
United States

Murthy Devarakonda
IBM T.J. Watson Research Center
19 Skyline Drive
Hawthorne, NY 10532
United States

Jack Dongarra
Computer Science Department
University of Tennessee
Knoxville, TN 37919
United States

Jan Dünnweber
Dept. of Computer Science
University of Münster
Einsteinstr. 62
Münster
Germany

Kaoutar El Maghraoui
Department of Computer Science
Rensselaer Polytechnic Institute
110 8th Street
Troy, NY 12180-3590
United States

Dietmar Erwin
John von Neumann-Institute for Computing
(NIC)
Forschungszentrum Jülich (FZJ)
52425 Jülich
Germany

Renato Ferreira
Departamento de Ciência
da Computacão
Universidade Federal de Minas Gerais
Belo Horizonte, MG
Brazil

Sandro Fiore
Department of Innovation Engineering
University of Lecce
Italy

Geoffrey Fox
Community Grids Lab
Indiana University
501 North Morton Street
Bloomington, Indiana
United States

Stefan Geisler
Clausthal, University of Technology
Department of Computer Science
Julius-Albert-Straße 4
38678 Clausthal-Zellerfeld
Germany

Gianpaolo Ghiani
Dipartimento di Ingegneria dell'Innovazione
Università degli Studi di Lecce
Via Arnesano
Lecce 73100
Italy

Sergei Gorlatch
Dept. of Computer Science
University of Münster
Einsteinstr. 62
Münster
Germany

Lucio Grandinetti
Center of Excellence on High-Performance
Computing
and Dipartimento di Elettronica,
Informatica e Sistemistica
Università della Calabria
Via P. Bucci 41C
Rende (CS) 87030
Italy

Emanuela Guerriero
Dipartimento di Ingegneria dell'Innovazione
Università degli Studi di Lecce
Via Arnesano
Lecce 73100
Italy

Francesca Guerriero
Center of Excellence on High-Performance
Computing
and Dipartimento di Elettronica,
Informatica e Sistemistica
Università della Calabria
Via P. Bucci 41C
Rende (CS) 87030
Italy

Shannon Hastings
Dept. of Biomedical Informatics
The Ohio State University
Columbus, OH, 43210
United States

Matt Haynos
IBM Systems and Technology Group
Route 100
Somers, NY 10589
United States

Felix Heine
Paderborn Center for Parallel Computing (PC^2)
Universität Paderborn
Germany

Matthias Hovestadt
Paderborn Center for Parallel Computing (PC^2)
Universität Paderborn
Germany

Kun Huang
Dept. of Biomedical Informatics
The Ohio State University
Columbus, OH, 43210
United States

C.R. Jesshope
Department of Computer Science
University of Amsterdam
Kruislaan 403
1098 SJ Amsterdam
The Netherlands

William E. Johnston
ESnet Manager and Senior Scientist, DOE
Lawrence Berkeley National
Laboratory MS
50B-2239, Berkeley
California
United States

Gerhard R. Joubert
Clausthal, University of Technology
Department of Computer Science
Julius-Albert-Straße 4
38678 Clausthal-Zellerfeld
Germany

Odej Kao
Paderborn Center for Parallel Computing (PC^2)
Universität Paderborn
Germany

Axel Keller
Paderborn Center for Parallel Computing (PC^2)
Universität Paderborn
Germany

George Kola
Computer Science Department
University of Wisconsin-Madison
1210 West Dayton Street
Madison, WI 53706
United States

Janusz Kowalik
Formerly The Boeing Company
and University of Washington
16477-107th PL NE
Bothell, WA 98011

Tevfik Kosar
Computer Science Department
University of Wisconsin-Madison
1210 West Dayton Street
Madison, WI 53706
United States

Tashin Kurc
Dept. of Biomedical Informatics
The Ohio State University
Columbus, OH, 43210
United States

Steve Langella
Dept. of Biomedical Informatics
The Ohio State University
Columbus, OH, 43210
United States

Wen-Syan Li
IBM Almaden Research Center
650 Harry Road
San Jose, CA 95120
United States

Y. Li
IBM China Research Laboratory
Haohai Building, #7, 5th Street
Shangdi, Beijing 100085
PRC

Thomas Lippert
John von Neumann-Institute for Computing
(NIC)
Forschungszentrum Jülich (FZJ)
52425 Jülich
Germany

Miron Livny
Computer Science Department
University of Wisconsin-Madison
1210 West Dayton Street
Madison, WI 53706
United States

D. Mallmann
John von Neumann-Institute for Computing
(NIC)
Forschungszentrum Jülich (FZJ)
52425 Jülich
Germany

Roger Menday
John von Neumann-Institute for Computing
(NIC)
Forschungszentrum Jülich (FZJ)
52425 Jülich
Germany

M. Mirto
Department of Innovation Engineering
University of Lecce
Italy

Indepal Narang
IBM Almaden Research Center
650 Harry Road
San Jose, CA 95120
United States

Scott Oster
Dept. of Biomedical Informatics
The Ohio State University
Columbus, OH, 43210
United States

Shrideep Pallickara
Community Grids Lab
Indiana University
501 North Morton Street
Bloomington, Indiana
United States

Tony Pan
Dept. of Biomedical Informatics
The Ohio State University
Columbus, OH, 43210
United States

Marlon Pierce
Community Grids Lab
Indiana University
501 North Morton Street
Bloomington, Indiana
United States

Jean-Pierre Prost
IBM EMEA Products and Solutions
Support Center
Rue de la Vieille Poste
34000 Montpellier
France

Michael Rambadt
John von Neumann-Institute for Computing
(NIC)
Forschungszentrum Jülich (FZJ)
52425 Jülich
Germany

Matheus Ribeiro
Departamento de Ciência da Computacão
Universidade Federal de Minas Gerais
Belo Horizonte, MG
Brazil

Morris Riedel
John von Neumann-Institute for Computing
(NIC)
Forschungszentrum Jülich (FZJ)
52425 Jülich
Germany

M. Romberg
John von Neumann-Institute for Computing
(NIC)
Forschungszentrum Jülich (FZJ)
52425 Jülich
Germany

Joel Saltz
Dept. of Biomedical Informatics
The Ohio State University
Columbus, OH, 43210
United States

B. Schuller
John von Neumann-Institute for Computing
(NIC)
Forschungszentrum Jülich (FZJ)
52425 Jülich
Germany

Keith Seymour
Computer Science Department
University of Tennessee
Knoxville, TN 37919
United States

S. Son
Computer Science Department
University of Wisconsin-Madison
1210 West Dayton Street
Madison, WI 53706
United States

Thomas Sterling
Center for Advanced Computing Research
California Institute of Technology 1200
E.California Blvd., MC158-79
Pasadena, CA
United States

Achim Streit
John von Neumann-Institute for Computing
(NIC)
Forschungszentrum Jülich (FZJ)
52425 Jülich
Germany

Bolelsaw K. Szymanski
Department of Computer Science
Rensselaer Polytechnic Institute
110 8th Street
Troy, NY 12180-3590
United States

Domenico Talia
DEIS, University of Calabria
Via P. Bucci, 41c
87036 Rende
Italy

James D. Teresco
Department of Computer Science
Williams College
47 Lab Campus Drive
Williamstown, MA 01267
United States

Paolo Trunfio
DEIS, University of Calabria
Via P. Bucci, 41c
87036 Rende
Italy

Jay Unger
IBM Systems and Technology Group
13108 Scarlet Oak Drive
Darnestown, MD 20878
United States

Carlos A. Varela
Department of Computer Science
Rensselaer Polytechnic Institute
110 8th Street
Troy, NY 12180-3590
United States

Dinesh C. Verma
IBM T.J. Watson Research Center
19 Skyline Drive

Hawthorne, NY 10532
United States

Philipp Wieder
John von Neumann-Institute for Computing
(NIC)
Forschungszentrum Jülich (FZJ)
52425 Jülich
Germany

Asim YarKhan
Computer Science Department
University of Tennessee
Knoxville, TN 37919
United States

Xi Zhang
Dept. of Biomedical Informatics
The Ohio State University
Columbus, OH, 43210
United States

TABLE OF CONTENTS

General Issues

Grid Computing: The New Frontier of High Performance Computing
Lucio Grandinetti (Editor)
3
© 2005 Elsevier B.V. All rights reserved.

The Advanced Networks and Services Underpinning Modern, Large-Scale Science: DOE's ESnet

William E. Johnston[a]

[a]ESnet Manager and Senior Scientist, DOE Lawrence Berkeley National Laboratory, MS 50B-2239, Berkeley, California, U.S.A.

Modern large-scale science requires networking that is global in extent, highly reliable and versatile, and that provides high bandwidth and supports sustained high volume traffic. These were some of the conclusions of a series of workshops conducted by the US Dept. of Energy's Office of Science that examined the networking and middleware requirements of the major science disciplines supported by the Office of Science. The requirements from the workshops have resulted in a new approach and architecture for DOE's Energy Sciences Network (ESnet), which is the network that serves all of the major DOE facilities. This new architecture includes elements supporting multiple, high-speed national backbones with different characteristics, redundancy, quality of service and circuit oriented services, and interoperation of all of these with the other major national and international networks supporting science. This paper describes the motivation, architecture, and services of the new approach. The approach is similar to, and designed to be compatible with, other research and education networks such as Internet2/Abilene in the United States and DANTE/GÉANT in Europe, and so the descriptions given here are at least somewhat representative of the general directions of the networking for the research and education community.

1.   ESnet's Role in the DOE Office of Science

"The Office of Science of the US Dept. of Energy is the single largest supporter of basic research in the physical sciences in the United States, providing more than 40 percent of total funding for this vital area of national importance. It oversees – and is the principal federal funding agency of – the Nation's research programs in high-energy physics, nuclear physics, and fusion energy sciences. [It also] manages fundamental research programs in basic energy sciences, biological and environmental sciences, and computational science. In addition, the Office of Science is the Federal Government's largest single funder of materials and chemical sciences, and it supports unique and vital parts of U.S. research in climate change, geophysics, genomics, life sciences, and science education." [1]

Within the Office of Science (OSC) the ESnet mission is to provide interoperable, effective, reliable, and high performance network communications infrastructure and selected leading-edge Grid-related services in support of OSC's large-scale, collaborative science.

2.   Office of Science Drivers for Networking

ESnet is driven by the requirements of the science Program Offices in DOE's Office of Science. Several workshops [2, 3, 4] examined these requirements as they relate to networking and middleware.

In the first Office of Science workshop (August, 2002) the goal was to examine the network needs of major OSC science programs. The programs considered were climate simulation, the Spallation Neutron Source facility, the Macromolecular Crystallography facility, high energy physics experiments, magnetic fusion energy sciences, chemical sciences, and bioinformatics. Except for nuclear physics and the two DOE supercomputer facilities (which were considered separately), this is a fairly complete representation of the major OSC programs.

The workshop approach was to examine how the science community believed that the process of doing science had to change over the next 5-10 years in order to make significant advances in the various science disciplines. The resulting future environment and practice of science was then analyzed to characterize how much network bandwidth and what new network and collaboration services would be needed to enable the future environment of science.

Qualitatively, the conclusions were that modern, large-scale science is completely dependent on networks. This is because unique scientific instruments and facilities are used through remote access by researchers from many institutions. Further, these facilities create massive datasets that have to be archived, catalogued, and analyzed by distributed collaborations. The analysis of such datasets is accomplished, e.g., using the approach of Grid managed resources that are world-wide in scope. [5]

The next sections describe two typical science scenarios that drive the networking requirements. They are abstracted from [2].

2.1. Distributed Simulation

To better understand climate change, we need better climate models providing higher resolution and incorporating more of the physical complexity of the real world. Over the next five years, climate models will see a great increase in complexity, for example in work such as the North American Carbon Project (NACP), which endeavors to fully simulate the terrestrial carbon cycle.

These advances are driven by the need to determine future climate at both local and regional scales as well as changes in climate extremes—droughts, floods, severe storm events, and other phenomena. Over the next five years, climate models will also incorporate the vastly increased volume of observational data now available (and even more in the future), both for hind casting and intercomparison purposes. The result is that instead of tens of terabytes of data per model instantiation, hundreds of terabytes to a few petabytes (10^{15} bytes) of data will be stored at multiple computing sites, to be analyzed by climate scientists worldwide. Middleware systems like the Earth System Grid [9], and its descendents, must be fully utilized in order access and manage such large, distributed, and complex pools of observational and simulation data.

In the period five to ten years out, climate models will again increase in resolution, and many more components will be integrated. These enhanced simulations will be used to drive regional-scale climate and weather models, which require resolutions in the tens to hundreds of meters range, instead of the hundreds of kilometers resolution of today's Community Climate System Model (CCSM) and Parallel Climate Model (PCM).

Better climate modeling requires that the many institutions working on various aspects of the climate be able to easily describe, catalogue, and seamlessly share the knowledge and the vast amounts of data that underlay the knowledge in order to facilitate the required interdisciplinary collaboration. Further, all of the sub-models must interoperate in ways that represent how the elements that make up the climate interact.

As climate models become more multidisciplinary, scientists from oceanography, the atmospheric sciences, and other fields, will collaborate on the development and examination of more realistic climate models. Biologists, hydrologists, economists, and others will assist in the creation of additional components that represent important but as-yet poorly understood influences on climate that must be coupled with the climate models.

There will be a true carbon cycle component, where models of biological processes will be used, for example, to simulate marine biochemistry and fully dynamic vegetation. These scenarios will include human population change, growth, and econometric models to simulate the potential changes in natural resource usage and efficiency. Additionally, models representing solar processes will be integrated to better simulate the incoming solar radiation.

The many specialized scientific groups that work on the different components that go into a comprehensive, multi-disciplinary model, build specialized software and data environments that will almost certainly never all be homogenized and combined on a single computing system. Almost all such multidisciplinary simulation is inherently distributed, with the overall simulation consisting of software and data on many different systems combined into a virtual system by using tools and facilities for building distributed systems.

This paradigm relies on high bandwidth networks for managing massive data sets, quality of service to ensure smooth interoperation of widely distributed computational

6

Grid components, and various (Grid) middleware to interconnect and manage this widely distributed system.

2.2. Collaboration and Data Management

The major high energy physics (HEP) experiments of the next twenty years will break new ground in our understanding of the fundamental interactions, structures and symmetries that govern the nature of matter and space-time. Among the principal goals are to find the mechanism responsible for mass in the universe, and the "Higgs" particles associated with mass generation, as well as the fundamental mechanism that led to the predominance of matter over antimatter in the observable cosmos.

The largest collaborations today, such as CMS [10] and ATLAS [11] that are building experiments for CERN's Large Hadron Collider program (LHC [12]), each encompass some 2000 physicists from 150 institutions in more than 30 countries. The current generation of operational experiments at Stanford Linear Accelerator Center (SLAC) (BaBar [13]) and Fermilab (D0 [14] and CDF [15]), as well as the experiments at the Relativistic Heavy Ion Collider (RHIC, [16]) program at Brookhaven National Lab, face similar challenges.

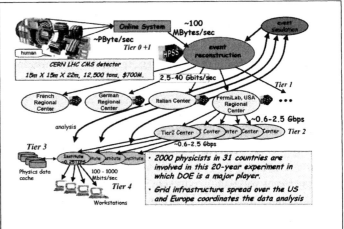

Figure 1. High Energy Physics Data Analysis

This science application epitomizes the need for collaboratories supported by Grid computing infrastructure in order to enable new directions in scientific research and discovery. The CMS situation depicted here is very similar to Atlas and other HEP experiments. (Adapted from original graphic courtesy Harvey B. Newman, Caltech.)

BaBar, for example, has already accumulated datasets approaching a petabyte.

The HEP (or HENP, for high energy and nuclear physics) problems are among the most data-intensive known. Hundreds to thousands of scientist-developers around the world continually develop software to better select candidate physics signals from particle accelerator experiments such as CMS, better calibrate the detector and better reconstruct the quantities of interest (energies and decay vertices of particles such as electrons, photons and muons, as well as jets of particles from quarks and gluons). These are the basic experimental results that are used to compare theory and experiment. The globally distributed ensemble of computing and data facilities (e.g., see Figure 1), while large by any standard, is less than the physicists require to do their work in an unbridled way. There is thus a need, and a drive, to solve the problem of managing global resources in an optimal way in order to maximize the potential of the major experiments to produce breakthrough discoveries.

Collaborations on this global scale would not have been attempted if the physicists could not plan on high capacity networks: to interconnect the physics groups throughout the lifecycle of the experiment, and to make possible the construction of Data Grids capable of providing access, processing and analysis of massive datasets. These datasets will increase in size from petabytes to exabytes (10^{18} bytes) within the next decade. Equally as important is highly capable middleware (the Grid data management and underlying resource access and management services) to facilitate the management of world wide computing and data resources that must all be brought to bear on the data analysis problem of HEP [5].

2.3. Requirements for Networks and Services Supporting Science

The results of these workshops are surprisingly uniform across the scientific programs represented. Their networking requirements fell into four major areas: bandwidth, reliability, quality of service, and network embedded data cache and computing elements.

The primary network requirements to come out of the Office of Science workshops were

- Network bandwidth must increase substantially, not just in the backbone but all the way to the sites and to the attached computing and storage systems
- The 5 and 10 year bandwidth requirements mean that current network bandwidth has, on average, to more than double every year
- A highly reliable network is critical for science – when large-scale experiments depend on the network for success, the network may not fail
- There must be network services that can guarantee various forms of quality-of-service (e.g., bandwidth guarantees).

The bandwidth required by DOE's large-scale science projects over the next 5 years is characterized in the Roadmap workshop (June, 2003) [4]. Programs that have currently defined requirement for high bandwidth include High Energy Physics, Climate (data and computations), NanoScience at the Spallation Neutron Source , Fusion Energy, Astrophysics, and Genomics (data and computations), and Nuclear Physics , and the OSC supercomputer centers. A summary of the bandwidth requirements are given in Table 1.

Additionally, the applications involved in these science areas must move massive amounts of data in a predictable way. That is, both network reliability and quality of service are critical. Further, achieving high bandwidth end-to-end for distributed applications, on-line instruments, etc., requires new network services and extensive monitoring and diagnosis in the network in order to provide feedback for both debugging and operation.

8

Table 1 – Projected Network Requirements for DOE Science				
Science Areas	Today *End2End* Throughput	5 year timeframe End2End Documented Throughput Requirements	5-10 year timeframe End2End *Estimated* Throughput Requirements	Remarks
High Energy Physics	0.5 Gb/s	100 Gb/s	1000 Gb/s	high bulk throughput
Climate (Data & Computation)	0.5 Gb/s	160-200 Gb/s	N x 1000 Gb/s	high bulk throughput
SNS NanoScience	Not yet started	1 Gb/s	1000 Gb/s + QoS for control channel	remote control and time critical throughput
Fusion Energy	0.066 Gb/s (500 MB/s burst)	0.198 Gb/s (500MB/ 20 sec. burst)	N x 1000 Gb/s	time critical throughput
Astrophysics	0.013 Gb/s (1 TBy/week)	N*N multicast	1000 Gb/s	computational steering and collaborations
Genomics Data & Computation	0.091 Gb/s (1 TBy/day)	100s of users	1000 Gb/s + QoS for control channel	high throughput and steering

3. Interlude: How Do IP Networks Work?

There are four basic aspects to wide-area networking:
The physical architecture, the communication elements and how they are organized, the basic functioning of IP networks, and the logical architecture (how are the interfaces to other networks organized and how is reachability information managed).

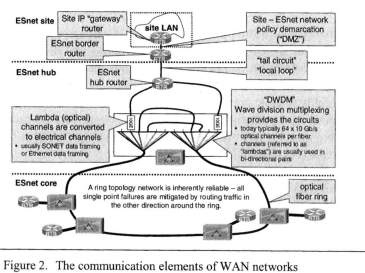

Figure 2. The communication elements of WAN networks

Looking at these in this order, consider first the physical architecture. There are two aspects of this – what is the relationship of the communication elements to each other, and what is the overall structure of the communication elements.

Most wide-area networks make use of the communication elements as indicated in Figure 2.

The wide area communication is accomplished by wave (frequency) division multiplexing of optical signal channels that are mixed and carried through optical fiber. Equipment that is typical today multiplexes 64, 10 Gb/s to 40 Gb/s data channels onto a single optical fiber. For data communication networks the channels are almost always used in pairs to provide full duplex communication. The electrical signals are put onto the optical channels using transponders/transmitters that have particular electrical interfaces (e.g. OC192 SONET (United States) / STM-64 SDH (Europe) or 10 Gigabit Ethernet). The optical signal for each channel is about 0.5 nm wide, the mixed signals (channels) are 17.5-32 nm wide and are carried on a base frequency of 1530-1560 nm (near infrared). This process is called Dense Wave Division Multiplexing. Ignored in this discussion are the optical amplifiers and dispersion correctors that are needed for the long distance (hundreds to thousands of km) propagation of the optical signals.

The relationship of groups of communication elements to each other (e.g. systems of interconnected, self-healing rings) is described in the section on the new ESnet architecture, below.

The SONET / SDH or Ethernet circuits implemented by DWDM equipment are point-to-point circuits that connect switches and/or IP routers.

The basic functions of IP networks are to provide addressing, routing, and data transport. IP packets are used by higher level protocols, such as TCP, to provide reliable, stream-oriented data communication. Routers forward IP packets received on one interface to another interface that will get the packet "closer" to its destination. This apparently stateless routing works because the routers exchange reachability information with their neighbors that specifies which interface actually will get the packet closer to its destination. The reachability information is managed by special protocols of which the Border Gateway Protocol (BGP) is most common in the wide area.

In terms of the network protocol architecture stack, application level protocols like HTTP and FTP utilize transport protocols such as TCP that implement semantics such as reliable streams, that, as noted, use IP (as do all Internet protocols) for addressing and routing. While not fundamental, the Domain Name Service (DNS) that translates between human readable addresses and IP addresses is sufficiently ubiquitous and deeply integrated into applications, that it is now also "essential" for the Internet.

For example, describing Figure 3

- Accessing a Grid service, a Web server, FTP server, physics data analysis server, etc., from a client application and client computer (e.g. a Web browser on a laptop) involves
  o Providing the target host names (e.g. google.com) where the service is located
  o Determining the IP addresses (e.g. 131.243.2.11 – via DNS)
  o Identifying the service on the target machine (the "port" number of the application server that distinguishes it from other servers that might be running on the same machine)

o Routing (getting the packets from source, through the Internet, to destination – the service)
- The Internet transports data packets from source to destination (multiple destinations in the case of multicast)
- The overall architecture of the Internet is focused on connectivity, routing, and inter-domain routing policy management
  o Domains ("Autonomous Systems") = large sites and Internet Service Providers (transit networks like ESnet)
  o Policy = Internet Service Provider (ISP) routing strategy and site security

In Figure 3 there are several instances of paired routers. In the case of the site gateway-ISP border router, the site gateway router typically implements security policy (e.g. via firewall rules) and the border router implements the ISP routing policy (e.g., only routes from the site that are for systems at the site will be accepted by the ISP).

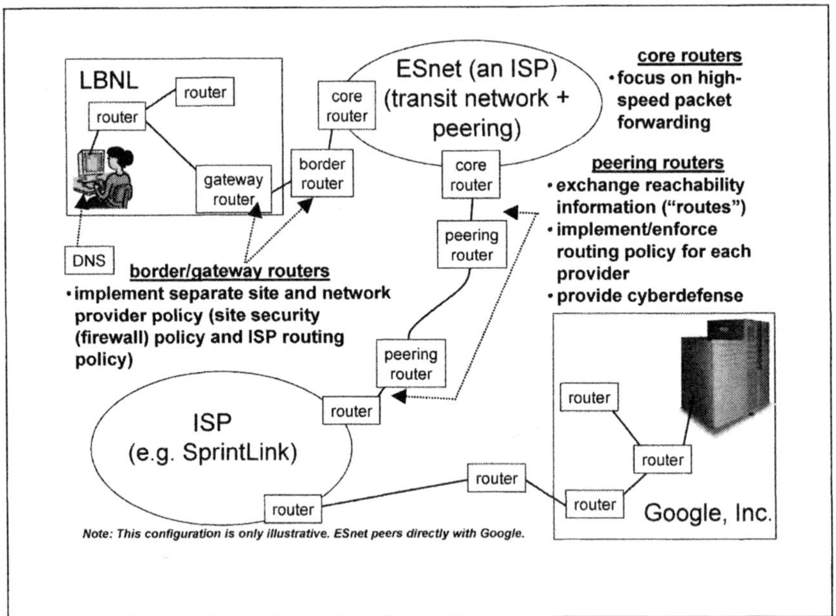

In the case of the peering router – peering router pairing between ISPs, the ISPs will accept some routes (claims of

Figure 3. How do IP networks work?

reachability for remote networks) and reject others. This selectivity is because the ISP may (frequently does) have multiple ways of getting to a given network and host, and it will use the one that is best suited for its connectivity. ("Best may mean fastest, least expensive, etc.)

"Peering" is the agreements and physical interconnects between two networks that exchange routing information. In order to reach the entire Internet it requires about 160,000 IPv4 routes. There are several dozens of major peering points where networks exchange routing information and packets. Each route provides reachability information for blocks of address space in the network that says "how do I get packets closer to their destination." The routes are obtained by "peering" (exchanging routing information) with other networks at one or more physical locations. Each peering point provides all of the routes for systems that it believes that it can reach. However, there are frequently multiple ways to reach a given host and the receiver selects the routes based on what it believes is the "best" path to the various networks.

4. What Does ESnet Provide?

All three of the research and education communities mentioned here – those associated with ESnet, Abilene and the U.S. regional nets, and GÉANT and the NRENS – serve institutions that have requirements for, and access to, a common set of Internet services. However, as mentioned, exactly which of the several networks associated with a given institution provides the services varies. ESnet, while it has a substantial user base (more than 30,000 users in the 42 served sites), is small compared to the U.S. higher education community served by Abilene or the overall European R&E community served by GÉANT. However, ESnet provides a convenient microcosm in which to describe the services provided by various network organizations to the scientific community. (While not excluding the education community, ESnet does not serve that community and the services ESnet provides to its customer base may not map

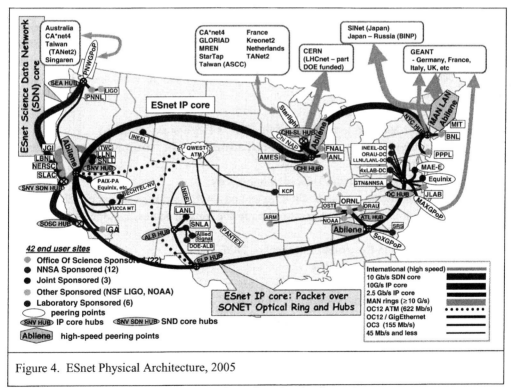

Figure 4. ESnet Physical Architecture, 2005

one to one with services offered to higher education institutes.)

One of the characteristics of science oriented networks is that they must provide a relatively small number of sites with very large amount of bandwidth. (As opposed to commodity ISPs like AOL or EarthLink which are tailored to provide a huge number of users a relatively small amount of bandwidth.) In particular, ESnet must provide high bandwidth access to DOE sites and to DOE's primary science collaborators in the science community. This is accomplished by a combination of high-speed dedicated circuits that connect the end sites and by high-speed peerings with the major R&E network partners.

ESnet builds and operates a comprehensive IP network infrastructure (IPv4, IP multicast, and IPv6, peering, routing, and address space management) based on commercial and R&E community circuits. The current physical architecture is shown in Figure 4 which illustrates the extent and diversity of the circuits.

ESnet provides full and carefully optimized access to the global Internet. This is essential, as mentioned above, for the best possible access to the sites where collaborators are located. In order to accomplish this ESnet has peering agreements with many commercial and non-commercial networking. Those agreements result in routes (reachability information) being exchanged between all of the networks needed to provide comprehensive (global) Internet site access.

As noted above, in order to provide DOE scientists access to all Internet sites, ESnet manages the full complement of Global Internet routes. This requires about 160,000 IPv4 routes from 180 peers. (The peering policy mentioned above selects these 160,000 routes from about 400,000 that are offered at all of the peering points.) These peers are connected at 40 general peering points that include commercial, research and education, and international networks. With a few of ESnet's most important partner networks (notably Abilene and GÉANT), direct peering (core router to core router) is done to provide high performance.

In summary, ESnet provides:
- An architecture tailored to accommodate DOE's large-scale science
  - Move huge amounts of data between a small number of sites that are scattered all over the world
- Comprehensive physical and logical connectivity
  - High bandwidth access to DOE sites and DOE's primary science collaborators: Research and Education institutions in the United States, Europe, Asia Pacific, and elsewhere
  - Full access to the global Internet for DOE Labs
- A full suite of network services
  - IPv4 and IPv6 routing and address space management
  - IPv4 multicast (and soon IPv6 multicast)
  - Prototype guaranteed bandwidth and virtual circuit services
  - Scavenger service so that certain types of bulk traffic will use all available bandwidth, but will give priority to all other traffic when it shows up
- A highly collaborative and interactive relationship with the DOE Labs and scientists for planning, configuration, and operation of the network
  - ESnet and its services evolve continuously in direct response to OSC science needs

- Comprehensive user support, including "owning" all trouble tickets involving ESnet users (including problems at the far end of an ESnet connection) until they are resolved – 24 hrs/day x 365 days/year coverage
  - ESnet's mission is to enable the network based aspects of OSC science, and that includes troubleshooting or otherwise managing network problems wherever they occur
- Cybersecurity in the WAN environment (ESnet sites are responsible for site cybersecurity)
- Collaboration services and Grid middleware supporting collaborative science
  - Federated trust services with science oriented policy
  - Audio and video conferencing

5. Drivers for the Evolution of ESnet

The predictive requirements that have been laid out by the scientific community, and that are discussed above, are backed up by observed traffic growth and patterns in ESnet.

5.1. Observed Traffic Growth is Exponential

The total traffic handled by ESnet has been growing exponentially for the past 15 years and currently ESnet handles more than 400 Terabytes/month of data. This

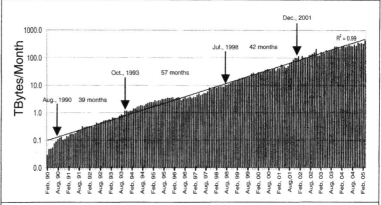

Figure 5. ESnet total traffic trends, Feb., 1990 – Mar., 2005, with markers indicating factors of 10 increase

growth is somewhat uneven month to month, but over 10 years the ESnet traffic has increased, on average, by a factor of 10 every 46 months.

This growth is qualitatively consistent with the predictions of the science community, and there should be nothing surprising about this growth. In a sense it is just tracking Moore's law. As computers get bigger, they run larger simulations that generate more data – an exponential process; many sensor based instruments, e.g. telescope CCDs, are also experiencing Moore's law growth of the sensors, and the data volume goes up correspondingly, etc.

5.2. A Small Number of Science Users Account for a Significant Fraction of all ESnet Traffic

Another aspect of large-scale science noted above is that it is inherently collaborative. One reason for this is that the instruments of large scale science are so large and expensive that only one or two may be built and all of the scientist in that filed must share the instrument. As noted above, for example, the "instruments" (detectors) at the LHC accelerator at CERN, in Switzerland, cost almost $U.S. 1 billion each (there are two major detectors on the LHC) and the scientific teams consists of several thousand physicists who are located all over the world.

The effects of this sort of large-scale collaboration are reflected in the data flow patterns in ESnet.

Over the past few years there has been a trend for very large flows (host-to-host data transfers) to be an increasingly large fraction of all ESnet traffic. These very large flows of individual

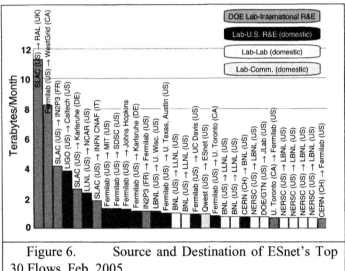

Figure 6.   Source and Destination of ESnet's Top 30 Flows, Feb. 2005

science projects now represent the dominate factor driving the planning for the evolution of the network. This trend is clearly illustrated in Figure 6 which shows host-to-host flows. In fact, 17 of the top 20 flows are from only three ESnet sites, all of which are high energy physics Labs.

The current predominance of international traffic is due to high-energy physics – the BaBar (SLAC) and D0 (Fermilab) experiments both have major analysis sites in Europe. However, all of the LHC U.S. Tier-2 data analysis centers are at U.S. universities, and as the Tier-2 centers come on-line, the ESnet traffic from U.S. Tier-1 centers (Fermilab and Brookhaven) to U.S. Tier-2 centers at various universities will increase enormously.

High energy physics is several years ahead of the other science disciplines in data generation. Several other disciplines and facilities (e.g. the supercomputer centers, driven by climate modeling) will contribute comparable amounts of additional traffic in the next few years.

6. 6   ESnet, Abilene, NLR, GÉANT, and LHC Networking

A large fraction of all of the national data traffic supporting U.S. science is carried by two networks – ESnet and Internet-2/Abilene, and on layer 1 services from National Lambda Rail. These three entities fairly well represent the architectural scope of science oriented networks.

ESnet is a network in the traditional sense of the word. It connects end user sites to various other networks. Abilene is a backbone network. It connects U.S. regional networks to each other and International networks. NLR is a collection of light paths or lambda channels that are used to construct specialized R&E networks.

ESnet serves a community of directly connected campuses – the Office of Science Labs – so ESnet interconnects the LANs of all of the Labs. Esnet also provides the peering and routing needed for the Labs to have access to the global Internet. Abilene serves a community of regional networks that connect university campuses. These regional networks – NYSERNet (U.S. northeast), SURAnet (U.S. southeast), CENIC (California), etc., – have regional aggregation points called GigaPoPs and Abilene interconnects the GigaPoPs. Abilene is mostly a transit network – the universities and/or the regional networks provide the peering and routing for end-user Internet access. This is also very similar to the situation in Europe where GÉANT (like Abilene) interconnects the European National Research and Education Networks that in turn connect to the LANs of the science and education institutions. (The NRENs are like the US regionals, but organized around the European nation-states).

The top level networks – ESnet, Abilene, GÉANT, etc. – work closely together to ensure that they have adequate connectivity with each other so that all of the connected institutions have high-speed end-to-end connectivity to support their science and education missions. ESnet and Abilene have had joint engineering meetings for several years (Joint Techs) and ESnet, Abilene, GÉANT, and CERN have also formed an international engineering team ("ITechs") that meets several times a year.

The goal is that connectivity from DOE Lab to US and European Universities should be as good as Lab to Lab and University to University connectivity. The key to ensuring this is constant monitoring. Esnet has worked with the Abilene and the US University community to establish a suite of monitors that can be use to provide a full mesh of paths that continuously checks all of the major interconnection points. Similarly, the ESnet to CERN connection is monitored, and key European R&E institutions will soon be included.

The networking to support the analysis of the massive data analysis required for the several experiments associated with the LHC (see section 2.2) is a special case. The LHC community is essentially building a three continent, lambda based network for the data distribution. By mid-summer, 2005 there will be two 10 Gb/s paths from CERN to the United States to support the Tier-1 data centers at Fermi National Accelerator Laboratory (Fermilab) and Brookhaven National Lab, both of which are ESnet sites. Many of the immediate requirements for the near-term evolution of ESnet arise out of the requirements of the LHC networking and both United States and international design and operations groups have been established.

7. 7   How the Network is Operated

The normal operation of a network like ESnet involves monitoring both the state of the logical network (connectivity to the rest of the Internet) and the state of the physical network (the operational status of the network links, switches, routers, etc.).

Managing the logical network entails ensuring that there are paths from the systems at the DOE Labs to every other system connected to the Internet. This is accomplished by having a comprehensive set of routes to all of the active IP address space through the peering process described above.

Managing these routes in order to provide high quality access to the global Internet is a never ending task because ISPs come and go and change their relationship to other ISPs, etc.

The physical network is managed largely through extensive, continuous monitoring. The eleven hubs and 42 end sites are monitored minute by minute at more than 4400 physical and logical interfaces. This includes every aspect of the operating state of the equipment and the traffic flowing over every interface. All of this information is simultaneously analyzed by a network monitoring system and entered into a database that is accessible to the ESnet engineers at various locations around the country.

7.1. Scalable Operation is Essential

R&E networks like ESnet are typically operated with a small staff. The key to this is that everything related to the operation of the network and related services must be scalable. The question of how to manage a huge infrastructure with a small number of people dominates all other issues when looking at whether to support new services (e.g. Grid middleware): Can the service be structured so that its operational aspects do not scale as a function of the user population? If not, then the service cannot be offered.

In the case of the network itself, automated, real-time monitoring of traffic levels and operating state of some 4400 network entities is the primary network operational and diagnosis tool. Much of the analysis of this information (generated in real-time with sample intervals as short as minutes or generated asynchronously as alarms) is automatically analyzed and catalogued as to normal or abnormal, urgent or not. Urgent abnormal events filter up through a hierarchy of operational and engineering staff. The entire ESnet network is operated 24x7x365 by about 16 people.

7.2. What Does the Network Actually Look Like?

The ESnet core consists of 11 hubs and sub-hubs. A typical ESnet hub ("AoA" - 32 Avenue of the Americas, NYC, in this case) is illustrated in Figure 7. The core routers have the primary job of high-speed forwarding of packets. They have the high-speed interfaces for the 2.5 and 10 Gb/s cross-country circuits, and for circuits to Abilene and GÉANT. At AoA the core router has a 10 Gb/s circuit to Chicago and 2.5 Gb/s to Washington, DC and a 2.5 Gb/s circuit to Brookhaven Lab, an ESnet site.

There are also several direct connections for high-speed peerings on the core router: MAN LAN (Manhattan Landing) provides 10 Gb/s connections to several R&E

networks – currently Abilene, NYSERNet (New York R&E network), SInet (Japan), CANARIE (Canada), HEAnet (Ireland), and Qatar. Most ESnet hubs also have a peering router that connects to the core router and to the peers that happen to have presence in that hub ("AoA Hub Peer" in the figure). The separation of the peering function from the core routing function simplifies management and allow for a more effective cyber security stance.

The router labeled "AoA Hub" is used for low-speed, long-haul interfaces such as OC3 (155 Mb/s) and T3 (45 Mb/s) that have to interface with Telco equipment at the

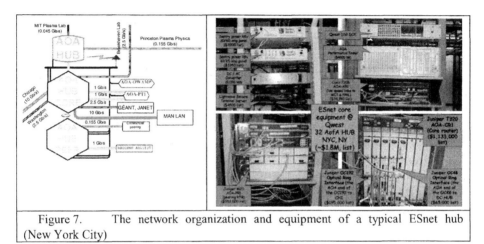

Figure 7.   The network organization and equipment of a typical ESnet hub (New York City)

sites.

Supporting and auxiliary equipment consists of a secure terminal server (the triangle and lighting bolt) that provides access of last resort by telephone modem, a power controller that allows for remote power cycling of all of the other equipment, and one or more performance testing systems. At AoA ESnet has two types of performance testing systems: The Performance Center systems provide for interactive diagnostics and are available to ESnet engineers, to site network engineers, and to end users. The OWAMP server is used for the DOE Lab to University site testing described in section 6. There is also a local management network.

8. Operating Science Mission Critical Infrastructure

ESnet is a visible and critical piece of DOE science infrastructure. There are several tens of thousands users at DOE facilities and many others who are collaborators. Further, like most modern enterprises, the business operation of DOE Labs depends on network access for many types of interactions with the outside world. This requires high reliability and high operational security in the systems that are integral to the operation and management of the network. Making the network and the science support robust involves both network design and operational issues.

As mentioned elsewhere in this paper, a new network architecture is being implemented that is intended to provide as close to fully redundant network connectivity for the DOE Labs as is practical. Beyond this there are several broad categories of operational functions that must be addressed.

- Secure and redundant mail and Web systems are central to the operation and security of ESnet
  - o ˜trouble tickets are by email
  - o ˜engineering communication by email
  - o ˜engineering database interfaces are via Web
- Secure network access to Hub routers
- Backup secure telephone modem access to Hub equipment
- 24x7x365 help desk and 24x7x365 on-call network engineer
- trouble@es.net (end-to-end problem resolution)

Disaster recovery and stability is essential and part of the basic network architecture. The engineering and operating infrastructure for ESnet is being replicated in a secure telecommunications facility in New York (the primary Network Operations Center – NOC – is in California). The replicated systems currently include

- Spectrum (network monitoring and alarm system)
- Engineering web server and databases providing network log management, IPv4 and IPv6 address administration, and other functions
- Domain Name Server
- Network device configuration management and load server.
- Web server www.es.net

The second phase will replicate the Remedy trouble ticket system and e-mail capabilities (scheduled for completion is 3QCY05). When complete this will allow ESnet to be operated independently by any of the engineers at the four NOC locations (two in California, one in Iowa, and one in New York) even in the event of a complete failure of the primary NOC in California.

In order to maintain science mission critical infrastructure in the face of cyber attack ESnet must also provide responsive, tailored, and defensive cybersecurity that results in a coordinated response to cyber attacks that both protects the Labs and keeps them on-line. This is accomplished with a Phased Response Cyberdefense Architecture that is intended to protect the network and the ESnet sites from a class of attacks like large-scale denial-of-service attacks. The phased response ranges from blocking certain site traffic to a complete isolation of the network that allows the sites to continue communicating among themselves in the face of the most virulent attacks. This is accomplished by separating ESnet core routing functionality from external Internet connections by means of a "peering" router that can have a policy different from the core routers, providing a rate limited path to the external Internet that will insure site-to-site communication during an external denial of service attack, and proving "lifeline" connectivity for downloading of patches, exchange of e-mail and viewing web pages (i.e.; e-mail, dns, http, https, ssh, etc.) with the external Internet prior to full isolation of the network.

9. Enabling the Future: ESnet's Evolution over the Next 10-20 Years

Based both on the projections of the science programs and the changes in observed network traffic and patterns over the past few years, it is clear that the network must evolve substantially in order to meet the needs of DOE's Office of Science mission needs.

The current trend in traffic patterns – the large-scale science projects giving rise to the top 100 data flows that represent about 1/3 of all network traffic – will continue to evolve.

As the LHC experiments ramp up in 2006-07, the data to the Tier-1 centers (FNAL and BNL) will increase 200-2000 times. A comparable amount of data will flow out of the Tier-1 centers to the Tier-2 centers (U.S. universities) for data analysis.

The DOE National Leadership Class Facility supercomputer at ORNL anticipates a new model of computing in which simulation tasks are distributed between the central facility and a collection of remote "end stations" that will generate substantial network traffic.

As climate models achieve the sophistication and accuracy anticipated in the next few years, the amount of climate data that will move into and out of the NERSC center will increase dramatically (they are already in the top 100 flows)

Similarly, the experiment facilities at the new Spallation Neutron Source and Magnetic Fusion Energy facilities will start using the network in ways that require fairly high bandwidth with guaranteed quality of service.

This evolution in traffic patterns and volume will result in the top 100 - 1000 flows accounting for most of the traffic in the network, even as total ESnet traffic volume grows: The large-scale science data flows will overwhelm everything else on the network.

The current, few gigabits/sec of average traffic on the backbone will increase to 40 Gb/s (LHC traffic) and then increase to probably double that amount as the other science disciplines move into a collaborative production simulation and data analysis mode on a scale similar to the LHC. This will get the backbone traffic to 100 Gb/s as predicted by the science requirements analysis three years ago.

The old hub and spoke architecture (to 2004) would not let ESnet meet these new requirements. The current core ring cannot be scaled to handle the anticipated large science data flows at affordable cost. Point-to-point, commercial telecom tail circuits to sites are neither reliable nor scalable to the required bandwidth.

9.1. ESnet's Evolution – The Requirements

In order to accommodate this growth, and the change in the types of traffic, the architecture of the network must change. The general requirements for the new architecture are that it provide:

1) High-speed, scalable, and reliable production IP networking, connectivity for University and international collaboration, highly reliable site connectivity to support Lab operations as well as science, and Global Internet connectivity

2) Support for the high bandwidth data flows of large-scale science including scalable, reliable, and very high-speed network connectivity to DOE Labs

3) Dynamically provisioned, virtual circuits with guaranteed quality of service (e.g. for dedicated bandwidth and for traffic isolation)

In order to meet these requirements, the capacity and connectivity of the network must increase to include fully redundant connectivity for every site, high-speed access to the core for every site (at least 20 Gb/s, generally, and 40-100 Gb/s for some sites) and a 100 Gbps national core/backbone bandwidth by 2008 in two independent backbones.

9.2. ESnet Strategy – A New Architecture

The new architecture that will meet the requirements consists of three elements.

1) Metropolitan Area Network (MAN) rings with multiple channels to provide dual site connectivity for reliability, much higher site-to-core bandwidth, and support for both production IP and circuit-based traffic.

2) A Science Data Network (SDN) core for provisioned, guaranteed bandwidth circuits to support large, high-speed science data flows. This new core network will provide for very high total bandwidth, for multiply connecting the MAN rings for protection against hub failure in the IP core, and as an alternate path for production IP traffic.

3) A high-reliability IP core (e.g. the current ESnet core) to address general science requirements, Lab operational (business) requirements, provide some level of backup for the SDN core, and act as a vehicle for science collaboration services.

These elements are structured to provide a network with fully redundant paths for all of the OSC Labs. The IP and SDN cores are independent of each other and both are ring-structured for

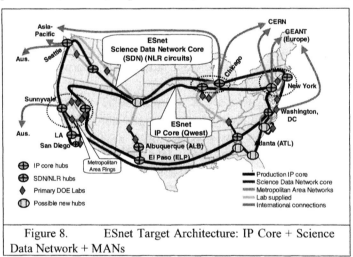

Figure 8.   ESnet Target Architecture: IP Core + Science Data Network + MANs

resiliency. These two national cores are interconnected at several locations with ring-structured metropolitan area networks that also incorporate the DOE Labs into the ring. This will eliminate all single points of failure except where multiple fibers may be in the same conduit (as is frequently the case between metropolitan area points of presence and the physical sites). In the places where metropolitan rings are not practical (e.g. the geographically isolated Labs) resiliency is obtained with dual connections to one of the core rings. (See Figure 8.)

The theoretical advantages of this architecture are clear but it must also be practical to realize an implementation. That is, how does ESnet get to the 100 Gbps multiple backbones and the 20-40 Gbps redundant site connectivity that is needed by the OSC community in the 3-5 yr time frame?

Only a hybrid approach is affordable.

The core IP network that carries the general science and Lab enterprise traffic should be provided by a commercial telecom carrier in the wide area in order to get the >99.9% reliability that certain types of science and the Lab CIOs demand.

Part, or even most, of the wide area bandwidth for the high impact science networking (SDN) will be provided by National Lambda Rail – an R&E community network that is much less expensive than commercial telecoms.

The Metropolitan Area Networks that get the Labs to the ESnet cores are a mixed bag and somewhat opportunistic – a combination of R&E networks, dark fiber networks, and commercial managed lambda circuits will be used.

9.3. ESnet Strategy: MANs

The MAN architecture is designed to provide at least one redundant path from sites to both ESnet cores, scalable bandwidth options from sites to the ESnet cores, and

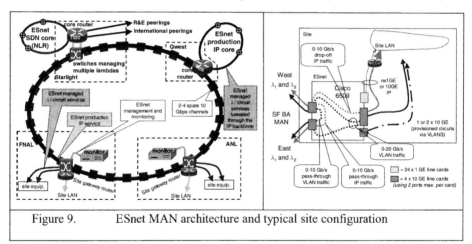

Figure 9.   ESnet MAN architecture and typical site configuration

support for high-bandwidth point-to-point provisioned circuits.

The MANs are also intended to provide independent connections to each of the two national core networks. This will ensure that no single failure, even of a core router, will disrupt all of the connectivity of any ESnet site. The architecture is illustrated in Figure 9.

In a partnership with Qwest Communications, the ESnet MAN architecture has first been realized in the San Francisco Bay Area. Qwest has provided a fiber network that provides a logical ring consisting of at least two independent fibers (the so-called "east" and "west" directions of the ring) into and out of each of five Bay Area sites, to the IP core hub and the SDN core hub. Qwest provides a "managed lambda" service and ESnet initially makes use of two lambda rings delivered as 10 Gb/s Ethernet channels (Figure 9). Each site has a layer2/3 switch/router that manages the Ethernet channels of the SDN and provides the production IP service (Figure 9).

9.4. Science Data Network

The Science Data Network (SDN) will be ESnet's second national core ring. SDN is intended to provide most of the bandwidth for high-impact science traffic and serve as a backup for the production IP network.

Most of the bandwidth needed in the next few years is between sites and peering points that are near paths along the West and East coasts and across the northern part of the United States, and so multiple lambda paths are planned for these paths.

National Lambda Rail (NLR) is "a major initiative of U.S. research universities and private sector technology companies to provide a national scale infrastructure for research and experimentation in networking technologies and applications." (www.nlr.net) ESnet will use NLR lambdas to provide 30-50 Gbps along the path described above and a single 10 Gb/s ring around the country by 2008. Closing the SDN ring in the south to provide resilience at 10 Gbps is a compromise driven by economic considerations that, however, provides a measure of redundancy for the second core.

9.5. High Reliability IP core

The ESnet production IP core is currently provided by Qwest Communications and is a highly reliable infrastructure that consistently provides > 99.9% reliability. This level of reliability is the norm for commercial telecommunications infrastructure and results from the redundancy, diversity, and dynamic circuit management at all levels. Such a high reliability infrastructure will probably always be the basis of the ESnet production IP service.

10. New Network Services

New network services are also critical for ESnet to meet the needs of large-scale science.

One of the most important new network services identified by the Roadmap workshop [5] is dynamically provisioned virtual circuits that provide traffic isolation that will enable the use of non-standard transport mechanisms that cannot co-exist with TCP based transport and provide guaranteed bandwidth.

Guaranteed bandwidth was identified as important in three specific situations.

The first situation is that it is the only way that we currently have to address deadline scheduling – e.g. where fixed amounts of data have to reach sites on a fixed schedule in order that the processing does not fall so far behind that it could never catch up. This is very important for experiment data analysis

The second situation is where remote computing elements are involved in control of real-time experiments. Two examples of this were cited in the applications requirements workshop [2] – one from magnetic fusion experiments and the other from the Spallation Neutron Source. The magnetic fusion situation is that theories are tested with experiments in Tokamak fusion reactors. The experiments involve changing the many parameters by which the reactor can operate and then triggering plasma generation. The "shot" (experiment) lasts a few 10s of milliseconds and generates hundreds of megabytes of data. The device takes about 20 minutes to cycle for the next shot. In that 20 minutes the data must be distributed to the remote collaborators, analyzed, and the results of the analysis fed back to the reactor in order to set up the next experiment (shot). In order to have enough time to analyze the data and use the parameters to set up the next experiment, 200-500 Mb/s of bandwidth must be guaranteed for 2-5 minutes to transmit the data and leave enough time to do that analysis. The situation with the SNS is similar.

The third situation is when Grid based analysis systems consist of hundreds of clusters at dozens of universities that must operate under the control of a workflow manager that choreographs complex workflow. This requires quality of service to ensure a steady flow of data and intermediate results among the systems. Without this, systems with many dependencies and with others dependent on them would stop and start with the interruptions propagating throughout the whole collection of systems creating unstable and inefficient production of analysis results that would reduce the overall throughput necessary to keep up with the steady generation of data by the experiment. (This is of particular concern with the huge amount of data coming out of the LHC experiments.)

10.1. OSCARS: Guaranteed Bandwidth Service

DOE has funded the OSCARS (On-demand Secure Circuits and Advance Reservation System) project to determine how the various technologies that provide dynamically provisioned circuits and that provide various qualities of service (QoS) can be integrated into a production net environment.

The end-to-end provisioning will initially be provided by a combination of Ethernet switch management of λ (optical channel) paths in the MANs and Ethernet VLANs and/or MPLS paths (Multi-Protocol Label Switching and Label Switched Paths - LSPs) in the ESnet cores.

The current scope of OSCARS is intra-domain – that is, to establish a guaranteed bandwidth circuit service within the boundary of the ESnet network. The Reservation Manager (RM) has being developed in the first phase of the project pertains only to the scheduling of resources within the ESnet domain.

Setting up inter-domain guaranteed bandwidth circuits is not a trivial task. Differences in network infrastructure (e.g. hardware, link capacity, etc.) may not provide consistent service characteristics (e.g. bandwidth, delay, and jitter) across domains. Differences in policies, such as Acceptable Use Policies (AUPs), Service Level Agreements (SLAs) and security requirements, may not allow the provisioning of inter-domain circuits. None-the-less, inter-domain circuits are of considerable interest, especially between ESnet, Internet2/Abilene, and GÉANT.

The MPLS mechanism provides good control over the path configuration. The Resource Reservation Setup Protocol (RSVP) is used to establish the state in the routers, and RSVP packets may either be routed using the default IP routing, or can set up paths along specified links. The label switching used by MPLS avoids the routing mechanism and QoS may be accomplished by assigning the paths to non-standard queues in the router – for example, expedited forwarding will provide bandwidth guarantees by giving the MLPS packet priority over the best-effort queuing of normal IP packets. Although there are typically only a small number of available queues, multiple virtual circuits with QoS are possible by limiting the total allocated QoS bandwidth to the available QoS bandwidth, and by enforcing QoS circuit bandwidth limits at the ingress points. That is, if a given path can accommodate 5 Gb/s of priority traffic (leaving, say, 5 Gb/s available for best-effort traffic) then $5 - 1$ Gb/s, guaranteed bandwidth user virtual circuits can be accommodated by enforcing a limit of 1 Gb/s at each circuit ingress point. The ingress policing is something that is always done because that is the mechanism of enforcing policy based sharing of bandwidth between best-effort and expedited traffic. The enforcing of bandwidth limits on multiple expedited virtual circuits is just an extension of that approach that is managed by the reservation manager that allocates and establishes the circuits in the first place.

With endpoint authentication, these MPLS paths are private and intrusion resistant circuits, so they should be able to bypass site firewalls if the endpoints trust each other.

MPLS is supported on all ESnet routers (and in most routers used in the cores of the R&E networks) and it allows for "stitching together" of paths across domains.

Since OSCARS facilitates the reservation of valuable shared resources, allocation management must be taken into account. Guaranteed bandwidth circuits that go across the country or beyond will be a scarce resource, and therefore an allocation mechanism including how allocations are assigned and managed must be considered.

When OSCARS is put into production, an allocation management framework (similar to that for allocating supercomputing time) must also be put in place.

The allocation management framework is beyond the scope of the current project, however the AAA subsystem is being designed to facilitate contacting an allocation management systems as part of the authorization process.

The Reservation Manager (RM) Components

A Web-Based User Interface (WBUI) will prompt the user for a username/password and forward it to the AAA system. The WBUI will operate in an HTTPS mode and the servers will be within the trusted domain of the RM.

WBUI then places the reservation request and user's authenticated identifier into a signed SOAP message and forward it to the AAAS.

The Authentication, Authorization, and Auditing Subsystem (AAAS) will handle access, enforce policy, and generate usage records. It will accept reservation requests in the form of signed SOAP messages, and then extracts the authenticated ID and passes it to a policy server that will interface with an allocation management system to authorize the request.

Authorized requests are sent to the Bandwidth Scheduler Subsystem for scheduling.

The AAAS also generates usage records for auditing, accounting, and allocation management purposes.

The Bandwidth Scheduler Subsystem (BSS) will track reservations and map the state of the network (present and future). BSS will preserve state including the current network topology (links in the network) and bandwidth reservations. The BBS will determine the path that will be taken and reserve the bandwidth by updating the reservation database.

BBS will also reschedule link reservations in the event of planned and unplanned network outages.

Just prior to the reservation time, the BBS will trigger the Path Setup Subsystem to setup the LSP. BBS will also trigger the teardown of the LSP when the reservation has expired.

The Path Setup Subsystem (PSS) will setup and teardown the on-demand paths (LSPs). Prior to path setup, PSS will validate the route the LSP will use, and query routers along the path to check for "illegal" active LSPs that could conflict with bandwidth reservation. To setup and teardown the LSP, PSS will change the router configuration on the start-end of the path.

All of the modules have well defined interfaces and are designed to be called from applications other than the Web-Based User Interface.

Operation of the System – Making A Reservation

The user will make reservations through the Web-Based User Interface. (Subsequently, user applications may talk directly to the AAAS to make a reservation.)

Information which uniquely identifies the stream (e.g. source/destination IP addresses, source/destination port numbers, protocol), along with the duration and bandwidth requirement are entered.

A notice is returned as to whether the reservation is accepted or denied.

Operation of the System – Claiming the Reservation

At the time when the reservation becomes active, the user simply sends traffic from the source to the destination (the source address and port are specified as part of the reservation process).

The packets are filtered on the ESnet ingress router and those conforming to a reservation are injected into an LSP that was setup by the PSS when the reservation became active.

Implementation

OSCARS is being implemented in three phases each with duration of about one year. Phase 1 (completed by Jun 2005) consists of
- Test and deploy MPLS, RSVP, and QoS in the ESnet production environment
- Implement web-based user interface.
- Implement basic access-control security for AAAS.
- Develop simple scheduling algorithms for BSS.
- Test and implement access methods for PSS.

- Test at least one user-level application using the QoS service.

Phase 2

- Create tools to monitor LSP setup/teardown and bandwidth usage.
- Test and deploy DOEGrids certificate authentication for AAAS.
- Evaluate the AAAS with one or more user communities

Phase 3

- Test and deploy authorization and auditing mechanisms for AAAS.
- Develop rescheduling algorithms for BSS to address network changes during a reservation.
- Evaluate the BSS with a user community.
- Test and develop policy server and client for AAAS and BSS.
- Test and deploy Generalized MPLS (GMPLS) to include optical cross connect equipment in LSP if applicable.

Current Status

MPLS paths have been established through the core between two pairs of ESnet sites Fermi Lab and Brookhaven, and General Atomics and the NERSC supercomputer center.

These tests have shown – unsurprisingly – that policing has a detrimental effect on unshaped TCP flows. The burstiness of the TCP flow causes the policer to discard multiple back-to-back packets, triggering TCP's congestions control mechanism. Flow shaping to ensure that packets are delivered to the virtual circuit within the allowed bandwidth is something that needs to be done prior to injecting the packets into the network. Unfortunately this cannot be done by the user at the application level because a TCP window's worth of IP packets are injected all at once at the network interface cards (NIC) line rate (and in a TCP instance tuned for cross-country distances this is a lot of packets). Shaping usually must be done in the OS of the system that talks to the network or on the NIC. Approaches to ameliorate this situation are being investigated, but are mostly outside the scope of the OSCARS project.

One possible alternative would be to utilize less loss sensitive (and typically less compatible with commodity TCP) protocols when using OSCARS LSPs (e.g. UDP rate-based transport).

Collaborations

The Bandwidth Reservation for User Work (BRUW) project is a part of Internet2's Hybrid Optical and Packet Infrastructure (HOPI) project that will allow authorized users to reserve bandwidth across the Abilene backbone network with minimal human intervention in the process to support advanced applications and research.

The OSCARS and BRUW projects are jointly developing code, which is possible because OSCARS and BRUW have very similar architectures. Among other things, this is intended to ensure compatibility between Internet2 and ESnet communities. There is also close cooperation with the DANTE/GÉANT virtual circuit project ("lightpaths – Joint Research Activity 3 project).

A demonstration of dynamic setup of an inter-domain LSP circuits between ESnet and Internet2 is targeted for the SC05 conference. One motivation for this is as a prototype for U.S. LHC Tier-1 (DOE Labs) – Tier-2 (U.S. universities) data transfers.

10.2. ESnet Grid and Middleware Services Supporting Science

The two key workshops whose results are guiding the evolution of ESnet ([2] and [5]) both identified various middleware services that had to be in place, in addition to the network and its services, in order to provide an effective distributed science environment.

In addition to the high-bandwidth network connectivity for DOE Labs, ESnet provides several of the middleware services that are critical for collaboration. These services are called "science services" – services that support the practice of science. Examples of these services include:

- Trust management for collaborative science
- Cross site trust policies negotiation
- Long-term PKI key and proxy credential management
- Human collaboration communication
- End-to-end monitoring for Grid / distributed application debugging and tuning
- Persistent hierarchy roots for metadata and knowledge management systems

There are a number of such services for which an organization like ESnet has characteristics that make it the natural provider. For example, ESnet is trusted, persistent, and has a large (almost comprehensive within DOE) user base. ESnet also has the facilities to provide reliable access and high availability of services through assured network access to replicated services at geographically diverse locations.

However, given the small staff of an organization like ESnet, a constraint on the scope of such services is that they must be scalable in the sense that as the service user base grows, ESnet interaction with the users does not grow.

There are three types of such services that ESnet offers to the DOE and/or its collaborators.

- Federated trust
  - policy is established by the international science collaboration community to meet its needs
- Public Key Infrastructure certificates for remote, multi-institutional, identity authentication
- Human collaboration services
  - video, audio, and data conferencing

10.3. Authentication and Trust Federation Services

Cross-site identity authentication and identity federation is critical for distributed, collaborative science in order to enable routine sharing computing and data resources, and other Grid services. ESnet provides a comprehensive service to support secure authentication.

Managing cross-site trust agreements among many organizations is crucial for authorization in collaborative environments. ESnet assists in negotiating and managing the cross-site, cross-organization, and international trust relationships to provide policies that are tailored to collaborative science.

ESnet Public Key Infrastructure

ESnet provides Public Key Infrastructure and X.509 identity certificates that are the basis of secure, cross-site authentication of people and Grid systems. The ESnet root Certification Authority (CA) service supports several CAs with different uses and policies that issue X.509 identity certificates after validating the user request against the policy of the CA. For example, the DOEGrids CA has a policy tailored to accommodate international science collaboration, the NERSC (DOE Office of Science supercomputer center) CA policy integrates CA and certificate issuance with NERSC user accounts management services, and the FusionGrid CA supports the policy of the DOE magnetic fusion program's FusionGrid roaming authentication and authorization services, providing complete key lifecycle management.

The DOEGrids CA (www.doegrids.org) was the basis of the first routine sharing of HEP computing resources between United States and Europe.

Federation and Trust management

ESnet has been working with the international Grid community develop policies and processes that facilitate the establishment of multi-institutional and cross-site trust relationships. This effort led to the development of two key documents used by the community and published by the Global Grid Forum (GGF): CA Policy Management Authority guidelines, and a reference Certificate Policy and Certification Practices Statement (CP/CPS). Policy Management Authorities (PMAs) encode, manage, and enforce the policy representing the trust agreements that are worked out by negotiation. The PMA guidelines outline how to establish a PMA. The CP/CPS guidelines were written to outline issues of trust that must be addressed when setting up a CA.

These documents are used by the regional CA providers to organize their management and to specify their policies. The European, EU Grid PMA, and the Asia Pacific, AP PMA, both use these documents for their communities.

The Americas Grid PMA

ESnet represents the DOE and NSF Grid user community by participation as a full member on the EUGrid PMA. This is a requirement because of the need to collaborate between the two user communities. However, with the successful deployment of the EU and AP PMAs, there has been pressure on the Americas to form their own regional PMA. The number of users in the Americas has continued to grow, but the only PMA that could handle their trust needs was the European PMA. The increasing number of users from the Americas that need to form similar trust relationships with the Europeans was beginning to stress the capacity of European Grids community. To better serve the Americas Grid community, and to help off load certification by the EU Grid PMA, ESnet has helped establish The Americas Grid PMA (TAGPMA).

International Grid Trust Federation

The formation of the EU, AP PMA, and Americas Grid PMAs has created a need to coordinate these regional efforts to insure a common, global trust based federation. The IGTF was fostered by ESnet to help coordinate the global efforts of trust management. In March 2003, ESnet met in Tokyo with a number of international PMAs, this led to the establishment of the IGTF (www.GridPMA.org). The IGTF has grown to include the three major regional PMAs: www.EUGridPMA.org, www.APGridPMA and the new www.TAGPMA.org (Americas). It will be the publishing point for various policies and official points of contact (POC).

OCSP Service for Grids

The Online Certificate Status Protocol (OCSP) (RFC 2560) is a simple query protocol that relieves PKI clients of the burden of managing and maintaining lists of revoked certificates. ESnet engineers are co-authoring an OCSP requirement document for GGF and have built a pilot OCSP service (http://amethyst.es.net/) for use by Grids and other users of ESnet PKI services.

Wide Area Net RADIUS and EAP

ESnet has developed considerable expertise in the use of RADIUS (RFC 2865) across ESnet, and in tandem with RADIUS is investigating the Extensible Authentication Protocol (EAP) (RFC 2864) to support secure authentication services for distributed computing applications. Authentication methods supported include one-time password services, PKI (as used in Grids and possibly in the US government's Personal Identity Verification (PIV) project [17]), and conventional password services. Applications supported include Grid credential stores like MyProxy, sshd, web servers, and UNIX login.

PGP Key Server

The ESnet PGP keyserver (http://www.es.net/pgp) provides an access and distribution service for PGP keys in the ESnet community, and with other PGP users. The PGP key server is a node in a mesh of worldwide PGP key servers, supporting over two million PGP keys.

10.4. Voice, Video, and Data Tele-Collaboration Service

Another important and highly successful ESnet Science Service are audio, video, and data teleconferencing services that are very important for supporting human collaboration in geographically dispersed scientific collaborators.

ESnet provides the central scheduling and ad-hoc conferencing services that are essential for global collaborations, and that serve more than a thousand DOE researchers and collaborators worldwide. The services consist of ad-hoc H.323 (IP) videoconferences (5000 port hours per month are used), scheduled audio conferencing (2000 port hours per month used), and data conferencing (50 to 100 port hours per month).

Web-based, automated registration and scheduling for all of these services provide the central coordination that makes the service valuable to a large, world-wide community (http://www.ecs.es.net).

11. Conclusions

ESnet is an infrastructure that is critical to DOE's science mission, both directly and in supporting collaborators. It is focused on the Office of Science Labs, but serves many other parts of DOE.

ESnet is implementing a new network architecture in order to meet the science networking requirements of DOE's Office of Science. This architecture is intended to provide high reliability and very high bandwidth.

Grid middleware services for large numbers of users are hard – but they can be provided if careful attention is paid to scaling. ESnet provides PKI authentication services and world-wide video and audio conferencing to DOE scientists and their collaborators.

12. Acknowledgements

The ESnet senior network engineering staff that are responsible for the evolution of ESnet consists of Joseph H. Burrescia, Michael S. Collins, Eli Dart, James V. Gagliardi, Chin P. Guok, Yvonne Y. Hines, Joe Metzger, Kevin Oberman and Michael P. O'Connor. The staff responsible for Federated Trust includes Tony J. Genovese, Michael W. Helm, and Dhivakaran Muruganantham (Dhiva). The staff responsible for the Tele-Collaboration services includes Stan M. Kluz, Mike Pihlman, and Clint Wadsworth. This group of people contributed to this paper.

ESnet is funded by the US Dept. of Energy, Office of Science, Advanced Scientific Computing Research (ASCR) program, Mathematical, Information, and Computational Sciences (MICS) program. Mary Anne Scott is the ESnet Program Manager and Thomas Ndousse-Fetter is the Program Manager for the network research program that funds the OSCARS project.

ESnet is operated by Lawrence Berkeley National Laboratory, which is operated by the University of California for the US Dept. of Energy under contract DE-AC03-76SF00098.

13. Notes and References

1. http://www.energy.gov/, Science and Technology tab.
2. High Performance Network Planning Workshop, August 2002
   http://www.doecollaboratory.org/meetings/hpnpw
3. DOE Workshop on Ultra High-Speed Transport Protocols and Network Provisioning for Large-Scale Science Applications, April 2003 http://www.csm.ornl.gov/ghpn/wk2003
4. DOE Science Networking Roadmap Meeting, June 2003
   http://www.es.net/hypertext/welcome/pr/Roadmap/index.html
5. LHC Computing Grid Project http://lcg.web.cern.ch/LCG/

6. http://www.sc.doe.gov/ascr/20040510_hecrtf.pdf (public report)
7. ASCR Strategic Planning Workshop, July 2003 http://www.fp-mcs.anl.gov/ascr-july03spw
8. Planning Workshops-Office of Science Data-Management Strategy, March & May 2004 http://www-user.slac.stanford.edu/rmount/dm-workshop-04/Final-report.pdf
9. ESG - Earth System Grid. http://www.earthsystemgrid.org/   ESG - Earth System Grid. http://www.earthsystemgrid.org/
10. CMS - The Compact Muon Solenoid Technical Proposal. http://cmsdoc.cern.ch/
11. The ATLAS Technical Proposal. http://atlasinfo.cern.ch/ATLAS/TP/NEW/HTML/tp9new/tp9.html
12. LHC - The Large Hadron Collider Project. http://lhc.web.cern.ch/lhc/general/gen_info.htm
13. The BaBar Experiment at SLAC. http://www-public.slac.stanford.edu/babar/
14. The D0 Experiment at Fermilab. http://www-d0.fnal.gov/
15. The CDF Experiment at Fermilab. http://www-cdf.fnal.gov/
16. The Relativistic Heavy Ion Collider at BNL. http://www.bnl.gov/RHIC/
17. http://csrc.nist.gov/piv-project/

Grid Computing: The New Frontier of High Performance Computing
Lucio Grandinetti (Editor)
© 2005 Elsevier B.V. All rights reserved.

NetSolve: Grid Enabling Scientific Computing Environments

Keith Seymour[a], Asim YarKhan[a], Sudesh Agrawal[a], and Jack Dongarra[ab]

[a]Computer Science Department, University of Tennessee, Knoxville, TN 37919 USA

[b]Computer Science and Mathematics Division, Oak Ridge National Laboratory, Oak Ridge, TN 37831 USA

The purpose of NetSolve is to create the middleware necessary to provide a seamless bridge between the simple, standard programming interfaces and desktop systems that dominate the work of computational scientists and the rich supply of services supported by the emerging Grid architecture, so that the users of the former can easily access and reap the benefits (shared processing, storage, software, data resources, etc.) of using the latter.

1. Introduction

Researchers today are becoming increasingly reliant on the availability of computational resources to assist in their research and quantify their findings. The creation of Grids has helped increase the availability of such resources by combining the computing power and storage resources of many computers into one. However, harnessing these combined resources is still a challenge and out of reach for many scientists. As a mechanism for providing access to various distributed hardware and software resources, NetSolve reduces the complexity of locating, accessing, and using the computational resources necessary for conducting timely research. To accomplish this goal, NetSolve provides the middleware necessary to provide a seamless bridge between the simple, standard programming interfaces and desktop systems that dominate the work of computational scientists and the rich supply of services supported by the emerging Grid architecture, so that the users of the former can easily access and reap the benefits (shared processing, storage, software, data resources, etc.) of using the latter. This vision of the broad community of scientists, engineers, research professionals and students, working with the powerful and flexible tool set provided by their familiar desktop computing environment, and yet able to easily draw on the vast, shared resources of the Grid for unique or exceptional resource needs, or to collaborate intensively with colleagues in other organizations and locations, is the vision that NetSolve is designed to realize.

2. Overview of NetSolve

NetSolve is a client-agent-server system which provides remote access to hardware and software resources from a variety of scientific problem solving environments such as Matlab, Mathematica, and Octave, as well as traditional programming languages like C and Fortran. In this section, we provide an overview of the architecture and features of NetSolve.

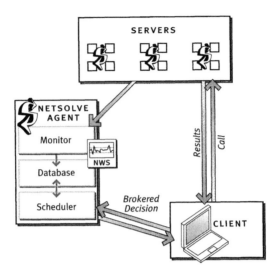

Figure 1. Overview of NetSolve

2.1. NetSolve Architecture

A NetSolve system consists of three entities, as illustrated in Figure 1.

- The *Client*, which needs to execute some remote procedure call. As we mentioned, the client may be invoked from an interactive problem solving environment or by a standalone program written in a traditional programming language.

- The *Server* executes functions on behalf of the clients. The server hardware can range in complexity from a uniprocessor to a MPP system and the functions executed by the server can be arbitrarily complex. Server administrators can straightforwardly add their own services without affecting the rest of the NetSolve system.

- The *Agent* is the focal point of the NetSolve system. It maintains a list of all available servers and performs resource selection for client requests as well as ensuring load balancing of the servers.

In practice, from the user's perspective the mechanisms employed by NetSolve make the remote procedure call fairly transparent. However, behind the scenes, a typical call to NetSolve involves several steps, as follows:

1. The client queries the agent for an appropriate server that can execute the desired function.

2. The agent returns a list of available servers, ranked in order of suitability.

3. The client attempts to contact a server from the list, starting with the first and moving down through the list. The client then sends the input data to the server.

4. Finally the server executes the function on behalf of the client and returns the results.

In addition to providing the middleware necessary to perform the brokered remote procedure call, NetSolve aims to provide mechanisms to interface with other existing Grid services. This can be done by having a client that knows how to communicate with various Grid services or by having servers that acts as a proxies to those Grid services. NetSolve provides some support for the proxy server approach, while the client-side approach would be supported by the emerging GridRPC standard API [1]. We briefly discuss these two approaches here.

Normally the NetSolve server executes the actual service request itself, but in some cases it can act as a proxy to specialty mechanisms such as Condor, MPI, and ScaLAPACK. The primary benefit is that the client-to-server communication protocol is identical so the client does not need to be aware of every possible back-end service. A server proxy also allows aggregation and scheduling of resources, such as the machines in a cluster, on one NetSolve server.

The GridRPC API represents ongoing work to standardize and implement a portable and simple remote procedure call (RPC) mechanism for grid computing. This standardization effort is being pursued through the Global Grid Forum Research Group on Programming Models [2]. The initial work on GridRPC reported in [1] shows that client access to existing grid computing systems such as NetSolve and Ninf [3] can be unified via a common API, a task that has proved to be problematic in the past. In its current form, the C API provided by GridRPC allows the source code of client programs to be compatible with different Grid services, provided that service implements a GridRPC API. We describe the capabilities of the GridRPC API in Section 3.

The combination of these technologies will allow NetSolve to provide seamless client access to a diverse set of Grid services.

2.2. Strengths of NetSolve
2.2.1. Ease of Use

The primary design goal of NetSolve is to make it easy to access grid resources, even for users who do not have much expertise in programming. We have accomplished this by providing interfaces to interactive scientific computing environments (Matlab, Octave, and Mathematica) which themselves are easy to use and place a low burden on the casual user. This design philosophy extends to the interfaces for traditional programming languages, which match the original function calls as closely as possible, thus reducing the amount of effort required to convert software to use NetSolve. For example, a direct call from Fortran77 to the LAPACK routine DGESV looks like:

```
CALL DGESV( N, 1, A, LDA, IPIV, B, LDB, INFO )
```

The equivalent call using NetSolve is:

```
CALL FNETSL( 'DGESV()', STATUS,
             N, 1, A, LDA, IPIV, B, LDB, INFO )
```

In addition, because NetSolve dynamically determines the calling sequence, no stub code needs to be linked with the client. In typical RPC systems, there is a formal description of the calling sequence of the procedure which is used to generate stub code. On the client side, the user calls the stub instead of the actual procedure. The client stub handles marshalling the arguments to

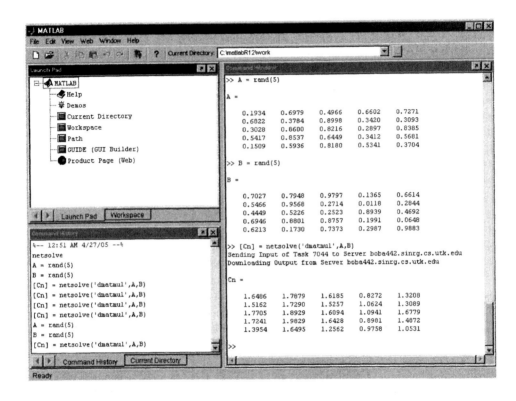

Figure 2. Example of Using NetSolve from Matlab

and from the remote server. Since the client stub must be compiled and linked with the user's code before it can be called, calling dynamically installed procedures from interactive environments is difficult. In contrast, the NetSolve client library determines the calling sequence at run-time by downloading a specification from the server. This specification is used to determine how to marshall the arguments to and from the server. Therefore, the user never needs to link stub code with their application, making it straightforward to use NetSolve from within interactive environments.

An example of the ease of using NetSolve from Matlab is shown in Figure 2. In this case, we generate two matrices using the Matlab random number generator and pass them to NetSolve to be multiplied using the dmatmul service. The result is assigned back to a Matlab variable and can be used in subsequent operations as usual.

2.2.2. Pre-configured Numerical Routines

In order to make the system immediately useful, NetSolve comes with pre-configured interfaces to a variety of numerical routines including dense linear algebra (from BLAS and LAPACK), sparse linear algebra, parallel solvers, and other miscellaneous examples. These problems can be selectively enabled by the server administrator depending on which libraries are available on the machine. In an attempt to provide a useful service to users who cannot start their own servers, the publicly available NetSolve grid running at the Univeristy of Tennessee has all the problems enabled. These pre-configured interfaces also serve as examples of how to integrate external software into NetSolve.

2.2.3. Agent as Resource Broker

One of the difficulties inherent in Grid computing is locating the best resources available to execute the requested service. In agent based scheduling, the NetSolve agent uses knowledge of the requested service, information about the parameters of the service request from the client, and the current state of the resources to score the possible servers and return the servers in sorted order.

When a service is started, the server informs the agent about services that it provides and the computational complexity of those services. This complexity is expressed using two integer constants a and b and is evaluated as aN^b, where N is the size of the problem. At startup, the server notifies the agent about its computational speed (approximate MFlops from a simple benchmark) and it continually updates the agent with information about its workload. The bandwidth and latency of communication between the server and the agent are also monitored, and are used as an estimate of the communication capacity between the client and server. When an agent receives a request for a service with a particular problem size, it uses the problem complexity and the server status information to estimate the time to completion on each server providing that service. It orders the servers in terms of fastest time to completion, and then returns the list of servers to the client. This scheduling heuristic is known as *Minimum Completion Time* and it works well in many practical cases. Each service request would be assigned to the server that would complete the service in the minimum time, assuming that the currently known loads on the servers will remain constant during the execution.

2.2.4. Resource Aggregation

Another of NetSolve's goals is to provide a middleware infrastructure that can be used to simplify access to complicated software, such as parallel or distributed programs. As we introduced in Section 2.1, in this approach NetSolve creates server-proxies to delegate the client requests to external scheduling and execution services such as batch systems, Condor, ScaLAPACK, or LFC (LAPACK for Clusters). The other NetSolve components see the server-proxy as a single entity, even though it can represent a large number of actual resources.

The key to this approach lies in the way services are defined. Each NetSolve service is defined by a formal description of the calling sequence, including the arguments, data types, and dimensions. This is generally referred to as an Interface Definition Language. Based on this description, both the client and server know how to marshall and unmarshall the input and output data. The actual implementation of the service is contained in an external library and is linked in with the service at compilation time. Therefore, any library with the same calling sequence can be linked using the same IDL, leaving the communication protocol unchanged. This allows having multiple NetSolve servers that implement the same service in vastly different ways. For example, a matrix multiplication service could be implemented on one machine using a vendor-tuned linear algebra library and on another machine using the reference BLAS [4]. Because the NetSolve communication protocol is the same for both, the client does not need to be concerned with which server is selected for the request.

This server-proxy approach has been used to provide simple access to parallel MPI jobs, as well as aggregate resources managed by LSF [5], Condor-G [6], and LFC [7]. In this way, we can bring the power of these aggregate resources to the user's familiar Matlab or Mathematica environment while leaving the server administrator free to optimize or modify the implementation without concern for the client.

2.2.5. Transparent Fault Tolerance

There are a variety of reasons a server may be unable to satisfy a client's request. In some cases, it is caused by policy decisions rather than technical problems. For instance, the server may have already accepted the maximum number of jobs the administrator configured it to handle or the server may be configured to require authentication and the client does not have the proper credentials. In those cases, the server is operating normally, but policy requires rejecting those requests. In other cases, however, the problem may be caused by genuine technical problems, such as the machine going down, the NetSolve server being stopped, network connectivity problems, or a poorly implemented service that crashes before the solution is computed.

The NetSolve approach to handling these problems is to automatically resubmit the job to another server. When the client initially submits a request to the agent, rather than returning a single server, it returns a list of servers. The client starts with the first server on the list and if a failure is encountered, it resubmits to the next server on the list. This continues until there are no servers remaining. The process is completely transparent to the user, so they only see a call fail if all servers that implement that service have failed.

2.2.6. Request Sequencing

As the size of data sets increases, the ability to specify the flow of data becomes more important. It would be inefficient to force intermediate results to be transmitted back and forth between the client and servers when those results will not be used again on the client and are needed at the server during the future steps of the computation. Our aim in *request sequencing* is to decrease network traffic between client and server components in order to decrease overall request response time. Our design ensures that (i) no unnecessary data is transmitted and (ii) all necessary data is transferred. This is accomplished by performing a data flow analysis of the input and output parameters of every request in the sequence to produce a directed acyclic graph (DAG) that represents the tasks and their execution dependences. This DAG is then sent to a server in the system where it is scheduled for execution.

In the current version of request sequencing, the NetSolve agent assigns the entire sequence to a single server. The server is selected based on the sum of the predicted run times of all the tasks. We execute a node if all its inputs are available and there are no conflicts with its output parameters. Because the only mode of execution we currently support is using a single NetSolve server, NetSolve is prevented from exploiting any parallelism inherent in the task graph. However, distributing independent tasks to different machines makes the scheduling and data management more important (and complicated) than in the single server scenario. This limitation would also be a problem when no single server has all the software required to execute the entire sequence. Therefore, we will need to extend the NetSolve scheduling and execution infrastructure to make more efficient use of the available resources when executing a sequenced request.

As a simple demonstration to show the effectiveness of request sequencing, we submit a sequence of three NetSolve requests, each dependent on the results of the previous request:

DGEMM $\Rightarrow$ DLACPY $\Rightarrow$ DGEMM. DGEMM is a matrix multiply routine and DLACPY copies a matrix. Because of the sequential nature of this task graph, even when multiple servers are available, the tasks cannot execute in parallel. Submitting this sequence to a dual processor 933MHz Pentium 3 machine as three individual requests took 4.43 seconds on average, while submitting it as one sequence only took 3.07 seconds because some data movement was avoided. Of course, if the task graph contained some inherent parallelism, using a non-sequenced series of requests would allow us to execute on multiple machines, possibly closing the performance gap. However, the difference in performance depends on the amount of parallelism that we could exploit and the communication overhead that we would avoid by using request sequencing.

2.2.7. Task Farming in NetSolve

Task Farming represents an important class of distributed computing applications, where multiple independent tasks are executed to solve a particular problem. Many algorithms fit into this framework, for example, parameter-space searches, Monte-Carlo simulations and genome sequence matching. This class of applications is highly suited to Grid computing, however, scheduling task farming applications efficiently can be difficult since the resources in a Grid may be highly variable and the tasks may take different amounts of time.

Without using a special task farming API, a naïve algorithm could be implemented by using the standard NetSolve interface and letting the NetSolve agent handle the scheduling. A user would make a series of non-blocking requests, probe to see if the requests have completed, and then wait to retrieve the results from completed requests. However this leads to problems with regard to scheduling, especially if the number of tasks is much larger than the number of servers. Alternatively, the user could try to handle the details of scheduling, but this solution requires a knowledge of the system that is not easily available to the user, and it ignores the NetSolve goal of ease-of-use.

In order to provide an efficient and easy to use interface to task farming, NetSolve implements a special API. In the farming interface, the user converts the parameters for requests into an arrays of parameters, indexed by an iterator string. Figure 3 shows an example of the task farming interface. The task farming API only adds 4 calls to NetSolve, namely 3 calls for constructing arrays of different data types, and 1 call for the actual farming. More details about the API can be found in the Users Guide to NetSolve [8].

One problem with the current task farming API is that it only returns when the all the tasks have been completed. That is, it does not allow the user to get results when a subset of the tasks have been completed, so the user cannot visualize, guide or cancel during the execution. These are things that we are working to address in the current development version of NetSolve (known as GridSolve).

2.2.8. Distributed Storage Infrastructure

As the size of the data sets used in scientific computing continues to increase, storage management becomes more important for grid applications. In the normal NetSolve RPC model, the client has all the input data resident in memory or in a local file. The client sends the data directly to the server and retrieves the results directly from the same server. Of course, the main limitation of this model is that the data set cannot exceed the storage capacity of the client, which could be a very severe restriction. In these cases, some form of remote storage management will be essential.

The Distributed Storage Infrastructure (DSI) is an attempt towards achieving coscheduling

40

```
Using standard non-blocking NetSolve API
requests1 = netslnb('iqsort()',size1, ptr1,sort1);
requests2 = netslnb('iqsort()',size2, ptr2,sort2);
...
requests200 = netslnb('iqsort()',size200, ptr200,sorted200);
for each request probe for completion with netslpr()
for each request wait for results using netslwt()
```

```
Using task farming API
int sizearray[200];
void *ptrarray[200];
void *sortedarray[200];
sizearray[0] = size1;
ptrarray[0] = ptr1;
sortedarray[0] = sorted1;
...
statusarray = netsl_farm("i=0,199","iqsort()",
ns_int_array(sizearray,"$i"), ns_ptr_array(ptrarray,"$i"),
ns_ptr_array(sortedarray,"$i"));
```

Figure 3. Task Farming Example: A integer quicksort routine is implemented using standard non-blocking calls (top) and then converted to using the task farming interface (bottom).

of the computation and data movement over the NetSolve Grid. The DSI API helps the user in controlling the placement of data that will be accessed by a NetSolve service. This is useful in situations where a given service accesses a single block of data a number of times. Instead of multiple transmissions of the same data from the client to the server, the DSI feature helps to transfer the data from the client to a storage server just once, and relatively cheap multiple transmissions from the storage server to the computational server. Thus the present DSI feature helps NetSolve to operate in a cache-like manner. Presently, only the Internet Backplane Protocol (IBP) [9] is used for providing the storage service. IBP provides middleware for managing and using remote storage, but we hide the specifics of the IBP interface behind the DSI layer. This will allow us to integrate other commonly available storage service systems in the future without requiring changes to client code already written using DSI.

3. GridRPC API

GridRPC is a standardized, portable, and simple programming interface for remote procedure call (RPC) over the Grid. NetSolve provides a GridRPC layer on top of the normal API, but in the future, GridRPC will be the primary end-user API. In this section, we informally describe the GridRPC model and the functions that comprise the API. The current Global Grid Forum Recommendation Draft for GridRPC [10] contains a detailed listing of the function prototypes, however the version currently implemented by NetSolve is described in detail in [1].

3.1. Function Handles and Session IDs

Two fundamental objects in the GridRPC model are *function handles* and *session IDs*. The function handle represents a mapping from a function name to an instance of that function on a particular server. The GridRPC API does not dictate the mechanics of resource discovery since different underlying GridRPC implementations may use vastly different protocols. Once a particular function-to-server mapping has been established by initializing a function handle, all RPC calls using that function handle will be executed on the server specified in that binding. A session ID is an identifier representing a particular non-blocking RPC call. The session ID is used throughout the API to allow users to obtain the status of a previously submitted non-blocking call, to wait for a call to complete, to cancel a call, or to check the error code of a call.

3.2. Initializing and Finalizing Functions

The initialize and finalize functions are similar to the MPI initialize and finalize calls. Client GridRPC calls before initialization or after finalization will fail.

- grpc_initialize reads the configuration file and initializes the required modules.

- grpc_finalize releases any resources being used by GridRPC.

3.3. Remote Function Handle Management Functions

The *function handle management* group of functions allows creating and destroying function handles.

- grpc_function_handle_default creates a new function handle using a default server. This could be a pre-determined server name or it could be a server that is dynamically chosen by the resource discovery mechanisms of the underlying GridRPC implementation, such as the NetSolve agent.

- grpc_function_handle_init creates a new function handle with a server explicitly specified by the user.

- grpc_function_handle_destruct releases the memory associated with the specified function handle.

- grpc_get_handle returns the function handle corresponding to the given session ID (that is, corresponding to that particular non-blocking request).

3.4. GridRPC Call Functions

The four GridRPC call functions may be categorized by a combination of two properties: blocking behavior and calling sequence. A call may be either blocking (synchronous) or non-blocking (asynchronous) and it may use either a variable number of arguments (like printf) or an *argument stack* calling sequence. The argument stack calling sequence allows building the list of arguments to the function at runtime through elementary stack operations, such as *push* and *pop*.

- grpc_call makes a blocking remote procedure call with a variable number of arguments.

- grpc_call_async makes a non-blocking remote procedure call with a variable number of arguments.

- grpc_call_argstack makes a blocking call using the argument stack.

- grpc_call_argstack_async makes a non-blocking call using the argument stack.

3.5. Asynchronous GridRPC Control Functions

The following functions apply only to previously submitted non-blocking requests.

- grpc_probe checks whether the asynchronous GridRPC call has completed.

- grpc_cancel cancels the specified asynchronous GridRPC call.

3.6. Asynchronous GridRPC Wait Functions

The following five functions apply only to previously submitted non-blocking requests. These calls allow an application to express desired non-deterministic completion semantics to the underlying system, rather than repeatedly polling on a set of sessions IDs. (From an implementation standpoint, such information could be conveyed to the OS scheduler to reduce cycles wasted on polling.)

- grpc_wait blocks until the specified non-blocking requests to complete.

- grpc_wait_and blocks until *all* of the specified non-blocking requests in a given set have completed.

- grpc_wait_or blocks until *any* of the specified non-blocking requests in a given set has completed.

- grpc_wait_all blocks until *all* previously issued non-blocking requests have completed.

- grpc_wait_any blocks until *any* previously issued non-blocking request has completed.

3.7. Error Reporting Functions

Of course it is possible that some GridRPC calls can fail, so we need to provide the ability to check the error code of previously submitted requests. The following error reporting functions provide error codes and human-readable error descriptions.

- grpc_get_last_error returns the error code for the last invoked GridRPC call.

- grpc_get_error returns the error code associated with a given non-blocking request.

- grpc_perror prints the error string associated with the last GridRPC call.

- grpc_error_string returns the error description string, given a numeric error code.

3.8. Argument Stack Functions

When describing the GridRPC call functions, we mentioned that there is an alternate calling style that uses an *argument stack*. With the following functions it is possible to construct the arguments to a function call at run-time. When interpreted as a list of arguments, the stack is ordered from bottom up. That is, to emulate a function call f(a, b, c), the user would push the arguments in the same order: push(a); push(b); push(c);.

- grpc_arg_stack_new creates a new argument stack.

- grpc_arg_stack_push_arg pushes the specified argument onto the stack.

- grpc_arg_stack_pop_arg removes the top element from the stack.

- grpc_arg_stack_destruct frees the memory associated with the specified argument stack.

4. GridSolve: The Future of NetSolve

Over time, many enhancements have been made to NetSolve to extend its functionality or to address various limitations. Task farming, request sequencing, and security are examples of enhancements made after the original implementation of NetSolve. However, some desirable enhancements cannot be easily implemented within the current NetSolve framework. Thus, our ongoing work on NetSolve involves redesigning the framework from the ground up to address some of these new requirements.

Based on our experience developing NetSolve we have identified several requirements that are not adequately addressed in the current NetSolve system. These new requirements - coupled with the requirements for the original NetSolve system - will form the basis for our next generation middleware, known as GridSolve.

The overall goal is to address three general problems: server-side ease of use, interoperability, and scalability. Improving server-side ease of use primarily refers to improving the process of integrating external code and libraries into a GridSolve server. Interoperability encompasses several facets, including better handling of different network topologies (such as those including NATs), better support for parallel libraries and parallel architectures, and better interaction with other Grid computing systems such as Globus [11] and Ninf [3]. Scalability in the context used here means that system performance does not degrade as a result of adding components or increasing the number of requested services in the GridSolve system.

This section describes some of the specific solutions to the general problems discussed above.

4.1. Network Address Translators

As the rapid growth of the Internet began depleting the supply of IP addresses, it became evident that some immediate action would be required to avoid complete IP address depletion. The IP Network Address Translator [12] is a short-term solution to this problem. Network Address Translation presents the same external IP address for all machines within a private subnet, allowing reuse of the same IP addresses on different subnets, thus reducing the overall need for unique IP addresses.

As beneficial as NATs may be in alleviating the demand for IP addresses, they pose many significant problems to developers of distributed applications such as GridSolve [13]. Some of the problems as they pertain to GridSolve are: IP addresses may not be unique, IP address-to-host bindings may not be stable, hosts behind the NAT may not be contactable from outside, and NATs may increase network failures.

To address these issues we have developed a new communications framework for GridSolve. To avoid problems related to potential duplication of IP addresses, the GridSolve components will be identified by a globally unique identifier specified by the user or generated randomly. In a sense, the component identifier is a network address that is layered on top of the real network address such that a component identifier is sufficient to uniquely identify and locate any GridSolve component, even if the real network addresses are not unique. This is somewhat similar to a machine having an IP address layered on top of its MAC address in that the protocol to obtain the MAC address corresponding to a given IP address is abstracted in a lower layer. Since NATs may introduce more frequent network failures, we have implemented a mechanism that allows a client to submit a problem, break the connection, and reconnect later at a more convenient time to retrieve the results.

An important aspect to making this new communications model work is the *GridSolve proxy*, which is a component that allows servers to exist behind a NAT. Since a server cannot easily accept unsolicited connections from outside the private network, it must first register with a proxy. The proxy acts on behalf of the component behind the NAT by establishing connections with other components or by accepting incoming connections. The component behind the NAT keeps the connection with the proxy open as long as possible since it can only be contacted by other components while it has a control connection established with the proxy. To maintain good performance, the proxy only examines the header of the connections that it forwards and it uses a simple table-based lookup to determine where to forward each connection. Furthermore, to prevent the proxy from being abused, authentication may be required.

4.2. Scheduling Enhancements

GridSolve will retain the familiar agent-based and server-based scheduling of resources, but in many cases the client has the most accurate knowledge about how to select the best resource. Therefore we are implementing an infrastructure that allows filtering and scheduling to be optionally performed by the client.

In the current NetSolve system, the only filter that affects the selection of resources is the problem name. Given the problem name, the NetSolve agent filters to select the servers that can solve that problem, then chooses the "best" server. However, the notion of which server is best is entirely determined by the agent. In GridSolve, we are extending this behavior. We allow the user to provide constraints on the filtering and selection process. These selection constraints imply that the user has some knowledge of which characteristics will lead to a better solution to the problem (most likely in terms of speed), for example, a minimum memory requirement. Also we will allow the user to have access to the complete list of resources and their characteristics so that the client can implement comprehensive scheduling algorithms in addition to simple filtering.

To make this functionality useful, the GridSolve servers should provide as much information as possible to the agent, in turn providing a flexible environment to the client for its request. To make the best selection for the client, the agent uses this information stored in the form of resource attributes and performs the filtering on behalf of the client. Furthermore, we allow the service providers (that is, those organizations that provide GridSolve servers) to specify constraints on the clients that can access that service. For example, an organization may want to restrict access to a certain group of collaborators. This information is also specified in the resource attributes of the service.

Since the GridSolve agent currently maintains information about all resources in the entire system, it can be viewed as the main performance bottleneck as more resources are added. The natural approach to this problem is to use multiple agents such that the load on each agent is reduced. However, this distributed approach leads to some interesting scheduling issues since each agent might only store information about its local domain. While each agent may prefer to schedule jobs within its domain, it may actually be more efficient to send the job to another agent if the computational and network communication requirements warrant. Thus, some agent-to-agent communication will certainly be required when using multiple agents.

4.3. IDL Improvements
One of the original design goals of NetSolve was to eliminate the need for client-side stubs for each procedure in a remote procedure call (RPC) environment. However, this design decision tends to push the complexity to the servers. Integrating new software into NetSolve required writing a complex server side interface definition (Problem Description File), which specifies the parameters, data types, and calling sequence. Despite several attempts to create a user-friendly tool to generate the Problem Description Files, it can still be a difficult and error-prone process.

Therefore, we have implemented a simple technique for adding additional services to a running server. The interface definition format itself has been greatly simplified and the services are compiled as external executables with interfaces to the server described in a standard format. The server re-examines its own configuration and installed services periodically or when it receives the appropriate signal. In this way it becomes aware of any additional services that are installed without re-compilation or restarting.

Integrating parallel software has been difficult in some cases because the Problem Description File format does not support it in a general way. Additionally, some parallel software has required using a customized server. Making parallel software easier to integrate into GridSolve hinges on two issues: the server should support it in a general way and the interface definition language should be extended to allow specifying additional parameters, such as the number of processors to be used. We are continuing to work on these issues.

5. Applications using NetSolve

The desire to make software available through a computational grid may be motivated by several factors. In some cases, the goal is to parallelize the computation to reduce the total time to solution. Grid middleware can also help increase overall resource utilization by balancing the load among the available servers. In other cases the goal is simply to provide remote access to software that is not feasible to run on the user's machine, perhaps because of high resource requirements, dependence on specialized libraries, or source code portability. In this section, we describe a diverse set of applications that have been grid-enabled using NetSolve.

5.1. Environmental Modeling

A tremendous amount of planning goes into an undertaking as large as restoring the Everglades. Studies must first be done to determine what areas need to be restored and how best to do so without further damaging an already delicate ecosystem. To aid in this planning, a group at the University of Tennessee led by Dr. Lou Gross has collaborated on the development of a suite of environmental models called ATLSS (Across Tropic Level System Simulation) [14]. These models provide comparisons of the effects of alternative future hydrologic plans on various components of the biota.

This package has proven itself quite useful in the planning efforts, however it requires extensive computational facilities that are typically not available to the many stakeholders (including several federal and state agencies) involved in the evaluation of plans for restoration that are estimated to cost $8 billion. To allow greater access and use of computational models in the South Florida stakeholder community, a grid-enabled interface to the ATLSS models has been developed and is currently being used on SInRG resources. This interface provides for the distribution of model runs to heterogeneous grid nodes. The interface utilizes NetSolve for model run management and the LoRs (Logistical Runtime System) [15] toolkit and library for data and file movement. Integration of the grid interface with a web based launcher and database provides a single interface for accessing, running, and retrieving data from the variety of different models that make up ATLSS, as well as from a variety of different planning scenarios.

ATLSS, in conjunction with NetSolve and LoRS, is the first package we are aware of that provides transparent access for natural resource managers through a computational grid to state-of-the-art models. The interface allows users to choose particular models and parameterize them as the stakeholder deems appropriate, thus allowing them the flexibility to focus the models on particular species, conditions or spatial domains they wish to emphasize. The results can then be viewed within a separate GIS tool developed for this purpose.

5.2. Statistical Parametric Mapping

Statistical Parametric Mapping (SPM) is a widely used medical imaging software package. The SPM web site [16] describes the technique as follows.

> Statistical Parametric Mapping refers to the construction and assessment of spatially extended statistical process used to test hypotheses about [neuro]imaging data from SPECT/PET & fMRI. These ideas have been instantiated in software that is called SPM.

Although SPM has achieved widespread usage, little work has been done to optimize the package for better performance. In particular, little effort has gone into taking advantage of the largely parallel nature of many parts of the SPM package.

Through continuing research by Dr. Jens Gregor and Dr. Michael Thomason at the University of Tennessee, preliminary work has been done to enhance the SPM package to utilize grid resources available through NetSolve and IBP by way of the NetSolve-to-IBP library. NetSolve-to-IBP is a library built on top of LoRS and ROLFS (Read-Only Logistical File System) that allows the sharing of files between the NetSolve client and server processes, using IBP repositories as intermediate storage. This allows programs that need access to a common set of files (e.g. SPM) to export some of their functionality to a NetSolve server without having to use a shared filesystem, such as NFS.

The grid-enabled version of SPM is still under development, but executions of the preliminary version have been timed to run in one half to one third the time of unmodified code in some simulations. Once completed, the SPM software will be distributed across the SInRG resources for use in medical research, providing doctors and researchers a faster time to completion, something often critical in medical imaging analysis.

5.3. Image Compression

An image compression application using singular value decomposition was built to demonstrate how the C# interface can be used from within .NET. Singular Value Decomposition (SVD) [17] is a useful mathematical tool for finding and removing information stored in matrix form based on its significance to the rest of the data. Image compression is one of many uses of SVD.

Images are represented as matrices with values in the elements to describe the intensity of the color. Color images are actually a composite of matrices representing different colors; generally red, green, and blue. When the image is decomposed into the form UDV^T by SVD, the singular values are representative of the clarity of the image. When some of the values are discarded the image loses clarity, but this loss in precision is made up for by the reduction in space needed to store the image.

Currently, the prototype NetSolve web service implements dgesvd (a singular value decomposition routine from the LAPACK [18] mathematical library) in a non-blocking fashion. Invoking the dgesvd web method creates a new thread and immediately returns. The dgesvd call ships the image as a .NET DIME [19] attachment to the web service side. The web service then decomposes the image into three matrices representing red, green, and blue. Each of the matrices is then submitted to NetSolve using the dgesvd problem and solved. Image reconstruction is done as soon as the client receives enough information from the web service to reconstruct the requested image(s).

5.4. Vertex Cover and Clique Problems

A widely-known and studied problem in computer science and other disciplines is the Vertex Cover problem, which asks the following question.

> Given a graph G=(V,E) and an integer k, does G contain a set S with k or fewer vertices that covers all of the edges in G, where an edge is said to be covered if at least one of its endpoints are contained in S?

Vertex Cover is NP-complete in general, but solvable in polynomial time when k is fixed. The applications for this problem are far-reaching, including applications in bioinformatics, such as phylogeny, motif discovery, and DNA microarray analysis. The problem, however, is inherently difficult and time-consuming to solve, so efficient software packages for solving Vertex Cover are very desirable.

Research conducted by Dr. Michael Langston of the University of Tennessee aims to create an efficient software package for solving Vertex Cover. Dr. Langston and his student researchers are interested mainly in the duality between the Vertex Cover problem and the Clique problem. The Clique problem asks the following question.

> Given a graph G=(V,E) and an integer k, does G contain a set S of k nodes such that there is an edge between every two nodes in the clique?

By exploiting the duality between these two problems, they have been able to solve extremely large instances of Clique (graphs containing greater than 104 vertices). To achieve reasonable times to solution, Dr. Langston's team has developed a parallel version of their software, which is being actively run on SInRG (Scalable Intracampus Research Grid) [20] resources. The team has taken several approaches to making their application grid-aware, ranging from developing a custom scheduler and starting jobs via Secure Shell (SSH) to using popular grid middleware, such as Condor. The team has implemented a prototype version of their software that uses NetSolve to efficiently access a large number of computational resources.

5.5. Genetic Algorithms

Because of their durability and fuel efficiency, diesel engines are installed in many kinds of vehicles ranging from compact cars to large trucks. With increasing environmental concerns and legislated emission standards, current research is focused on reduction of soot and NOx simultaneously while maintaining reasonable fuel economy. In this research, the optimization system designs a diesel engine with small amounts of Soot and NOx along with high fuel efficiency [21]. There are three components: the phenomenological diesel engine model, the Genetic Algorithm, and NetSolve.

HIDECS (Hiroyasu Diesel Engine Combustion Simulation) [22] is the most sophisticated phenomenological spray-combustion model currently available, originally developed at the University of Hiroshima. It has already demonstrated potential as a predictive tool for both performance and emissions in several types of direct injection diesel engines. Genetic Algorithm (GA) is an optimization algorithm that imitates the evolution of living creatures. In nature, creatures inadaptable to an environment meet extinction, and only adapted creatures can survive and reproduce. A repetition of this natural selection spreads the superior genes to conspecifics and then the species prospers. GA models this process of nature on computers.

GA can be applied to several types of optimization problems by encoding design variables of individuals. Searching for the solution proceeds by performing three genetic operations on the individuals: selection, crossover, and mutation, which play an important role in GA. Selection is an operation that imitates the survival of the fittest in nature. The individuals are selected for the next generation according to their fitness. Crossover is an operation that imitates the reproduction of living creatures. The crossover operation exchanges the information of the chromosomes among individuals. Mutation is an operation that imitates the failure that occurs when copying the information of DNA. Mutating the individuals with a proper probability maintains the diversity of the population.

Since it takes a lot of time to derive the optimum solution by GA, parallel processing is preferred. Fortunately GA is a very suitable algorithm for performing parallel processing and the *farming* function of NetSolve is very easy to apply to GA since it provides an easy way to submit a large number of requests to be executed in parallel. In this system, GA is performed on the client side. When the searching points are evaluated, the data is sent to the server and calculated using the faming function. A huge computational cost is required to derive these results. However, NetSolve farming helps this system to reduce the total calculation time.

6. Related Work

Several Network Enabled Servers (NES) provide mechanisms for transparent access to remote resources and software. Ninf-G [23] is a reference implementation of the GridRPC API [1] built on top of the Globus Toolkit. Ninf-G provides an interface definition language that allows services to be easily added, and client bindings are available in C and Java. Security, scheduling and resource management are left up to Globus.

The DIET (Distributed Interactive Engineering Toolbox) project [24] is a client-agent-server RPC architecture which uses the GridRPC API as its primary interface. A CORBA Naming Service handles the resource registration and lookup, and a hierarchy of agents handles the scheduling of services on the resources. An API is provided for generating service profiles and adding new services, and a C client API exists.

NEOS [25] is a network-enabled problem-solving environment designed as a generic application service provider (ASP). Any application that can be changed to read its inputs from files, and write its output to a single file can be integrated into NEOS. The NEOS Server acts as an intermediary for all communication. The client data files go to the NEOS server, which sends the data to the solver resources, collects the results and then returns the results to the client. Clients can use email, web, sockets based tools and CORBA interfaces.

Other projects are related to various aspects of NetSolve. For example, task farming style computation is provided by the Apples Parameter Sweep Template (APST) project [26], the Condor Master Worker (MW) project [27], and the Nimrod-G project [28]. Request sequencing is handled by projects like Condor DAGman [6].

However, NetSolve provides a complete solution for easy access to remote resources and software. It differs from the other NES implementation by including a tight, simple integration with a variety of client PSEs (Matlab, Mathematica, Octave). Interface descriptions for a variety of standard mathematical libraries is distributed with NetSolve, and it is easy for additional services to be added. The ability to use server-proxies to leverage additional resource management and scheduling environments also adds to NetSolve's strengths.

7. Conclusion

Since the inception of the NetSolve project, the paramount design goal has been ease of use. This has motivated us to develop interfaces to popular interactive scientific computing environments such as Matlab, Mathematica, and Octave. The existence of these interfaces serves to reduce the barrier to entry for Grid computing since users do not need significant programming expertise to use them. NetSolve's agent based scheduling eliminates the need for the user to know the location of resources capable of servicing the request and the fault tolerance mechanism allows selecting alternate resources without intervention from the user. The NetSolve server also hides complexity from the user by making it easier to invoke parallel programs or jobs on machines controlled by a batch queue.

We have described how NetSolve is being used by several projects to solve problems ranging from medical imaging to optimizing the emissions from diesel engines. As researchers continue to investigate feasible ways to harness computational resources, we hope the NetSolve system will continue to provide a useful paradigm for Grid computing.

8. Acknowledgments

We would like to thank the following people for describing the status of their research using NetSolve: Jens Gregor, Lou Gross, Tomo Hiroyasu, Michael Langston, Zhiao Shi, and Michael Thomason.

REFERENCES

1. K. Seymour, H. Nakada, S. Matsuoka, J. Dongarra, C. Lee, and H. Casanova. Overview of GridRPC: A Remote Procedure Call API for Grid Computing. In M. Parashar, editor, *GRID 2002*, pages 274–278, 2002.
2. Global Grid Forum Research Group on Programming Models. `http://www.gridforum.org/7_APM/APS.htm`.
3. Hidemoto Nakada, Mitsuhisa Sato, and Satoshi Sekiguchi. Design and Implementations of Ninf: Towards a Global Computing Infrastructure. In *Future Generation Computing Systems, Metacomputing Issue*, volume 15, pages 649–658, 1999.
4. C. Lawson, R. Hanson, D. Kincaid, and F. Krogh. Basic Linear Algebra Subprograms for Fortran Usage. *ACM Transactions on Mathematical Software*, 5:308–325, 1979.
5. Load Sharing Facility. `http://www.platform.com/products/LSF/`.
6. James Frey, Todd Tannenbaum, Ian Foster, Miron Livny, and Steve Tuecke. Condor-G: A Computation Management Agent for Multi-Institutional Grids. *Cluster Computing*, 5:237–246, 2002.
7. Z. Chen, J. Dongarra, P. Luszczek, and K. Roche. Self Adapting Software for Numerical Linear Algebra and LAPACK For Clusters. In *Parallel Computing*, volume 29, pages 1723–1743, 2003.
8. D. Arnold, S. Agrawal, S. Blackford, J. Dongarra, M. Miller, K. Seymour, K. Sagi, Z. Shi, and S. Vadhiyar. Users' Guide to NetSolve V1.4.1. Innovative Computing Laboratory. Technical Report ICL-UT-02-05, University of Tennessee, Knoxville, TN, June 2002.
9. A. Bassi, M. Beck, T. Moore, J. Plank, M. Swany, R. Wolski, and G. Fagg. The Internet Backplane Protocol: A Study in Resource Sharing. In *Future Generation Computing Systems*, volume 19, pages 551–561.
10. H. Nakada, S. Matsuoka, K. Seymour, J. Dongarra, C. Lee, and H. Casanova. A GridRPC Model and API for End-User Applications. `http://forge.gridforum.org/projects/gridrpc-wg/document/End-User_API_23%_Sept_04/en/1`, September 2004. Global Grid Forum Recommendation Draft.
11. Ian Foster and Carl Kesselman. Globus: A Metacomputing Infrastructure Toolkit. *International Journal of Supercomputer Applications*, 1997.
12. K. Egevang and P. Francis. The IP Network Address Translator (NAT). RFC 1631, May 1994.
13. K. Moore. Recommendations for the Design and Implementation of NAT-Tolerant Applications. Internet-draft, February 2002. Work in Progress.
14. D. M. Fleming, D. L. DeAngelis, L. J. Gross, R. E. Ulanowicz, W. F. Wolff, W. F. Loftus, and M. A. Huston. ATLSS: Across-Trophic-Level System Simulation for the Freshwater Wetlands of the Everglades and Big Cypress Swamp. National Biological Service Technical Report, 1994.

15. M. Beck, Y. Ding, S. Atchley, and J. S. Plank. Algorithms for High Performance, Wide-area Distributed File Downloads. *Parallel Processing Letters*, 13(2):207–224, June 2003.

16. Statistical Parametric Mapping. http://www.fil.ion.ucl.ac.uk/spm/.

17. G. Golub and C.F. Van Loan. *Matrix Computations*. Johns Hopkins University Press, 1996.

18. E. Anderson, Z. Bai, C. Bischof, S. Blackford, J. Demmel, J. Dongarra, J. Du Croz, A. Greenbaum, S. Hammarling, A. McKenney, and D. Sorensen. *LAPACK Users' Guide, Third Edition*. SIAM, Philadelphia, PA, 1999.

19. Direct Internet Message Encapsulation. http://www.gotdotnet.com/team/xml_wsspecs/dime/dime.htm.

20. Scalable Intracampus Research Grid. http://icl.cs.utk.edu/sinrg.

21. H. Hiroyasu, T. Hiroyasu, M. Miki, J. Kamiura, and S. Watanabe. Multi-Objective Optimization of Diesel Engine Emissions using Genetic Algorithms and Phenomenological Model. *JSAE (Society of Automotive Engineers of Japan) Paper No. 20025489*, November 2002.

22. H. Hiroyasu and T. Kadota. Models for Combustion and Formation of Nitric Oxide and Soot in Direct Injection Diesel Engines. *SAE Paper 760129*, 1976.

23. Y. Tanaka, H. Nakada, S. Sekiguchi, Suzumura Suzumura, and S. Matsuoka. Ninf-G: A Reference Implementation of RPC-based Programming Middleware for Grid Computing. *Journal of Grid Computing*, 1(1):41–51, 2003.

24. E. Caron, F. Desprez, F. Lombard, J.-M. Nicod, L. Philippe, M. Quinson, and F. Suter. A Scalable Approach to Network Enabled Servers (Research Note). *Lecture Notes in Computer Science*, 2400, 2002.

25. E. Dolan, R. Fourer, J. J. Moré, and Munson Munson. The NEOS Server for Optimization: Version 4 and Beyond. Technical Report ANL/MCS-P947-0202, Mathematics and Computer Science Division, Argonne National Laboratory, Argonne, IL, February 2002.

26. Henri Casanova, Graziano Obertelli, Berman Berman, and Rich Wolski. The AppLeS Parameter Sweep Template: User-Level Middleware for the Grid. In *Proceedings of Supercomputing'2000 (CD-ROM)*, Dallas, TX, Nov 2000. IEEE and ACM SIGARCH.

27. Jeff Linderoth, Sanjeev Kulkarni, Jean-Pierre Goux, and Michael Yoder. An Enabling Framework for Master-Worker Applications on the Computational Grid. In *Proceedings of the Ninth IEEE Symposium on High Performance Distributed Computing (HPDC9)*, pages 43–50, Pittsburgh, PA, August 2000.

28. David Abramson, Rajkumar Buyya, and Jonathan Giddy. A Computational Economy for Grid Computing and its Implementation in the Nimrod-G Resource Broker. *Future Generation Computer Systems*, 18(8):1061–1074, October 2002.

Grid Computing: The New Frontier of High Performance Computing
Lucio Grandinetti (Editor)
© 2005 Elsevier B.V. All rights reserved.

Operations Research Methods for Resource Management and Scheduling in a Computational Grid: a Survey

Andrea Attanasio [a], Gianpaolo Ghiani [b], Lucio Grandinetti [a],
Emanuela Guerriero [b], Francesca Guerriero [a]

[a] Center of Excellence on High-Performance Computing and
Dipartimento di Elettronica, Informatica e Sistemistica, Università degli
Studi della Calabria, Via P. Bucci 41C, Rende (CS) 87030, Italy

[b] Dipartimento di Ingegneria dell'Innovazione, Università degli Studi di
Lecce, Via Arnesano, Lecce 73100, Italy

Computational grids are emerging as the new generation computing paradigm for tackling large scale hard problems in a wide range of scientific fields. Grids are highly complex distributed systems (involving multiple organizations with different goals and policies) which aim at providing computing services without the users need to know the location and features of the required resources. While the current and previous research efforts have been mainly concentrated on architectures and protocols, this paper deals with quantitative methods for grid resource management. In particular, three main issues are considered: performance forecasting, local scheduling (i.e., job scheduling within a single administrative domain) and distributed mechanisms for coordinating grid resources within several administrative domains. For each such a topic, the current literature is reviewed and new research avenues are highlighted.

1. Introduction

A "computational grid" is a collection of geographically distributed, loosely coupled, heterogeneous, non-dedicated computing resources, belonging to several organizations, which provide computing services without users know the location and features of the involved resources [1] (Figure 1). The resources shared and aggregated in order to provide the required services may include: processors; nodes with arithmetic, vector, graphic, signal processing facilities; storage systems; data sources, etc. Grids are inspired by electricity power production, transmission and trading [2]. However, unlike power grids,

- computing services may have a relatively complex structure (e.g., a job may be constituted by several precedence constrained tasks, and may be characterized by a deadline and a budget);
- it is unlikely that individual resources (e.g., individual CPU, memory, databases, etc.) are useful on their own; therefore, resource allocation on a grid is mainly concerned with suitable combinations (*bundles*) of resources;
- resource proximity may be relevant in the resource selection process because of the finite bandwidth and latency.

In addition, it is worth noting that, while in a power grid both fixed and variable costs are relevant, in a computational grid variable costs are often negligible.

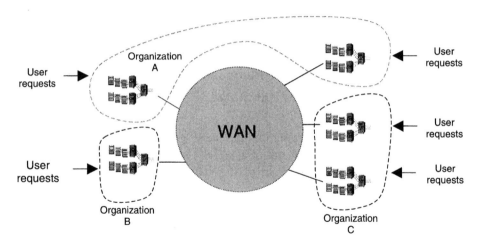

Figure 1. Grid Network.

In the long run it is expected that all the grids will be part of a unique *world wide grid* which will be a sort of generalization of the *world wide web*. In fact, in the same way an user reads a web page containing pieces of information located on multiple computers around the world (without knowing where these data come from), the world wide grid will allow using more advanced computing services without being aware of which resources are utilized. A grid user submits a task request by means of a Graphic User Interface (GUI), giving some high level specifications (e.g., a set of precedence constrained tasks, the applications to be used, input data requirements, a deadline, an available budget, etc.). The *Grid Resource Management System* (GRMS) plays the role of finding and allocating feasible resources (CPU cycles, storage, bandwidth, etc) in order to satisfy the user request. Then, the GRMS monitors the correct task processing, and notifies the user when the results are available. The GRMS must be able to utilize the residual resources of each organization being part of the grid (i.e., the resources left by internal users). As a consequence, an organization may act as a "grid resource provider" or as a "grid resource user" depending on whether its own "capacity" is less than or greater than its internal demand (Figure 2).

From an economic point of view, grids are motivated by the following observation: if user demands are uncorrelated, the aggregated capacity required by a grid system is significantly smaller than the sum of the capacities that the organizations would have in a traditional computing system. This phenomenon (known in the supply chain literature as *risk pooling*) can be explained qualitatively as follows: in a grid, if the demand from an organization is higher than the average, then there will probably be another organization whose demand is below average. Hence, capacity originally allocated to an organization can be reallocated to the other and, as a result, an lower overall capacity will be required.

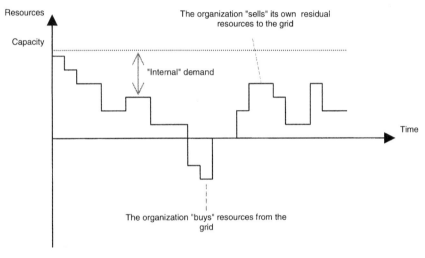

Figure 2. Available resources minus internal demand for a sample organization.

In a grid environment, a key issue is the optimization and the coordination of computing resource usage, which is the topic of this paper. Indeed allocation and scheduling approaches developed for massively parallel processor (MPP) schedulers are based on a number of hypotheses which are not satisfied in a grid environment:

- all resources lie within a single administrative domain;
- an MPP scheduler is in control of all resources;
- the resource pool is invariant;
- the impact caused by contention from other applications in the system on application execution performance is minimal;
- all computation resources and all communication resources exhibit similar performance characteristics.

The GRMS provides three fundamental services: resource dissemination and discovery as well as job scheduling [3]. This is accomplished in conjunction with other grid components such as applications, grid toolkits, native operating systems, billing and accounting systems, and security components (Figure 3). Grid toolkits (made up of

56

compilers, development environments and run time systems) allow applications to describe their resource requirements. The RMS uses the services of the native operating systems (OSs) to execute applications. In a grid environment, "local" users may submit jobs to nodes which are managed by the nodes' OSs (not by the GRMS). In addition, the GRMS interacts with a security component (that implements the authorization and authentication functions of the grid) and with the billing and accounting systems.

To meet the requirements of a grid environment, computer scientists in the mid-1990's began exploring the design and development of tailored methods for specifying application requirements, as well as translating these requirements into computational resources and network-level quality-of-service parameters, and arbitrating between conflicting demands. As shown in the subsequent sections, the current tools for resource management are relatively simple and do not allow to fully exploit the potential of computational grids. On the other hand, it is expected that Operations Research methods become necessary in order to support advanced features such as hard Quality of Service, a grid economy paradigm, etc.

The remainder of the paper is organized as follows. In Section 2 we introduce a taxonomy of GRMS and describe the currently available tools. In Section 3 we present a general framework for resource management in a grid economy, inspired by liberalized electricity markets, and describe the architecture of a GRMS. In Section 4 we survey the performance forecasting methods. In Section 5 we review local grid scheduling algorithms while in Section 6 we examine the coordination among different administrative domains. Finally, in Section 7 a blueprint for grid resource management is presented.

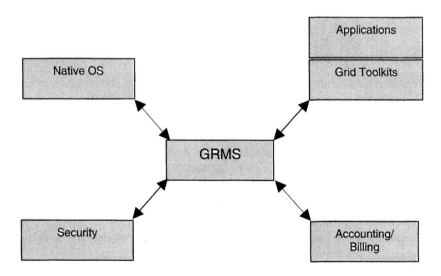

Figure 3. Resource Management System Context.

2. A Taxonomy of Grid Resource Management Systems

Several projects, such as Globus [4], Legion [5], AppleS [6], Condor [7] and Nimrod/G [8], are currently underway with the aim to design and implement a grid resource management system. This section summarizes the main features of such GRMSs while the remaining sections are mostly focused on methodological issues which need to be further exploited in the near future.

Our GRMS classification is based on the taxonomy described in [3] and divides the GRMSs according to the following features: application target, machine organization, resource model characterization and scheduling peculiarities. We first summarize the taxonomy [3].

Application target. Depending on the focus and application target, grids are classified into *computational grids, data grids and service grids*. A computational grid aggregates a large computational capacity in order to solve highly demanding applications (such as the ones utilized for solving grand challenge problems). Data grids provide an infrastructure for synthesizing new information from data repositories (e.g., digital libraries and data warehouses) distributed in a wide area network. Finally, service grids (including on demand, collaborative and multimedia grid systems) provide services that cannot be provided by any single machine.

Machine organization. Another meaningful classification is based on machine organization which affects the communication patterns and the scalability of the system. To this respect, grids may have a *flat, hierarchical* or *cell structure*. In a flat organization all machines can directly communicate with each other while in a hierarchical organization machines are subdivided into a number of levels and each machine can communicate with the machines directly above it or below it, or peer to it in the hierarchy. Finally, in a cell organization machines are clustered into cells and the machines within any cell can communicate between themselves using a flat organization. Moreover, a designated machine in each cell acts as a gateway.

Quality of service support. The level of support for extensive Quality of Service (QoS) will gain increasing relevance as soon as grid applications become more sophisticated and demanding. At present, sometimes jobs are queued in for hours before being actually processed, leading to degraded QoS. The QoS is not only concerned with network bandwidth but also extends to the processing and storage capabilities of the grid nodes. To this respect, GRMS can be of three types. A GRMS that provides the ability to specify QoS at job submission time and can reserve resources in advance accordingly is said to provide *hard QoS support*. At present most grid systems provide soft QoS since they cannot enforce non-network QoS guarantees. This is mainly due to non real-time operating systems which do not allow the specification of service levels for running jobs.

Scheduler organization. Grid scheduling systems can be classified into centralized, hierarchical and decentralized. In a centralized controller scheme, it is assumed that a single machine controls, or has sight of, the scheduling policies for all the nodes. In a hierarchical system, the resource controllers are organized as a hierarchy in which higher level resource controllers manage bigger units of resources while lower level controllers schedule smaller units of resources. Finally, in a fully decentralized approach there are no dedicated resource controller machines and the resource allocation and scheduling is done, e.g., on the basis of some sort of market trading. In a grid system each administrative domain is expected to have its own resource utilization policy. Broadly speaking, policies can be *system-centric* (if they try to maximize system throughput) or *application-centric* (if they try to minimize an application completion time or lateness). Because of the uncertainty affecting machine speeds, job processing efforts as well as request arrival times, schedules need to be re-examined and the job executions reordered from time to time. Rescheduling can be periodic or event driven (i.e., triggered by certain system events such as the arrival of a new job).

Table 1 reports a summary of the main features of the most popular systems. For the sake of brevity, we are not describing these systems in detail. Instead, we underline that grid resource management seems to be still in its infancy. In particular, most systems still use a centralized architecture.

While a centralized approach is suitable for cluster computing systems, it does not fit large grid environments with machines distributed across multiple organizations and administrative domains. Indeed, the main reasons for rejecting a centralized approach are:

- a centralized scheduler would be a bottleneck (allocation and scheduling problems to be solved are NP-hard and large scale so that huge computing resources would be necessary just for generating reasonably good feasible solutions);
- some organizations and administrative domains might not be available to share information on their capacity and/or their computing demand and/or their available budget.

On the basis of the previous analysis, the architectural design of grid scheduling system needs to be based on a decentralized or hierarchical approach. Indeed a GRMS should comprise both *local schedulers* (LS) and *external schedulers* (ES) (*superscheduler or metascheduler*). A LS (e.g., Condor [7] and PBS [9]) manages a single site (e.g., a cluster or a supercomputer) in a centralized way while an ES allocates jobs to sites according to a distributed mechanism. It is worth noting that at present LSs often employ very simple (and quite inefficient) scheduling policies based on a first come first served, priorized queue or round-robin policy, or on a greedy heuristic. Another drawback of most current LSs is that they consider a single conventional objective (e.g., the maximization of system throughput, the optimization of resource utilization, etc) and do not address QoS issues in a satisfactory way. The main effort toward this direction has been made at a local scheduler level by the economy-based scheduler Nimrod-G ([8]) (which is part of the GRACE project [10]). Originally developed for parameter-sweep applications, Nimrod-G makes use of two main scheduling strategies (depending on the user preferences):

- minimize job completion time with a give budget constraint (the so-called *time optimization*);
- minimize cost within a given deadline (the so-called *cost optimization*).

In order to manage QoS at a superscheduling level, an economy-driven resource management system needs to be set up. For an overview of economic models (i.e., commodity market model, posted price model, auctions, etc.) the reader is referred to [11]. In an economy-driven GRMS,

- resource providers pursuit the best possible return on their investment (or the maximization of their resource utilization);
- resource users try to have their problems solved within a specified timeframe and budget.

The price of resources vary over time (based on supply and demand), allowing important jobs to be scheduled during "peak" hours and less important jobs during "off peak" hours. Studies on grid economy are at a very preliminary stage. From a theoretical perspective [12], a quite general framework is given by the general equilibrium theory (GET) which aims at determining resource prices in such a way supply meets demand for each commodity and the different players optimize their use of resources at the current price levels. The GET describes conditions under which the existence and uniqueness of such a general Pareto-optimal solution hold.

Finally, most GRMS have been implemented following a monolithic architecture and are hard to extend to different applications.

3. Grid Economy and Resource Management

Current grid computing systems operate on a zero settlement basis (in which users give their resources for free in order to contribute to relevant research projects) or on the basis of an award process. However, it is expected that, as soon as commercial grids become a reality, resources will be traded on an economic basis which will be able to support a hard QoS.

3.1. Zero settlement basis grid

Examples of such projects are the SETI@home project [13], which aims at finding evidence of extraterrestrial life, the XPulsar@home project [14], which studies a mathematical model of a pulsar, the Intel CURE project [15], which aims at evaluating the curing potential of hundreds of millions of molecules in order to design new drugs, the FightAIDS@Home project [16], the RSA Factoring by Web project [17], etc.. In these projects, the overall job is subdivided into independent tasks. For instance, in the SETI@home project, a telescope located in Puerto Rico repeatedly scans about 25% of the sky and records a range of radio frequencies centered at the hydrogen line. This data is delivered to a server at the University of California, Berkeley. The data is decomposed into tasks each described using about 300 KB. Each task needs to be processed using a Fast Fourier Transformation to detect spikes of frequencies significantly above the noise level. Each task can be performed independently. The processing of one task takes about 10 hours on a typical personal computer. During the time when tasks are processed, new signals are received, and so new tasks continue being created.

60

Table 1. Existing GRMS main features.

System	Grid Type	Organization	GRMS Features
2K	On Demand Service Grid	Flat (Hierarchical in the Future)	Soft network QoS, one level hierarchical scheduler for network resources, decentralized scheduler for other resources
AppleS	Computational Grid		Resource model provided by the underlying Globus, Legion, or Netsolve middleware services. Centralized scheduler, predictive heuristic state estimation, online rescheduling
Bond	On Demand Service Grid	Flat	Hard QoS, decentralized scheduler, predictive pricing models, online rescheduling
CERN DataGrid	Data Grid Computational Grid	Hierarchical	No QoS, hierarchical schedulers, extensible scheduling policy
Condor	Computational Grid	Flat	No QoS, centralized scheduler
Darwin	Network Oriented Service Grid	Hierarchical	Hard QoS, hierarchical scheduler, non-predictive state estimation, online rescheduling
Globus	Grid Toolkit (for developing computational data, service Grids)	Hierarchical Cells	Soft QoS, lower level services for resource allocation or co-allocation including resource reservation. Higher-level tools (like Nimrod-G) perform scheduling
Lancaster DMRG	Multimedia Service Grid	Flat	Hard QoS, decentralized scheduler
MOL	Computational Grid	Hierarchical Cells	No QoS, decentralized scheduler
MSHN	Computational & Service Grids	Flat	Hard QoS, centralized scheduler, predictive heuristics for state estimation, event driven rescheduling

NetSolve	Computational & Service Grids	Hierarchical	Soft QoS
Nimrod/G & GRACE	High-throughput Computational and Service Grids	Hierarchical Cells	Resource model provided by the underlying Globus or Legion middleware services, soft and hard QoS depending on the availability on computational nodes, application-level scheduling policies driven by computational economy and deadline, hierarchical distributed scheduling model
Ninf	Computational & Service Grids	Hierarchical	No QoS, decentralized scheduler
Ninja	On Demand Service Grid	Hierarchical	No QoS
PUNCH	Computational & on Demand Service Grids	Hierarchical	Soft QoS, both hierarchical and decentralized, non-preemptive, adaptive scheduling

A client-server architecture is utilized in which the server can: register any volunteer and send there a client program that can process any task, send a task to a client program that contacted the server, and receive the result of processing of a task from a client program. Any client computer processes at most one task at any time. The server stores a database of about 2 million volunteers, half a million of which actively participate in the processing, and keeps track of which volunteer processed which task. A task is sometimes processed more than once (by different volunteers) to verify the results using an independent volunteer.

3.2. Award based grids

An example of such a project is the National Science Foundation's Partnerships for Advanced Computational Infrastructure (PACI) Program which manages a number of computing resources at several US research institutions (including the Distributed Terascale Facility). There are several ways of obtaining access to PACI resources [18]. A scientist, engineer or educator who has a joint appointment with a US university or a US Federal agency can obtain access to PACI resources [18] depending on his/her eligibility and requirements. Smaller allocations, including startup allocations, are handled by individual sites while larger applications are considered by the National Resource Allocations Committee (NRAC) twice annually. Requests should be clearly linked to the scientific goals and should be supported by providing performance and parallel-scaling information for the application(s) to be used. Currently, the PACI Program does not allocate resources other than CPU time. It is anticipated that the allocation of non-CPU resources (such as data storage or dedicated networking resources) may be required in the future. CPU resources are requested in the form of Service Units (SUs). In general, an SU is approximately equivalent to either one CPU hour or one wall clock hour on one CPU of the system of interest. The exact definition of an SU on each platform is defined in the technical documentation associated with each resource available through the listing of PACI resources at [19].

3.3. Economy-based grids

Economy-based GRMSs provide a distributed mechanism for allocating resources to jobs at a superscheduler level while enforcing QoS constraints. Market-based GRMSs force users to compete so that the different levels of importance they give to their job become explicit and resources can be allocated accordingly. Furthermore, market-based schedulers provide a feedback signal that prevents the user from submitting unbounded amounts of work. Negotiation may be done on a monetary basis or with a dummy currency in order to share the benefit of the cooperation among organizations. According to the economic theory, auctions are among the most suitable means for achieving this result. Auction design in a grid setting will be addressed in Section 6.

3.4. Architecture of a Grid Resource Management System

Grid users submit their jobs from any one of a number of entry points (EPs). Some privileged users have direct access to the resources of some administrative domain while others are managed by an ES. An ES acts as a broker, i.e. it is in charge of dividing the job into a number of tasks and allocating each task to a site (in such a way QoS constraints are satisfied). For each site (an administrative domain or a part of it), a LS is responsible for determining job sequencing, local resource allocation and data transfer scheduling. In general, on receipt of a job request, the ES interrogates a number of controlled LSs to ascertain whether the task can be executed on the available resources and meet the user-specified deadline (*feasibility check*). If this is not the case the ES attempts to locate a LS, managed by another ES, that can meet the task requirements.

If a LS cannot be located within a preset number of search steps, the task request is either rejected or passed to a scheduler that can minimize the deadline failure. When a suitable site is located, the task request is passed from the ES to the selected LS. The choice of specific algorithms for each component defines a particular GRMS.

In practice, the above described architecture can be expanded in order to improve its flexibility and/or to implement grid economy features. In particular, the following variants are expected to be considered in the near future:

- the ES might split an user job into a number of simpler tasks to be submitted to different LSs;
- the feasibility check performed by LSs might accept a job only if its price is greater than the value of the required resources;
- as new important and urgent local jobs are submitted, a LSs might try to re-allocate pending low-priority jobs to other LSs through an ES.

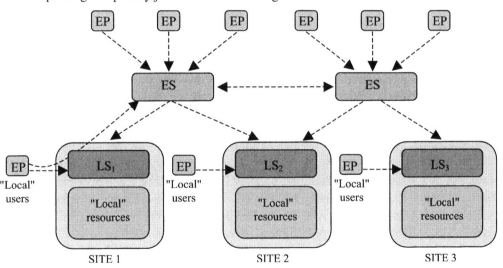

Figure 4. Grid scheduling architecture.

4. Performance Forecasting

Resource management on a computational grid requires accurate predictions of computing, data, and network resources. While it is straightforward to get a machine's static resource information (such as CPU frequency, memory size, network bandwidth, file system features, etc.), it is much more complex to get accurate estimations of run-time resources (such as CPU load, available memory and available network capacity) because of the dynamic nature of a grid environment.

It is well known that no forecasting method can be deemed to be superior to others in every respect. As a matter of fact, in order to generate a forecast, a performance measure must show some degree of regularity. Quantitative methods can be used every time there is sufficient demand history. Such techniques belong to two main groups: causal methods and time series extrapolation. Causal methods are based on the hypothesis that future demand depends on the past or current values of some variables. They include regression, econometric models, input-output models, computer simulation models and neural networks. For a general introduction of these techniques the reader is referred to Montgomery et al [20].

The major advantage of causal methods is their capability to anticipate variations in demand. As such, they are very effective for medium and long-term forecasts. However, it is difficult to find a variable that leads the forecasted variable in time. Vazhdukai [21] uses a regression technique to predict data transfer times in grid systems.

Time series extrapolation presupposes that some features of the past demand time pattern will remain the same. The demand pattern is then projected into the future. This can be done in a number of ways, including moving averages, exponential smoothing, the decomposition approach and the Box-Jenkins method. Such techniques are suitable for short and medium-term predictions, where the probability of a changeovers is low. The choice of the most suitable quantitative forecasting technique depends on the kind of historical data available and the type of parameter to be predicted.

The most known on-going project on performance prediction on a computational Grid gave rise to the *Network Weather Service* (NWS) [22]. The NWS is a distributed system that periodically monitors and dynamically forecasts the performance that various network and computational resources can deliver over a given time interval. The service operates a distributed set of performance sensors (network monitors, CPU monitors, etc.) from which it gathers readings of the instantaneous conditions. It then uses numerical models to generate forecasts of what the conditions will be for a given time frame. Adaptive scheduling methodology (such as The AppLeS [6]) makes extensive use of NWS facilities. Currently, the system includes sensors for end-to-end TCP/IP performance (bandwidth and latency), available CPU percentage, and available non-paged memory. The sensor interface, however, will be soon allowed to have new internal sensors to be configured into the system (see [23] for an update on the latest NWS release). The current set of supported forecasting methods treat successive measurements from each monitor as a time series.

The initial methods fall into three categories:
- mean-based methods that use some estimate of the sample mean as a forecast,

- median-based methods that use a median estimator, and
- autoregressive methods.

The system tracks the accuracy of all predictors (by using some accuracy measures), and uses the one exhibiting the lowest cumulative error measure at any given moment to generate a forecast. In this way, the NWS acts as a "meta-predictor" by automatically identifying the best forecasting technique for any given resource. Moreover, as new methods are added, they will automatically be used to forecast the resource performance for which they are the most accurate. Let $d(t)$, $t = 1, \ldots, T$, be the performance measure to be considered at time period t, where T indicates the time period associated to the latest entry available. Moreover, let $p_a(t,\tau)$, $\tau = 1, 2, \ldots$, be the τ periods ahead forecast made at time t (i.e., the forecast of $d(t+\tau)$ generated at time t) by procedure a. If $\tau = 1$, a one-period-ahead forecast has to be generated and the notation can be simplified to $p_a(t,1)=p_a(t+1)$. It is worth defining a forecast error in order to evaluate, a posteriori (i.e., once the forecasted parameter becomes known), the deviation of the performance measure from its forecast. The error made by using forecasting $p_a(t,\tau)$ instead of demand $d(t+\tau)$ is given by:

$$e_a(\tau) = d(t+\tau) - p_a(t,\tau).$$

As before, the notation can be simplified if $\tau = 1$: $e_a(t-1,1) = e_a(t)$. In order to select the most precise forecasting method at any moment in time t, a number of accuracy measures can be used. The most widely utilized are the mean squared error (MSE) and the mean absolute percentage deviation (MAPD) defined as follows:

$$MSE_{a,t} = \frac{\sum_{k=2}^{t} [e_a(k)]^2}{t-2}, \tag{1}$$

$$MAPD_{a,t} = \frac{\sum_{k=2}^{t} |e_a(k)|/d_k}{t-1}, \tag{2}$$

where we supposed for the sake of simplicity that $\tau = 1$. In the NWS, at any time t the different forecasting methods are compared through either the MSE or the MAPD, and the forecasting method achieving the most accurate predictions is selected.

Akioka and Muraoka [24] propose an alternative meta-predictor in which a Markov chain model is used to select the most accurate forecast at any time. Let a_t be the forecasting method selected at time t and let T be the current period. A *state* is associated with each sequence of prediction techniques $s=(a_{T-M+1}, a_{T-M+2}, \ldots, a_T)$ used during the last M time periods in order to predict $d_{T-M+1}, d_{T-M+2}, \ldots, d_T$. Every time a new measurement is taken, the meta-predictor checks which algorithm was best, and recalculates the probability distributions of the Markov model as follows. For each algorithm a, the conditional one step transition probability from state s to state s' is computed as follows:

$$p_{s,s'} = \frac{n_{s,s'}}{T}, \tag{3}$$

where $n_{s,s'}$ is the number of time periods in which the state changed from s to s' in T periods. In addition, for each algorithm a, the conditional one step transition probability from state s to state s' is computed as follows:

$$p_{s,s'|a} = \frac{n_{s,s'|a}}{n_{s,s'}},$$

(4)

where $n_{s,s'|a}$ is the number of times algorithm a provided the best prediction given that the state changed from s to s'. Computational results were derived on a real-world instance made up of the measurement of the throughputs between the Waseda University (Japan) and the University of Indiana (USA) roughly every minute between September 9–11, 2002. The comparison between the Akioka and Muraoka method and two versions of the NWS showed that the latter approaches slightly outperformed the former one. However the Markov chain based approach is viable only for very small values of M since the number of states $2M-1$ grows very fast as the M increases.

Other on-going projects on performance prediction include the PACE [25], ENV [26] and Remos [27] projects.

5. Local Scheduling

As pointed out in Section 1, computing services may have a relatively involved structure and may require a quite complex bundle of resources. For instance, a job may require a computing device with 8 processing nodes, 16 GB of available memory per node, a licensed software package for 2 hours between 10.00 and 16.00 GMT of the following day, a local visualization device during program execution, a minimum sustained bandwidth between the devices during program execution and a specified data set from a data repository as an input. In addition, it may be required that cost does not exceed a given budget (with a preference to a cheaper job execution over an earlier execution). Other relevant information may include the internal structure of the job (expressed by a set of tasks possibly constrained by precedence relationships) and the scalability of each task.

In a grid environment, each site may be a single PC, a workstation or a parallel computing system made up of expensive assets that are shared by several users. While single machine schedulers need to be simple and fast (since such schedulers are run on the same machines they are controlling), in case of parallel computing systems it is worth running much more "sophisticated" scheduling algorithms on a relatively unexpensive dedicated resource (e.g., a PC). In the former case, Operations Research (OR) is expected to play an important role, especially in order to support hard QoS. For an account of the OR literature over the last three decades, see [28]. Only recently, some new concepts have been proposed in order to deal with parallel application scheduling. In what follows, we survey the most interesting contributions. For the sake of clarity, we subdivide the most relevant paper into three main areas.

In deterministic scheduling, resource and job features are assumed to be known in advance while in stochastic and dynamic scheduling some parameters can be modelled as a random variable. Grid scheduling problems are stochastic and dynamic in nature (see Section 2) so that rescheduling plays a key role.

Depending on how a job can be divided, scheduling theory can be divided into two different areas: *divisible workload* scheduling (where a job workload can be divided into arbitrary-sized independent pieces or "chunks") and *fixed-sized task* scheduling (with or without precedence constraints).

Another relevant classification is based on the number of users: in a single user environment minimizing the makespan is a reasonable goal while in a multi-user context (like a grid setting) a most significant performance measure is a (possibly weighted) mean of the lateness of user jobs.

5.1. Divisible Workload Scheduling

Divisible workload scheduling (DWS) [29] arises in several application areas, such as image processing, scientific computing and data mining. The goal is to suitably utilize the communication and computation overlap in a distributed computing system.

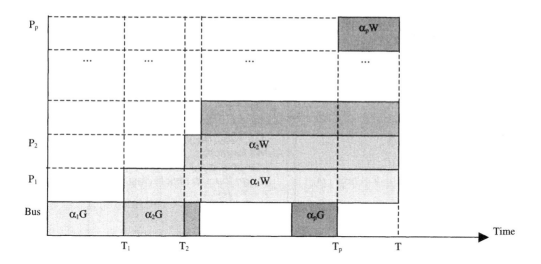

Figure 5. Single round divisible scheduling in case of identical processors ($W_j = W$, $j = 1, ..., p$).

Let $\{P_1, ..., P_p\}$ be the set of processors. In *single round* DWS [30], it is assumed there is a single bus and the workload is divided into p "chunks" α_i. The transmission time of the i-th chunk is given by $\alpha_i G$, where G is the inverse of the bus bandwidth, while the processing time of the i-th chunk on processor P_j is equal to $\alpha_i W_j$, where W_j is the inverse of the processor frequency. It is easy to show that in a single round DWS all processors finish working at the same time in any optimal solution. The scheduling decision to be taken is to determine the value of each chunk α_i ($i=1,2,...,p$) in such a way the makespan is minimized (Figure 5).

In *multi-round DWS* the workload assigned to a processor is distributed during several runs. The basic idea is to let as many as processors start computing as quickly as possible, then keep both the processors and the bus busy. Intuitively, in an optimal solution the chunks should be small during the first run, to get all processor started, then they should become larger in subsequent rounds, and finally they should decrease during the last rounds. Several DWS problems can be casted and solved as a linear programming (LP) problem with equality constraints. In addition, in some special cases the LP problem can be solved by a greedy procedure. See [30], [31], [32] and [33] for more details.

5.2. Fixed-sized task scheduling

Three greedy heuristics are often used for scheduling fixed-sized independent tasks (e.g., parameter sweep applications) in a single-user environment ([34], [35]): Min-min, Max-min and Sufferage. These procedures iteratively assign tasks to processors. At each step, the Min-min procedure allocates the task that can be completed the earliest. The Max-min heuristic chooses the unallocated task that can be completed the latest. Sufferage allocates the task that would suffer the most if not allocated to the most suitable host. Let T be the set of tasks to be scheduled and let c_{ij} be the estimated completion time of the *i-th* task on the *j-th* host. A more formal description of the three heuristic is given in the Figure 6.

```
Min-max heuristic
while (T ≠ ∅)
  foreach (i ∈ T)
    ĵ(i) = argminⱼ cᵢⱼ
  end foreach
  s=argmaxᵢ cᵢ ĵ*(i);
  assign the s-th task to host ĵ*(s);
  T = T \ {s}
end while
```

```
Min-min heuristic
while (T ≠ ∅)
  foreach (i ∈ T)
    ĵ(i) = argminⱼ cᵢⱼ
  end foreach
  s=argminᵢ cᵢ ĵ*(i);
  assign the s-th task to host ĵ*(s);
  T = T \ {s}
end while
```

```
Sufferage heuristic
while (T ≠ ∅)
  foreach (i ∈ T)
    ĵ*(i) = argminⱼ cᵢⱼ;
    ĵ**(i) = argminⱼ≠ĵ*(i) cᵢⱼ;
    sufferage(i) = cᵢ ĵ**(i) - cᵢ ĵ*(i);
  end foreach
  s=argmaxᵢ sufferage(i);
  assign the s-th task to host ĵ*(s);
  T = T \ {s}
end while
```

Figure 6. Three single-user environment greedy scheduling heuristics.

5.3. Scheduling with Communication Delays

Some issues related to scheduling with communication delay has been examined in [36], [37] and [38]. In the following we illustrate a particular problem considered in [39], where a number of (independent) parameter sweep tasks share common input files which reside at remote locations (Figures 7 and 8). In this context, local scheduling must take into account the impact of data transfer times. Casanova et al [39] are motivated by the need to run a micro-physiology application which uses multiple 3-D Monte Carlo simulations in order to study molecular bio-chemical interactions within living cells. A typical run is made up of tens of thousands tasks, each dealing with hundreds of MBytes of input and output data, with various task-file usage patterns. The authors assume that the grid can be modelled by a set of sites (with unlimited storage space) that are accessible via k distinct (logical) network links. They also assume that all input files are initially stored on the users' host where all output files must be returned, and there are no inter-cluster file exchanges.

Casanova et al [34] modify the Sufferage heuristic ([34], [35]) in order to exploit file locality issues without an a-priori analysis of the task-file dependence pattern. The basic idea is that if an input file required by a task is already available at a remote cluster, that task would "suffer" if not assigned to that site.

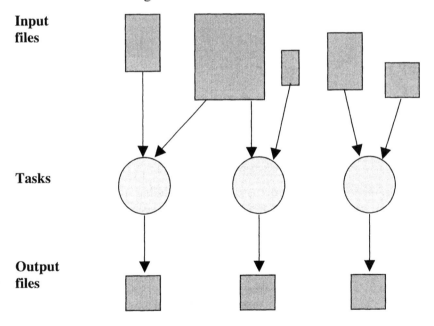

Input files

Tasks

Output files

Figure 7. Scheduling with data transfer.

5.4. Multiprocessor Task Scheduling

Unlike classical scheduling theory [28], several high performance computing applications contradict the assumption that a task is executed by a single processor at a time. This can be explained as follows. An application can be modelled by a Directed

Acyclic Graph (DAG) with the nodes representing the tasks and the arcs describing the precedence between pairs of tasks. However, DAGs are strongly data dependent, i.e. they are often known after job execution rather than before, and may have thousands of nodes. Since at the current state of technology schedulers are not able to handle, analyze and optimize such big structures, it is quite common that the operating system controls the number of processors granted to an application leaving the control of threads to the application (i.e., to the compiler and to the programmer) [40].

Drozdowski [41] surveys the current literature on multiprocessor task scheduling and extends the classical notation in order to accommodate the new features. In particular, he takes into account both fixed and variable profile tasks. The profile of a task is *fixed* if the set of required processors does not change during the execution of the task or *variable* otherwise.

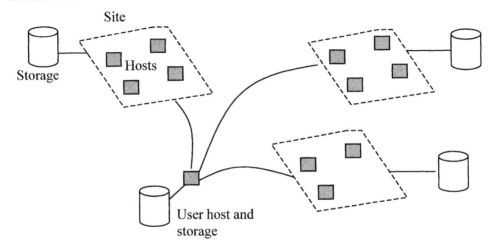

Figure 8. System architecture.

A recent and remarkable multiprocessor task scheduling problem is described by Caramia et al [42]. In this paper, a group of independent tasks have to be scheduled on a given site, within a given deadline. The site is characterized by a number of identical processing nodes and a limited storage. Tasks are not known in advance by the LS (see [43] and [44] for some basic results concerning on-line scheduling on parallel processors). Each task has specific resource requirements for its execution, e.g., duration, number of required processing nodes, and required dataset, which become known when the task is managed by the LS. A task can be executed by the site if it has idle suitable processing resources and dataset availability. All tasks have the same release times and deadlines. The aim is to schedule as many tasks as possible, thus maximizing the resource usage.

More specifically, the local scheduling problem is a multiprocessor task scheduling problem where a set of H processors, and a set J of non preemptive tasks are given; each task j J requires h_j processors for a certain time w_j with no preemption and must be executed within a deadline W. In the following we assume that processors are indexed, and restrict the subsets of processors assignable to task j to be formed by h_j

consecutive indexed processors. Caramia et al [42] model the processing time of a task and the required number of processors as the width and height of a rectangle, respectively. Therefore, scheduling task j corresponds to assigning a box of height h_j and width w_j in a bounded rectangular area of height H and width W, with the objective of using as much as possible such bounding area. This corresponds to a rectangle packing problem defined as follows. Given a set J of two-dimensional rectangular-shaped boxes, where each box j J is characterized by its width w_j and its height h_j, the problem consists in orthogonally packing a subsets of the boxes, without overlapping, into a single bounding rectangular area A of width W and height H, maximizing the efficiency ratio ρ ($[0,1]$) between the area occupied by the boxes and the total available area A, i.e., minimizing the wasted area of A. It is assumed that the boxes cannot be guillotined, and have fixed orientation, i.e., they cannot be rotated; it is also assumed that all input data are positive integers, with $w_j \leq W$ and $h_j \leq H$, for every j J. The rectangle (or two-dimensional) packing problem (see, for example, [45]) has been shown to be NP-complete [46], and is a special case of the two-dimensional cutting stock (or knapsack) problem, where each box has an associated profit, and the problem is to select a subset of the boxes to be packed in a single finite rectangular bin maximizing the total selected profit [47].

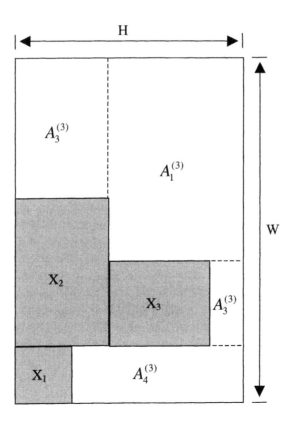

Figure 9. On-line multiprocessor task scheduling.

The authors provide two on-line algorithms, named PACK and PACKr. Given a list $L = \{1, 2, ..., n\}$ of jobs, an on-line algorithm A considers items in the order given by list L. In addition A considers each job i without knowledge of any subsequent job $j > i$ and never reconsiders a job already examined. Let $A^{(j-1)}$ be the unassigned area just before algorithm A decides whether to insert item j or not ($j=1, ..., n$). Area $A^{(j-1)}$ can be partitioned into j rectangles $A_1^{(j-1)}, ..., A_j^{(j-1)}$ ($A_r^{(j-1)} \cap A_s^{(j-1)} = \varnothing$ for $r \neq s \in \{1, ..., n\}$ and $\bigcup_{r=1}^{j} A_r^{(j-1)} = A^{(j-1)}$), where rectangle $A_r^{(j-1)}$ ($r=1, ..., j$) has width $W_r^{(j-1)}$ and height $H_r^{(j-1)}$. Clearly, $A^{(0)} = A$. Job j is accepted if there is a free rectangular area $A_r^{(j-1)}$ ($r=1,...,j$) such that $W_r^{(j-1)} \geq w_j$ and $H_r^{(j-1)} \geq h_j$. If such a condition is satisfied, let

$$A_{r*}^{(j-1)} = \min_{W_r^{(j-1)} \leq w_j,\ H_r^{(j-1)} \leq h_j} W_r^{(j-1)} H_r^{(j-1)}, \tag{5}$$

(ties are broken by selecting the area with the minimum index r). Job j is assigned to a subarea $A(j-1)$ in the north-west corner of $A_{r*}^{(j-1)}$ (see Figure 9). Such an insertion of job j creates one or two free rectangles, namely $A_{r*}^{(j)}$ and $A_{j+1}^{(j)}$ while the remaining free rectangles remain unchanged ($A^{(j)} = A^{(j-1)}$ $r=1, ..., r*-1, r*+1, ..., j$). The algorithm can be characterized by the *efficiency ratio* defined as follows:

$$= \frac{WH - \sum_{s=1}^{n+1} W_s^{(n)} H_s^{(n)}}{\min\{WH, \sum_{j=1}^{n} w_j h_j\}}. \tag{6}$$

In order to improve its empirical performance, the authors propose a variant of PACK (named PACKr) which is based on the observation that, as the algorithm progresses, the mechanism of creating new areas could create a division of the free area into very small parts so that some incoming jobs might be rejected even if there is room for their insertion. In order to overcome this drawback, PACKr tries to recombine pairs of adjacent areas in a bigger one (see [42] for more details). Extensive computational experiments showed that PACKr outperformed the off-line heuristics with rejection presented by Wu et al. in [48] on the rectangle packing benchmarks by Hopper and Turton [45]. In addition, the scheduling algorithms were tested in a simulated grid environment made up of $m=5$ computing sites, and two different processing environments: in the first one, all the sites have identical processing speeds; in the second one, the more realistic case in which each site has an own processing speed is considered. The authors also considered two different data scenarios. In the first one, datasets were replicated in all the sites while in the second one it exists exactly one copy of each dataset, stored in a certain site. In the former scenario, the algorithm schedules the jobs without considering the data availability whereas in the latter scenario a fetching operation (taking a time proportional to the data size) is performed just before executing a task. In this context a job cannot be executed unless its data transfer has been completed. The authors assumed that the dataset sizes were in the range 500MB-2GB and the bandwidth was equal to 100MB/sec, so that data fetch times lied in between 5 and 20 seconds. Finally, the authors assumed that the jobs were perfectly scalable (*malleable jobs*) in such a way for each task $j{\in}J$, w_j and h_j can be varied, subject to the constraint:

$$w_j h_j = constant. \tag{7}$$

The total grid efficiency was expressed by

$$\rho_{GRID} = \frac{\sum_{l=1}^{m} W_l H_l - \sum_{l=1}^{m}\sum_{s=1}^{n_l+1} W_{l,s}^{(n_l)} H_{l,s}^{(n_l)}}{\min\{\sum_{l=1}^{m} W_l H_l, \sum_{l=1}^{m}\sum_{j=1}^{n_l} w_{l,j} h_{l,j}\}}, \tag{8}$$

where an index l is associated to parameters corresponding to site l ($l=1,...,m$). Computational experiments performed on the simulated grid showed that ρ_{GRID} varied between 0.69 and 0.94 (Table 2).

6. Resource Coordination among multiple administrative domains

As explained in Section 4, economy-based GRMSs provide a distributed mechanism for allocating resources to jobs at a superscheduler level while enforcing QoS constraints.

Table 2. Average grid efficiency.

Instances			ρ_{GRID}
Non malleable jobs	Equal speeds	All Data are replicated	0.85
		All Data are centralized	0.85
	Different speeds	All Data are replicated	0.85
		All Data are centralized	0.85
Malleable jobs	Equal speeds	All Data are replicated	0.88
		All Data are centralized	0.88
	Different speeds	All Data are replicated	0.89
		All Data are centralized	0.88

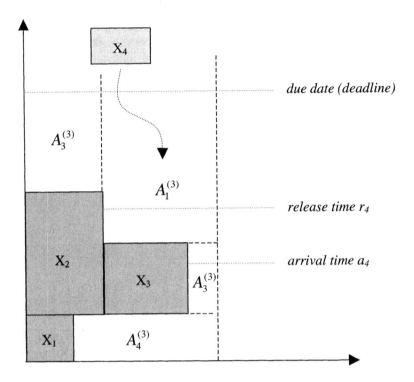

Figure 10. On-line multiprocessor task scheduling with arrival, release and due times.

Auctions are important market mechanisms, used since the earliest of times for the allocation of goods and services [50]. Auctions are used for products that have no standard value (e.g., when price depends on supply and demand at a specific moment in time). An auction consists of four parts: players, objects, payoff functions and strategies. Players are (potential) buyers and sellers each with his/her/its utility function. An auction may involve a single or large quantity of indivisible or divisible objects whose true value may or may not be known to the bidder. In addition, an object's value may vary among bidders. The payoff function may include an award mechanism, a reservation price, as well as a participation, preparation and information cost. A rational player chooses strategies that maximize his/her/its expected gain.

The basic type auction is the *bid auction*, where buyers submit bids and sellers may accept bids but cannot make offers. In an *offer auction* the roles of buyers and sellers are reversed. As a general rule, *one-side auctions* tend to favour the silent side, e.g. sellers in a bid auction and buyers in an offer auction.

From an economic perspective, a key feature of auctions is the presence of asymmetric information. In other words, each player has some private information that are not shared with other players.

Four basic types of bid auctions are widely used and analyzed: the *ascending-bid* auction (also called the *open* or oral or *English* auction), the *descending-bid* auction (also called the *Dutch* auction), the *first-price sealed-bid* auction, and the *second-price sealed-bid* auction (also called the Vickrey auction). For the sake of simplicity we describe these auctions in the case of a single item.

In the *English auction*, the price is successively raised until only one bidder remains, and that bidder wins the object at the final price. This auction can be run by having the sellers announce prices, or by having the bidders call out prices themselves, or by having bids submitted electronically with the best current bid posted. In the model most commonly used by auction theorists, the price rises continuously while bidders gradually quit the auction. In addition, bidders observe when their competitor quits and there is no possibility for one bidder to preempt the process by making a large jump bid. A dominant strategy is to stay in the bidding until the price reaches the player's value, that is, until the player is indifferent between winning and loosing. The winner will buy at a price equal to the value of the second-highest bidder. Antiques, artworks and houses are sold using versions of English auction.

The *Dutch action* works exactly in the opposite way: the auctioneer (i.e., the seller) starts at a very high price and then lowers the price continuously. The first bidder who accepts the current price wins the object at that price. Flowers are sold in a similar way in Netherlands, as is fish in Israel and tobacco in Canada.

In the *first-price sealed-bid* auction, each bidder independently submits a single bid, without seeing others' bid, and the object is sold to the bidder who makes the highest bid. Therefore the bidder who chooses the highest price wins. Thus this game is strategically equivalent to the Dutch auction and players' bidding functions are therefore exactly the same. Hence the Dutch auction is sometimes referred to as an open first price auction.

In the *second price sealed bid auction* [51], each bidder independently submits a single bid, without seeing others' bids, and the winner is the bidder who makes the highest bid. However, the price he pays is the second-highest bidder's bid, or "second price". Therefore in a English auction and in a second price sealed bid the winner pays the same price. This is why the English auction is also referred to as an open second price auction.

There exists a number of variations on the four standard forms presented above. First, a seller may discard all the bids whose price is less than a pre-fixed *reserve price*. Second, bidders could be allowed a limited amount of time to submit their bids. Third, an auctioneer might charge an entry fee to bidders for the right to participate. Fourth, a payment (a royalty) may be added to the overall price. Fifth, an auctioneer of the English auction may set a minimum acceptable increment to the highest existing bid.

In a grid environment, any distributed mechanism for resource coordination and scheduling must exhibit two main properties:

(i) the protocol must require minimal communication overhead;

(ii) the mechanism must not waste resources.

As far as issue (ii) is concerned, the solutions provided by the GRMS should be required

(ii.a) to maximize some social performance measure

or, at least,

(ii.a) to be Pareto optimal (i.e., no players can better off without harming other players).

Wellman et al [52] observe that straightforward distributed scheduling policies such as first-come first served, shortest job first, priority first, and combinations of thereof, do not generally possess these properties. The same authors present two auction mechanisms that compute optimal or near-optimal solutions to the single unit distributed scheduling problem in a computationally efficient manner. Other contributions related to this line of research include Attanasio et al [53] in which it is shown that there exist strong links between auction and Lagrangean-based decomposition. In addition, these authors describe and test different versions of the auction mechanism in case of independent jobs on parallel machines. A quite different approach is taken by Seredynski et al [54] that develop competitive coevolutionary genetic algorithms (loosely coupled genetic algorithms) for scheduling a parallel and distributed system.

6.1. Combinatorial auctions

Many modern auctions (including auctions arising in a grid environment) are "combinatorial" in nature, meaning that a long list of items is offered for sale and bidders are free to submit bids on packages of items from the list [55, 56]. Examples are airport time slots and delivery routes. Because of complementary (or substitutability) between different items, bidders have preferences not just for particular items but for sets (or *combinations* or *bundles*) of items. For this reason, economic efficiency is enhanced if bidders are allowed to bid on bundles of different items. Then a particular item can (and often does) add much to the price of one bundle, but little or nothing to the price of another. Combinatorial auctions are typically broken into a succession of "rounds," during each of which participants are free to bid on any unsold package, and at the end of which the auctioneer must either accept or reject each of the bids received. The process continues until a round occurs in which the auctioneer receives no acceptable bids. The first and most obvious difficulty in designing a combinatorial auction is that each bidder must submit a bid for every combination in which he/she/it is interested. In order to reduce the amount of information a bidder has to transmit to the auctioneer, most designs impose narrow restrictions on the number of bundles on which the bidder is permitted to bid. One approach is to specify a language in which the bidder's preference ordering over the subsets of items can be expressed. An alternative approach, not yet explored in depth, involves the use of "oracles" that are capable of computing the bid a given bidder would submit for any admissible package. In practice, an oracle is nothing else that the software implementation of a particular bidding strategy, which bidders could be required to submit in place of bids. With oracles in hand, the auctioneer needs only to invoke an oracle to learn what that bidder would quote for a given bundle.

After deciding on a language in which bids can be submitted, the auctioneer must still decide which bids to accept or reject (*winner determination problem*). It is possible to distinguish between one-sided auctions and multilateral ones. *One-sided auctions* correspond to trading situations in which there is (a) one seller and multiple buyers (the one-to-many case), or (b) many sellers and one buyer (the many-to-one case). Multilateral auctions, often designated by the name *exchanges*, involve many sellers and many buyers (the many-to-many case). In an exchange a player can be only a seller, only a buyer or both. In order to illustrate a sample optimization problem to be solved in a combinatorial auction, we now focus on the one-to-many auction and suppose that items are indivisible. In this configuration one seller has a set W of m indivisible items to sell to n potential buyers. Let us suppose first that items are available in single units. A bid made by buyer j, $1 \leq j \leq n$ is defined as a pair $(S, p_{j,S})$ where $S \subseteq W$ and $p_{j,S}$ is the amount of money buyer j is ready to pay to obtain bundle S. Define $x_{j,S}=1$ if S is allocated to buyer j, and 0 otherwise. The winner determination problem can be formulated as follows:

$$\text{Maximize} \quad \sum_{1 \leq j \leq n} \sum_{S \subseteq W} p_{j,S} x_{j,S} \tag{9}$$

s.t.

$$\sum_{1 \leq j \leq n} \sum_{S \subseteq W} {}_{i,S} x_{j,S} \leq 1 \qquad\qquad i \in W \tag{10}$$

$$\sum_{S \subseteq W} x_{j,S} \leq 1 \quad 1 \leq j \leq n \tag{11}$$

$$x_{j,S} \in \{0,1\} \quad S \subseteq W, 1 \leq j \leq n \tag{12}$$

where ${}_{i,S} =1$ if $i \in S$ and 0 otherwise. Constraints (10) establish that no single item is allocated to more than one buyer, while constraints (11) ensure that no buyer obtains more than one bundle. The objective (9) is to maximize the revenue of the seller given the bids made by buyers. This problem is an instance of the *Set Packing Problem* (SPP), a well-known combinatorial optimization problem [57]. The SPP is NP-hard and hence there are strong reasons for believing that no polynomial time algorithm exists for such a problem.

7. A blueprint for grid resource management

As pointed out in previous Sections, the literature on grid resource management is still in its infancy. As a result there are several research lines that deserve to be followed. In the remainder of this paper we report and discuss a list of the most remarkable issues.

Local scheduling. The research activity should be focused on devising enhanced semi on-line heuristics for the multiprocessor task scheduling problem ([41], [42], [49]). Unlike traditional sequential and parallel computing environments (where only "soft" QoS is guaranteed, and scheduling must be performed very quickly), in a grid environment it is worth spending a greater effort in order to obtain better schedules (i.e. schedule with a better trade-off between economic and QoS objectives). In order to improve the algorithms proposed in [42] and [49], our basic idea is to allow a modification of the current schedule any time a new user request arrives. In order to implement this strategy, new tailored metaheuristics [58] should be devised in order to provide much better solutions in a short amount of time. The so called metaheuristic algorithms can play a very important role in solving hard combinatorial problems. They include multistart methods, genetic algorithms, simulated annealing, tabu search, variable neighborhood descent, variable neighborhood search, and grasp. It is worth noting that, in order to provide good results, metaheuristics need to be tailored to handle the problem at hand.

Secondly, the research activity should be based on a number of meaningful generalizations of the on-line problems tackled in [42] and [49]. The main features of these problems are listed below:

- precedence constrained tasks;
- variable profile tasks (see Section 5.3);
- different processor classes (e.g., processors with/without vector facilities, etc);
- data transfer constraints;
- maximization of the overall net revenue (job price minus resource value).

Thirdly, the high degree of dynamism of computational grids should be taken into account explicitly in the resource management system. This requires that variations of resource availability (e.g., processor speed and network bandwidth) and service requests (e.g., job arrival times) are suitably characterized. Then such (probabilistic) characterizations need to be taken into account in computationally efficient rescheduling algorithms.

External scheduling. As explained in the previous sections, economy-based GRMSs provide a distributed mechanism for allocating resources to jobs at a superscheduler level while enforcing QoS constraints. Because of the peculiar nature of grid resources and services, combinatorial auctions are the most suitable mechanism. With this regard, three main research issues deserve attention. Firstly, a *grid bidding language* should be devised in such a way applications' agents are able to express alternative resource needs. Secondly, efficient *grid auction mechanisms* need to be developed. A mechanism is defined as the specification of all possible bidding strategies available to participants, and of an outcome function that maps these strategies to an allocation of resources (who gets what ?) and corresponding payments that participants need to make or receive. Finally, efficient heuristics should be devised for the winner determination problems associated to the selected auction mechanisms.

8. Acknowledgments

This research was partially supported by the Center of Excellence on High-Performance Computing, University of Calabria, Italy. This support is gratefully acknowledged.

References

1. I. Foster and C. Kesselman (editors), The Grid: Blueprint for a Future Computing Infrastructure, Morgan Kaufmann Publishers, San Francisco, USA, 1999.
2. M. Chetty and R. Buyya. Weaving computational Grids: How analogous are they with electrical Grids? Journal of Computing in Science and Engineering, 4, 61-71, 2001.

3. K. Krauter, R. Buyya and M. Maheswaran. A taxonomy and survey of grid resource management systems for distributed computing, Software - Practice & Experience, 32, 135-164, 2002.

4. I. Foster and C. Kesselman. Globus: A Metacomputing Infrastructure Toolkit. International Journal of Supercomputer Applications, 11, 115-128, 1997.

5. S. Chapin, J. Karpovich and A. Grimshaw. The Legion Resource Management System, Proceedings of the 5th Workshop on Job Scheduling Strategies for Parallel Processing, Birmingham, UK, 1999.

6. F. Berman and R. Wolski. The AppLeS Project: A Status Report, Proceedings of the 8th NEC Research Symposium, Berlin, Germany, 1997.

7. D. Thain, T. Tannenbaum and M. Livny. Distributed computing in practice: the Condor experience. Concurrency and Computation: Practice and Experience, 17, 323–356, 2005.

8. R. Buyya, D. Abramson and J. Giddy. Nimrod/G: An Architecture for a Resource Management and Scheduling System in a Global Computational Grid, International Conference on High Performance Computing in Asia-Pacific Region (HPC Asia 2000), Beijing, China. IEEE Computer Society Press, USA, 2000.

9. B. Bode, D. Halstead, R. Kendall, and D. Jackson. PBS: The portable batch scheduler and the maui scheduler on linux clusters. Proceedings of the 4th Linux Showcase and Conference, Atlanta, GA, USENIX Press, Berkley, CA, 2000.

10. GRACE (Grid Architecture for Computational Economy) project, http://www.gridbus.org/.

11. R. Buyya. Economic-based Distributed Resource Management and Scheduling for Grid Computing, Ph.D. Thesis, Monash University, Melbourne, Australia, 2002.

12. T. Sandholm. Distributed Rational Decision Making. In: G. Weiss (Editor), Multiagent Systems, The MIT Press, Cambridge, MS, 201-258, 1999.

13. Korpela, E., Werthimer, D., Anderson, D., Cobb and J., Lebofsky. Seti@home - massively distributed computing for SETI. Computing in Science & Engineering, 3, 78-83, 2001 (http://setiathome.ssl.berkeley.edu).

14. Weth, C., Kraus, U., Freuer, J., Ruder, M., Dannecker, R., Schneider, R., Konold, M. Ruder. XPulsar@home - Schools help Scientists. Proceedings of CCGrid, Brisbane, Australia, 588–594, 2001

15. The Intel(r) Philanthropic Peer-to-Peer Program. (http://www.intel.com/cure).

16. The Olson Laboratory FightAIDS@Home project. (http://www.fightaidsathome.org/discovery.asp).

17. The RSA Factoring By Web project (http://www.npac.syr.edu/factoring).

18. PACI and DTF Resource Allocations Policies, V1.0.a, Modified 09 March 2004, available at http://www.PACI.org/.

19. http://www.PACI.org/HardwareList.html

20. D. C. Montgomery, L. A. Johnson and J. S. Gradiner. Forecasting and Time Series Analysis, McGraw Hill, New York, MA, 1990.

21. S. Vazhkudai and J. M. Schopf. "Using regression techniques to predict large data transfers", The International Journal of High Performance Computing Applications 17, 24-31, 2003.

22. R. Wolski, N. T. Spring and Hayes, J. The network weather service: A distributed resource performance forecasting service for metacomputing, Journal of Future Generation Computing Systems, 15, 757-768, 1999.

23. Network Weather Service homepage, http://nws.cs.ucsb.edu/

24. S. Akioka and Y. Muraoka. The Markov Model Based Algorithm to Predict Networking Load on the Computational Grid, Journal of Mathematical Modelling and Algorithms 2: 251–261, 2003.
25. C. Junwei, S. Jarvis, D. Spooner, J. Turner, D. Kerbyson and G. Nudd. Performance prediction technology for agent-based resource management in grid environments. In 16th International Parallel and Distributed Processing Symposium(IPDPS '02 (IPPS and SPDP)), Tokyo, April 2002. IEEE. Available from http://www.dcs.warwick.ac.uk/~hpsg/html/downloads/public/docs/CaoJ.PPTARM.pdf.
26. G. Shao, F. Breman and R. Wolski. Using effective network views to promote distributed application performance. In: Proocedings of the 1999 International Conference on Parallel and Distributed Processing Techniques and Applications, New York, MA, 1999.
27. B. Lowekamp, N. Miller, D. Sutherland, T. Gross, P. Steenkiste and J. Subhlok. A resource query interface for network-aware applications. In: Proceedings of the 7th IEEE Symposium on High Performance Distributed Computing, Amsterdam, The Netherland, 1998.
28. M. Pinedo. Scheduling: Theory, Algorithms and Systems. Prentice Hall. Englewood Cliffs, NJ, 1995.
29. T. Robertazzi. "Ten Reasons to Use Divisible Load Theory", Computer, 36, 42-51, 2003.
30. O. Beaumont, A. Legrand, Y. Robert. Scheduling divisible workloads on heterogeneous platforms, Parallel Computing, 29, 1121-1152, 2003.
31. V. Bharadwaj, D. Ghose, V. Mani and T. Robertazzi. Scheduling Divisible Loads in Parallel and Distributed Systems, IEEE Computer Society Press, Los Alamitos CA, 1996.
32. V. Bharadwaj, D. Ghose, V. and Mani. Multi-installment Load Distribution in Tree Networks with Delays", IEEE Transactions on Aerospace & Electronic Systems, 31, 555-567, 1995.
33. Y. Yang. and H. Casanova. UMR: A Multi-Round Algorithm for Scheduling Divisible Workloads, Proceedings of the International Parallel and Distributed Processing Symposium (IPDPS'03), Nice, France, 2003.
34. O. H. Ibarra and C. E. Kim. Heuristic algorithms for scheduling independent tasks on nonidentical processors. Journal of the ACM, 24, 280-289, 1977.
35. T. Hagerup. Allocating Independent Tasks to Parallel Processors: An Experimental Study. Journal of Parallel and Distributed Computing, 47, 185-197, 1997.
36. P. Chrétienne. Tree Scheduling with Communication Delays. Discrete Applied Mathematics 49, 129-141, 1994.
37. J. Y. Colin and P. Chrétienne. C.P.M. Scheduling with Small Communication Delays and Task Duplication. Operations Research 39, 680-684, 1991.
38. V. J. Rayward-Smith. U.E.T. Scheduling with Interprocessor Communication Delays. Discrete Applied Mathematics 18, 55-71, 1987.
39. H. Casanova, A. Legrand, D. Zagorodnov and F. Berman. Heuristics for Scheduling Sweep Applications in Grid Environments, Proceedings of the 9th Heterogeneous Computing, Technical Report CS1999-0632, University of California, San Diego, CA, 1999.
40. J. Zahorjan, E. D. Lazowska and D. L. Eager. The effect of scheduling discipline on spin overhead in shared memory parallel systems, IEEE Transaction on Parallel and Distributed Systems 2, 180-198, 1991.
41. M. Drozdowski. Scheduling multiprocessor tasks. An overview, European Journal of Operations Research 94, 215-230, 1996.
42. M. Caramia, S. Giordani, A. Iovanella. Grid scheduling by on-line rectangle packing, Networks 44, 106-119, 2004.

43. A. Borodin and R. El-Yaniv. Online computation and competitive analysis, Cambridge University Press, Cambridge, UK, 1998.

44. D. Shmoys, J. Wien and D.P. Williamson. Scheduling parallel machines on-line, SIAM Journal of Computing 24, 1313-1331, 1995.

45. E. Hopper and B.C.H. Turton. An empirical investigation of meta-heuristic and heuristic algorithms for a 2D packing problem. European Journal of Operational Research 128, 34-57, 2001.

46. J. Leung, T. Tam, C.S. Wong, G. Young and F. Chin. Packing squares into square, Journal of Parallel and Distributed Computing 10, 271-275, 2001.

47. A. Lodi, S. Martello and M. Monaci, Two-dimensional packing problems: A survey, European Journal of Operational Research 141, 241-252, 2002.

48. Y. L. Wu, W. Huang, S. C. Lau, C. K. Wong and G. H. Young. An effective quasi-human based heuristic for solving the rectangle packing problem. European Journal of Operational Research 141, 341-358, 2002.

49. P. Festa, G. Ghiani, L. Grandinetti and E. Guerriero. Semi on-line multiprocessor task scheduling, Technical Report, Center of Excellence for High Performance Computing, Università della Calabria, 2005.

50. V. Krishna. Auction Theory, Academic Press, New York, MA, 2002.

51. W. Vickrey, Counter-speculation, auctions, and competitive sealed tenders, Journal of Finance, 16/1, 9-37, 1961.

52. M. P. Wellman, W. E. Walsh, P. R. Wurman and J. K. MacKieMason. Auction Protocols for Decentralized Scheduling, Games and Economic Behaviour 35, 271-303, 2001.

53. A. Attanasio, G. Ghiani, L. Grandinetti, F. Guerriero. "Auction Algorithms for Decentralized Parallel Machine Scheduling", forthcoming in Parallel Computing, 2005.

54. F. Seredynski. Competitive Coevolutionary Multi-Agent Systems: The Application to Mapping and Scheduling Problems, Journal of Parallel and Distributed Computing, 47, 39-57, 1997.

55. S. de Vries and R. Vohray. Combinatorial Auctions: A Survey, INFORMS Journal on Computing 15, 284-309, 2003.

56. J. Abrache, T. Crainic, M. Gendreau. Design issues for combinatorial auctions, 4OR 2, 1-34, 2004.

57. G. Nehmauser and L. Wolsey. Integer and combinatorial optimization, Wiley, New York, MA, 1972.

58. F. W. Glover, G. A. Kochenberger (Eds). Handbook of Metaheuristics (International Series in Operations Research & Management Science), Springer, Berlin, Germany, 2003.

Grid Computing: The New Frontier of High Performance Computing
Lucio Grandinetti (Editor)
© 2005 Elsevier B.V. All rights reserved.

Peer-to-Peer Protocols and Grid Services for Resource Discovery on Grids

Domenico Talia [a] and Paolo Trunfio [a]

[a]DEIS, University of Calabria
Via P. Bucci 41c, 87036 Rende, Italy

Resource discovery is a key issue in Grid environments, since applications are usually constructed by composing hardware and software resources that need to be found and selected. Classical approaches to Grid resource discovery, based on centralized or hierarchical approaches, do not guarantee scalability in large-scale, dynamic Grid environments. On the other hand, the Peer-to-Peer (P2P) paradigm is emerging as a convenient model to achieve scalability in distributed systems and applications. This chapter describes a protocol and an architecture that adopt a pure-decentralized P2P approach to support resource discovery in OGSA-compliant Grids. In particular, the chapter describes a modified Gnutella protocol, named *Gridnut*, which uses appropriate message buffering and merging techniques to make Grid Services effective as a way to exchange discovery messages in a P2P fashion. We present the design of Gridnut, and compare Gnutella and Gridnut performances under different network and load conditions. The chapter presents also an architecture for resource discovery that adopts the Gridnut approach to extend the model of the Globus Toolkit 3 information service.

1. INTRODUCTION

The Grid computing paradigm is today broadly applied to many scientific and engineering application fields, and is attracting a growing interest from business and industry. At the same time, *Peer-to-Peer* (*P2P*) computing is emerging as an important paradigm for developing distributed systems and applications.

Many aspects of today's Grids are based on centralized or hierarchical services. However, as Grids used for complex applications increase their sizes, it is necessary decentralize their functionalities to avoid bottlenecks and ensure scalability. As argued in [1], [2] and in other work, a way to improve scalability in large-scale Grids is to adopt P2P models and techniques to implement non-hierarchical decentralized services.

Within the Grid community, the *Open Grid Services Architecture* (*OGSA*) model is being widely adopted to achieve integration and interoperability among the increasing number of Grid applications. OGSA defines *Grid Services* as an extension of Web Services [3] to take advantage of important Web Services properties, such as service description and discovery, automatic generation of client and service code, compatibility with emerging standards and tools, and broad commercial support [4].

The OGSA model does not only support client-server applications, but it provides an opportunity to integrate P2P models in Grid environments since it offers an open cooperation model that allows Grid entities to be composed in a decentralized way. A core Grid functionality that could be effectively redesigned using the P2P paradigm is *resource discovery*. Resource discovery is a key issue in Grid environments, since applications are usually constructed by composing hardware and software resources that need to be searched, discovered and selected.

Although Grid Services are appropriate for implementing loosely coupled P2P applications, they appear to be inefficient to support an intensive exchange of messages among tightly-coupled peers. In fact, Grid Services operations, as other RPC-like mechanisms, are subject to an invocation overhead that can be significant in terms of memory consumption, processing time, and bandwidth requirements. The number of Grid Service operations that a peer can efficiently manage in a given time interval depends strongly on that overhead.

For this reason, pure decentralized P2P protocols based on a pervasive exchange of messages, such as Gnutella [5], are inappropriate on large OGSA Grids where a high number of communications take place among hosts. On the other hand, this class of protocols offer useful properties in dealing with the high heterogeneity and dynamicity of Grid resources.

To take advantage of the pure decentralized approach and, at the same time, controlling the bandwidth consumption rate, we proposed a modified Gnutella protocol, named *Gridnut* [6], which uses appropriate message buffering and merging techniques that make Grid Services effective as a way for exchanging discovery messages among Grid nodes in a P2P fashion. Gnutella defines both a protocol to discover hosts on the network, based on the *Ping/Pong* mechanism, and a protocol for searching the distributed network, based on the *Query/QueryHit* mechanism. Here we discuss only the Gridnut discovery protocol, even if we are also designing the Gridnut search protocol.

We simulated the protocol by implementing a Java prototype of a Gridnut peer, which can also work as a standard Gnutella peer for comparison purposes. To verify how significantly Gridnut reduces the workload of each peer, we evaluated the Gridnut and Gnutella behaviors in different network topologies and load conditions.

The Gridnut approach can be an effective way to discover active nodes and support resource discovery in OGSA Grids. We designed an architecture for resource discovery that adopts such an approach to extend the model of the Globus Toolkit 3 (GT3) information service.

The remainder of the chapter is organized as follows. Section 2 presents the main features of Grid Services and discusses their performances in supporting the exchange of messages among tightly-coupled applications. Section 3 discusses the use of P2P models and techniques for Grid resource discovery. Section 4 presents the design of the Gridnut protocol focusing on message routing and buffering rules. Section 5 compares the performance of Gridnut and Gnutella protocols under different network and load conditions. Section 6 discusses a P2P architecture for resource discovery that extends the model of the GT3 information service. Finally, Section 7 concludes the chapter.

2. GRID SERVICES FEATURES AND PERFORMANCES

The goal of OGSA is to provide a well-defined set of basic interfaces for the development of interoperable Grid systems and applications. The attribute "open" is used to communicate architecture extensibility, vendor neutrality, and commitment to a community standardization process [4].

OGSA adopts Web Services as basic technology. Web Services are an important paradigm focusing on simple, Internet-based standards. such as the *Simple Object Access Protocol (SOAP)* [7] and the *Web Services Description Language (WSDL)* [8], to address heterogeneous distributed computing. Web services defines techniques for describing software components to be accessed, methods for accessing these components, and discovery mechanisms that enable the identification of relevant service providers.

In OGSA every resource (e.g., computer, storage, program) is represented by a service, i.e., a network enabled entity that provides some capability through the exchange of messages. More specifically, OGSA represents everything as a *Grid Service*: a Web Service that conforms to a set of conventions and supports standard interfaces. This service-oriented view addresses the need for standard interface definition mechanisms, local and remote transparency, adaptation to local OS services, and uniform service semantics [9].

OGSA defines standard mechanisms for creating, naming, and discovering transient Grid Service instances; provides location transparency and multiple protocol bindings for service instances; and supports integration with underlying native platform facilities. OGSA also defines mechanisms required for creating and composing sophisticated distributed systems, including lifetime management, change management, and notification.

A first specification of the concepts and mechanisms defined in the OGSA is provided by the *Open Grid Services Infrastructure (OGSI)* [10], of which the open source *Globus Toolkit 3* [11] is the reference implementation.

The research and industry communities, under the guidance of the *Global Grid Forum (GGF)* [12], are contributing both to the implementation of OGSA-compliant services, and to evolve OGSA toward new standards and mechanisms. As a result of this process, the *WS-Resource Framework (WSRF)* was recently proposed as a refactoring and evolution of OGSI aimed at exploiting new Web Services standards, and at evolving OGSI based on early implementation and application experiences [13].

WSRF provides the means to express state as stateful resources and codifies the relationship between Web Services and stateful resources in terms of the *implied resource pattern*, which is a set of conventions on Web Services technologies, in particular XML, WSDL, and *WS-Addressing* [14]. A stateful resource that participates in the implied resource pattern is termed a *WS-Resource*. The framework describes the WS-Resource definition and association with the description of a Web Service interface, and describes how to make the properties of a WS-Resource accessible through a Web Service interface. Despite OGSI and WSRF model stateful resources differently - as a Grid Service and a WS-Resource, respectively - both provide essentially equivalent functionalities. Both Grid Services and WS-Resources, in fact, can be created, addressed, and destroyed, and in essentially the same ways [15].

As mentioned before. Grid Services operations are subject to an invocation overhead that can be significant both in terms of memory/processing consumption and bandwidth requirements. The goal of this section is to evaluate, in particular, the performances of Grid Services in supporting the exchange of messages among tightly-coupled applications. To this end we developed a Grid Service S and a client application C:

- S exports one operation, called `deliver`, which receives in input an *array of messages* to be delivered to it.

- C invokes the `deliver` operation to deliver one or more messages to S.

The client C was executed on a node N_c, while the service S was executed on a node N_s using the Globus Toolkit 3. By using a different number of input messages we measured both the generated *network traffic* and the *execution time* needed to complete a `deliver` operation. In particular, tests have been performed with a number of messages per operation ranging from 1 to 1024, where each message has a length of 100 bytes. Each single test was run 100 times. The traffic and time values reported in each row of Table 1 and Table 2 are computed as an average of the 100 values measured in the tests.

Table 1
Network traffic generated by a `deliver` operation for different number of messages.

Number of messages per deliver operation	Mean traffic per deliver operation (byte)	Mean traffic per message (byte)
1	2613	2613.0
2	2740	1370.0
4	2995	748.75
8	3635	454.38
16	4652	290.75
32	6948	217.13
64	11408	178.25
128	20330	158.83
256	37840	147.81
512	72134	140.89
1024	140988	137.68

Table 1 reports the network traffic measured between N_c and N_s when the `deliver` operation of S is invoked by C. The second column reports the mean traffic per operation, whereas the third column reports the mean traffic per message delivered. The values in the third column are obtained by dividing the mean traffic per operation by the number of messages per operation.

The traffic per operation is the sum of a fixed part (of about 2500 bytes) and a variable part that depends from the number of messages. For instance, the delivery of a single message (100 bytes) generates 2613 bytes of traffic, while the delivery of two messages (2×100 bytes) requires 2740 bytes. The fixed overhead is mainly due to the Grid

Service invocation mechanism, which uses SOAP messages for requests to the server and responses to the client. Obviously, by increasing the number of messages per operation the traffic per message decreases, since a single SOAP envelope is used to transport more application-level messages. In particular, the mean traffic per message passes from 2613 bytes for one message to 137.68 bytes for 1024 messages, as shown in Table 1.

Table 2
Execution time of a `deliver` operation for different number of messages.

Number of messages per deliver oper.	LAN		WAN	
	Mean time per deliver oper. (msec)	Mean time per message (msec)	Mean time per deliver oper. (msec)	Mean time per message (msec)
1	5.60	5.60	62.68	62.68
2	5.71	2.86	65.34	32.67
4	5.88	1.47	67.44	16.86
8	6.25	0.781	70.12	8.765
16	7.12	0.445	75.63	4.727
32	8.33	0.260	90.05	2.814
64	11.25	0.176	113.21	1.769
128	16.71	0.131	144.93	1.132
256	28.90	0.113	197.14	0.770
512	55.70	0.109	291.07	0.568
1024	107.38	0.105	558.86	0.546

Table 2 reports the time needed to complete a `deliver` operation, measured in two configurations:

- *LAN*: N_c and N_s are connected by a 100 Mbps direct link, with an average RTT (Round Trip Time) equal to 1.41 msec.

- *WAN*: N_c and N_s are connected by a WAN network, with a number of hops equal to 10, bottleneck bandwidth equal to 1.8 Mbps, and an average RTT equal to 28.3 msec.

For each configuration, execution times are reported in Table 2 both per operation and per message delivered.

In the LAN configuration the execution time of a `deliver` operation ranges from 5.60 msec for one message to 107.38 msec for an array of 1024 messages, whereas in the WAN configuration the execution time passes from 62.68 msec for one message to 558.86 msec for 1024 messages. As before, the execution time is the sum of a fixed part - that includes the network latency - and a variable part. As the number of messages per operation increases, the mean time per message decreases, ranging from 5.60 msec for one message to 0.105 msec for 1024 messages in the LAN configuration. This is even more evident in the WAN configuration, in which the mean execution time ranges from 62.68 msec for one message to 0.546 msec for 1024 messages.

To better evaluate the performances of Grid Services in supporting the delivery of messages, we can compare two opposite cases: i) n deliver operations are executed to deliver n messages (*one message per operation*); ii) one deliver operation is executed to deliver n messages (*n messages per operation*).

In the following, the term *serial time* indicates the sum of the times needed to execute n operations in sequence, and *parallel time* indicates the time needed to complete n operations executed concurrently. All the execution times are referred to the LAN configuration.

For instance, considering $n = 16$ messages to be delivered, we have the following performances:

- *one message per operation*: the overall traffic is $2613 \times 16 = 41808$ bytes; the serial time is $5.60 \times 16 = 89.6$ msec; the parallel time is 65.43 msec.

- *n messages per operation*: the overall network traffic is 4652 bytes (37156 bytes less than the first case, saving the 88.9% of traffic); the overall execution time is 7.12 msec (58.31 msec less than the parallel time of the first case, saving the 89.1% of time).

Moreover, considering $n = 64$ we have:

- *one message per operation*: the overall traffic is $2613 \times 64 = 167232$ bytes; the serial time is $5.60 \times 64 = 358.4$ msec; the parallel time is 186.6 msec.

- *n messages per operation*: the overall network traffic is 11408 bytes (saving the 93.2% of traffic); the overall execution time is 11.25 msec (saving the 94.0% of time).

Tests results show that by decreasing the number of processed Grid Service operations (for a given number of messages to be delivered), both the overall traffic generated and the delivery time are substantially reduced. The Gridnut protocol, described in Section 4, makes use of message buffering and merging techniques that produce significant performance improvements, both in terms of number and distribution of Grid Service operations processed, as discussed in Section 5.

3. P2P AND GRID RESOURCE DISCOVERY

While P2P and Grids share the same focus on harnessing resources across multiple administrative domains, they differ in many respects: Grids address support for a variety of applications and therefore focus on providing infrastructure with quality-of-service guarantees to moderate-sized, homogeneous, and partially trusted communities. In contrast, P2P systems concentrate on providing support for intermittent participation in vertically integrated applications for significantly larger communities of untrusted, anonymous individuals.

However, the convergence of the two systems is increasingly visible: the two research communities started to acknowledge each other by forming multiple research groups that study the potential lessons that can be exchanged; P2P research focuses more and more on providing infrastructure and diversifying the set of applications; Grid research is starting to pay particular attention to increasing scalability.

In [1] Foster and Iamnitchi compare and contrast Grid and P2P computing, reviewing their target communities, resources, scale, applications, and technologies. On the basis of this review, they argue that both Grids and P2P networks are concerned, in essence, with the same general problem: the organization of resource sharing within virtual communities. The complementary nature of the strengths and weaknesses of Grids and P2P suggests that an integration between the two computing models will tend to accelerate progress in both disciplines.

As pointed out before, the OGSA model provides an opportunity to integrate P2P models in Grid environments since it offers an open cooperation model that allows Grid entities to be composed in a decentralized way. As a significant example, Fox and colleagues explored the concept of a *Peer-to-Peer Grid* designed around the integration of Peer-to-Peer and OGSA models [16]. A Peer-to-Peer Grid is built in a *service* model, where a *service* is a Web Service that accepts one or more inputs and gives one or more results. These inputs and results are the messages that characterize the system. All the entities in the Grid (i.e., users, computers, resources, and instruments) are linked by messages, whose communication forms a distributed system integrating the component parts.

In a Peer-to-Peer Grid, access to services can be mediated by "servers in the core," or by direct Peer-to-Peer interactions between machines "on the edge." The server approach best scales within pre-existing hierarchical organizations, but P2P approaches best support local dynamic interactions. The Peer-to-Peer Grid architecture is a mix of structured (Grid-like) and unstructured dynamic (P2P-like) services, with peer groups managed locally and arranged into a global system supported by core servers. A key component of a Peer-to-Peer Grid is the messaging subsystem, that manages the communication among resources, Web Services, and clients to achieve the highest possible system performance and reliability.

In [2] we outlined some areas where a P2P approach can produce significant benefits in Grid systems. These include security, connectivity, fault tolerance, access services, resource discovery and presence management. In particular, the P2P model is proposed as a practical approach to implement resource discovery on the Grid.

Grid users and applications need to get information about dynamic resources status such as current CPU load, available disk space, free memory, job queue length, network bandwidth and load, and other similar information. All this information is necessary to efficiently configure and run applications on Grids. As the Grid size increases, hierarchical approaches to Grid information systems, do not guarantee scalability and fault tolerance. As mentioned before, a practical approach towards scalable solutions is offered by P2P models. Some P2P systems for resource discovery in distributed systems and Grid environments have been proposed (see for instance [17] [18] [19] [20]).

P2P resource sharing systems can be classified in two categories: *unstructured networks*, in which the placement of data is completely unrelated to the network topology, and *structured networks*, in which the topology is tightly controlled and pointers to data items are placed at precisely specified locations. Structured P2P networks generally make use of distributed hash tables (DHTs) to perform mappings from keys to locations in an entirely distributed manner. Examples of unstructured networks are Gnutella and Morpheus [21]; examples of structured networks include Chord [22], CAN [23] and Tapestry [24].

Structured P2P networks are designed to locate objects with complete identifiers. Some recent structured systems provide support also for keyword search, multi-attribute, and range queries [25] [20] [26]. However, structured approaches are not well suited to handle decentralized contents about dynamic Grid resources whose values change continuously over the time and that need to be computed when requested. For this reason, we adopt an unstructured P2P approach, which allow for handling highly dynamic information, at the cost of a high bandwidth requirement for searching the network. To control the bandwidth consumption we use appropriate buffering and merging techniques, as described in the next section.

4. PROTOCOL DESIGN

The two basic principles of the Gridnut protocol that make it different from Gnutella are

1. *Message buffering*: to reduce communication overhead, messages to be delivered to the same peer are buffered and sent in a single packet at regular time intervals.

2. *Collective Pong*: when a peer B must respond to a Ping message received from A, it waits to receive all the Pong messages from its neighbors, then merge them with its Pong response and send back the Pong collection as a single message to A.

Each peer in the network executes a Grid Service, called *Peer Service*, through which remote peers can connect and deliver messages to it.

The Peer Service is a persistent Grid Service, activated at the peer's startup and terminated when the peer leaves the network. Each Peer Service is assigned a globally unique name, the *Grid Service Handle* (*GSH*), that distinguishes a specific Grid Service instance from all other Grid Service instances. This handle is used within a Gridnut network to uniquely identify both the Peer Service and the peer to which it is associated. For instance, a valid handle could be:

```
http://node1.deis.unical.it:8080/ogsa/services/p2p/PeerService
```

The Peer Service supports four operations:

- connect: used by a remote peer to connect this peer. The operation receives the *handle* of the requesting peer and returns a *reject* response if the connection is not accepted (for instance, because the maximum number of connections has been reached).

- disconnect: used by a remote peer to disconnect this peer. The operation receives the *handle* of the requesting peer.

- `deliver`: used by a connected peer to deliver messages to this peer. The operation receives the *handle* of the requesting peer and an *array of messages* to be delivered to this peer.

- `query`: invoked by a client application to submit a query to this peer. Query responses are returned to the client through a notification mechanism.

4.1. Messages

A peer connects itself to the Gridnut network by establishing a connection with one or more peers currently in the network (a discussion of the connection and disconnection phases is given in Section 6). Once a peer joined successfully the Gridnut network, it communicates with other peers by sending and receiving Ping and Pong messages:

- A Ping is used to discover available nodes on the Grid; a peer receiving a Ping message is expected to respond with a Pong message.

- A Pong is a response to a Ping; it includes the URL of a set of reachable Peer Services, each one representing an available peer (or Grid node).

The logical structure of Ping and Pong messages is shown in Figure 1.

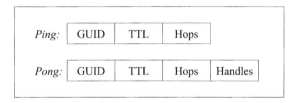

Figure 1. Structure of Gridnut messages.

The meaning of the fields in Figure 1 is the following:

- *GUID* (*Global Unique Identifier*): a string identifying the message on the network.

- *TTL* (*Time To Live*): the number of times the message will be forwarded by peers before it is removed from the network.

- *Hops*: the number of times the message has been forwarded by peers.

- *Handles*: an array of zero, one or more reachable Peer Services' URLs.

For the purposes of this chapter, Pong messages do not include further information because here we use the discovery protocol to locate all the active peers (i.e., all the active nodes on the Grid). The search protocol we are designing (not discussed in the chapter) will be used for host characterization, discovery of needed services, etc.

4.2. Data structures

Each peer uses a set of logical data structures to perform its functions.

A *connection list* (*CL*) is used to maintain a reference to all directly connected Peer Services. Entries into the CL are updated by the `connect` and `disconnect` operations.

A *routing table* (*RT*) is used to properly route messages through the network. The RT contains a set of records having a structure [*GUID, Handle*], used to route messages with a given *GUID* to a Peer Service with a given *Handle*.

The results of the discovery tasks are stored into a *result set* (*RS*).

Finally, each peer uses a set of internal *transmission buffers*, in which messages are stored and processed before to deliver them to the proper Peer Service. In particular, a peer S_0 uses two separated transmission buffers for each of its neighbors:

- A *pong buffer* (B_p), in which Pong messages with the same GUID are merged before the delivery. The notation $B_p(S_k)$ indicates the pong buffer in which S_0 inserts Pong messages directed to a Peer Service S_k.

- A *fast buffer* (B_f), used for Ping and Pong messages that are to be fast delivered to a given Peer Service. We use the notation $B_f(S_k)$ to indicate the fast buffer in which S_0 inserts messages directed to a Peer Service S_k.

A thread T_k is associated to each couple of buffers $B_p(S_k)$ and $B_f(S_k)$. T_k periodically delivers the buffered messages to S_k, on the basis of the rules described below.

4.3. Routing rules

In Gridnut, like in Gnutella, Ping messages are forwarded to all directly connected peers, whereas Pong messages are sent along the same path that carried the incoming Ping message. The Hops value is increased each time a Ping is forwarded, and whenever a Pong is sent in response to a Ping, the Hops value is assigned to the TTL field, so that the TTL will hold the number of hops to reach the source of the Ping. Hence, the TTL will be 0 when the result reaches the source of the discovery message.

However, there are two main differences between Gnutella and Gridnut message routing and transmission modalities:

1. In Gnutella implementations, messages are sent as a byte stream over TCP sockets, whereas Gridnut messages are sent through a Grid Service invocation (by means of the `deliver` operation).

2. In standard Gnutella implementations (based on version 0.4 of the protocol [5]), each message is forwarded whenever it is received, whereas Gridnut messages, as mentioned before, are buffered and merged to reduce the number of Grid Service invocations and routing operations executed by each peer.

Consider a peer S_0 having a set of neighbors $S_1...S_n$. When a neighbor delivers an array of messages to S_0, each message is processed separately by S_0 as specified below. Let us suppose that S_0 received from S_k the message *Ping*[GUID=g, TTL=t, Hops=h] (this notation means that g, t, and h are the actual values of GUID, TTL and Hops of this Ping); S_0 performs the following operations:

```
t = t - 1; h = h + 1;
if (RT contains a record with GUID=g)
    insert a Pong [GUID=g, TTL=h, Hops=0, Handles=Ø] into B_f(S_k);
else if (t == 0)
    insert a Pong [GUID=g, TTL=h, Hops=0, Handles=S_0] into B_f(S_k);
else {
    insert a record [GUID=g, Handle=S_k] into RT;
    insert a Pong[GUID=g, TTL=h, Hops=0, Handles=S_0] into B_p(S_k);
    for (i:1..n; i ≠ k)
        insert a Ping [GUID=g, TTL=t, Hops=h] into B_f(S_i);
}
```

First of all - as shown above - the TTL and Hops values of this message are up-dated. Then, if the message is a duplicated Ping (since the routing table already contains its GUID), a "dummy Pong" (i.e., having Handles=Ø) is fast delivered to S_k. Else, if this Ping terminated its TTL, it is not further forwarded, and a Pong response is fast delivered to S_k. In the last case, first the routing table is updated, then a Pong response is inserted into the pong buffer, and finally the Ping is forwarded to all the neighbors, except the one from which it was received.

Let us suppose that S_0 received from S_k the message $Pong$[GUID=g, TTL=t, Hops=h, Handles=H] (where H is a set of Peer Services' handles); the following operations are performed by S_0:

```
t = t - 1; h = h + 1;
if (t == 0)
    insert H into RS;
else if (RT contains a record R with GUID=g) {
    S_r = value of the Handle field of R;
    insert a Pong [GUID=g, TTL=t, Hops=h, Handles=H] into B_p(S_r);
}
```

As before, the TTL and Hops fields are updated. Then, if this Pong terminated its TTL (and so this peer is the final recipient), its handles are inserted into the result set. Else, the Pong is forwarded, through the corresponding pong buffer, to the proper peer, as specified by the routing table.

Finally, to start a new discovery task, S_0 must perform the following operations:

```
clear RS;
g = globally unique string;
t = initial TTL;
insert the record [GUID=g, Handle=S_0] into RT;
for (i:1..n)
    insert a Ping [GUID=g, TTL=t, Hops=0] into B_f(S_i);
```

As described above, the result set is reset before anything else. Then, a Ping message is created (with a new GUID and a proper TTL) and forwarded to all the neighbors through the corresponding fast buffers. The discovery task is completed when the result set contains the handles of all the reachable peers in the network.

4.4. Buffering rules

Consider again a peer S_0 connected to a set of N peers $S_1...S_n$. Within a pong buffer $B_p(S_k)$, a set of counters are used. A counter C_g counts the number of Pong messages with GUID=g till now inserted in $B_p(S_k)$.

When a Pong $P_1 = Pong[$GUID=g, TTL=t, Hops=h, Handles=$H_1]$ is inserted into $B_p(S_k)$, the following operations are performed:

```
Cg = Cg + 1;
if (Bp(Sk) contains a Pong P0 with GUID=g) {
    add H1 to the current Handles set of P0;
    if (Cg ≥ N)
        mark Pong P0 as ready;
}
else {
    insert Pong P1 into Bp(Sk);
    if (Cg ≥ N)
        mark Pong P1 as ready;
}
```

Whenever a Pong message is marked as *ready*, it can be delivered to the peer S_k. To avoid blocking situations due to missed Pong messages, a Pong could be marked as ready also if a *timeout* has been reached. In the following we do not consider failure situations, therefore no timeouts are used.

Differently from a pong buffer, messages inserted into a fast buffer $B_f(S_k)$ are immediately marked as ready to be delivered to S_k.

As mentioned before, a thread T_k is used to periodically deliver the buffered messages to S_k. In particular, the following operations are performed by T_k every time it is activated:

```
get the set of ready messages M from Bp(Sk) and Bf(Sk);
deliver M to Sk through a single deliver operation;
```

The time interval I_a between two consecutive activations of T_k is a system parameter. In the worst case, exactly a `deliver` operation can be invoked by S_0 for each of its N neighbors. Therefore, the maximum number of `deliver` operations invoked by S_0 during an interval of time I is equal to $(I \div I_a) \times N$. Obviously, increasing the value of I_a the number of `deliver` operations can be reduced, but this could produce a delay in the delivery of messages. In our prototype we use $I_a = 5$ msec.

5. PERFORMANCE EVALUATION

In this section we compare some experimental performance results of Gridnut and Gnutella protocols. To perform our experiments we developed a Java prototype of a Peer Service, which can also work as a standard Gnutella peer for comparison purposes. In our prototype the Peer Service is an object accessed through Remote Method Invocation (RMI). The goal of our tests is to verify how significantly Gridnut reduces the workload - number of Grid Service operations - of each peer. In doing this, we compared Gridnut and Gnutella by evaluating two parameters:

1. ND, the average number of `deliver` operations processed by a peer to complete a discovery task. In particular, $ND = P \div (N \times T)$, where: P is the total number of `deliver` operations processed in the network, N is the number of peers in the network, and T is the overall number of discovery tasks completed.

2. $ND(d)$, the average number of `deliver` operations processed by peers that are at distance d from the peer S_0 that started the discovery task. For instance: $ND(0)$ represents the number of `deliver` operations processed by S_0; $ND(1)$ represents the number of `deliver` operations processed by a peer distant one hop from S_0.

Both ND and $ND(d)$ have been evaluated considering seven different network topologies. We distinguish the network topologies using a couple of numbers $\{N, C\}$, where N is the number of peers in the network, and C is the number of peers directly connected to each peer (i.e., each peer has exactly C neighbors). The network topologies we experimented are characterized by $\{N, C\}$ respectively equal to $\{10,2\}$, $\{10,4\}$, $\{30,3\}$, $\{30,4\}$, $\{50,4\}$, $\{70,4\}$ and $\{90,4\}$. Notwithstanding the limited number of used peers, the number of exchanged messages among peers was extremely high and performance trends are evident.

Resulting networks were connected graphs, that is each peer can reach any other peer in the network in a number of steps lower or equal than TTL.

5.1. Number of `deliver` operations

For each network topology, we measured ND under four load conditions. We use R to indicate the number of discovery tasks that are initiated in the network at each given time interval. The following values for R have been used: 1, 3, 5 and 10. In particular,

- $R = 1$ indicates that, at each time interval, only one discovery task is initiated, therefore only messages with a given GUID are simultaneously present in the network;

- $R = 10$ indicates that, at each time interval, ten discovery tasks are initiated, therefore messages with up to ten different GUID are simultaneously present in the network.

Table 3 and Table 4 report the ND measured in Gnutella and Gridnut networks, respectively. ND values are measured for network topologies ranging from $\{10,2\}$ to $\{90,4\}$, under load conditions ranging from $R = 1$ to $R = 10$.

Table 3
ND in Gnutella networks.

	{10,2}	{10,4}	{30,3}	{30,4}	{50,4}	{70,4}	{90,4}
R=1	3.60	4.53	4.91	5.49	6.00	6.27	6.52
R=3	3.61	4.54	4.95	5.48	6.01	6.32	6.53
R=5	3.61	4.55	4.96	5.47	6.01	6.35	6.54
R=10	3.60	4.54	4.99	5.49	6.02	6.35	6.53

In Gnutella (see Table 3), ND is not influenced by the R factor, apart from little variations due to measurements errors. This is because in Gnutella no buffering strategies are adopted, and one `deliver` operation is executed to move exactly one message in the network. Obviously, the value of ND increases with the size of the network, ranging from an average value of 3.61 in a {10,2} network, to an average value of 6.53 in a {90,4} network.

Table 4
ND in Gridnut networks.

	{10,2}	{10,4}	{30,3}	{30,4}	{50,4}	{70,4}	{90,4}
R=1	2.12	5.91	3.86	5.74	5.75	5.72	5.73
R=3	1.96	4.54	3.48	4.81	4.76	4.70	4.89
R=5	1.85	3.98	3.11	4.28	4.22	4.16	4.03
R=10	1.70	2.93	2.52	3.19	3.22	3.10	2.91

In Gridnut (see Table 4), ND depends from both network topology and load condition. For a given value of R, ND mainly depends from the value of C (number of connections per peer), whereas it varies a little with the value of N (number of peers). For instance, if we consider the value of ND for $R = 1$, we see that it varies in a small range (from 5.72 to 5.91) for all the networks with $C = 4$.

If we consider networks with the same value of N, we see that ND decreases when the value of C is lower. For instance, the ND for a network {10,2} is lower than the ND for a network {10,4}, with any value of R. Moreover, because a single `deliver` operation is performed to deliver more buffered messages, for a given topology the value of ND decreases when R increases.

Comparing the results in Tables 3 and 4 we can see that the number of `deliver` operations is lower with Gridnut in all the considered configurations. In particular, when the number of discovery tasks increases, the Gridnut strategy maintains the values of ND significantly low in comparison with Gnutella.

5.2. Distribution of `deliver` operations

Table 5 and Table 6 report the value of $ND(d)$ measured in Gnutella and Gridnut networks, respectively. Notice that in the {10,4} network the maximum distance between any couple of peers is 2, therefore no values have been measured for $d > 2$. For analogous reasons, there are no values for $d > 4$ in $\{30,3\}$, $\{30,4\}$ and $\{50,4\}$ networks.

Table 5
ND(d) in Gnutella networks.

	$\{10,2\}$	$\{10,4\}$	$\{30,3\}$	$\{30,4\}$	$\{50,4\}$	$\{70,4\}$	$\{90,4\}$
d=0	9.00	9.00	29.00	29.00	49.00	69.00	89.00
d=1	4.50	4.08	9.67	7.82	12.44	17.28	22.50
d=2	3.50	4.00	4.39	4.32	5.53	6.72	8.20
d=3	2.50	-	3.04	4.00	4.11	4.41	4.46
d=4	2.00	-	3.00	4.00	4.00	4.01	4.02
d=5	2.00	-	-	-	-	4.00	4.00

In Gnutella (see Table 5) the value of $ND(0)$ is always equal to $N-1$. This is because S_0 receives, through its neighbors, a Pong message from each of other peers in the network, and each of those messages are delivered to S_0 by means of a separated deliver operation. $ND(1)$ is always greater or equal than $ND(0)$ divided by C. The equality is obtained only for networks in which C is sufficiently little compared to N, as in $\{10,2\}$ and $\{30,3\}$ networks. In general, the value of $ND(d)$ decreases when d increases, and it reaches the minimum value, equal to C, on the peers more distant from S_0.

Table 6
ND(d) in Gridnut networks.

	$\{10,2\}$	$\{10,4\}$	$\{30,3\}$	$\{30,4\}$	$\{50,4\}$	$\{70,4\}$	$\{90,4\}$
d=0	2.00	4.00	3.00	4.00	4.00	4.00	4.00
d=1	2.00	5.35	3.00	4.51	4.07	4.04	4.22
d=2	2.00	6.76	3.07	5.40	5.20	4.89	4.52
d=3	2.01	-	4.05	6.40	5.84	5.61	5.50
d=4	2.34	-	4.80	6.82	6.65	6.32	6.26
d=5	2.82	-	-	-	-	6.78	6.67

In Gridnut (see Table 6) the value of $ND(0)$ is always equal to C, because S_0 must process exactly a deliver operation for each peer directly connected to it. The value of $ND(d)$ increases slightly with d, reaching its maximum on the peers more distant from S_0. $ND(d)$ increases with d because the number of "dummy Pong" messages increase moving away from S_0. Anyway, the value of $ND(d)$ remains always of the order of C, even for d equal to TTL.

Comparing the results in Tables 5 and 6 we can see that Gridnut implies a much better distribution of deliver operations among peers in comparison with Gnutella. In

Gnutella, the peer that started the discovery task and its closest neighbors must process a number of Grid Service operations that becomes unsustainable when the size of the network increases to thousands of nodes. In Gridnut, conversely, the number of Grid Service operations processed by each peer remains always in the order of the number of connections per peer. This Gridnut behavior results in significantly lower discovery times since communication and computation overhead due to Grid Services invocations are considerably reduced as shown in Tables 5 and 6. For example, considering a {90,4} network with R ranging from 1 to 10, Gnutella discovery experimental times vary from 2431 to 26785 msec, whereas Gridnut times vary from 2129 to 8286 msec.

6. A P2P ARCHITECTURE FOR GRID RESOURCE DISCOVERY

The Gridnut approach can offer an effective model to discover active nodes and support resource discovery in OGSA Grids. In this section we describe a framework for resource discovery that adopts such an approach to extend the model of the Globus Toolkit 3 (GT3) information service [27].

In the OGSA framework each resource is represented as a Grid Service, therefore resource discovery mainly deals with the problem of locating and querying information about useful Grid Services.

In GT3 information about resources is provided by *Index Services*. An Index Service is a Grid Service that holds information (called *service data*) about a set of Grid Services registered to it. A primary function of the Index Service is to provide an interface for querying aggregate views of service data collected from registered services. There is typically one Index Service per *Virtual Organization* (*VO*). When a VO consists of multiple large sites, very often each site runs its own Index Service that indexes the various resources available at that site. Then each of those Index Services is included in the VO's Index Service.

From the perspective of the GT3 information service, the Grid can be seen as a collection of VOs, each one indexed by a different Index Service. As mentioned before, Index Services of different sites can be included in a common higher-level Index Service that holds information about all the underlying resources. However, for scalability reasons, a multi-level hierarchy of Index Services is not appropriate as a general infrastructure for resource discovery in large scale Grids. Whereas centralized or hierarchical approaches can be efficient to index resources structured in a given VO, they are inadequate to support discovery of resources that span across many independent VOs. The framework described here adopts the P2P model to support resource discovery across different VOs.

Figure 2 shows the general architecture of the framework. Some independent VOs are represented; each VO provides one top-level *Index Service* (*IS*) and a number of lower-level Index Services.

A *P2P Layer* is defined on top of the Index Services' hierarchy. It includes two types of specialized Grid Services: *Peer Services* (introduced before), used to perform resource discovery, and *Contact Services*, that support Peer Services to organize themselves in a P2P network.

There is one Peer Service per VO. Each Peer Service is *connected* with a set of Peer Services, and exchanges query/response messages with them in a P2P mode. The connected

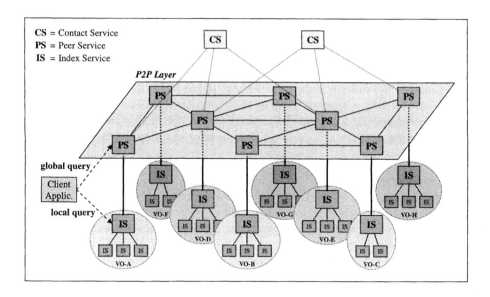

Figure 2. Framework architecture.

Peer Services are the *neighbors* of a Peer Service. A *connection* between two neighbors is a logical state that enables they to directly exchange messages. Direct communication is allowed only between neighbors. Therefore, a query message is sent by a Peer Service only to its neighbors, which in turn will forward that message to their neighbors. A query message is processed by a Peer Service by invoking the top-level Index Service of the corresponding VO. A query response is sent back along the same path that carried the incoming query message.

To join the P2P network, a Peer Service must know the URL of at least one Peer Services to connect to. An appropriate number of Contact Services is distributed in the Grid to support this issue. Contact Services cache the URLs of known Peer Services; a Peer Service may contact one or more well known Contact Services to obtain the URLs of registered Peer Services.

As shown in Figure 2, a *Client Application* can submit both *local* and *global* queries to the framework. A local query searches for information about resources in a given VO. It is performed by submitting the query to the Index Service of that VO. A global query aims at discovering resources located in possibly different VOs, and is performed by submitting the query to a Peer Service at the P2P Layer. As mentioned before, the Peer Service processes that query internally (through the associated Index Service), and will forward it to its neighbors as in typical P2P networks.

The main difference between a hierarchical system and the framework described here is the management of global queries. Basically, in a hierarchical information service two alternative approaches can be used:

- the query is sent separately to all the top-level Index Services, that must be known by the user;

- the query is sent to one (possibly replicated) Index Service at the root of the hierarchy, that indexes all the Grid resources.

Both these approaches suffer scalability problems. In the P2P approach, conversely, global queries are managed by a layer of services that cooperate as peers. To submit a global query, a user need only to know the URL of a Peer Service in the Grid.

In the next subsection the design of the Peer Service and Contact Service components is discussed.

6.1. Services design

Both Peer Service and Contact Service instances are identified by a globally unique GSH.

Each Peer Service supports four operations: `connect`, `disconnect`, `deliver`, and `query`, as described in Section 4.

A Contact Service supports just one operation:

- `getHandles`: invoked by a Peer Service to register itself and to get the handles of one or more registered Peer Services.

Figure 3 and Figure 4 describe, respectively, the main software components of Peer Services and Contact Services.

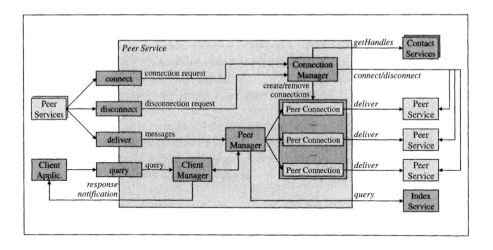

Figure 3. Peer Service software components.

The Peer Service (see Figure 3) is composed by three main modules: *Connection Manager*, *Peer Manager*, and *Client Manager*.

The goal of the Connection Manager is to maintain a given number of connections with neighbor Peer Services. A *Peer Connection* object is used to manage the connection and the exchange of messages with a given Peer Service. A Peer Connection includes the *Grid Service Reference (GSR)* of a given Peer Service, and a set of *transmission buffers* for the different kinds of messages directed to it. The Connection Manager both manages connection/disconnection requests from remote Peer Services, and performs connection/disconnection requests (as a client) to remote Peer Services. Moreover, it may invoke one or more Contact Services to obtain the handles of Peer Services to connect to.

The Peer Manager is the core component of the Peer Service. It both manages the messages delivered from other Peer Services, and interacts with the Client Manager component to manage client requests and to provide responses. It performs different operations on delivered messages: some messages are simply forwarded to one or more Peer Connections, whereas query messages need also a response (that in general is obtained by querying the local Index Service). Moreover, the Peer Manager generates and submits query messages to the network on the basis of the Client Manager requests.

The Client Manager manages the query requests submitted by client applications. It interacts with the Peer Manager component to submit the query to the network, and manages the delivery of query results to the client through a notification mechanism.

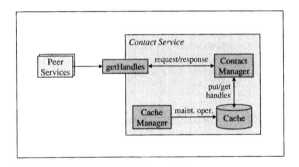

Figure 4. Contact Service software components.

The Contact Service (see Figure 4) is composed by two software modules: *Contact Manager* and *Cache Manager*.

The Contact Manager manages the execution of the `getHandles` operation. Basically, it receives two parameters: the handle h of the invoker, and the number n of handles requested by the invoker. The Contact Manager first inserts (or updates) the handle h into a *Cache*, then it extracts (if available) n distinct handles from the Cache and returns them to the invoker. The handles can be extracted from the Cache on the basis of a given policy (e.g., randomly). If a Peer Service does not receive the requested number of handles, it can try to invoke the Contact Service later.

The Cache Manager performs maintenance operations on the Cache. For instance, it removes oldest (not recently updated) handles, performs content indexing, etc.

7. CONCLUSIONS

Although P2P and Grid computing are still considered two different research areas, an integrated approach based on the merging of these two models will be profitable for the development of scalable distributed systems and applications. As Grids become very large and pervasive, the use of P2P approaches can be exploited to achieve scalability.

An important Grid functionality that could be effectively redesigned using the P2P paradigm is resource discovery. To this end, we designed a Gnutella-like discovery protocol, named *Gridnut*, which uses appropriate message buffering and merging techniques to make OGSA-compliant services effective as a way to exchange discovery messages in a P2P fashion. We compared Gridnut and Gnutella performance considering different network topologies and load conditions. Experimental results show that appropriate message buffering and merging strategies produce significant performance improvements, both in terms of number and distribution of Grid Service operations processed.

The Gridnut approach can be an effective way to discover active nodes and support resource discovery in OGSA Grids. The chapter described an architecture for resource discovery that adopts such an approach to extend the model of the Globus Toolkit 3 information service. In particular, a P2P Layer of specialized Grid Services is defined to support discovery queries on Index Services of multiple VOs in a P2P fashion. Since the proposed architecture adopts a general P2P service-based approach, it can be also used as a model for designing an information service in future P2P-based Grid programming environments.

REFERENCES

1. I. Foster and A. Iamnitchi, On Death, Taxes, and the Convergence of Peer-to-Peer and Grid Computing. Proc. 2nd International Workshop on Peer-to-Peer Systems, Berkeley, USA (2003).
2. D. Talia and P. Trunfio, Toward a Synergy between P2P and Grids. IEEE Internet Computing, vol. 7, n. 4, pp. 94-96 (2003).
3. The World Wide Web Consortium, Web Services Activity. http://www.w3.org/2002/ws.
4. I. Foster, C. Kesselman, J. Nick, and S. Tuecke, The Physiology of the Grid. In: F. Berman, G. Fox, and A. Hey (eds.), Grid Computing: Making the Global Infrastructure a Reality, Wiley, pp. 217-249 (2003).
5. Clip2, The Gnutella Protocol Specification v.0.4. http://www9.limewire.com/developer/gnutella_protocol_0.4.pdf.
6. D. Talia and P. Trunfio, A P2P Grid Services-Based Protocol: Design and Evaluation. Proc. European Conference on Parallel Computing (EuroPar 2004), Pisa, Italy, LNCS 3149, pp. 1022-1031 (2004).
7. D. Box et al., Simple Object Access Protocol (SOAP) 1.1, W3C Note 08 May 2000. http://www.w3.org/TR/2000/NOTE-SOAP-20000508.
8. E. Christensen, F. Curbera, G. Meredith and S. Weerawarana, Web Services Description Language (WSDL) 1.1, W3C Note 15 March 2001. http://www.w3.org/TR/2001/NOTE-wsdl-20010315.

9. I. Foster, C. Kesselman, J. M. Nick and S. Tuecke, Grid Services for Distributed System Integration. IEEE Computer, vol. 35, n. 6, pp. 37-46 (2002).
10. S. Tuecke et al., Open Grid Services Infrastructure (OGSI) Version 1.0. http://www-unix.globus.org/toolkit/draft-ggf-ogsi-gridservice-33_2003-06-27.pdf.
11. The Globus Alliance, Globus Toolkit 3. http://www.globus.org/toolkit.
12. The Global Grid Forum (GGF). http://www.ggf.org.
13. K. Czajkowski et al., The WS-Resource Framework Version 1.0. http://www-106.ibm.com/developerworks/library/ws-resource/ws-wsrf.pdf.
14. D. Box et al., Web Services Addressing (WS-Addressing), W3C Member Submission 10 August 2004. http://www.w3.org/Submission/2004/SUBM-ws-addressing-20040810.
15. K. Czajkowski et al., From Open Grid Services Infrastructure to WS-Resource Framework: Refactoring & Evolution. http://www-106.ibm.com/developerworks/library/ws-resource/ogsi_to_wsrf_1.0.pdf.
16. G. Fox, D. Gannon, S. Ko, S. Lee, S. Pallickara, M. Pierce, X. Qiu, X. Rao, A. Uyar, M. Wang, and W. Wu, Peer-to-Peer Grids. In: F. Berman, G. Fox, and A. Hey (eds.), Grid Computing: Making the Global Insfrastructure a Reality, Wiley, pp. 471-490 (2003).
17. A. Iamnitchi, I. Foster, and D. Nurmi, A Peer-to-Peer Approach to Resource Discovery in Grid Environments. Proc. 11th Int. Symposium on High Performance Distributed Computing (HPDC 11) (2002).
18. A. Andrzejak and Z. Xu, Scalable, Efficient Range Queries for Grid Information Services. Proc. 2nd Int. Conference on Peer-to-Peer Computing (P2P2002) (2002).
19. A.R. Butt, R. Zhang, and Y.C. Hu, A Self-Organizing Flock of Condors. Proc. Supercomputing Conference (SC2003) (2003).
20. M. Cai, M. Frank, J. Chen, and P. Szekely, MAAN: A Multi-Attribute Addressable Network for Grid Information Services. Journal of Grid Computing (to appear).
21. K. Truelove and A. Chasin, Morpheus Out of the Underworld. http://www.openp2p.com/pub/a/p2p/2001/07/02/morpheus.html.
22. I. Stoica, R. Morris, D. Karger, F. Kaashoek, and H. Balakrishnan, Chord: A Scalable Peer-to-peer Lookup Service for Internet Applications. Proc. SIGCOMM 2001, pp. 149-160 (2001).
23. S. Ratnasamy, P. Francis, M. Handley, R. Karp, and S. Shenker, A Scalable Content-Addressable Network. Proc. SIGCOMM 2001, pp. 161-172 (2001).
24. B.Y. Zhao, J. Kubiatowicz, and A.D. Joseph, Tapestry: An infrastructure for fault-tolerant wide-area location and routing. Technical Report UCB/CSD-01-1141, Computer Science Division, University of California, Berkeley (2001).
25. P. Reynolds and A. Vahdat, Efficient Peer-to-Peer Keyword Searching. Proc. Int. Middleware Conference (Middleware 2003), Rio de Janeiro, Brazil (2003).
26. A. Crainiceanu, P. Linga, J. Gehrke, and J. Shanmugasundaram, PTree: A P2P Index for Resource Discovery Applications. Proc. 13th Int. Conference on World Wide Web (WWW 2004) (2004).
27. D. Talia and P. Trunfio, Web Services for Peer-to-Peer Resource Discovery on the Grid. Proc. 6th Thematic Workshop of the EU Network of Excellence DELOS, S. Margherita di Pula, Italy (2004).

Data Placement in Widely Distributed Environments

T. Kosar[a], S. Son[a], G. Kola[a], and M. Livny[a]

[a]Computer Sciences Department, University of Wisconsin-Madison
1210 West Dayton Street, Madison WI 53706
Email: {kosart, sschang, kola, miron}@cs.wisc.edu

The increasing computation and data requirements of scientific applications, especially in the areas of bioinformatics, astronomy, high energy physics, and earth sciences, have necessitated the use of distributed resources owned by collaborating parties. While existing distributed systems work well for compute-intensive applications that require limited data movement, they fail in unexpected ways when the application accesses, creates, and moves large amounts of data over wide-area networks. Existing systems closely couple data movement and computation, and consider data movement as a side effect of computation. In this chapter, we propose a framework that de-couples data movement from computation, allows queuing and scheduling of data movement apart from computation, and acts as an I/O subsystem for distributed systems. This system provides a uniform interface to heterogeneous storage systems and data transfer protocols; permits policy support and higher-level optimization; and enables reliable, efficient scheduling of compute and data resources.

1. Introduction

The computational and data requirements of scientific applications have increased drastically over the recent years. Just a couple of years ago, the data requirements for an average scientific application were measured in Terabytes, whereas today we use Petabytes to measure them. Moreover, these data requirements continue to increase rapidly every year. A good example for this is the Compact Muon Solenoid (CMS) [1] project, a high energy physics project participating in the Grid Physics Network (GriPhyN). According to the Particle Physics Data Grid (PPDG) deliverables to CMS, the data volume of CMS, which is currently a couple of Terabytes per year, is expected to subsequently increase rapidly, so that the accumulated data volume will reach 1 Exabyte (1 million Terabytes) by around 2015 [2]. This is the data volume required by only one application, and there are many other data intensive applications from other projects with very similar data requirements, ranging from genomics to biomedical, and from metallurgy to cosmology.

The problem is not only the enormous I/O needs of these data intensive applications, but also the number of users who will access the same datasets. For each of the projects, number of people who will be accessing the datasets range from 100s to 1000s. Furthermore, these users are not located at a single site, rather they are distributed all across the country, even the globe. So, there is a prevalent necessity to move large amounts of data around wide area networks to complete the computation cycle, which brings with it the problem of efficient and reliable data placement. Data needs to be located, moved to the application, staged and replicated; storage should be allocated and de-allocated for the data whenever necessary; and everything should be cleaned up when the user is done with the data.

Just as compute resources and network resources need to be carefully scheduled and managed, the scheduling of data placement activities all across the Grid is crucial, since the access to data has the potential to become the main bottleneck for data intensive applications. This is especially the case when most of the data is stored on tape storage systems, which slows down access to data even further due to the mechanical nature of these systems.

The common approach to solve this problem of data placement has been either doing it manually, or employing simple scripts, which do not have any automation or fault tolerance capabilities. They cannot adapt to a dynamically changing distributed computing environment. They do not have a single point of control, and generally require baby-sitting throughout the process. There are even cases where people found a solution for data placement by dumping data to tapes and sending them via postal services [3].

The Reliable File Transfer Service(RFT) [4] and the Lightweight Data Replicator (LDR) [5] were developed to allow fast and secure replication of data over wide area networks. Both RFT and LDR make use of Globus [6] tools to transfer data, and work only with a single data transport protocol, which is GridFTP [7].

There is an ongoing effort to provide a unified interface to different storage systems by building Storage Resource Managers (SRMs) [8] on top of them. Currently, a couple of data storage systems, such as HPSS [9], Jasmin [10] and Enstore [11], support SRMs on top of them. On the other hand, the SDSC Storage Resource Broker (SRB) [12] aims to provide a uniform interface for connecting to heterogeneous data resources and accessing replicated data sets. SRB uses a Metadata Catalog (MCAT) to provide a way to access data sets and resources based on their attributes rather than their names or physical locations.

There has also been some efforts to provide reliability and fault tolerance for data placement in distributed systems. Thain et. al. proposed the Ethernet approach [13] to distributed computing, in which they introduce a simple scripting language which can handle failures in a manner similar to exceptions in some languages. The Ethernet approach is not aware of the semantics of the jobs it is running, its duty is retrying any given job for a number of times in a fault tolerant manner.

GFarm [14] provided a global parallel filesystem with online petascale storage. Ocean-Store [15] aimed to build a global persistent data store that can scale to billions of users. BAD-FS [16] was designed as a batch aware distributed filesystem for data intensive workloads.

In this chapter, we present a new approach to handle these problems. This new approach comes with a totally new concept: "Data placement activities must be first class citizens in widely distributed environments just like the computational jobs." They need to be queued, scheduled, monitored, and even check-pointed. It must be made sure that they complete successfully and without any need for human intervention. In other approaches, data placement is generally not considered part of the end-to-end performance, and requires lots of baby-sitting. In this new approach, the end-to-end processing of the data is completely automated, so that the user can just launch a batch of computational/data placement jobs and then forget about it [17].

On the other hand, data placement jobs should be treated differently from computational jobs, since they have different semantics and different characteristics. Data placement jobs and computational jobs should be differentiated from each other and each should be submitted to specialized schedulers that understand their semantics. For example, if the transfer of a large file fails, we may not simply want to restart the job and re-transfer the whole file. Rather, we may prefer transferring only the remaining part of the file. Similarly, if a transfer using one protocol fails, we may want to try other protocols supported by the source and destination hosts to perform the transfer. We may want to dynamically tune up network parameters or decide concurrency level for specific source, destination and protocol triples. A traditional computational job scheduler does not handle these cases. For this purpose, we have developed a "data placement subsystem" for distributed computing systems [18], similar to the I/O subsystem in operating systems. This subsystem includes a specialized scheduler for data placement, a higher level planner aware of data placement jobs, a resource broker/policy enforcer and some optimization tools.

In addition to the scheduling and management of data placement activities, the heterogeneous and multi-administrative nature of the widely distributed systems introduces several other problems. Different storage systems and data transfer protocols need to be accessed, firewalls need to be passed, network fluctuations need to be considered, and all kinds of failures need to be handled. In this chapter, we also discuss how we address all of these problems. We start by highlighting the challenges for data placement activities in widely distributed systems.

2. Data Placement Challenges in Widely Distributed Systems

The widely distributed environments provide researchers with enormous resources, but they also bring some challenges with them. Below are some of the data placement related challenges we will be addressing in this chapter.

Heterogeneous Resources. In the widely distributed environments, many different storage systems, different data transfer middleware and protocols coexist. And it is a fundamental problem that the data required by an application might be stored in heterogeneous repositories. It is not an easy task to interact with all possible different storage systems to access the data. So there should be a negotiating system through which you can access all different kinds of storage systems, and also you can make use of all different underlying middleware and file transfer protocols.

Hiding Failures from Applications. The widely distributed systems bring failed network connections, performance variations during transfers, crashed clients, servers and storage systems with them. But generally the applications are not prepared to these kind of problems. Most of the applications assume perfect computational environments like failure-free network and storage devices, unlimited storage, availability of the data when the computation starts, and low latency. We cannot expect every application to consider all possible failures and performance variations in the system, and be prepared for them.

Instead, we should be able to hide these from the application by a mediating system.

Different Job Requirements. Each job may have different policies and different priorities. Scheduling should be done according to the needs of each individual job. Global scheduling decisions should be able to be tailored according to the individual requirements of each job. Using only global policies may not be affective and efficient enough. The job description language used should be strong and flexible enough to support job level policies. And the job scheduler should be able to support and enforce these policies.

Overloading Limited Resources. The network and storage resources that an application has access to can be limited, and therefore they should be used efficiently. A common problem in distributed computing environments is that when all jobs submitted to remote sites start execution at the same time, they all start pulling data from their home storage systems (stage-in) concurrently. This can overload both network resources and the local disks of remote execution sites. It may also bring a load to the home storage systems from where the data is pulled.

One approach would be to pre-allocate both network and storage resources before using them. This approach works fine as long as the pre-allocation is supported by the resources being used, and also if the user knows when and how long the resources will be used by the application beforehand.

A more general solution would be to control the total number of transfers happening anytime between any given two sites. Most job schedulers can control the total number of jobs being submitted and executed at any given time, but this solution is not sufficient always and it is not the best solution in most cases either. The reason is that it does not do any overlapping of CPU and I/O, and causes the CPU to wait while I/O is being performed. Moreover, the problem gets more complex when all jobs complete and try to move their output data back to their home storage systems (stage-out). In this case stage-ins and stage-outs of different jobs may interfere, especially overloading the network resources more. An intelligent scheduling mechanism should be developed to control the number of stage-in and stage-outs from and to any specific storage systems anytime, and meanwhile do not cause any waste in CPU time.

Changing Conditions. Many tunable parameters depend on the current state of the network, server, and other components involved in the pipeline. Ideally, the system should be able to figure this out and adapt the application. A low-level example is that the TCP buffer size should be set equal to the bandwidth delay product to utilize the full bandwidth. A higher-level example is that to maximize throughput of a storage server, the number of concurrent data transfers should be controlled taking into account server, end host, and network characteristics. Current systems do not perform automated tuning.

Efficient Utilization of Available Bandwidth. Wide-area network bandwidth is increasing. Unfortunately, many of the applications are unable to use the full available bandwidth. New data transport protocols are capable of using almost the entire bandwidth, but tuning them to do so is difficult. Further, users want the ability to give different bandwidth to different applications. Currently, this is very difficult to accomplish.

Connectivity. Firewalls/NATs provide many benefits such as network protection, a solution to IPv4 address shortage, and easy network planning. However, these devices come with prices as well, notably non-universal (and asymmetric) connectivity of the Internet. Because of the connectivity problem, a data may not be moved to a desired

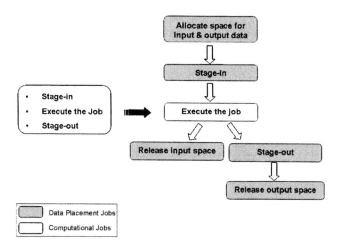

Figure 1. Separating data placement form computation. *Computation at a remote site with input and output data requirements can be achieved with a new five-step plan, in which computation and data placement are separated. This is represented as a six node DAG in the figure.*

place, no matter how a scheduler tries hard. Reconnecting and trying other protocol may not help in this case. For computational jobs, the problem can be mitigated by extra movements of jobs to the places that the final destination can communicate with. However, the extra movements may not be affordable to the data placement, considering the size of data being moved. Even if no extra copies need to be made, data must flow some strategic points to reach a final destination. The constraints imposed by underlying fabric may make data placement efforts we will discuss less effective or even useless.

Several traversal systems that enable applications to communicate over firewalls/NAT have been developed. However, each system has a unique security and other characteristics and supports only its intended use cases. Organizations use different firewalls/NATs and have different network settings, security concerns, performance requirement, etc. Different organizations want to or have to allow traffic into their networks in different ways. In data placement, one site must be able to communicate with multiple sites over time or in a single moment. This multi-organizational and multi-party communication pattern makes previous traversal systems almost useless.

In order to utilize the resources in the widely distributed environments efficiently, researchers have to overcome these challenges first.

3. A New Concept

Most of the data intensive applications in widely distributed environments require moving the input data for the job from a remote site to the execution site, executing the job,

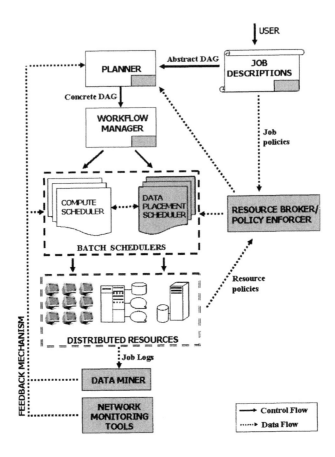

Figure 2. Components of the Data Placement Subsystem. *The components of our data placement subsystem are shown in gray color in the figure.*

and then moving the output data from execution site to the same or another remote site. If the application does not want to take any risk of running out of disk space at the execution site, it should also allocate space before transferring the input data there, and release the space after it moves out the output data from there.

We regard all of these computational and data placement steps as real jobs and represent them as nodes in a Directed Acyclic Graph (DAG). The dependencies between them are represented as directed arcs, as shown in Figure 1.

In our framework, the data placement jobs are represented in a different way than computational jobs in the job specification language, so that the high level planners (i.e. Pegasus [19], Chimera [20]) can differentiate these two classes of jobs. The high level planners create concrete DAGs with also data placement nodes in them. Then, the planner submits this concrete DAG to a workflow manager (i.e. DAGMan [21]). The workflow manager submits computational jobs to a compute job queue, and the data placement jobs to a data placement job queue. Jobs in each queue are scheduled by the corresponding scheduler. Since our focus in this work is on the data placement part, we do not get into details of the computational job scheduling.

The data placement scheduler acts both as a I/O control system and I/O scheduler in a distributed computing environment. Each protocol and data storage system have different user interface, different libraries and different API. In the current approach, the users need to deal with all complexities of linking to different libraries, and using different interfaces of data transfer protocols and storage servers. Our data placement scheduler provides a uniform interface for all different protocols and storage servers, and puts a level of abstraction between the user and them.

The data placement scheduler schedules the jobs in its queue according to the information it gets from the workflow manager and from the resource broker/policy enforcer. The resource broker matches resources to jobs, and helps in locating the data and making decisions such as where to move the data. It consults a replica location service (i.e. RLS [22]) whenever necessary. The policy enforcer helps in applying the resource specific or job specific policies, such as how many concurrent connections are allowed to a specific storage server.

The log files of the jobs are collected by the data miner. The data miner parses these logs and extracts useful information from them such as different events, timestamps, error messages and utilization statistics. Then this information is entered into a database. The data miner runs a set of queries on the database to interpret them and then feeds the results back to the scheduler and the resource broker/policy enforcer.

The network monitoring tools collect statistics on maximum available end-to-end bandwidth, actual bandwidth utilization, latency and number of hops to be traveled by utilizing tools such as Pathrate [23] and Iperf [24]. Again, the collected statistics are fed back to the scheduler and the resource broker/policy enforcer.

The components of our data placement subsystem and their interaction with other components are shown in Figure 2. The most important component of this system is the data placement scheduler, which can understand the characteristics of the data placement jobs and can make smart scheduling decisions accordingly. In the next section, we present the features of this scheduler in detail.

4. A New Scheduler: Stork

We have implemented a prototype of the data placement scheduler we are proposing. We call this scheduler Stork. Stork provides solutions for many of the data placement problems encountered in the widely distributed environments.

Interaction with Higher Level Planners. Stork can interact with higher level planners and workflow managers. This allows the users to be able to schedule both CPU resources and storage resources together. We made some enhancements to DAGMan, so that it can differentiate between computational jobs and data placement jobs. It can then submit computational jobs to a computational job scheduler, such as Condor [25] or Condor-G [26], and the data placement jobs to Stork. Figure 3 shows a sample DAG specification file with the enhancement of data placement nodes, and how this DAG is

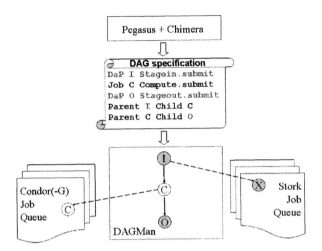

Figure 3. Interaction with Higher Level Planners. *Our data placement scheduler (Stork) can interact with a higher level planners and workflow managers. A concrete DAG created by Chimera and Pegasus is sent to DAGMan. This DAG consists of both computational and data placement jobs. DAGMan submits computational jobs to a computational batch scheduler (Condor/Condor-G), and data placement jobs to Stork.*

handled by DAGMan.

In this way, it can be made sure that an input file required for a computation arrives to a storage device close to the execution site before actually that computation starts executing on that site. Similarly, the output files can be removed to a remote storage system as soon as the computation is completed. No storage device or CPU is occupied more than it is needed, and jobs do not wait idle for their input data to become available.

Interaction with Heterogeneous Resources. Stork acts like an I/O control system (IOCS) between the user applications and the underlying protocols and data storage servers. It provides complete modularity and extendibility. The users can add support for their favorite storage system, data transport protocol, or middleware very easily. This is a very crucial feature in a system designed to work in a heterogeneous distributed environment. The users or applications may not expect all storage systems to support the same interfaces to talk to each other. And we cannot expect all applications to talk to all the different storage systems, protocols, and middleware. There needs to be a negotiating system between them which can interact with those systems easily and even translate different protocols to each other. Stork has been developed to be capable of this. The modularity of Stork allows users to insert a plug-in to support any storage system, protocol, or middleware easily.

Stork already has support for several different storage systems, data transport protocols, and middleware. Users can use them immediately without any extra work. Stork can interact currently with data transfer protocols such as FTP [27], GridFTP [28], HTTP

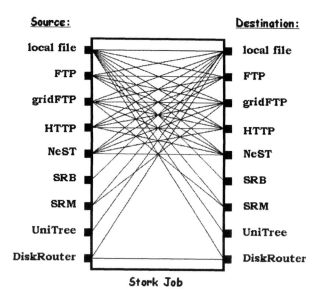

Figure 4. Protocol Translation using Stork Memory Buffer or Third-party Transfers. *Transfers between some storage systems and protocols can be performed directly using one Stork job via memory buffer or third-party transfers.*

and DiskRouter [29]; data storage systems such as SRB [12], UniTree [30], and NeST [31]; and data management middleware such as SRM [8].

Stork maintains a library of pluggable "data placement" modules. These modules get executed by data placement job requests coming into Stork. They can perform inter-protocol translations either using a memory buffer or third-party transfers whenever available. Inter-protocol translations are not supported between all systems or protocols yet. Figure 4 shows the available direct inter-protocol translations that can be performed using a single Stork job.

In order to transfer data between systems for which direct inter-protocol translation is not supported, two consecutive Stork jobs can be used instead. The first Stork job performs transfer from the source storage system to the local disk cache of Stork, and the second Stork job performs the transfer from the local disk cache of Stork to the destination storage system. This is shown in Figure 5.

Flexible Job Representation and Multilevel Policy Support. Stork uses the ClassAd [32] job description language to represent the data placement jobs. The ClassAd language provides a very flexible and extensible data model that can be used to represent arbitrary services and constraints.

Figure 6 shows three sample data placement (DaP) requests. The first request is to allocate 100 MB of disk space for 2 hours on a NeST server. The second request is to transfer a file from an SRB server to the reserved space on the NeST server. The

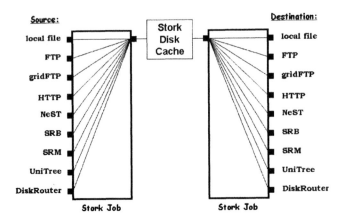

Figure 5. Protocol Translation using Stork Disk Cache. *Transfers between all storage systems and protocols supported can be performed using two Stork jobs via an intermediate disk cache.*

third request is to de-allocate the previously reserved space. In addition to the "reserve", "transfer", and "release", there are also other data placement job types such as "locate" to find where the data is actually located and "stage" to move the data from a tertiary storage to a secondary storage next to it in order to decrease data access time during actual transfers.

Stork enables users to specify job level policies as well as global ones. Global policies apply to all jobs scheduled by the same Stork server. Users can override them by specifying job level policies in job description ClassAds. The example below shows how to override global policies at the job level.

```
[
  dap_type = ''transfer'';
  ...
  ...
  max_retry  = 10;
  restart_in = ''2 hours'';
]
```

In this example, the user specifies that the job should be retried up to 10 times in case of failure, and if the transfer does not get completed in 2 hours, it should be killed and restarted.

Dynamic Protocol Selection. Stork can decide which data transfer protocol to use for each transfer dynamically and automatically at the run-time. Before performing each transfer, Stork makes a quick check to identify which protocols are available for both the source and destination hosts involved in the transfer. Stork first checks its own host-protocol library to see whether all of the hosts involved in the transfer are already in the library or not. If not, Stork tries to connect to those particular hosts using different data transfer protocols, to determine the availability of each specific protocol on that particular

```
[
    dap_type      = "reserve";
    dest_host     = "db18.cs.wisc.edu";
    reserve_size = "100 MB";
    duration      = "2 hours";
    reserve_id    = 3;
]

[
    dap_type = "transfer";
    src_url    = "srb://ghidorac.sdsc.edu/home/kosart.condor/1.dat";
    dest_url  = "nest://db18.cs.wisc.edu/1.dat";
]

[
    dap_type   = "release";
    dest_host = "db18.cs.wisc.edu";
    reserve_id = 3;
]
```

Figure 6. Job representation in Stork. *Three sample data placement (DaP) requests are shown: first one to allocate space, second one to transfer a file to the reserved space, and third one to de-allocate the reserved space.*

host. Then Stork creates the list of protocols available on each host, and stores these lists as a library:

```
[
  host_name = "quest2.ncsa.uiuc.edu";
  supported_protocols = "diskrouter, gridftp, ftp";
]
[
  host_name = "nostos.cs.wisc.edu";
  supported_protocols = "gridftp, ftp, http";
]
```

If the protocols specified in the source and destination URLs of the request fail to perform the transfer, Stork will start trying the protocols in its host-protocol library to carry out the transfer. The users also have the option not to specify any particular protocols in the request, letting Stork to decide which protocol to use at run-time:

```
[
  dap_type = "transfer";
  src_url  = "any://slic04.sdsc.edu/tmp/foo.dat";
  dest_url = "any://quest2.ncsa.uiuc.edu/tmp/foo.dat";
]
```

In the above example, Stork will select any of the available protocols on both source and destination hosts to perform the transfer. Therefore, the users do not need to care about which hosts support which protocols. They just send a request to Stork to transfer a file from one host to another, and Stork will take care of deciding which protocol to use.

The users can also provide their preferred list of alternative protocols for any transfer. In this case, the protocols in this list will be used instead of the protocols in the host-protocol library of Stork:

```
[
  dap_type = "transfer";
  src_url  = "drouter://slic04.sdsc.edu/tmp/foo.dat";
  dest_url = "drouter://quest2.ncsa.uiuc.edu/tmp/foo.dat";
  alt_protocols = "nest-nest, gsiftp-gsiftp";
]
```

In this example, the user asks Stork to perform the a transfer from slic04.sdsc.edu to quest2.ncsa.uiuc.edu using the DiskRouter protocol primarily. The user also instructs Stork to use any of the NeST or GridFTP protocols in case the DiskRouter protocol does not work. Stork will try to perform the transfer using the DiskRouter protocol first. In case of a failure, it will switch to the alternative protocols and will try to complete the transfer successfully. If the primary protocol becomes available again, Stork will switch to it again. Hence, whichever protocol is available will be used to successfully complete user's request.

Run-time Protocol Auto-tuning. Statistics for each link involved in the transfers are collected regularly and written into a file, creating a library of network links, protocols and auto-tuning parameters.

```
[
  link = "slic04.sdsc.edu - quest2.ncsa.uiuc.edu";
  protocol = "gsiftp";

  bs      = 1024KB;      //block size
  tcp_bs  = 1024KB;      //TCP buffer size
  p       = 4;           //parallelism
]
```

Before performing every transfer, Stork checks its auto-tuning library to see if there are any entries for the particular hosts involved in this transfer. If there is an entry for the link to be used in this transfer, Stork uses these optimized parameters for the transfer. Stork can also be configured to collect performance data before every transfer, but this is not recommended due to the overhead it would bring to the system.

Failure Recovery. Stork hides any kind of temporary network, storage system, middleware, or software failures from user applications. It has a "retry" mechanism, which can retry any failing data placement job any given number of times before returning a failure. It also has a "kill and restart" mechanism, which allows users to specify a "maximum allowable run time" for their data placement jobs. When a job execution time exceeds this specified time, it will be killed by Stork automatically and restarted. This feature overcomes the bugs in some systems, which cause the transfers to hang forever and never return. This can be repeated any number of times, again specified by the user.

Efficient Resource Utilization. Stork can control the number of concurrent requests coming to any storage system it has access to, and makes sure that neither that storage system nor the network link to that storage system get overloaded. It can also perform space allocation and deallocations to make sure that the required storage space is available on the corresponding storage system. The space reservations are supported by Stork as long as the corresponding storage systems have support for it.

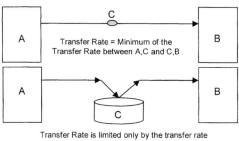

Figure 7. Advantage of buffering at an intermediate node.

5. High Throughput Data Transfers

The steady increase in data sets of scientific applications, the trend towards collaborative research and the emergence of grid computing have created a need to move large quantities of data over wide-area networks. The dynamic nature of network makes it difficult to tune data transfer protocols to use the full bandwidth. Further, data transfers are limited by the bottleneck link and different links become the bottleneck at different times resulting in under-utilization of other network hops. To address these issues, we have designed *DiskRouter*, a flexible infrastructure that uses hierarchical main memory and disk buffering at intermediate points to speed up transfers. The infrastructure supports application-level multicast to reduce network load and enables easy construction of application-level overlay networks to maximize bandwidth.

We present the functions that DiskRouter currently performs.

Store and Forward Device/Wide-area Unix Pipe. DiskRouter in its simplest form is a store and forward device. It uses buffering to match the speed of sender and receiver. It is smart to use main memory first and then disk to perform the buffering. It is slightly different from the normal UNIX pipe in that it provides a tagged block abstraction instead of a continuous stream abstraction. The tagged blocks may arrive out-of-order and the DiskRouter clients at the end-points handle the re-assembly.

Figure 7 shows a case where such a store and forward device improves throughput. A source A is transferring large amounts of data to destination B, and C is an intermediate node between A and C. Placing a DiskRouter at C improves throughput if the bandwidth fluctuation between A and C is independent of the bandwidth fluctuation between C and B. When the bandwidth in the path between A and C is higher than the bandwidth between C and B, data gets buffered at C and when the bandwidth between C and B is higher than the bandwidth between A and C, the buffer drains. Such scenarios occur quite often in real world where A and B are in different time zones and C is an intermediate point.

Data Mover. DiskRouter functions as a data mover. Typically, compute nodes want to get rid of the generated data as quickly as possible and get back to computation. They do not want to spend time waiting for the wide-area transfers to complete and this time

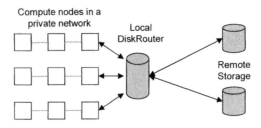

Figure 8. Streaming data via a local DiskRouter.

can be non-deterministic in the presence of failures. In such cases, the computation nodes can write to a local DiskRouter and expect it to take care of pushing the data to the destination. In this function, DiskRouter behaves similar to Kangaroo [33]. It is more efficient, because the data does not have to traverse the disk.

The data mover is very useful when the compute nodes are in a private network and only the head node is accessible outside. In this case, we can deploy DiskRouter on the head-node and use it to stream data to/from the compute nodes. Figure 8 shows this process.

DiskRouter has a significant performance advantage over simply writing the data to disk on the head node and then transferring it because for large amounts of data, disk becomes the bottleneck. Further, the head node may not have enough storage to accommodate all the data. DiskRouter has dynamic flow control whereby it can slow or stop the sender if it runs out of buffer space and make the sender resume sending data when the buffer space becomes available.

Application-level Overlay Network. DiskRouter enables easy construction of application-level overlay network to maximize the throughput of the transfers. While other application-level overlay networks like Resilient Overlay Network (RON) help in reducing latency, DiskRouter overlay-network helps in maximizing bandwidth. Below, we give a concrete example of where this is useful.

In the UW-Madison wide-area network, we have two physical paths to go to Chicago. The direct path has a lower latency but the bandwidth is limited to 100 Mbps. There is an another path to Chicago via Milwaukee which has a bandwidth of 400 Mbps. Unfortunately, because of limitations of current networking(we cannot use two paths and dynamically split data between them), we can use only one path and the current networking based on reducing latency chooses the lower latency (and lower bandwidth) path.

We have been able to deploy a DiskRouter at Milwaukee and exploit the combined bandwidth of 500 Mbps for the data transfer. DiskRouter is able to split the data and dynamically determine the fraction that has to be sent directly and the fraction that has to be sent via Milwaukee. The DiskRouter client reassembles the data and passes the complete data to the application. We find similar cases in other environments as well.

DiskRouter overlay network can also be used to route around failures. Users can build more complex overlay networks and may even dynamically build an overlay network and re-configure it.

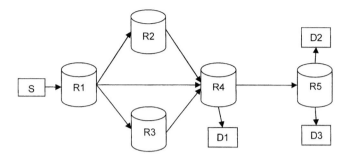

Figure 9. Source S uses a DiskRouter overlay network with DiskRouters R1-R5 to multi-cast data to destinations D1-D3.

Application-level Multicast. Large collaborative projects have a number of participating sites. The source data needs to be moved to the different participating sites. Some of the participating sites are physically located close by. For example, scientist in NCSA Urbana-Champagne, Illinois and Yale, Connecticut needs the data from Palomar telescope in California.

Unfortunately, IP multicast is not available over this wide-area. The only viable alternative is to build an overlay network with application-level multicast capability. DiskRouter helps accomplish that. Since the DiskRouter has buffering capabilities, not all the end-points need have the same bandwidth.

In this scheme, a DiskRouter at Chicago would provide the necessary buffering, make copies of the data, and send one copy to NCSA and the other copy to Yale. If terabytes of data are being moved, the network bandwidth saving is quite significant.

Figure 9 shows an application-level multicast overlay network created using DiskRouters R1-R5 for transferring data from source S to destinations D1-D3. The routing here is a little complex. First, the source sends data to DiskRouter R1. R1 dynamically splits the data and sends fractions of the data to R2, R3 and R4. R2 and R3 send all the data received from R1 to R4. R4 sends the data to destination D1 and to the next DiskRouter R5. R5 sends a copy of data to destinations D2 and D3.

Running Computation on Data Streams. DiskRouter allows uploading filters to choose incoming data. Recipients can run choose to run arbitrary computation on the specified amount of data before deciding whether to accept it. Users can use DiskRouters ability to make on-the-fly copies to perform computation on the nodes close to each DiskRouter and then distribute the result through the DiskRouter overlay network. It is also possible to combine data movement and data processing using DiskRouters.

Network Monitor/Dynamic TCP tuning. By using *pathrate* [23] to estimate the network capacity and observing actual transfers, DiskRouter dynamically tunes the TCP buffer size and the number of sockets needed for the transfer to utilize the full bandwidth. Pathrate uses packet dispersion techniques to estimate the network capacity. DiskRouter tunes the buffer size to be equal to the bandwidth delay product. For every 10 ms of latency, DiskRouter adds an extra stream. This is an empirical value that is known to

120

work well [34]. If multiple streams are being used, the buffer size is split equally among the streams.

It is also possible to regulate the bandwidth used by DiskRouter and the bandwidth used by each DiskRouter stream. At this point, this works by limiting the TCP buffer size.

Since DiskRouter performs this periodic latency and network capacity estimation, it can function as a network monitor.

Integration with Higher Level Planners. DiskRouter has features that enable easy integration with higher-level planners. We believe that this ability is the key to addressing failure and fault tolerance issues. For instance, it is possible when using DiskRouter overlay network that a wide-area network outage disconnects one of the nodes. The DiskRouter client has a tunable time-out and if some pieces are missing after the timeout, it can directly fetch them from the source.

While this handling works, to make better decisions and dynamically reconfigure the overlay network, higher-level planners need this information. DiskRouters and DiskRouter clients pass this information and a summary of the different link status (bandwidth, failures encountered) to higher-level planners, which can then use this information to plan data movement strategies.

In real-world experiments, we have integrated DiskRouter into a data placement framework managed by Stork [17]. Data placement schedulers can make better scheduling decision using the information provided by DiskRouters.

6. Connectivity

Many organizations still resort to a very insecure approach to get around the connectivity problem of the Internet caused by firewalls/NATs. As a data movement becomes necessary, the network administrator manually opens the firewall/NAT for the address quadruples that are believed to be used during the movement. However, it is very difficult to know those quadruples a priori. Especially in the automated data placement, where protocols are dynamically selected and the number of streams is dynamically determined, knowing the exact addresses that a data movement will use is almost impossible. Therefore, to be safe but less secure, the administrator must open more addresses than actually used. These extra openings can be exploited by attackers to sneak into the network.

Previous systems target a specific network setting and/or firewall/NAT behavior. For instance, the approach used by many file sharing software assumes that firewalls/NATs allow web traffic (port 80). Some systems assume that certain components can be installed on firewall/NAT machines or on the boundaries of networks. Organizations use different types of firewalls/NATs and have different network settings, security concerns, performance requirement, etc. Therefore, networks owned by different organizations must be traversed in different ways. For this reason, no previous system satisfies every organization.

In a data placement, one site may have to communicate with multiple sites over time or in a single moment. Those peer sites may have to be traversed in different ways as explained above. Because of this multi-organizational and multi-party communication pattern, we need to have various sorts of traversal systems. Furthermore, we need an integrated system that combines those systems so that two organizations having different network settings and security criteria can communicate each other. At our best knowledge, UCB (Unified Connection Brokering) is the only system that satisfies these requirements.

UCB is an integrated system that combines 3 component systems, each of which supports unique network settings and use cases. With UCB, an organization can choose one from those component mechanisms and can still talk with others using different component systems. This is very similar to that, in Stork, data can be moved from an organization using a protocol to another using a different protocol. To support as many organizations as possible, we have chosen UCB's component systems very carefully. Instead of adding component systems in ad hoc ways, we classified representative ways to open firewalls/NATs and then invented component systems for each class. The component systems are GCB (Generic Connection Brokering) [35], CODO (Cooperative On-Demand Opening) [36], and XRAY (middleboX traversal by RelAYing).

6.1. Overview

In UCB, each network chooses a component mechanism based upon its network situation and other criteria. Yet, two networks using different component mechanisms can communicate each other. Figure 10 shows a typical topology of UCB. The figure shows a situation that a client in an organization using CODO makes a connection to a server in another organization using GCB.

If a server network does not allow inbound connections, then it has to have one or more agents that arrange connections toward authorized server applications. Similarly, a client network that does not allow outbound connections from arbitrary clients must have one or multiple agents that arrange connections from authorized clients. A UCB agent configured to use GCB as its component mechanism is called a GCB agent. Other types of agents are called similarly. Not every place can an organization install its agents. The places on which agents can (or must) be installed mainly depend on the factors that an organization chooses its component mechanism based upon. For example, GCB must be used when end users (researchers) do not have a control relationship to the firewalls/NATs on a communication path. Since they cannot control the devices, agents cannot be installed on the devices. In this case, researchers normally do not have privilege to install entities on the boundary of the network, either. For this reason, GCB agents are generally installed on the public network as shown in the figure 10.

When a server application creates a socket, UCB library linked with the server (the server library for short) contacts the agent of the server network (the server agent for short) and registers the socket information to the agent. Through this registration process, the agent checks if the server is authorized to accept inbound communications.

To make a connection to a server, a client behind a firewall/NAT contacts the agent of the client network (the client agent for short) and asks for the arrangement of a connection to the server. Next, the client agent, on behalf of the client, contacts the server agent and asks for an inbound connection to the server. If the client network allows outbound connections by arbitrary clients, i.e. the client does not have an agent to arrange outbound connections (as the client in the bottom of figure 10), then the client itself contacts the server agent.

Upon receiving a connection request to a server, the server agent checks if the server

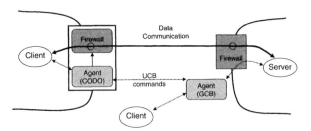

Figure 10. Typical topology of UCB. *A server network on the right has a GCB agent outside of it. A client network on the left has a CODO agent running on the firewall machine.*

and the client (or its agent) are authorized to accept and make inbound connections, respectively. If the test passes, it creates a pinhole or a relay point and replies success to the client agent with the information such as how and to what address the client agent can make the connection.

When the client agent receives the reply from the server agent, it creates a pinhole or a relay point. Then, the client agent notifies the client the result of the arrangement. The server agent also notifies the server, if an action must be triggered by the server. To allow only authorized applications to communicate through a firewall/NAT, a strong security mechanism is used to exchange UCB commands.

The important points of the connection setup process in UCB are (1) that each network opens its firewall/NAT using its component mechanism and (2) that two component mechanisms are glued together through the cooperation of agents.

6.2. Component mechanisms
6.2.1. GCB (Generic Connection Brokering)

GCB is a component system of UCB and supports the cases that end users (usually called researchers in grid) can not control (either manually or programmatically) the firewall/NAT of the server network. For example, if a researcher has a grid pool behind a firewall of the campus network, then (s)he may not be able to control the campus firewall.

Today, most networks allow outbound but block inbound communications. Most NATs allow outbound communications (and their replies). Most firewalls are factory-configured to allow outbound communications. GCB exploits this common configuration. From a different perspective, GCB tries to bring the symmetry back to the Internet. With the traditional socket layer, the first packet, e.g. SYN packet, is always sent from a client to a server. Therefore, the direction of a connection is decided by the role–who the client (or the server) is in a communication. The main idea of GCB is to make the Internet symmetric by decoupling the direction from the role. GCB decides the direction of a connection based upon the relative topology of communicating parties, instead of who calls connect. Because of the decoupling, the role is still decided by application programmers. Thus, in GCB, it is possible that a connection is made from a server that calls accept to a client calling connect.

To make a connection to a server, a client sends a connection request to the agent of the server. Upon receiving the request, the agent decides the direction of the connection and notifies the client and the server, if necessary. If a client is in the public network and a server is behind a firewall/NAT, the connection is made from the server to the client. If both are behind firewalls/NATs, then both parties make outbound connections to a relay point that the agent creates.

6.2.2. CODO (Cooperative On-Demand Opening)

CODO is used when the firewall/NAT of the network can be programmatically controlled. A CODO agent running on the firewall/NAT machine dynamically creates and deletes pinholes at the device upon requests from applications. CODO controls outbound as well as inbound communications. Therefore, networks need not allow outbound communications to use CODO.

When a client behind a firewall/NAT wants to connect to a server also behind another firewall/NAT, it contacts the client agent and asks for outbound connection toward the server. The client agent then contacts the server agent and asks for inbound connection. Using the API that each firewall/NAT provides, the client and server agents create pinholes for outbound and inbound, respectively, for the quadruple (client's IP, client's port, server's IP, server's port).

Other systems that support similar network settings as CODO creates pinholes with wildcard client address. On the other hand, CODO creates pinholes with full addresses of the client and the server. This results in firewalls/NATs opened as narrow and short as possible, because pinholes are made so that only intended pairs can get through and only when there are authorized client-server pairs. CODO involves more interactions between applications and agents than other systems because it opens firewalls/NATs with more address information. To support organizations that want efficient traversal at the expense of security, it provides efficient but less secure mode, called promiscuous mode. In this mode, CODO operates the same way as other systems.

6.2.3. XRAY (middleboX traversal by RelAYing)

XRAY is used when the firewall/NAT of the network can be manually controlled. The firewall/NAT is configured to allow traffic to/from XRAY agents that are usually installed inside the network. The XRAY agents relay communications for authorized applications, but drop packets from unauthorized ones. Therefore, we can regard that the firewall/NAT trusts the agents and delegates them a part of policy enforcement. Like CODO, XRAY controls both inbound and outbound communications.

A connection is established in a very similar way as with the CODO case. The only difference is that XRAY agents create relay points instead of making pinholes at the firewall/NAT. Application data units are transferred from the client to the relay point in the client network to the relay point in the server network and finally to the server, and vice versa. Relay points terminate overlay link at the application layer. Each overlay link is secured by security negotiation between hops terminating the link. Therefore, every application data unit is authenticated and authorized by each hop.

In addition to the fact that XRAY does not require programmatic control of the firewall/NAT, it can provide the most secure traversal. In CODO, pinholes are made only when authorized applications request so. However, communications through the pinholes are not secured by the traversal mechanism. On the contrary, XRAY creates relay points such that only authorized applications can communicate via those relay points.

One drawback of relay-based approach is the performance. Hop-by-hop encryption/decryption slows down communication. At replay points, packets must traverse the protocol stack up and down. However, these are inevitable costs to achieve secure traversal.

6.2.4. Unifying component mechanisms

To integrate component mechanisms, UCB uses the model that a network uses one mechanism to enable communications into and out of it, while an endpoint uses any mechanism chosen by the network that it wants to communicate into or out of. With this model, we just need to show how UCB connects two mechanisms used by each network to provide an end-to-end communication channel. The followings show how two mechanisms are glued in UCB for each combination of mechanisms used by the client and the server network. Each combination is denoted as "from A to B", where A is the mechanism the client network uses and B used by the server network. We do not have the cases that the client network uses GCB because GCB is not used to control outbound communications.

From CODO to GCB: The agent of the client network (client agent for short) creates a pinhole for inbound from the server to the client. The end-to-end connection is made from the server to the client through the hole.

From CODO to XRAY: The agent of the server network (server agent for short) creates a relay point and the client agent creates a pinhole for outbound from the client to the relay point. The end-to-end connection consists of two connections: one from the client to the relay point (through the hole) and the other from the relay point to the server.

From CODO to CODO: The client and server agent create pinholes for outbound and inbound, respectively, from the client to the server. The end-to-end connection is made from the client to the server.

From XRAY to GCB: The client agent creates a relay point with passive sockets for both client and server sides. The end-to-end connection consists of two connections: one from the client to the relay point and the other from the server to the relay point.

From XRAY to CODO: The client agent creates a relay point and the server agent creates a pinhole for inbound from the relay point to the server. The end-to-end connection consists of two connections: one from the client to the relay point and the other from the relay point to the server through the hole.

From XRAY to XRAY: The client and server agent create relay points. The end-to-end connection consists of three connections: one from the client the relay point in the client network, another from the relay point in the client network to the relay point in the server network, and the other from the relay point in the server network to the server.

7. Conclusions

Existing systems closely couple data movement and computation. This results in re-computation if the output data transfer fails, or re-transfer of the data if the computation fails. This is especially undesirable for data intensive applications, where the transfers have a higher likelihood of failure due to the large amounts of data moved. We have presented a framework that de-couples data movement from computation, and acts as an I/O subsystem for distributed systems. This system provides a uniform interface to heterogeneous storage systems and data transfer protocols; permits policy support and higher-level optimization; and enables reliable, efficient scheduling of compute and data resources.

The current approaches consider data movement as a side effect of computation. There is no scheduling of data movement. This has resulted in thrashing and crashing of storage servers when there are uncontrolled number of requests to them; uneven and inefficient utilization of the network links; and decreased end-to-end performance of data intensive applications. Just as computation and network resources need to be carefully scheduled and managed, the scheduling of data movement across distributed systems is crucial, since the access to data is generally the main bottleneck for data intensive applications. We have presented an approach which regards data movement as a full-fledged job just like computational jobs. In this approach, data movement can be queued, scheduled, monitored, and even check-pointed. We have also introduced the first specialized scheduler for data movement, which we call Stork.

While work has been done on making computation adapt to changing conditions, little work has been done on making the data movement adapt to changing conditions. Many tunable parameters depend on the current state of the network, server, and other components involved in the data movement. Ideally, the system should be able to figure this out and adapt the application. A low-level example is that the TCP buffer size should be set equal to the bandwidth delay product to utilize the full bandwidth. A higher-level example is that to maximize throughput of a storage server, the number of concurrent data transfers should be controlled taking into account server, end host, and network characteristics. I have presented an infrastructure that observes the environment and enables run-time adaptation of data placement jobs.

We have introduced a flexible infrastructure called DiskRouter that uses hierarchical buffering at intermediate points to aid in large-scale data transfers. It supports easy construction of application level overlay network and can perform routing. It performs dynamic TCP tuning to improve throughput. It supports application level multicast to help lower the network load and improve the system throughput, and it has been integrated into a data placement framework managed by Stork.

Because of its multi-organizational, multi-party, and huge amount of communications, data placement may be the field most damaged from the connectivity problem of the Internet. We have introduced an integrated system, UCB, which handles the problem. Just as Stork is able to handle diverse protocols, middleware, and storage systems, UCB handles the diversity of network settings, types of firewalls/NATs, security concerns of organizations. UCB provides three component mechanisms each of which supports unique use cases and has different characteristics such as performance, security, and deployability. An organization can choose a component mechanism to use based upon its requirements and constraints. Still, organizations using different component mechanisms can communicate each other.

126

REFERENCES

1. CMS, The Compact Muon Solenoid Project, http://cmsinfo.cern.ch/.
2. PPDG, PPDG Deliverables to CMS, http://www.ppdg.net/archives/ppdg/2001/doc00017.doc.
3. W. Feng, High Performance Transport Protocols, Los Alamos National Laboratory (2003).
4. R. Maddurri, B. Allcock, Reliable File Transfer Service, http://www-unix.mcs.anl.gov/ madduri/main.html (2003).
5. S. Koranda, B. Moe, Lightweight Data Replicator, http://www.lsc-group.phys.uwm.edu/lscdatagrid/LDR/ overview.html (2003).
6. I. Foster, C. Kesselmann, Globus: A Toolkit-Based Grid Architecture, in: The Grid: Blueprints for a New Computing Infrastructure, Morgan Kaufmann, 1999, pp. 259–278.
7. B. Allcock, J. Bester, J. Bresnahan, A. Chervenak, I. Foster, C. Kesselman, S. Meder, V. Nefedova, D. Quesnel, S. T. ke, Secure, efficient data transport and replica management for high-pe rformance data-intensive computing, in: IEEE Mass Storage Conference, San Diego, CA, 2001.
8. A. Shishani, A. Sim, J. Gu, Storage Resource Managers: Middleware Components for Grid Storage, in: Nineteenth IEEE Symposium on Mass Storage Systems, 2002.
9. SDSC, High Performance Storage System (HPSS), http://www.sdsc.edu/hpss/.
10. I. Bird, B. Hess, A. Kowalski, Building the mass storage system at Jefferson Lab, in: Proceedings of 18th IEEE Symposium on Mass Storage Systems, San Diego, California, 2001.
11. FNAL, Enstore mass storage system, http://www.fnal.gov/docs/products/enstore/.
12. C. Baru, R. Moore, A. Rajasekar, M. Wan, The SDSC Storage Resource Broker, in: Proceedings of CASCON, Toronto, Canada, 1998.
13. D. Thain, , M. Livny, The ethernet approach to grid computing, in: Proceedings of the Twelfth IEEE Symposium on High Performance Distributed Computing, Seattle, Washington, 2003.
14. Y. Morita, H. Sato, Y. Watase, O. Tatebe, S. Sekiguchi, S. Matsuoka, N. Soda, A. Dell'Acqua, Building a high performance parallel file system using grid datafarm and root i/o, in: Proceedings of the 2003 Computing in High Energy and Nuclear Physics (CHEP03), La Jolla, CA, 2003.
15. J. Kubiatowicz, D. Bindel, Y. Chen, S. Czerwinski, P. Eaton, D. Geels, R. Gummadi, S. Rhea, H. Weatherspoon, W. Weimer, C. Wells, B. Zhao, Oceanstore: An architecture for global-scale persistent storage, in: Proceedings of the Ninth international Conference on Architectural Support for Programming Languages and Operating Systems (ASPLOS 2000), 2000.
16. J. Bent, D. Thain, A. Arpaci-Dusseau, R. Arpaci-Dusseau, Explicit control in a batch-aware distributed file system, in: Proceedings of the First USENIX/ACM Conference on Networked Systems Design and Implementation, 2004.
17. T. Kosar, M. Livny, Stork: Making Data Placement a First Class Citizen in the Grid, in: Proceedings of the 24th Int. Conference on Distributed Computing Systems, Tokyo, Japan, 2004.

18. T. Kosar, M. Livny, A framework for reliable and efficient data placement in distributed computing system s, Journal of Parallel and Distributed Computing.

19. E. Deelman, J. Blythe, Y. Gil, C. Kesselman, Pegasus: Planning for execution in grids, in: GriPhyN technical report, 2002.

20. I. Foster, J. Vockler, M. Wilde, Y. Zhao, Chimera: A virtual data system for representing, querying, and automating data derivation, in: 14th International Conference on Scientific and Statistical Database Management (SSDBM 2002), Edinburgh, Scotland, 2002.

21. D. Thain, T. Tannenbaum, M. Livny, Condor and the Grid, in: Grid Computing: Making the Global Infrastructure a Reality., Fran Berman and Geoffrey Fox and Tony Hey, editors. John Wiley and Sons Inc., 2002.

22. L. Chervenak, N. Palavalli, S. Bharathi, C. Kesselman, R. Schwartzkopf, Performance and scalability of a Replica Location Service, in: Proceedings of the International Symposium on High Performance Distributed Computing Conference (HPDC-13), Honolulu, Hawaii, 2004.

23. C. Dovrolis, P. Ramanathan, D. Moore, What do packet dispersion techniques measure?, in: INFOCOMM, 2001.

24. NLANR/DAST, Iperf: The TCP/UDP bandwidth measurement tool, http://dast.nlanr.net/Projects/Iperf/ (2003).

25. M. J. Litzkow, M. Livny, M. W. Mutka, Condor - A Hunter of Idle Workstations, in: Proceedings of the 8th International Conference of Distributed Computing Systems, 1988, pp. 104–111.

26. J. Frey, T. Tannenbaum, I. Foster, S. Tuecke, Condor-G: A Computation Management Agent for Multi-Institutional Grids, in: Proceedings of the Tenth IEEE Symposium on High Performance Distributed Computing, San Francisco, California, 2001.

27. J. Postel, FTP: File Transfer Protocol Specification, RFC-765 (1980).

28. W. Allcock, I. Foster, R. Madduri, Reliable data transport: A critical service for the grid, in: Building Service Based Grids Workshop, Global Grid Forum 11, 2004.

29. G. Kola, M. Livny, Diskrouter: A flexible infrastructure for high performance large scale data transfers, Tech. Rep. CS-TR-2003-1484, University of Wisconsin (2003).

30. M. Butler, R. Pennington, J. A. Terstriep, Mass Storage at NCSA: SGI DMF and HP UniTree, in: Proceedings of 40th Cray User Group Conference, 1998.

31. Condor, NeST: Network Storage, http://www.cs.wisc.edu/condor/nest/ (2003).

32. R. Raman, M. Livny, M. Solomon, Matchmaking: Distributed resource management for high throughput computing, in: Proceedings of the Seventh IEEE International Symposium on High Performance Distributed Computing (HPDC7), Chicago, Illinois, 1998.

33. D. Thain, J. Basney, S. Son, M. Livny, The kangaroo approach to data movement on the grid, in: Proceedings of the Tenth IEEE Symposium on High Performance Distributed Computing, San Francisco, California, 2001.

34. G. Kola, T. Kosar, M. Livny, Run-time adaptation of grid data-placement jobs, Parallel and Distributed Computing Practices.

35. S. Son, M. Livny, Recovering internet symmetry in distributed computing, in: Proceedings of the 3rd International Symposium on Cluster Computing and the Grid, Tokyo, Japan, 2003.

36. S. Son, B. Allcock, M. Livny, Codo: Firewall traversal by cooperative on-demand pening, in: Proceedings of the Fourteenth IEEE Symposium on High Performance Distributed Computing, Research Triangle Park, NC, 2005.

Grid Computing: The New Frontier of High Performance Computing
Lucio Grandinetti (Editor)
© 2005 Elsevier B.V. All rights reserved.

The Grid Relational Catalog Project

G. Aloisio[a], M. Cafaro[a], S. Fiore[a] and M. Mirto[a]

[a] Department of Innovation Engineering, University of Lecce, Italy

Today many DataGrid applications need to manage and process a very large amount of data distributed across multiple grid nodes and stored into heterogeneous databases.
Grids encourage and promote the publication, sharing and integration of scientific data (distributed across several Virtual Organizations) in a more open manner than is currently the case, and many e-Science projects have an urgent need to interconnect legacy and independently operated databases through a set of data access and integration services.
The complexity of data management within a Computational Grid comes from the distribution, scale and heterogeneity of data sources.
A set of dynamic and adaptive services could address specific issues related to automatic data management providing high performance and transparency as well as fully exploiting a grid infrastructure. These services should involve data migration and integration, discovery of data sources and so on, providing a transparent and dynamic layer of data virtualization.
In this paper we introduce the Grid-DBMS concept, a framework for dynamic data management in a grid environment, highlighting its requirements, architecture, components and services. We also present an overview about the Grid Relational Catalog Project (GRelC) developed at the CACT/ISUFI of the University of Lecce, which represents a partial implementation of a Grid-DBMS for the Globus Community.

1.INTRODUCTION

Many e-Science projects need to manage and process a huge amount of data distributed across multiple nodes and stored into heterogeneous databases. Several research activities related to Computational Grids [1,2] have been generally focused on applications where data is stored in files (i.e. DataGrid project [3]), but nowadays there is an urgent need to interconnect legacy and independently operated databases [4,5,6].
Database Management Systems (DBMSs) represent a reliable, accepted and powerful instrument to store persistent data but, to date, they are not grid enabled (with the notable exception of Oracle [7]), that is, there is not data grid middleware, based on standard protocols (i) satisfying basic requirements such as security, availability and

transparency, (ii) fully exploiting the power of a computational grid and (iii) supplying grid applications with adaptive, high level and dynamic data management functionalities. Lastly, many efforts have been concentrating in this direction, basically providing *static* services for data access and integration [8,9,10], but for really exploiting a grid infrastructure for data management it is necessary to introduce a set of *dynamic* services, i.e., a more complex and adaptive (with respect to the existent ones [11]) framework.

This work presents a preliminary version of the Grid-DBMS specification [12], illustrating an open and distributed framework for dynamic data management in a grid environment and then it presents an overview about the Grid Relational Catalog Project [13,14], which is a reference implementation of a Grid-DBMS.

The outline of the paper is as follows. In Section 2 we briefly recall related work, whereas in Section 3 we introduce the Grid-DBMS concept and related basic definitions. In Section 4 we present the main challenges, whereas in Section 5 we highlight the basic components of a Grid-DBMS. Section 6 describes the main Grid-DBMS services, whilst Section 7 illustrates the overall architecture. In Section 8 we discuss the most important issues related to a Grid-DBMS whereas in Section 9 we present the GRelC project. We finally conclude the paper in Section 10.

2.RELATED WORK

The Spitfire Project [15] is part of the Work Package 2 in the European Data Grid Project and provides a means to access relational databases from the grid. It is a very thin layer on top of an RDBMS (by default MySQL) that provides a JDBC driver. It is using Web Service technology (Jakarta Tomcat) to provide SOAP-based RPC (through Apache Axis) to a few user-definable database operations.

The Open Grid Services Architecture Data Access and Integration (OGSA-DAI [16]) is another project concerned with constructing middleware to assist with access and integration of data from separate data sources via the grid. It is engaged in identifying the requirements, designing solutions and delivering software that will meet this purpose. The project was conceived by the UK Database Task Force and is working closely with the Global Grid Forum DAIS-WG and the Globus team.

These two projects are strongly related to data access and integration services, but to date they do not address the dynamic data management as described in the Grid-DBMS specification.

The Storage Resource Broker (SRB) [17] was designed to provide applications with uniform access to distributed storage resources. Its main focus is file-based data and it provides several features including a Metadata Server, a logical naming scheme for datasets, automatic replica creation and maintenance, etc., but it does not solve the problem of integrating databases into a grid.

In [11] the authors propose a long term vision of a layer of grid data virtualization services which aims at providing a high level of transparency and dynamism as we address in our work. Some differences are related to additional services such as accounting & billing or data monitoring and concurrency control.

3.BASIC DEFINITIONS

This paper presents the Grid-DBMS concept, a system for dynamically managing data sources in a grid environments. Before describing the Grid-DBMS requirements and architecture, we need to formally introduce some basic concepts providing the elementary definitions for Grid-DBMS, Grid-DataBase and Logical Data Space.

In our vision a "*Grid-DBMS is a distributed system which automatically, transparently and dynamically reconfigures at runtime components such as Data Resources, according to the Grid state, in order to maintain a desired performance level. It must offer an efficient, robust, intelligent, transparent, uniform access to Grid-Databases*".

By dynamic reconfiguration we mean three elementary operations:

✓ data source relocation (a data source can be moved from one node of the grid to another one which is more performant in terms of access time, cost, etc.);

✓ data source replication (a data source can be replicated on different nodes of the grid to increase performance, availability and fault tolerance of the overall system);

✓ data source fragmentation (a data source can be partitioned on different nodes of the grid to speedup searches and complex screening operations by performing them in parallel).

The three operations, listed before, represent the basic primitives for more complex data reconfiguration processes in a distributed environment.

In the Grid-DBMS definition we referred to the Grid-Database concept, which "*is a collection of one or more databases logically interrelated (distributed over a grid environment) which can also be heterogeneous and contain replica, accessible through a Grid-DBMS front end. It represents an extension and a virtualization of the Database concept in a grid environment*".

The last definition, that we need to introduce, is related to the Logical Data Space which refers to "*the virtualized physical space in which a Grid-Database can be managed*".

Finally, the three concepts can be brought together as follows:

"*A Grid-Database is dynamically managed by the Grid-DBMS within its Logical Data Space*".

4.CHALLENGES

A dynamic framework such as the Grid-DBMS has to face several challenges, in a grid environment. In this Section we present the most representative ones highlighting their importance and related issues. In the following we discuss about security, transparency, heterogeneity, efficiency and dynamicity. The main challenges are:

1) Security: data security is a fundamental requirement of a Grid-DBMS that aims at protecting data against unauthorized accesses. It includes: data protection and user control.

The former is required to prevent unauthorized users from understanding the physical content of data, so that data encryption must be used both for information stored on disk and to protect data exchanged on the network. The latter is required to perform authentication and authorization processes.

Authentication is required to check the user's identity, whilst authorization control (centralized or distributed) determines whether a user has the right to perform a specific operation (i.e. read/write) on a database object (the object represents a subset of a database). Object is intended to be used in different ways by different users, thus we need to consider access rights. These specify who is allowed to perform what operations on an object (i.e., who is allowed to read or change its status).

2) Transparency: it refers to separation of the higher-level semantics of a system from low-level implementation issues. There are various possible forms of transparency within a distributed environment. Starting form the ANSA Reference Manual [18] and the International Standards Organization's Reference Model for Open Distributed Processing (RM-ODP) [19] we highlight the most important forms of transparency for a Grid-DBMS:

✓ *location transparency*: the user must know nothing about the physical location of a database on the grid. This way mechanisms which move (totally or partially) a data source can be entirely transparent to the user (data relocation transparency);

✓ *access transparency*: it enables local or remote data sources to be accessed using identical operations (it represents an important issue for data virtualization);

✓ *fragmentation transparency*: fragmentation of data consists of dividing database information into smaller fragments and treating each one of them as a separate unit. This process allows the system to improve global performance, availability and reliability. Moreover, fragmentation increases the level of concurrency and therefore the system throughput;

✓ *performance and mobility transparency*: it allows the system to be reconfigured (i.e. moving data sources – data relocation transparency) to improve the performance of the entire system as the grid state varies;

✓ *replication transparency*: replication of data improves performance, reliability and fault tolerance of the overall system. It is worth noting here that the user must not be aware of the existence of multiple copies of the same logical information.

3) Heterogeneity: many different DBMSs exist (i.e. ORACLE, IBM/DB2, PostgreSQL [20], MySQL [21], etc). Moreover, an increasing number of applications interact with flat files and/or unstructured data sources. Access, integration and sharing of data belonging to legacy systems may be difficult for several reasons: different data types, physical supports, data format, data model, etc. The Grid-DBMS has to conceal heterogeneity performing a data virtualization process. This way, for instance the access mechanism will be independent (transparent) of the actual implementation of the data sources and data will be presented in an unified manner. In order to support different data format/type/domain and other issues related to data integration, we need additional information bridging the syntactic and semantic gaps among the individual data sources and the user.

4) Efficiency: from the performance point of view, the Grid-DBMS must provide high throughput, concurrent accesses, fault tolerance, reduced communication overhead, etc. Three factors have strong impact on the performance of a Grid-DBMS:

- ✓ *data localization*, that is the ability to store/move data in close proximity to its point of use. This can lead to: reduced query response time (due to data fragmentation) and better exploitation of distributed resources (using for different portion of a database, different CPUs and I/O services);
- ✓ *query parallelism* due basically to data distribution (intra-query parallelism) and concurrent accesses to the Grid-DBMS (inter-query parallelism);
- ✓ *high level queries*: in grid environments new kind of queries can improve global performance (reducing connection time and/or amount of data transferred) exploiting advanced and efficient data transport protocols (i.e. protocols supporting parallel data streams), compression mechanisms, and so on.

5) Dynamicity: as we stated in our definition a Grid-DBMS must be dynamic in the sense that according to the state of the grid resources, it has to reconfigure its components (data sources) in order to provide high performance, availability and efficiency. So, relocation of data sources, fragmentation (which consequently leads to the fragment allocation problem) and replication of databases are the three basic pillars which can be jointly used by the Grid-DBMS to perform more complex and dynamic data management activities. A Grid-DBMS must provide some intelligent components in order to carry out the dynamic mechanisms cited before. In the Grid-DBMS architecture that we envision, we basically need two kinds of schedulers:

- ✓ *data scheduler*, which must address (i) relocation of data sources, (ii) replication of the data sources and (iii) fragment allocation choosing the "best" nodes of the grid (taking into account system optimization performance parameters/goals);
- ✓ *query scheduler*, which has to (i) provide an engine for distributed query optimization which must find, in a grid environment, the best node (computational resource) on which critical operations (join, semi-join, union, cartesian product, etc.) can be performed and (ii) choose, from a set of replicated catalogues, the "best" replica of the dataset to use, in order to maximize throughput, provide load balancing, minimize response time and communication overhead.

5.MAIN COMPONENTS OF THE GRID-DBMS

In this Section we briefly discuss about the two main components of a Grid-DBMS. At the highest level the Grid-DBMS consists of two components (see Figure 1): one mainly hardware and another one specifically software. They are:

- Legacy System: it brings together hardware elements (pc, workstations, storage, network, etc.) of the grid infrastructure (named Enterprise Grid - EG) as well as legacy software for data management (i.e. DBMSs already installed).

- Grid-DBMS middleware: distributed middleware which allows managing, accessing, integrating, optimizing and reconfiguring data sources installed within a Legacy System.

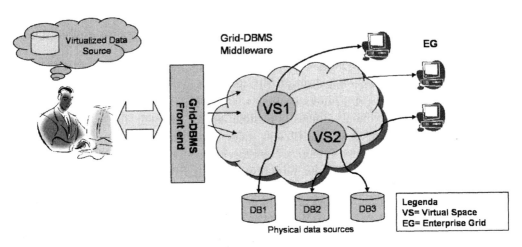

Figure 1. Grid-DBMS Components.

6.GRID-DBMS SERVICES

The Grid-DBMS represents a valid, self-optimizing and self-configuring solution. It does not represent a new kind of DBMS and it is not just a set of data access and integration services, but rather a dynamic and complex environment. In this Section we present the basic services connected with the Grid-DBMS architecture: Data Access, Data Gather, Static Management, Data Monitoring, Data Optimizer and Dynamic Reconfiguration.

The Grid-DBMS must provide the following core services:

• *Data Access Service* (DAS): a layer providing a standard interface for relational and not-relational (i.e. textual) data sources. It is placed between grid applications and DataBase Management Systems. It has to conceal many physical details such as the physical database location, database name, DBMS, etc. It must also hide the DBMS heterogeneity offering a uniform access interface to data sources, thus providing a first level of virtualization (data access virtualization);

• *Data Gather Service* (DGS): the main purpose of this service (placed on top of DAS) is to allow the user to look at a set of distributed databases (fragments), as a single logical data source, that is, a Grid-DataBase. Hence, it has to hide the number of fragments, the DAS physical locations, etc., providing a second level of virtualization (data integration virtualization). This layer must offer the capabilities of data federation [22] and distributed query processing (DQP) [23,24], providing the illusion that a single database is being accessed, whereas, in fact, several distributed databases are being accessed;

• *Static Management Service* (SMS): this layer has to provide the basic primitives to move, split and copy a data source. It is placed on top of DAS and it is extensively used by the higher levels connected with dynamic data management. At this layer it is necessary to define a cross-DBMS data format used to move structured data from one location to one or more others;

• *Data Monitoring Service* (DMS): a service which aims at monitoring the entire Enterprise Grid (hosts and databases performance) in order to obtain information snapshots useful for making decision processes. Exceeding critical thresholds can, in turn, trigger higher level data management processes aimed at re-establishing (by means of reconfiguration activities) a desired level of application performance;

• *Dynamic Reconfiguration Service* (DRS): a service which is responsible for automatically reconfiguring (replicating, relocating and partitioning) data sources using the services offered by the SMS and considering:
  ✓ information (statistics) coming from the DMS;
  ✓ administrator-defined parameters (minimum performance level, number of concurrent accesses, CPU/memory and disk usage level, etc.);

• *Data-Optimizer Service* (DOS): a service which aims at optimizing the performance related to data sources (creating views, indexes, etc., exploiting the DAS) based on information coming from the DMS.

7.GRID-DBMS ARCHITECTURE

In this paragraph we introduce the Grid-DBMS architecture presenting the main layers which are directly involved in data management activities. For each level many primitives and/or services could be defined but these details are out of the scope of this Section.

As shown in Figure 2, the Grid-DBMS architecture is composed of several layers, each one taking into account important issues.

In the Grid-DBMS architecture, the lower layers 1 and 2 are strongly related to the Legacy System component, whereas the upper layers 3, 4 and 5 are connected with the Grid-DBMS middleware (see Section 5).

Let us go now into more details about the Grid-DBMS architecture:

• *Fabric* layer (level 1) comprises the underlying systems of the Enterprise Grid, that is storage (containing data sources), computers, operating systems, computational resources, networks, routers and so on;

• *DBMS* layer (level 2), consists of a set of applications (DBMSs) useful to interact with specific data sources (DBMSs, by definition, are powerful tools or complex software packages designed to store and manage databases). At this level we can find both commercial database products (i.e. ORACLE 10g, IBM/DB2, etc.) and Open

Source database software (PostgreSQL, UnixODBC [25], etc.) which support data management offering different solutions and functionalities.

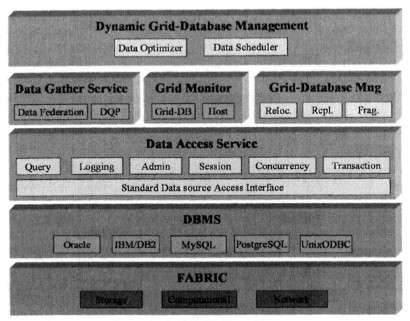

Figure 2. Grid-DBMS architecture.

• Data Access layer (level 3), must provide basic and uniform primitives to get access to and interact with different data sources. It has to hide, from the higher levels, the DBMSs heterogeneity performing a basic kind of data virtualization. This layer (which can be considered as a set of static services) is composed of two sub-layers:

   ✓ Standard Data source Access Interface (SDAI), sublevel 3.1, strongly related to the data source connectivity facilities. It provides a set of primitives to directly establish and manage a connection with several data sources (both structured and unstructured). Different DBMSs, sometimes do not implement completely and often with several variations, the SQL99 standard; furthermore exceptions and errors from the database back-end are not standardized. The DAS must ensure, through a translation process, uniform exceptions and standardized errors handling, uniform APIs and data types. Unstructured data need to be accessed too, by means of specific wrappers able to provide the basis for access, integration/federation and other data management activities. At this level it is very important to define an interchange format, that is a data structure useful to move information among different data sources (it can also be considered as a one shot ingestion mechanism or a higher level of data representation).

Moreover, it should be able to take into account links among information stored within a Grid-DataBase (preserving referential integrity constraint).

✓ Set of components (sublevel 3.2), which exploit the SDAI and so, provide a set of high level services connected with session control, user management and data access control policy, data privacy, concurrency and transaction management, advanced query submission leveraging compression mechanisms and efficient protocols for data delivery, etc.

• fourth layer (level 4) consists of three joint subcomponents:

✓ the first is the Data Gather Service (DGS) which is responsible for offering capabilities of data federation and DQP. Within this layer we find the *query scheduler* previously introduced (see Section 4). Data integration, federation and reconciliation are some of the most important topics connected with this level but they are not addressed in this work.

✓ the second is the Grid Monitor, which is responsible for monitoring Host (resource consumption information, i.e. CPU load average, free memory, etc.) and Grid-Database performance (query response time, etc.). All of this metadata are then stored over time into a system performance database, to supply information for decision making processes and diagnosis tools at the higher levels. Suite tests for database performance, forecasting models, classification of host and network information are topics strongly related to this level;

✓ the third is the Grid-Database Management which provides basic services for dynamic data management. In particular this level offers relocation, replication and fragmentation primitives. It must exploit some data source interchange format (defined at level 3) useful to move data from one location to one or more others. Moreover it must offer efficient data transport protocol (using for instance, parallel streams, etc.) to reduce the data transfer time and consequently to improve the performance of the overall system;

• fifth layer is the Dynamic Grid-Database Management which has to dynamically, transparently and automatically reconfigures (exploiting level 4 primitives) data sources. At this level we find the *data scheduler* previously introduced (see Section 4) and also the Data Optimizer which improves system performance by means of views, indexes, etc. dynamically created.

In this work we mainly focus on the Data Access layer both from a specification and an implementation point of view (see Section 9). For this reason additional details about the Data Gather Service, Grid-Monitor and Dynamic Grid-DB Management which represent, each one, complex topics and interesting challenges will not be addressed in this paper.

8.GRID & GRID-DBMS ISSUES

In this Section we propose some of the most important issues connected both with the Grid-DBMS framework and the Enterprise context. These issues motivate why the Grid-DBMS can represent a good choice for an Enterprise environment.

Exploiting a Grid-DBMS, an Enterprise could:

✓ reuse the existing physical framework (Legacy System), optimizing the usage of physical resources in terms of storage and computational power. This way, reusing the EG infrastructure (a low-cost solution), buying new large and expensive computing systems (high cost solution) can be avoided;

✓ improve the performance of the entire system in terms of efficiency, reliability and availability moving, replicating and distributing data sources over the most performant machines of the EG (the Grid-DBMS is able to support changing workload by dynamically exploiting the reconfiguration processes of data sources);

✓ transparently and securely access/join/manage data stored in heterogeneous and widespread data sources providing a real data virtualization in a grid environment;

✓ easily extend the physical framework adding and/or deleting resources without either turning off the system or activating complex reconfiguration processes;

✓ automatically monitor all the physical resources (EG) and data sources (Grid-DB), providing self-diagnosis instruments aimed at reducing the human interaction. All of these monitoring information are also stored into internal repositories to support further analysis.

9.THE GRELC PROJECT

In this Section, we introduce the Grid Relational Catalog Project (GRelC), that is a reference implementation of the Grid-DBMS specification, developed at the CACT/ISUFI Laboratory at the University of Lecce. Our main focus, in this work, is to present the middleware related to Data Access (GRelC Service), which is a set of interfaces providing the basic primitives to easily get access to and interact with data sources in a grid environment (level 3 of the Grid-DBMS architecture). Moreover we have also developed other services related to data integration [26,27] (level 4), but they are out the scope of this paper.

In the following we present the GRelC Project talking about some basic concepts (related to security, service interface, network protocol), middleware and programming language, query support (basic and advanced), main components (GRelC Service, library and protocol), test suite (environment, results and discussion) and web service approach.

9.1.Basic Concepts

The GRelC middleware is built on top of the Globus Toolkit [28]; the user can build its own client application, using a rich set of interfaces and high-level APIs, without knowing any low level details about the Globus APIs, the XML library [29], the DBMS connection APIs, etc. (transparency requirement).

The *security of the connection*, between client applications and the GRelC Service (see Figure 3), is provided by the Grid Security Infrastructure (GSI) [30], whereas the security of the connection between the GRelC Service and the RDBMS relies entirely on the ODBC drivers used.

The security mechanism is carried out as a two steps process: first, there is a mutual authentication (grid-user/GRelC Service) based on the public key infrastructure which leverages the X509.v3 certificates and secondly, there is an authorization based on the Access Control List properly defined by the GRelC Service Administrator (this check is performed using the subject name of the user's certificate, e.g., /O=Grid/O=Globus/OU=unile.it /CN=Sandro Fiore). If the user belongs to the set of currently trusted users, this leads to a correctly opened session during which the user will be able to perform queries of any sort based on Data Access Policies (properly defined by the Administrator).

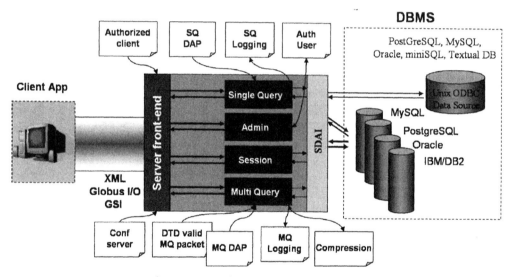

Figure 3. GRelC Data Access Service.

In this context, the local users/groups disappear. Indeed, all the grid users are mapped onto a local database user and data access control activities are performed by the GRelC Service (on behalf of grid users) and not by the DBMS (on behalf of local users). For each Grid-Database one or more grantors are responsible for assigning the rights to the grantees (data access policies). More flexible, complex and decentralized forms of control will be provided in the next releases of the middleware. Moreover, data encryption for information stored on disk will be utilized in order to improve data security/privacy.

The *network protocol* is fully GSI enabled and it is based on the eXtensible Markup Language (XML) standard, for payload definition. So, the GRelC Service and the client applications interact, using the canonical XML data format that is widely considered as an established standard, representing flexible data interoperability and exchange.

The *service interface* is abstract, transparent and high-level, allowing the users to get access and interact with distributed and heterogeneous data resources.

Furthermore, the GRelC Service allows concurrent, efficient and scalable access to databases. The GRelC Service uses ODBC connection drivers to achieve good performance w.r.t. efficiency and throughput. Indeed, as we pointed out in our tests, the proposed solution performs well w.r.t. stability, efficiency and scalability. We will present these issues after (see subsection 9.5).

It is worth noting here that we keep track of all the server activities using proper logging and bookkeeping. In this way, the administrator can access the information related to connection trials and their outcomes, submitted queries, connected users, timestamp and result of these operations and even more. This is also useful for debugging purposes.

9.2. Middleware

The GRelC library is built on top of the Globus Toolkit and the XML library. We chose the Globus Toolkit as grid middleware because it represents a "de facto" standard, released under a public license and is successfully used in many important Grid projects. Moreover, we can transparently take advantage of the uniform access to distributed resources using Globus.

Security is provided by the Grid Security Infrastructure (GSI), that is a layer based on public key technology which leverages the X.509v3 digital certificates.

In order to allow a robust and efficient transfer we decided to use the grb-gsiftp library [31] developed at the CACT/ISUFI of the University of Lecce. This library wraps the GridFTP protocol [32,33] and provides the user with the capability of starting a parallel third-party file transfer, transferring single file or directory.

9.3. Queries

The main functionalities of the GRelC Service are strongly related to the queries that is what the users can do using the proposed middleware. In the following we describe into details the queries provided by the GRelC software:

1. Basic Single Query (BSQ): it represents the most basic and intuitive kind of query. Some examples are SELECT, INSERT, UPDATE and DELETE operations;

2. SingleQuery GridFTP (SQFTP): it is used for a SELECT query in which the user redirects the resultset to an XML file, transferring it back to the client using the GridFTP protocol;

3. SingleQuery Zipped GridFTP (SQZipFTP): it is similar to the previous kind of query. The only difference is that the XML file is first compressed and then transferred back to the client (using the GridFTP protocol);

4. SingleQuery Remote (Zipped) GridFTP: it is the same as case 2 (respectively case 3). The only difference is that the user can select another final destination for the XML file;

5. MultiQuery (MQ): the MultiQuery is a GRelC proprietary kind of query/format used to efficiently update into a data source a massive amount of data. The rationale behind this kind of query is that the user does not directly transfer the update query

(INSERT, UPDATE and DELETE), but just the data (in XML format) from which the XML/SQL translator (a component of the GRelC Service) is able to infer the query itself (translating logical links into physical ones). This kind of query represents a basic primitive for moving huge amount of data among several data sources (providing support for relocation and/or replication processes).

To fully understand how this query works, let us suppose to have a huge amount of data, that need to be updated in a database. There are two different ways to do that. The first one is represented by many SingleQuery with multiple interactions between client and GRelC-Service. The second one is just a MultiQuery. In this case, the user has to send to the GRelC-Service a MQ XML file containing all the data. Obviously this file must be compliant with the Document Type Definition of the user's Grid-Database (that is, a DTD representing the schema of the Grid-Database; it is based on a fixed structure in which for each data source the user adds some particular specifications strongly connected with relations, attributes names and types, table names and so on). So, for each MultiQuery XML file, at first the GRelC Service performs a validation process using the right DTD and then a translation process (from XML data to SQL queries). In this way the user will be able to update in her database all of the data present in the MultiQuery XML file. Due to the nature, mechanism and performance of this query, the Multiquery is strongly recommended to populate relational Information Services (for example it is extensively used within the Dynamic Grid Catalog Information Service (DGC) [34,35] and the iGrid Information Service [36,37]). The MQ presents several advantages, because it allows:

- ✓ to compute in only one shot (also atomically by using transactions support) many insert, update and delete queries (indeed in the same MQ XML file the user can specify information related to several records of multiple tables);
- ✓ to reduce the interactions between client and GRelC Service (for a MQ submission there is only one feedback, whereas N SQs produces N feedbacks);
- ✓ to transfer on the GRelC Service side the queries submission process (reducing the connection time between client and GRelC Service and speeding up the entire updating process);
- ✓ to be considered as an interoperable and cross-DBMS format useful to move huge amount of data (entire databases) among several nodes of a computational grid.

Additional information related to a performance analysis in an European testbed of the MultiQuery can be found in [38];

6. Multi Query GridFTP (MQFTP): it is like the previous kind of query. The only difference is that the MQ XML file is transferred from the client to the GRelC Service using the GridFTP protocol and hence using multiple parallel streams to improve performance;

7. Multi Query Zipped GridFTP (MQZipFTP): in this case the MQ XML file is first compressed and then transferred from the client to the GRelC Service using the GridFTP protocol. The compression lead to reduced transfer time;

8. Multi Query Third Party (Zipped) GridFTP: it is the same as case 6 (respectively case 7). The only difference is that the user can speficy another source (different by the

host on which the client application runs) for the MQ XML file; this involves a third-party transfer;

9. Multi Single Query (MSQ): in this case the user can send a sequence of not SELECT queries (that is INSERT, UPDATE and DELETE queries) to the GRelC Service in one shot, thus reducing the interactions between the client application and the GRelC Service and increasing the system throughput.

9.4. Components

In the following subsections we present the most important components of the GRelC architecture that is (i) the GRelC Service, (ii) the GRelC library and (iii) the GRelC Protocol, talking about their properties and features.

9.4.1 GRelC Service

The GRelC Service is placed among client applications and data sources. It is responsible for establishing connections and managing interactions with databases. As shown in Figure 3, its main subcomponents are:

a) *Server front-end*: it listens for incoming request from the client applications and performs the client's authentication/authorization. Moreover it creates the user's environment, sets up the user data access policies and forks a requests manager, responsible for managing the entire user data session;

b) *Session*: this component is responsible for properly establishing and closing the communications among client applications and data resources;

c) *SingleQuery*: this component provides Single Query (SQ) support. By SQ, we mean a query such as a SELECT, INSERT, UPDATE and DELETE operation. More specifically, for each SQ requests coming from the client applications, this component:

  ✓ performs a query analysis in order to reject queries for which further processing is either impossible or unnecessary. This step is fundamental because a query could be "type incorrect", that is containing some attribute/relation names not defined in the grid-database schema or containing some operation applied to attributes of the wrong type,

  ✓ if the query is type correct the SQ submits it, through the SDAI, to the data sources retrieving the operation results and finally,

  ✓ SQ sends back to the client the query results, that is both the operation result (always) and the data retrieved from the database (when the query is a SELECT one);

d) *MultiQuery*: this component provides MQ support (see Section 9.3).

e) *Standard Data source Access Interface*: it implements the sublevel 3.1 of the Grid-DBMS architecture (see Section 7). The SDAI represents the lowest level in our architecture and it is responsible for dynamic binding with the physical data sources hiding the DBMS heterogeneity, the data format differences, etc. From an implementation point of view, the SDAI is a set of DBMS-specific wrappers (shared libraries) which (i) provide access to different classes of data sources and (ii) mask any kind of heterogeneity.

f) *Administration*: this component is strongly related to the system administration. Indeed, for each Grid-Database, the administrator can set (activate/deactivate) the authorization policy, define the Access Control List (ACL - which is the list containing all of the principals), the Data Access Policies (DAP - that is the rules which map principals to privileges), set the connection parameters, which are the values for physical connection with database (database location, login and password, DBMS listening port and database name) and define the Grid-DBMS name and listening port.

9.4.2 GRelC Library

In this subsection we introduce the GRelC library [39] which allows the user to build its own client application interacting with the GRelC Service.

As shown in Figure 4, it is placed on top of the core libraries (Globus libraries, grb-gsiftp library and XML library). This new layer provides a lot of transparency because it hides many technological details such as, for instance, the physical location of the databases, the low level connection, etc. allowing the user to query and update data transparently.

It is composed of many APIs (more than 80 functions) which can be classified in five categories:

- *Connection*: using these APIs, the user can set the channel (client-GRelC Service) properties, and open and close a connection with the Grid-DBMS;
- *Data Manipulation*: using these APIs, the user can manipulate the data retrieved from the data resources. She can move through the entire recordset, finding some records containing particular data, controlling the EOF and the BOF of the recordset, etc;
- *Core*: this category contains the APIs for Single Query submission. These functions implement the common SQL operations such as the SELECT, INSERT, UPDATE or DELETE query;
- *Administration*: this category contains all the APIs which are strongly connected with the system administration. For instance, the administrator can (remotely and securely) update the ACL or DAP related to the users. As we stated before, the privileges associated with these APIs are different from and less than the privileges associated with the physical database administrator. A basic set of these privileges are showed in Table 1;

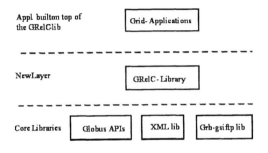

Figure 4. A new software layer, the GRelC Library.

- *High Level*: these APIs are related to higher functionalities. For instance using these APIs the user can (i) submit a simple Multi Query (ii) use the GridFTP protocol (for SQ-GridFTP and MQ-GridFTP submission (iii) start/commit/abort and rollback a transaction.

Two interesting features are added in the library to improve performance: GridFTP and Compression. The GridFTP protocol is used in order to transfer back to the client the XML file containing the resultset of a SELECT query or to send from the client to the GRelC Service a MultiQuery XML file. Compression can also be performed before sending a file. These features can also be jointly used. This would turn out to reduce the connection time between client application and GRelC Service leading to a better performance in terms of efficiency and throughput.

Using the GRelC library we developed a textual and interactive environment named SQLGRelC (like psql or mysql) useful to interact with a generic relational data source located in a computational grid without any kind of low level knowledge connected with the Globus Toolkit, the GRelC middleware or the XML libraries.

Table 1. Data Access Policies

DAP	If true it allows the user to...
CREATE_DB	create new database
DROP_DB	drop database
CREATE_TABLE	create new table
DROP_TABLE	drop table
MQ	perform a MultiQuery (MQ)
GRIDFTPMQ	perform a MQ GridFTP
GRIDFTPSQ	perform a SQ GridFTP
TRANSACTION	perform a transaction
INSERT	submit an insert query
UPDATE	submit an update query
DELETE	submit a delete query
ADMIN	change the DAPs of the users

9.4.3 GRelC Protocol

The GRelC protocol allows communication between each client application and the GRelC Service within the client/server architecture. In this protocol the packet's payload definition is based on the XML standard format. This protocol provides the main functionalities such as opening/closing a connection with the Grid-DBMS, submitting a SingleQuery or a MultiQuery to the Grid-DBMS, using the GridFTP support and so on.

Let us now go into more details about the most important packets designed in our protocol:

Init Session: it is used to open a connection with the Grid-DBMS. It contains the Grid-Database name with which the user wants to open a session. After opening the connection, a *Result* packet is returned to the client with the operation result;

End Session: it is used to close a connection with the Grid-DBMS. A *Result* packet is then returned to the client with the operation result;

SingleQuery Select: it is used to submit a SELECT query to the GRelC Service. It contains the SELECT query string. A *Result* packet containing the resultset is then returned to the client. This packet contains (i) the resultset schema that is the number, names and types of the attributes (ii) the query result (query-ok, query-failed), (iii) the resultset, that is the number of records and the records themselves;

SingleQuery Not Select: it is used to submit a DELETE, UPDATE or INSERT query to the GRelC Service. It contains the query string. A *Result* packet is then returned to the client with the operation result;

SingleQuery GridFTP: it is used to submit a Single Query GridFTP that is a SELECT query whose resultset is first stored in an XML file and then sent back to the client.

SingleQuery Remote GridFTP: it looks like the previous packet. The only difference is that the XML file can be transferred to another host of the Grid different from the client. A *Result* packet is then returned to the client. This packet contains (i) the transfer result (transfer-ok or transfer-failed), (ii) the query result (query-ok, query-failed);

MultiQuery: this packet contains the MQ data (in XML format) that must be inserted in the data resources. A *Result* packet containing the validation data result is then sent back to the client;

MultiQuery GridFTP: it contains the name of the MQ file already transferred (using the GridFTP protocol) to the GRelC Service. A *Result* packet is then returned to the client. This packet contains (i) the transfer result (transfer-ok, transfer-failed), (ii) the validation data result (validation-ok, validation-failed);

MultiQuery Third Party GridFTP: it looks like the previous packet. The only difference is that the XML file can be transferred from another host of the Grid different from the client. A *Result* packet which is exactly the same as the previous case is then returned to the client.

System Management: in this Section we group several packets which are involved in the system management in order to (i) add/delete users, (ii) change the data access policies associated with a specific user, (iii) set the authorization policy and (iv) change the parameters related to the physical location of the data resources, their names, etc.
For each functionality, a *Result* packet containing the operation result is sent back to the client.

9.5. European Testbed

In this Section, we present some experimental results related to a performance comparison among the three kinds of SingleQuery illustrated before (BSQ, SQFTP, SQZipFTP), considering a GRelC Service installed in Cardiff (UK) and several client applications in Potsdam (DE).
In the first subsection we present a GridFTP bandwidth analysis connected with the machines considered in our European testbed, whereas, in the second and third one we

show some experimental results related to the SingleQueries comparison considering sequential and concurrent tests.

9.5.1 GridFTP Bandwidth Analysis

The GridFTP Bandwidth was measured by transferring a set of files (from Cardiff to Potsdam) with a dimension ranging from 1KB to 1GB using the GridFTP protocol (see Figure 5).

The experiments were repeated several times during the day (peak time for computing resource with high workload) and late during the night (off-peak time, low workload) and we did not appreciate relevant differences. The received data rates, were averaged to address accuracy test requirement and for each file size a related standard deviation was also computed in order to provide a short term variability index.

The application test was developed in C language, for performance reasons, and in order to address a robust and efficient file transfer, we decided to use the grb-gsiftp library. This library wraps the GridFTP protocol and provides the user with the capability of starting a parallel third-party file transfer, transferring single files or directories, using parallel streams etc.

We obtained a bandwidth of 900KB/sec, considering in our test only one stream for the data transfer. It is worth noting here that this result, represents a lower bound for the GridFTP bandwidth. Indeed testing our applications with 2, 4, 8 and 16 parallel streams (see Figure 6) we obtained better results (more than 1MB/sec with 4 and 8 streams, that is, a 11% improvement w.r.t. 1 stream). Additional details and motivation about the GridFTP behaviour using different parallel streams can be found in [31].

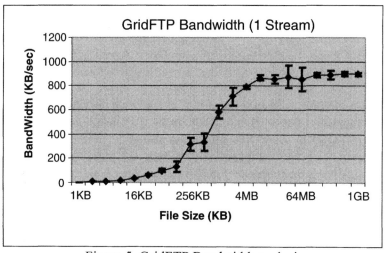

Figure 5. GridFTP Bandwidth analysis.

9.5.2 Single Queries Testbed (Sequential Tests)

In this subsection, we present some experimental results related to a performance comparison among the SingleQueries (BSQ, SQFTP, SQZIPFTP). We just consider in the sequential test only one client application submitting several kinds of SingleQueries. These tests can give us some information about the efficiency of the new proposed kind of queries (SQFTP and SQZIPFTP), whereas the concurrent tests in the next Section will give us information about global performance (efficiency, stability and throughput) of SQFTP and SQZIPFTP, in a real case study, compared with BSQ.

In our European testbed the GRelC Service ran on a linux machine (1.0GHz processor, 1,5GB of main memory, Linux Operating System - kernel 2.4 - and a 38GB HD) in which we also installed the DBMS and the test database (we used a free RDBMS - PostgreSQL 7.4.2 - but this is not a strict constraint in our system implementation because the GRelC middleware allows the use of any RDBMS as for instance Oracle, MySQL, etc.).

The client application ran on a linux machine (2.8GHz processor, 4GB of main memory, Linux Operating System - kernel 2.4 - and a 1,3TB HD) and was developed using the C language.

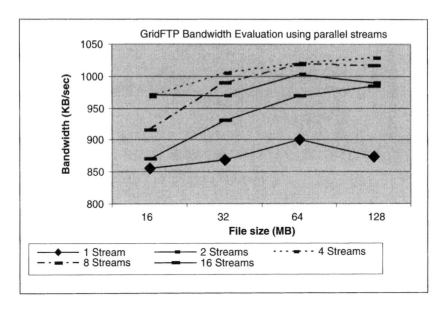

Figure 6. GridFTP bandwidth analysis with different number of parallel streams.

Our goal was to perform a SELECT query in three different ways, that is, comparing BSQ, SQFTP and SQZIPFTP.

In this experiment, we considered our own relational version of the Swiss-Prot data bank [40] (we translated the sprot44.dat flat file available at the site: ftp://ftp.ebi.ac.uk/pub/ databases/swissprot /release/ - about 575MB, containing 153.000 sequences - in a relational data model), considering the following fields: sequence identifier, authors, creation date, last sequence update, last annotation update, reference field, sequence field and other minor information.

We added additional 47 thousand tuples in order to run our tests on an overall number of tuples equal to two hundred thousand (this is a feasible value reachable in the next few months if we take into account the rate of growth of this kind of data bank).

In our tests, we considered a relational database because we have been investigating the performance in the use of the relational approach w.r.t the use of the textual data format to perform efficiently high throughput parameter sweep applications such as Blast tool [41] (which need just the sequence information) available at the NCBI [42]; however this is out of the scope of this paper and we will analyze it in a future work.

We ran several tests considering N, the number of retrieved records, in the following two classes:

SMALL: N ranging from one thousand to ten thousand;
LARGE: N ranging from ten thousand to two hundred thousand.

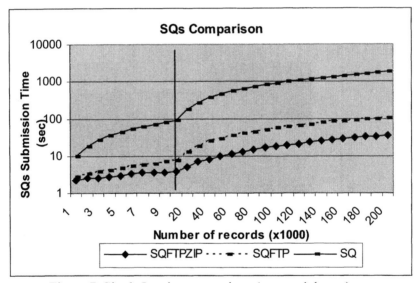

Figure 7. SingleQueries comparison (sequential tests).

The sizes of the resulting XML files for the SQFTP and SQZIPFTP are shown in Table 2. As we can see in this table, introducing compression mechanisms, we can strongly reduce the number of Kbytes to be transferred from the GRelC Service to the client application - for N greater than 100000 records, we obtained a compression ratio of 1:9, that is 11% of original file size. This interesting result is due to the nature of the file (text file with an high data correlation degree) and the compression algorithm utilized (Lempel-Ziv77 and Huffman coding). So we can expect different results comparing the BSQ with the SQFTP or the SQZIPFTP w.r.t. the total time of query submission.

The experiment was repeated several times during the day (peak time) and late during the night (off-peak time) and we did not appreciate relevant differences. For every client applications results were averaged in order to address accuracy test requirement.

Referring to Figure 7 it is worth noting that the SQFTP and SQZIPFTP are more performant w.r.t. the BSQ. As expected, the GridFTP and the compression mechanisms introduce a speedup which is relevant in the SMALL case as well as in the LARGE one. For N greater than 50 thousand the speedup is almost 17 for the SQFTP and 50 for the SQZIPFTP providing in the LARGE case a stable ratio between SQFTP and SQZIPFTP equal to 2,9.

On the contrary (see Figure 8), BSQ is more stable w.r.t the SQFTP and SQZIPFTP. We analyzed (for N ranging from one thousand to two hundred thousand) the ratio between the standard deviation and the query submission time (average value) considering the three kind of queries both in the LARGE and in the SMALL case.

As expected, the SQFTP and SQZIPFTP introduce a higher percentage variability w.r.t. the BSQ. This result can be easily explained considering that the SQFTP and SQZIPFTP take less time than BSQ and so considerably suffer any network performance fluctuations. The bigger is N, the better is the result in terms of relative standard deviation.

Table 2. SQFTP, SQZIPFTP Files Sizes and % of original size

N tuples	FileSize$_{SQFTP}$ (MB)	FileSize$_{SQZIPFTP}$ (MB)	% of original size
1000	0,4	0,1	25%
10000	4	0,8	20%
50000	19	3,4	18%
100000	38	4,2	11%
150000	57	6,8	11%
200000	76	7,6	10%

9.5.3 Single Queries Testbed (Concurrent Tests)

In this subsection, we present the experimental results related to a performance comparison between the SingleQueries (BSQ, SQFTP, SQZIPFTP) considering twelve client applications each one retrieving a number of records ranging from one thousand to ten thousand. This is a feasible scenario in which several clients try to carry out a protein-to-protein comparison on a subset of the SWISSPROT database.

In this European testbed the GRelC Service was the same as the previous case whereas the client applications ran on several linux machines as in the previous tests.

The experiments were repeated several times during the day (peak time) and late during the night (off-peak time) and even in this case, we did not appreciate relevant differences.

Referring to Figure 9 it is worth noting that in this case too, the SQFTP and SQZIPFTP are more performant w.r.t. the BSQ. As expected, the GridFTP and the compression mechanisms introduce a speedup which is strongly relevant for each number, of

150

retrieved data items analysed. Considering the case N equal to ten thousand records (for each client) the speedup is almost 13 for the SQFTP and 42 for the SQZIPFTP.

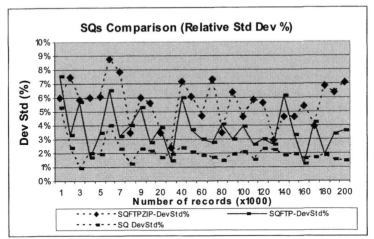

Figure 8. SingleQueries comparison of relative standard deviation (%).

In all of the performed tests the GRelC Service was able to supply the clients with correct answers, without any crashes or failures satisfying the robustness requirement of our DAS implementation. Other intensive tests performed continuously for many days (with a growing number of clients applications) confirmed this important issue. Additional information about these tests can be found in [43].

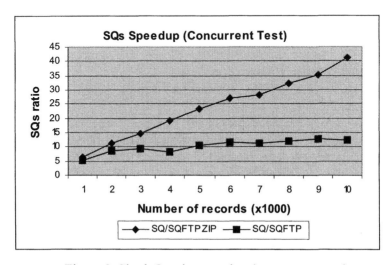

Figure 9. SingleQueries speedup (concurrent tests).

9.6.GRelC Web Service

To date two versions of the GRelC Service are available: the former (depicted in this paper) leverages a client/server architecture whereas the latter exploits GSI enabled Web Services (we used the gSOAP toolkit [44] and added GSI support - available as a gSOAP plug-in [45,46] - in order to guarantee a secure data channel between client applications and the GRelC Service).

The GRelC Web Service provides all of the functionalities described in this paper such as the SQ, MQ and so on. The migration from client/server to web service architecture was very easy and fast due to the modularity of the middleware developed before (indeed the core libraries related to *SDAI, query submission, administration*, etc. are the same).

Moreover we designed a GRelC Proxy C++ class embedding all of the methods of the GRelC Web Service. This class easies the development of client applications interacting in a grid environment with data sources because it hides all of the low level details connected with the Web Service interaction, GSI, Globus libraries, DBMS and so on. This class virtualizes the connection to a data source allowing the user to interact and manage a database within a computational grid virtually like a locally available one.

The XGRelC Enterprise Manager is a GUI built on top of the GRelC Proxy C++ class and Qt libraries which allows the user to interact with a generic relational data source located in a computational grid without any kind of low level knowledge of the Globus Toolkit, the GRelC Web Service, SOAP protocol, SDAI, DBMSs APIs and so on. This console provides (i) several wizards for database/user creation, stored procedure and (ii) other high level interfaces to make easy the database management activities. In Figure 10 we show the deployment diagram related to the GRelC middleware.

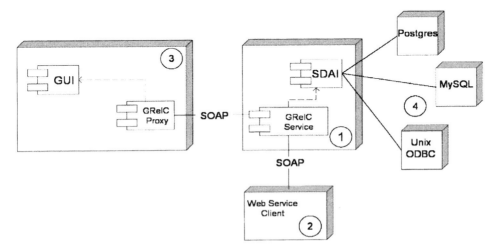

Figure 10. Deployment diagram (1 - Web Service Server; 2 – Generic client;
3 – Advanced XGRelC GUI; 4 – DBMS layer).

10. CONCLUSIONS

Nowadays, several data grid applications need to access, share, manage and integrate a massive amount of data distributed across heterogeneous and geographically spread grid resources. Such applications could improve their performance and quality of results by using efficient, robust and secure data services for a grid environment.

Database Management Systems represent a reliable, accepted and powerful instrument to store persistent data but currently (with the notable exception of Oracle) they are not grid enabled. Lastly, many efforts have been basically providing only static services for data access and integration. Our aim is to provide a more complex framework supporting both static (access and integration) and dynamic (management) services in grid environments. This leads to the Grid-DBMS concept, which has been extensively defined and discussed in this paper. It provides the basic services/primitives for dynamically, transparently and automatically managing data sources in grids. We plan in the future to extend the Grid-DBMS architecture including new services, functionalities and capabilities to take into account a wider range of issues related to grid data management.

In this paper we also presented an overview about the Grid Relational Catalog project, which provides a set of high level and grid-enabled data services for relational and not relational repositories. We discussed about the Data Access Service presenting some experimental results related to a performance comparison, within an European testbed, among the BSQ and the proposed SQFTP and SQZIPFTP.

In future releases, we will move towards a Grid Services architecture paying special attention to the Open Grid Service Architecture [47,48] and to the emerging WSRF [49], in order to develop a real dynamic and adaptive framework able to offer more functionalities and new and high level services in the data management area.

REFERENCES

1. I. Foster, C. Kesselman, The Grid: Blueprint for a New Computing Infrastructure. Morgan Kaufmann, (1998).
2. The Anatomy of the Grid: Enabling Scalable Virtual Organizations. I. Foster, C. Kesselman, S. Tuecke. International J. Supercomputer Applications, 15(3), 2001.
3. The European DataGrid Project, URL: [http://eu-datagrid.web.cern.ch/eu-datagrid/].
4. M.T. Özsu, P. Valduriez, Principles of Distributed Database Systems, 2nd edition, Prentice Hall (Ed.), Upper Saddle River, NJ, USA (1999).
5. D. Bell and J. Grimson (1998). Distributed Database Systems. Addison Wesley (Ed.)
6. E. K. Clemons (1985). Principles of Database Design, Vol. 1, Prentice Hall (Ed.).

7. Oracle Grid Computing Technologies URL: [http://otn.oracle.com/products/oracle9i /grid_computing/index.html].
8. Database Access and Integration Services WG, URL: [https://forge.gridforum.org/projects/dais-wg].
9. N. W. Paton, M. P. Atkinson, V. Dialani, D. Pearson, T. Storey, P. Watson, "Database Access and Integration Service on the Grid", Global Grid Forum OGSA-DAIS WG. Technical Report (2002).
10. P. Watson, Databases and the Grid. Technical Report CS-TR-755, University of Newcastle, 2001.
11. V. Raman, I. Narang, C. Crone, L. Haas, S. Malaika, T. Mukai, D. Wolfson, C. Baru. "Data Access and Management Services on Grid", Technical Report Global Grid Forum 5 (2002).
12. G. Aloisio, M. Cafaro, S. Fiore, M. Mirto, The Grid-DBMS: Towards Dynamic Data Management in Grid Environments, Proceeding of the IEEE International Conference on Information Technology (ITCC 2005), April 2005, Las Vegas, Vol. II, pp. 199-204.
13. The GRelC Project: An Easy Way to Manage Relational Data Sources in the Globus Community. URL: [http://gandalf.unile.it/].
14. G. Aloisio, M. Cafaro, S. Fiore, M. Mirto, The GRelC Project: Towards GRID-DBMS, Proceedings of Parallel and Distributed Computing and Networks (PDCN) IASTED, Innsbruck (Austria) February 2004.
15. The Spitfire Project URL: [http://edg-wp2.web.cern.ch/edg-wp2/spitfire/].
16. Open Grid Services Architecture Data Access and Integration, URL: [http://www.ogsadai.org.uk/].
17. SRB (2000). Storage Resource Broker Documentation v.1.1.8. URL: [http://www.npaci.edu-/DICE/SRB/CurrentSRB/SRB.htm].
18. ANSA (1989). The Advanced Network System Architecture (ANSA) Reference Manual. Castle Hill, Cambridge, England: Architecture Project Management.
19. International Standard Organization (1992). Basic Reference Model of Open Distributed Processing, Part 1: Overview and Guide to use. ISO/IEC JTC1/SC212/WG7 CD 10746-1, International Standards Organization, 1992.
20. Postgresql, URL: [www.postgresql.org].
21. MySQL URL: [www.mysql.com].
22. A. P. Sheth, J. A. Larson, Federated Database Systems for Managing Distributed, Heterogeneous and Autonomous Databases. ACM Computing Survey 22(3): 183-236, (1990).
23. J. S. A, Gounaris, P. Watson, N. W. Paton, A.A.A. Fernandes, and R. Sakellariou. Distributed query processing on the grid. In Proceedings of the 3rd International Workshop on Grid Computing (GRID 2002), pages 279-290. LNCS 2536, Springer-Verlag, 2002.
24. L. Haas, D. Kossmann, E.L. Wimmers and J. Yang, Optimizing Queries Across Diverse Data Sources. In proc. VLDB, pages 276-285, Morgan-Kaufmann, 1997.

25. UnixODBC, URL : [www.unixodbc.org].

26. G. Aloisio, M. Cafaro, S. Fiore, M. Mirto, A Gather Service in a Health Grid Environment, CD-Rom of Medicon and Health Telematics 2004, IFMBE Proceedings, Volume 6, July 31 – August 05, Island of Ischia, Italy.

27. G. Aloisio, M. Cafaro, S. Fiore, G. Quarta, A Grid-Based Architecture for Earth Observation Data Access, accepted to *The 20th Annual ACM Symposium on Applied Computing*, Santa Fe, New Mexico, March 13 -17, 2005.

28. The Globus Project, URL: [http://www.globus.org/].

29. Extensible Markup Language (XML) URL: [http://www.w3.org/XML/].

30. S. Tuecke (2001). Grid Security Infrastructure (GSI) Roadmap. Internet Draft 2001. URL: [www.gridforum.org/security/ggf1_-200103/drafts/draft-ggf-gsi-roadmap02. pdf].

31. G. Aloisio, M. Cafaro, I. Epicoco, Early experiences with the GrifFTP protocol using the GRB-GSIFTP library. North-Holland: Future Generation Computer Systems. Special Issue on Grid Computing: Towards a New Computing Infrastructure. 18(8), 1053-1059, (2002).

32. Grid Forum GridFTP Introduction URL: [http://www.sdsc.edu/GridForum/Remote Data/Papers/gridftp_intro_gf5.pdf].

33. GridFTP Protocol. URL: [http://www-fp.mcs.anl.gov/dsl/GridFTP-Protocol-RFC-Draft.pdf].

34. G. Aloisio, M. Cafaro, E. Blasi, I. Epicoco, S. Fiore, M. Mirto, Dynamic Grid Information Catalog, Proceedings of First European Across Grid Conference, Lecture Notes in Computer Science, Springer-Verlag, Santiago de Compostela, Spain, 2003.

35. G. Aloisio, M. Cafaro, S. Fiore, I. Epicoco, M. Mirto, S. Mocavero, A performance Comparison between GRIS and LDGC Information Services, *Proceedings of SCI2003, 27-30 July, Orlando, florida*, Volume XII, pp. 416-420, 2003.

36. G. Aloisio, M. Cafaro, I. Epicoco, S. Fiore, D. Lezzi, M. Mirto and S. Mocavero, iGrid, a Novel Grid Information Service, to appear in Proceedings of the First European Grid Conference, Lecture Notes in Computer Science, Springer-Verlag, 2005.

37. G. Aloisio, M. Cafaro, I. Epicoco, S. Fiore, D. Lezzi, M. Mirto and S. Mocavero, Resource and Service Discovery in the iGrid Information System, to appear in Proceedings of the 2nd International Workshop on Grid Computing and Peer-to-Peer Systems (GPP'05), Singapore, May 9-12, 2005.

38. G. Aloisio, M. Cafaro, S. Fiore, M. Mirto, Early Experiences with the GRelC Library, Journal of Digital Information Management, Vol. 2, No. 2, pp 54-60, June 2004. Digital Information Research Foundation (DIRF) Press.

39. G. Aloisio, M. Cafaro, S. Fiore, M. Mirto, The GRelC Library: A Basic Pillar in the Grid Relational Catalog Architecture, Proceedings of Information Technology Coding and Computing (ITCC), April 5 to 7, 2004, Las Vegas, Nevada, Volume I, pp.372-376.

40. B. Boeckmann, A. Bairoch, R. Apweiler, M. Blatter, A. Estreicher, E. Gasteiger, M. J. Martin, K. Michoud, C. O'Donovan, I. Phan, S. Pilbout, and M. Schneider. The Swiss-Prot protein knowledgebase and its supplement TrEMBL. Nucleic Acids Research 31: 365-370 (2003). Site address: http://www.ebi.ac.uk/swissprot/.

41. Altschul, F. Stephen, Gish Warren, Webb Miller, Eugene W. Myers, and David J. Lipman (1990). Basic local alignment search tool. J. Mol. Biol. 215:403-410.

42. National Center for Biotechnology Information. URL: [http://www.ncbi.nlm.nih.gov/].

43. G. Aloisio, M. Cafaro, S. Fiore, M. Mirto, Advanced Delivery Mechanisms in the GRelC Project, Proceeding of 2nd International Workshop on Middleware for Grid Computing (MGC 2004), ACM, October 2004, Toronto, Ontario, Canada pp. 69-74.

44. R.A. Van Engelen, K.A. Gallivan, The gSOAP Toolkit for Web Services and Peer-To-Peer Computing Networks, Proceedings of IEEE CCGrid Conference, May 2002, Berlin, pp. 128-135.

45. M. Cafaro, D. Lezzi, R.A. Van Engelen, The GSI plugin for gSOAP, URL: [http://sara.unile.it/~cafaro/gsi-plugin.html].

46. G. Aloisio, M. Cafaro, I. Epicoco, D. Lezzi and R.A. Van. Engelen , The GSI plug-in for gSOAP: Enhanced Security, Performance, and Reliability, Proceeding of the IEEE International Conference on Information Technology (ITCC 2005), April 2005, Las Vegas, Volume I, pp. 304-309.

47. I. Foster, C. Kesselman, J. Nick, and S. Tuecke. Open Grid Services Architecture: A Unifying Framework for Distributed System Integration. Technical Report, Globus Project, 2002. URL: [www.globus.org/research/papers/-ogsa.pdf].

48. I. Foster, C. Kesselman, J. Nick, S. Tuecke, The Physiology of the Grid: An Open Grid Services Architecture for Distributed System Integration. Technical Report for the Globus project. (2002) URL: [http://www.globus.org/-research/papers/ ogsa.pdf].

49. Web Service Resource Framework (WSRF). Site address: http://www.globus.org/wsrf/.

Performance

© 2005 Elsevier B.V. All rights reserved.

The "MIND" Scalable PIM Architecture

Thomas Sterling and Maciej Brodowicz

Center for Advanced Computing Research, California Institute of Technology
1200 E.California Blvd., MC158-79, Pasadena, CA, USA

MIND (Memory, Intelligence, and Network Device) is an advanced parallel computer architecture for high performance computing and scalable embedded processing. It is a Processor-in-Memory (PIM) architecture integrating both DRAM bit cells and CMOS logic devices on the same silicon die. MIND is multicore with multiple memory/processor nodes on each chip and supports global shared memory across systems of MIND components. MIND is distinguished from other PIM architectures in that it incorporates mechanisms for efficient support of a global parallel execution model based on the semantics of message-driven multithreaded split-transaction processing. MIND is designed to operate either in conjunction with other conventional microprocessors or in standalone arrays of like devices. It also incorporates mechanisms for fault tolerance, real time execution, and active power management. This paper describes the major elements and operational methods of the MIND architecture.

1. INTRODUCTION

The immediate future of commercial computing is challenged by the combined trends of 1) the incoming disparity between memory bandwidth and processor speeds known as the "memory wall", and 2) the use of multicore processor chips. Processor clock speeds continue to grow at a rate substantially greater than memory access rates, widening the gap between processor demand rates and memory data delivery. At the same time, memory chip capacity continues to track Moore's law, increasing by about a factor of 4 every 3 years. Together, these trends are increasing the total time (measured in processor cycles) required to touch every word on a memory chip. This imposes a hard barrier on the continued effective performance gain for real world applications. The migration to multicore is a response to the upper bound of efficient use of increased number of transistors in a single processor design and the power penalty due to increased clock rate. As the number of transistors has increased in ever more complicated processor designs (e.g., Intel Itanium2) the number of operations per transistor has declined. At the same time, attempts to continue to increase clock rates have resulted in prohibitive power consumption while sustained performance has not improved proportionally. Multicore structures putting multiple processors on the same chip increase the number of operational ALUs without increasing the clock rate or the degree of instruction level parallelism (ILP) that the compiler needs to successfully exploit limited to single instruction stream issue. MIND is a next-generation Processor in Memory (PIM) architecture that addresses both challenges. It exploits the very high on-chip memory bandwidth of DRAM (or SRAM) dies to attack the memory barrier while supporting a parallel model of computation through hardware mechanisms to achieve scalable computing through a potentially large array of custom multicore processors. This paper describes the MIND PIM architecture, its microarchitecture organization, and its parallel instruction set and execution model.

MIND (Memory, Intelligence, and Network Device) is an advanced parallel computer architecture for high performance computing and scalable embedded processing. It is a Processor-in-Memory architecture (PIM) that exploits those semiconductor fabrication processes capable of integrating both DRAM bit cells and CMOS logic devices on the same silicon die. MIND is distinguished from other PIM architectures in that it incorporates mechanisms for efficient support of a global parallel execution model based on the semantics of message-driven, multithreaded, split-transaction processing. MIND is designed to operate either in conjunction with other conventional microprocessors or in standalone arrays of like devices. MIND can support conventional parallel programming practices including MPI and OpenMP, or more advanced parallel programming models being explored such as UPC and Co-Array Fortran. However, its rich support mechanisms for efficient parallel computing lends itself to new programming models that can exploit its diverse capabilities for superior efficiency and scalability. MIND reflects a global shared memory model without cache coherence. Any element of a MIND component array can directly reference any part of the system memory address space without software intervention, thus providing an efficient single system image.

MIND is intended for future systems that either incorporate a very large number of components or for very long duration operation in remote regimes. To meet the reliability requirements for both extremes, MIND employs a strategy of graceful degradation for fault tolerance that allows individual elements of the MIND parallel system to fail while the rest of the system remains functional. Mechanisms for fault detection and fault isolation in the hardware are combined with runtime software for rollback, recovery, and restart of application execution. MIND is power-aware, benefiting from the low-power attributes intrinsic to the PIM while incorporating mechanisms for selectively controlling deactivation/activation of sub sections of the global parallel array to adapt power consumption to computer resource usage based on demand. Finally, limited real time response capability is provided through thread priority scheduling and guaranteed local execution time of thread operation.

The objective of this chapter is to give the reader an understanding of the MIND architecture physical organization, the basic semantic elements and governing execution model, and the principal mechanisms incorporated to support efficient parallel execution. The next section provides an overview of the MIND-based system architecture, its primary components, and their interrelationships. The most relevant examples of prior art architectures that have influenced the MIND design are discussed in Section 3. Section 4 presents a high level view of the ParalleX model of parallel execution that provides a methodology for managing computation of application concurrency on the highly replicated elements of the MIND components. Section 5 discusses the major semantic elements of the instruction set architecture. Section 6 describes the component architecture. Section 7 describes the system wide architecture of a MIND based system to define the key components and the alternative organizations that can be supported, as well as the core building block, the memory/logic "node", which manages the execution of the application and of which many instances are integrated on a single module (or chip). The remaining sections focus on the major individual components of the MIND node: Section 8 describes the register organization, Section 9 the wide ALU, Section 10 the thread manager, Section 11 the memory manager, and finally Section 12 the parcel handler.

2. AN OVERVIEW OF THE MIND SYSTEM ARCHITECTURE

The MIND architecture involves three levels of structure. The top level is the system, an ensemble of MIND components or "modules" and possibly other devices integrated by one or more interconnection networks. The bottom level is the "node", a bank of memory combined with the necessary logic to perform message-driven ("parcel") multithreaded execution. The intermediate level is the MIND "module" that is a collection of MIND nodes tightly connected by means of a local network and interrelated to the rest of the system by means of one or more parcel interfaces that communicate messages between modules and to other system components.

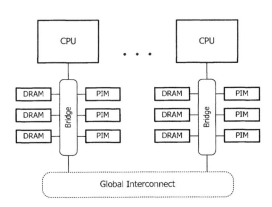

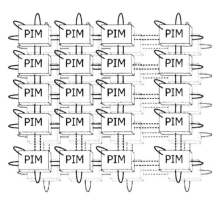

Figure 2.1. Heterogeneous system with PIMs.

Figure 2.2. "Sea of PIMs".

MIND systems may either combine MIND modules with other classes of components (e.g., conventional microprocessors) to share the computation responsibilities or comprise an array of only MIND modules with perhaps one or more external service support processors. The former is illustrated in Figure 2.1 as a system of a cluster of microprocessors, each with a heterogeneous memory subsystem of conventional DRAM chips and MIND modules. In this class of MIND-based system, the microprocessors perform the compute intensive work and the MIND modules are allocated data-oriented work as well as some overhead tasks. The latter class of MIND-based system is sometimes referred to as a "sea of PIMs" system in which the only active component is the MIND module. This kind of system could incorporate many thousand MIND modules interconnected by a network such as a degree-6 toroidal mesh topology as shown in Figure 2.2. Here too there are conventional microprocessors in the system but only a very few and their only responsibility is to run certain parts of the operating system such as job control and the file system, providing such high level external interface services to the MIND array. In both cases, a special kind of message is employed to communicate between MIND modules. Referred to as "parcels", these messages move not only data from one module to another but also commands, dictating actions to be performed remotely. This supports a message-driven split-transaction model of parallel computation that is intrinsically latency hiding for high efficiency.

The MIND module contains all the memory, logic, and communications interfaces required to perform coordinated parallel computation. Organized as a set of interconnected nodes, the module connects the nodes to the external parcel interfaces and to shared resources accessible to all nodes on the chip. An incident parcel will be transferred from the external parcel interface to the target node containing the destination data, invoking an action by that node related to the selected data. Similarly, the module will route a parcel instigated by any of its nodes to the appropriate parcel interface, directing it to the remote target module. The module also provides access to its shared resources by its local nodes. Different module designs can include different mixes of shared resources but may include one or more high speed pipelined floating point units, large shared instruction cache, system configuration tables, module status and control registers, and external real-time signal interface ports.

The MIND node is the core functional unit of the MIND module and system. It includes main memory, functional arithmetic units, and control logic designed to exploit the accessibility of the wide data path from the row buffer as will be shown in Figure 7.2. The MIND node is multithreaded and is message driven. Threads can be instantiated by the arrival of a parcel message from a remote MIND module. The memory employs virtual addresses locally and to all module nodes in the system. The MIND node employs a variable length binary instruction set to reduce instruction pressure, understood as the combined effect of the required memory bandwidth and the spatial overhead associated with instruction caching. It supports multiple operations per cycle on a multi-field structure. A node can be isolated from the rest of the module in the case of failure and incorporates fault detection mechanisms in the memory, internal data paths, and some of the arithmetic function units. Highly replicated elements within the node can also be isolated from the rest of the node to permit continued operation with degraded capability even in the presence of a fault. A node clock can be reduced in rate for slower low power operation and the entire node can be powered down temporarily for active power management. The node permits limited real time execution with guaranteed response time for small local sequential tasks.

3. RELATED RESEARCH IN THE FIELD

Prior work in the disciplines of PIM and parallel computing models over the last two decades (and possibly more) has contributed greatly to the development of the MIND architecture. Here, a few highlights do inadequate justice to the rich panoply of experiences, concepts, projects, and contributors that have constituted the intellectual environment from which this work has emerged.

The idea of smart memories goes back to the days of content addressable memory and associative processors. These predated high-density semiconductor integration but explored the potential performance opportunities of intimate association of logic and memory in single structures. STARAN [1] is one example of example of such architectures followed by other SIMD architectures as the Goodyear MPP [2], the MasPar MP-1 & MP-2 [3,4], and the TMC CM-2 [5].

The term PIM was coined by Ken Iobst in the late 1980s who led the IDA Terasys [6] project, another SIMD architecture with a wide row of bit level processors on the memory chip, each servicing a single column of the memory block. Peter Kogge, then at IBM, developed the Execube [7] at about the same time, which was the first MIMD PIM component, incorporating eight banks of memory, each with a dedicated processor of simple design but independent control. Execube also had a mode in which all processors could be operated in SIMD mode from an external controller.

The IRAM [8] project at UC Berkeley led by Dave Patterson developed a PIM architecture for multimedia applications to be employed in otherwise conventional systems such as workstations and servers. The DIVA architecture [9] was developed by Draper, Hall, and others at USC ISI to provide a multicore scalable PIM architecture for a wide array of general applications including scalable embedded applications. This PIM architecture incorporated a simple mechanism for message (parcel) driven computation and supported a network that permitted the interconnection of a number of such components to work together in parallel on the same application. Two generations of the DIVA chip have been fabricated.

Message driven computation has a long history. In the late 1970s, Hewitt developed the Actor model [10], an object oriented computing model employing message-driven computation. Daly, Keckler, and Noakes at MIT developed the J-Machine [11] at MIT, a highly parallel architecture with individual processors that were message-driven. Yelick and Culler at UC Berkeley developed the active message model [12] and split-C language [13] for message driven computation for distributed memory machines through software. The DIVA architecture incorporated a variant of the parcels message driven protocol initially devised for the HTMT architecture [14]. Parcels have continued to be used as the basis for the Gilgamesh MIND architecture [15] developed by Sterling and the Cascade architecture under development by Cray Inc.

Halstead at MIT in the late 1970s developed reference trees for management of distributed virtual address spaces, possibly with copies, and later incorporated this in the early 1980s in the MultiLisp language [16] and multiprocessor implementation. Sterling has developed a variant of reference trees for address management and translation for the MIND architecture. These techniques with important advances are being employed in MIND.

The *futures* synchronization construct was also developed by Hewitt as part of the Actors model and employed very successfully by Halstead in his implementation of MultiLisp. A variant of futures was devised by Arvind in the 1980s initially at UC Irvine and then at MIT as part of the dataflow language Id Nouveau [17]. Burton Smith of Tera (now Cray) incorporated hardware mechanisms in support of futures in the MTA architecture [18] for efficient producer-consumer computation.

Multithreaded computation has a long tradition with an early implementation by Smith at Denelcor in the HEP computer [19] and then at Tera in the MTA. Gao at McGill (now University of Delaware) developed the Earth system [20] (no relation to the Japanese Earth Simulator) which was a software implementation of a multithreaded execution model. Culler at Berkeley developed the treaded abstract machine or TAM [21] for conventional multiple-processor systems.

4. PARALLEX EXECUTION MODEL

MIND departs from conventional sequential microprocessor architecture in that it is conceived from the beginning to provide for a global parallel execution model for efficient scalable computing. Clusters and MPPs use sequential processors that through software middleware support a coarse-grained distributed execution strategy of concurrent communicating sequential processes employing basic message passing that matches the distributed memory I/O-based hardware capabilities of its constituent components. In contrast, MIND based systems employ the MIND memory architecture that supports an intrinsic parallel model of computation enabling dynamic adaptive resource management, efficient synchronization and task management, and latency hiding to effectively exploit the high degree of available memory bandwidth and logic throughput.

4.1. Shared memory

The MIND architecture supports a distributed shared memory name space. Any element of the parallel MIND system can refer to any data within the entire system directly without software intervention at the remote location of the addressed data. This is similar to the T3E and like that earlier system does not imply cache coherency. Any caching in the MIND architecture is local to the elements and memory on a given chip. The address space of the MIND architecture is virtual and is more flexible than most. Any virtually named object can be stored in any part of the system or near it depending on resource availability. A system of virtual to physical address translation is supported by the MIND architecture through a combination of hardware and software mechanisms.

The address space is partitioned into a number of distinct contexts for protection and security. Contexts are a logical resource provided by the hardware that can not be duplicated or counterfeited by software. Jobs can not touch addresses outside their own context except through an explicit protocol (beyond the scope of this paper) or between supervisor and user jobs under supervisor control. This is a limited application of capability based systems.

4.2. Continuations

The MIND parallel computing model is based on the concept of ephemeral continuations. A continuation is a set of related data that fully specifies a next computation to be performed. It must refer to some descriptive of a program and a specific entry of that descriptive that will govern the type of operation that is to be performed. It must refer to an active process (in the broadest sense) that defines the context of the computation in which the action is to be performed. Within that context, the continuation may identify argument variables upon which the action is to be performed and that may be modified as a consequence of the specified action. The continuation may also identify local or private variables accessible only to the continuation itself. A continuation is a first class object. It has a name in the global address space and it can be manipulated as such. A continuation is ephemeral. It is created at some event during the program execution and may terminate upon completion of the specific action set (not necessarily a sequence). The effect of a continuation is reflected by the change in global mutable state either directly or indirectly, including the modification to the control state of the executing program.

The MIND architecture supports three kinds of continuations that are employed for different modes of parallel flow control. The three forms of continuations are:

1. Active thread
2. Parcel
3. Lightweight control object

Although distinct in form, they represent the same basic types of information needed to govern the computation. Indeed, one form of continuation can be transformed in to one of the other forms, when circumstances warrant.

A thread is the only kind of continuation that actually causes operations to occur on a per cycle basis on MIND hardware. It is only a thread that in its own form can control MIND hardware directly for instruction issue and execution. The exception to this is that parcels can invoke atomic memory operations directly. A thread, like other continuations contains the necessary state to govern execution of a set of actions. A thread is temporally dynamic but spatially static. Once instantiated, it exists throughout its life at a single execution site.

A parcel is the only kind of continuation that moves through a system. Once instantiated, it travels to the physical location holding the virtually named data or object that is its destination target operand. A parcel carries all of the information required to invoke a remote action. Some of those actions are primitive atomic memory operations that are performed directly on the contents of the target operand in which case the effect is direct without the need for continuation transformation. When a more complex task is to be invoked remotely, the parcel causes a thread to be instantiated at the site of the target data. The parcel designates the thread code block to be executed at the remote site and provides additional operand values that may be used for the computation. It also conveys information about the action to be performed upon its completion such as the destination variable to send a resulting value from the invoked computation. A parcel may also update the last kind of continuation, the lightweight control object.

The last form of the continuation is the lightweight control object (LCO). The LCO coordinates multiple events, conditioned on a specified criterion (or criteria) that, when satisfied, will cause an action to be performed. An LCO is not an executing entity nor does it migrate through the system. It is a smart conditional that is event driven and maintains private state between successive events, which may arrive out of order. LCOs can take on a number of forms. In fact, they can even be a snap shot of either a thread or a parcel. They serve this role when either is suspended and buffered in memory. A suspended thread is an LCO as is a suspended parcel. Although they are not performing in their normal mode, they can accept updates while suspended as LCOs and may be reactivated as a result. A couple of special LCOs are of express interest for purposes of synchronization. One is the dataflow object. This LCO, known as a *template* in the dataflow community, accepts result values from other computations and when all of the precedence constraints have been satisfied, instantiates a designated action in the form of a thread. The template LCO keeps the result value until requested, sends the result via a parcel to a specified variable, or sends it to another template LCO. Another LCO supports the *futures* construct for memory based synchronization. The futures LCO captures requests for a variable value before it has been written. When the value is finally stored, the LCO returns that value to all pending requests.

4.3. Split-transaction processing

The MIND architecture is designed to perform lightweight transaction processing. This is a dramatic departure from conventional sequential processes oriented computing. Where a conventional microprocessor-based distributed system will instantiate a single process per processor that exists for the life of the application, MIND elements process transactions in reaction to the incidence of directed requests for actions to be taken. A transaction is initiated by the arrival of such a request, conducted by the local resources on local data possibly altering the content of that data. At the termination of a transaction, one or more continuations may be generated to spawn future parallel tasks that involve, at least in part, the results of the transaction execution. In the vast majority of cases, a transaction does not make remote memory or service requests to be satisfied within its life time. While this is not true for absolutely all instances of transactions, to do so causes delays and waste of resources. Instead, such remote service requirements are satisfied by decomposing a task in to two or more tasks, one at the initiating site, and one at the remote site. This splitting of a task in two or multiple dependent components is referred to as "split transaction" processing for decoupled computation. Work is almost always performed locally and when involvement of remote data, services, or resources is required, a new transaction is created at a remote site. When a transaction is terminated, the local hardware immediately begins to process the next pending transaction. Thus, assuming there is sufficient parallelism in the application and bandwidth within the hardware interconnection fabric, there are no delays in execution due to waiting for response from remote sites. Split transaction processing provides a powerful method of parallel system latency hiding that scales with system and application size.

Split transaction processing is enabled through the classes of continuations discussed above. An active transaction task is carried out by a thread continuation at a specific local execution site. This transaction thread was initiated by one of several events. A thread continuation can instantiate another transaction thread at the same local site. A parcel continuation can instantiate a transaction at a remote site. And, a lightweight control object continuation can cause a transaction either by instantiating a local thread or by eliciting a parcel at a remote site.

It is assumed that when a parcel is incident at a MIND execution site but there is contention for the necessary resources at that time, that some action is taken to defer the intended computation. In the case of MIND, the parcel is stored as a LCO in the local memory bank. It is converted again as a thread when resources become available. Threads also can be suspended as LCOs until resources are available to service them. In the worst case, when buffer space in memory is not available, a new parcel can be created that converts to an LCO at a remote site whose only value is that it has available space. Thus, the entire system can serve as a buffer of pending work in the form of LCOs.

5. INSTRUCTION SET ARCHITECTURE

The MIND instruction set architecture combines conventional, scalar, register-to-register operations employed within threads with operations for managing application and system parallelism not found in typical sequential instruction sets in support of the ParalleX model of computation. There are also a set of wide-register instructions that support multiple operations on the related fields of the wide registers to atomically manipulate structures through compound operations, called "struct processing". In addition, auxiliary instructions provide the means for managing the system resources for fault tolerance, active power management, and real time operation. This section introduces some of the attributes and features of the MIND instruction set.

5.1. Intra-thread functional scalar instructions

A thread performs a sequence of operations. MIND is a register oriented architecture in that the arithmetic and logical functions are performed mostly on the contents of the registers. These are either register fields within the thread frame for scalar values or wide registers of other designated frames, which will be discussed in the next subsection. The thread frame fields are fixed length of 64-bits but can serve any supported data type of that size or less. These include:

- Boolean
- Logical bit vectors
- Signed and unsigned integers of 8, 16, 32, and 64 bit lengths
- IEEE 754 floating point, 32 and 64 bit format
- Address pointers

The intra-thread functional instructions are typical of the majority of RISC ISAs on these data types and include the following classes:

1. Full set of bit-wise logical operations
2. Integer add, subtract, multiply, and compare
3. Floating point add, subtract, multiply, and compare
4. Boolean operations
5. Branches and jumps

Most arithmetic operations have a test version which alters the set of condition flags. There are separate flags for positive, zero, carry, overflow, NaN, parity and additional special cases. Branches are predicated on these condition flags. A number of more common combinations of the condition codes are represented by explicit branch instructions. In addition, there is a general branch instruction with an immediate mask argument that can represent any combination of codes both in true and zero valued in Boolean sum or Boolean product relations. All instruction addresses are contiguous within a thread and checked for boundedness.

5.2. Struct processing

In addition to fields in a thread frame, the thread may reference one or more other frames within the local node. A frame may be treated as a wide register and any sub-field of that wide register may be accessed by the thread. A wide register is treated as part of the context of the thread and can hold an entire row of the memory bank. This is large enough to contain 256 bytes and hold the entire contexts of most instances of the complex data structure alternatively referred to as "records" (in Fortran) or "structs" (in C). The format of a struct is determined by user software. The wide ALU can process multiple fields simultaneously for some (but not all) operations and can perform an operation of one field of a struct conditioned on the value of another field within the same struct. This permits a number of sophisticated compound atomic actions to be performed. Examples include:

- vectors – a contiguous sequence of single typed values upon which the same operations are to be performed,
- associative searches – a set of structs, each comprising one or more data elements with a tag field, such that the value of the tag field of each struct is tested and if satisfying the criterion causes an action to be performed on one or more fields of the struct,
- in-memory synchronization – a field of one or more bits is used to manage synchronization information, either for maintaining mutual exclusion for the struct and associated data, or for general parallel flow control,
- histogramming – involving two different struct types: one a large block of equivalent structs, and the second an integer vector that holds counts of the first block for each category of a designated field,
- generic types – a data element has an associated field that specifies the type of the remainder of the struct, to determine the exact operation performed in response to a general (generic) operation. Can be extended to user defined complex data types and operation sequences,
- data driven computing – a lightweight control object that specifies an operation to be performed on arriving argument values and a destination for the result(s),
- directed graph traversal including tree-walking – with each node in the data structure represented as a struct including meta-data designating the other immediately adjacent nodes in an otherwise sparse, irregular, and possibly non-ergodic data structure,

- circular queue and stack control – control data including upper and lower bounds, head and tail offsets, empty and full condition flags (for example) of a diverse set of useful compound (but usually contiguous) data structures,
- futures synchronization – a powerful mechanism for addressing read-before-write conflicts when the consumers of a computed value do not know who the producing tasks are and vice versa.

5.3. Parallel flow control

The logical executing agent is the thread, a fixed format data structure that when allocated to one of the thread frames can cause a sequence of instruction issues by its hosting node. Instructions are provided by which a thread can be created, terminated, suspended, and synchronized. A child thread can be blocking or non-blocking but is always local to the parent thread. If a remote thread is required, i.e., a thread is to be instantiated using data at a remote site storing the target data, then instructions are used that will create an appropriate parcel. These instructions can be either implicit or explicit. An explicit parcel instruction demands the formulation of a parcel, independent of its destination and some instructions provide in-depth control of the parcel contents. Implicit instructions are generalized functional applicative commands that will create a thread if the operand is local and a parcel if the operand is remote. A set of instructions are available to test this condition to permit user application control of what to do in either case. For example, if an argument is remote, the user program (or compiler) may decide to suspend the parent thread or take other actions that could enhance overall efficiency of operation.

A set of instructions is available for the use of lightweight control objects to support this third form of continuation as described in Section 4. These include the definition of the LCO, the methods that are associated with it to control its operation. Examples, as mentioned above, include suspended threads, data flow templates, and futures. The futures is particularly important as it permits decoupled asynchronous computation with multiple producers and consumers but without prior coordination. A futures object is centered around a variable element or structure. Referencing parcels, when finding that the necessary values have been provided, treat it as a regular data element for efficient access. But when the values have yet to be committed to the location, a representation of the requesting parcel is stored locally and linked to the variable (different methods for this are used). When the requested value(s) is delivered, the pending entries in the future are reissued with the referenced value. In this way the producing and consuming tasks are synchronized without having to know about each other.

The futures construct is one example of in-memory synchronization that is used effectively by the MIND architecture and for which instructions are provided to manage the execution flow control. Most architectures use barriers sparingly and usually for coarse-grained synchronization because of the overheads involved. Some architectures have been implemented that provide hardware tag bits with supporting logic for this purpose, including older data flow architectures and the Tera MTA multithreaded architecture. MIND does not include hardware tags. But it does provide hardware and instructions for in-memory synchronization even without explicit dedicated hardware synchronization bits. Instead, these instructions operate on fields within user defined structs, providing hardware performance and low overhead with the flexibility of software defined structures. The result is a highly flexible and highly efficient near-fine grain method of parallel flow control.

6. ARCHITECTURAL DESIGN FOR POWER, RELIABILITY, AND RESPONSE

The MIND architecture incorporates additional capabilities beyond those implied by the semantics of the instruction set to provide for highly robust operation over long periods without maintenance intervention. To further the system effectiveness, the MIND architecture is also power aware to reduce average power consumption and enhance power efficiency through active power management. For certain critical code segments of embedded applications, bounded response time is essential and the MIND architecture incorporates limited real time computing on a per thread basis. These additional capabilities significantly extend the breadth of roles and dramatically reduce the risk of operation of MIND based systems.

6.1. Graceful degradation

A system characterized by single point failure modes will experience catastrophic failure (the system ceases to operate) if any of its components suffer a hard fault. Thus the mean time between failures (MTBF) of the system is a function of the mean time between failure of the components and the number of components of which it is composed. Where there are many like elements, a time versus space tradeoff can be promoted to let working subsystems fulfill the requirements of a computation even as other similar subsystems fail. The rate of computation declines as constituent elements fail, thus delivering degraded performance, but the operational lifetime of the system is substantially extended. Statistical parametric tradeoff studies have shown that MIND-like PIM organizations can achieve between three and four orders of magnitude improvement of MTBF with respect to comparable systems that exhibit single point failure modes.

In order to deliver graceful degradation of performance in the presence of faults, MIND incorporates two kinds of mechanisms. The first is isolation through reconfiguration switches. Ordinarily on, these switches can be permanently disabled through external signals to disconnect a failed memory/logic node or key duplicated elements of such nodes from the remaining system. Additional configuration state allows the control logic to operate around the missing pieces. This works well for registers, memory rows, and some redundant data paths. Arithmetic and control logic are more difficult. Because MIND memory/logic nodes incorporate wide ALUs, there are duplicate logic paths that can be exploited and time shared, assuming the permutation network is intact. This is not the case for control logic. Therefore, the fundamental Boolean formulation of the control logic is defined with the possibility of single bit or signal line errors included and the logic still finding its correct state sequence.

The second mechanism class is fault detection. Here prior art is leveraged in the typical structures of memory and data paths through error bit encoding. These are included in all hardware of the MIND components. More challenging is detecting errors in the arithmetic logic, especially transient errors. Redundant computation with scalar operations is made possible for many but not all such operations through the replicated arithmetic logic resources and additional checking logic that is included. This does require higher power and can be turned off for power conservation, a difficult tradeoff: correctness or power conservation. On a cycle available basis, background testing is performed. For the memory, this is memory scrubbing that catches bit errors early, tests the memory to determine if these are hard or soft errors and, if possible, to correct in place. Also, in background using introspective threads is a set of test suites with test vectors through the ALU and ancillary logic to check for hard faults. In spite of this aggressive mosaic of complementing mechanisms, 100% fault detection is not achieved in MIND and critical sections of the computation for which errors are unacceptable may resort to duplicate computing on separate nodes with comparison of critical results at the end. While this is brute force, the loss of a factor of two in performance may be acceptable when orders of magnitude performance scalability is achieved.

6.2. Active power management

Power consumption is emerging as a dominant constraint on the scale and density, as well as performance and capacity, of high end computing platforms. It is additionally of considerable concern for those environments for which power is a precious resource, such as deep space missions (e.g., Mars rovers "Spirit" and "Opportunity"). For computing systems planned for the end of this decade in the low Petaflops performance regime, power budgets in excess of 10 Megawatts are anticipated, precluding their use to all but a few high-profile national laboratories.

MIND benefits from intrinsic properties of PIM resulting from several effects that combine to make the computation more power efficient. The most important factor is that operations performed in memory by local logic do not involve the external interface pins or drivers which consume much power. A second factor is that because the logic is so close to the sense amps or row buffers on the memory chip that little data movement is required reducing the on-chip data path power expended. When there is spatial locality, only one access request to a given row is required as all the data of that row can be processed without subsequent accesses to that row for the same data. Because the clock rate is approximately half that of conventional processors of the same technology generation, the energy consumed per operation is reduced as well. Generally, MIND processors are much simpler than conventional processor architectures, with approximately one tenth the numbers of gates or even less. Far fewer gates are involved in the computation thus reducing the average power consumption further. PIMs usually do not support a traditional cache layer thus eliminating that source of power demand also. Additional lesser properties of MIND also contribute to additional energy savings.

The MIND strategy for active power management employs two mechanisms of hardware control. The first provides for clock slowing. The logic of a given node has its own clocking for distribution and skew control. (Each chip has a master clock but the individual nodes even on the same semiconductor die operate asynchronously with respect to each other.) This node clock can operate at a number of speeds of factors of 2. The memory access timing control circuits can be separately adjusted as well. Only the parcel handler is maintained at full clock rate for message assimilation. Slower clocking reduces power consumption and permits low power idling when workload is low and requests are few. The second mechanism powers down MIND nodes with the exception again of the parcel handler. A node can be temporarily isolated from the rest of the MIND chip and the power cut off to stop essentially all power consumption for that node while in this state. This can also enhance long term system reliability as powered down subsystems are less likely to experience failures. While a fully shut down node will consume less power than the slowed clock, it takes much longer to restart and a local boot process must be engaged. Therefore, both mechanisms are incorporated in the MIND architecture. A third software method can temporarily discontinue certain background introspective thread processing and some redundant operations used for fault tolerance. This exposes the tradeoff between power consumption and reliability.

6.3. Real time response

For embedded computing applications responsible for sensor data assimilation and real time control of mechanical actuators, as well as some time-critical service functions in high performance computers, bounded response time is essential. Most conventional mainstream microprocessors do not support real-time computing. MIND does, to a limited degree. Each memory/processor node can dedicate a single thread to a real time task. This thread, referred to as a *time-thread*, can be assigned to a specific I/O signal (e.g., a signal pin on a MIND chip). Except for actions triggered by catastrophic failure events, the time-thread has highest priority and guarantees action completion in bounded and predictable time. While the limitation of only a single time-thread to each node may seem over constraining, this is one of the true features of the MIND architecture. Since each MIND chip can have a substantial number of nodes and a system may comprise multiple MIND chips, each real time task can be allocated its own execution unit, ensuring that no two (or more) real-time tasks demand the same physical resources, thus avoiding any delays due to contention.

7. MIND MODULE AND MIND NODE ARCHITECTURE

In this section, we highlight the relevant features of the MIND architecture and of its constituting components, while rationalizing our design choices. We first describe the architecture of the MIND module, and then describe the architecture of the MIND nodes within a module and of the components within a MIND node.

7.1. MIND module architecture

A MIND module consists of a set of MIND nodes with accompanying interfaces and infrastructure. Such a module can be fabricated either as silicon chips or integrated further into multi-chip modules (MCMs). The number of nodes per package depends on available process technology rules and practical die sizes; the current estimates place it between 16 and 128, but we envision modules with hundreds or thousands of nodes before the middle of the next decade. The internal structure of a MIND module is depicted in Figure 7.1.

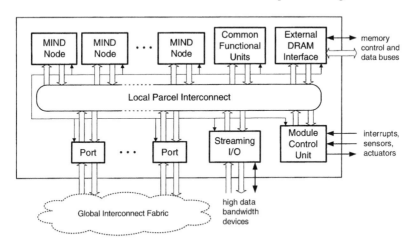

Figure 7.1. Architecture of a MIND module.

In their raw format the nodes alone cannot handle all aspects of computational tasks and communications expected. As seen in Figure 7.1, several additional subcomponents are required to provide full functionality:

- *Local Parcel Interconnect.* This is a high-bandwidth, low latency network that connects all components within a module. It is the only intra-module parcel transport medium in the module and attaches directly to parcel handlers at the nodes. This interconnect must achieve a very low latency (e.g., only a few clock cycles between issuing a request at the local node and the initialization of, for instance, the corresponding memory operation at a remote node). While low latency for accessing the functionality of a remote node is a clear requirement for nodes in the same "neighborhood" (as defined by the interconnect topology), the latency for interactions involving any two components within the module should not be much higher either. Given these requirements, although a bus-oriented topology may be sufficient for a nominal number of components, the need to alleviate contention suggests a more hierarchical organization for the local parcel interconnect.

- *Communication Ports.* These ports provide an interface between the local interconnect and the global interconnect, enabling parcel exchange between all modules. Parcels traversing the global interconnect must be "wrapped" inside packets/frames of the communication protocol proprietary to that interconnect. In contrast, the local parcel interconnect network communicates parcel content as is. The role of the ports is to facilitate parcel communication among these two networks by converting between the two parcel representations. The number of ports is typically smaller than the number of internal nodes, and is selected to satisfy the bandwidth requirements of the communication traffic incident on the module. In addition, the ports also perform buffering of messages and handle message fragmentation and reassembly in order.

- *External DRAM Interface.* This interface makes it possible to increase the available RAM capacity in the system by attaching standard "dumb" memory modules to PIM devices, thus allowing flexible platform configurations. Internally, the interface connects to the local parcel interconnect and emulates responses to remote memory access requests of a regular node. The external signaling interface conforms to industry standard protocols, such as DDR and its variants. Since the PIM nodes are capable of processing atomic memory requests locally, the interface incorporates a simplified ALU to enable this feature without undue overhead.

- *Data Streaming I/O.* This is used to communicate with external high-bandwidth streaming devices, such as mass storage (file I/O), video interfaces (cameras), or specialized processors (e.g., DSP engines). To minimize the number of dedicated external pins, most likely a form of serial, low-voltage swing differential signaling will be adopted. However, other standardized interfaces (HDMI, SATA, IEEE 1394) may be considered as well.

- *Common Functional Units.* These units complement the processing capabilities of the MIND nodes either by adding functions not directly supported by the nodes, or by implementing dedicated units to increase the performance of specific tasks. For example, if the cost of implementing a pipelined IEEE 754-compliant FPU in every node proves to be prohibitive, a number of such FPUs may be combined in a separate subcomponent, shared by all nodes.

- *Module Control Unit.* This entity monitors a number of external signal lines, processes changes in their status and distributes this information to PIM nodes and other components. The unit stores low level information describing the function and relation of the MIND module relative to the rest of the system. Besides reacting to low-level control inputs, such as global reset and interrupts, the control unit may also receive signals over a dedicated set of configurable I/O lines as well as drive them to control simple external devices (sensor arrays, mechanical actuators, etc.). Of course, different implementation versions of MIND modules may vary the availability and the nature of configurable I/O features.

7.2. MIND node architecture

The internal structure of a MIND node embeds all the functionality necessary to provide efficient memory access, extra-node communications, and multithreaded processing. The overriding design principles aim at maintaining a high degree of autonomy of individual subcomponents as well as at maximizing local memory bandwidth, while attempting contention avoidance in component interactions. As depicted in Figure 7.2, there are five fundamental components in a MIND node:

- *Frame Cache.* This cache provides local low-latency frame storage for various key data, including thread data (active register file/stack frame), instruction stream data, auxiliary data registers (vectors and structs), runtime and system management data, and temporary data. Since the chances of access contention from various components need to be minimized, the frame cache operates with single-cycle access latency and features multiple wide data I/O buses. Additionally, the frame cache controls the allocation and deallocation of individual frames for use by other components.

- *Wide ALU.* This ALU performs permutations, arithmetic, and logical operations on data. In addition to standard processing of scalar values, the ALU can also apply SIMD-style or heterogeneous struct operations to 256-bit wide vectors of elements up to 64 bit in size each. The ALU supports both coarse-grain (element boundary) and fine-grain (bit boundary) vector element replication, permutations, and masking to take the most advantage of processing capabilities during a single pass through the ALU pipeline. To increase the effective floating-point throughput, the ALU may be augmented with a standard double-precision FPU.

- *Thread Manager.* This manager is responsible for the local execution of multithreaded code. The centerpiece of this component is a *thread scheduler* that maintains a table of active threads and selects threads for execution on a cycle-by-cycle basis, subject to resource availability, scheduling priorities, privilege level, and exception and instruction caching status. The thread manager also includes instruction fetch engines for transferring the currently executing code fragments to the frame cache, as well as execution pipelines that interface directly with the resources visible from the node and exception handler.

- *Memory Manager.* This block combines a sophisticated request handler with a fairly standard DRAM macro. Its role is fourfold: (i) handling of local memory accesses; (ii) ensuring atomicity of read-modify-write requests; (iii) internal data and metadata buffer management; (iv) application of optimization techniques, such as access combining; and (v) data replication on register boundary to comply with the intra-node bus and destination register organization.

- *Parcel Handler.* This component controls parcel traffic originating from and arriving at the node. The handler maximizes both the incoming and outgoing stream bandwidths, effectively processing a rudimentary parcel in a single cycle per stage. The receive pipeline decodes the parcel contents, extracts the data or request operands and deposits them in a pre-allocated frame registers. Conversely, the output stages can accept a proto-parcel specification residing anywhere in the frame cache or directly from the memory manager, and form and emit the outgoing parcel. Since some parcels may effect thread creation, parcel handler interfaces directly with the thread manager.

The organization of datapaths within the MIND node provides the necessary interconnect bandwidth and a high degree of independence in interfacing with internal components. At the heart of the node's floor plan resides the frame cache with multiple wide (256 bits), but relatively short unidirectional buses attached to other major components. Such an organization alleviates latencies typically associated with recharging parasitic capacitances inherently associated with long buses and eliminates the need for costly (in terms of die area and switching latency) multiplexer arrays. The access control is also vastly simplified compared to bi-directional mode. Each of the data buses can operate independently and since the requestors typically either access different frames in the cache, or the accesses to the same registers are disjoint in time, the write contentions occur with very low probability and can thus be handled by simple hardware. In this arrangement, the frame cache plays effectively the role of a high-bandwidth switch with the added benefit of single-cycle accessible storage.

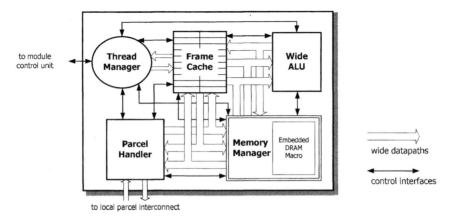

Figure 7.2. Architecture of a MIND node.

The control interfaces are routed point-to-point between the interacting entities. Any required arbitration is performed by the resource owner when multiple conflicting requests are received simultaneously. Since the amount of control information is miniscule compared to the volume of data, the use of unidirectional control buses does not pose significant problems.

In the next four sections we provide a detailed description of the Frame Cache, the Wide ALU, the Thread Manager, the Memory Manager, and the Parcel Handler.

8. FRAME CACHE

The Frame Cache is a central, register-level, instruction and data repository for the node. The storage space is partitioned into frames (2048 bit wide registers), each of which can be assigned to hold a single thread's state, cache currently accessed fragments of instruction stream, configured as temporary hardware buffer, or assigned as an auxiliary data register visible to the active threads. The frames are further subdivided into eight 256-bit wide registers, which naturally match the widths of I/O data paths and can be used to handle and transfer non-scalar data efficiently. For the purpose of standard fine-grain register access, a frame may also be viewed as a collection of 32 general purpose 64-bit registers addressable from threads. The total frame count is expected to be no lower than 64.

To minimize contention, the frame cache is multi-ported for both read and write accesses, using standard SRAM technology. The multiplexing is performed directly at bit-cell level by activating one of multiple word lines to select which of the bit lines will drive the cell's inputs for writes, or conduct the bit values stored in the cell to the sense amplifiers during reads. The only downside of this approach is the increased size of the memory cell because of additional data and control lines with associated switching transistors.

Due to the organization of wide buses, reads and writes always operate on 256-bit data chunks. However, the threads frequently require finer-grain access to registers. While the necessary alignment hardware is present in every component block connected to the frame cache outputs, the writes require only a simple replication of a scalar over 256-bit space; the target 64-bit register is selected by write control logic activating only the required subset of word lines. The frame cache also features an internal selection and replication logic attached to a dedicated pair of input and output buses, which is used to perform efficient register to register moves. This results in much improved latency of such operations compared to using the ALU and it doesn't consume any additional cycles or resources in components external to the frame cache.

There are currently two competing solutions to incorporate the instruction caching gracefully. The first assumes that each frame is equally available to be used as a data or instruction store. Hence, the OS may dynamically partition the frame cache and adjust the size of the portion allocated for instruction stream depending on the characteristics of the executing code. This approach, while flexible, potentially wastes significant die area due to multiporting. The second solution is based on the observation that since the instruction caching hardly requires multiple access buses, the optimized implementation could fit more bit cells per area unit if the code was actually stored in a dedicated, minimal I/O, structure. This has also the added benefit of removing the instruction path as another port from the data cache and offers an option of exact matching the widths of the instruction buses to the interfacing units: higher level cache on the input (capable of handling bursty traffic involving transfer of cache lines) and instruction decoder in thread manager on the output (requiring reduced width, but contiguous stream every cycle). The viability of each solution will be determined through simulation.

Besides providing physical storage, the frame cache also tracks the usage of individual frames, providing *allocate* and *deallocate* functions to the neighboring components. Since frame reservations are hardly ever performed en masse, the control automaton may be quite simple and handle such requests within a cycle. The ownership and associated responsibility to deallocate the frame when no longer in use is assigned to the original requestor, but with the possibility of OS override if problems arise.

9. WIDE ALU

Analogously to traditional processors, the MIND ALU performs all non-trivial arithmetic and logical processing on data passing through the node. Unlike many CPUs, however, it features wide operand inputs and output, extensive range of data permutations, operand masking, extended set of logical operations, unary vector, scalar-vector and vector-vector operations on many vector element sizes, and struct processing. The ALU is fully pipelined and accepts 256-bit arguments with transparent support for scalar (64-bit) operations. The vectors may be composed of elements ranging from one to eight bytes in size, packed within the 256-bit field, while scalars are right-adjusted in the rightmost 64-bit scalar field of wide operand, which complies with the data alignment applied in thread registers.

The arguments originate either from the frame cache or internal memory manager registers. The latter is necessary to implement atomic memory operations (AMOs), in which the memory has a master control over processing applied to a chunk of memory data before the result is committed back to the memory. In either case, the transfer of control is uniform and represented as a specially formed request token, naming the operation(s), argument number, types and location as well as the destination of the result. The ALU is capable of accessing the data registers of both the memory manager and the frame cache using standardized interfaces. Since control bits are decoupled from data, the tokens may be decoded before fetching the operands, which enables a convenient setup of the processing pipeline and minimizes the intermediate data buffer space. The result of processing is either a vector or a 64-bit scalar, in which case a built-in alignment network is used to adjust its location within the 256-bit output field. Besides the data outcome, the ALU generates the condition codes, which are typically stored in the thread status register by the final stages of the instruction execution pipeline, or examined directly by the requestor if the operation was triggered by an external entity, e.g., through a parcel, to determine its validity and possibly signal an exception. The condition codes are wrapped in a return token, whose additional function is to provide notification for the completion of computations. Indeed, the result write operation may be performed asynchronously without the knowledge of the requestor.

The ALU components include the coarse-grain permutation network, integer vector unit, scalar multiply-divide unit, floating point unit, and the distribution and selection network. Each of these is described in more detail below.

9.1. Coarse permutation network

The role of the coarse permutation network (CPN) includes preconditioning of the operands for the operation to be performed in the subsequent stages, rearranging the byte order in the 64-bit component subfields, and masking out the unnecessary portions of the input. The processing is performed in two largely independent pipelines, one for each of the input arguments. The operand preconditioning involves alignment of the scalar arguments, which are right-adjusted in the 256-bit field (so that the 64-bit functional units can fetch them from a predetermined subfield), and replication of scalars to form a vector of uniform elements. The latter is required for scalar-vector operations, as they are executed as vector-vector operations. The replication and alignment logic, which is organized as a set of 64-bit wide 4-way demultiplexers can also be applied to realize the coarse part of high-count bit shifts (i.e., by more than 64 positions).

The second level of permutation hardware consists of four independent modified Banyan networks, each processing a 64-bit chunk of the input vector with the 8-bit granularity in three stages. This allows an independent implementation of shifts and rotations on all four scalar fields (the final high-resolution shifting takes place in another functional block). The Banyan switch also performs arbitrary permutations and replications of vector components smaller than 8 bytes, thus reusing the same hardware structure for another task.

Finally, the output of the Banyan network is passed through the masking logic, which nullifies unwanted portions of arguments (again, on a byte boundary). Its second purpose is to provide correct sign extensions of the shifted/rotated integer vector components.

9.2. Integer vector unit

The most complex functional block of the ALU is the integer vector unit, which in turn can be subdivided into three major components: fine-grain permutation network (FPN), logical unit and vector arithmetic unit. The fine-grain network essentially helps finalize shift and masking operations initialized in the coarse permutation unit. It consists of two stacked stages, each of which is a limited range (zero, one or two bits in either direction) shift-rotate unit combined with a masking logic. Note that superposition of FPN operations together with those of the coarse permutation network yields the full range of shift-rotate counts. The masking logic has a bit resolution and may also accept bit patterns supplied by the programmer.

The logical unit performs all typical unary (*not*) and binary bitwise (*and, or, xor, implication* with complements) operations on vectors treated as contiguous groups of bits, as well as population counts (both zeroes and ones), leading and trailing bit counts and parity in each component of the vector. This functionality is distributed across both argument's data paths, as many of these operations are mutually exclusive and require quite different processing logic. To reduce the number of logic stages, and thus the effective latency, a crossover network is used to divert operands onto secondary path when necessary.

The final processing steps in the integer vector unit are performed by a three-stage vector arithmetic unit. Besides integer adders and comparators handling argument widths of up to 64 bits, the arithmetic unit features a sophisticated reduction network, including both arithmetic and logical operations. Thanks to distribution of computing logic over both operand flows, the arithmetic unit is capable of delivering a result of bitwise logical reduction or a sum of all elements in a full vector every cycle, even if their type size is as small as byte.

9.3. Integer multiply-divide unit

The multiply-divide unit was separate from the main vector pipeline for a couple of reasons. Firstly, the latency of operations (especially division) is significantly higher than that of any elementary calculations performed in the vector pipeline. Secondly, the amount of logic implementing the desired functionality is substantial, which makes its replication to support vector operations consume rather large portion of chip die area. With the progress of process technology it is anticipated that moving at least a rudimentary multiplier to the vector unit becomes possible, while significantly lesser used functions, such as division, would be delegated to a standalone scalar unit.

The unit features two separate Wallace-tree multiply and carry-lookahead cellular array divide pipelines. Each of these operations produces 128 bits of result from the input pair of scalars, since the division yields both quotient and remainder.

9.4. Floating point unit

The FPU operates on double-precision IEEE 754 number representations. Its implementation is pipelined and supports a standard set of floating-point calculations, such as addition, subtraction, multiplication, comparison and operand conversion. More sophisticated algorithms for division and square root approximation are also planned.

9.5. Selection and distribution logic

The purpose of this final ALU stage is to identify and choose fairly the ready results from one of the parallel pipelines, and perform the data alignment before sending them to the register file. The output selection algorithm, whose scaled-down version is also used in the multiply-divide unit, provides nearly starvation-free operation with a vastly reduced level of stall back-propagation from processing pipelines to the input stages.

Each of the computing blocks described above produces results of different sizes. While the full 256-bit vectors are handled directly by the frame cache logic, scalars and 128-bit long data are replicated to be correctly written to the intended target register or register set.

10. THREAD MANAGER

The multithreaded execution model, which provides the basis for MIND programming, relies heavily on the efficient implementation and hardware support for threads. The threads are named objects, which can reside anywhere in the virtual address space. For convenience, a thread name is synonymous with the virtual address of memory holding its frame. Frames are encapsulations of the local thread state; they include contents of the register window and thread execution status with such details as current instruction pointer, condition codes, priority and privilege levels, interrupt mask, synchronization information and environment linkage. A frame occupies 2048 bits of storage (typical size of a memory row) and thus can be efficiently transferred between node's register space and memory. The frames of all threads associated with a node, executing or not, are collected in internally linked pools of memory that are pre-allocated and initialized by the operating system.

10.1. Thread management and execution

Every actively executing thread must be present in the node's frame cache and is supervised by the *thread manager*. By contrast, threads whose state has been removed from the cache, and committed to memory, are suspended. The thread manager controls all aspects of thread creation, suspension, termination, scheduling and execution, which demands a number of auxiliary tasks, such as allocation of thread entries, storage and updates of the state of active threads, instruction stream handling, monitoring resource availability, management of execution pipelines, exception processing, inter-thread synchronization, and detection and workarounds for stalls and faults. The active threads are selected for execution based on their relative priority, immediate availability of the next decoded instruction and status of the primary target resource indicated by the instruction. This eliminates priority inversion problems, in which a high-priority thread may obtain a static execution slot, but is unable to progress due to unavailability of the target resource, thus blocking an unprivileged thread. To avoid stalls inherent to a single execution pipeline dispatching requests to multiple resources with different response times, every major resource has a dedicated pipeline, which receives predecoded requests when allowed to do so by the scheduler. The optimal-FIFO-depth issue pertinent to this scenario when processing time at the resources can vary drastically is resolved by a split-phase transaction strategy. In this strategy, buffering effectively occurs directly at the resource site, or along the conduit leading to it, in a distributed fashion (e.g., in the parcel handler and interconnect buffers). Split-phase transactions also shorten the execution pipelines and their control. The pipelines dedicated to very short latency and high availability services don't need to rely on split transaction approach.

The thread manager contains a single instruction decoder for all threads; its role is to determine quickly what class of operation is to be performed and identify the target resource. Such predecoded information is stored in a relevant field of the *thread table* and retained there until the thread is scheduled for further execution. This happens when the dynamic priority value is higher than that of other active threads and the status line of the primary resource specified in the instruction signals readiness to process requests. The relevant portions of the instruction and its operand(s), including the not yet decoded fragments, are then passed to the appropriate execution pipeline for the resource. When the decoding is complete, the pipeline also generates a request token, which can be directly understood and consumed by the resource. In split-transaction pipelines, the shipping off of the token to the target execution site signifies the end of the first phase of the transaction. The second phase starts when the return token is received from the site and thus the execution pipe can learn the status of the operation with possible exceptions incurred during the execution. At this moment, the dynamic priority of the thread is decreased (scheduling fairness policy) and the updated state information, including the new IP value and condition codes, is written to the thread's frame. Note that the instructions causing non-maskable exceptions do not perform the state write-back. Instead, their thread's entry is flagged as blocked (to remove it from the scheduler's view), relevant information is passed to an exception handler and the corresponding stage of the execution pipeline invalidated. The handler thread can analyze the information (the IP of the offending instruction can still be found in the thread's frame) and, depending on the severity of the exception, terminate the thread, suspend it, or unblock it.

Since at any time each thread has only at most one instruction being processed, the complex hazard detection and resolution circuitry known from superscalar CPUs is unnecessary. This also guarantees that instructions executed by each thread are processed in order. The threads in a group, however, may proceed at different relative speeds, affected by the response rate of resources they access and individual scheduling parameters. To allow the operating system to monitor the progress of program execution and detect potentially hazardous situations and faults, several counters capable of triggering timeout exception have been integrated with every thread's entry. Hence, if a remote processing site becomes unresponsive, this fact will eventually become known to the local runtime system. Similarly, some counters are linked to the scheduling priority computation, thus enabling reasonably efficient emulation of custom scheduling policies, or identification of cases when underprivileged threads cannot make progress.

10.2. Components of the thread manager

The functionality of the thread manager is distributed over several internal blocks:

- The *Thread Scheduler,* which maintains an internal *thread table*. The thread table contains information about active threads that is volatile and mostly invisible to the programmer. The table contains one entry per active thread, with the estimated total number of entries not exceeding 16. The thread data include, among other, the updated value of instruction pointer, indices to thread register and instruction frames, status flags (active, running, blocked, waiting for instruction, etc.), scheduling attributes (static and dynamic priorities, privilege level, timeout value, execution counter and scheduler control flags), predecoded instruction field and exception attributes. The scheduler determines which thread to run based on parallel lookup of all entries in the table. The lookup, as well as updates of the fields in thread entries take one cycle.

- The *Thread Control Unit*, which provides an external interface to the thread manager, accommodating high-level thread oriented requests such as thread creation, suspension and termination, which are produced by or relayed from other components of the MIND node. It also generates control signals to other subcomponents (particularly the thread scheduler) and coordinates them. Finally, it allocates and frees the individual frames from thread pools in memory via a dedicated free-list manager, thus mapping and unmapping thread objects in virtual namespace.

- The *Execution Engine*, which is an aggregation of all pipelines conditioning requests associated with supported resources. The engine directs output from the thread scheduler containing the next predecoded instruction to run and injects it into the relevant pipeline. The final stages of all pipelines share the bus delivering the state update data to the thread table. Currently, the supported resources include frame cache, memory manager, parcel handler, wide ALU, common functional unit, external I/O queue and external DRAM.

- The *Instruction Cache Frame Prefetch*, which initializes cache line transfers from the shared instruction repository and stores them in the frame cache. This operation is triggered as soon as the computation of the next IP during the instruction execution refers to the address outside the span of text cached in the instruction frame(s) for the thread. Since the prefetch is activated ahead of time, there exists a good chance that the new line will arrive before the next instruction is needed. Note that since cache lines and frames do not have to be of the same size, the prefetch sequence may require multiple lines to be streamed per fetch.
- The *Instruction Fetch and Predecode*, which performs two functions: it extracts individual instructions from the local instruction frame and passes them to the decoder. Compared to the frame prefetch machine, the fetch operation is much simpler (it requires one access to the frame cache, followed by an alignment step). The decoder is fairly primitive as well, since it has to determine only basic parameters of instruction execution. Both fetch automata have the authority to unblock a thread as soon as the operation completes.
- The *Exception Handler*, which has a threefold purpose: it provides an entry point for the external exceptions routed from the module control unit, it arbitrates the invocation order of the exception handlers based on predefined priorities, and it buffers parameters of simultaneously occurring exceptions. The exception handler interfaces to the final stages of the execution pipes, where the exception description returned by the executing resources may be decoded and used.
- The *Frame Cache Arbiter*, which is a minor supporting block whose function is to admit access to the frame cache to selected competing components of the thread manager. While the arbitration only minimally increases the average request turnaround time, it drastically reduces the number of supporting data buses while increasing their utilization. The arbiter caches the most recent access history internally to increase the fairness of its decisions.

11. MEMORY MANAGER

The memory manager provides the means of accessing the dynamic memory embedded in a PIM node. It services memory read and write primitives with data sizes ranging from 64-bit scalars and 256-bit vectors to 2048-bit wide memory rows/frames. To aid the PIM integration in systems employing traditional CPUs, some provisions for adjustable size cache line transfers has been made as well. Both physical and virtual addressing modes are supported. The memory manager also supervises atomic memory operations, in which a memory datum is offloaded to the wide ALU to be processed in an uninterruptible sequence. The conflicting accesses to the same memory location are guaranteed to be delayed until the result is computed and stored back. This direct support of AMOs is one of the architectural elements enabling an efficient implementation of distributed synchronization algorithms.

The design of the memory manager was driven by the need to both extract the maximum of the available memory bandwidth and provide efficient mechanisms to deal with the inherently high latency of memory accesses. The first requirement assures that the DRAM macros are utilized to their potential; the latter promotes pre-staging and early initialization of memory request processing, memory access combining (reducing the raw number of memory accesses), and efficient arbitration for multiple access channels. While the dynamic memory blocks are typically well optimized for use in standalone modules, there are possibilities of improving their efficiency in some situations based on the spatial relationship of addresses accessed in sequence. This is possible due to unhindered access to the decoder circuits in PIM. The bandwidth may also be increased by using multiple memory macros per node or changing their internal organization; however, routing an excessive number of bit line sets and multiplexing the wide outputs of memories may prove to be too expensive in terms of space required. The variation of the last approach is to decompose a single memory block into banks that can handle the scalar data independently of each other. If scalar accesses temporarily dominate the request stream, this modification could help reclaim at least some part of the wasted bandwidth. During vector access, all address decoders and data lines remain tightly coupled.

The second set of optimizations deals with issues related to the interfacing with the requesting entities (arbitration), buffering (the internal register space has to accommodate all data supplied by the pending writes, as well as the data read from memory using dynamic allocation of buffers), request combining (where the issue is the optimal size of the working set), request processing (decoding and setup of incoming requests should overlap the memory array access as much as possible), and memory operation retirement (streaming out the results, with possible post-conditioning). While most of these are fairly straightforward, if not mundane, a clever integration of these tasks is expected to lower further the effective average memory access latency.

12. PARCEL HANDLER

The parcel handler is a communication center of the MIND node; it shapes all aspects of inbound and outbound parcel traffic. Its main functions include:
- Assimilation of parcels from the local interconnect, with the emphasis on maintaining the incoming parcel bandwidth and thus preventing the stalls of the input link. It also implies reconstruction of large parcels from elementary transfer units (flits) used directly by the communication medium.
- Parcel decoding and conversion to data aggregations understood by other node components. This involves identification of the parcel type, extraction of the local destination of the embedded request, extraction of the request itself with its arguments and repackaging of the reply address if a response to the request is expected.
- Function dispatch based on request type, which may range from a simple physical register access, through memory operations (including AMOs and page transfers) to thread instantiation. While the operations in physical space are trivial enough to be performed by the handler directly and instantly, memory and thread manager requests additionally involve register allocation and deposition of their arguments in the frame cache.
- Outgoing parcel assembly and its emission onto the interconnect. The output parcel may be generated as a result of inbound parcel processing (e.g., memory read request), or explicitly assembled by a local thread. The proto-parcel arguments supplied in each of these scenarios are different enough to require customized approaches.
- Invocation of exception handlers in case of faults or errors.
- Buffering of unprocessed parcels in the available space of the local node. While the parcel handler has only a minimal buffer space to support the request flow, it can act as a conduit and allocator to store the parcel data in the frame cache or, in the worst case, in memory. In theory, this mechanism could also be used to offload the parcel traffic to an underutilized node, should the original destination node become a communication hotspot.

The design of the parcel handler was dictated primarily by the parcel throughput requirements on both I/O links. Both input and output flows have their dedicated pipelines with a crossover bus connecting the end stage of the receive logic with the input of the

182

transmit pipe. The purpose of the crossover is to enable a quick route for the parcels which require minimal processing with reply, such as a physical register read, thus minimizing their turn-around time. In general, the incoming parcel traffic has a higher processing priority over the requests generated within the node. This is reasonable given that parcels are received in fragments and cannot continuously block the access to the resources from internal components. Some of the arbitration logic may therefore be simplified by not having to implement the fully qualified fairness algorithms. Analogously, the quick turn-around path is allowed to block the parcels originating from anywhere in the node when competing for the output pipeline, since otherwise the stall could back-propagate and back up the input link.

The secondary processing priority is associated with extracting the maximal memory bandwidth, and thus additional provisions have been made in the input stages to assure a quick dispatch of memory requests, such as a dedicated channel to memory manager and an auxiliary request buffer to independently retain the parcel information when arbitrating the memory access. This also alleviates the contention with other parcel-initiated actions, such as thread spawn requests, for which waiting for the preceding memory request to come through may significantly increase the latency if the memory manager is busy. Such requests rely on access to the register file only and then relinquish the control to the thread manager in a minimal number of cycles.

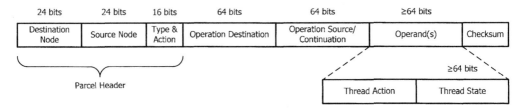

Figure 12.1. Basic parcel format.

The fundamental structure of a parcel is shown in Figure 12.1. Even parcels of this basic format can already perform a variety of actions: physical register accesses, simple thread creations, operations on scalars in memory. Frequently, all elements required to build a simple parcel can be stored within a single 256-bit datum, taking advantage of very fast transfers from the frame cache. More complex and larger parcels are formed by reusing the basic parcel's header and extending the sizes of other fields.

ACKNOWLEDGMENTS

The authors would like to express their deep gratitude to William D. Whittaker of NASA/JPL for lending his unparalleled expertise in the field of logic and VLSI design, and countless hours spent in discussions leading to the refinement of the architectural components of the MIND system. Our thanks also extend to Susan Powell, who assisted and significantly helped to shape this document into its final form. We also thank Prof. Henri Cassanova of UCSD for his substantial contributions in editing this document.

REFERENCES

1. K. Batcher, STARAN Parallel Processor System Hardware. *Proc. AFIPS Conference 43 (1974) 405-410.*

2. K. Batcher, Design of a Massively Parallel Processor. *IEEE Trans. on Computers 29:9 (1980) 836-840.*

3. T. Blank, The MasPar MP-1 Architecture. *IEEE Compcon (1990) 20-24.*

4. MasPar Corporation, Sunnyvale, California, MasPar System Overview. *Doc. 9300-0100, Rev. A3, March 1991.*

5. W. Hillis, The Connection Machine. *MIT Press, Cambridge, Mass., 1985.*

6. M. Gokhale, B. Holmes and K. Iobst, Processing In Memory: the Terasys Massively Parallel PIM Array. *IEEE Computer (1995) 23-31.*

7. P. Kogge, The EXECUBE Approach to Massively Parallel Processing. *Proc. Int. Conference on Parallel Processing 1 (1994) 77-84.*

8. D. Patterson, T. Anderson, N. Cardwell, R. Fromm, K. Keeton, C. Kozyrakis, R. Thomas and K. Yelick, A Case for Intelligent RAM: IRAM. *IEEE Micro (1997) 34-44.*

9. J. Draper, J. Chame, M. Hall, C. Steele, T. Barrett, J. LaCoss, J. Granacki, J. Shin, C. Chen, C. Woo Kang, I. Kim and G. Daglikoca, The Architecture of the DIVA Processing-In-Memory Chip. *Proc. ICS '02 (2002).*

10. C. Hewitt and H.G. Baker, Actors and Continuous Functionals. *Proc. IFIP Working Conference on Formal Description of Programming Concepts (1977) 367-390.*

11. M. Noakes, D. Wallach and W. Dally, The J-Machine Multicomputer: An Architectural Evaluation. *Proc. 20th Int. Symp. on Computer Architecture, 1993.*

12. T. von Eicken, D. Culler, S. Goldstein and K. Schauser, Active Messages: A Mechanism for Integrated Communication and Computation. *Proc. 19th Int. Symp. on Computer Architecture (1992) 256-266.*

13. D. Culler, A. Dusseau, S. Goldstein, A. Krishnamurthy, S. Lumetta, T. von Eicken and K. Yelick, Parallel Programming in Split-C. *Proc. SC99 (1999).*

14. G. Gao, K. Likharev, P. Messina and T. Sterling, Hybrid Technology Multithreaded Architecture. *Proc. 6th Symp. on the Frontiers of Massively Parallel Computation (1996) 98-105.*

15. T. Sterling and H. Zima, Gilgamesh: A Multithreaded Processor-In-Memory Architecture for Petaflops Computing. *Proc. SC02 (2002).*

16. R. Halstead, Jr., Multilisp: A Language for Concurrent Symbolic Computation. *ACM Trans. Programming Languages and Systems 7:4 (1985) 501-538.*

17. R. Nikhil, S. Pingali and Arvind, Id Nouveau. *Tech. Rep. Memo 265, Computational Structures Group, Laboratory for Computer Science, MIT, July 1986.*

18. R. Alverson, D. Callahan, D. Cummings, B. Koblenz, A. Porterfield and B. Smith, The Tera Computer System. *Proc. ICS '90 (1990) 1-6.*

19. B. Smith, Architecture and Applications of the HEP Multiprocessor Computer System. *Proc. SPIE - Real Time Signal Processing IV 298 (1981) 241-248.*

20. H. Hum, O. Maquelin, K. Theobald, X. Tian, G. Gao and L. Hendren, A Study of the EARTH-MANNA Multithreaded System. *J. Int. Parallel Programming 24 (1996) 319-347.*

21. D. Culler, S. Goldstein, K. Schauser and T. von Eicken, TAM - A Compiler Controlled Threaded Abstract Machine. *J. Parallel and Distributed Computing 18:3 (1993) 347-370.*

22. T. Sterling, J. Brockman and E. Upchurch, Analysis and Modeling of Advanced PIM Architecture Design Tradeoffs. *Proc. SC04 (2004).*

Grid Computing: The New Frontier of High Performance Computing
Lucio Grandinetti (Editor)
185
© 2005 Elsevier B.V. All rights reserved.

SLA-aware Job Migration in Grid Environments

F. Heine[a], M. Hovestadt[a], O. Kao[a] and A. Keller[a]

[a]Paderborn Center for Parallel Computing (PC²), Universität Paderborn, Germany,
{fh,maho,okao,kel}@upb.de

Grid Computing promises an efficient sharing of world-wide distributed resources, ranging from hardware, software, expert knowledge to special I/O devices. However, although the main Grid mechanisms are already developed or are currently addressed by tremendous research effort, the Grid environment still suffers from a low acceptance in different user communities. Beside difficulties regarding an intuitive and comfortable resource access, various problems related to the reliability and the Quality-of-Service while using the Grid exist.

Users should be able to rely, that their jobs will have certain priority at the remote Grid site and that they will be finished upon the agreed time regardless of any provider problems. Therefore, QoS issues have to be considered in the Grid middleware but also in the local resource management systems at the Grid sites. However, most of the currently used resource management systems are not suitable for SLAs, as they do not support resource reservation and do not offer mechanisms for job checkpointing/migration respectively. The latter are mandatory for Grid providers as rescue anchor in case of system failures or system overload.

This paper focuses on SLA-aware job migration and presents a work, which is being performed in the EU supported project HPC4U.

1. Introduction

Current Grid architectures and implementations lack essential capabilities necessary for a future large scale Grid system. For that reason, a group of experts has been convened by the European Commission, to identify research priorities for realizing the Next Generation Grids (NGG) [1].

Applications in these NGGs will demand the Grid middleware for mechanisms to enable a flexible negotiation of specific levels of Quality of Service (QoS). In this context, a QoS guarantee may range from the reservation of resources for a given time span, which is required for the orchestrated usage of distributed resources, up to guarantees for an advanced level of Fault Tolerance (FT).

A Service Level Agreement (SLA) is a powerful instrument for describing job requirement profiles [2]. It is the exact statement of all obligations and expectations within the business partnership between the resource provider and the Grid user as its customer. It describes which resources should be provided, in what amount, for how long, and in which quality. It also encompasses the price for resource consumption, respectively the penalty fee for violating the agreement.

Many research projects already focus on SLA functionality within the Grid middleware. However, it is not sufficient to add SLA mechanisms like negotiation or monitoring to Grid middleware systems only. As Grid middleware systems base on local Resource Management Systems (RMS) for the execution of Grid jobs, these RMSs also have to be able to guarantee the contents of a negotiated SLA [3]. Comparing the capabilities of current resource management systems on the one side and the requirements of future Grid systems on the other, a gap between both sides becomes apparent.

HPC4U (HPC4U stands for "Highly Predictable Cluster for Internet Grids") is an EU-funded project [4], which started in June 2004 and will end in May 2007. The partners are Meiosys SA (FR), Fujitsu Systems Europe Ltd (UK), Seanodes SA (FR), Dolphin Interconnect Solutions AS (NO), Scali AS (NO), Paderborn Center for Parallel Computing (DE), CETIC (BE), and National Supercomputer Centre (SE).

The primary goal of the HPC4U project is to realize a resource management system, that – unlike to today's resource management systems – allows the Grid user to rely on jobs which are computed on an HPC4U cluster middleware system. The HPC4U system will provide predictability by allowing the user to negotiate on Service Level Agreements (SLA). Within such an SLA the user can specify exactly which QoS services the HPC4U system should provide and how it should react in case of failures, e.g. resource outages on compute nodes.

The HPC4U results will provide Next Generation Grids with the possibility to guarantee the completion of Grid jobs, thus leveraging a larger uptake of Grid environments. The HPC4U software will be customizable and interoperable with future Grid middleware systems. It will open new perspectives to the usage of Grids for additional services as they are strongly required by the industry today. HPC4U will extend well accepted technologies and integrate them with innovative features (such as Grid embedded Fault Tolerance), for all the components required for a dependable Grid (storage, communication, resource management, or application environment).

The outcomes of HPC4U will be a mix of open source and proprietary software embedded in two outcomes (rf. Figure 1). The SLA-aware and Grid-enabled resource management system includes SLA negotiation, multi-site SLA-aware scheduling, and interfaces for storage, checkpointing, and networking support. It will be available as open source. The second HPC4U outcome will be a vertically integrated commercial product with proprietary Linux-specific developments for storage, networking and checkpointing. This outcome will demonstrate the entire, ready-to-use HPC4U functionality (job checkpointing, migration, and restart) for Grids based on Linux architectures.

The rest of the paper is organized as follows. After a brief overview of the problems to solve for increasing the fault tolerance of a cluster, we present an overview about related work done in this area. Section 4 focuses on the HPC4U architecture with its different subsystems, including a discussion about compatibility issues when migrating between different clusters. Section 5 describes the Grid-scale migration of jobs. Before concluding in the last section, we introduce the VRM concept in section 6.

2. Problem Definition

As outlined in the introduction, future applications will demand the Grid middleware to provide a reliable and fault tolerant service. For executing these high-demand applications, Grid systems utilize resource management systems, which are connected to the Grid infrastructure. Hence, these attached resource management systems also have to provide an advanced level of service quality. The goal of the HPC4U project is to provide such a fault tolerance, SLA-aware cluster middleware. HPC4U will provide two basic service levels: *run to completion* and *guaranteed deadlines*.

Run to completion ensures that a job will be finished, no matter which failures happen during the execution. Based on this service level HPC4U will assure the user that his job will be finished until a fixed point in time (i.e. a deadline). For this purpose, the user has to specify a maximum job runtime. It will be interpreted like "this job will run on the specified hardware no longer than the given time".

However, the HPC4U software will not only provide this basic service levels to the user, it will also negotiate with the user about the QoS level and respect a contract in form of an SLA, specifying the level both parties have agreed upon. Thinkable SLAs are guarantees for a minimal communication bandwidth, a storage capacity, or a file access bandwidth.

The service level *run to completion* is a real challenge. The nodes where the job executes may crash, the interconnect network between the nodes may break, or a hard drive used to write the job's temporary data may fail. Since it is impossible to avoid such failures, one has to checkpoint the applications state. HPC4U will provide *application-transparent checkpointing*. Checkpointing will be done in periodic, selectable intervals. These checkpoints then will be used when restarting the job, so that only the computation done since the latest checkpoint is lost.

Checkpointing a sequential job is easy, parallel jobs are the crunchpoint. Here the checkpoint encompasses not only the processes but also the handling of in-transit network packets and the contents of related storage partitions. For this purpose HPC4U has distinct *subsystems*, which detect and handle failures on the process, the network, and the storage level. The process subsystem virtualizes the application to decouple it from the underlying hardware and thereby provides stateful application relocation. The storage subsystem creates a unified high-performance storage space using available disks in the cluster nodes. The network subsystem supports the other two subsystems and provides bandwidth regulation, dedicated virtual subnets, and enhanced MPI error handling.

The cooperation of these subsystems is coordinated by the RMS. If the subsystems are not able to handle a failure, they notify the RMS which then has to decide what to do. The HPC4U RMS is planning based. This means that it does not only regard the present, like queuing systems do. It also plans future resource usage. For example, if scheduling a deadline it is not sufficient to plan the required resources. The scheduler also has to take into account the additional overhead for checkpointing, possible losses of computation due to a failure and the time consumed by a restart from a checkpoint.

There might be cases where the local cluster does not have enough resources to restart a checkpointed job after a failure of some nodes. In this case the job has to be migrated to either another cluster in the same administrative domain, or even another system in the Grid, if the systems in the local domain are unable to finish the job. Within the

HPC4U project, we only consider migration to other clusters which are also operated with the HPC4U software. However, in case this is too restrictive, a virtual layer above the different RMS like Platform LSF, PBS, etc. is needed to unify the different capabilities of these systems and to steer the policies under which they operate. This is addressed by the virtual resource manager (VRM) in section 6.

3. Related Work

Beside many commodity Grid systems, general purpose toolkits exist such as UNI-CORE [5] or Globus [6]. Although Globus represents the de-facto standard for Grid toolkits, all these systems have proprietary designs and interfaces. To ensure future interoperability of Grid systems as well as the opportunity to customize installations, the OGSA (Open Grid Services Architecture) working group within the GGF [7] aims to develop the architecture for an open Grid infrastructure [8].

The Next Generation Grid aims at supporting resource-sharing in virtual organizations all over the world [1]. One of its goals is to attract commercial users to use the Grid, to develop Grid enabled applications, and to offer their resources in the Grid. Mandatory prerequisites are flexibility, transparency, reliability, and the application of SLAs to guarantee a negotiated level of QoS.

An architecture that supports the co-allocation of multiple resource types, such as processors and network bandwidth, was presented in [9]. The Globus Architecture for Reservation and Allocation (GARA) provides "wrapper" functions to enhance a local RMS not capable of supporting advance reservations with this functionality. This is an important step towards an integrated QoS aware resource management. However, the GARA component of Globus currently does neither support the definition of SLAs, nor does it support resilience mechanisms to handle resource outages or failures. In HPC4U, we enhance the "wrapping" approach by SLA and monitoring facilities and use a planning based RMS [10]. These enhancements are needed in order to guarantee the compliance with all accepted SLAs. This means, it has to be ensured that the system works as expected at any time, not only at the time a reservation is made.

The requirements and procedures of a protocol for negotiating SLAs were described in SNAP [11]. However, the important issue of how to map, implement, and assure those SLAs during the whole lifetime of a request on the RMS layer remains to be solved. This issue is also addressed by the architecture presented in this paper.

The Grid community has identified the need for a standard for SLA description and negotiation. This led to the development of WS-Agreement/WS-AgreementNegotiation [12]. These upcoming standards rely upon the new Web Services Resource Framework (WSRF) [13] which will supersede the OSGI specification. We are following these developments closely and will stick to these standards.

4. Architecture

The HPC4U system is built of three layers: an interface to Grid middleware, a resource management system, and subsystems for storage-, process-, and network-management.

At the upper level, the HPC4U cluster middleware provides an interface, which can be used by Grid middleware systems to negotiate on SLAs. To ensure a maximum compati-

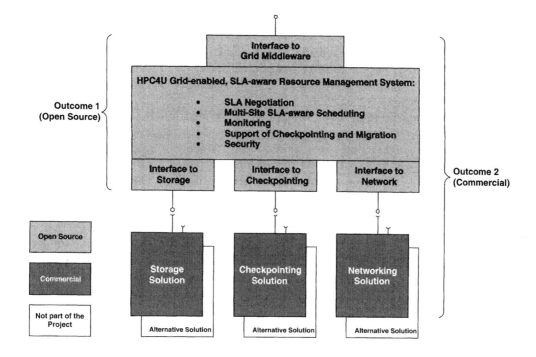

Figure 1. Outcomes of the HPC4U project.

bility with other research projects and software developments, HPC4U will follow existing standards of the Global Grid Forum (GGF), e.g. the Grid Resource Allocation Agreement Protocol (GRAAP) working group of the GGF.

4.1. Resource Management System

According to Figure 1 the RMS plays a central role in the HPC4U architecture. It not only has to negotiate on SLAs, it also has to ensure the assured level of QoS during the applications runtime. In case of resource outages the RMS has to locate suitable spare resources for resuming concerned jobs. Therefore, the resource management system has to have a monitoring subsystem to scan for resource outages. Additionally the RMS has to steer the HPC4U subsystems and has to react on events thrown by them.

4.1.1. Requirements and Architecture

The term Service Level Agreement implies the process of negotiating the service levels between provider and customer. Here the RMS is the Service provider. To be able to negotiate a service level, the RMS has to have knowledge about resource usage for the present and the future.

However, today almost all resource management systems are queuing based. Several queues with different limits are used for the submission of resource requests. Jobs within a queue are ordered according to a scheduling policy like FCFS (first come, first served). Queues might be activated only for specific times (e. g. prime time, non prime time, or weekend). Examples for queue configurations are found in [14,15].

The task of a queuing system is to assign free resources to waiting requests. It is remarkable that queuing based RMSs do not necessarily need information about the duration of requests, unless backfilling is applied.

Although queuing systems are commonly used, they have drawbacks which are inherent to their design. No information is provided that answers questions like "Is resource x available between 8am and 4pm next Tuesday?" or "When will my request be started?". However this knowledge is mandatory for negotiating SLAs. This inability of queuing based RMSs led to the decision to use a planning based RMS for the HPC4U project.

Planning based systems [10] do resource planning for the present and future, which results in an assignment of start times to all requests. A mandatory prerequisite for planning based systems is the specification of the maximum job runtime. There are no queues in planning based RMSs. Every incoming request is planned immediately. Advanced reservations are easily possible and may be submitted by all users. Planning based systems are not restricted to scheduling policies like FCFS, SJF (shortest job first), or LJF (longest job first). Backfilling is implicitly done during the replanning process. As requests are placed as soon as possible in the current schedule, they might be placed in front of already planned requests. Depending on the used scheduling policy already planned requests may be delayed in the backfilling phase.

Controlling the usage of the machine as it is done with activating different queues, e. g. for prime and non prime time in a queuing based system has to be done differently in a planning based system. One way is to use time dependent constraints for the planning process (refer to Figure 2). For example "during prime time no requests with more than 75% of the machines resources are placed". Project or user specific limits are also possible so that the machine size is virtually and time dependent decreased.

To be able to plan requests with assigned SLAs (e. g. a guaranteed minimal bandwidth) an RMS scheduler not only has to count free resources (like PEs), it also has to keep in mind system specific constraints like the topology of a high speed network. The RMS used in the HPC4U project does this by splitting the scheduling process into two parts, a hardware-dependent called Machine Manager (MM) and a hardware-independent part called Planning Manager (PM). This separation allows to consider system specific requirements (e. g. location of I/O-nodes or network topologies) at which the MM part may be adapted to different resource configurations without changing the basic scheduling part (i.e. the PM). The MM verifies, whether or not a schedule computed by the PM can be realized with the available hardware. The MM checks this by mapping the user given specification with the static (e.g. topology) and dynamic (e.g. node availability) information on the system resources. Information provided by the subsystems are incorporated in this mapping procedure. If the MM is not able to find an SLA conform mapping of the jobs onto the resources at the time scheduled by the PM it tries to find an alternative time. The resulting conflict list is sent back to the PM which in turn accepts the schedule or computes a new one based on the schedule given by the MM.

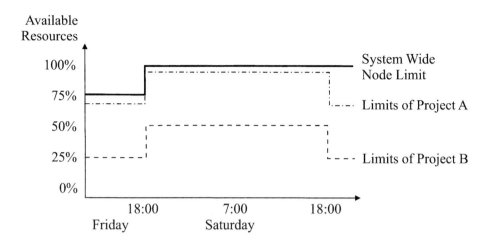

Figure 2. Time dependent limits in a planning based RMS.

4.1.2. Monitoring

SLA-aware RMSs have to observe the jobs during their whole lifetime. For this purpose, the MM monitors the running jobs and the affected resources. In case of an error (e. g. a resource failure) the MM is able to migrate the job to another matching resource. Since the MM always knows the current schedule this may be done without violating the current schedule.

The RMS also has interfaces to the three mentioned HPC4U subsystems. These interfaces are located in the MM part of the RMS since the MM also controls the execution of jobs. Using the interfaces the RMS may subscribe callback routines which are called in case a subsystem notices an error and is not able to solve the problem alone and therefore needs help by the RMS. For instance we assume a job with an SLA which guarantees a minimal bandwidth. It may now happen that due to a resource failure (not necessarily used by the concerned application) the networking subsystem is impelled to change its routing tables. The subsystem tries to fulfill the mentioned SLA since the RMS started the application with this constraint. If the networking subsystem is not able to keep the agreed minimal bandwidth it informs the RMS about the problem. The RMS then has to decide what to do: migrating the concerned application or suspending another one.

4.2. Process Subsystem

If the resource management system agrees on a specific SLA, it assigns a specific partition of the system for the computation of the job bound to this SLA. Assuming that this SLA demands for adherence with a given deadline, the resource management system has to ensure that the job has completed before this deadline. We presume that the requestor specified a runtime estimate for his application and that the application does not void this estimate.

As long as all resources operate normally, the resource management system is able to guarantee the adherence with all agreed SLAs, since these SLAs have been considered within the planning process. If a resource outage (e. g. a power failure) occurs at runtime of such an SLA bounded job on any of the assigned compute nodes, the job normally aborts. The resource management system now has to restart the application from the very beginning, which implies that all computational results are lost. As a matter of fact, this may cause the violation of the agreed deadline and the agreed SLA.

Checkpointing mechanisms are saving the current state of a given application. Using such mechanisms, applications still are aborted in case of resource outages, but now they can resume at the last checkpointed state. Therefore, only the computational results between the time of the last checkpoint and the time of resource failure are lost. By increasing the checkpoint frequency, this loss can be minimized. However, the choice of a checkpoint frequency is a tradeoff between lost computational results in case of failures and the delay of the application caused by the checkpointing process.

Some applications provide their own checkpointing mechanisms. The user can start these applications, specifying that the application should regularly generate checkpoints (e. g. generate a checkpoint every 60 minutes). If the application has to be restarted, the user will specify the latest checkpoint, so that the application can resume at that point. Unfortunately, only a minority of applications is able to generate such application level checkpoints. Hence, the application has to be checkpointed externally.

Such process checkpointing mechanisms are well known and established techniques. They all create an image of the whole running process. This does not only include the main memory used by the checkpointed process, but also other relevant information, e. g. program counter, process id, or cpu registers. Many different implementations of such checkpointing mechanisms exist, as to mention implementations of Platform LSF [16] and Condor [17]. However, these products require the recompilation of the application which should be checkpointed at runtime, since specific checkpointing libraries of these products need to be linked into the application. Therefore, these checkpointing solutions are not transparent to the applications. Especially in commercial Grid scenarios this is a major drawback, since the source code of commercial applications normally is not available, so that these applications can not benefit from being checkpointed.

In HPC4U, process checkpointing will be application-transparent. For that, the process subsystem will create a "virtual bubble" around the process, presenting a virtual environment, e. g. consisting of virtual network devices, and virtual process IDs. This virtual environment allows the checkpointing of a process without the necessity of linking additional special purpose libraries into the environment. It is remarkable, that the virtual bubble has only minimal impact on the runtime of a job.

Since no recompilation is required, arbitrary applications can be checkpointed and benefit from an increased level of fault tolerance. Hence, also in commercial Grid environments, the resource management system can guarantee the adherence with given deadlines.

In the first phase of the HPC4U project, this process subsystem is only capable of creating a virtual bubble around non-parallel jobs. Within the HPC4U project, this checkpointing mechanism will be extended to also cover parallel applications running on multiple nodes. At this, the process subsystem will utilize mechanisms of the network subsystem to ensure that also in-transit packets are handled, which are transmitted over the network at checkpoint time.

A major task within the process subsystem is the retrieval of compatible resources for a given checkpoint. Only if the target system is compatible to the source system, where the checkpoint has been generated, the checkpoint will be able to restart. This problem is described in Section 4.5.1.

The process subsystem will generate a requirement profile of each checkpointed job. In such a profile all relevant characteristics of a job are stated, e.g. CPU type, kernel version, and versions of loaded libraries. This profile will then be used by the resource management system for querying compatible resources.

4.3. Storage Subsystem

The checkpointing capabilities of the process subsystem are a powerful instrument in realizing a high level of fault tolerance. However, providing checkpointing mechanisms alone is not yet enough for realizing fault tolerant cluster middleware.

Nearly each application accesses a local data storage partition at runtime, e.g. for reading input data, and saving temporary and output data. As long as the cluster is at normal operation, the storage subsystem solely has to ensure, that the running application is able to access the storage partition at the guaranteed level of QoS as agreed within the content of the SLA, e.g. to guarantee that the agreed storage capacity is available, or performance characteristics like average I/O transfer rate are met.

If resource outages occur on used compute nodes, the resource management system will detect this exceptional situation and utilizes its fault tolerance mechanisms to assure the adherence with agreed SLAs. For this, it has periodically checkpointed the application, so that it can take the latest checkpoint, query for compatible resources and resume the application at the checkpointed state on the discovered spare resource.

However, a checkpoint of the process containing an image of the main memory used by the process is not enough. As the process might write temporary or result files, also the state of the storage partition for the process has to be saved. Thus, every process checkpoint must be accompanied by a storage checkpoint to avoid inconsistencies between the state of the process and the state of the storage.

To achieve this consistency, the process subsystem uses data containers to provide storage capacity to running applications. A data container is assigned to exactly one application. If an application is checkpointed, the resource management system first requests the process subsystem to freeze the application, so that its state is stable and does not change. The process subsystem then generates a checkpoint of the virtual bubble, which is encapsulating the freezed application. After this, the resource management system requests the storage subsystem to generate a snapshot of the data container, holding the storage partition of the freezed application. Since the application did not make any computational steps between checkpointing and snapshotting, both datasets are consistent. Now the application can be unfreezed and resume with computation.

If the application needs to be restarted from a checkpoint at some time, this restart will restore the original state of the application, both including process image and storage partition. Furthermore it is feasible to transfer checkpoint and snapshot datasets to remote clusters, if the computation can not be continued on the original cluster machine, e.g. due to a lack of suitable spare resources. Using these datasets, the entire environment can be reestablished on arbitrary machines.

This is of major importance, because the HPC4U project does not only focus on fault tolerance on a single cluster. It also envisages to use resources from multiple clusters within a single administrative domain, or even resources from the Internet Grid. Hence, a job may be resumed on resources of a completely different cluster system. At this, not only the data of the checkpointed process has to be transferred to the new system, but also the according checkpoint of the storage partition. As storage partitions may be huge, this might be a time consuming process which would prevent to meet the agreed deadline of a job. Therefore the storage subsystem will provide mechanisms for a background replication of storage data to remote systems.

4.4. Network Subsystem

The network subsystem will not only provide network-related mechanisms for fault tolerance, but will also support the other subsystems in providing their mechanisms. The resource management system will query the network subsystem for dynamic information about the network, e. g. currently available bandwidth. This information is necessary for SLA negotiation and scheduling.

The commercial outcomes of the HPC4U project will be tailored to specific commercial products, which are developed and provided by HPC4U partners. Therefore the network subsystem will use the SCI network as interconnect between the compute nodes of an HPC4U cluster system. Some functions of the network subsystem will be SCI specific. However, it will be possible to integrate arbitrary network interconnects into an HPC4U enabled cluster system, if the specific network subsystem provides the required interfaces.

As described in 4.2, the process subsystem will not only create checkpoints of single-node applications, but also from parallel applications running on multiple nodes. If a parallel application is running on multiple nodes, each node may send messages to the other nodes of the applications. According to the frequency of these messages such applications are called loosely or tightly coupled. If such an application is checkpointed, a node might have just sent a message to another node. This message might have already left the sender node, but not yet reached the recipient. Such a packed is called in-transit.

To ensure consistency, the network subsystem must be able to handle these in-transit packets. The procedure is as follows: At checkpoint time, the process subsystem will first freeze the application, so that its state is stable and does not change. Now the network subsystem is invoked to check all stacks for network packets. Also the network itself is checked for currently transmitted packets. All these packets are saved in a network dataset file. Thereafter, the process subsystem can continue with the checkpoint of the freezed application. If an application is to be resumed from a checkpointed state, this network dataset file is used to restore the network situation at checkpoint time.

Furthermore, the network subsystem will provide mechanisms for a fault-tolerant message passing interface (MPI). It will allow the resource management system to initialize the application, so that in case of failures the application will not immediately be informed. Instead, the network subsystem will invoke callback functions of the resource management system, so that failure handling mechanisms of the RMS can take place. Without this procedure, the application would be immediately informed about an MPI error and cancel the execution.

Another feature of the network subsystem will be transparent failover. If network connections fail, the network subsystem will detect this problem and switch immediately to other network connections (i.e. reroute the network). Agreed network SLAs (e. g. a minimal bandwidth) are concerned. Even a failover to other available networks is feasible, e. g. Gigabit ethernet. Of course, this failover will be compliant to the general initialization of the resource management system and the actual network conditions. This means, that the RMS can restrict the failover to specific network cards or network segments. Constraints like bandwidth limits will be regarded. At runtime, the network subsystem will monitor the consumed network bandwidth of a job and enforce bandwidth limits, if specified.

In case the failover does not solve the problem, the resource management system is informed. The RMS now can decide to relocate running applications from affected nodes to spare resources, which are not affected by this problem. This way, the HPC4U system can also react on network problems, which only slow down the network communication, but do not hinder the communication completely.

4.5. Migrating jobs between clusters

With the mechanisms presented in the previous sections, an HPC4U cluster middleware system is able to negotiate service levels, and to monitor the environment, in which a job is executed. In case of occurring resource outages, the HPC4U system utilizes its subsystems according to the agreed SLA to provide fault tolerance. At this, the main instrument is the resume of a checkpointed job on a spare resource.

It is obvious, that the availability of suitable spare resources is the limiting factor of this mechanism. Presuming that a spare resource is always available, the system can guarantee the compliance with every agreed SLA - with no impact of current system load. Thus, the pool of resources, which will be queried for spare resources, should be as big as possible, since the probability of finding suitable resources increases with the number of available systems.

As a consequence, HPC4U will not be restricted to a single cluster system when searching spare resources. It also may use remote cluster resources for migration. If the cluster middleware detects a resource outage which may violate an agreed SLA, the resource management system first tries to resolve this conflict internally, using the presented mechanisms on fault tolerance of process-, storage-, and network-subsystem. If no spare resources are available (e. g. the affected job is deadline bounded, but due to high utilization no local resources would be available early enough, so that the agreed deadline can be met), the resource management system queries other cluster systems for suitable resources. Since the job in question is bound to an SLA, its requirement profile is known. From the point of the Grid customer it makes no difference, which resource is actually used for computation.

4.5.1. Compatibility of Resources

When migrating jobs between different, inhomogeneous clusters, it is important to ensure that the target cluster will be able to resume the checkpointed application. For this purpose we have to concern the *compatibility* of the clusters with respect to the job being migrated. As we do application-transparent checkpointing, the compatibility has to be very tight. We also have to distinguish between jobs which are migrated before they are started (e. g. because the allocated resources crashed beforehand) and those jobs which are already running when being migrated. They might have even more restrictions concerning the target system as – for example – some libraries might be opened and mapped to specific addresses. Thus such libraries must be available on the target machine in exactly the same version.

We expect that the SLA contains all hardware and software requirements for the application to start. This might include the specification of the CPU architecture, required frequency, special features of the CPU like hyper threading, a list of libraries required to run the program, an operating system type, kernel version, etc.

The RMS matches its resources against this requirement list to find resources suitable to execute the job. Further negotiation about QoS levels makes only sense if the resource will be able to execute the job. In order to be not too restrictive, the RMS records general compatibility information like library versions, kernel versions, CPU architectures, etc. This information is integrated in the matching process to find as much resources as possible.

In case the job has to be migrated to a different target resource, the checkpointing subsystem generates a so-called *profile*, which contains more detailed information about the requirements of this checkpoint. This includes all libraries which are already open, and thus have to be available in exactly the same version. Here, no compatible version is allowed, as it might have a different memory layout, thus preventing the restarted job to function correctly.

In the context of large Grid environments with millions of resources, the question how to find compatible resources is an interesting research topic. A possible architecture is outlined in [18].

5. Grid Scope

In its final stage the HPC4U project will expand the fault tolerance capabilities of the HPC4U systems. In case local resource outages can not be compensated by suitable spare resources, the SLA does not have to be violated. Instead, the HPC4U system then will actively use the available Grid infrastructure by querying the Grid for suitable spare resources. If such resources can be found, the HPC4U system will try to migrate the affected job to the remote Grid resource. At this, security becomes vital. Without providing, guaranteeing and enforcing security policies and mechanisms, the user will not accept Grid migration of his job.

5.1. Security

The first step to integrate the HPC4U system into an Internet Grid will be the implementation of all necessary security aspects connected to Internet Grids.

Security and nondisclosure aspects of job processing are major requirements for commercial users to develop and apply Grid applications. These issues are already addressed by a multitude of research groups worldwide, thus a lot of proposals are already published but not yet standardized. Implementing the currently established security GGF standards will satisfy these demands. Users then will be able to stage-in and stage-out the job data in a secure way, which will be provided using existing or future techniques such as the PKI based data transport mechanism gridFTP. HPC4U will support the valid security standards and thus allow a seamless integration of HPC4U in worldwide Grids. This guarantees that the HPC4U middleware will be able to act as a part of the Internet Grid, thus being interoperable with any other GGF-compliant middleware, which implements and follows the current GGF or related security standards for authentication, accounting and data transfer.

5.2. Policies

In an administrative domain a given set of policies is valid. These policies define, how the resources in such a domain can be used (e. g. which external users are allowed to use specific internal resources), which information is published (e. g. which resources are visible to the outside world) or what should happen in case of resource outages.

Access policies may be tailored to specific user groups. For security reasons and customization purposes, the administrator may further define the granularity of the information that is published. If privacy is not a key issue, it is possible to publish all available information about the internal infrastructure. However, this is not reasonable in most cases.

However a policy does not only define the general operation of resources within an administrative domain. At negotiation time, service requestor and service provider may also agree on specific policies. Such policies can imply all aspects of job computation, e. g. which security constraints regarding used compute nodes exist, which information may be published about this job, or which nodes may be used as spare resource for migration in case of failures.

In the context of policy management, some concepts for describing policies already have been established, like work from the IETF Policy Framework working group [19] or the Common Open Policy Service (COPS) [20]. These concepts also focus on detecting and solving conflicts between policies. They can be used in the HPC4U system to analyze incoming SLA requests, and to map them to local policies. With policy support enabled, a job may only be accepted, if the required policy profile can be supported. However, within the HCP4U project, only a subset of policies will be integrated.

6. The Virtual Resource Manager

The HPC4U system presented in the previous sections is already able to cope with demands of future Grid applications and future Grid middleware systems. However, just adding fault tolerance mechanisms for providing an agreed level of QoS is not yet sufficient. Likewise, it is essential to consider the requirements of the resource providers which are interested in a smooth integration of existing RMS installations into an SLA-aware environment. Important aspects are the retention of existing administrative responsibilities, and a fine-grained limitation of information published about the local infrastructure.

6.1. VRM

The *Virtual Resource Manager* (VRM) is a powerful instrument for closing this gap [3]. It copes with these requirements and has been designed on top of existing RMS for clusters and networks. The design provides different functionalities for QoS management which can be deployed on top of local RMS. The granularity for the deployment of these components can be selected by the local administrators.

The VRM conceals the underlying structures and components of the local systems such that it is possible to provide *virtual resources*. This is done by establishing so called

198

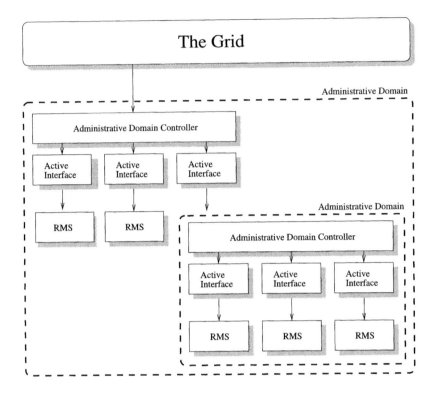

Figure 3. Hierarchical Administrative Domain Structure.

Administrative Domains (AD). ADs may be seen as a pool of resources with the same set of policies. Such policies describe which resources are visible and accessible from what kind of entity and how this access can be provided. ADs may be nested and resources within an AD may be combined to form virtual resources (see Fig. 3). The VRM architecture comprises three layers as depicted in Fig. 4.

The *Administrative Domain Controller* (ADC) is the topmost element in the VRM architecture. It establishes an administrative domain by enforcing a given set of policies regarding security, access, information, or job migration. For the outside world, the ADC provides an interface for connecting and negotiating. This enables the local administrator to keep control about the way how remote Grid users may access and use internal resources, and what should happen in case of resource failures. For instance it is possible to specify policies describing which internal resources are available at what time and to what extend. The administrator may also define that resource failures are not immediately published to the Grid. This way, the system first may try to find suitable spare resources within the own administrative domain, as long as the adherence with the given SLA still can be guaranteed.

Furthermore, the ADC publishes information about topology and actual condition of internal resources, according to the current policy set. At this, the ADC may join phys-ically existing resources to virtual resources, or recombine them to resource classes. The administrator may publish information of these virtual resources and resource-classes to the outside world, thereby hiding the exact layout of the internal topology. Incoming requests then will be mapped to existing resources.

Comprising, the ADC acts as a gateway between the internal resources and the outside Grid system. However, the inside world may be heterogeneous. Many different resource management systems may exist, each of them offering different capabilities and different interfaces. *Active Interfaces* (AI) then act as brokers between the demands of the ADC and the different capabilities of the underlying RMS.

At this, the AI does not simply encapsulate the underlying RMS. It may also be used to improve the level of QoS provided by the RMS. For example, the AI may try to map a certain subset of SLA-mechanisms to existing RMS capabilities. This approach is well known and similar to GARA's approach of emulating advance reservations.

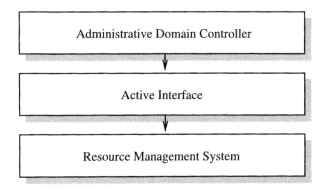

Figure 4. Layers of the VRM Architecture.

With this encapsulation mechanism, the ADC has a uniform view on the underlying RMS. Hence, the SLA negotiation process between the ADC and the underlying RMS is independent of the actually targeted RMS. If the RMS is not capable of negotiating on SLAs, the AI negotiates on behalf of the RMS, using the available interfaces of the RMS to determine if the contents of the SLA can be fulfilled. If the RMS is SLA-aware, the AI just forwards the incoming SLA requests, using appropriate functions in the API of the RMS. At runtime, the AI may also monitor the underlying components, to detect exceptional situations. In such a case, the AI will provide feedback to the ADC, which then may react to prevent the violation of an agreed SLA.

At the lowest level of the VRM architecture, local resource management systems provide access to various kinds of locally available physical resources. Here it is possible to integrate another VRM as an RMS, thus building up hierarchical structures, each operating their own VRM installation. However, within the HPC4U project, only cluster RMSs will be supported.

7. Conclusion

In this paper we have outlined the basic ideas and components of the application transparent HPC4U cluster middleware system. It assures, unlike to today's resource management systems, job completion, no matter which failures happen during the execution on the process, storage, or network layer. The HPC4U system allows the user to negotiate on Service Level Agreements (SLA). Within such an SLA one can exactly specify which level of service quality the HPC4U system should provide (e.g. a minimal bandwidth, deadlines, etc.) and how it should react in case of failures.

For this purpose HPC4U is based on a planning based RMS and distinct *subsystems*, which detect and handle failures. The process subsystem virtualizes a resource to decouple the application from the underlying hardware and provides application transparent checkpointing of sequential and parallel applications. The storage subsystem creates a unified high-performance storage space using available disks in the cluster nodes. The network subsystem supports the other two subsystems and provides bandwidth regulation, dedicated virtual subnets, and enhanced MPI error handling. Job migration may be done within one cluster, using several clusters in one domain, or by using available Grid resources.

The HPC4U software will be customizable and interoperable with other Grids and will open new perspectives to the usage of Grids for additional services as they are today strongly required by the industry. An initial version of the HPC4U system has already been successfully completed. It provides application transparent fault tolerance for single-node running jobs and supports the migration of such jobs within a single cluster system. Hence, if a running application if affected by a resource outage, the HPC4U system migrates the job transparently to a suitable spare resource. In the next step, this system will be extended to also cover parallel jobs and inter-cluster Grid migration.

REFERENCES

1. H. Bal et al, Next Generation Grids 2: Requirements and Options for European Grids Research 2005-2010 and Beyond, ftp://ftp.cordis.lu/pub/ist/docs/ngg2_eg_final.pdf (2004).
2. A. Sahai, S. Graupner, V. Machiraju, A. v. Moorsel, Specifying and Monitoring Guarantees in Commercial Grids through SLA, Tech. Rep. HPL-2002-324, Internet Systems and Storage Laboratory, HP Laboratories Palo Alto (November 2002).
3. L.-O. Burchard, M. Hovestadt, O. Kao, A. Keller, B. Linnert, The Virtual Resource Manager: An Architecture for SLA-aware Resource Management, in: 4th Intl. IEEE/ACM Intl. Symposium on Cluster Computing and the Grid (CCGrid) 2004, Chicago, USA, 2004.
4. Highly Predictable Cluster for Internet Grids (HPC4U), IST 511531, http://www.hpc4u.org.
5. UNICORE Forum e.V., http://www.unicore.org.
6. Globus Alliance: Globus Toolkit, http://www.globus.org.
7. Global Grid Forum, http://www.ggf.org.

8. GGF Open Grid Services Architecture Working Group (OGSA WG), Open Grid Services Architecture: A Roadmap (April 2003).

9. I. Foster, C. Kesselman, C. Lee, R. Lindell, K. Nahrstedt, A. Roy, A Distributed Resource Management Architecture that Supports Advance Reservations and Co-Allocation, in: 7th International Workshop on Quality of Service (IWQoS), London, UK, 1999.

10. M. Hovestadt, O. Kao, A. Keller, A. Streit, Scheduling in HPC Resource Management Systems: Queuing vs. Planning, in: Job Scheduling Strategies for Parallel Processing: 9th International Workshop, JSSPP 2003 Seattle, WA, USA, 2003.

11. K. Czajkowski, I. Foster, C. Kesselman, V. Sander, S. Tuecke, SNAP: A Protocol for Negotiating Service Level Agreements and Coordinating Resource Management in Distributed Systems, in: D. Feitelson, L. Rudolph, U. Schwiegelshohn (Eds.), Job Scheduling Strategies for Parallel Processing, 8th International Workshop, Edinburgh, 2002.

12. A. Andrieux, K. Czajkowski, A. Dan, K. Keahey, H. Ludwig, J. Pruyne, J. Rofrano, S. Tuecke, M. Xu, Web Services Agreement Negotiation Specification (WS-AgreementNegotiation) (2004).

13. I. Foster, S. Graham, S. Tuecke, K. Czajkowski, D. Ferguson, F. Leymann, M. Nally, I. Sedukhin, D. Snelling, T. Storey, W. Vambenepe, S. Weerawarana, Modeling Stateful Resources with Web Services (2002).

14. K. Windisch, V. Lo, R. Moore, D. Feitelson, B. Nitzberg, A Comparison of Workload Traces from Two Production Parallel Machines, in: 6th Symposium Frontiers Massively Parallel Computing, 1996, pp. 319–326.

15. D. G. Feitelson, M. A. Jette, Improved Utilization and Responsiveness with Gang Scheduling, in: D. G. Feitelson and L. Rudolph (Ed.), Proc. of 3rd Workshop on Job Scheduling Strategies for Parallel Processing, Vol. 1291 of Lecture Notes in Computer Science, Springer Verlag, 1997, pp. 238–262.

16. Platform Checkpointing, http://www.science-computing.de/manuals/lsf/5.0/sdk_5.0/checkpoint.html.

17. Condor Checkpointing, http://www.cs.wisc.edu/condor/checkpointing.html.

18. F. Heine, M. Hovestadt, O. Kao, Towards Ontology-Driven P2P Grid Resource Discovery, in: 5th IEEE/ACM International Workshop on Grid Computing, 2004.

19. IETF Policy Framework Working Group, http://www.ietf.org/html.charters/OLD/policy-charter.html.

20. Common Open Policy Service (COPS), http://www.eion.com/protocols_traffic_cops_h.html.

Grid Computing: The New Frontier of High Performance Computing
Lucio Grandinetti (Editor)
© 2005 Elsevier B.V. All rights reserved.

MICROGRIDS - The Exploitation of Massive On-chip Concurrency

C. R. Jesshope

Department of Computer Science, University of Amsterdam,
Kruislaan 403, 1098 SJ Amsterdam, The Netherlands
E-mail: jesshope@science.uva.nl

In this paper a general model for instruction-level distributed computing is described. This model provides an explicit description of instruction-level concurrency and allows for scalable implementations of various types of wide-issue multiprocessors. The model is based on microthreading, a hardware-supported multithreading paradigm that schedules small fragments of code dynamically. This model is a replacement for out-of-order issue, currently used in superscalar processors, in order to expose higher levels of concurrent instruction issue. The model describes parametric concurrency, based on loops, and produces schedule-independent binary code. Moreover, this model can be implemented in a fully scalable manner and it is shown here that the instruction issue logic, the distributed register-files and communication structures all scale linearly with issue width. Out-of-order issue has the distinct advantage of backward compatibility in binary code execution as the concurrency is implicit but the scalability disadvantages will eventually outweigh this; in the out-of-order-issue model there is a square-law scaling in the size of issue logic with issue width and a cube law scaling of the global register-file with issue width. Microthreading does not yield concurrency unless existing code is recompiled using the concurrency controls introduced by this model. However, backward compatibility is still possible and some speedup on legacy code may be achieved by binary-code translation.

1 Where did all the transistors go?

Current microprocessors use out-of-order issue as a mechanism for dynamically extracting concurrency from legacy, sequential, binary code. This method is highly speculative, which ultimately has implication for both performance, which is lower than the issue width would imply and power consumption, which increases with speculative failure. Indeed, it is well known that significant performance loss (and wasted power) is associated with miss-prediction and any associated cleanup. However, there is another major problem, which is currently being masked by the exponential increase in transistor packing density. This problem is that the logic required for out-of-order issue does not scale well with issue width and will eventually be a major obstacle to the use of this approach.

The so-called billion-transistor chip has been on the agenda for seven years now [1] and in another seven years, according to the ITRS 2003 road map [2], we will have this level of chip density in mainstream products and will be looking to support massive on-chip concurrency in our computer systems. To put this in perspective, the INMOS T800 transputer [3] was a 32-bit integer/64-bit floating-point microprocessor with 4KByte of on-chip RAM and four fast communication channels, which provided hardware support for concurrency (at the process level). This system was implemented in a half a million transistors. At that time, parallel computers were constructed with thousands of these chips as building blocks without any external RAM, except for the host, and connected only by their on-chip communications channels. Such a system, i.e. thousands of T800 transputers, could be integrated onto a single billion-transistor chip. While such a system is attractive in its scalability, this concurrency must be explicitly programmed and is at a relatively coarse grain. An ideal architecture would provide this same scalability but would support as much of that concurrency as possible at the instruction level, derived implicitly from existing user code but not necessarily at run time. At the same time such an architecture should flexibly encompass other levels of concurrency.

To compare the above scaling with that found in recent microprocessors, it seems that we are unable to efficiently exploit even the current levels of transistor density. Today's 100 million transistor chips should be supporting hundreds concurrent instruction issues, whereas actual issue widths are less than ten and effective IPC is typically not much more than two. It is a conjecture of this paper that the barriers to achieving these levels of concurrency are largely two-fold and can both be avoided using the concurrency model described in this paper. The barriers are the complexity of the out-of-order instruction issue and the amount of on-chip cache required to mitigate against the memory wall. Typically 20-30% of the chip area is dedicated to the former and 50-75% to the latter. A third and as yet uncritical issue is the scaling of the central register file but if issue widths had scaled with packing density, this would also be a critical issue today.

It may be unfair to compare the T800 with a pipelined, RISC processors but even if we look at the history of a single microprocessor family, we still have a very similar picture. Consider the twelve-year history of the PPC processor (see http://www.rootvg.net/RSmodels.htm). It can be seen that the PPC does not achieve the levels of concurrency in instruction issue that Moore's law would predict (a packing density increase of 256 in that period). The PPC has evolved from a 32-bit, single-instruction issue design to a 64-bit, five-way issue design. Circuit density has grown as predicted in this period but has not contributed to on-chip concurrency, where we see only a factor of ten (a factor of 2 in bit-level issue and of 5 in instruction-level issue). On the other hand, the clock rate has increased from from 33Mhz to 1Ghz or roughly twice the predicted 16-fold increase we would expect from Moore's law, given that a CMOS transistor's speed is inversely proportional to its length. This faster-than-predicted clock speed is due to a finer slicing of the pipeline, which is detrimental to overall power consumption. The smaller than predicted concurrency, a factor of up to 25, is more worrying and is a key motivation for this work.

2 A Strategy for Performance

Relying on clock speed as a means to provide increased performance, especially for a given power level, is a poor design strategy (although it may be a good marketing strategy for consumer processors). There are several reasons for this. The first is that increasing clock speed by super-pipelining actually increases the problems associated with the so-called memory wall, i.e. the divergence between processor speed and that of the main off-chip memory [4]. The second issue is power dissipation. The dynamic power of a CMOS chip is proportional to its frequency but is also proportional to the square of the supply voltage, $(V_{dd})^2$. It may be thought that the linear increase in power with frequency is neutral, as doubling either frequency or concurrency would double both performance and power. However, for optimum power management, it is possible to reduce the supply voltage with frequency. Circuit delay is known to be inversely proportional to $(V_{dd} - V_t)^2$ and frequency is inversely proportional to circuit delay, hence frequency is proportional to $(V_{dd} - V_t)^2$, where V_t is the threshold voltage. Embedded and portable systems already use both voltage and frequency scaling to conserve power and this practice is likely to become more widespread. If voltage scaling with frequency is used, power scaling is closer to frequency squared. Both memory-wall and power issues would indicate that increased concurrency is a much better strategy to follow than simply increasing clock frequency in order to increase performance.

Any strategy must assume a linear increase in performance with either frequency or concurrency but this is not always possible. The issue with increasing processor frequency thorough super-pipelining is that the increased relative latency for memory access limits the generality of the model to applications with regular access patterns or reduces performance from one related to processor frequency to one related to memory frequency, which diverges exponentially from processor frequency. The issue with using concurrency is performance scalability and relates to the loss of performance due to the additional overheads of communication and synchronisation between concurrent units, be they instructions, threads or processes.

In out-of-order issue, synchronisation between dependent instructions constrains issue and contributes to the square-law growth in instruction issue area; the communication is defined by the register specifiers in the binary code, in conjunction with any subsequent renaming. It is difficult to implement this communication on anything but a global register file or some distributed structure that emulates one. In the worst case of a single register file, the size of the register file grows as the cube of the issue width as cell area grows with the square of the number of ports, which is linearly related to issue width, and there is a linear increase in number of locations with issue width. At best, using a distributed solution, a constant delay switch would grow as the square of the issue width and complex logic would be required to distribute the variables in order to minimise delays in scheduling due to this communication.

This paper describes a technique for instruction-level concurrency based on the concept of microthreading [9-12], which yields scalable, distributed implementations, with asynchronous communication between the distributed components. Moreover, the technique is based on simple additions to an existing ISA. It also allows a compiler to partition the variables used into classes that allow an optimisation of the communication between the distributed components. It is shown that only a simple, ring network and a broadcast bus are required to implement this communication. Instruction issue in this model is distributed and scales linearly with the issue width. It also provides good latency-tolerance characteristics, which ameliorate any problems associated with the memory wall and indeed in the latency of communicating results between the distributed components. These components can be single-issue, in-order pipelines, a heterogeneous collection of in-order pipelines or indeed VLIW pipelines.

3 Concurrency in Microprocessors

There are a number of critical issues in the exploitation of on-chip, instruction-level concurrency in a microprocessor design, two have already been raised in the introductory sections, namely communication and synchronisation between instructions executed. Another is the nature of the concurrency controls used in the execution model, which may be implicit or explicit. These controls will determine the extent of concurrency, how it is managed and possibly provide other primitive operations such as global synchronisation. Finally there is the commercial issue of ISA compatibility.

3.1 Speculative architectures

The current superscalar approach of issuing instructions out of order from a sequential stream of instructions (i.e. a completely implicit approach to concurrency) has the overwhelming advantage of totally compatibility for any ISA, as no concurrency controls are introduced. The dataflow graph that specifies dependencies in the code is reconstructed in the instruction-issue window using a namespace that is limited by the address range of the ISA's register-specifier field. However, sequential reuse of this namespace through renaming is necessary, in order to expose sufficient concurrency but at additional cost. The problems with this approach are inefficient use of chip area and poor power-scaling. Proposals to partition the instruction-issue window have been made in [5] but this does not address the problem of communication via a central register file. Another speculative model, based on both block and instruction speculation is proposed in [6]. Superficially, this has similar distribution properties to the micro-threaded model described here, in that it allows a distribution of register files and requires a ring network for dependencies. However, it is unlikely that any speculative model will give scalable performance and power dissipation as concurrency increases. The former as is apparent from the limits observed in existing wide-issue superscalar processors, the latter due to the additional logic required to control instruction issue. In such an approach, not only does performance fail to scale with issue width but more importantly, miss-prediction, and the attendant cleanup that this requires, both consume power without producing any tangible results.

3.2 Distributed architectures

Quite separately, the problem of scaling register files has been addressed in [7], where (not surprisingly) it is shown that the ideal scaling of registers in a CMP distributes the registers to the ALU input ports, with a switching network routing results from the ALU to the next input port required. Although such an implementation is appropriate for regular, streaming applications, as considered by that paper, it does not support a general-purpose model of computation, where a static allocation of instructions to ALUs is not generally possible.

More recently, a more general variant of the same approach has been proposed in [8], which outlines the EDGE model of concurrency and an implementation of the TRIPS instruction set. TRIPS is a dataflow ISA, which is used to explicitly describe dependencies within a block of code. In this model, these instructions are statically allocated to processors in a cluster. Input and output to the block is performed by register or memory read/write operations but internally, register reads and writes are replaced by tag matching using an explicit token store. In this ISA the tag is a triple, which identifies the coordinate in a two-dimensional array of processors where the instruction will be executed plus a matching location in that processor. In the proposed implementation, a matching store of 64 locations allows 8 hyper-blocks of up to 8 instructions to execute concurrently in each of the 16 processors.

This approach exploits the efficiency of the ETS direct-match mechanism, proposed by Greg Papadopoulos in his thesis from MIT [22]. By eliminating loops and procedure calls from the dataflow mechanism, the complexity associated with the dynamic allocation of the tag address space is eliminated completely, giving an efficient, statically-mapped and dynamically-scheduled form of concurrency. The disadvantage however, is that the blocks created must be large, they are called hyper-blocks and are compiled by unrolling loops, predicating any conditionals within the loop and in-lining any functions called there. Hyper-blocks are then executed speculatively, based on branch prediction, albeit at a less frequent rate than in a superscalar architecture, i.e. at a rate of one prediction in at most eight machine cycles. This model still poses potential problems in power-efficiency and performance due to miss-prediction as well as to any failed predication. It is not clear from this paper how large the impact on performance will be, certainly it will be reduced compared to instruction-by-instruction speculation.

Scalability and compatibility in this model seems less well developed. Binary code will not be compatible under a scaling to more processors in the cluster as instructions are mapped statically to processor by the compiler. Hence any increases in the number of processors used to execute the hyperblock will require recompilation or at the very least binary-to-binary translation. It is known that any instability in ISA is very disruptive to both the manufacturer and users of computer systems and this issue needs to be carefully considered. Of course it can be solved by increasing the number of hyper-block cores used to execute the code but this relies on implicit rather than explicit concurrency and will have the same adverse scaling as found in superscalar processors, due to data dependency management and renaming. Thus for a given ISA width, a fixed scaling factor is achieved, in this case 16 and therefore in four more doubling periods, i.e. six to eight years, this model will require a new broader ISA or suffer from the same problems superscalar architecture does today.

3.3 Architectures with explicit concurrency controls

There are already a number of architectures that use explicit, instruction-level concurrency. Typically they schedule instructions explicitly to separate functional units using a very long instruction word (VLIW). This class of architecture also includes EPIC, jointly developed by HP and Intel, where the concurrency exposed in the ISA is decoupled from that of the execution hardware, i.e. the binding stage between instruction and execution unit is delayed until runtime. In both cases, one instruction combines a number of operations that can be executed simultaneously. By delegating the scheduling of instructions to the compiler [9], the scaling problems associated with hardware schedulers found in superscalar architecture are avoided; the scaling problems associated with the register file are not. These static schedules are also a poor choice of concurrency control unless all instructions execute deterministically. This is generally not the case, as control dependencies, and some data dependencies, such as memory accesses, cannot be scheduled statically. Normally instructions are scheduled for a cache hit but if this fails, the entire instruction packet must be stalled. EPIC introduces solutions to some of these problems. For example, using predicated instruction execution and binding pre-fetches on memory accesses. Again power may be dissipated for no tangible work performed.

3.4 Threaded models

Thread-based concurrency is orthogonal to that used in VLIW and can be exploited together with it. Also simultaneous multithreading SMT [20] combines both thread concurrency with out-of-order issue to increase the concurrency exposed in the instruction window but does not solve the scaling problems. Multithreading defines many sequences of instructions that execute concurrently but does not fix a schedule between instructions in different threads. Because of this dynamic scheduling, threaded models provide a solution to the problems of non-deterministic events in instruction execution. Switching between threads on a single pipeline can hide the latency of a non-deterministic event by continuing to execute instructions from other independent threads. Generally, the level of concurrency found in a threaded model is low and at a higher level of granularity than that used in instruction-level models of concurrency. It also requires explicit, user-level concurrency in the software. Microthreading on the other hand, expresses concurrency at the instruction level by defining many *very small* sequences of instructions, from sequential code, which can execute concurrently. This is the same process as occurs in hardware in out-of-order issue but in this case is compiled into the binary code using explicit concurrency controls.

The microthreaded model was first proposed in 1996 [10] and has been further refined and evaluated in subsequent papers [11-13]. Other similar models have been proposed, the earliest being nano-threads in [14], a limited form of microthreading using only two contexts to tolerate memory latency. There is now a relatively large body of similar work describing the usage of threads for pre-fetching and tolerating memory latency [15-19]. More recently, in [20], a thread model called mini-threads was evaluated to increase concurrency in SMT without increasing register-file size. SMT uses threads that require their own context and architectural register set, and the argument given is that by sharing the architectural register set of one thread between two or more mini-threads (two were investigated in [20]), concurrency is increased without requiring additional registers. It is not at all clear however, that increasing concurrency by the use of mini-threads does not put pressure on the register pool but then that is an application-related rather than an architectural constraint. Last but not least, threading has been used in a broader context with a single shared register set in dataflow architectures, see for example [21].

4 The Microthreaded Model

The microthreaded model of concurrency adds a few instructions to a base ISA in order to implement explicit concurrency controls. The concurrency defined by these instructions is in the form of fragments of code, which can be scheduled concurrently. This concurrency is applied within a single context and the code fragments comprise the code for that context. They share data via registers in a synchronised manner and via memory using bulk synchronisation. Compilation to microthreads does not require explicit concurrency in the source code and instruction-level concurrency is extracted by a compiler analysis of sequential code, especially that including loop structures. This is also a source of concurrency in the VLIW, superscalar and EDGE models of concurrency. The scheduling of code fragments can provide parallel slackness and hence latency tolerance in a single pipeline or can be used to schedule instructions simultaneously to multiple processors to achieve speedup. Because the controls added are explicit, it is necessary to recompile the source code in order to obtain any advantages such as speedup using this model but it is possible to execute legacy binary code based on the base ISA without recompilation. It is even possible to obtain speedup on legacy code using binary-to-binary translation in order to expose explicit concurrency.

The instructions required to implement the concurrency controls are *Cre* to create one or more microthreads, *Swch* and *Kill* to signal when to context switch (with the later signalling the last instruction in a fragment). There are also some synchronisation instructions, a barrier, *Bsync*, to support bulk synchronisation on memory and a break instruction, *Brk*, to terminate all thread-level concurrency.

All instruction-level models of concurrency use loops as a source of concurrency. VLIW and TRIPS compilers will unroll loops statically to extract higher levels of concurrency up to their execution width (and beyond this in EPIC). In a superscalar microprocessor, loops are unrolled dynamically in the instruction window by branch prediction, up to limits imposed by the size of the instruction window or of the renaming buffer. In both models there are limits to the concurrency that can be exposed. Conversely, in the microthreaded model, parametric concurrency based on loops can be expressed through the ISA, using a control block associated with the Cre instruction. This was first proposed in [11]. The concurrency is not therefore limited by hardware constraints. The concurrency can even have a dynamic range, i.e. where a loop bound is a variable, not known at compile time; this can be written to the control block by user code. Currently, the proposed implementations of this model restrict the concurrency described to that exposed by a single level of loop, including the specification of any constant-strided, loop-carried dependencies. A more general model could execute multiple, nested loops as a single family of micro-threads. This would be similar to the Bourroughs BSP [23], a vector computer designed by Steve Chen, which was optimised to exploit triply-nested DO loops from FORTRAN.

Micro-threading is not strictly a vector model, although it shares much in common with one. In addition to loop concurrency, instruction-level concurrency within a block can also be expressed directly as code fragments. However, because the dependency pattern will not be regular, such concurrency is mapped to a single processor and is used to tolerate latency rather than increase issue width.

4.1 An introduction to microthreaded code generation

To understand how both loop and in-line forms of concurrency are expressed in this model, consider the code generated from the simple loop given below:

```
For i=1,n Do
  C[i] := A[i]²+B[i]²;
```

First note that in this loop, it is possible to execute all values of i independently as it is what vector compilers would call vectorisable. Secondly note that both A[i] and B[i] can be squared quite independently. The loop can therefore be executed using a family of microthreads comprising 2n threads. For each i, one thread loads and computes $A[i]^2$, and another computes $B[i]^2$, waits for $A[i]^2$, completes the summation and stores the result. This is a partitioning of the dataflow graph for the loop body, which is shown in Figure 1. These two threads are then repeated for all values of i, giving the 2n threads shown in Figure 2.

Instructions in these threads execute in order and no branch prediction is required, indeed the loop branch is removed in this model as the loop is iterated in hardware. Threads are distributed to multiple pipelines and multiple threads on a single pipeline are interleaved according to explicit context switch instructions generated by the compiler. Where operands to instructions are deterministically defined, the compiler creates a static schedule of instructions and where they are not, for example following a cache access or a communication from another thread, then the compiler must signal a context switch immediately following a read of such variables. The model provides synchronisation on registers and uses a blocking read. The context switch allows different fragments to be interleaved following a potential blocking.

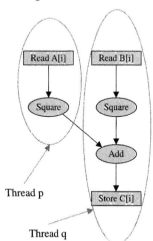

Figure 1. Dataflow diagram of the code analysed in section 4.1

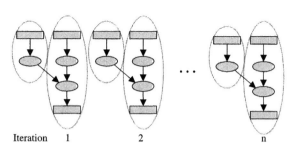

Figure 2. Concurrency exposed by iterating all loops in parallel

For thread p in Figure 1, the compiler would generate the assembler code given below, where the lower-case letters represent register variables

```
p:      Lw  a  A(i)
        Mul  t  a  a
        Kill
```

This code fragment loads the register 'a' with the value A[i] and squares it. The *Kill* instruction in this code causes the required context switch and is required for two reasons; first the *Mul* is the last executable instruction in the fragment and second it has a non-deterministic operand 'a', which may not be defined in this schedule due the possibility of a cache miss. In an implementation, the context switch fills the pipeline with instructions from other threads (if there are any) so that instruction processing may continue uninterrupted. Then, if the read to register 'a' fails on the *Mul* instruction, a reference to the issuing thread is saved in the empty register until the data is produced (in this case by the memory system). At that stage, the thread is rescheduled using the stored reference and the failing instruction is reissued and is now guaranteed to succeed. This form of local synchronisation is based on an i-structure and requires two state bits to implement. Restricting the register to store only a single continuation makes this a scalable method of synchronising between dependencies at the instruction level.

The code for thread q completes the loop body by squaring B[i], summing the two squares, 't' and 'u' and storing the result in C[i]:

```
q:      Lw  b  B(i)
        Mul  u  b  b
        Swch
        Add  c  t  u
        Swch
        Sw  c  C(i)
        Kill
```

In this fragment, there are two explicit context switches in addition to the *Kill* instruction. One is required to synchronise 'b' with the memory load and one is required to synchronise 'u' produced by thread p. Depending on the processor implementation, the static scheduling of instructions within a thread may vary. For example, a single-issue pipeline would probably require a one-cycle delay to bypass the result from the Lw for A[i], which could be achieved by placing the Lw instruction for B in thread p. In this example, no specific assumptions are made about the kind of processor but the compiler will need this information to generate good static schedules.

The 2n threads to execute this loop are generated by executing a single *Cre* instruction, which references a parameter block for this thread family. This is called the *thread control block* or *TCB*. Also a *Bsync* instruction may be required if there is any dependency between data written by this family of threads and any sub sequent threads created. The parameters for the thread control block in this example are given below. Only a subset is used here and this comprises the loop bounds and two pointers to the threads that execute the body of the loop.

```
        .data
loop    .word 2         #threads per iteration
        .word 1         #start
        .word n         #limit
        .word 1         #step
        .word p         #pointer 1
        .word q         #pointer 2

main:   Cre loop
        Bsync
```

This example is based on an affine loop with no loop-carried dependencies but it should be noted that neither of these are restrictions on the model. A further example is given in section 4.6.

4.2 Deadlock

This paper's contribution to the microthreaded model previously defined is the set of pointers used to define the loop body. Namely, the ability to define multiple code fragments that comprise the loop body and thus to represent the concurrency within the loop's body, for example threads p and q in the example above. Using previously published models [11-13], this in-line concurrency could have been expressed by having q create p but the static alternative proposed here provides better management of resource deadlock.

Our research into code generation and scheduling microthreads has revealed problems with the previous approach. The underlying issue is the synchronisation name space, which is potentially much larger than the register resources available on any implementation. The creation of a subordinate thread (e.g. q from p) is subject to the model's dynamic scheduling and hence can never be guaranteed to occur while resources are available. Resource deadlock will occur if synchronisation is required between a thread and its subordinate, where the subordinate cannot be created due to a lack of resources and the producer of the data cannot release its resources until the subordinate has read the data. Note that even though a thread may have been killed, its resources cannot be released until the dependent thread has read the data, which in a conservatively implementation, is deemed to be when it has also terminated.

The static alternative proposed here uses multiple threads to represent the loop body and allows the thread scheduler to distribute iterations to processors avoiding resource deadlock. All microthreads representing one basic block are allocated simultaneously to a single processor prior to any subsequent iterations being allocated. Further iterations are then allocated in iteration order, which is also the order of any loop-carried dependencies. The control block will contain the information needed to allocate resources and map dependencies. This information can be used to determine any potential for resource deadlock prior to allocation, which can then be managed by some system-level functionality (i.e. allocating more resources to the loop family). This solution maps all in-line concurrency to a single processor and is only a minor restriction but it does simplify dependency management and also minimises traffic between processors. In this model, only loop-carried dependencies will ever generate an inter-processor communication.

A global schedule, i.e. an allocation of iterations to a *profile* of processors, can be determined locally in each processor using the TCB and a few other parameters, namely the number of processors, the number of local registers and a processor ordering. The TCB address can be broadcast to all processors via a broadcast bus, thereafter scheduling is completely local. Resource deadlock can be analysed either statically if the number of processors, n, in known at compile or dynamically if n is unknown or indeed if n is a function of some operating system interaction in a reconfigurable system.

4.3 Register namespace

As already indicated, the microthreaded model uses registers for synchronisation. This is the only viable option to provide efficient control over the dynamic scheduling used and is consistent with most instruction-level models of concurrency. It raises two further issues that are not addressed in section 4.1. The first is how to create a namespace that includes all iterations of the loop and the second is how to create a binding between variables in two iterations, where necessary, in order to achieve synchronisation on loop-carried dependencies.

A solution to both issues has been described in [11], which proposed the dynamic allocation of registers to microthreads based loop iteration and also specified an offset in the index space, the *dependency distance*, which defines any loop-carried dependencies. Register addressing then uses a base-offset mechanism, where the base address is a component of a thread's state and the offset is from the register address in the binary code. A partitioning of this namespace was also proposed in that paper, indicating the type of communication required. This is one of the most significant features of this model, as it allows communication to be optimised using a static analysis of the code, while dynamic and target-specific information, such as loop bounds, dependency distance, number of processors and number of registers per processor can be used by the schedulers to optimise thread placement and avoid deadlock.

4.4 Partitioning the register namespace

In the microthreaded model, the register namespace is partitioned according to the type of communication being performed [11]. An implementation would then map each partition onto an appropriate register file and associated access mechanisms. In [13] it was shown that all classes of register window based on this partitioning can be mapped to distributed register files using the unmodified register specifier from the base ISA, giving complete scalability with respect to issue width in an implementation, as each local register file has a constant number of ports. The four classes of register window are defined according to variable type:

- loop invariants, give rise to broadcast communication, where these variables can be written to and read from in any microthread. They are called *Global* registers in this model and are represented by a specifier $Gi in the assembler;
- loop-carried dependencies, give rise to pair-wise communication between two iterations. The producer writes to the *Shared* registers, represented by a specifier $Si and the consumer reads from the *Dependent* registers, represented by a specifier $Di. Note that $Di in the consumer thread is mapped onto $Si in the producer thread either directly if both map to the same processor or via a cache window if mapped to different processors.

- all other variables are *Local* and are used to communicate data between variables within one iteration of a loop and with the memory system. These are represented by $Li. Note that the local thread scheduler writes the value of the loop index for each iteration into the first local register location ($L0) for that iteration.

The implementation proposed in [13] maps these four windows onto a conventional RISC ISA, where the $Gi are mapped to the lower 16 locations of a 5-bit register specifier and, for each iteration, the $Li, $Si and $Di variables are mapped to the upper 16 addresses. Only writes to $Gi and reads from $Di need to be trapped to alternate access mechanisms, all other accesses are to the processor's local register file via the normal pipeline ports. The upper 16 addresses in the main or static thread cannot be read by any dynamic thread and are therefore local it.

Distributing writes to $Gi from any processor is implemented using the same broadcast bus used to create a global schedule. It replicates a value written to $Gi by any processor to all other processors. A read to the $D window uses a ring network to copy a value from a remote processor's $S window if producer and consumer are mapped to different processors. Figure 5 illustrates a possible implementation of this distributed solution to the global register file problem.

The code generated from the affine loop, with no loop-carried dependencies, given in section 4.1 can now be completed using these register specifiers just defined. This is given in table 1. The thread control block must store parameters defining the resources required per iteration, in order to perform dynamic register allocation. It defines the number of local registers and the number of shared registers. The total number of registers allocated per iteration is the number of locals plus the number of shared registers or twice this figure, if the dependent thread is on another processor. This is bounded above by 16 in the implementation described in [13]. Other implementations are possible that do not provide backward compatibility to a base ISA.

It should also be noted that implementations of the *Swch* and *Kill* instructions do not require a pipeline slot. [13] described several possible implementations of encoding these instructions from explicit instructions that execute completely in the first stage of the pipeline to implicit solutions that require this information to be stored in the thread control block. The result is that that the number of instructions executed per iteration in this model is actually less than would be required using conventional code. This comes about because the global schedule is iterated in hardware, and index increment and branch instructions are not required.

4.5 Setting up and finishing off a loop

The code from section 4.1 is very simple, all iterations in the loop compiled are independent and there are no loop-carried dependencies. The communication model however, is designed to support loop-carried dependencies and such loops can still be executed concurrently on multiple processors. Instruction scheduling is determined by dataflow constraints between processors' local register files and of course concurrency is diminished.

Thread control block		Code fragments	

```
Thread control block                        Code fragments
        .data                               main:  Cre loop
loop:  .word 2 #threads per iteration               Bsync
       .word 0 #dependency distance
       .word 1 #loop start                  p:     Lw $L1 A($L0)
       .word n #loop limit                         Mul $L2 $L1 $L1
       .word 1 #loop step                          Kill
       .word 5 #number of local registers
       .word 0 #number of shared registers  q:     Lw $L3 B($L0)
       .word p #pointer to code fragment           Mul $L4 $L3 $L3
       .word q #pointer to code fragment           Swch
                                                    Add $L3 $L2 $L4
                                                    Swch
                                                    Sw $L3 C($L0)
                                                    Kill
```

Table 1. Complete code for the independent loop from section 4.1

Loops that carry dependencies usually require special action in the first one or more iterations, the last one or more iterations or both. This could be achieved using the conditional execution of code from a single instance of the code for the loop body, based on the index value stored in $L0. Better code density and execution efficiency can be obtained by augmenting the thread control block to define code to execute both a pre-amble and post-amble to the loop. Pointers are therefore added to the thread control block to define these additional threads with parameters defining the number of repetitions of each. Dependencies are then carried from the pre-amble, through the main body of the loop and finally through the post-amble, with no other dependencies between threads other than though local or global windows. For example, dependencies between multiple threads executing a loop body can be defined on local variables on one processor and initialisation and termination boundary conditions to the loop can use global variables. A full definition of the fields required in the loop control block is given in Table 2.

Name	Description
Threads per iteration	Number of threads per iteration
Dependency distance	No of iterations prior to this one for loop carried dependencies
Pre-amble iterations	Number of iterations using preamble code
Post-amble iterations	Number of iterations using post-amble code
Start	Start of loop index value
Limit	Limit of loop index value
Step	Step between loop indices
Locals	Number of local registers dynamically allocated to each iteration
Shared	Number of shared registers dynamically allocated to each iteration
Pre-amble pointers*	One pointer for each thread in pre-amble code
Main body pointers*	One pointer for each thread in main-body code
Post-amble pointers*	One pointer for each thread in post-amble code

Table 2. Fields required in the loop control block

4.6 Scheduling issues

Figure 3 shows another example loop, which contains a loop-carried dependency and that requires both pre-amble and post-amble code fragments. This code uses a while loop to search a list of objects of type *box*, until either end-of-list is detected or a box is located which is positioned over the input parameters, x and y. The code generated for this source is given in table 3. In this code, some multiple of the number of processors, n, is used to define the number of iterations in the family of threads. This is a mild form of speculation that trades off the overhead of thread creation with the execution of a few instructions that check a pointer for *nil* and then kill themselves if there are no more elements in the list. In this example, the *Cre* instruction creates ten threads per processor. The pre-amble initiates the dependency chain by passing the *start* parameter (from $G13) to the shared variable $S0. It also passes a token through the shared variable $S1, to maintain the sequential termination semantics of the code, which may or may not be necessary. The first instruction in the pre-amble sets *next* relative to the *nil* pointer to zero. This allows the inter-thread dependency to be expressed in one lw instruction, which loads the next address to $S0 using the current address from $D0. This device allows *nil* to be passed to the remaining threads created, following the discovery of the end of list by a thread.

```
struct box {int next;int x1;int x2;int y1;int y2;}
struct box start;
struct box locate( int x; int y; start)
{while (start.next != nil)
{if (x >= start.x1)
      if (y >= start.y1)
            if (x <= start.x2)
                  if (y<= start.y2)
                        return start;      /*match*/
start := start.next}
return -1;}                               /*fail*/
```

Figure 3. Example code requiring pre-amble and post-amble

The loop body and post-amble are very similar, the difference is that the latter is responsible for creating a new family of 10n threads. There are two dependencies chains in this code. The first using $S0/$D0 passes the address of the next box element in the first instruction. The second using $S1/$D1 passes a token between iterations as the last instruction on failing. No iteration can succeed until it has this token and it is only received if all prior iterations have failed. This is required to force the loop to terminate in list order.

An iteration first checks for end of list and only continues if it has a valid box element, otherwise the thread is killed. The geometric tests are then performed on the input coordinate (passed as parameters) for inclusion in the box. If any of the four tests fail, the thread terminates after passing the termination token to the next iteration. If all tests succeed, the iteration waits for the token before setting the return value, $G14, to the current list pointer and issuing a return, which will terminate all remaining threads. One difference between the main body and the post-amble is that in the post-amble, the next address is passed via a global, $G13, which gets picked up in the following family's pre-amble to continue the next dependency chain. Note that in order to reuse and synchronise on G13 again, it has to be set to empty, *reset $G13*. Note that *reset* is a pseudo instruction that loads a non-existent address.

Control block/Main/Pre-amble	Loop body	Post-amble
`.data`	`body: lw $S0 next($D0)`	`post: lw $G13 next($D0)`
`loop: .word 1 #threads`	`swch`	`swch`
`.word 1 #dep dist`	`bne $S0 $G0 ok`	`bne $G13 $G0 ok`
`.word 1 #pre rep`^{n}	`kill`	`kill`
`.word 1 #post rep`^{n}	`ok:  lw $L1 x1($S0)`	`ok:  lw $L1 x1($S0)`
`.word 2 #locals`	`blt $G11 $L1 fail`	`blt $G11 $L1 fail`
`.word 2 #shared`	`swch`	`swch`
`.word 1 #start`	`lw $L1 y1($S0)`	`lw $L1 y1($S0)`
`.word 10n #limit`	`blt $G12 $L1 fail`	`blt $G12 $L1 fail`
`.word 1 #step`	`swch`	`swch`
`.word pre`	`lw $L1 x2($S0)`	`lw $L1 x2($S0)`
`.word body`	`bge $G11 $L1 fail`	`bge $G11 $L1 fail`
`.word post`	`swch`	`swch`
	`lw $L1 y2($S0)`	`lw $L1 y2($S0)`
`Main: cre loop`	`bge $G12 $L1 fail`	`bge $G12 $L1 fail`
`Bsync`	`swch`	`swch`
	`mv $L1 $D1`	`mv $L1 $D1`
`Pre:  sw $G0 next($G0)`	`swch`	`swch`
`mv $S0 $G13`	`mv $G14 $S0`	`mv $G14 $S0`
`reset $G13`	`jr`	`jr`
`mv $S1 $G0`	`fail: mv $S1 $D1`	`fail: cre loop`
`kill`	`kill`	`kill`

Table 3. Code generated for the while loop.

This coding technique uses speculatively created threads to generate concurrency but each thread immediately suspends until the pointer to its data is made available. Only if the pointer is not *nil* will the thread perform any computation. Then if it succeeds it will wait for all prior threads to fail before it returns its results. Because of these two dependencies, the source code is not "vectorisable" but in this model, instruction-level concurrency is distributed to multiple processors and will provide some speedup.

All iterations except the pre-amble and any that locate a box, execute between 5 and 9 instructions between these two dependencies. On average therefore, 7 instructions can be executed concurrently to amortise the propagation latency across an iteration slice distributed to n-processors. If a modulo scheduling algorithm is adopted, where iteration i is allocated to processor $|i/M|_n$, sequences of M iterations are allocated to one processor. This minimises the propagation latency for all but the Mth iteration in each processor, which must communicate to the neighbouring processor. It is therefore unlikely that a large speedup will be possible. The only way to overcome sequential dependencies and still provide good speedup is to schedule further independent instructions, either by chaining loops sequentially without a barrier synchronisation or by interleaving multiple loops into one family. Of course, the dependency can be removed entirely by distributing an independent outer loop if one exists. Loop reordering is an optimisation frequently used by vectorising compilers.

4.7 Diversity and constraint

This model of concurrency shares the benefits of multithreading in providing latency tolerance but combines this with the efficiency in execution of a vector model. The result is a combination of static scheduling within a single thread and dynamic scheduling between threads. Two types of concurrency can be specified, basic-block concurrency, which carries

218

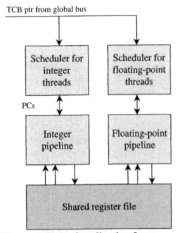

TCB ptr from global bus

Scheduler for integer threads

Scheduler for floating-point threads

PCs

Integer pipeline

Floating-point pipeline

Shared register file

Figure 4. Unit of replication for a chip multiprocessor comprising a heterogeneous cluster of processors.

dependencies via local registers and is used only for latency tolerance and parametric concurrency in the form of families of loops, which are distributed across multiple processors. One key issue in this model is that the concurrency is parametric and that the binary code is schedule independent, i.e. the same binary code can be scheduled on one or to many processors. It is even possible to statically analyse the potential concurrency and perhaps use this for the dynamic allocation of processors to families of threads to maximise speedup or to minimise power dissipation.

In this model, there are constraints on the manner in which dependencies can be mapped. A single dependency distance for loop-carried dependencies (and a single level of loop nesting) means that inter-loop dependencies must be regular and of the form A[i+k], where k is a loop invariant. There is no restriction on intra-loop dependencies, which are carried by local registers nor through dependencies carried by global registers, which can be used in the pre-amble and post-amble to loops.

There are other constraints in this model used to enforce the good behaviour of code when exposing parametric concurrency. In this model, registers act as synchronisers. In a dataflow model or even in other instruction-level models that use some kind of data-flow scheduling e.g. [8], there may be many target instructions requiring a data value produced by one instruction. In microthreading, the registers are scalable i-structures [10] and can only store a single reference to a suspended thread. Thus, whenever the compiler cannot determine the schedule of a value in a register, such when loading data from memory or through dependencies between threads, then that variable must not have concurrent readers (until it is known to be defined). In microthreading, this restriction can be enforced simply by statically scheduling instructions reading the variable to a single thread, where the first reader will suspend the thread until the data is produced. This requires a strict in-order execution of instructions from a thread.

Although this specific constraint on execution could be recognised in hardware to enable wide issue of instructions, such solutions would become unscalable and the alternative of wide issue using VLIW scheduling is far more appropriate for microthreaded pipelines. The main disadvantage of VLIW is that a scheduling failure in any component of an instruction will halt instruction processing until the data becomes available. Microthreading, on the other hand, can flag any instruction having a non-deterministic operand to context switch and thus avoid the problem completely. There is a practical limit to VLIW instruction width when using microthreaded extensions, due to the increased number of potential synchronisation failures. A one-cycle overhead is incurred for the reissue of any instruction, which fails to find all of its operands defined. In a single-issue pipeline, an operation with two non-deterministic operands might suspend and be reissued twice. In a w-way VLIW instruction, this could be to

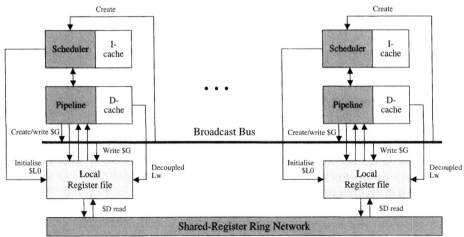

Figure 5. A microthreaded multi-processor, which communicates by local register files using a global write bus and a ring network.

up to 2w times, depending on constraints in the instruction set and the dynamic schedule taken.

In embedded systems, heterogeneous multiprocessors with different instruction sets are quite common. The microthreaded model can also support such architectures, see Figure 4, showing a processor cluster, which can be replicated if required. This example has independent fixed-point and floating-point processors and requires the compiled code to be separated into fragments for each type of processor, which can be scheduled concurrently onto the different processor types.

It can be seen that the microthreaded model is very flexible. It can support single-issue, VLIW or clusters of heterogeneous processors, which can all be replicated to exploit loop-level concurrency.

5. A DISTRIBUTED CHIP MULTIPROCESSOR

In this model of concurrency, scheduling is shared between the compiler and the schedulers, which allocate iterations to cores and control the instruction-level schedules that are defined by control and data dependencies. The compiler determines the static schedule of instructions within a thread. Although context switching is compiler determined, the local schedulers can choose which of any active threads to run at a context switch. This division of scheduling allows compact and power-efficient processors to be used, i.e. in-order pipelines with relatively few stages, which in turn minimises the effects of the memory wall. The schedulers also provide latency tolerance and given enough resources and concurrency can eliminate this problem entirely. Replicating processors then speeds up iterative code. Implementations of this model are scalable in issue width because instruction-issue logic, the distributed register files and the inter-processor connection network all have area, which grows linearly with the issue width.

220

To scale performance in a distributed multi-processor requires two important design parameters to be met. The first is to provide an even balancing of load, the second is to minimise the communication and/or synchronisation overhead, perhaps more importantly to tolerate any latency associated with that. In the microthreaded model, load balancing is achieved by the even distribution of many small fragments of code (the iterations). The fact that the granularity of those units is small helps enormously in load balancing, the fragments are not place holders for code but are uniform units that are created and destroyed frequently. The overhead for distribution and creation is low. Concerning communications, the register partitioning and scheduling constraints optimise communication and mean that only loop-carried dependencies (if they exist) and globals are communicated between processors. Communication should not stall the pipeline and it is imperative therefore to decouple the operation of the local pipeline or cluster from any remote register reads. Microthreading does decouple cores into asynchronous domains with latency tolerance to amortise any delay.

Prior published work on this model has used three states in implementing the synchronising registers. These represent an empty state, one containing a continuation and one containing valid data. This needs to be extended in a distributed and asynchronous chip multiprocessor to differentiate between two types of continuation. If the $S and $D windows are allocated to different processors, then both windows must be physically allocated and the implementation must maintaining coherency between the $S window and the $D window, which implements a cache of the producer thread's $S window. This is performed on demand. A thread reading its $D window must context switch and be suspended locally. A read-request is then generated to the adjacent processor, where the corresponding $S window is located. If the data has not yet been written to the required location, the remote read request will suspend there and await the required data. When the data is written it is returned to the requesting processor and is stored in the $D window, where it can be accessed directly until reset. This requires us to differentiate between a local read, which stores the thread reference in the register as a continuation and a network read, which must store the location to which data must be returned for caching. Once the remote data arrives, the continuation to the thread that caused the remote read reactivates that thread. This requires four synchronisation states on all registers during various phases of this synchronisation. These are given in table 4.

State	Description	Contains
Empty	All registers are allocated empty	Nothing
	A Lw sets a register empty	
Waiting-local	A thread reference is suspended	Reference to the suspended thread
Waiting-remote	A network request is suspended	Remote register address
Full	Contains data that can be read	User data

Table 4. Synchronisation states on each register

Figure 5 gives a block diagram of a distributed implementation of a chip multiprocessor based on the microthreaded model. Its reflects the two asynchronous types of communication defined in section 4. Local communication, within iterations, is performed via the local register files. Global communication is performed by writing to the local register file and having these writes broadcast to all processors on the *global bus*. Arbitration is required for the use of this bus and hence a remote writes may be delayed with respect to the local write but the synchronised read avoids any inconsistency in program state. Finally, the pair-wise communication between dependent iterations allocated to different processor is achieved by allocating both $S and $D windows to each iteration and maintaining consistency between these windows on demand, using a remote register read, which uses a ring network. There is one further global communication required. This implements the *Cre* and requires the pointer to the TCB to be broadcast to all processors. This can also use the broadcast bus but must be differentiated from a $G write. Both global write and *Cre* are low-frequency events [13].

The issue of memory hierarchy is deliberately avoided here, as it is not clear that a conventional L1/L2/L3/memory hierarchy is what is required for this model. It is anticipated that a more likely memory model might be L1 cache communicating with a large distributed memory using communication-channels.

We predict a mixture of instruction-level and task-level concurrency executed on chip within a 5-10 year timeframe, with upwards of 1000 processors, some local memory and both on- and off-chip communication channels, giving what is referred to in the title of this paper as micro-grids. Concurrency at the instruction level would be implicit in the source code and extracted and captured during compilation using the microthreaded model. Concurrency at the task level would be based on explicit concurrency in the software via threads or processes in an application. This would require a reconfigurable arrangement of processors with broadcast and ring networks being partitionable between different profiles of processors used for each thread of control. This requires some model of system environment management to take requests and allocate processors to each thread. As each thread of control (context) can have a varying concurrency requirement, the TCB might contain static or dynamic information on the concurrency required at each create, based on the maximum useful concurrency that can be exploited by the code on a loop-by-loop basis. Such a dynamically reconfigurable processor would be able to trade off issues such as performance, power dissipation etc. as unused processors, whether by partitioning or by virtue of active thread state may be powered down awaiting work or data respectivly.

Note that the model has all the attributes required for the efficient execution of code. The delay imposed by communication, whether between processors or between a processor and distributed memory can exploit latency tolerance at the instruction level to minimise impact on performance and scalability. Moreover, the level of latency tolerated is large, being bounded either by the parametric concurrency or by the size of a processor's register file. Higher-level context switching is complicated somewhat in this model by the synchronisation state of each register, the state of the local scheduler for that context and the requirement to manage communication on a per-context basis. However there are solutions to this if required or alternatively, as processors can be powered down asynchronously, single processors can be used as place holders for contexts with additional processors being added as required for performance. Thus processor allocation, rather than time-slicing would become the means of managing resources in such a system.

This mixture of task and instruction-level concurrency then, has the potential to efficiently exploit massive on-chip concurrency. Implementations based on simple, in-order processors will already provide an order of magnitude jump in on-chip concurrency using today's technology and has the potential to scale with chip packing density well into the next decade or in all likelihood to the end of silicon CMOS technology.

5 Conclusions

In this paper a model of instruction-level concurrency has been presented and analysed. It is shown that the model has parametric concurrency. It is also shown that a partitioning of the synchronisation namespace according to the kinds of communication found in concurrent computers, namely local, broadcast and pair-wise makes for an efficient and scalable implementation of the model as a chip multiprocessor. The unit of replication in such implementations can be a single-issue microprocessor, a VLIW processor or even a heterogeneous cluster of microprocessors.

The model is based on microthreading, which decomposes code into small code fragments that can be scheduled concurrently to provide parallel slackness for latency tolerance and for distribution to multiple processors. Various constraints on this model are analysed and include the mapping of concurrency from a single loop body to a single processor to simplify dependency management and to eliminate the need for a general switching network. Instead a ring network can implement the remaining loop-carried dependencies, which are constrained in the implementation discussed to be a constant distance across the iteration space. Given sufficient resources, modulo scheduling based on this distance can be applied, which makes all communication in the ring network local.

Other significant features of the model are that it describes parametric concurrency, is schedule invariant and can be applied to an existing ISA by simply adding a handful of instructions to create and control the concurrency. This means that existing binary code will run, albeit at single-processor performance. Recompilation of the source code or translation of the binary code will add the concurrency controls and enable speed-up and latency tolerance to be achieved.

6 References

1. D. Burger and J. R. Goodman (Eds.) (1997) *IEEE computer*, Theme Feature on "Billion Transistor Architectures", **30** (9).
2. ITRS (2003) International Technology Roadmap for Semiconductors, 2003 Edition http://public.itrs.net/Files/2003ITRS/Home2003.htm
3. M. Homewood, D. May, D. Shepherd and R. Shepherd (1987) The IMS T800 Transputer *IEEE Micro*, October 1987, pp10-26.
4. W. A. Wulf and S. A. McKee (1995) Hitting the Memory Wall: Implications of the Obvious, in *Computer Architecture News*, 23(1):20-24, March 1995.
5. K. I. Farkas et. al. (1997) The multicluster architecture: reducing cycle time through partitioning, *Proc 30th ann. IEEE/ACM Intl. Symp. on Microarchitecture* (MICRO-30), pp149-159, IEEE.
6. G. S. Sohi, S. E. Breach and T. N. Vijaykumar (1995) Multiscaler processors, *Proc 22nd Intl. Symp. Computer Architecture* (ISCA 95) pp414-425, IEEE.

7. Scott Rixner, et al. (2000) Register organization for media processing, In *Proceedings of the 6th International Symposium on High-Performance Computer Architecture* (January 2000), pp 375—386, IEEE.

8. D. Berger et. al. (2004) Scaling to the end of silicon with EDGE architectures, *IEEE Computer*, **37** (7), pp44-55, IEEE.

9. J. A. Fisher et. al. (1984) Parallel processing: a smart compiler and a dumb machine, *Proc 1984 SIGPLAN Symp. Compiler Construction,* pp37-47, ACM Press.

10. A Bolychevsky, C R Jesshope and V B Muchnick, (1996) Dynamic scheduling in RISC architectures, *IEE Trans. E, Computers and Digital Techniques* ,**143**, pp309-317.

11. C. R. Jesshope (2001) Implementing an efficient vector instruction set in a chip multi-processor using microthreaded pipelines, Proc. ACSAC 2001, *Australia Computer Science Communications*, **Vol 23**, No 4., pp80-88, IEEE Computer Society (Los Alimitos, USA), ISBN 0-7695-0954-1, Brisbane, Australia, 29-30 Jan 2001.

12. Luo B. and Jesshope C. (2002) Performance of a Microthreaded Pipeline, *in Proc. 7th Asia-Pacific conference on Computer systems architecture* , **Volume 6** , (Feipei Lai and John Morris Eds.), pp83-90, Australian Computer Society, Inc. (Darlinghurst, Australia), ISSN:1445-1336 , ISBN 0-909925-84-4, Melbourne, Australia, 28 Jan - 2 Feb, 2002..

13. C. R. Jesshope (2003) Samos

14. L. Gwennap, (1997) DanSoft develops VLIW design. *Microproc. Report 11*, 2 (Feb. 17), 18–22.

15. Yan Solihin, Jaejin Lee and Josep Torrellas, (2003) Correlation Prefetching with a User-Level Memory Thread, *IEEE Trans. on Parallel and Distributed Systems*, **vol. 14**, no. 6.

16. R. Balasubramonian, S. Dwarkadas, and D. H. Albonesi (2001) Dynamically allocating processor resources between nearby and distant ILP. In *Proc. Intl. Symp. on Computer Architecture*

17. R. Chappell, J. Stark, S. Kim, S. Reinhardt, and Y. Patt (1999) *Simultaneous subordinate microthreading* (SSMT). *Proc. Intl. Symposium on Computer Architecture.*

18. J. Redstone, S. J. Eggers and H. M.Levy, (2000) An analysis of operating system behavior on a simultaneous multithreaded architecture, *Intl. Conf. on Architectural Support for Programming Languages and Operating Systems.*

19. C. Zilles and G. Sohi (2001) Execution-based prediction using speculative slices, *Proc. Intl. Symposium on Computer Architecture.*

20. J. Redstone, S. Eggers and H. Levy (2003) Mini-threads: increasing TLP on small-scale SMT processors, *Proc 9th Intl. Symp. On High Performance Computer Architecture (HPCA-9)*, p19, IEEE.

21. R. S. Nikhil, G. M. Papadopoulos and Arvind (1992) *T: A multithreaded massively parallel architecture. *Proc. Intl. Symposium on Computer Architecture.*

22. G. M. Papadopoulos (1991) *Implementation of a general-purpose dataflow multiprocessor*, ISBN 0-273-08835-1, The MIT Press, Cambridge MA.

23. J. H. Austin Jr. (1979) The Burroughs Scientific Processor, *Infotech State of the Art report: Supercomputers*, **Vol 2** (Eds. Jesshope and Hockney) Maidenhead UK, pp1-31.

Autonomous Performance and Risk Management in Large Distributed Systems and Grids[*]

Marc Brittan[a] and Janusz Kowalik[b]

[a] Mathematics and Computing Technology, Boeing Phantom Works P.O. Box 3707, MS 7L-20, Seattle WA 98124, USA

[b] Former Boeing Company and University of Washington 16477-107th PL NE, Bothell, WA 98011, USA

1. Introduction

Problems in performance, risk, and resource management have been at the core of distributed processing since the advent of this technology. A key problem in building real time performance and risk management tools into distributed operating systems is that the classic problems in distributed system design, like problems in queuing theory, combinatorial optimization, cost, and failure analysis, must now be confronted by the operating system in near real time. One of the things that prolongs the design phase for large distributed systems is that these problems are combinatorial in nature (Job/server/processor assignment, routing, Number of CPU's per host, etc.), and are classically intractable (NP-Complete, #P-Complete). This complicates the problem of incorporating performance and risk management into an operating system, since the underlying problems in distributed design are themselves computationally expensive. Given the significant advances in processor speed and algorithms in recent years, we have reached a point where many hard problems in distributed system design and grid management can be solved in near real time for large systems. This ability to model real

[*] Sponsored by: Defense Advanced Research Projects Agency, Information Exploitation Office, UltraLog Program, Issued by DARPA/CMO Under Contract No. MDA972-02-C-0025, Distribution Statement A: Approved for Public Release, Distribution Unlimited.

world systems in near real time opens up new opportunities to address performance and risk management problems in a distributed and parallel environment.

To take advantage of real time performance and risk management capabilities, we also need a flexible architecture that allows the jobs and workloads to be moved around the system. This mobile architecture is needed to take advantage of underutilized resources, and to take advantage of lower risk services in a high risk environment. In this paper we will present some of the techniques being investigated for state management in the DARPA Ultralog project on survivable distributed systems, along with suggested enhancements for improved state management of future systems. The Ultralog program is currently focused on logistics applications, although the architecture is generally applicable to most applications in grid computing. Although the Ultralog system uses agents to achieve the required task/job mobility, any system of task sharing and task mobility will confront these fundamental problems in real time design and state management. Many of the core problems in the mathematics of distributed processing management are common to high performance computing, grid computing, and standard distributed system design.

The logistics application is worthy of note since the DARPA Ultralog program is using as a target application one of the world's largest and most complex distributed computing applications, military logistics. In this application domain, the program must continue to carry out its critical operations meeting performance and risk demands during both normal low risk operation, and during high risk operations where components are under electronic or physical attack. After an attack or loss of computing resource on a grid the system is designed to either reconfigure itself to protect itself from further attack, or to reconfigure itself to improve a mix of risk, cost, and performance metrics. While the "Survivability" aspect of the Ultralog system places an emphasis on risk management, the automated state manager must also address the classic problems of CPU and memory management, inter-process communications, and other details of state management.

The system is designed to update its operating state on a periodic basis during normal operations, and arrange itself to either defend against the next attack or component failure, or configure itself to improve performance and other metrics of grid quality. In today's world of distributed denial of service attacks and physical attacks on corporate assets, the distributed computing architecture used in Ultralog can also be useful in commercial distributed computing applications. The underlying problems in state management are common to all distributed computing applications with mobile tasks, which is the topic of this paper.

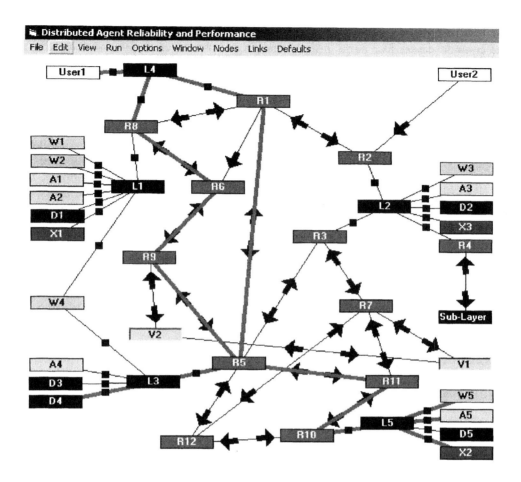

Figure 1: Physical view of servers and routers (rectangles) in an example system connected by directional data links (lines with arrows) The current optimal solution is highlighted with thick black lines. This multi-tiered system has web servers *Wn*, application servers *An*, data servers *Dn*, routers *Rn*, LAN hubs *Ln*, auxiliary servers *Xn*, and users *Usern*. A common problem in distributed system design and grid computing is to design a system with tasks assigned to a variety of server types to meet goals and constraints in response time, cost, reliability, and security.

In Figure 1 we have constructed an example network of web and data servers, routers, and links to illustrate a typical distributed system where users interact in multi-threaded transactions. The users should be understood in general terms, and may themselves be other programs or agents that spawn a sequence of distributed computations across the grid. The "users" are simply the points where response and performance are being tracked, and are the start of the transaction tree of jobs spawned across the grid.

It is common for large problems in distributed processing to take days to complete, and in some cases (like large military campaigns) weeks or months to complete, so robust distributed computation is vital. To avoid having a component failure force a restart of a lengthy calculation it is necessary to generate periodic checkpoint data for a process or task to ensure that restarts of failed processes are based on recent states of the system.

In DARPA Ultralog, the computing tasks are performed by a set of mobile programs or agents. The agent architecture that is being used is the Cougaar agent architecture [1], and was originally developed to deal with large scale logistics applications. The Ultralog extensions to the Cougaar architecture were developed by a team of about 75-100 people in about 20 different organizations, with the primary focus on improving *survivability* of the system [2]. The agents are allowed to move their processing to any eligible server on the network. It is the job of the state manager (topic of this paper) to describe how this workload is managed to improve performance and reduce risk.

We will define a *state* of a grid or general distributed system as a set of agent/server assignments, and the required routing to support the inter-agent messaging. It is the job of the state manager to choose an operating state for the system that optimizes various measures of risk and performance. State management can be accomplished by a global or centralized manager, or distributed with decisions on agent movement made at the local level. In the Ultralog program we used a combination of distributed and global state management. Decisions are made via heuristics at the local level for agent assignment when resources are plentiful and risk is low. When resources are scarce or risk is high, then the global solver is invoked for state management.

In deployment, the Ultralog system is a large *society* of agents, with the overall society broken down into smaller groups called *enclaves*. We are targeting a typical enclave for our state optimizer of about 150 agents on 75 servers. On this size of problem our solver for the state optimizer returns a good solution in 10 seconds or less on an 800 mhz Linux pc. This solver response time has been more than adequate, given the time it takes to move agents to new servers. This run time in the seconds range is possible for small networks up to the size of a class C (250+ hosts) with a few hundred agents. Because of this size limit for state management, our current approach is to break the larger Ultralog society into multiple smaller groups called enclaves, and manage performance and risk at the subsystem or enclave level.

2. Operational Modes and Defense Strategies

To configure grid operations we need to know both the environment in which the grid will operate, and the operational requirements of the users or jobs/tasks of the system. In many cases the differing operational requirements and goals will produce radically different system configurations or states. It is the job of the state manager or controller to interpret environmental data and requirements and then select a mode of operation for the system. For example, if a high risk situation is detected, then the state manager might choose to configure the system to minimize risk. If a low risk situation is detected, then the state manager might choose a configuration that improves response time for the selected set of tasks.

Information on resource availability along with threat and risk information from the agent community is used by a management agent to select a strategy or mode of operation for the system. These strategies are designed to minimize risk or improve performance of the system by placing the system into a particular state. Several strategies are discussed in this paper with differing objective functions for each strategy.

The Ultralog system is naturally divided into enclaves with each enclave managed in its own local environment. If the risk level for an enclave is perceived by the state manager to be high, then the management agent would have the state optimizer find a state that minimizes risk for that enclave. In a high risk situation the default procedure is to reduce risk using a two-pass procedure in the state optimizer. In the first pass the solver removes high risk nodes and links in the system (find the safest set of hosts/links) which minimizes the probability of state failure from all causes. Since a break in a component either forces agents to move, or routes to change, then we try to minimize overall state failure in the first pass of a risk based strategy. In the second pass of a high risk strategy we spread the agents around the remaining servers and level out the risk profiles for each server. In this second pass our goal is to minimize the maximum expected damage from a single point attack. This approach places more agents on low risk servers, and fewer agents on high risk servers. The two pass risk strategy minimizes the overall failure rate for the state and then levels out the risk profiles on the remaining servers.

If an enclave was at risk for corrupted communications, then the controller might choose another strategy for that part of the system, and operate that particular subsystem under a minimize remote messaging strategy (described below). In this case, the solver will find a state that reduces traffic between servers, and places agents with high rates of communication on the same servers. Still another strategy might be chosen by the controller if an enclave appeared to be low risk. In this case, the controller might choose a standard load balancing strategy to improve performance for the enclave.

In Figure 2 we have illustrated the decisions being made by the state manager. In this simplified example the state manager must choose a state for grid operations from four available management strategies labeled *Balance Resource Usage*, *Minimize Failure*, *Improve Security*, and *Reduce Remote Messaging*. Each of these strategies represents a different problem in state optimization, and will have a different objective function for the state optimizer. To make this strategy decision, the state manager must interpret the environmental situation based on threats to security, physical threats, planned workload, quality of service demands like response time, and of course the budget.

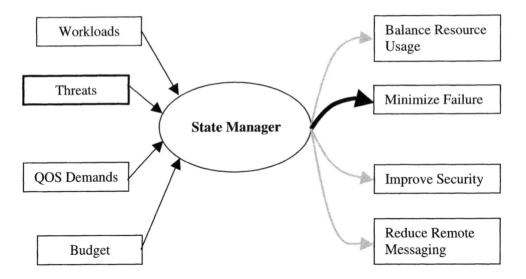

Figure 2: A State Manager evaluates the current situation based on Quality of Service demands (QOS), Threat conditions, Workloads, Budgets, and other environmental parameters and chooses a state or strategy for the system. In this example, the threat level is perceived to be high, so the State Manager has chosen the "Minimize Failure" strategy.

3. Agents and Distributed Computing

Agent based systems have become increasingly popular over the last few years and are now being deployed in a variety of applications in commercial and scientific works. While mobile tasks and load balancing have been around for many years, the development of agent technology has formalized this task and made the process of building an agent system accessible for both common and exotic processes. The networked agent system brings with it the potential for parallelism and autonomy, and of course the headaches of performance management in a network where everything moves during processing.

The use of mobile agents and grid computing in the design of a distributed calculation now serves as an effective complement to our adaptive routing methods that have been in use for years. While networks have long had the ability to adjust to damage to communications links and routers by "routing around the damage", most current systems do not have this ability to move jobs around the system in near real time. The

DARPA Ultralog architecture is designed as a marriage between a flexible software agent architecture and a flexible hardware architecture, with jobs and messages moving and adjusting in real time to performance needs and system risks. Of course this puts new demands on our state manager since it must obtain resource availability, usage, and risk information for a system, and then have the state optimizer solve a number of NP-Hard problems in state management using this data.

Although the distributed system design problem has many NP-Complete sub-problems, it is relatively easy in a resource-rich environment where there is large server power and bandwidth compared to job and messaging requirements. A simple greedy search usually works well for system design problems with abundant resources. The full NP-Completeness (and difficulty) of the problem is felt in resource-marginal situations, where there is little excess capacity in the system. This is where techniques in simulated annealing, genetic algorithms, and other specialized search techniques are frequently used to find good solutions in reasonable time. Since the UltraLog goal is to build a system capable of withstanding 45% destruction to its infrastructure, then the state solver must be prepared for "resource-marginal" situations.

Of course this new computing model comes at a cost. One of the costs for this implementation is that our agents must generate checkpoint information for their internal process state, and store this information on a remote host for a possible restart after an attack or system crash of the current host. The checkpoint information is currently stored on a single remote host in Ultralog, although there was some investigation of the problems in moving the system into a distributed checkpoint mode of operation. The actual process of generating and storing checkpoint data for states of the system is managed by the *persistence engine* and can be extremely involved for large complex systems like the current logistics application. The checkpoint storage problem and associated problem of moving a system from its current state to a new state is at least NP-Hard for systems with distributed persistence.[3]

In future work we hope to address this problem of distributed persistence and the complex problems in moving a system from its current state to a new state in a cost-effective manner. Note that a state transition is only profitable if the benefits of moving to the new state outweigh the costs of moving to the new state. During Ultralog development we investigated this state transition time. It is mainly comprised of two components, the time to move agents, and the time to *rehydrate* the agents on the new servers and place the system back into operation. One of the topics that we investigated was the mean system rehydration time, or the time on average that is spent in a current state moving and rehydrating agents on alternate servers given the probabilistic failure rates of the servers and links supporting the state. One possible goal for a system state would be to place the system into a state that minimizes the expected time moving and rehydrating agents. This is a much more involved state management scheme than a standard "maximize uptime" scheme since it requires information on the size of each agent's stored state from the persistence engine, and probabilistic estimates of where this state might be rehydrated in the event of a failure. Although this would be a reasonable design goal, there was not enough time to pursue the automated data mining needed to support this type of state management strategy. We believe that this mean system rehydration approach to state management will be an excellent topic for future work.

3.1. Implications for Security

This flexible architecture has positive implications for security, since we are now presenting our attackers with a moving target. In conventional systems, the attacker could study the patterns of access to the servers and use that information to infer the types of software running on the servers. Fixed architectures make excellent fixed targets for those intent on cracking into your system. The mobile agent architecture creates a moving target for attackers by continually changing task/server assignments, ports, protocols, and other parameters of the system in real time. This means our attackers must now try to crack into a system before the system changes its configuration and addressing scheme. While this creates a complex moving target for attackers which is useful in high security situations, this places an additional burden on the state management solver, since the solver must be capable of finding new high quality states in real time to allow for this job-hopping needed to create a moving target.

The security aspects of Ultralog are highly developed since secure operation in a faulty environment is the target operating environment. While this is not a paper about security, it is important to note that by design the system is secure. Note that while the movement of tasks may create a moving target for an attacker, it also has the potential for revealing partial information to an attacker. For example, the actual data movement in moving agents opens up new opportunities for attack, and may reveal the size of agent-states being moved which can be useful information for an attacker.

4. Specific Strategies for the State Optimizer

In this section we will present a few of the major strategies and operational considerations that are present in our state optimizer. The actual state search engine has several strategies beyond those listed here, and is capable of mixed strategies in addition to the pure strategies. As with all multi-objective optimization problems, the pure strategies are the easiest to understand and evaluate, while the mixed strategies have tradeoffs between conflicting objectives that complicate the state management evaluation.

Note that conflicting goals will force compromises in state management. For example, in moving a system to a state that minimizes risk, we may be forcing the system into a state that has longer run times for all of the users or tasks of interest. The actual selection of strategies for state management is itself a complex problem. If there are adversaries that can be modeled that are trying to attack the system then this is a good application for game theory. We will discuss an algorithm in a later section that analyzes the state performance space and then uses this information to have the state manager attack itself. In future work we hope to expand on this approach along with other game theory techniques to resource and risk management, since the selection of a strategy or goal of operation is as important as the implementation of that strategy.

4.1. Reducing Inter-Host Communications

One of the common design goals in building healthy distributed systems and grids is to minimize remote messaging between the servers involved in a distributed computation. This approach is frequently used in distributed database design, and uses a technique in mathematics known as graph partitioning, which is NP-Complete.[4] Graph partitioning can be an effective tool for improving response time and performance in situations where the inter-host messaging time is significant compared to processing time at the servers. In a data grid environment this strategy is frequently a reasonable approach to state management. Distributed database transactions are typically comprised of a collection of low CPU transactions combined with inter-host messaging, with the messaging component dominating the response time. As with any operational model, to use this strategy we will need to know how the various data components and agents are used in an application, and the messaging loads between the data components and agents. The data acquisition and monitoring can itself place a significant burden on the system, since a system with N agents has N*(N-1)/2 possible directed communications paths between agent pairs. For a sparse communications matrix this is not a burden on the system, but it can be a burden when we have a full matrix of communication between all agent pairs. However in most cases, a full communications matrix is also a signal of a poor architectural design to the underlying problems being solved by the system

The graph partitioning strategy may also be selected by the defense controller or management agent when it is perceived that there are significant errors in transmission (low effective bandwidth). In this case a reduction in faulty inter-host messaging is reflected in improved response time for the system since the agents involved in messaging do not have to resend messages to remote servers. Another application of graph partitioning is to enhance security by minimizing the remote messaging for an enclave. The objective function for the graph partitioning problem is given below, where the sum is taken over all agent pairs that are assigned to different servers:

Minimize Remote Messaging Strategy (graph partitioning):

$$\text{Minimimize} \quad \left\{ \sum_{i,j} \text{Msg}(i,j) \right\}$$

where Msg(i, j) = Messaging rate between agents i and j, where agents i and j are on different servers

234

While graph partitioning may be effective in data grids and transaction based systems, the graph partitioning technique is only a surrogate for the most common goal of interest, response time. Graph partitioning may be capable of reducing remote messaging, but reduced inter-host messaging does not necessarily mean reduced response time. Response time is measured by tracking the time-length of all parallel threads spawned by an initial event, such as a user query or job submission. Clearly there can be many situations where we minimize remote messaging on the system and increase response time. We will discuss response time in greater detail in a later section.

A two server graph partitioning problem is illustrated in Figure 3. In this example we have six agents labeled A through F that are to be assigned to the servers such that the server CPU and memory constraints are satisfied, and such that the inter-host messaging is minimized. Each of the links in the figure represents inter-agent communications, with a weighting factor that represents the degree of messaging (e.g., bytes per second). In this example the two servers on the left have an inter-host messaging rate of 180, which is high since the agents with high communications rates are on different servers. By switching agents B and E we arrive at the configuration on the right where we are able to reduce the inter-host messaging to 15. Dramatic reductions in remote messaging like this are frequently associated with significant improvements in response time.

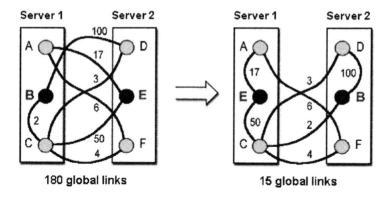

Figure 3: A graph partitioning problem for two servers with six agents (A - F). Inter-agent communication is illustrated with weighted links to reflect messaging rates. By switching agents B and E we reduce the remote messaging from 180 to 15.

4.2. Server Health and Constraints

In many cases we lack detailed knowledge of how the system will be used and are limited to estimates of current use or requirement of CPU and memory for an agent. We can use this limited information to find states of the system that are within the *healthy* operational limits of the system's components. The assignment problem of assigning agents to servers such that CPU and memory constraints are satisfied is a variant of the two dimensional bin packing problem and is NP-Complete [4]. A four server bin packing problem is illustrated in Figure 4, where the state manager is trying to fit eleven agents onto four servers with varying CPU and memory parameters. In resource-rich situations where we have abundant CPU and memory, the bin packing problem can be solved by a variety of fast heuristic techniques. The bin packing problem of assigning jobs to servers can be difficult in a resource-starved situation where the job requirements are close to system capacity. The problem is complicated by the fact that this bin packing must take place within context of other goals and constraints on the system.

Depending on the types of workloads on the system we may try to keep resource utilization levels below about 80%. This is typically the beginning of the "knee-of-the-curve" in M/M/c queuing theory - the point where long lines of jobs/tasks start piling up in queues waiting for service at an overloaded resource. When the CPU Utilization levels are high (e.g., above 80%), we see large increases in task response time due to queuing at the CPU processors in systems involving random workload arrivals. CPU is treated as a constraint in all Ultralog strategies, and is included as a direct component of the objective function for strategies based on CPU load balancing.

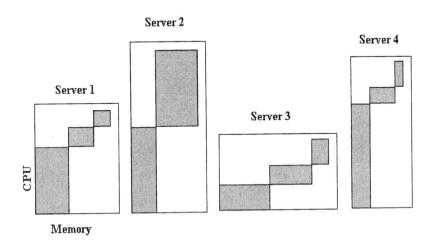

Figure 4: To ensure healthy operations we try to assign agents/jobs to servers so that each agent gets its requested CPU and Memory. In this example of a four server system we have 11 agents (smaller solid blocks) that must be divided among 4 servers. CPU is the vertical dimension and Memory is the horizontal dimension.

This 80% resource utilization is a common design point in distributed processing with random task arrivals in single processor systems. In Figure 5 we have illustrated a typical response time curve from M/M/1 queuing theory where the system is showing clear signs of saturation at the 80% utilization level. For multi-processor systems with a number "c" of processors it is common to run the system at much higher levels of utilization since the knee of the response time curve in M/M/c queuing theory occurs at higher utilization levels with multiple parallel processors.

While it makes sense to use queuing theory for systems where there is a random component to task arrival, in CPU intensive tasks a grid user may schedule a portion of the processing cycles up to 100%. Regardless of how a CPU utilization limit is derived, it is certainly less than or equal to 100%, so the task scheduler or state manager still has a packing problem that needs to be accomplished in the system along with other problems in state management.

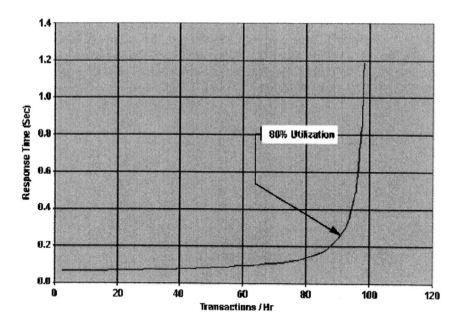

Figure 5: An M/M/1 queuing system illustrating saturation of a server. As the server utilization approaches 80% the response time begins to degrade rapidly.

To manage performance of a grid system we will also need to account for agent memory consumption in the agent/server assignment problem. In our current memory model we calculate the total memory consumption on a given host in the system by adding the memory requirements for each agent on that server. Our current Ultralog model does not treat shared memory, although that would be a useful extension that would not increase the computational complexity of the problem. We would like our servers to have enough memory to keep the servers in their healthy zones of operation. When an agent or program is starved for memory, it means that some pieces of data or code must be read from disk and saved to disk (page faults and virtual RAM). This disk retrieval is a much slower process than reading from RAM, hence the importance of memory management in choosing a state of the system.

4.3. Response Time and Performance Thread Tracking

In a response time model of a system we model the sequences of calls or subtasks generated by an initial function call or agent task. The response time is defined as the time-length of the longest running thread in the set of all threads generated by the initial call or task. For example, a user or agent might initiate a task that is handled by a variety of agents performing subtasks. Each of these subtask agents may themselves have subtasks, thus forming a series of threads/trees of agent tasks. We have not implemented thread tracking and optimization in UltraLog since the availability of the real-time job arrival and job size information needed for thread tracking and queuing theory was not yet available, although our state optimizer is capable of thread modeling.

The state optimizer for DARPA UltraLog was built from the core of a complex Boeing program for designing large distributed systems. Boeing has several large distributed systems with tens of thousands of users actively involved in complex multi-server distributed processing tasks. To ensure performance and quality for the computing customers, Boeing has maintained an active distributed system design and research effort for many years, with a special focus on the performance and scalability aspects of large systems, [5,6] and on the intractable problems in distributed design that are discussed in this paper and previous works. [7] Since NP-hard problems are only truly "hard" for large systems, then it was natural for Boeing to get involved in the research of large systems, where they developed tooling for automated design of distributed systems. The distributed system design program had a special emphasis on the intractable parts of the system design problem which are especially difficult for large systems. The Boeing solver was automated to run in the UltraLog distributed agent environment, and programmed to run in real time to manage performance and risk of the agent system.

In the Boeing software for distributed design the optimizer tracks threads (with queuing theory estimates) generated from initial user queries to estimate response time. The design tool performs this thread tracking in a TCP/IP environment with packetization of messaging. In this thread tracking model the solver searches out the design space to minimize the length of the longest thread generated by an initial user query or agent task.[7] The objective function for the thread response time strategy is defined below, where we minimize the time-length of the longest running thread. Although thread modeling was not implemented in Ultralog due to time constraints, a small prototype system was built during the project using a queuing network model of a system. In our Boeing tool the threads used by the model are generated from user-defined inputs that describe the performance threads and software calling architecture of the system. Multiple levels of synchronous and asynchronous calls are allowed by the tool and can be tracked by the solver for response time estimates.

Minimize Thread Response Time Strategy:

Minimize   { Max [T(i)] }

$T[i]$ = Time-length of i'th thread in test set of threads

One of the most common techniques for estimating response time of a system is to build a simulation model. To simulate a computer system we have computer models of artificial users generating jobs according to some random distribution. These jobs in the simulation model will place loads on the servers and links, and begin building queues as necessary due to random arrivals of workloads. Each of these virtual jobs may spawn new jobs and generate a threaded set of calls that are tracked in the simulation. A simulation model frequently samples millions of artificial jobs submitted by thousands of artificial users in the simulation, and measures the average user response times along with other systems performance parameters like CPU utilization and memory. While a detailed simulation model may be the preferred modeling technique for complex random processes it is also a computationally lengthy task. A simulation model of one specific state of a distributed system (agent/server and routing)   may take hours to complete on a fast workstation. This might be useful for a careful detailed study of a system, but in our distributed design problem we may have an exponentially large number of possible design options that need to be explored. A typical agent system may involve a thousand agents in a complex network with hundreds of hosts. The large number of discrete design options is a problem with classic simulation since we may end up trying to simulate an exponentially large number of design options - this is not a good choice for real-time automated performance and risk management of a grid!

We can quickly prune this design space using a variety of heuristics, but the overall number of possible design options is still extremely large. While a solver based on the global simulation of a system might appear ideal, it is not feasible with current processor technology. Since there were a number of discrete NP-Hard problems at the core of distributed design we have developed a variety of fast approximations for the core solver. To get a fast first estimate of a system state, including queuing effects associated with random job arrivals and random job sizes, we have been using fast analytic estimates from queuing theory to build queuing networks that model random user or agent tasks. This combination of fast analytic queuing plus global optimization based on simulated annealing with fast heuristics has allowed us to build a near real-time tool for distributed agent management. During the project we experimented with both open and closed queuing network models. Closed queuing network models require iteration, and we found that our experimental prototype models converged to three significant figures within three iterations. Due to the lack of data availability and monitoring needed to estimate agent task arrivals and task sizes, the queuing network approach was not pursued in Ultralog. The major focus of our state management efforts was on supplying a variety of risk and health management strategies for the system. This mixture of combinatorial optimization with fast queuing networks does appear to be a fruitful area for further research.

A standard performance model such as those built in simulation models of distributed computation is built from a set of threads of interest in the larger system. The choice of performance threads is quite complex in the general case, although special cases like classic three or four tier architectures can be modeled with a few basic threads to represent types of user transactions. For the objective function in a response time model we first calculate the time length of each thread in the set of thread samples and then sum the overall weighted thread times. During the search for an optimal state a penalty function is used to penalize solutions where a sample thread has response time that exceeds the maximum allowable response time.

In response time management of medium to large systems we are confronted with a number of NP-Hard problems in state management that have plagued the distributed computing industry for years. These same problems in state management are now at the core of grid computing and grid management. To deal with this need for improved thread modeling for real time tools, we have developed a variety of heuristics for thread selection and heuristics for state transitions that involve threads. The selection of threads typically involves identifying a set of "user centers" or places where agents may initiate tasks. If we are not tracing the entire transaction (i.e., not tracing all threads generated from the initial task), then we need to select a set of sub-threads which we believe dominate the response time for major tasks of interest.

The selection of sub-threads for a performance model may involve looking at the traffic matrix for inter-agent messaging and identifying compute intensive or message intensive threads buried in the overall set of threads. Once we have selected a set of threads for our performance model, the next step is to build these threads into our objective function, and choose a set of state transitions to be used by the optimizer in its search. The key, as with most optimization problems, is to structure the solver so that it captures the essence of the problem. In a later section we will describe a basic set of moves in the solution space that help the solver find good solutions to thread-based optimization problems in reasonable time. In the case of thread tracking there is considerable structure in the problem that can be captured in the solver. Since the simulated annealing algorithm used by our solver is based on the theory of inhomogeneous Markov chains, then we need to be careful when we design our solver to design a reasonable state transition matrix for state moves along the chain. In the case where we are allowed to move agents and messaging around a network in a thread-based model, there is enough structure in the physical problem to explore several opportunities in the design of the state transition matrix used by our solver. In many cases, like the thread modeling case discussed in section 6 of this paper, "Neighborhood Structure in Simulated Annealing", the state transitions used to expedite the search are fairly natural, and a good fit between the search algorithm and the underlying physical problem.

4.4. Modeling Risk

The UltraLog system is designed to self-adjust when it detects a threat and move jobs and communications to protect the system. One of the primary tasks of our automated performance/risk manager is to propose designs that minimize failure, since failure of a component forces agents to move which delays processing. In a high risk situation we may want to eliminate a risky server from active service, or deploy fewer agents on that server.

To minimize state failure and other risk measures in UltraLog we implement a mixed strategy that initially eliminates high risk nodes and links from use, and then minimizes the agents at risk from a single point attack on the remaining nodes. We currently assume that failures in the system are statistically independent. The objective function for the first phase of this two pass mixed strategy is the probability that one or more component failures occurs anywhere in the set of components supporting the state. This objective is calculated by first calculating the probability that there are no failures, which is just the standard product, over all physical components in the state, of the probability of that component being operational. This is the standard "uptime" calculation for the state of a system, so reducing failures will tend to eliminate servers and links from the design (unless constrained) since they represent risk. In this first phase, called the "Minimize State Risk" strategy, we are reducing the risk of the state to some acceptable minimum, and minimizing our exposure to risky components that can break the current state of the system:

Minimize State Risk Strategy:

$$Minimize \quad \left\{ 1 - \prod_{object \, \in \, State} (1 - Pfail(object)) \right\}$$

Pfail(object) = Probability of failure for node or link object

The objective function for the second phase of our mixed risk strategy, called the "Minimize Expected Single-Point Risk" strategy, is given below. In the actual implementation we perform a leveling of risk among the servers after minimizing the maximum expected single-point risk which produces a smoother risk profile for the overall state:

Minimize Expected Single-Point Risk Strategy:

Minimize { Max$_{(inod \in system)}$ [Pfail(inod) * NumAgents(inod)] }

Pfail(inod) = Probability of failure for node number inod

NumAgents(inod) = Number of Agents on node number inod

Note that we have described a number of strategies for the state management problem having different objective functions. Since the state management problem is intrinsically a problem in multi-objective optimization this means there are tradeoffs. The state optimizer currently offers a variety of pure strategies like "Minimize State Risk", "Minimize Remote Messaging", and "Minimize Expected Single-Point Risk", and some mixed strategies like our previously described two pass strategy for Minimize State Risk followed by Minimize Expected Single-Point Risk. Each of these strategies represents a different problem to our state optimizer. In the next section we will discuss how the optimization engine actually searches out the state space of distributed computation.

5. Building the Solver, and Solver Self-Attack

One of the key design goals in DARPA Ultralog is to design a system that can withstand damage or loss to 45% of the system infrastructure and suffer no more than 30% performance degradation after this damage or loss. In the Ultralog project statement the performance aspect of the system is generally measured in units of time to complete a set of test jobs. The capacity of the system is a measure of the number of concurrent users or tasks assigned to a system in a test period. To build this self-healing design goal into a real time system we must address a number of distributed system design problems in near real time. As discussed in the sections above on strategies and goals for the state optimizer, the state model for a distributed system or grid must deal with a number of NP-Hard problems in optimization and constraint satisfaction mixed with classic hard problems in queuing and cost modeling. The state search engine is also required to deal with issues in failure and reliability analysis, with the reliability problem known to be #P-Complete. Since we cannot possibly generate a full reliability study with all possible solutions in *real time*, we have designed a fast approach which studies the solution space and performs a series of smart attacks on the system to find key weaknesses in near real time, adding a "tabu" flavour to the annealing search.

Since the stated goal of the Ultralog project was to build a system that could lose 45% of its infrastructure and suffer no more than 30% performance degradation, then a natural question is "which 45% of the system components should we destroy before testing performance?". Clearly we cannot search over all possible failure combinations (up to 45% of system), since that is exponentially large.

To get a fast estimate of system hardness and build diversity into the solver we have developed an attack plan that uses sampling from our solver to estimate attack points in a distributed system. The attack is based on a sequence of attacks that terminates after the system fails to find a viable state (i.e., performance has degraded by more than 30%). At each step in the attack sequence a single physical component involved in supporting the current state is mathematically broken in the computer model of the system. Some of the physical components that support the current state will occur in many other high quality states of the system (e.g., well connected routers), while other components (e.g., small servers) may be involved in only a few possible states of the system. At each point of the attack we attempt to choose the single component in the state that has the highest quality-weighted frequency of occurrence in the set of all failover plans for the system. By breaking this component we break the current optimal state at the physical point in the state that also breaks the greatest number of quality weighted failover plans. This attack plan both attacks the optimal solution and performs a semi-greedy attack on the failover system. Once we have mathematically broken a component we find the next new optimal state of the system, and then plan another attack. This process of planning an optimal state, attacking the state, planning a new optimal state, and attacking the state is repeated until the solver fails to find a viable solution state for the distributed agent problem. This attack sequence is an effective test of system hardness. In example tests this attack on the grid performance solution space has been extremely effective at locating vulnerable points in a system.

The attack part of the algorithm uses the solver to run a sensitivity analysis on the solution space, looking for physical components that occur in a large number of possible states of the system. Since the solver samples from tens of thousands to millions of possible solutions to the distributed system design problem, then we can use information from the sample set to estimate points of attack on the system. While the solver is busy looking for an optimal state solution, it is also tracking the frequency of component use for each sampled state of the system. It uses this to build a real time "reliability and performance map" of the design space during the solution process. The actual map is a set of numbers, $P(\Im, objectid)$, representing the weighted frequency of occurrence of the individual servers, links, and routers in the set of feasible solutions sampled by the solver in the distributed agent assignment problem.

$\Im$ = Set of non-unique solutions found by the solver that meet hard constraints

$\Im_{\#}$ = Set of all possible unique solutions meeting constraints

$P(\Im, objectid)$ = Probability that random selection from $\Im$ contains $objectid$

where $objectid$ is a Link, Router, Server, or other component of physical topology

In the simulated annealing algorithm the solution will converge at very low temperatures to the estimate of the globally optimal state of the system. At high temperatures the annealing solver will move randomly about the distributed system performance space sampling a broad range of low quality to high quality solutions.

At medium and lower temperatures the higher quality states will be preferentially sampled. We use this preferential sampling in the annealing algorithm to build our estimate of quality weighted frequency of use for physical objects in the solution space.

We are using the well known Metropolis algorithm [8,9] for this annealing algorithm in which we accept downhill moves with probability one, and uphill moves with a probability that is exponentially damped with respect to the change (degradation) in the objective function.

The terms in the exponent for the state change probabilities are the change DE in the objective function in moving from the current state to the proposed state, and the temperature T, which is a measure of randomness in the annealing algorithm.

Metropolis Algorithm: *downhill moves always accepted*
                                uphill moves exponentially damped

P(State Change) $\propto$ exp(-DE/T)   (uphill move probability for case DE > 0)

The set $\Im\#$ is the set of all unique solutions to the state configuration problem. We use the # sign in the notation as a reminder of the underlying enumeration problem and the related #P-Complete network reliability problem.

The set $\Im$ is the set of all solutions found by the solver during an annealing phase without regard to uniqueness of solution, but knowing that higher quality solutions in multiple states will be preferentially sampled by the solver.

We do not have the computing power to calculate $P(\Im\#, objectid)$ in real time since the underlying state enumeration problem is #P-Complete, so we build $P(\Im, objectid)$ as a fast real time estimate of the frequency of occurrance of a physical component in the set of all solutions sampled by the solver.

For each object in the system we are going to sum the number of times that object appears in the set of solutions sampled by the solver. We do this by dividing the cooling region in the annealing algorithm into several steps (10 steps in our solver) between a "hot" temperature *Thot* and the "cold" temperature *Tcold* where the system has converged to its estimate of the global solution.

At each step of this cool down process, we calculate a quantity conceptually related to $P(\Im, objectid)$, which we will label $P_{anneal}(\Im, objectid, T)$, which is the frequency of occurrence of an object in the set of solutions sampled by the annealing solver at the temperature T. While we cool the system during the annealing process, for each physical component we build these counts of the number of times that component has been used in a successfully sampled state.

During the cooling phase of the annealing algorithm we calculate the overall map of system usage as a weighted average over the temperature regions sampled by our solver:

$$P_{anneal}(\Im, objectid) = C \sum_{T=Tlow}^{Thot} W(T) * P_{anneal}(\Im, objectid, T)$$

C = Normalization constant,   W(T) = Weighting function

We use this smoothing technique to estimate the component's weighted frequency of use in the sample set. The weighting is by solution quality, since higher quality solutions are sampled more often in the annealing algorithm.

We have tried a few different weighting functions W(T) and methods of averaging the samples $P_{anneal}(\Im, objectid, T)$ such as moving averages throughout the cooling schedule, although for simplicity W(T) = 1 is frequently used. A map of the performance and risk solution space can be generated in near real time with this procedure, and can be viewed in a graphics format in real time as the solver searches out the solution space.

The links in Figure 6 are weighted according to the values of $P_{anneal}(\Im, objectid)$. This is the initial view of the system before an attack with all links and servers operational. As the annealing progresses from high to low temperatures the solver preferentially samples states of the system with higher quality, with an exponential sampling preference dictated by the Metropolis algorithm. This gives a real time view of the weighted solution space that can be used to test the system for robustness in the attack phase of the algorithm.

flexibility and robustness the simulated annealing algorithm has been applied to a wide variety of industrial applications. The technique draws heavily from statistical physics and the theory of inhomogeneous Markov chains, and has a rich and active literature with a number of techniques for improving the speed of the annealing algorithm and automating the cooling schedule used during the search.

The annealing techniques require care in designing moves about the search space and in defining the cooling schedule, [9,11] but once implemented the annealing algorithms usually work well and are easy to modify. Annealing techniques are known for being slow at times (like all algorithms applied to NP-Complete problems), but can be accelerated with heuristics to become competitive with other techniques. Annealing algorithms are quite famous, however, for being robust, and we believe the technique is particularly well suited for this application (combinatorial optimization in a faulty queuing network), where the objective function is so complex that many classic optimization techniques fail to perform, or are not applicable.

Attempts to design reliable and robust networks have a long history. In 1964 Paul Baran from RAND considered several network architectures capable of withstanding atomic attacks. More recently Albert-Laszlo Barabasi and his collaborators [12] introduced the scale-free topology which preserves network connectivity after severe random damages. Havlin and his colleagues [13,14] proved that the scale-free topology networks are robust under certain circumstances. Dorogovtsev and Mendes provide a good overview on some of the modern theories and properties of large scale networks found in many areas of nature and human activities. [15]

Since scale free networks have a number of well connected nodes they tend to be robust against random damage to the network, and can withstand substantial damage. For random damage this network topology may be robust, but a scale free topology is susceptible to attacks on those well connected points that give it its scale free characteristic.

While robustness against random failure is important, the focus of this paper has been on the automated risk and performance management of a system, and the damage that can be done to a system from a smart attack on the solution space. In future work we plan to consider the challenging task of combining topological robustness with the optimization approaches described in this paper.

6. Neighbourhood Structure in Simulated Annealing

A key problem in designing effective annealing algorithms is defining the neighbourhood structure of the search space. Our Markov chain in the annealing algorithm is based on moves from any given state to a neighbouring state. Defining this neighbourhood structure is a complex and application dependent problem. The application dependence of the annealing algorithm means that each new problem type (Traveling Salesman Problem, Graph Partitioning, Distributed System Design) presents new problems in moving about the solution space.

For example, the classic k-opt moves of the Traveling Salesman problem are good examples of defining topologically close states that capture the essence of the problem, with a neighbourhood structure that allows efficient moves through the solution space [16]. For our distributed design problem we are also going to define some basic moves through the solution space that capture the structure of the space and help the solver find quality solutions in a reasonable amount of time.

One of the most basic state moves in the solver is to choose a single random host, and select a subset of jobs on the server to move to other random servers in the system. In this host selection step we occasionally make heuristic state change proposals to the annealing solver. For example, in the mixed minimize risk strategy described earlier, a common step is to identify servers at high risk, and move agents from the high risk servers to the low risk servers.

Another basic state transition in the spirit of the k-opt moves for the traveling salesman problem is to pick a set of k servers and either exchange agents among the servers, or more generally moves agents onto or off the selected servers. This k-server state transition may also have heuristic variants depending on the strategy.

By our definition of single state failure, the system will have failed regardless of whether a failed host had a single function running on it, or had all functions in the system running on it. Although we want our system to be capable of probabilistically exploring all possible task/host assignments, it is especially important for our failure analysis that the system be capable of reaching the empty server state (no running jobs) in a reasonable number of steps in the Markov chain.

As a practical matter it is useful to design one of these basic state moves as a state change that moves *all* agents on a given random server to other eligible servers in the system in a single step of the Markov chain. This is a practical requirement for the failure component of the objective function, since we do not want our state moves that add agents to a server to overwhelm the state moves that are trying to empty a server.

The next set of moves in our state space is defined by selecting a random subset of functions/agents on a random set of hosts involved in a randomly selected thread in the performance model.

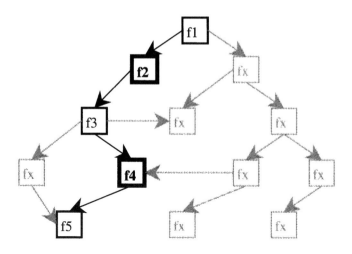

Figure 8: By selecting agents from a thread in a performance model, a set of state space moves are generated that capture the essence of the solution space. The selected thread is illustrated in black. A subset of functions (agents) on the selected thread are selected for movement to other servers. In this example the agents/functions f2 and f4 (illustrated with bold black outlines) have been selected for movement in a state transition proposal passed to the Metropolis algorithm.

In Figure 8 we have highlighted the selection of a single random thread of function calls embedded in a complex calling sequence initiated by an initial function or agent f1. The steps in our process for defining these threaded state moves are defined below:

1.) Select a single random thread $\mathcal{T}$ in the system. The thread $\mathcal{T}$ is a sequence of ordered pairs listing the functions and hosts in the thread, with [f(1), H(1)] being the first function or agent call in the threaded set of calls, and hosted on host H(1).

$$\mathcal{T} = \{ \ [f(1),H(1)] \ , \ [f(2),H(2)] \ , \ ... \ [f(n),H(n)] \ \}$$

> where:
> f(i) = i'th function call or agent in thread
> H(i) = host associated with i'th function call in thread

2.) Select a random subset $\mathcal{T}sub$ of function/host pairs in $\mathcal{T}$.

3.) For each member of $\mathcal{T}sub$ randomly change the function/server assignment for each function in the sub-thread. For example if [f(i), H(i)] is in $\mathcal{T}sub$, then randomly change H(i) to one of the other eligible servers capable of hosting function f(i). As an option, randomly move one or more of the functions on H(i) (other than f(i)) to other servers, leaving f(i) fixed, which also changes the thread environment, a key requirement of good state moves.

When thread-based response time is formally part of the distributed system design goal, then this thread-based state change is an effective means of moving about the performance solution space and captures the nature of the problem in the set of state moves. For optimizing response time, these basic threaded state moves are an especially good set of state moves since the overall response time of a job is equal to the length of the longest running thread in the set of threads generated by the initial task. By focusing on correlated state moves associated with calls within a thread, we are more likely to remove any large scale design errors in thread assignment in a reasonable number of steps by the solver.

In our basic thread move we take a specific thread of calls, and move a selected set of agents in the thread to other servers. This state move does a good job of covering the threadlike structure of our performance model. We have experimented with the use of smart state moves, like greedy heuristics for agent/server assignment in the annealing steps, and the preferential sampling of agents in a thread, and have found considerable speedup using careful selection and design of the state change operators. This is to be expected since the state changes define the local neighbourhood structure of the solution space (topological closeness of one state to another state). By choosing our state moves to sample more heavily in the basic logical components of the problem (threads, risky servers, overloaded servers, etc.), we are able to get good solutions from an annealing algorithm in a reasonable amount of time.

It is possible to implement other basic state moves to improve solver speed for the state optimizer, such as selecting a set of trees in the calling hierarchy and moving selected agents on these calling trees to other servers. This tree-like basic step would help in situations with complex multi-threaded logic where the overall process tree has considerable parallel branching in the calling and processing architecture. A tree-like state transition allows annealing state moves that more closely match the treelike calling architecture of many thread tracking problems. While we have implemented the thread-like state changes described above, we have only begun experimenting with tree-like state changes and hope to explore this area in future work. It is also possible to generalize the threaded state move by selecting a set of threads { $\mathcal{T}i$ }, and performing multiple exchanges between threads as a basic state move. Since the solution space for a distributed system is extremely complex, anything we can do to improve the way we move about the space will improve the speed of the state optimizer. In this regard, annealing is similar to most algorithms, where a carefully designed and tuned algorithm that captures the nature of the problem can usually outperform other more general purpose techniques.

7. Conclusions

The DARPA UltraLog project has built and deployed a large scale experimental distributed mobile agent system designed to improve distributed system performance and survivability. The system is designed to self-adjust to meet performance and risk goals and constraints in a changing environment. It is built on the Cougaar architecture of mobile agents that perform their tasks from multiple points on the network. The issue of performance and risk in an agent based system arises as it does with any distributed system or grid, and is complicated by the autonomous and mobile nature of agents in a society. The natural parallelism present in many large scale problems makes them good candidates for an agent based solution with autonomous self-healing capabilities. The large logistics applications that are used as a test bed for DARPA Ultralog serve as testimony to the ability of large agent based systems to solve some of the world's most complex tasks in grid computing. Furthermore, the agent systems do this in a distributed and autonomous fashion, obtaining a solution speedup through parallel tasking in the agent environment, and improving survivability and security through the mobile agent architecture.

The design of a modern grid system or general distributed system must make effective use of resources to build a system that meets capacity, response time, risk, and cost goals. The same intractable problems that we encounter in distributed system design are now being confronted by real-time solvers in the pursuit of real-time management of system performance and risk. This real-time design problem (or redesign after attack or failure) is complicated by the frequently conflicting goals in performance versus survivability and risk. In a survivable system we try to spread the agents among several remote servers so we do not have major parts of the system vulnerable to attack on any given host. From a performance perspective, we try to assign the agents to a few servers that are close together, or even assign the agents to one server to minimize delays from remote messaging.

The UltraLog system is designed to be a highly flexible and robust computing architecture that can meet requirements in performance and reliability and withstand attacks. In this system the attackers will need to have considerable knowledge about the performance space if they are to have any hope of impacting the system. In the UltraLog system we have matched a flexible software architecture with a flexible hardware architecture to create a system that is survivable, testable, and meets performance demands in a distributed environment. In this paper we have described the techniques we have used to build tooling for real time management of performance and risk of large distributed agent systems. We have also outlined some of the steps in the solution process, and some of the basic state changes, or basic moves in the solution space that are used to improve solver speed for the state optimization problem.

At the core of high performance computing, grid computing, general distributed computing, and the Ultralog distributed agent system is the important problem of automated management of the system. This means managing for performance, risk, response time, capacity, CPU, Memory, messaging, bandwidth, connectivity/routing, cost, and other state parameters. In the past, this was a formidable task for the designer of a distributed system or parallel algorithm. As processing speeds increase we will find that centralized solver techniques will be capable of managing very large systems in a hierarchical fashion as is done with Ultralog. The Ultralog project which is focused on military logistics as an example application is demonstrating that one of the world's largest software applications can be managed using the techniques discussed in this paper.

The flexible agent architecture is an excellent fit to modern grid architectures, and allows tasks to be readily reassigned to take advantage of computing cycles, memory, and other resources on the grid. The combined CPU/Memory/Bandwidth constraint satisfaction problems, mixed with the numerous other problems in streaming, latency, processing speed, and cost means that the objective function is an extremely complex mix of goals. Our current Ultralog solver has a variety of "Strategies" for various modes of operation with varying levels of risk and performance requirements. The strategies themselves are managed in a higher level "gaming solver" that is used to predict moves of attackers, and plan counter moves as defenses of the system. The next generation of autonomous grids will both war-game with themselves to design improved states of the system, and self-design the system's own monitoring subsystem by placing detectors in optimal positions to detect flaws or intrusions of the system.

In the process of building this system we are confronted with some of the most difficult problems in computational mathematics, problems which must now be solved in near real time. The interesting blend of advanced mathematics, agent systems, and classic distributed system design is now being applied to one of our most critical problems in today's world of computing - the problem of designing robust grid systems that can self-configure themselves to improve performance, or self-configure to survive a smart attack.

REFERENCES

[1] Cougaar Web Site (http://www.Cougaar.org)

[2] Brinn M, Berliner J, Helsinger A, Wright T, Dyson M, Rho S, Wells D. Extending the limits of DMAS survivability: the Ultralog project. IEEE Intelligent Systems, Sep-Oct 2004;19(5)

[3] Kraus S, Tas C, Subrahmanian VS. Probabilistically Survivable Multiagent Systems. Proc. 2003 Intl. Joint Conf. on Artificial Intelligence. p. 789-795.

[4] Garey MR, Johnson DS. Computers and intractability, a guide to the theory of NP-Completeness. New York: W.H. Freeman and Company; 1979.

[5] Aries JA, Banerjee S, Brittan MS, Dillon E, Kowalik JS, Lixvar JP. Capacity and performance analysis of distributed enterprise systems. Communications of the ACM, Jun 2002;45(6):100-105.

[6] Aries J, Brittan M, Dillon E, Korncoff A, Kowalik J, Lixvar J. Capacity planning for and performance analysis of large distributed transaction systems. In: Kowalik J, editor. Design, performance and scalability of the distributed enterprise systems. New York: Nova Science Publishers, Inc.; 2001. p. 21-49.

[7] Brittan M, Kowalik J. Performance, optimization, & complexity in the design of large scale distributed systems. Parallel and Distributed Computing Practices, Dec 2000;3(4)

[8] Aarts E, Korst J. Simulated annealing and Boltzmann machines. New York: Wiley; 1989.

[9] Kirkpatrick S, Gelatt CD Jr., Vecchi MP. Optimization by simulated annealing. Science, 1983;220:671-680.

[10] Ersoy C, Panwar SS, Topological design of interconnected LAN/MAN networks. IEEE Journal on Selected Areas in Communications, Oct. 1993; p. 1172-1182.

[11] Salamon P, Sibani P, Frost R. Facts, conjectures, and improvements for simulated annealing. Philadelphia: SIAM; 2002.

[12] Barabasi A, Albert R. Emergence of scaling in random networks. Science, 1999;286:509-512.

[13] Callaway DS, Newman MEJ, Strogatz SH, Watts DJ. Network robustness and fragility: percolation on random graphs. Physical Review Letters, 2000;85:5468-5471.

[14] Cohen R, Erez K, ben-Avraham D, Havlin S. Resilience of the Internet to random breakdowns. Physical Review Letters, 2000;85:4626.

[15] Dorogovtsev SN, Mendes JFF. Evolution of Networks: From Biological Nets to the Internet and WWW. Oxford: Oxford University Press; 2003.

[16] Lin S, Kernighan B. An effective heuristic algorithm for the traveling salesman problem. Operations Research, 1973;21:498-516.

Grid Computing: The New Frontier of High Performance Computing
Lucio Grandinetti (Editor)
© 2005 Elsevier B.V. All rights reserved.

Optimization Techniques for Skeletons on Grids

Marco Aldinucci[a], Marco Danelutto[b], Jan Dünnweber[c] and Sergei Gorlatch[c]

[a]Italian National Research Council (ISTI–CNR),
Via Moruzzi 1, Pisa, Italy

[b]Dept. of Computer Science – University of Pisa
Largo B. Pontecorvo 3, Pisa, Italy

[c]Dept. of Computer Science – University of Münster
Einsteinstr. 62, Münster, Germany

Skeletons are common patterns of parallelism, such as farm and pipeline, that can be abstracted and offered to the application programmer as programming primitives. We describe the use and implementation of skeletons on emerging computational grids, with the skeleton system Lithium, based on Java and RMI, as our reference programming system. Our main contribution is the exploration of optimization techniques for implementing skeletons on grids based on an optimized, *future-based RMI* mechanism, which we integrate into the macro-dataflow evaluation mechanism of Lithium. We discuss three optimizations: 1) a lookahead mechanism that allows to process multiple tasks concurrently at each grid server and thereby increases the overall degree of parallelism, 2) a lazy task-binding technique that reduces interactions between grid servers and the task dispatcher, and 3) dynamic improvements that optimize the collecting of results and the work-load balancing. We report experimental results that demonstrate the improvements due to our optimizations on various testbeds, including a heterogeneous grid-like environment.

1. Introduction

Parallel and distributed computer systems have recently become less expensive and easier to build from the engineering point of view. However, the development of correct and efficient software for such systems remains a complicated and error-prone task. Most application programs are still being written at a low level of the C or Java programming language, combined with a communication library or mechanism like MPI or RMI. For performance reasons, programs are often tuned towards one specific machine configuration.

In sequential programming, low-level coding for a specific machine also prevailed three decades ago. The software engineering solution to overcome this problem was to introduce levels of abstraction, effectively yielding a tree of refinements, from the problem specification to alternative target programs [1]. In the parallel setting, high-level programming constructs and a refinement framework for them would be very desirable, because of the inherent difficulties in maintaining the portability of low-level parallelism [2].

Since the 1990s, the "skeleton approach" [3] deals with high-level languages and methods for parallel programming; see [4] for the current state of the art. In this approach, parallel algorithms are characterised and classified by their adherence to generic patterns of computation and interaction. For example, many applications from different fields share the well-known pipeline structure of control and/or data flow, probably in somewhat different flavours. Skeletons express and implement such common patterns and can be used as program building blocks, which can be customized to a particular application to express its particular flavour of the generic pattern.

Traditionally, skeletons are used to extend existing sequential programming languages or parallel programming frameworks (e.g., C+MPI or Java+RMI). Examples of available parallel libraries that support skeletal programming include, among others: *SKElib* [5], SKiPPER [6], *Lithium* (see Section 3), and *eSkel* [7]. Several real world applications have been programmed and experimented with to validate the effectiveness of the approach. Application fields where skeletons have proven to be useful include computational chemistry [8], massive data-mining [9], remote sensing and image analysis [10,11], numerical computing [12], and web search engines, e.g., Google [13].

In this work, we focus on the performance issues arising when skeletons are put into modern heterogeneous and highly dynamic distributed environments, so-called *grids*. The particular contribution of this paper is a set of novel optimization techniques that aim at solving some of the performance problems of skeleton-based programming that originate from the specific characteristics of grids. In particular, we develop optimizations in the context of Lithium, a Java-based skeleton programming library [14]. Lithium uses Java-RMI [15] to coordinate and distribute parallel activities, such that we were able to integrate our recently developed optimizations of RMI presented in [16] into Lithium.

In Section 2 and 3 we motivate our work and describe the Lithium system. Section 4 explains an optimized RMI mechanism, *future-based RMI*, which is used in Section 5 to implement the three proposed optimizations in Lithium. We describe our experiments in Section 6, where we study the performance improvement of an image processing application due to the proposed optimizations. We compare our results to related work and discuss the general applicability of our approach in Section 7.

2. Motivation for Optimizing Skeletons on Grids

Skeletons [3] are commonly used patterns of parallel or distributed computation and communication. The idea is to employ skeletons as pre-implemented, ready-to-use components that are customized to a particular application by supplying suitable parameters (data or code) [17,18]. Correspondingly to the frequently used control structures in parallel programming, the most popular skeletons are: pipeline, farm, reduce, scan and divide&conquer.

Our motivation in this paper is the performance of parallel skeletons in emerging distributed environments like grids [19]. A specific property of grids is the varying latency and bandwidth of communication between involved machines, i.e. clients and high-performance servers. Moreover, in grid environments, it is difficult to make definite assumptions about the load and the availability of individual computers. This raises new, challenging problems in using and implementing skeletons efficiently, as compared to traditional multiprocessors.

Our goal is to develop specific optimization techniques that aim at improving the coordination and communication between the servers of the grid during the execution of a skeletal program. There are two extreme levels of abstraction, at which such optimizations are in principle possible:

- at the high level of algorithmic design: such semantics-preserving transformations were studied by ourselves, e.g., in [20];

- at the low level of the particular communication mechanism.

Our approach is to take the middle path between these two alternatives, which has not been covered by previous research. This corresponds also nicely to the general philosophy of skeletons: patterns are abstracted and provided as a programmer's toolkit, with specifications which transcend architectural variations but implementations which recognize these to enhance performance. Our optimizations demonstrate that skeletons

- enhance portability and re-use by absolving the programmer of responsibility for detailed realization of the underlying patterns;

- offer scope for static and dynamic optimization, by explicitly documenting information on algorithmic structure (e.g., data dependencies) which would often be impossible to extract from equivalent unstructured programs.

Apart from "embarrassingly parallel" programs, distributed applications often involve data and control dependencies that need to be taken into account by the skeletons' evaluation mechanism. Our further objective is to present optimizations that are applicable for programs both with and without dependencies between tasks and data.

3. Skeleton-based Programming in Lithium

Our reference skeleton programming system is Lithium [14]. Lithium is a full Java library that provides the programmer with a set of parallel nestable skeletons. The skeletons implemented in Lithium include the `Farm` skeleton, modeling task farm computations, the `Pipeline` skeleton, modeling computations structured in independent stages, the `Map` skeleton, modeling data parallel computations with independent subtasks and the `DivideConquer` skeleton, modeling divide&conquer computations. All these skeletons process *streams* of *input tasks* to produce streams of *results*.

Figure 1 shows the structure of a typical Lithium application: the programmer first declares the program to be executed, then instantiates a controller/scheduler for the application; he requires the parallel execution of the program after providing the input data, and eventually processes the results computed.

Lithium implements the skeletons according to the *Macro Data Flow* (MDF) execution model [21]. Skeleton programs are first compiled into a data flow graph: each *Macro Data Flow instruction* (MDFi, i.e.,each node of the MDF graph) is a plain data flow instruction. It processes a set of input tokens (Java `Object` items in our case) and produces a set of output tokens (again Java `Object` items) that are either directed to other data flow instructions in the graph or directly presented to the user as the computation results.

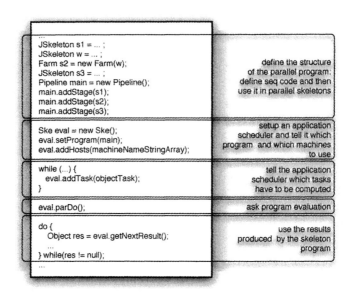

```
...
JSkeleton s1 = ... ;
JSkeleton w = ... ;
Farm s2 = new Farm(w);
JSkeleton s3 = ... ;
Pipeline main = new Pipeline();
main.addStage(s1);
main.addStage(s2);
main.addStage(s3);
```
define the structure
of the parallel program:
define seq code and then
use it in parallel skeletons

```
Ske eval = new Ske();
eval.setProgram(main);
eval.addHosts(machineNameStringArray);
```
setup an application
scheduler and tell it which
program and which machines
to use

```
while (...) {
    eval.addTask(objectTask);
}
```
tell the application
scheduler which tasks
have to be computed

```
eval.parDo();
```
ask program evaluation

```
do {
    Object res = eval.getNextResult();
    ...
} while(res != null);
...
```
use the results
produced by the skeleton
program

Figure 1. Sample Lithium code

An MDFi may represent large portions of code, rather than only simple operators or functions; therefore the term *Macro* Data Flow [22–25] is used.

The skeleton program is transformed into an MDF graph transparently to the programmer as a consequence of the `eval.setProgram` call. Lithium also allows to statically optimize the MDF graph associated with the skeleton program, such that a more compact and efficient MDF graph (the MDF "normal form") is actually executed. These optimizations are not taken into account in this work; we refer to [14,26] for further details on this subject.

The skeleton program is then executed by running the scheduler (`eval`) on the local machine and a remote server process on each of the available remote hosts. The task pool manager creates a new MDF graph for each new input task added via the `eval.addTask` call and dispatches fireable MDFi (that is, MDFi with all the input tokens available) to the remote servers. The remote servers execute the fireable MDFi in the graph(s) and dispatch the results back to the task pool manager. The task pool manager stores the results in the proper place: intermediate results are delivered to other MDFi (that, as a consequence, may become fireable); final results are stored, such that subsequent `eval.getResult` calls can retrieve them.

Remote servers are implemented as Java RMI servers, see Figure 2. The scheduler forks a control thread for each remote server. Such a control thread looks up a reference to one

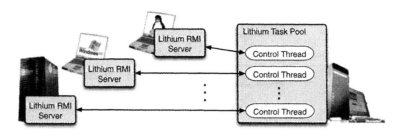

Figure 2. Lithium implementation outline.

server in the RMI-registry, by issuing a call to the static lookup-method of the standard java.rmi.Naming-class. Then it sends the MDF graph to be executed and eventually enters a loop. In the loop body, the thread fetches a fireable instruction from the task pool that is joined to the scheduler on the local machine, asks the remote server to execute the MDFi and deposits the result in the task pool.

4. Future-Based RMI

Using the RMI (*Remote Method Invocation*) mechanism in distributed programming has the important advantage that the network communication involved in calling methods on remote servers is transparent for the programmer: remote calls are coded in the same way as local calls.

4.1. The Idea of Future-Based RMI

Since the RMI mechanism was developed for traditional client-server systems, it is not optimal for systems with several servers where server/server interaction is required. We illustrate this with an example of a pipeline application: here, the result of a first call evaluating one stage is the argument of a second call (lithiumServer1 and lithiumServer2 are remote references):

```
partialResult = lithiumServer1.evalStage1(input);
overallResult = lithiumServer2.evalStage2(partialResult);
```

Such a code is not directly produced by the programmer, but rather by the run-time support of Lithium. In particular, any time a Pipeline skeleton is used, such code will be executed by the run-time system of Lithium to dispatch data computed by stage i (partialResult) to stage $i + 1$.

When executing this example composition of methods using standard RMI, the result of the remote method invocations will be sent back to the client, as shown in Figure 3 a). When evalStage1 is invoked (arrow labeled by ①), the result is sent back to the client, (②), and then to LithiumServer2 (③). Finally, the result is sent back to the client (④). For applications consisting of many composed methods like multistage pipelines, this schema results in a quite high time overhead.

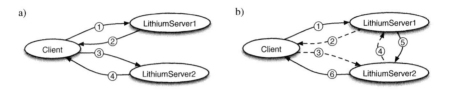

Figure 3. Method composition: a) using plain RMI, and b) using future-based RMI.

To eliminate this overhead, we have implemented a *future-based RMI*, based on the concepts that have been proven useful for other programming languages and communication technologies [27–29]. As shown in Figure 3 b), an invocation of the first method on a server initiates the method's execution. The method call returns immediately (without waiting for the method's completion) carrying a reference to the (future) execution result (②). This future reference is then used as a parameter for invoking the second method (③). When the future reference is dereferenced (④), the dereferencing thread on the server is blocked until the result is available, i. e. until the first method actually completes. The result is then sent directly to the server dereferencing the future reference (⑤). After the completion of the second method, the result is sent to the client (⑥).

Compared with traditional RMI, the future-based mechanism can substantially reduce the amount of data sent over the network, because only a reference to the data is sent to the client, whereas remote data itself is communicated directly between the servers. Moreover, communications and computations overlap, thus hiding latencies of remote calls.

4.2. Implementation of Future-Based RMI

In future-based RMI, a remote method invocation does not directly return the result of the computations. Remote hosts immediately start the execution of each call, but rather than waiting for its completion, an opaque object representing a (remote, future) reference to the result is returned. The opaque object has type `RemoteReference`, and provides two methods:

```
public void setValue(Object o) ...;
public Object getValue() ...;
```

Let us suppose that `fut` is a `RemoteReference` object. The `fut.setValue(o)` method call triggers the availability of the result and binds `Object o` to `fut`, which has been previously returned to the client as the result of the execution of a remote method. The `fut.getValue()` is the complementary method call. It can be issued to retrieve the value bound to `fut` (`o` in this case). A call to `getValue()` blocks until a matching `setValue(o)` has been issued that assigns a value to the future reference.

The `getValue()` method call can be issued either by the same host that executed `setValue(...)` or by a different host, therefore `RemoteReference` cannot be implemented as remote (RMI) class. It is rather implemented as a standard class acting as a proxy. There are two possible situations:

1. If matching methods `setValue(...)` and `getValue()` are called on different hosts, the bound value is remotely requested and then sent over the network. In order to remotely retrieve the value, we introduce the class `RemoteValue` (having the same methods as `RemoteReference`), accessible remotely. Each instance of `RemoteReference` has a reference to a `RemoteValue` instance, which is used to retrieve an object from a remote host if it is not available locally. The translation of remote to local references is handled automatically by the `RemoteReference` implementation.

2. If, otherwise, matching methods `setValue(...)` and `getValue()` are called on the same host, no data is sent over the network to prevent unnecessary transmissions of data over local sockets. A `RemoteReference` contains the IP address of the object's host and the (standard Java) hashvalue of the object, thus uniquely identifying it. When `getValue()` is invoked, it first checks if the IP address is the address of the local host. If so, it uses the hashvalue as a key for a table (which is static for class `RemoteReference`) to obtain a local reference to the object. This reference is then returned to the calling method. A remote call for retrieving a value from a `RemoteReference`, is only executed, if the object holding the value is actually located at a remote server.

Internally, remote references handle the availability of results using a simple boolean flag. Once a `RemoteReference`'s `setValue` method was called for the first time, this object's `getValue`-method will not wait anymore. It is in general not a good practice to issue subsequent calls to `setValue` for resetting `RemoteReferences`, because `RemoteReferences` can not be cached properly using a simple hash table when they are assigned more than once, nor does the class provide any kind of multistage notification mechanism. As `RemoteReferences` are cached by the servers, they are not garbage collected automatically. The scheduler explicitly causes a permanent deletion of a `RemoteReference`, once the corresponding MDFi has no more successors in the MDF graph, i.e. there is no remote post-processing necessary

5. Optimization Techniques Applied to Skeletons

In this section, we describe three optimization techniques for the Lithium skeleton system, which are based on the future-based RMI mechanism presented in the previous section. All three enhancements are transparent to the application programmer, i.e. an existing Lithium application does not require any changes to benefit from them.

5.1. Task Lookahead on RMI servers

We call our first optimization technique "task lookahead": a server will not have to get back to the task pool manager every time it is ready to process a new task. The immediate return of a remote reference enables the scheduler to dispatch multiple tasks instead of single tasks. When a server is presented with a new set of tasks, it starts a thread for every single task that will process this task asynchronously, producing a reference to the result. This is particularly important if we use multi-processor servers, because it allows the multithreaded implementation to exploit all available processors. However, even a single-processor server benefits from look-ahead, because transferring multiple tasks right at the beginning avoids idle times between consecutive tasks.

A Lithium program starts its execution by initializing the available servers and binding their names to the local `rmiregistry`. Then the servers wait for RMI calls. There are two kinds of calls that can be issued to a server:

- `setMDFGraph`, used within the `setProgram`-method of the scheduler to send a macro data flow graph to a server. This remote call happens transparently to the programmer, who uses `setProgram` as shown in Section 3. The information in the transferred graph is used to properly execute the MDFi that will be assigned later to the server for execution.
- An `execute` call is used to force the execution of MDFi on a remote node. Also this remote method is never called by the programmer directly, but it is called by the control threads during the evaluation of the `parDo`-call shown in Section 3.

In the original Lithium, each control thread performs the following loop [14]:

```
while (!taskPool.isEmpty() && !end) {
    tmpVal = (TaskItem[])taskPool.getTask();
    taskPool.addTask(Ske.slave[im].execute(tmpVal));
}
```

i. e. it looks for a fireable instruction (a *task* according to Lithium terminology), invokes the `execute` method on the remote server and puts the resulting task back to the task pool for further processing. Actually, each control thread and its associated server work in sequence; the behavior is sketched in Figure 4. Therefore, each Lithium server has an idle time between the execution of two consecutive tasks:

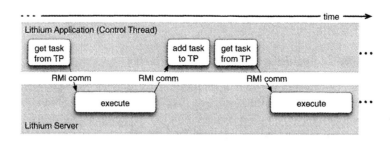

Figure 4. Server's idle time in original Lithium implementation.

The lookahead-optimization aims at avoiding idle times at the servers. Servers are made multithreaded by equipping them with a thread pool. As soon as a server receives a task execution request, it selects a thread from its pool and starts it on the task. After this invocation (and before the thread completes the task), the server returns a handle to its control thread, thus completing the RMI call. In this way, the control thread may continue to run, extracting as many new fireable tasks from the task pool as currently available and assigning them to the same server. Simultaneously, some of the server's threads may be still running on previous tasks. As we shall see in Section 5.3, the amount of tasks looked ahead can be bounded within a heuristically chosen range in order to prevent load unbalance among servers.

As a result, we can have many threads running on a single server, thus exploiting the parallelism of the server. In any case, we eliminate control thread idle time by overlapping useful work in each server with running its control thread. Since having multiple threads per server also increases the control thread pressure, the MDFi computational grain should be not too small w.r.t. communication grain. MDFi computational grain directly depends on code enclosed within sequential skeletons (run method of `JSkeleton` coded by the programmer), while communication grain depends on their input and output data size. In general, finding a communication/computation balance is the programmer's responsibility. However, even if this has not been done, Lithium can coarsen the computational grain in the server by collapsing many MDFi(s) into a single one. This transformation converts tokens passing thru collapsed MFDi (i.e. communications) in local memory operations thus coarsening computational grain. The full description of this technique (a.k.a task normalization) is beyond the scope of this paper [14,26].

5.2. Server-to-Server Lazy Binding

Our second optimization technique is called "lazy binding": a remote server will only execute a new MDFi from the graph if necessary; analogously, the scheduler will not wait for a remote reference to produce the future result.Here, we use remote references to avoid unnecessary communications between control threads and remote servers. Our implementation of remote references uses hash tables as local caches, which leads to the caching of intermediate results of the MDF evaluation. The system will identify chains in which each task depends on previous ones and make sure that such sequences will be dispatched to a single remote machine. Thus, a sequence of dependent tasks will be processed locally on one server, which leads to a further reduction of communication.

If no post-processing of an MDFi is specified in the MDF graph, then it does not need to be cached anymore. Once such an MDFi has been processed, the associated `RemoteReference` is removed from the cache by the server, which makes it eligible for garbage collection.

Let us consider again the evaluation of the sequence of two functions, f and g, on a stream of data as in our first example in Section 3. The program can be expressed using the `Pipeline` skeleton, whose two stages evaluate f and g, respectively. The behavior of the original Lithium system on this program is shown in Figure 5 a):

(i) The control thread fetches a fireable MDF-instruction and sends it to the associated server (①). The MDF-instruction includes a reference to the function $\uparrow f$ and the input data x_i.
(ii) The Lithium server executes the instruction and sends the resulting data y_i back to the control thread (②).
(iii) The control thread deposits the result in the task pool that makes another MDF-instruction $\uparrow g(y_i)$ fireable. It will be then fetched by either the same or another

control thread and sent to the server (③).

(iv) After the evaluation, the whole execution $z_i = g(f(x_i))$ is completed (④).

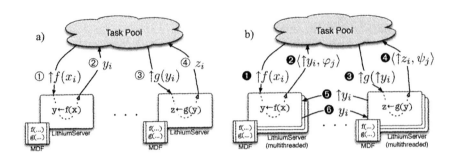

Figure 5. Communications between the Task Pool and Servers. a) Original Lithium. b) Optimized implementation using lazy binding.

The goal of the lazy binding optimization is reducing the size of communications ② and ③. Without lazy binding both, the reference to the function to be executed and its input data are transmitted in these communications, the latter being the large part. Since the input data might be computed in a previous step by the same server, we can communicate a handle (the RemoteReference) for the input/output data instead of their actual values. In this way, each server retains computed values in its cache until these values are used. If they are used by the same server, we greatly reduce the size of round trip communication with the control thread. If they are used by another thread, then we move the values directly between servers, thus halving the number of large-size communications.

The optimized behavior is shown in Figure 5 b):

(i) The control thread fetches an MDF-instruction and sends it to a server (❶).

(ii) The Lithium server assigns the work to a thread in the pool and, immediately, sends back the result handle $\uparrow y_i$ (❷). The message may be extended with the completing token φ_j for a previously generated handle j ($i > j$) in order to make the control thread aware of the number of ongoing tasks.

(iii) The control thread deposits the result in the task pool that makes another MDF-instruction $\uparrow g(\uparrow y_i)$ fireable; it will be fetched by either the same or another control thread and sent to its associated server (❸). Let us suppose the instruction is fetched by another control thread.

(iv) The server immediately returns the handle to the control thread (❹).

(v) To evaluate $\uparrow g(\uparrow y_i)$, the server invokes getValue() on $\uparrow y_i$ (❺).

(vi) Value y_i arrives at the server (❻), thus enabling the evaluation of $g(y_i)$.

Note that if f and g are evaluated on the same server, then the communications ❺ and ❻ do not take place at all, since references are resolved locally.

Lazy Binding for Data-Parallel Computations.

The execution of skeletons like `Map` or `Farm` with no dependencies between data elements are performed as data-parallel computations, i.e. these skeletons are parallelized by partitioning the input data and processing all partitions in parallel, which is carried out in Lithium as follows:

- a task x is divided into a set of (possibly overlapping) n subsets $x_1 \cdots x_n$;
- each subset is assigned to a remote server;
- the results of the computation of all the subsets are used to build the overall result of the data-parallel computation.

This implies the following communication overhead (see Figure 6 a):

- n communications from the task pool control thread to the remote servers are needed to dispatch subsets;
- n communications from the remote servers to the task pool control threads are needed to collect the subsets of the result;
- one communication from the control thread to a remote server is needed to send the subsets in order to compute the final result;
- one communication from the remote server to the task pool control thread is needed to gather the final result of the data-parallel computation.

The lazy-binding optimization implies the following behavior (Figure 6 b):

- each time a data-parallel computation is performed, the task pool control thread generates and dispatches all "body" instructions, i. e. instructions that compute a subset of the final result. The remote servers immediately return handles $\uparrow y_1 \cdots \uparrow y_n$ (`RemoteReferences`) representing the values still being computed;
- after receiving all handles, the control thread dispatches the "gather" MDFi (i. e. the instruction packing all the sub-results into the result data structure) to the remote server hosting the major amount of references to sub-results. Thereby, the dispatcher assigns the gathering task to the server that already holds the largest number of references. When this instruction is computed, the result is sent back to the task pool.

Thus, we avoid moving the intermediate results back and forth between the task pool threads and the servers in both the execution and gathering phases.

5.3. Load-Balancing

In this section, we describe how the load-balancing mechanism of Lithium is adapted to the optimized evaluation mechanisms presented above, in order to achieve a stable level of parallelism on all servers. This is accomplished by measuring the number of active threads on the servers.

Our asynchronous communications lead to a multithreaded task evaluation on the servers. The scheduler can dispatch a task by sending it to a server, which is already evaluating other tasks, so that the server will start evaluating the new task in parallel. We implemented this server-side multithreading using a thread pool, which is more efficient than spawning a new thread for each task. However, tasks may differ in size, and

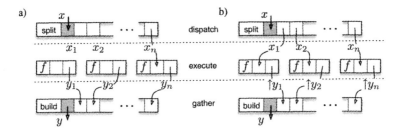

Figure 6. Executing a data-parallel skeleton: a) original Lithium; b) optimized.

machines in a Grid are usually heterogeneous. Without a suitable load-balancing strategy, this may lead to an inefficient partitioning of work.

To balance the load in the system, we measure the current load of each grid server. One possibility would be to use a new remote method, which, however, implies additional remote communication. Instead, we exploit the fact that the scheduler already communicates frequently with the remote servers when it dispatches tasks. We extend communicated data records by a value that reports to the scheduler the actual work-load on the server. So, every time the scheduler sends a task to a server, it gets the number of threads currently running on that server. The scheduler can re-check this number and, if there is already much load on this server, it can decide to release the task again and wait instead. Accordingly, another scheduler thread will process the task by sending it to another server.

So, dispatching tasks and measuring work-load can be done in one remote communication as shown in Figure 7: Here, we have a maximum number of six active threads per server. Dispatching tasks to server 1 and server n yields the actual work-load (five active threads at server 1, six active threads at server n), which means that the scheduler can continue to dispatch tasks to these servers. But for a server that has already reached the maximum number of active threads (server 2 in the figure), the scheduler waits until the number of active threads has fallen below the limit.

With many remote servers and, correspondingly, control threads running in the scheduler, the measured value may already be obsolete when the next task is sent. However, since asynchronous communication causes tasks to be dispatched with a high frequency, the suggested technique is precise enough for an efficient load balancing. This has also been proved by our experiments that included checkpointing.

6. Experiments

For the evaluation of our optimizations, we conducted performance measurements on three different distributed platforms:

(i) A dedicated Linux cluster at the University of Pisa. The cluster hosts 24 nodes: one node devoted to cluster administration and 23 nodes (P3@ 800MHz) exclusively devoted to parallel program execution. Described in Section 6.1.

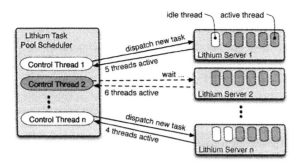

Figure 7. Communication schema for the load balancing mechanism.

(ii) A distributed execution environment including Linux and Sun SMP machines. The client runs on a Linux machine in Münster and the servers run on a set of Sun SMP machines in Berlin. Described in Section 6.2.

(iii) A Grid-like environment, including two organizations: the University of Pisa *(di.unipi.it)* and an institute of the Italian National Research Council in Pisa *(isti.cnr.it)*. The server set is composed of several different Intel Pentium and Apple PowerPC computers, running Linux and Mac OS X respectively (The detailed configuration is shown in Figure 10 left). The comparison of computing power of machines is performed in terms of BogoPower, i.e. the number of tasks per second which a given machine can compute running the sequential version of the application. Described in Section 6.3.

The three testing environments represent significantly different scenarios:
(i) is characterized by uniform computing power and high-bandwidth communications across the whole system (client and servers);
(ii) has low latency and high bandwidth for server-to-server communication, while the client is connected to the servers with a fairly slow connection.
(iii) shows a heterogeneous distribution of computing power and interconnection speed, typical for grids.

The image processing application we used for our tests employs the Pipeline skeleton, which applies two filters in sequence to 30 input images. All input images are true-color (24 bit color depth) of 640x480 pixels size. We used filters from the Java Imaging Utilities (available at http://jiu.sourceforge.net) that add a blur effect and an oil effect. Note that these are *area filter operations*, i.e. the computation of each pixel's color does not only impact its direct neighbors, but also an adjustable area of neighboring pixels. By choosing five neighboring pixels in each direction as filter workspaces, we made the application more complicated and enforced several iterations over the input data within each pipeline stage, which makes our filtering example a good representative for a compute intensive application.

Despite its simplicity, the application presented here, which is based on a single pipeline, represents a significant and complete test for our optimizations. Indeed, the Pipeline is the simplest skeleton among all the skeletons offered by Lithium that exhibits control dependencies and a compositional behavior, like described in Figure 3 and Figure 5. This kind of interaction is typical for the MDF evaluation mechanism of Lithium and occurs in more sophisticated application repeatedly, but with no technical differences concerning the communication schema (see [14]). Actually, the only programs that do not interact like shown in Figure 3 and Figure 5 are applications composed of the plain Farm skeleton only, which can not benefit from Lazy Binding since it does not involve any Server-to-Server interaction.

Load-balancing for the future-based version was adjusted to the maximum of six concurrent threads per node. The lower limit was set to two threads. These values enable the exploitation of both task-lookahead optimization and thread parallelism on standard SMP systems, while not introducing excessive overhead due to multithreading management. All experiments were performed using the Sun J2SE Client VM SDK version 1.4.1.

As shown in the following sections, the optimized Lithium demonstrates a clear time advantage over the standard version along all tested configurations.

6.1. Dedicated Cluster (environment i)

Figure 8 (left) shows the measured time in seconds, for both the original Lithium and the optimized version running on the dedicated cluster in Pisa. The speedup in the right part of the figure is calculated with respect to the plain Java sequential version of the application running on one node of the same cluster (execution time 446 Sec). The plots show that the future-based version performs approximately twice as fast as standard Lithium.

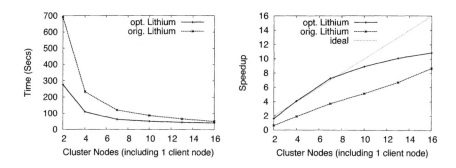

Figure 8. Measured execution times and speedup on the cluster (i).

In the example application, three kinds of activities take place: communication, computation, and data I/O. Task lookahead allows to overlap these activities, while lazy binding ensures that the whole data transfer between the stages of the pipeline takes place on the server side without client interaction.

6.2. Distributed Environment (ii)

Figure 9 shows the execution time for both the original Lithium and the optimized version running in the environment (ii). The tests demonstrate a clear increase in performance due to our optimizations, in particular to the lazy-binding mechanism.

By introducing server-to-server communication, the transmission of data between client and servers is reduced considerably. The fastest connections of the network (the interconnection between the servers in Berlin) are used for handling the biggest part of data exchange instead of tracing back each communication to the scheduler host with a much slower connection.

6.3. Heterogeneous Environment (iii)

Figure 10 compares the optimized version against the standard one in the heterogeneous environment (iii), whose composition is listed in Figure 10 left. To take the varying computing power of different machines into account, the performance increase is documented by means of the *BogoPower* measure, which enables the comparison between application's actual parallel performance and the application ideal performance (Figure 10 right).

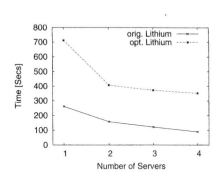

Figure 9: Run times in environment (ii)

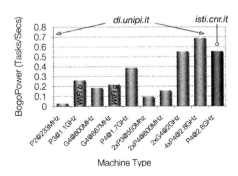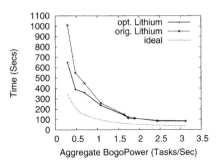

Figure 10. Left: Test environment (iii). Right: Execution times vs. increasing (Bogo-)powerful ordered server set.

Parallel speedup usually assumes that all machines in the running environment have the same computational power, which is often not true in grid-like environments. The BogoPower measure describes the aggregate BogoPower of a heterogeneous distributed system as the sum of individual BogoPower contributions (Figure 10 left). Application

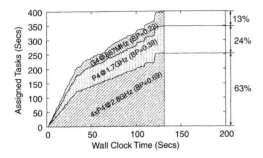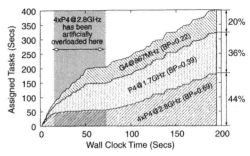

Figure 11. Detailed history of tasks scheduling. Left: All machines are dedicated to the experiment. Right: One of the machines is externally overloaded from time 10 to 70.

ideal performance curve is evaluated w.r.t. a system exploiting a given BogoPower rank, assuming both an optimal scheduling of tasks and zero communication costs.

We use environment (iii) for studying to what extent the heterogeneity challenge of grids is met by our improved load-balancing strategy. The Lithium runtime system continuously monitors the servers' states and raises or drops the number of threads correspondingly. To demonstrate the dynamic load-balancing behavior of the scheduler, we performed two identical experiments with differing load on one of the involved machines.

First (Figure 11 left) all machines were dedicated to the experiment. Then, in the second experiment (Figure 11 right) fewer tasks are dispatched to the most powerful machine, because this machine was heavily loaded by another application.

Figure 12 shows the history of threads issued to the overloaded machine: When the machine load grows too much, the scheduler drops the number of active threads (which range from 2 to 12 in the experiment). This decision is supported by the system-wide historical statistics, maintained by the load-balancing module of the client.

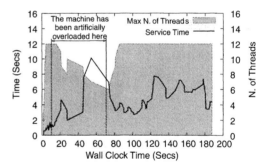

Figure 12: Throttling in task scheduling.

7. Related Work and Conclusions

In this paper, we have described three optimization techniques aimed at an efficient implementation of parallel skeletons in distributed grid-like environments with high communication latencies. As a reference implementation, we took the Lithium skeleton library.

We studied the effects of three optimizations based on the asynchronous, future-based

RMI mechanism: (1) dispatching batches of tasks, rather than single tasks, to remote servers ("task lookahead"); (2) caching intermediate results on the remote servers, thus allowing to reduce the communication overhead ("lazy binding"); (3) adapting the load-balancing strategy to the multithreaded evaluation mechanism initiated by the task lookahead and implementing it without a large increase in remote communication: the messages carry one additional value, but the number of messages remains unchanged.

Several research projects investigated asynchronous RMI in Java [16,30,31]. In almost all of them, the programmer is responsible for writing the asynchronous invocations. In contrast, our future-based implementation encapsulates the modified communication schema into the skeleton evaluation mechanisms of the Lithium system, without demanding from the programmer to take care of the internal changes. Internally, our implementation uses the future-mechanism introduced in [16], but these core methods could also be replaced by e.g. ProActive that implements concepts described in [30], without affecting the high-level interface provided by Lithium. In [32], RMI calls are optimized using call-aggregation, where a server can directly invoke methods on another server. While this approach optimizes RMI calls by reducing the amount of communicated data, the method invocations are not asynchronous as in our implementation: they are delayed to find as many optimization possibilities as possible.

All three optimization techniques have been integrated into Lithium transparently to the user; i. e., applications developed on top of the original framework can directly use the optimized version without any changes in the code. The presented optimizations can easily be applied to other skeleton programming environments than Lithium. Furthermore, they are not restricted to RMI as a communication mechanism.

The broad applicability of our optimizations is confirmed by the fact that currently we are considering the adoption of these techniques in ASSIST [33], a system that exploits in part the experiences gained from Lithium and that runs upon different kinds of modern grid middleware (plain TCP/IP and POSIX processes/threads, CORBA and the Globus Toolkit [34]).

Acknowledgments

We are grateful to the anonymous referee of the draft version of this paper for very helpful remarks, and to Julia Kaiser-Mariani for her help in improving the presentation. This research was partially supported by the FP6 Network of Excellence *CoreGRID* funded by the European Commission (Contract IST-2002-004265) and by a travel grant from the German-Italian exchange programme *Vigoni*.

REFERENCES

1. D. L. Parnas, On the design and development of program families, IEEE Trans. on Software Engineering SE-2 (1) (1976) 1–9.
2. M. Cole, S. Gorlatch, J. Prins, D. Skillicorn (Eds.), High Level Parallel Programming: Applicability, Analysis and Performance, Dagstuhl-Seminar Report 238, Schloß Dagstuhl, 1999.
3. M. Cole, Algorithmic Skeletons: Structured Management of Parallel Computations, Research Monographs in Parallel and Distributed Computing, Pitman, 1989.

4. F. A. Rabhi, S. Gorlatch (Eds.), Patterns and Skeletons for Parallel and Distributed Computing, Springer-Verlag, 2002.
5. M. Danelutto, M. Stigliani, SKElib: parallel programming with skeletons in C, in: A. Bode, T. Ludwing, W. Karl, R. Wismüller (Eds.), Proc. of Euro-Par 2000, no. 1900 in LNCS, Springer-Verlag, 2000, pp. 1175–1184.
6. J. Sérot, D. Ginhac, Skeletons for parallel image processing: an overview of the SKiP-PER project, Parallel Computing 28 (12) (2002) 1685–1708.
7. M. Cole, Bringing skeletons out of the closet: A pragmatic manifesto for skeletal parallel programming, Parallel Computing 30 (3) (2004) 389–406.
8. S. Crocchianti, A. Laganà, L. Pacifici, V. Piermarini, Parallel skeletons and computational grain in quantum reactive scattering calculations, in: G. R. Joubert, A. Murli, F. J. Peters, M. Vanneschi (Eds.), Parallel Computing: Advances and Current Issues. Proceedings of the International Conference ParCo2001, Imperial College Press, 2002, pp. 91–100.
9. M. Coppola, M. Vanneschi, High performance data mining with skeleton-based structured parallel programming, Parallel Computing 28 (5) (2002) 793–813.
10. G. Sardisco, A. Machì, Development of parallel paradigms templates for semi-automatic digital film restoration algorithms, in: G. R. Joubert, A. Murli, F. J. Peters, M. Vanneschi (Eds.), Parallel Computing: Advances and Current Issues. Proceedings of the International Conference ParCo2001, Imperial College Press, 2002, pp. 498–509.
11. A. Giancaspro, L. Candela, E. Lopinto, V. A. Lorè, G. Milillo, SAR images co-registration parallel implementation, in: Proc. of the International Geoscience and Remote Sensing Symposium and the 24th Canadian Symposium on Remote Sensing (Igarss 2002), IEEE, 2002.
12. P. D'Ambra, M. Danelutto, D. di Serafino, M. Lapegna, Integrating MPI-based numerical software into an advanced parallel computing environment, in: Proc. of the 11th Euromicro Conference on Parallel, Distributed and Network-Based Processing, IEEE, 2003, pp. 283–291.
13. J. Dean, S. Ghemawat, MapReduce: Simplified data processing on large clusters., in: 6th Symp. on Operating System Design and Implementation (OSDI 2004), 2004, pp. 137–150.
14. M. Aldinucci, M. Danelutto, P. Teti, An advanced environment supporting structured parallel programming in Java, Future Generation Computer Systems 19 (5) (2003) 611–626.
15. C. Nester, R. Philippsen, B. Haumacher, A more efficient RMI for Java, in: Proc. of the Java Grande Conference, ACM, 1999, pp. 152–157.
16. M. Alt, S. Gorlatch, Future-based RMI: Optimizing compositions of remote method calls on the grid, in: H. Kosch, L. Böszörményi, H. Hellwagner (Eds.), Proc. of the Euro-Par 2003, no. 2790 in LNCS, Springer, 2003, pp. 427–430.
17. H. Kuchen, A skeleton library, in: B. Monien, R. Feldmann (Eds.), Proc. of Euro-Par 2002, no. 2400 in LNCS, Springer-Verlag, 2002, pp. 620–629.
18. S. Pelagatti, Structured Development of Parallel Programs, Taylor&Francis, 1998.
19. I. Foster, C. Kesselmann (Eds.), The Grid: Blueprint for a New Computing Infrastructure, Morgan Kaufmann, 1998.

20. S. Gorlatch, Optimizing compositions of components in parallel and distributed programming, in: Christian Lengauer et al. (Ed.), Domain-Specific Program Generation, Vol. 3016 of Lecture Notes in Computer Science, Springer-Verlag, 2004, pp. 274–290.
21. M. Danelutto, Efficient support for skeletons on workstation clusters, Parallel Processing Letters 11 (1) (2001) 41–56.
22. Ö. Babaoglu, L. Alvisi, A. Amoreso, R. Davoli, L. A. Giachini, Paralex: An environment for parallel programming in distributed systems, in: 6th ACM International Conference on Supercomputing, 1992.
23. R. F. Babb, Parallel processing with large-grain data flow techniques, in: IEEE Computer, 1984, pp. pp. 55–61.
24. A. S. Grimshaw, Object-oriented parallel processing with Mentat, Information Sciences 93 (1) (1996) 9–34.
25. V. Sarkar, J. Hennessy, Compile-time partitioning and scheduling of parallel programs, in: Proceedings of the 1986 SIGPLAN symposium on Compiler contruction, ACM Press, 1986, pp. 17–26.
26. M. Aldinucci, M. Danelutto, Stream parallel skeleton optimization, in: Proc. of the 11th IASTED Intl. Conference on Parallel and Distributed Computing and Systems (PDCS'99), IASTED/ACTA press, Cambridge, MA, USA, 1999.
27. A. L. Ananda, B. H. Tay, E. K. Koh, A survey of asynchronous remote procedure calls, ACM SIGOPS Operating Systems Review 26 (2) (1992) 92–109.
28. K. A. Hawick, H. A. James, A. J. Silis, D. A. Grove, K. E. Kerry, J. A. Mathew, P. D. Coddington, C. J. Patten, J. F. Hercus, F. A. Vaughan, DISCWorld: An Environment for Service-Based Metacomputing, Future Generation Computer Systems 15 (5) (1999) 623–635.
29. B. Liskov, L. Shrira, Promises: linguistic support for efficient asynchronous procedure calls in distributed systems, in: Proc. of the ACM SIGPLAN conference on Programming Language design and Implementation, ACM Press, 1988.
30. D. Caromel, A general model for concurrent and distributed object-oriented programming., SIGPLAN Notices 24 (4) (1989) 102–104.
31. D. Caromel, W. Klauser, J. Vayssiere, Towards seamless computing and metacomputing in Java, Concurrency Practice and Experience (1998) 10 (11–13).
32. K. C. Yeung, P. H. J. Kelly, Optimising Java RMI programs by communication restructuring, in: D. Schmidt, M. Endler (Eds.), Middleware 2003: ACM/IFIP/USENIX Intl. Middleware Conference, Springer-Verlag, 2003.
33. M. Aldinucci, M. Coppola, M. Danelutto, M. Vanneschi, C. Zoccolo, ASSIST as a research framework for high-performance Grid programming environments, in: J. C. Cunha, O. F. Rana (Eds.), Grid Computing: Software environments and Tools, Springer, 2005, (to appear, draft available as University of Pisa Tech. Rep. TR-04-09).
34. I. Foster, C. Kesselman, J. M. Nick, S. Tuecke, Grid services for distributed system integration, Computer 35 (6) (2002) 37–46.
    URL http://www.computer.org/computer/co2002/r6037abs.htm;

Grid Computing: The New Frontier of High Performance Computing
Lucio Grandinetti (Editor)
© 2005 Elsevier B.V. All rights reserved.

Towards a Middleware Framework for Dynamically Reconfigurable Scientific Computing

Kaoutar El Maghraoui[a], Travis Desell[a], Boleslaw K. Szymanski[a], James D. Teresco[b], and Carlos A. Varela[a]

[a]Department of Computer Science, Rensselaer Polytechnic Institute,
110 8th Street, Troy, NY 12180-3590, USA

[b]Department of Computer Science, Williams College,
47 Lab Campus Drive, Williamstown, MA 01267, USA

Computational grids are appealing platforms for the execution of large scale applications among the scientific and engineering communities. However, designing new applications and deploying existing ones with the capability of exploiting this potential still remains a challenge. Computational grids are characterized by their dynamic, non-dedicated, and heterogeneous nature. Novel application-level and middleware-level techniques are needed to allow applications to reconfigure themselves and adapt automatically to their underlying execution environments. In this paper, we introduce a new software framework that enhances the performance of Message Passing Interface (MPI) applications through an adaptive middleware for load balancing that includes process checkpointing and migration. Fields as diverse as fluid dynamics, materials science, biomechanics, and ecology make use of parallel adaptive computation. Target architectures have traditionally been supercomputers and tightly coupled clusters. This framework is a first step in allowing these computations to use computational grids efficiently.

1. Introduction

Computational grids [1] have become very attractive platforms for high performance distributed applications due to their high availability, scalability, and computational power. However, nodes in grid environments (e.g., uniprocessors, symmetric multiprocessors (SMPs), or clusters) are not necessarily dedicated to a single parallel or distributed application. They experience constantly changing processing loads and communication demands. Achieving the desired high performance requires augmenting applications with appropriate support for reconfiguration and adaptability to the dynamic nature of computational grids. Since they span a wider range of geographical locations and involve large numbers of computational nodes, the potential for failures and load fluctuations increases significantly.

Computationally-demanding scientific and engineering applications that arise in diverse disciplines such as fluid dynamics, materials science, and biomechanics often involve solving or simulating multi-scale problems with dynamic behavior. Solution procedures use sophisticated adaptive methods underlying data structures (e.g., meshes) and numerical methods to achieve specified levels of solution accuracy [2]. This adaptivity, when used for parallel solution procedures, introduces load imbalance which can be corrected using application-level dynamic load balancing techniques [3]. These applications generally deal with huge amounts of data and require extensive computational resources, but they usually assume a fixed number of cooperating processes running in a dedicated and mostly homogeneous computing environment. Running such applications on computational grids, with their dynamic, heterogeneous, and non-dedicated resources, makes it difficult for application-level load balancing alone to take full advantage of available resources and to maintain high performance. Application-level load-balancing approaches have a limited view of the external world where the application is competing for resources with several other applications. Middleware is a more appropriate location where to place resource management and load balancing capabilities since it has a more global view of the execution environment, and can benefit a large number of applications.

MPI [4] has been widely adopted as the de-facto standard to implement single-program multiple-data (SPMD) parallel applications. Extensive development effort has produced many large software systems that use MPI for parallelization. It's wide availability has enabled portability of applications among a variety of parallel computing environments. However, the issues of scalability, adaptability and load balancing still remain a challenge. Most existing MPI implementations assume a static network environment. MPI implementations that support the MPI-2 standard [5,6] provide partial support for dynamic process management, but still require complex application development from end-users: process management needs to be handled explicitly at the application level, which requires the developer to deal with issues such as resource discovery and allocation, scheduling, load balancing, etc. Additional middleware-support for application reconfiguration is therefore needed to relieve application developers from such concerns. Augmenting MPI applications with automated process migration capabilities is a necessary step to enable dynamic reconfiguration through load balancing of MPI processes among geographically distributed nodes. We initially address dynamic reconfiguration through process migration for the class of iterative applications since a large number of legacy MPI applications have this property.

The purpose of this paper is two-fold: first we demonstrate how we achieve process migration in applications that follow the MPI programming model. The adopted strategy does not require modifying existing MPI implementations. Second we introduce the design of a middleware infrastructure that enhances existing MPI applications with automatic reconfiguration in a dynamic setting. The Internet Operating System (IOS) [7,8] is a distributed middleware framework that provides opportunistic load balancing capabilities through resource-level profiling and application-level profiling. MPI/IOS is a system that integrates IOS middleware strategies with existing MPI applications. MPI/IOS adopts a semi-transparent checkpointing mechanism, where the user needs only to specify the data structures that must be saved and restored to allow process migration. This approach does not require extensive code modifications. Legacy MPI applications can benefit from load balancing features by inserting just a small number of calls to a simple application programming interface. In shared environments where many applications are running, having application-level resource management is not enough to balance the load of the entire system efficiently. A middleware layer is the natural place to manage the resources of several distributed applications running simultaneously.

Providing simple application programmer interfaces (APIs) and delegating most of the load distribution and balancing to middleware will allow smooth and easy migration of MPI applications from static and dedicated clusters to highly dynamic computational grids. This framework is more beneficial for long running applications involving large numbers of machines, where the probability of load fluctuations is high. In such situations, it will be helpful for the running application to have means by which to evaluate its performance continuously, discover new resources, and be able to migrate some or all of the application's cooperating processes to better nodes. We target initially highly synchronized iterative applications that have the unfortunate property of running as slow as the slowest process. Eliminating the slowest processor from the computation results or migrating its work to a faster processor can, in many cases, lead to a significant overall performance improvement.

The remainder of the paper is organized as follows. Section 2 presents motivating application scenarios for reconfigurable execution. Section 3 discusses the requirements and benefits of dynamically reconfigurable parallel and distributed applications. In Section 4, we describe our methodology for enabling reconfiguration of distributed and parallel applications using the MPI programming model. We then present IOS resource model and load balancing strategies in Section 5. Section 6 details the architecture of the MPI/IOS framework and presents experimental results. Section 7 presents related work. We conclude with discussion and future work in Section 8.

2. Dynamically Changing Computations

In a grid environment, one of the following scenarios might happen:

1. The application can predicts initially its resource requirements and the allocated resources' utilization and availability do not change drastically over time.

2. The application has a dynamic nature. The initial resource requirements of the application are hard to predict or the application's problem size can grow or shrink over time.

3. The execution environment is dynamic. This is usually the case of dynamic grid environments where resources are shared and they experience varying loads and availability.

In the first case, a good initial resource allocation might suffice to provide the desired performance throughout the lifetime of the application. However in the second and third cases, adaptive execution is needed to either cope with the dynamic nature of the application and/or adapt to the dynamic nature of the execution environment. The last two scenarios are expected to be the rule and not the exception in dynamic grids. Therefore, providing the necessary support for reconfiguration is indispensable. The rest of this section describes the characteristics of mesh-based adaptive scientific computation, a motivating application scenario for reconfigurable applications.

Adaptive scientific computation is dynamic by nature. A typical simulation begins with a small initial mesh, and adaptive refinement produces finer meshes (i.e., meshes with larger number of elements) in regions where interesting solution features are present, and does this as part of the simulation process. As these solution features arise and dissipate or move through the domain, some of the refined mesh may be coarsened. Thus, the locations in the domain where the finer mesh is needed as well as the total mesh size change throughout the computation.

When using the traditional MPI model, the computing resources are allocated initially and simulations begin with a partitioning of the (small) initial mesh. Dynamic load balancing procedures are then applied periodically to redistribute the mesh among the cooperating processes on the allocated processors. The computing resources assigned to the problem remain the same throughout, but the workload is redistributed among them. Even when the problem size is small and the solution would be more efficient on fewer processors (because of reduced communication volume), all of the allocated processors are used, in part because it is difficult to add or remove processes using the MPI model.

In the more dynamic environments we target and that the middleware described herein is intended to support, resources may be added to or removed from the computation as the simulation proceeds. This sort of reconfiguration may be in response to the changing computational needs of the simulations or to the changing availability of resources. Parts of the computation that can be executed more efficiently on fewer processors may do so, leaving other resources available for other purposes. Additional resources can be requested and the computation can be reconfigured to take advantage of those resources when the computation grows sufficiently large.

3. Reconfigurable Distributed and Parallel Applications

Grid computing thrives to provide mechanisms and tools to allow decentralized collaboration of geographically distributed resources across various organizations in the Internet. One of its main goals is to maximize the use of underutilized resources and hence offer efficient and low cost paradigms for efficiently executing distributed applications. Grid environments are highly dynamic, shared, and heterogeneous. Running distributed or parallel applications on such platforms is not a trivial task. Applications need to be able to adapt to the various dynamics of the underlying resources through dynamic reconfiguration mechanisms. Dynamic reconfiguration implies the ability to modify the application's structure and/or modify the mapping between physical resources and application's components while the application continues to operate without any disruption of service.

Grid applications have several needs:

- **Availability:** The ability of the application to be resilient to failures.

- **Scalability:** The ability of the application to use new resources while the computation is taking place.

- **High Performance:** The ability to adapt to load fluctuations, which results in high performing applications.

Several resource management requirements need to be addressed to satisfy applications' demands in grid environments such as: 1) resource allocation, 2) reallocation or reconfiguration of these resources, and 3) resource profiling for an optimal reconfiguration. All of these resource management issues are beyond the scope of applications and should be embodied in smart middleware that is capable of harnessing available resources and allocating them properly to running applications.

3.1. Resource Allocation and Reallocation

Resource discovery and allocation have been some of the paramount issues in the grid community. Several applications may be competing for resources. Some sort of admission control needs to be established to ensure sufficient resources exist before admitting any new resource requests. The initial allocation of resources may not be the final configuration to achieve the desired performance. The dynamic nature of grids necessitates a constant evaluation of the application's needs, of resources' availability, and an efficient reallocation strategy.

Being able to change the mapping of applications' components to physical resources requires having the ability to migrate whole or parts of the application's processes or data at runtime. Process migration requires being able to save the current state of the running application, ensuring no loss of messages while migration is in progress, and then restoring the state. Data migration, on the other hand, requires programming support from developers. Migration is an expensive procedure and should be performed only if it will yield gains in the overall performance of the running application. Process or data migration capabilities allow also load balancing.

3.2. Resource Profiling

Understanding the behavior of the application's topology helps to provide a good partitioning and an optimal placement of its components over decentralized heterogeneous resources. One of the important characteristics of distributed/parallel applications are the communication patterns between their several components. Applications can range from highly synchronized where components communicate frequently to massively parallel. An optimal mapping of application's components to physical resources must try to maximize the utilization of resources (CPU, memory, storage, etc.) while minimizing communication delays across links.

Changing effectively the configuration of running applications entails understanding the computational and communication requirements of their various components. One approach is to infer this information statically from performance models supplied by the users. The problem with this approach is that it may not be very accurate. Additionally several applications do not render themselves nicely to mathematical models due to their complexity. One way to address this issue is by learning the topology of the application at runtime through application-level profiling. This approach requires modifying existing applications to include profiling and might incur some overhead.

4. Dynamically Reconfigurable MPI Applications

Traditional MPI programs are designed with dedicated resources in mind. Developers need to know initially what resources are available and how to assign them to MPI processes. To permit a smooth migration of existing MPI applications to dynamic grid environments, MPI runtime environments should be augmented with middleware tools that free application developers from concerns about what resources are available and when to use them. Simply acquiring the resources is not enough to achieve peak MPI performance. Effective scheduling and load balancing decisions need to be performed continuously during the lifetime of a parallel application. This requires the ability to profile application behavior, monitor the underlying resources, and perform appropriate load balancing of MPI processes through process migration.

Process migration is a key requirement to enable malleable applications. We describe in what follows how we achieve MPI process migration. We then introduce our middleware-triggered reconfiguration.

4.1. Application Support: MPI Process Migration

MPI processes periodically get notified by the middleware of migration or reconfiguration requests. When a process receives a migration notification, it initiates checkpointing of its local data in the next synchronization point. Checkpointing is achieved through library calls that are inserted by the programmer in specific places in the application code. Iterative applications exhibit natural locations (at the beginning of each iteration) to place polling, checkpointing and resumption calls. When the process is first started, it checks whether it is a fresh process or it has been migrated. In the second case, it proceeds to data and process interconnectivity restoration.

In MPI, any communication between processes needs to be done as part of a *communicator*. An MPI communicator is an opaque object with a number of attributes, together with simple functions that govern its creation, use and destruction. An *intra-communicator* delineates a communication domain which can be used for point-to-point communications as well as collective communication among the members of the domain, while an *intercommunicator* allows communication between processes belonging to disjoint intracommunicators. MPI process migration requires careful update of any communicator that involves the migrating process. A migration request forces all running MPI processes to enter a reconfiguration phase where they all cooperate to update their shared communicators. The migrating process spawns a new process in the target location and sends it its local checkpointed data. Figure 1 describes the steps involved in managing the MPI communicators for a sample process migration. In the original communicator, communicator 1, P7 has received a migration request. P7 cooperates with the processes of communicator 1 to spawn the new process P0 in communicator 2, which will eventually replace it. The intercommunicator that results from this spawning is merged into one global communicator. Later, the migrating process is removed from the old communicator and the new process is assigned rank 7. The new process restores the checkpointed data from its local daemon and regains the same state of the migrating process. All processes then get a handle to the new communicator and the application resumes its normal execution.

4.2. Middleware-triggered Reconfiguration

Although MPI processes are augmented with the ability to migrate, middleware support is still needed to guide the application as to when it is appropriate to migrate processes and where to migrate them. IOS middleware analyzes both the underlying physical network resources and the application communication patterns to decide how applications

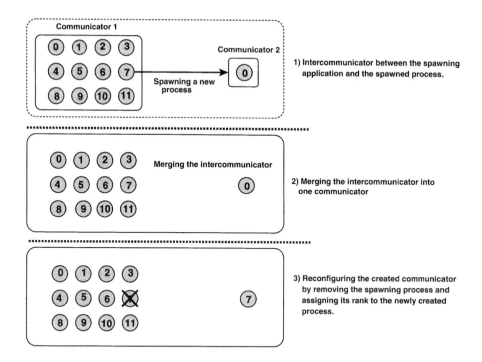

Figure 1. Steps involved in communicator handling to achieve MPI process migration.

should be reconfigured to accomplish load balancing through process migration and other non-functional concerns such as fault tolerance through process replication. Resource profiling and reconfiguration decisions are embodied into middleware agents whose behavior can be modularly modified to implement different resource management models. Figure 2 shows the architecture of an IOS agent and how it interacts with applications. Every agent has a profiling component that gathers both application and resource profiled information, a decision component that predicts based on the profiled information when and where to migrate application entities, and a protocol component that allows inter-agent communication. Application entities refer to application components. In the case of MPI applications, they refer to MPI processes.

The middleware agents form a virtual network. When new nodes join the network or existing nodes become idle, their corresponding agents contact peers to steal work [9]. We have shown that considering the application topology in the load balancing decision procedures dramatically improves throughput over purely random work stealing [7]. IOS supports two load-balancing protocols: 1) application topology sensitive load balancing and 2) network topology sensitive load balancing [7,8]. More details about IOS virtual network topologies and its load balancing strategies are presented in Section 5.

Applications communicate with the IOS middleware through clearly defined interfaces that permit the exchange of profiled information and reconfiguration requests. Applica-

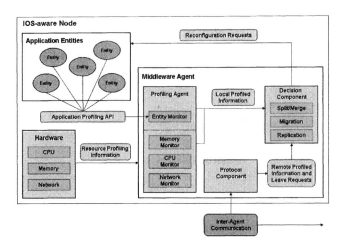

Figure 2. Architecture of a node in the Internet Operating System middleware (IOS). An agent collects profiling information and makes decisions on how to reconfigure the application based on its decisions, protocol, and profiling components.

tions need to support migration to react to IOS reconfiguration requests.

5. Middleware-level Load Balancing Policies

The IOS architecture has a decentralized architecture to ensure robustness, scalability and efficiency. Each IOS-ready node is equipped with a *middleware agent*. Agents organize themselves in various virtual network topologies to sense the underlying physical environment and trigger accordingly applications' reconfiguration. Decision components are embodied in each agent to evaluate the surrounding environment and decide based on a resource sensitive model (RSM) how to balance the resource consumption of the application's entities in the physical layer. In what follows we describe RSM, the different virtual topologies of the IOS agents, and the various load balancing policies implemented as part of the the IOS framework.

5.1. Resource Sensitive Model

A resource sensitive model has been used to reconfigure application's entities. A weight is assigned to each resource type (i.e, memory, processing power, storage, or bandwidth.) depending on its importance to the application. For instance, if the application is computation intensive, the CPU processing power's weight will dominate the other resources' weights. Similarly if the application is more communication intensive, more weight will be given to the communication resources such as bandwidth.

The purpose of this model is to balance the resource consumption among executing entities. The model has a decentralized approach whereby reconfiguration decisions are done at the level of each grid node. Each entity is profiled to gather its message sending

Notation	Explanation
A	A group of application entities.
$\mathcal{A}_{r,f}$	The amount of available resource r at node f.
$\mathcal{U}_{r,l,A}$	The amount of resource r used by A at node l.
R	The set of all resources to be considered by the resource sensitive model.
w_r	A weight for a given resource r, The weight is associated with a resource type, where $\sum w_r = 1$ over all the used resource types.
$\mathcal{C}_{l,f,A}$	The cost of migrating the set of application entities A from l to f in seconds
$\mathcal{E}_A$	The average life expectancy of the set of application entities A in seconds. We assume that $\mathcal{E}_A \geq 1$ s
$\Delta_{r,l,f,A}$	The overall improvement in performance the application would receive in terms of resource r by migrating the set of entities A from node l to node f, where $\Delta_{r,l,f,A}$ is normalized between -1 and 1. $\Delta_{r,l,f,A} = \frac{\mathcal{A}_{r,f} - \mathcal{U}_{r,l,A}}{\mathcal{A}_{r,f} + \mathcal{U}_{r,l,A}}$
$gain(l,f,A)$	A normalized measure of the overall improvement gained by migrating a set of entities A from local node l to foreign node f. $gain(l,f,A) = (\sum_r w_r * \Delta_{r,l,f,A}) - (\frac{\mathcal{C}_{l,f,A}}{(10 + log(\mathcal{E}_A))})$

Figure 3.   The resource sensitive model (RSM) used by the IOS decision component to determine which entities to migrate between nodes.

history with peer entities. This information is used to guide the reconfiguration decision to keep highly communicating entities as closely collocated as possible. The model provides a normalized measure of the improvement in the resource availability an entity or a group or entities would receive by migrating between nodes (see Figure 3 for details). The life expectancy of an entity is taken into consideration while trying to decide whether to migrate or not. The intuition behind this is that entities who are expected to have a short remaining life should not be migrated if the migration cost will exceed the remaining life expectancy. This is reflected in the used gain formula through amortizing the cost of migration over the life expectancy.

5.2. Virtual Network Topologies

We are considering *network sensitive* virtual network topologies which adjust themselves according to the underlying network topologies and conditions. We present two types of representative topologies: a *peer-to-peer* (p2p) topology and a *cluster-to-cluster* (c2c) topology. The p2p topology consists of several heterogeneous nodes inter-connected in a peer-to-peer fashion while the c2c topology imposes more structure on the virtual

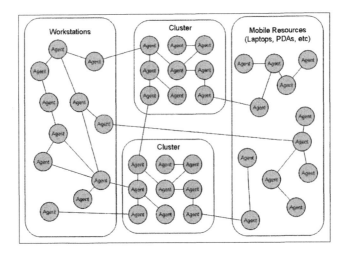

Figure 4. The peer-to-peer virtual network topology. Middleware agents represent heterogeneous nodes, and communicates with groups or peer agents. Information is propagated through the virtual network via these communication links.

network by grouping homogeneous nodes with low inter-network latencies into clusters.

A Network Sensitive Peer-to-Peer Topology (NSp2p)

Agents initially connect to the IOS virtual network either through other known agents or through a *peer server*. Peer servers act as registries for agent discovery. Upon contacting a peer server, an agent registers itself and receives a list of other agents (peers) in the virtual network. Peer servers simply aid in discovering peers in a virtual network and are not a single point of failure. They operate similarly to gnutella-hosts in Gnutella peer-to-peer networks [10]. After an agent has connected to the virtual network, it can discover new peers as information gets passed across peers. Agents can also dynamically leave the virtual network. Previous work discusses dynamic addition and removal of nodes in the IOS middleware [7].

A Network Sensitive Cluster-to-Cluster Topology (NSc2c)

In NSc2c, agents are organized into groups of virtual clusters (VCs), as shown in Figure 5. Each VC elects one agent to act as the cluster manager. VCs may reconfigure themselves as necessary by splitting or merging depending on the overall performance of the running applications. Cluster managers view each other as peers and organize themselves as a NSp2p virtual network topology.

5.3. Autonomous Load Balancing Strategies

IOS adopts two load balancing strategies depending on the kind of virtual topology used by the middleware agents.

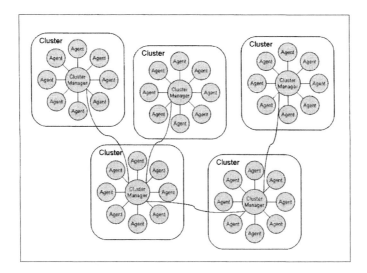

Figure 5. The cluster-to-cluster virtual network topology. Homogeneous agents elect a cluster manager to perform intra and inter cluster load balancing. Clusters are dynamically created and readjusted as agents join and leave the virtual network.

Peer-to-peer Load Balancing

Peer-to-peer load balancing is based on a simple but effective work stealing algorithm described by [9]. Agents configuring themselves in the NSp2p topology keep a list of peers and arrange these peers into four groups based on communication latency [11]: 1) local (0 to 10 ms), 2) regional (11 to 100 ms), 3) national (101 to 250 ms), and 4) global (251 ms and higher).

Agents on nodes which are *lightly loaded* (have more resources available than are currently being utilized) will periodically send reconfiguration request packets (RRPs) containing locally profiled information to a random peer in the local group. The decision component will then decide if it is beneficial to migrate entities to the source of the RRP according to the RSM. If it decides not to migrate any entities, the RRP is propagated to a local peer of the current agent. This progresses until the RRP's time to live has elapsed, or the desired entities have been migrated. If no migration happens, the source of the RRP will send another RRP to a regional peer, and if no migration occurs again, an RRP is sent nationally, then globally. As reconfiguration is only triggered by lightly loaded nodes, no overhead is incurred when the network is fully loaded, and thus this approach is stable [12].

Cluster-to-cluster Load Balancing

The cluster-to-cluster strategy attempts to utilize central coordination within VCs in order to obtain an overall picture of the applications' communication patterns and resource consumption as well as the physical network of the VC. A cluster manager acts as the central coordinator for a VC and utilizes this relatively global information to provide both intra- and inter-VC reconfiguration.

Every cluster manager sends periodic profiling requests to the agents in its respective VC. Every agent responds with information from its profiling component about the local entities and their resource consumption. The cluster manager uses this information to determine which entities should be migrated from the node with the least available resources to the node with the most available resources. Let n_1 and n_2 be the number of entities running on two nodes, and $r_{i,j}$ be the availability of resource i on node j with a resource weight w_i. The intra-cluster load balancing continuously attempts to achieve the relative equality of application's entities on nodes according to their relative resource availability: $\frac{n_1}{n_2} = \frac{\sum w_i r_{i,1}}{\sum w_i r_{i,2}}$.

For inter-cluster load balancing, NSc2c uses the same strategy as peer-to-peer load balancing, except that each cluster manager is seen as a peer in the network. The cluster managers decision component compares the heaviest loaded node to the lightest loaded node at the source of the RRP to determine which entities to migrate.

Migration Granularity

Our resource model supports both single migration and group migration of application entities. In single migration, the model is applied to determine an estimation of the gain that would be achieved from migrating an entity from one node to another. If the gain will be achieved by migrating a group of entities, single migration attempts to migration one entity at a time while group migration strategy will migrate a group of entities simultaneously. One advantage of group migration is that it helps to speed up load balancing. However it might cause trashing behavior if the load of the nodes fluctuates very frequently.

5.4. Experimental Evaluation

We have evaluated IOS different load balancing strategies using benchmarks that represent various degrees of computation to communication ratios. The benchmarks have been developed using Java and SALSA [13], a dialect of Java with high level programming abstractions for universal naming, asynchronous message passing, and coordination strategies. Both hypercube and tree application topologies represent applications that have a high communication to computation ratio. While the sparse and tree application topologies represent applications with a low communication to computation ratio.

The experiments were evaluated using two different physical environments to model Internet-like networks and Grid-like networks. The first physical network consists of 20 machines running Solaris and Windows operating systems with different processing power and different latencies to model the heterogeneity of Internet computing environments. The second physical network consists of 5 clusters with different inter-cluster network latencies. Each cluster consists of 5 homogeneous SUN Solaris machines. Machines in different clusters have different processing power.

Figures 6 and 7 show that the p2p topology performs better in Internet-like environments that lack structure for highly synchronized parallel and distributed applications, while the c2c topology is more suitable for grid-like environments that have a rather

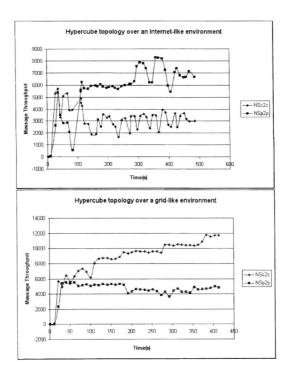

Figure 6. Message throughput for the hypercube application topology on Internet- and Grid-like environments.

hierarchical structure.

For a more thorough evaluation of IOS load balancing strategies, readers are referred to [8].

6. MPI Process Migration and Integration with IOS Middleware

MPI/IOS is implemented as a set of middleware services that interact with running applications through an MPI wrapper. The MPI wrapper uses a Process Checkpointing and Migration (PCM) library [14]. The MPI/IOS runtime architecture consists of the following components (see Figure 8): 1) the PCM-enabled MPI applications, 2) the wrapped MPI that includes the PCM API, the PCM library, and wrappers for all MPI native calls, 3) the MPI library, and 4) the IOS runtime components.

6.1. Process Checkpointing and Migration API

PCM is a user-level process checkpointing and migration library that acts on top of native MPI implementations and hides several of the issues involved in handling MPI communicators and updating them when new nodes join or leave the computation. This work does not alter existing MPI implementations and hence, allows MPI applications to

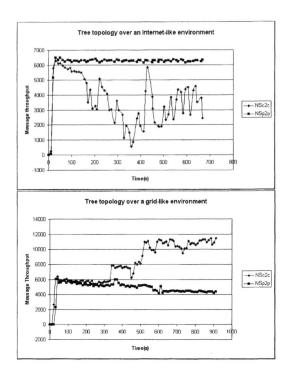

Figure 7. Message throughput for the tree application topology on Internet- and Grid-like environments.

continue to benefit from the various implementations and optimizations while being able to adapt to changing loads when triggered by IOS middleware load balancing agents.

MPI/IOS improves performance by allowing running processes to migrate to the processors with the best performance and collocating frequently communicating processes within small network latencies. The MPI-1 standard does not allow dynamic addition and removal of processes from MPI communicators. MPI-2 supports this feature; however existing applications need extensive modification to benefit from dynamic process management. In addition, application developers need to explicitly handle load balancing issues or interact with existing schedulers. The PCM runtime system utilizes MPI-2 dynamic features, however it hides how and when reconfiguration is done. We provide a semi-transparent solution to MPI applications in the sense that developers need to include only a few calls to the PCM API to guide the underlying middleware in performing process migration. Figures 10 and 11 show a skeleton of an MPI program and its modified version with the PCM calls to interface with IOS middleware.

Existing MPI applications interact with the PCM library and the native MPI implementation through a wrapper as shown in Figure 8. The wrapper MPI functions are provided to perform MPI-level profiling of process communication patterns. This profiled

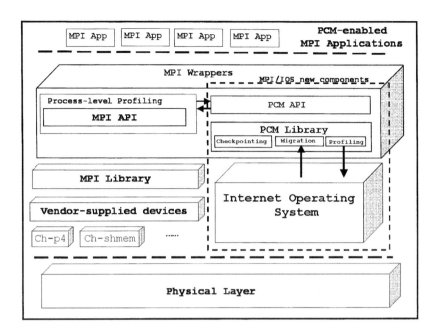

Figure 8. The layered design of MPI/IOS which includes the MPI wrapper, the PCM runtime layer, and the IOS runtime layer.

information is sent periodically to the IOS middleware agent through the PCM runtime daemon.

6.2. The PCM Library

Figure 9 shows an MPI/IOS computational node running MPI processes. A PCM daemon (PCMD) interacts with the IOS middleware and MPI applications. A PCMD is started in every node that actively participates in an application. A PCM dispatcher is used to start PCMDs in various nodes and used to discover existing ones. The application initially registers all MPI processes with their local daemons. The port number of a daemon is passed as an argument to mpiexec or read from a configuration file that resides in the same host.

Every PCMD has a corresponding IOS agent. There can be more than one MPI process in each node. The daemon consists of various services used to achieve process communication profiling, checkpointing and migration. The MPI wrapper calls record information pertaining to how many messages have been sent and received and their source and target process ranks. The profiled communication information is passed to the IOS profiling component. IOS agents keep monitoring their underlying resources and exchanging information about their respective loads.

When a node's available resources fall below a predefined threshold or a new idle node joins the computation, a *work steal* packet is propagated among the actively running

290

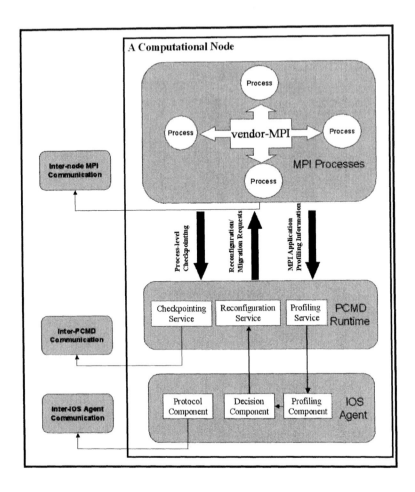

Figure 9. Architecture of a node running MPI/IOS enabled applications.

nodes. The IOS agent of a node responds to work stealing requests if it becomes overloaded and its decision component decides according to the resource management model which process(es) need(s) to be migrated. Otherwise, it forwards the request to an IOS agent in its set of peers. The decision component then notifies the reconfiguration service in the PCMD, which then sends a migration request to the desired process(es). At this point, all active PCMDs in the system are notified about the event of a reconfiguration. This causes all processes to cooperate in the next iteration until migration is completed and application communicators have been properly updated. Although this mechanism imposes some synchronization delay, it ensures that no messages are being exchanged while process migration is taking place and avoids incorrect behaviors of MPI communicators.

```
#include <mpi.h>
...

int main(int argc, char **argv) {
   //Declarations
   ....

   MPI_Init( &argc, &argv );

   MPI_Comm_rank( MPI_COMM_WORLD, &rank );
   MPI_Comm_size( MPI_COMM_WORLD, &totalProcessors );

   current_iteration = 0;

   //Determine the number of columns for each processor.
   dataWidth = (WIDTH-2) / totalProcessors;

   //Initialize and Distribute data among processors
   ...

   for(iterations=current_iteration; iterations<TOTAL_ITERATIONS; iterations++){

      // Data Computation.
      ...

      //Exchange of computed data with neighboring processes.
      // MPI_Send() || MPI_Recv()
      ...
   }

   // Data Collection
   ...
   MPI_Barrier( MPI_COMM_WORLD );

   MPI_Finalize();
   return 0;
}
```

Figure 10. Skeleton of the original MPI code of a heat diffusion problem.

6.3. Experimental Results

We have used an MPI program that computes a two-dimensional heat distribution matrix to evaluate the performance of process migration. This application models iterative parallel applications that are highly synchronized and therefore require frequent communication between the boundaries of the MPI processes. The original MPI code was manually instrumented by inserting PCM API calls to enable PCM checkpointing. It took 10 lines of PCM library calls to instrument this application, which consists originally of 350 lines of code.

The experimental test-bed consists of a multi-user cluster that consists of a heterogeneous collection of Sun computers running Solaris. We used a cluster of 20 nodes that consist of 4 dual-processor SUN Blade 1000 machines with 750 MHz per processor and 2 GB of memory, and 16 single-processor SUN Ultra 10 machines with 400MHz and 256 MB of memory. We used MPICH2 [15], a freely available implementation of the MPI-2 standard. Most of the experiments conducted try to demonstrate the usefulness of process migration when the allocated resources' load varies during the lifetime of the running application.

The goal of the first experiment was to determine the overhead incurred by the PCM

```
#include "pcm.h"
...

MPI_Comm PCM_COMM_WORLD;

int main(int argc, char **argv) {
   //Declarations
   ....
   int spawnrank=-1, current_iteration;
   PCM_Status pcm_status;
   MPI_Init( &argc, &argv );
   PCM_COMM_WORLD = MPI_COMM_WORLD;
   PCM_Init(PCM_COMM_WORLD);

   MPI_Comm_rank( PCM_COMM_WORLD, &rank );
   MPI_Comm_size( PCM_COMM_WORLD, &totalProcessors );

   spawnrank = PCM_Process_Status();

   if(spawnrank <= 0){
      current_iteration = 0;

      //Determine the number of columns for each processor.
      dataWidth = (WIDTH-2) / totalProcessors;

      //Initialize and Distribute data among processors
      ...
   }
   else{
      PCM_Load(spawnrank, "iterator",&current_iteration);
      PCM_Load(spawnrank, "datawidth", &dataWidth);
      prevData = (double *)calloc( (dataWidth+2)*WIDTH,sizeof(double) );
      PCM_Load(spawnrank, "myArray",prevData);
   }

   for(iterations=current_iteration; iterations<TOTAL_ITERATIONS; iterations++){
      pcm_status = PCM_Status(PCM_COMM_WORLD);
      if(pcm_status == PCM_MIGRATE){
         PCM_Store(rank, "iterator", &iterations, PCM_INT, 1);
         PCM_Store(rank, "datawidth", &dataWidth, PCM_INT, 1);
         PCM_Store(rank,"myArray", prevData, PCM_DOUBLE, (dataWidth+2)*WIDTH);

         PCM_COMM_WORLD = PCM_Reconfigure(PCM_COMM_WORLD,"mpiheat");

      }
      else if(pcm_status == PCM_RECONFIGURE)
      {
         PCM_COMM_WORLD =  PCM_Reconfigure(PCM_COMM_WORLD,"mpiheat");
         MPI_Comm_rank(PCM_COMM_WORLD, &rank);
      }

      // Data Computation.
      ...

      //Exchange of computed data with neighboring processes.
      // MPI_Send() || MPI_Recv()
      ...
   }

   // Data Collection
   ...
   MPI_Barrier( PCM_COMM_WORLD );

   PCM_Finalize(PCM_COMM_WORLD);
   MPI_Finalize();
   return 0;
}
```

Figure 11. Skeleton of the instrumented MPI code of a heat diffusion problem with PCM calls.

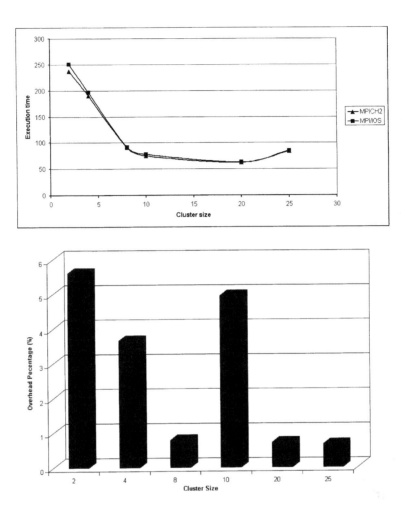

Figure 12. Overhead of the PCM library: Execution time of the heat application using different numbers of nodes with and without the PCM layer. The top figure shows the overall execution time while the bottom figure shows the percentage of the overhead of the PCM library

API. The heat distribution program was executed using both MPICH2 and MPI/IOS with several numbers of nodes. We run both tests under a controlled load environment to make sure that the machine load is somehow balanced and no migration will be triggered by the middleware. Both implementations demonstrated similar performance. Figure 12 shows that the overhead of the PCM library is less than 5% for several sizes of the cluster.

The second experiment aims at evaluating the impact of process migration. The cluster of 4 dual-processor nodes was used. Figures 13 and 14 show the breakdown of the itera-tions' execution time of the heat application using MPICH2 and MPI/IOS respectively.

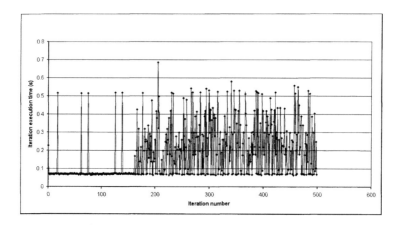

Figure 13. Breakdown of execution time of two-dimensional heat application iterations on a 4-node cluster using MPICH2.

The load of the participating nodes was controlled to provide the same execution environment for both runs. The application was allowed to run for a few minutes, after which the load of one of the nodes was artificially increased substantially. In Figure 13, the overall execution time of the application's iterations increased. The highly synchronized nature of this application forces all the processes to become as slow as the one assigned to the slowest processor. The application took 203.97 seconds to finish. Figure 14 shows the behavior of the same application under the same load conditions using MPI/IOS. At iteration 260, a new node joined the computation. This resulted in migration of an MPI process from the overloaded node to the available new node. Figure 14 shows how migration corrected the load imbalance. The application took 115.27 seconds to finish in this case, which is almost a 43% improvement over the non-adaptive MPICH2 run.

In a third experiment, we evaluated the adaptation of the heat application to changing loads. Figure 15 shows the behavior of the application's throughput during its lifetime. The total number of iterations per second gives a good estimate of how good the application is performing for the class of highly synchronized applications. We run the heat program using the 4 dual-processor cluster and increased the load in one of the participating nodes. MPI/IOS helped the application to adapt by migrating the process from the slow node to one of the cooperating nodes. The application was using only 3 nodes after migration; however, its overall throughput improved substantially. The application execution time improved with 33% compared to MPICH2 under the same load conditions. In Figure 16, we evaluated the impact of migration when a new node joins the computation. In this experiment, we used 3 fast machines and a slow machine. We increased the load of the slow machine while the application was running. The throughput of the application increased dramatically when the slow process migrated to a fast machine that joined the IOS network. The performance of the program improved with 79% compared with MPICH2.

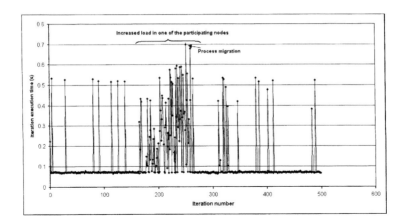

Figure 14. Breakdown of execution time of two-dimensional heat application iterations on a 4-node cluster using MPI/IOS prototype.

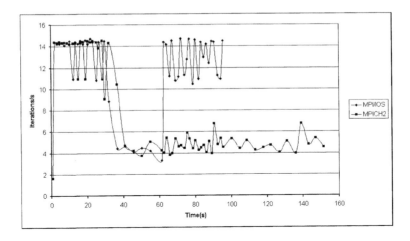

Figure 15. Measured throughput of the two-dimensional heat application using MPICH2 and MPI/IOS. The applications adapted to the load change by migrating the affected process to one of the participating nodes in the case of MPI/IOS.

To evaluate the cost of reconfiguration, we varied the problem data size and measured the overhead of reconfiguration in each case. In the conducted experiments, we started the application on a local cluster. We then introduced artificial load in one of the participating machines. One execution was allowed to reconfigure by migrating the suffering process to an available node that belongs to a different cluster, while the second execution was

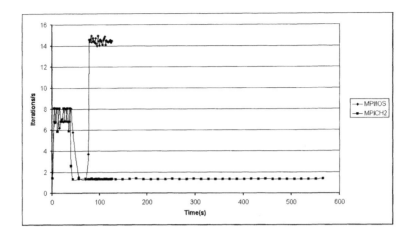

Figure 16. Measured throughput of the two-dimensional heat application using MPICH2 and MPI/IOS. The applications adapted to the load change by migrating the affected process to a fast machine that joined the computation in the case of MPI/IOS.

not allowed to reconfigure itself. The experiments in Figure 17 show that in the studied cases, reconfiguration overhead was negligible. In all cases, it accounted for less than 1% of the total execution time. The application studied is not data-intensive. We also used an experimental testbed that consisted of 2 clusters that belong to the same institution. So the network latencies were not significant. The reconfiguration overhead is expected to increase with larger latencies and larger data sizes. However, reconfiguration will still be beneficial in the case of large-scale long-running applications. Figure 18 shows the breakdown of the reconfiguration cost. It consists of checkpointing, loading checkpoints, and the synchronization involved in re-arranging the communicators in the case of MPI-based applications.

7. Related Work

There are a number of conditions that can introduce computational load imbalances during the lifetime of an application: 1) the application may have irregular or unpredictable workloads from, e.g., adaptive refinement, 2) the execution environment may be shared among multiple users and applications, and/or 3) the execution environment may be heterogeneous, providing a wide range of processor speeds, network bandwidth and latencies, and memory capacity. Dynamic load balancing (DLB) is necessary to achieve a good parallel performance when such imbalances occur. Most DLB research has targeted the application level (e.g., [3,16,17]), where the application itself continuously measures and detects load imbalances and tries to correct them by redistributing the data, or changing the granularity of the problem through domain repartitioning. Although such approaches have proved beneficial, they suffer from several limitations. First they are not

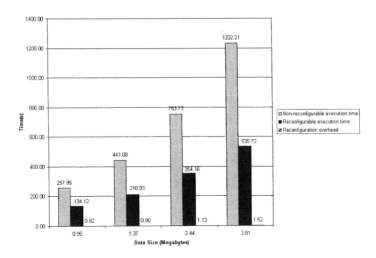

Figure 17.   Execution time for a reconfigurable and non-reconfigurable execution scenarios for different problem data sizes. The graph shows also the reconfiguration overhead for each problem size.

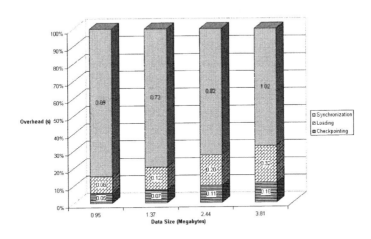

Figure 18.   Breakdown of the reconfiguration overhead for the experiment of Figure 17.

transparent to application programmers. They require complex programming and are domain specific. Second, they require applications to be amenable to data partitioning, and therefore will not be applicable in areas that require rigid data partitioning. Lastly, when these applications are run on the more dynamic grid, application-level techniques which have been applied successfully to heterogeneous clusters [16,18] may fall short in coping with the high fluctuations in resource availability and usage. Our research targets middleware-level DLB which allows a separation of concerns: load balancing and resource management are transparently dealt with by the middleware, while application programmers deal with higher level domain specific issues.

Several recent efforts have focused on middleware-level technologies for the emerging computational grids. Adaptive MPI (AMPI) [19,20] is an implementation of MPI on top of light-weight threads that balances the load transparently based on a parallel object-oriented language with object migration support. Load balancing in AMPI is done through migrating user-level threads that MPI processes are executed on. This approach limits the portability of process migration across different architectures since it relies on thread migration. Process swapping [21] is an enhancement to MPI that uses over-allocation of resources and improves performance of MPI applications by allowing them to execute on the best performing nodes. Our approach is different in that we do not need to over-allocate resources initially. Such a strategy, though potentially very useful, may be impractical in grid environments where resources join and leave and where an initial over-allocation may not be possible. We allow new nodes that become available to join the computational grid to improve the performance of running applications during their execution.

Other efforts have focused on process checkpointing and restart as a mechanism to allow applications to adapt to changing environments. Examples include CoCheck [22], starFish [23], and the SRS library [24]. Both CoCheck and starFish support checkpointing for fault-tolerance, while we provide this feature to allow process migration and hence load balancing. SRS supports this feature to allow application stop and restart. Our work differs in the sense that we support migration at a finer granularity. Process checkpointing is a non-functional concern that is needed to allow dynamic reconfiguration. To be able to migrate MPI processes to better performing nodes, processes need to save their state, migrate, and restart from where they left off. Application-transparent process checkpointing is not a trivial task and can be very expensive, as it requires saving the entire process state. Semi-transparent checkpointing provides a simple solution that has been proved useful for iterative applications [21,24]. API calls are inserted in the MPI program that informs the middleware of the important data structures to save. This is an attractive solution that can benefit a wide range of applications and does not incur significant overhead since only relevant state is saved.

8. Discussion and Future Work

This paper introduced several enhancements to MPI to allow for application reconfiguration through middleware-triggered dynamic load balancing. MPI/IOS improves MPI runtime systems with a library that allows process-level checkpointing and migration. This library is integrated with an adaptive middleware that triggers dynamic reconfiguration based on profiled resource usage and availability. The PCM library has been initially introduced in previous work [14]. We have made major redesign and improvements over the previous work, where the PCM architecture was centralized and supported only application-level migration. The new results show major improvements in flexibility, scalability, and performance. Our approach is portable and suitable for grid environments with no need to modify existing MPI implementations. Application developers need only insert a small number of API calls in MPI applications.

Our preliminary version of MPI/IOS has shown that process migration and middleware support are necessary to improve application performance over dynamic networks. MPI/IOS is a first step in improving MPI runtime environments with the support of dynamic reconfiguration. Our implementation of MPI process migration can be used on top of any implementation that supports the MPI-2 standard. It could also be easily integrated with grid-enabled implementations such as MPICH-G2 [25] once they become MPI-2 compliant. Our load balancing middleware could be combined with several advanced checkpointing techniques (e.g., [22,26–28]) to provide a better integrated software support for MPI application reconfiguration.

Future work includes: 1) using the MPI profiling interface to discover communication patterns in order to provide a better mapping between application topologies and environment topologies, 2) evaluating different resource management models and load balancing decision procedures, 3) extending MPI/IOS to support non-iterative applications, 4) changing the granularity of reconfiguration units through middleware-triggered splitting and merging of executing processes, and 5) targeting more complex applications.

Providing the necessary tools to allow reconfigurability of complex scientific applications in highly dynamic environments such as grids has become a primordial research direction. Reconfigurable grid computing will open up new frontiers and possibilities for scientists by providing the ability to simulate and solve larger and more interesting problems and to get involved in scientific collaborations at the national and international scale. This work, among others, is an important step in achieving this goal.

9. Acknowledgments

The authors would like to acknowledge the members of the Worldwide Computing Laboratory at Rensselaer Polytechnic Institute. In particular, our special thanks go to Joseph Chabarek and WeiJen Wang for their careful readings and comments. Any errors or omissions remain our own. The machines used in our experiments have been partially supported by two IBM SUR Awards. This work has been partially supported by NSF CAREER Award No. CNS-0448407.

REFERENCES

1. I. T. Foster, The anatomy of the grid: Enabling scalable virtual organizations, in: Euro-Par '01: Proceedings of the 7th International Euro-Par Conference Manchester on Parallel Processing, Springer-Verlag, 2001, pp. 1–4.
2. K. Clark, J. E. Flaherty, M. S. Shephard, Appl. Numer. Math., special ed. on Adaptive Methods for Partial Differential Equations 14.
3. J. D. Teresco, K. D. Devine, J. E. Flaherty, Numerical Solution of Partial Differ-

ential Equations on Parallel Computers, Springer-Verlag, 2005, Ch. Partitioning and Dynamic Load Balancing for the Numerical Solution of Partial Differential Equations.

4. Message Passing Interface Forum, MPI: A message-passing interface standard, The International Journal of Supercomputer Applications and High Performance Computing 8 (3/4) (1994) 159–416.

5. W. Gropp, E. Lusk, Dynamic process management in an MPI setting, in: Proceedings of the 7th IEEE Symposium on Parallel and Distributeed Processing, IEEE Computer Society, 1995.

6. Message Passing Interface Forum, MPI-2: Extensions to the Message-Passing Interface (1996).
   URL `citeseer.ist.psu.edu/396449.html`

7. T. Desell, K. E. Maghraoui, C. Varela, Load balancing of autonomous actors over dynamic networks, in: Hawaii International Conference on System Sciences, HICSS-37 Software Technology Track, Hawaii, 2004.

8. K. E. Maghraoui, T. Desell, C. Varela, Network sensitive reconfiguration of distributed applications, Tech. Rep. CS-05-03, Rensselaer Polytechnic Institute (2005).

9. R. D. Blumofe, C. E. Leiserson, Scheduling Multithreaded Computations by Work Stealing, in: Proceedings of the 35th Annual Symposium on Foundations of Computer Science (FOCS '94), Santa Fe, New Mexico, 1994, pp. 356–368.

10. Clip2.com, The Gnutella protocol specification v0.4 (2000).
    URL `http://www9.limewire.com/developer/gnutella_protocol_0.4.pdf`

11. T. T. Kwan, D. A. Reed, Performance of an infrastructure for worldwide parallel computing, in: 13th International Parallel Processing Symposium and 10th Symposium on Parallel and Distributed Processing, San Juan, Puerto Rico, 1999, p. 379.

12. N. G. Shivratri, P. Kreuger, M. Ginghal, Load distributing for locally distributed systems, IEEE Computer 25 (92) 33–34.

13. C. Varela, G. Agha, Programming dynamically reconfigurable open systems with SALSA, ACM SIGPLAN Notices. OOPSLA'2001 Intriguing Technology Track Proceedings 36 (12) (2001) 20–34, `http://www.cs.rpi.edu/~cvarela/oopsla2001.pdf`.

14. K. E. Maghraoui, J. E. Flaherty, B. K. Szymanski, J. D. Teresco, C. Varela, Adaptive computation over dynamic and heterogeneous networks, in: R. Wyrzykowski, J. Dongarra, M. Paprzycki, J. Wasniewski (Eds.), Proc. Fifth International Conference on Parallel Processing and Applied Mathematics (PPAM 2003), Vol. 3019 of Lecture Notes in Computer Science, Springer Verlag, Czestochowa, 2004, pp. 1083–1090.

15. Argone National Laboratory, MPICH2, `http://www-unix.mcs.anl.gov/mpi/mpich2`.

16. R. Elsasser, B. Monien, R. Preis, Diffusive load balancing schemes on heterogeneous networks, in: Proceedings of the twelfth annual ACM symposium on Parallel algorithms and architectures, ACM Press, 2000, pp. 30–38.

17. J. E. Flaherty, R. M. Loy, C. Özturan, M. S. Shephard, B. K. Szymanski, J. D. Teresco, L. H. Ziantz, Parallel structures and dynamic load balancing for adaptive finite element computation, Applied Numerical Mathematics 26 (1998) 241–263.

18. J. D. Teresco, J. Faik, J. E. Flaherty, Resource-aware scientific computation on a heterogeneous cluster, Computing in Science & Engineering 7 (2) (2005) 40–50.

19. M. A. Bhandarkar, L. V. Kaleé;, E. de Sturler, J. Hoeflinger, Adaptive load balancing

for MPI programs, in: Proceedings of the International Conference on Computational Science-Part II, Springer-Verlag, 2001, pp. 108–117.
20. C. Huang, O. Lawlor, L. V. Kaleé, Adaptive MPI, in: Proceedings of the 16th International Workshop on Languages and Compilers for Parallel Computing (LCPC 03), College Station, Texas, 2003.
21. O. Sievert, H. Casanova, A simple MPI process swapping architecture for iterative applications, International Journal of High Performance Computing Applications 18 (3) (2004) 341–352.
22. G. Stellner, Cocheck: Checkpointing and process migration for MPI, in: Proceedings of the 10th International Parallel Processing Symposium, IEEE Computer Society, 1996, pp. 526–531.
23. A. Agbaria, R. Friedman, Starfish: Fault-tolerant dynamic MPI programs on clusters of workstations, in: Proceedings of the The Eighth IEEE International Symposium on High Performance Distributed Computing, IEEE Computer Society, 1999, p. 31.
24. S. S. Vadhiyar, J. J. Dongarra, SRS - a framework for developing malleable and migratable parallel applications for distributed systems, in: Parallel Processing Letters, Vol. 13, 2003, pp. 291–312.
25. N. T. Karonis, B. Toonen, I. Foster, MPICH-G2: a grid-enabled implementation of the Message Passing Interface, J. Parallel Distrib. Comput. 63 (5) (2003) 551–563.
26. R. Batchu, A. Skjellum, Z. Cui, M. Beddhu, J. P. Neelamegam, Y. Dandass, M. Apte, MPI/FTTM: Architecture and taxonomies for fault-tolerant, message-passing middleware for performance-portable parallel computing, in: Proceedings of the 1st International Symposium on Cluster Computing and the Grid, IEEE Computer Society, 2001.
27. G. Bosilca, A. Bouteiller, F. Cappello, S. Djilali, G. Fedak, C. Germain, T. Herault, P. Lemarinier, O. Lodygensky, F. Magniette, V. Neri, A. Selikhov, MPICH-V: toward a scalable fault tolerant MPI for volatile nodes, in: Proceedings of the 2002 ACM/IEEE conference on Supercomputing, IEEE Computer Society Press, 2002, pp. 1–18.
28. G. E. Fagg, J. Dongarra, FT-MPI: Fault tolerant MPI, supporting dynamic applications in a dynamic world, in: Proceedings of the 7th European PVM/MPI Users' Group Meeting on Recent Advances in Parallel Virtual Machine and Message Passing Interface, Springer-Verlag, 2000, pp. 346–353.

Applications

Grid Computing: The New Frontier of High Performance Computing
Lucio Grandinetti (Editor)
© 2005 Elsevier B.V. All rights reserved.

Messaging in Web Service Grid with Applications to Geographical Information Systems

Geoffrey Fox, Shrideep Pallickara, Galip Aydin and Marlon Pierce

Community Grids Lab, Indiana University,
501 North Morton Street, Bloomington, Indiana, United States

Several efforts to design globally distributed computing systems have converged to the principles of message-centric, service-oriented architectures. As realized through several Web Service specifications, these provide the scaling, robustness, and reliability for delivering distributed capabilities that collectively form virtual organizations. Service architectures are based a clean separation between service implementations and their communication patterns. In this article, we examine several consequences of this separation. First, services should exist on a general purpose, software messaging substrate. Services (and their containers) inherit various qualities of service directly from this substrate: we implement message level security, reliability, events, and notifications in the message routing middleware. Second, all communications involving services should be treated as messages. This applies not only to remote procedure call-style messages and notifications, but to streaming data as well. Finally, services are often domain-specific, but collective applications are cross-domain. Using message-based Geographical Information Systems as an example, we illustrate how a Grid of services is really a Grid of Grids: a composition of capabilities developed independently of specific end applications.

1. Introduction

As standards such as SOAP 1.2, WSDL 2.0, and WS-Addressing become widely implemented and deployed, the initial concepts and implementations of Web Services as "remote procedure calls for the Web" are giving way to a more message-oriented, service-oriented approach. Such systems place an emphasis on managing secure, reliable messages that may be delivered in any number of ways across multiple routing SOAP intermediaries.

As we discuss in this article, all communications in SOA-based systems are messages. Further, a powerful way to implement these systems is to place the service "islands" on a software-level messaging substrate that implements efficient routing, security, reliability and other qualities of service. As we will show, such systems support messages of all types, from infrequent update notification events to continuous streams. We suggest that in the complex evolving technology scene today, not only services but their collection into systems of higher functionality should be as decoupled as possible in architecture and tight timing constraints. This we call the principle of building "Grids of Grids of Simple Services"

Many important Grid applications in real-time data mining involve all of these message types. We discuss a GIS (Geographical Information System) example from our SERVOGrid (Solid earth Research Virtual Observatory) work that uses the NaradaBrokering messaging system for managing data streams from GPS stations. We are in the process of connecting these to RDAHMM, a time series data analysis program useful for mode change detection. These streaming services form one sub-Grid in the "Grid of Grids" system supporting solid earth science and also containing (sub)-Grids involving code execution services and information/metadata services.

2. Service Oriented Architectures for Grids

With the advent of the Open Grid Computing Architecture (OGSA) [1] and the UK e-Science program, Grid computing has aligned itself with Web Service standards activities: Grid infrastructure will be Web Service infrastructure, although the aggressiveness in developing and adopting extensions is a matter of debate. The current general consensus is that Web and Grid Services should follow Service Oriented Architecture (SOA) principles, such as discussed by the World Wide Web Consortium's Web Service Architecture working group. We summarize key SOA features as follows, following Ref. [2]:

1. SOAs are composed of services that present programmatic access to resources to remote client applications. Typical basic (atomic) services include data access (logically wrapping storage technologies such as databases and file systems) and the ability to run and manage remote applications. More complicated services may be composed of these basic services using workflow expression languages coupled with workflow engines.
2. Services communicate using messages. Messages are usually encoded using SOAP [26]. The asynchronous nature of messaging is one of the keys to Grid and Web Service scalability beyond the intranets.
3. SOAs are metadata rich. We must describe service interfaces, provide descriptions of services so that we know how to use them, provide look-up registries to find service URLs, and so forth.

Much debate has gone into refining concepts such as stateful conversations and stateful resources accessed through services [3]. However, we believe that the other two characteristics, messaging and metadata, have been somewhat overlooked. In this paper, we are particularly interested in the messaging infrastructure needed to realize such things as the SOAP message processing model (particularly in SOAP 1.2), which allows for multiple intermediaries that will need to process header information required by WS-Addressing and WS-Security.

These issues have direct relevance to scientific Grid applications, which need to go beyond remote procedure calls in client-server interactions to support integrated distributed applications that couple databases, high performance computing codes, and visualization codes with real time streaming data [4, 5]. These coordinated, composite applications are asynchronous by their nature: applications may take hours or days to complete. Message-based Grids, events, and service coordination are not just abstract Grid research issues: they are needed to meet the requirements of real science application Grids, as we discuss below.

In our discussion of these topics, we emphasize the message orientation of SOAs and Web Service Grids. Messages may range from infrequent notification events to remote method invocations/responses to streaming data. Various Web Service specifications (Sections 2 and 3) are intended to provide the underpinnings of such a system, allowing for asynchronous communication, reliability, message routing, and security. We discuss our implementation of these specifications on top of NaradaBrokering, a general purpose messaging software substrate (Sections 4 and 5). The implication of SOA principles is that service implementations will proliferate in various domains, which may be composed in various ways for specific applications. We have dubbed this composition of services as a "Grid of Grids," discussed in Section 6. Finally, in Sections 7 and 8 we present an example application within a Grid of Grids: streaming data control of GPS stations to support real-time data mining.

3. Messaging in Web/Grid Environments

Messaging is a fundamental primitive in distributed systems. Entities communicate with each other through the exchange of messages, which can encapsulate information of interest such as application data, errors and faults, system conditions, search and discovery of resources. A related concept is that of *notifications* where entities receive messages based on their registered interest in certain occurrences or situations. Messaging and notifications are especially important in the Service Oriented Architecture (SOA) model engendered by Web Services. Here, Web Services interact with each other through the exchange of messages.

In this section, we first discuss message exchange patterns and also briefly review two specifications in the area of notifications. There are two main entities involved in a notification: the *source* which is the generator of notifications and the *sink* which is interested in these notifications. A sink first needs to register its *interest* in a situation, this operation is generally referred to as a *subscribe* operation. The source first wraps *occurrences* into notification messages. Next, the source checks to see if the message satisfies the constraints specified in the previously registered subscriptions. If so, the source routes the message to the sink. This routing of the message from the source to the sink is referred to as a notification. It should be noted that there could be multiple sources and sinks within the system. Furthermore, each sink could register its interests with multiple sources, while a given source can manage multiple sinks. The complexity of the subscriptions registered by a sink could vary from simple strings such as "Weather/Warnings" to complex XPath or SQL queries. Some application examples are given in Section 8.

We take the point of view that all communications within an SOA-based Grid should be treated as messages. This applies equally well to event notifications as to data streams. The capabilities of the messaging substrate, and the associated Web Service standards that define qualities of service, may be applied equally to all of these messages.

3.1 WSDL Message Exchange Patterns

Messaging is fundamental to Web Services, and WSDL [6], which describes these services, facilitate the description of various message exchange patterns (hereafter MEP) that are possible between service endpoints. Since these MEPs are defined to be part of the WSDL document, any node wishing to interact with the service knows both the *sequence* and the

308

cardinality of messages associated with a given WSDL operation. WSDL 1.1 defined a basic set of MEPs; this has been expanded upon in WSDL 2.0.

WSDL 1.1 describes four MEPs defining the sequence and cardinality of abstract messages –– *In, Out, Fault* – that are part of a WSDL operation. The MEPs governing the exchanges between a service **S** and a node **N** are *one-way, request/response, notification* and *solicit*. A one-way message comprises a single *Out* message from a service **S** to node **N**. A request/response comprises an *In* message sent by a node **N** that is followed by an *Out* message by the service **S**. The notification MEP is simply an *Out* message from a service **S** to a node **N**. Finally, a solicit MEP is an *Out* message from service **S** followed by an *In* message from node **N**. It must be noted that the *Out* message in the notification MEP and the *In* message in the solicit MEP can also be a Fault message.

WSDL 2.0 has defined 4 additional MEPs *Robust In-Only, In-Optional-Out, Robust Out-Only* and *Out-Optional-In* which are extensions to the four MEPs that were defined in WSDL 1.1. These patterns occur because of the new fault propagation rules that are part of WSDL 2.0. The MEPs with the *optional* tag within them are patterns that comprise one or two messages, with the second message being a *Fault* that was triggered because of the first message in the pattern. The MEPs with the *robust* tag within them are patterns with exactly one message, however a fault may be triggered because of the first message.

3.2 WS-Eventing

Figure 3 depicts the chief components in WS-Eventing [7] a specification from Microsoft and IBM. When the sink subscribes with the source, the source includes information regarding the subscription manager in its response. Subsequent operations –– such as getting the status of, renewing and unsubscribing –– pertaining to previously registered subscriptions are all directed to the subscription manager. The source sends both notifications and a message signifying the end of registered subscriptions to the sink.

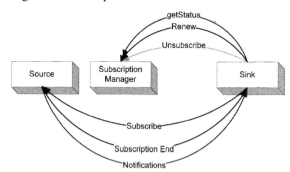

Figure 1: WS-Eventing - Chief components

3.3 WS-Notification

The WS-Notification specification refers to a set of specifications comprising WS-BaseNotification [8], WS-Brokered Notification [9] and WS-Topics [10]. WS-BaseNotification standardizes exchanges and interfaces for producers and consumers of notifications. WS-Brokered Notification facilitates the deployment of Message Oriented Middleware (MOM) to enable brokered notifications between producers and consumers of the notifications. WS-Topics deals with the organization of subscriptions and defines dialects associated with subscription expressions; this is used in the conjunction with exchanges that take place in WS-BaseNotification and WS-Brokered Notification. WS-Notification currently also uses two related specifications from the WSRF specification; WS-ResourceProperties [11] to describe data associated with resources, and WS-ResourceLifetime [12] to manage lifetimes associated with subscriptions and publisher registrations (in WS-BrokeredNotifications).

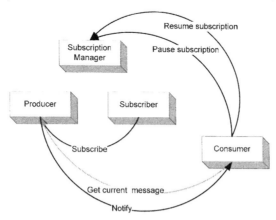

Figure 2: WS-BaseNotification - Chief components

Figure 1 depicts the chief components of the WS-BaseNotification specification. Also, depicted in this figure are the interactions (along with the directions) that these components have with each other. In WS-BaseNotification, a subscriber registers a consumer with a producer, which in turn includes information regarding the subscription manager in its response. Consumers can pause and resume subscriptions, with no messages being delivered while the subscription is in a paused state. Resumption of subscriptions after a pause can entail replay of all notifications that occurred in the interim. After a disconnect, either due to a scheduled downtime or failure, a consumer may also retrieve the last message issued by a producer. Finally, notifications from the producer are issued directly to the consumer. In WS-Notification each subscription is considered to be a resource (more appropriately a WS-Resource [13]). A consumer can use WS-ResourceLifetime or WS-ResourceProperties to manage lifetimes and properties associated with these subscriptions.

310

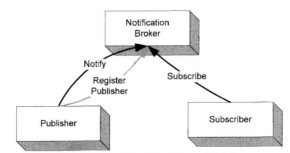

Figure 3: WS-BrokeredNotification - Chief components

Figure 2 depicts the chief components of the WS-BrokeredNotification specification. The notification broker interface performs the function of an intermediary between the producers and consumers of content. The broker is responsible for managing the subscriptions and also for routing the notifications to the subscriber. Furthermore, the broker also maintains a topic space (based on the WS-Topics specification) that allows consumers to review the list of topics to which publishers publish. It should be noted that each topic is also a resource and can be inspected for its properties such as *dialect* and *topic expressions*.

4. Reliable Messaging in Web/Grid Environments

As web services have become dominant in the Internet and Grid systems landscape, a need to ensure guaranteed delivery of interactions (encapsulated in messages) between services has become increasingly important. This highly important and complex area was previously being addressed in the Web Services community using homegrown, proprietary, application specific solutions. It should be noted that the terms guaranteed delivery and reliable delivery tend to be used interchangeably to signify the same concept.

Reliable delivery of messages is now a key component of the Web Services roadmap, with two promising, and competing, specifications in this area viz. WS-Reliability (hereafter WSR) [14] from OASIS and WS-ReliableMessaging (hereafter WSRM) [15] from IBM and Microsoft among others

4.1 WS-ReliableMessaging and WS-Reliability

The specifications – WSR and WSRM – both of which are based on XML, address the issue of ensuring reliable delivery between two service endpoints. Both the specifications use positive acknowledgements to ensure reliable delivery. This in turn implies that error detections, initiation of error corrections and subsequent retransmissions of "missed" messages can be performed at the sender side. A sender may also proactively initiate corrections based on the non-receipt of acknowledgements within a pre-defined interval. WSRM also incorporates support for negative acknowledgements which facilitates sender side error corrections.

The specifications also address the related issues of ordering and duplicate detection of messages issued by a source. A combination of these issues can also be used to facilitate exactly once delivery. Both the specifications facilitate guaranteed exactly-once delivery of messages, a very important quality of service that is highly relevant for transaction oriented applications; specifically banking, retailing and e-commerce.

Both the specifications also introduce the concept of a group (also referred to as a sequence) of messages. All messages that are part of a group of messages share a common group identifier. The specifications explicitly incorporate support for this concept by including the group identifier in protocol exchanges that take place between the two entities involved in reliable communications. Furthermore, in both the specifications the qualities of service constraints that can be specified on the delivery of messages are valid only within a group of messages, each with its own group identifier.

The specifications also introduce timer based operations for both messages (application and control) and group of messages. Individual and group of messages are considered invalid upon the expiry of timers associated with them. Finally, the delivery protocols in the specifications also incorporate the use of timers to initiate retransmissions and to time out retransmission attempts.

In terms of security both the specifications aim to leverage the WS-Security [16] specification, which facilitates message level security. Message level security is independent of the security of the underlying transport and facilitates secure interactions over insecure communication links.

The specifications also provide for notification and exchange of errors in processing between the endpoints involved in reliable delivery. The range of errors supported in these specifications can vary from an inability to decipher a message's content to complex errors pertaining to violations in implied agreements between the interacting entities.

5. Messaging Infrastructures for SOA

The SOAP processing model supports a general purpose messaging strategy of multiple, distributed SOAP processing nodes that can act as intermediaries, routing nodes, and final destinations. This model goes well beyond the standard client-server, remote procedure call methodology that many current Web Service implementations use. In this section, we review the general requirements for building a message oriented middleware (MoM) that will realize the SOAP processing model as well as several Web Service extensions. A more detailed discussion of these topics is given in [17]. Such middleware messaging substrates may, in addition, provide additional levels of support that are logically separate from services and messages, such as performance, fault tolerance, and reliability. The Community Grids Lab has for several years been developing a messaging substrate NaradaBrokering [18]-24. NaradaBrokering is an open-source, distributed messaging infrastructure. The smallest unit of this distributed messaging infrastructure intelligently processes and routes messages, while working with multiple underlying communication protocols. We refer to this unit as a *broker*. In NaradaBrokering communication is asynchronous and the system can support different interactions by encapsulating them in specialized messages, which we call *events*. Events can encapsulate information pertaining to transactions, data interchange, method invocations, system conditions and finally the search, discovery and subsequent sharing of resources. NaradaBrokering places no constraints on the size, rate, or scope of the interactions encapsulated within these events or the number of entities present in the system.

In NaradaBrokering we impose a hierarchical, cluster-based structure on the broker network [19]. This cluster-based architecture allows NaradaBrokering to support large heterogeneous client configurations. The routing of events within the substrate is very efficient [21] since for every event, the associated targeted brokers are usually the only ones involved in disseminations. Furthermore, every broker, either targeted or en route to one, computes the shortest path to reach target destinations while eschewing links and brokers that have failed or have been failure-suspected.

5.1 Services within Messaging Infrastructures

In messaging systems, entities should be able to specify constraints on the Quality of Service (QoS) related to the delivery of messages. The QoS pertain to the reliable delivery, order, duplicate elimination, security and size of the published events and their encapsulated payloads. We have researched these issues for delivery [22] of events to authorized/registered entities. The delivery guarantee is satisfied in the presence of both link and node failures. Entities are also able to retrieve events that were missed during failures or prolonged disconnects. The scheme also facilitates exactly-once ordered delivery of events.

5.1.1 Reliable Delivery Service and Replay of events

The NaradaBrokering substrate's reliable delivery guarantee holds true in the presence of four conditions.

1. Broker and Link Failures: The delivery guarantees are satisfied in the presence of individual or multiple broker and link failures. The entire broker network may fail. Guarantees are met once the broker network (possibly a single broker node) recovers.
2. Prolonged Entity disconnects: After disconnects an entity can retrieve events missed in the interim.
3. Stable Storage Failures: The delivery guarantees must be satisfied once the storage recovers.
4. Unpredictable Links: Events can be lost, duplicated or re-ordered in transit over individual links.

The scheme also facilitates ordered and *exactly once* delivery of events. More recently the reliable delivery framework has been extended to incorporate support for multiple replications. Any of these replicas could be used for recovery from failures or to ensure reliable delivery. The replicas themselves may fail and a recovering replica arrives at a consistent after exchanging a series of control messages with the other replicas.

The NaradaBrokering reliable delivery scheme has been extended to provide support replays of events. A variety of replay requests formats are supported. Furthermore, a time differential service which preserves the time-spacing between successive events in the replay is also available.

5.1.2 Dealing with large payload sizes: Compression/Fragmentation

Web Service messaging systems that support science Grids should provide a means for managing very large data transmissions. Compression and decompression are obviously desirable capabilities. Additionally, message fragmentation/coalescence can be used to verify completed and uncorrupted large transmissions, and also support partial re-transmissions in the case of failures. The latter efficiently eliminates the need to re-transmit the entire message in the case of a few incorrectly delivered fragments. Fragmentation also allows for parallel transmission within the MoM.

This capability in tandem with the reliable delivery service was used to augment GridFTP to provide reliable delivery of large files across failures and prolonged disconnects. The recoveries and retransmissions involved in this application are very precise. Additional details can be found in Ref [23]. Here, we had a proxy collocated with the GridFTP client and the GridFTP server. This proxy, a NaradaBrokering entity, utilizes NaradaBrokering's fragmentation service to fragment large payloads (> 1 GB) into smaller fragments and publish fragmented events. Upon reliable delivery at the server-proxy, NaradaBrokering reconstructs original payload from the fragments and delivers it to the GridFTP server.

5.1.3   Time and Buffering Services

Proper time sequence ordering of messages and events is of utmost importance in many applications, such as audio/video collaboration systems. The NaradaBrokering system provides this capability through an implementation of the Network Time Protocol (NTP). The NaradaBrokering TimeService [24] allows NaradaBrokering processes (brokers and entities alike) to synchronize their timestamps using the NTP algorithm with multiple time sources (usually having access to atomic time clocks) provided by various organizations, like NIST and USNO. The NaradaBrokering time service plays an important role in collaborative environments and can be used to time order events from disparate sources. The substrate includes a buffering service which can be used to buffer replays from multiple sources, time order these events and then proceed to release them.

5.1.4   Security Services

Messaging systems possess many interesting requirements not present in client-server systems. The latter may be suitably handled by transport level security, but in MoMs the messages may pass through many intermediaries and may be destined for multiple recipients. The NaradaBrokering security framework [25] provides a scheme for end-to-end secure delivery of messages between entities within the system. The scheme protects an event in its traversal over multiple, possibly insecure, transport hops. Entities can verify the integrity and source of these events, before proceeding to process the encrypted payload.

5.2   Broker Discovery

Since accesses to services are mediated through the distributed broker substrate it is essential that an entity connect to a broker that maximizes its ability to utilize the hosted services. Furthermore, since the broker network is a very dynamic and fluid system, where broker processes may join and leave the broker network at arbitrary times and intervals, it is not possible for an entity to assume that a given broker is available at all times. Static solutions to this problem might result in a certain known remote broker being accessed over and over again. This in turn causes degradations due to poor bandwidth utilizations. The broker discovery process in the NaradaBrokering substrate operates on the current state of the broker network and ensures that a discovered broker is the *nearest* available one; where nearest corresponds to network proximities or latencies. In this scheme newly added brokers within overloaded broker *clusters* in the substrate are assimilated faster since the discovery process allows these brokers to be preferentially selected. This scheme thus allows brokers to be added to enable to the system to scale.

5.3 Support for Web/Grid Service specifications

The substrate has recently incorporated support for Web/Grid Services. The substrate incorporates support for several Web/Grid service specifications such as WS-Eventing, WS-ReliableMessaging and WS-Reliability. Work on the implementation of the WS-Notification suite of specifications is currently an on-going effort. It must be noted that almost all Web/Grid Service specifications leverage the SOAP [26] specification. We are currently also incorporating support for SOAP within the substrate. This would allow the substrate to perform certain services for SOAP messages, function as a SOAP intermediary, and also facilitate the routing of SOAP messages. Web/Grid Services can then send SOAP messages directly to the substrate. Another area that we intend to research further is the support for high-performance transport of SOAP messages.

6. Support for SOAP within messaging substrates

SOAP has emerged as the de facto standard for encapsulating and transporting various Web Services interactions. SOAP, along with WSDL and UDDI [27], has been included as part of the WS-I Basic Profile [18]. Addressing support for SOAP within the substrate is thus central to our strategy. Subsequent sub-sections describe our approach to providing support for Web Services within the substrate. By incorporating the SOAP processing stack into the substrate applications residing in different hosting environments (C++ based gSOAP, .NET-based WSE, or Perl-based SOAP::Lite) can interact with the substrate. Furthermore, so long as these Web Services are connected to the substrate they can partake from all the QoS provided to the NaradaBrokering clients. This includes features such as failure resilience and recovery from failures. This approach requires the substrate to function as a SOAP node which conforms to the SOAP processing model governing the actions that need to taken upon receipt of a SOAP message. Specifically in SOAP 1.2 the substrate needs to deal with the role (in SOAP 1.1 this corresponds to the actor attribute), mustUnderstand and the relay attributes. The substrate will issue a fault if the message contains any headers targeted to its role, with the mustUnderstand attribute set, which it cannot process.

Finally it must be noted that the substrate may forward or interact with other SOAP intermediaries inside or outside the substrate to accomplish certain functions. The SOAP 1.2 model allows the relay attribute to be incorporated into SOAP message headers to facilitate such an interaction. In some cases, such as WS-Eventing and WS-Notification, the substrate can provide support for delegated interactions such as information regarding the list of topics, management of subscriptions and their lifetimes, and replays of notification messages to recovering endpoints. Another related capability is that of a *proxy* where the substrate can interact with other Web Services on behalf of a non-Web Service endpoint.

6.1 Federation of competing specifications

The substrate can facilitate federation between competing specifications in the same target area. Examples of such scenarios include WS-ReliableMessaging (WSRM) and WS-Reliability in the reliable delivery area and WS-Eventing and WS-Notification in the area of notifications. Such a federation would enable service endpoints from competing specifications to interoperate with each other. This capability requires the substrate to map not only the structural elements of the SOAP messages but do so while ensuring that the semantics encapsulated within the original message are also mapped accordingly. It is entirely possible that in some cases it might not be possible to find a semantically equivalent operation in a target specification; here we may either throw faults or provide for custom extensions.

6.2   Functioning as a SOAP intermediary

The substrate can provide a variety of services to SOAP messages. This includes support for compressing and decompressing, fragmenting and coalescing data encapsulated in the SOAP body, and logging of messages for subsequent replays among others. A substrate operates in variety of roles. A SOAP message can include such processing directives for the substrate through SOAP headers targeted to it as a SOAP intermediary. Additionally the substrate can provide support for conversion between different encoding schemes that may be employed in a SOAP message.

6.3   Support for Filters/Handlers

In this section we include a brief description of the typical deployment of services and accesses to these services. We also discuss extensions that most hosting environments provide for augmenting the behavior and functionality of service endpoints. This lays the groundwork for our strategy for making the substrate permeate service endpoints.

To facilitate incremental addition of capabilities to service endpoints one can also configure *filters* (examples include filters for encryption, compression, logging etc.) in the processing path between the service endpoints. Since the service endpoints communicate using SOAP messages these filters operate on SOAP messages. Several of these filters can be cascaded to constitute a *filter pipeline*. Services are generally hosted within a hosting environment also known as a *container*. The container provides a variety of services which the service implementation can use. For example, a service implementation need not worry about communication details since this necessary functionality would be implemented within a *container component* such as servlets in the Java J2EE environment. This component in tandem with the container *support classes* is responsible for packaging data received over the wire into data structures that can be processed by the service implementation. An instance of the web component is typically automatically generated by the container during the *deployment* phase of the Web Service. This scenario is depicted in Figure 1. It is possible to deploy services without a container. In the simplest case one may simply use the TCP protocol for communications and reconstruct SOAP messages from byte packets received over a socket; a custom deployment component can used to configure filter pipelines.

316

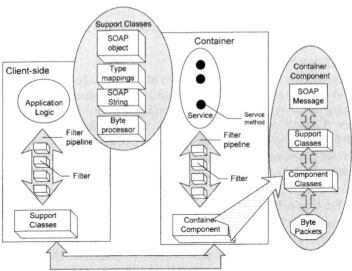

Figure 4: Deployment of services and filter-pipelines

Filters within a pipeline operate on SOAP messages encapsulating invocation requests or responses. In the case of a service this pipeline is configured between the container component and the service, while in the case of clients this is configured between the support classes and the application logic. It should also be noted that individual filters are autonomous entities that have access to the entire SOAP message encapsulating the request/invocation. Individual filters are allowed to modify both the header and body elements of SOAP messages. The order in which filters operate on messages needs to be consistent, for example the stages at which encryption/decryption and compression/decompression take place at the service endpoints should be consistent otherwise unpredictable results/behavior may ensue.

There are three advantages to utilizing the filter approach. First, it entails no changes to the service endpoints: this facilitates incremental addition of capabilities. Second, filters can be developed and tested independent of the service endpoints thus providing greater robustness. Finally, the filter approach promotes code reuse since different filters corresponding to security, compressions, logging or timestamps can be utilized by multiple services.

The substrate can provide additional capabilities by permeating a service endpoint. Specially designed filters allow the incremental addition of capabilities to existing services. These filters encapsulate several of the substrate's capabilities and in some cases allow for richer interaction with the substrate. A heart-beat filter would send a message at regular intervals to the substrate indicating that it is alive; this in turn helps discovery services within the substrate to identify live service instances. A performance monitoring filter would in turn notify the substrate at regular intervals about the load that it is experiencing. This in turn allows the substrate to load balance service requests by routing them to the least overloaded service instance. A filter may also automatically generally service advertisements along with information related to the transports available at the service endpoint. Additionally, these filters can also leverage the substrate's capabilities to communicate across NAT (Network Address Translator), firewall and proxy boundaries.

6.4 High performance transport of SOAP

The substrate provides support for a very wide array of transports (TCP, UDP, Multicast, SSL, HTTP and ParallelTCP among others). Depending on the size of SOAP message and the nature of continuing interactions appropriate transports will be deployed for communications. The nature of continuing interactions are dictated by issues such as whether the service exchanges messages at a high rate for a long time or whether the service considers reliable delivery to be more important than timely delivery. Filters at an endpoint can negotiate the best possible transport between itself and the substrate. The choice of the transport protocol being deployed is a function of the reliability, volume, rate and security requirements at the endpoint. The transport negotiations are carried out using a set of SOAP messages some of which are used to determine performance metrics such as latency, bandwidth, loss rates and jitters.

Note that the SOAP messages being transported can be based either on the traditional RPC style request/response message or the asynchronous one-way messaging. In the former case of RPC the substrate will facilitate correlations between requests and responses over transports, such as UDP, that do not naturally support a request/response based interaction that is at the heart of HTTP. The substrate will generate a UUID for such messages and include this as a header in the SOAP message. This message identifier when included in responses allows correlation with the original request.

Another area that we intend to research further is the support for high-performance transport of SOAP messages. Here we will leverage the XML Infoset; by separating the SOAP message context from its XML syntax, we can freely move between the binary and classic angle-bracketed representations of SOAP messages without content loss. Another area for further investigation is the efficient binary representations of XML Infosets such as SOAP Message Transmission Optimization Mechanism (MTOM) [28] and XML-binary Optimized Packing (XOP) [29]. We are developing schemes which allow two endpoints to first negotiate the best-available transport and then proceed to use it for transfers. To accommodate legacy systems that do not use the XML format, the Data Format Description Language (DFDL) [30] is an XML-based language that describes the structure of binary and character-encoded files and data streams so that their format, structure, and metadata can be exposed. This can also be used in tandem while transferring binary data using SOAP.

These latter topics are particularly important in several application areas. We have primarily been interested in efficient message representation in order to support PDA and other end clients, which are typically reached over much lower speed networks and have limited memory and processing power. However, the same ideas should scale up for Web Service-based scientific computing, since efficient message compression and high performance processing are required for moving non-trivial data sets and messages. Finally, these transport mechanisms are also important to real-time processing. As we have emphasized, all communications are messages moving through the substrate. These messages may range from infrequent events to remote method invocations to negotiated streams of time-sequenced data.

318

7. Grids of Grids

We may view it as a collection of capabilities provided by different organizations that have banded together to form a "Virtual Organization" [24]. A capability is just a Web Service, and Grids may be built from collections of Web Services. A Grid service is just a Web Service, although it may follow more restrictive conventions defined by OGSA. It is actually better to define a Grid by how it is used rather than how it is built. In this section we investigate some of the issues involved in building Grids of Grids.

We recommend two sets of services to facilitate such a scenario. Services provided within the substrate constitute the Internet-on-Internet (IOI) services. It is referred to as IOI since it enables us to build an application-level "Internet" of services connected by a messaging substrate that replicates in the application layer many of the desirable features (security, guaranteed delivery, optimal routing) that are normally found in the TCP/IP stack. See Ref [31] for a discussion of why TCP/IP is not enough, and thus why IOIs are necessary for SOAP messages. These services have been described in detail in sections 2 and 3.

The IOI services will be invisible to the applications that run in it. Applications would simply specify the QoS constraints and the substrate would deal with the complexity of satisfying these constraints. There are a number of higher level services and capabilities that do not belong in the IOI layer: these services typically extend the capabilities available through the IOI layer and are more specifically needed for Web Service management and apply to specific domains. Typical examples include service information and metadata management. We refer to this collection of capabilities as the Context and Information Environment (CIE). CIE services broadly fall into the following 5 categories.

1. Collaboration: Some collaborative applications may place a premium on the ability to pause/replay live streams rather than timely delivery. It is easy to see how the buffering strategies may vary in such scenarios. Strategies for the demarcation and subsequent retrieval of major and minor events may vary in different domains.
2. Authorization and authentication interfaces: Depending on the domain authentication schemes may span the wide spectrum from bio-metrics to text-based passwords. Same is true for trust propagation.
3. Support for specifications in various domains: Prime examples of this include WS-Discovery which is suitable for ad-hoc networks, and WS-Context which maintains contexts for a distributed computation.
4. Metadata Management: Different domains may have different formats for storing metadata and constraints regarding their exchange. In some scenarios custom solutions may be used or some endpoints may choose to use WS-Metadata exchange which facilitates exchange of metadata between two end points.
5. Portal Services: This involves allowing access to all metadata, the management of system deployments, firewall tunnels, performance information, and error-logs. Additionally a portal service may aggregate a set of services and provide a domain specific view of the state of these services.

Grids of Grids are composed of applications and services from many different domains. In the next section, we take an extended example from Geographical Information Services, which combine streaming data sources with data filters and online data mining applications.

8. Applications to Earthquake Science and Geographical Information Systems Grids

8.1 A Motivating Example: Data Mining Live GPS Streams

SERVO Grid [4, 5] is a Grid system for earthquake modeling and simulation and includes a diverse set of applications, but we will focus on Robert Granat's Regularized Deterministic Annealing Hidden Markov Model (RDAHMM) application [32]. An earlier, non-streaming version of this application was discussed in [33]. RDAHMM may be used to analyze arbitrary time ordered data, such as GPS position measurements and seismic records, to identify underlying modes of the system. This occurs in three distinct methods of operation:

1. **Training and mode analysis:** this phase applies to historical data. The RDAHMM application is applied to a particular data set (i.e. an archived time sequence from a GPS station) in order to determine the historical modes. These may be compared to known physical processes, but the mode identification process does not involve fixed parameters.

2. **Change detection:** once RDAHMM has initially identified a system's historical modes (a one-time operation), it can be used to detect mode changes in new, incoming data streams. Typically we need one logical RDAHMM application per data source (i.e. GPS station). RDAHMM clones may be periodically retrained on the updated historical data sets.

3. **Event Accumulation and Notification:** Methods of operation (1) and (2) apply to specific data sources, but we will also be interested in network-wide events. For example, there may be several causes for individual GPS stations to undergo mode transitions, but simultaneous mode change events in several stations in the same geographic region may be associated with underlying seismic events. Such network-wide changes need to spawn additional notifications, to both humans and other application codes.

Data mining of live data streams [34, 35, 36, 37] is an important scientific Grid application in many areas of crisis management and homeland security. As we have outlined in the previous sections of this chapter, Service Oriented Architecture-based Grids implemented with Web Service standards will meet many of the requirements of real-time Grids, providing a system based open and extensible standards. As we have emphasized above, messages are a key component of SOA systems, and a software messaging substrate such as NaradaBrokering may be used to implement the qualities of service demanded by sophisticated Grids. As we emphasize again here, there is no difference between notifications, events, and data transfers from the point of view of the messaging substrate. Substrates such as the NaradaBrokering system may be applied equally well to problems in Web Service Eventing/Notification and to streaming data. Web Service Architectures likewise may be adapted to streaming applications and associated message patterns, just has they have been applied to remote procedure call-style patterns.

For the problem at hand, we may identify several important components, which we review in more detail below. First, the GPS station network is an example of a Geographical Information System (GIS). It requires a diverse set of services for such tasks as accessing archival data, accessing streaming data, querying metadata that describes various members of the GPS network, and so on. These may be coupled to more traditional science Grid services for running and managing applications. Second, we have a diverse set of messages and services in the system: GPS stations provide streaming data, but we must also manage a) metadata services that describe individual stations in the network, b) less frequent messages (change events) that indicate a station has changed modes (which may occur only a few times per year), c) other GIS services for generating maps used for user interfaces; and d) services for managing application codes (such as RDAHMM) that are in the loop.

8.2   Geographic Information Systems and GIS Grids

Advances in Internet and distributed systems helped academia, governments and businesses to provide access to a substantial amount of geospatial data. The GIS community must face the following challenges:

1. Adoption of universal standards: Over the years organizations have produced geospatial data in proprietary formats and developed services by adhering to differing methodologies;
2. Distributed nature of geospatial data: Because the data sources are owned and operated by individual groups or organizations, geospatial data is in vastly distributed repositories,
3. Service interoperability: Computational resources used to analyze geospatial data are also distributed and require the ability to be integrated when necessary.

The Open Geospatial Consortium, Inc (OGC) represents a major effort to address some of these problems. The OGC is an international industry consortium of more than 270 companies, government agencies and universities participating in a consensus process to develop publicly available interface specifications. OGC Specifications support interoperable solutions that "geo-enable" the Web, wireless and location-based services, and mainstream IT. OGC has produced many specifications for web based GIS applications such as Web Feature Service (WFS) [38] and the Web Map Service (WMS) [39]. Geography Markup Language (GML) [40] is widely accepted as the universal encoding for geo-referenced data. In addition to the more traditional HTTP request/response style services, the OGC is also defining the SensorML family of services [41].

The GIS community quite obviously represents a major sub-domain in the "Grid of Grids" picture. By architecting GIS services using Web Services, and be placing these services within a SOA messaging substrate, we may integrate GIS Grid Services with other applications. Our work on GIS services as Web Services is described in more detail in [4, 5].

GIS applications developed by various vendors and academic institutions have become more complex as they are required to process larger data sets, utilize more computing power and in some cases need to collect data from distributed sources. Traditionally GIS applications are data centric: they deal with archived data. However, with sensor-based applications gaining momentum the need of integrating real-time data sources such as sensors, radars, or satellites with high end computing platforms such as simulation, visualization or data mining applications introduces several important distributed computing challenges to GIS community.

Although commercial GIS applications provide various solutions to these problems, most of the solutions are based on more traditional distributed computing paradigms such as static server-client approaches. Traditional point to point communication approaches tend to result in more centralized, tightly coupled and synchronous applications which results in harder management practices for large scale systems. Modern large scale systems on the other hand require more flexible asynchronous communication models to cope with the high number of participants and transfer of larger data sets between them.

Defining a Common Data Format

The first step for building such services is to decide appropriate encodings for describing the data. The importance of the data format lies in the fact that it becomes the basic building block of the system which in turn determines the level of interoperability. Use of a universal standard like XML greatly increases the number of users from different backgrounds and platforms who can easily incorporate our data products into their systems. Furthermore, services and applications are built to parse, understand and use this format to support various operations on data. So in a sense the type and variety of the tools being used in the development and data assimilation processes depend on the format initially agreed.

For these reasons we use GML, a commonly accepted XML based encoding for geospatial data, as our data format in GIS-related applications. One important fact about GML is that, although it offers particular complex types for various geospatial phenomena, users can employ a variety of XML Schema development techniques to describe their data using GML types. This provides a certain degree of flexibility both in the development process and in the resulting data products. For instance, depending on the capability of the environment schema developers may exclusively use certain XML Schema types and choose not to incorporate more obscure ones because of incompatibility issues. As a result a particular geospatial phenomenon can be described by different valid GML schemas.

By incorporating GML in our systems as de facto data format we gain several advantages:

1. It allows us to unify different data formats. For instance, various organizations offer different formats for position information collected from GPS stations. GML provides suitable geospatial and temporal types for this information, and by using these types a common GML schema can be produced. (See http://www.crisisgrid.org/html/servo.html for sample GML schemas for GPS and Seismic data)
2. As more GIS vendors are releasing compatible products and more academic institutions use OGC standards in their research and implementations, OGC specifications are becoming de facto standards in GIS community and GML is rapidly emerging as the standard XML encoding for geographic information. By using GML we open the door of interoperability to this growing community.
3. GML and related technologies allow us to build general set of tools to access and manipulate data. Since GML is an XML dialect, any XML related technology can be utilized for application development purposes. Considering the fact that in most cases the technologies for collecting data and consecutively the nature of the collected data product

would stay the same for a long period of time the interfaces we create for sharing data won't change either. This ensures having stable interfaces and libraries.

8.2.1 Data Binding

Establishing XML or some flavor of it as the default message/data format for the global system requires consideration of a Data Binding Framework (DBF) for generating, parsing, marshalling and un-marshalling XML messages. Marshalling and un-marshalling operations convert between XML-encoded formats and (typically Java) binding classes that can be used to simplify data manipulation.

Being able to generate XML instances and parsing them in a tolerable amount of time is one of the criteria while choosing such a framework, because message processing time would affect overall system performance as well as the performance of the individual XML processing component.

Another criterion to consider is the ability of the binding framework to successfully generate valid instances according to the Schema definitions. This is a major problem for DBFs since not all of the XML Schema types can be directly mapped to Object Oriented Programming constructs. Some of the XML Schema types (such as Substitution Groups which are heavily used in GML Schemas) do not correspond to types in Object Oriented world and this causes difficulties while processing the XML documents. Various Data Binding Frameworks offer different solutions, some of which are more elaborate than the other and depending of the nature of the data a suitable framework must be chosen.

8.2.2 Data Services

GIS systems are supposed to provide data access tools to the users as well as manipulation tools to the administrators. In principle the process of serving data in a particular format is pretty simple when it is made accessible as files on an HTTP or FTP server. But additional features like query capabilities on data or real-time access in a streaming fashion require more complicated services. As the complexity of the services grows, the client's chance of easily accessing data products decreases, because every proprietary application developed for some type of data require its own specialized clients. Web Services help us overcome this difficulty by providing standard interfaces to the tools or applications we develop.

No matter how complex the application itself, its WSDL interface will have standard elements and attributes, and the clients using this interface can easily generate methods for invoking the service and receiving the results. This method allows providers to make their applications available to others in a standard way.

The usefulness of Web Services is constrained by several factors. They can be used in several cases such as
- The volume of data transferred between the server and the client is not high. Actual amount of data can be transferred depends on a number of factors like the protocol being used to communicate or maximum allowed size by HTTP;
- Time is not a determining factor. Despite the obvious advantages, current HTTP-based implementations do not provide desirable results for systems that require fast response and

high performance. This is simply due to the delays caused by data transfer over network, network constraints, and HTTP request-response overhead.

Most scientific applications that couple high performance computing, simulation or visualization codes with databases or real-time data sources require more than mere remote procedure call message patterns. These applications are sometimes composite systems where some of the components require output from others and they are asynchronous, it may take hours or days to complete. Such properties require additional layers of control and capabilities from Web Services which introduces the necessity for a messaging substrate that can provide these extra features.

9. SOPAC GPS Services: Real Time Streaming Support for Position Messages

To demonstrate the use of technologies discussed earlier we describe GPS Services developed for the Scripps Orbit and Permanent Array Center (SOPAC) GPS data networks. Two of SOPAC's GPS networks are distributed in San Diego Counties and Riverside/Imperial Counties, respectively, and provide publicly available data. Raw data from the GPS stations are continuously collected by a Common Link proxy (RTD server) and archived in RINEX files.

The data collected from the GPS stations are served in 3 formats:
- **RAW**: For archiving and record purposes, not interesting for scientific applications, not available in real-time.
- **RTCM**: Published real-time and no records are kept. This is useful for RTCM capable GPS receivers as reference.
- **Positions**: Positions of the stations. Updated and presented every second. GPS Time Series can be produced using these positions and they can be in different epochs such as hourly, daily, etc.

Position information is used by RDAHMM and other applications. The RTD server however outputs the position messages in a binary format called RYO. This introduces another level of complexity on the client side because the messages have to be converted from binary RYO format.

To receive station positions, clients are expected to open a socket connection to the RTD server. An obvious downside of this approach is the extensive load this might introduce to the server when multiple clients are connected.

After the RTD server receives raw data from the stations it applies filters and for each network generates a message. This message contains a collection of position information for every individual station from which the position data has been collected in that particular instant. In addition to the position information there are other measurements in a message such as quality of the measurement, variances etc. For each GPS network, the RTD server broadcasts one position message per second through a port in RYO format. This is depicted on the left hand sides of Figures 5 and 6.

As we discuss below, to make the position information available to the clients in a real-time streaming fashion we are using the NaradaBrokering messaging system. Additionally we developed applications to serve position messages in ASCII and GML formats. This allows applications to choose the format that they want for applications will additionally allow us to implement more finely grained network subscriptions: users and applications don't have to process an entire network's stream to receive the subset of GPS stations that they want. RDAHMM provides a specific example for this: we need to apply RDAHMM change detection to individual GPS station signals.

9.1.1 Decoding RYO Messages

As shown in Figures 5 and 6, the incoming data streams must be converted into various formats. This is done by using developed specialized services that subscribe to specific topics and republish the decoded data to topics associated with the new format.

For example, the RYO Message Type 1 starts with a 5-byte Header which is followed by a 47-byte GPS Position message. Three types of optional blocks may follow the Position Message and a 2-byte checksum is located at the end of the message.

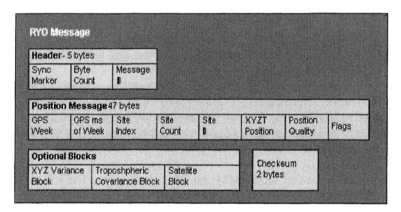

A non-blocking Java Socket connection is made to RTP server to collect RYO messages. We use thread programming techniques for this purpose. An RYO Decoder application which uses binary conversion tools converts RYO messages into text messages. Furthermore since we do not expect clients to know about the GPS time format we convert GPSWeek and GPSmsOfWeek values to Gregorian calendar format (i.e. 2005-19-07/04:19:44PM-EST). Additionally since we anticipate some clients to expect position information in terms of Latitude and Longitude, we calculate Latitude, Longitude and Height values from XYZT Position.

9.1.2 GML Schema for Position Messages and Data Binding

We have developed a GML conformant Schema to describe Position Messages. The Schema is based on RichObservation type which is an extended version of GML 3's Observation model. This model supports Observation Array and Observation Collection types which are useful in describing SOPAC Position messages since they are collections of multiple individual station positions. We follow strong naming conventions for naming the elements to make the Schema more understandable to the clients.

We used Apache XML Beans for data binding purposes: these convert ASCII data streams into XML. SOPAC GML Schema and sample instances are available here: http://www.crisisgrid.org/schemas

9.1.3   Integrating NaradaBrokering with Streaming GPS Measurements

After we have services for decoding position information into three different formats we may integrate these services with NaradaBrokering to provide real-time access to data. The following figures depict the use of NaradaBrokering topics in the system. Figure 5 depicts the flow of data to interested subscribers: applications like RDAHMM, databases for permanent storage, and portal systems (such as QuakeSim) for human interaction. To support these various consumers, we must provide different versions of the data stream.

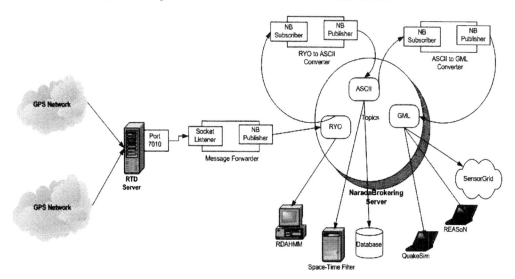

Figure 5 GPS streams are delivered to interested end clients.

Figure 6 expands Figure 5 to illustrate the basic routing techniques. The GPS network data streams are collectively made available by Scripps through ports 7010 and 7011. These two ports serve all the data from two distinct networks, each with 15 stations. The data is published in RYO format. We intercept this data through Java proxies that act as publishers on the topics RYO1 and RYO2 to a NaradaBrokering node. Subscribers to this topic may be any number of applications capable of handling these binary formats, including translation programs. As shown in Figure 6, these streams are translated into ASCII text formats by RYO Decoders. These decoders then publish the data back to the broker network on new topics, Positions/Text1 and Positions/Text2 in the figure. Any number of listening applications may receive this data, including (as shown in the figure), GML Converters that transform the ASCII streams into GML suitable for GIS applications.

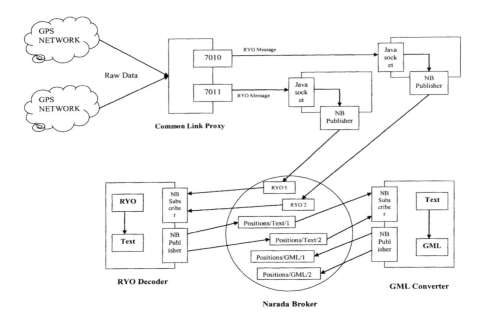

Figure 6 GPS network integrated with NaradaBrokering.

Currently the system is being tested for San Diego Counties and Riverside/Imperial Counties GPS networks. The following tables show the current information for NaradaBrokering Server and topic names:

NaradaBrokering Server address: *xsopac.ucsd.edu:3045*

Format	Topic Name
RYO	*SOPAC/GPS/Positions/SanDiego/RYO*
Text	*SOPAC/GPS/Positions/SanDiego/Text*
GML	*SOPAC/GPS/Positions/SanDiego/GML*

San Diego County

Format	Topic Name
RYO	*SOPAC/GPS/Positions/Riverside/RYO*
Text	*SOPAC/GPS/Positions/Riverside/Text*
GML	*SOPAC/GPS/Positions/Riverside/GML*

Riverside/Imperial County

We may add more filters to the data and develop more finely grained topics. For example, after decoding the binary stream, we may publish the individual GPS station data streams to individual topics.

9.2 Building a Sensor Grid

We are developing a Service Oriented Architecture to support real-time integration of sensor data with scientific applications such as simulation, visualization or data mining software.

Scientific applications that require processing of huge data sets are increasing in number with the evolution of computing resources, network bandwidth, and storage capabilities etc. At the same time some of the applications are being designed to run on real-time data to provide near-real time results; such applications are gaining ground in systems like Crisis Management or Early Warning Systems because they allow authorities to take action on time. Earthquake data assimilation tools are good examples of this group since they use data from Seismic or GPS sensors. However, in SERVO Grid, most of these tools currently consume data from repositories and they do not have access to real-time data due to several reasons.

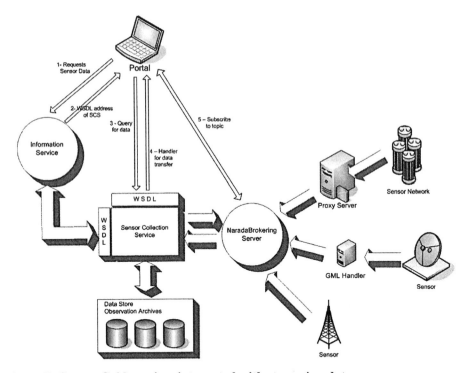

Figure 7: Sensor Grid services integrated with streaming data sources.

A Sensor Grid architecture will couple data assimilation tools with real-time data using GIS standards and Web Services methodologies. The system will use NaradaBrokering as the messaging substrate and this will allow high performance data transfer between data sources and the client applications. The Standard GIS interfaces and encodings like GML will allow data products to be available to the larger GIS community.

Figure 7 shows the major components of Sensor Grid using SensorML components. The client discovers the related Sensor Collection Service (SCS) information by using search interfaces provided by Information Service (IS). IS returns a handler which contains the WSDL address of the SCS that has access to the particular sensor client requests. The client then sends a getData query to SCS. Depending on the nature of the query SCS may take two actions; if the query is for archived sensor data then it requests data from the Observation Archives and returns it to the client. But if the client wants to access real-time data then it returns a data handler which contains the broker information and topic name for the sensor. Also depending on the size of the archived data SCS may choose one of two options for data transfer; if the result size is relatively small then it is returned via SOAP message, otherwise NaradaBrokering is used. SCS also keeps information about the sensors themselves. This information is encoded in SensorML. After receiving the broker address and the topic name, client may subscribe to the NaradaBrokering server to receive real-time data.

10. Conclusions

As standards such as SOAP 1.2, WSDL 2.0, and WS-Addressing become widely implemented and deployed, the initial concepts and implementations of Web Services as "remote procedure calls for the Web" are giving way to a more message-oriented, service-oriented approach. Such systems place an emphasis on managing secure, reliable messages that may be delivered in any number of ways across multiple routing SOAP intermediaries.

As we have discussed in this article, all communications in SOA-based systems are messages. Further, the correct way to implement these systems is to place the service "islands" on a software-level messaging substrate that implements efficient routing, security, reliability and other qualities of service. As we have shown, such systems support messages of all types, from infrequent update notification events to continuous streams.

Many important Grid applications in real-time data mining involve all of these message types. We have discussed a GIS example from our SERVOGrid work that uses the NaradaBrokering messaging system for managing data streams from GPS stations. We are in the process of connecting these to RDAHMM, a time series data analysis program useful for mode change detection. These streaming services are part of a more comprehensive system involving code execution services and information/metadata services.

References

[1] I. Foster, C. Kesselman, J. Nick, S. Tuecke, "The Physiology of the Grid: An Open Grid Services Architecture for Distributed Systems Integration." Open Grid Service Infrastructure WG, Global Grid Forum, June 22, 2002. Available from http://www.globus.org/research/papers/ogsa.pdf.

[2] D. Booth, H. Haas, F. McCabe, E. Newcomer, M. Champion, C. Ferris, and D. Orchard, "Web Services Architecture." W3C Working Group Note 11 February 2004. Available from http://www.w3.org/TR/2004/NOTE-ws-arch-20040211/.

[3] I. Foster (ed), J. Frey (ed), S. Graham (ed), S. Tuecke (ed), K. Czajkowski, D. Ferguson, F. Leymann, M. Nally, I. Sedukhin, D. Snelling, T. Storey, W. Vambenepe, S. Weerawarana, "Modeling Stateful Resources with Web Services v. 1.1." March 5, 2004.

Available from http://www-106.ibm.com/developerworks/library/ws-resource/ws-modelingresources.pdf.

[4] Andrea Donnellan, Jay Parker, Geoffrey Fox, Marlon Pierce, John Rundle, Dennis McLeod Complexity Computational Environment: Data Assimilation SERVOGrid 2004 Earth Science Technology Conference June 22 - 24 Palo Alto.

[5] Andrea Donnellan, Jay Parker, Greg Lyzenga, Robert Granat, Geoffrey Fox, Marlon Pierce, John Rundle, Dennis McLeod, Lisa Grant, Terry Tullis The QuakeSim Project: Numerical Simulations for Active Tectonic Processes 2004 Earth Science Technology Conference June 22 - 24 Palo Alto.

[6] Web Services Description Language (WSDL) 1.1 http://www.w3.org/TR/wsdl

[7] Web Services Eventing. Microsoft, IBM & BEA.
http://ftpna2.bea.com/pub/downloads/WS-Eventing.pdf

[8] Web Services Base Notification (WS-BaseNotification). IBM, Globus, Akamai et al.
ftp://www6.software.ibm.com/software/developer/library/ws-notification/WS-BaseN.pdf

[9] Web Services Brokered Notification Notification (WS-BrokeredNotification). IBM, Globus, Akamai et al. ftp://www6.software.ibm.com/software/developer/library/ws-notification/WS-BrokeredN.pdf

[10]   Web Services Topics (WS-Topics). IBM, Globus, Akamai et al.
ftp://www6.software.ibm.com/software/developer/library/ws-notification/WS-Topics.pdf

[11]   WS-Resource Properties. IBM, Globus, USC et al. http://www-106.ibm.com/developerworks/library/ws-resource/ws-resourceproperties.pdf

[12]   Web Services Resource Lifetime. IBM, Globus, USC et al. http://www-106.ibm.com/developerworks/library/ws-resource/ws-resourcelifetime.pdf

[13]   I. Foster (ed), J. Frey (ed), S. Graham (ed), S. Tuecke (ed), K. Czajkowski, D. Ferguson, F. Leymann, M. Nally, I. Sedukhin, D. Snelling, T. Storey, W. Vambenepe, S. Weerawarana, "Modeling Stateful Resources with Web Services v. 1.1." March 5, 2004. Available from http://www-106.ibm.com/developerworks/library/ws-resource/ws-modelingresources.pdf.

[14]   Web Services Reliable Messaging TC WS-Reliability. http://www.oasis-open.org/

[15]   Web Services Reliable Messaging Protocol (WS-ReliableMessaging) ftp://www6.software.ibm.com/software/devel oper/library/ws-reliablemessaging200403.pdf

[16]   Web Services Security. OASIS. http://www.oasis-open.org/committees/tc_home.php?wg_abbrev=wss

[17]   Geoffrey Fox, Shrideep Pallickara and Savas Parastatidis Towards Flexible Messaging for SOAP Based Services. To appear, proceedings of ACM/IEEE Conference on Supercomputing Applications 2004.

[18]   The NaradaBrokering Project at the Community Grids Lab:
http://www.naradabrokering.org

[19]   Shrideep Pallickara and Geoffrey Fox. NaradaBrokering: A Middleware Framework and Architecture for Enabling Durable Peer-to-Peer Grids. Proceedings of ACM/IFIP/USENIX International Middleware Conference Middleware-2003.

[20]   Shrideep Pallickara et. al. Performance of a Possible Grid Message Infrastructure. (To appear) Journal of Concurrency and Computation: Practice & Experience. UK e-Science meeting on Grid Performance Edinburgh, UK.

[21]   Shrideep Pallickara and Geoffrey Fox. On the Matching Of Events in Distributed Brokering Systems. Proceedings of IEEE ITCC Conference on Information Technology. April 2004. pp 68-76 Volume II.

[22]   Shrideep Pallickara and Geoffrey Fox. A Scheme for Reliable Delivery of Events in Distributed Middleware Systems. Proceedings of the IEEE International Conference on Autonomic Computing. 2004.

[23]   G. Fox, S. Lim, S. Pallickara and M. Pierce. Message-Based Cellular Peer-to-Peer Grids: Foundations for Secure Federation and Autonomic Services. (To appear) Journal of Future Generation Computer Systems.

[24]   Hasan Bulut, Shrideep Pallickara and Geoffrey Fox. Implementing a NTP-Based Time Service within a Distributed Brokering System. ACM International Conference on the Principles and Practice of Programming in Java. Pp 126-134.

[25]   Pallickara et al. A Security Framework for Distributed Brokering Systems. Available from http://www.naradabrokering.org.

[26]   Gudgin, M., Hadley, M., Mendelsohn, N., Moreau, J.-J., and Nielsen, H. (2003), SOAP Version 1.2 Part 1: Messaging Framework.   W3C Recommendation 24 June 2003. Available from http://www.w3c.org/TR/soap12-part1/

[27]   Universal Description, Discovery and Integration UDDI.

[28]   SOAP Message Transmission Optimization Mechanism. Microsoft, IBM and BEA. http://www.w3.org/TR/2005/REC-soap12-mtom-20050125/

[29]   XML-binary Optimized Packing. Microsoft, IBM and BEA. http://www.w3.org/TR/2005/REC-xop10-20050125/ .

[30]   The Data Format Description Language (DFDL) working group. https://forge.gridforum.org/projects/dfdl-wg/.

[31]   W. Vogels, "Web Services Are Not Distrubted Objects." IEEE Internet Computing, vol. 7 (6), pp59-66, 2003.

[32]   Robert Granat, Regularized Deterministic Annealing EM for Hidden Markov Models, Doctoral Dissertation, University of California Los Angeles, 2004.

[33]   Harshawardhan Gadgil, Geoffrey Fox, Shrideep Pallickara, Marlon Pierce, Robert Granat A Scripting based Architecture for Management of Streams and Services in Real-time Grid Applications Proceedings of the IEEE/ACM Cluster Computing and Grid 2005 Conference (CCGrid 2005). Cardiff, UK May 2005.

[34]   Robert L. Grossman, Yunhong Gu, Chetan Gupta, David Hanley, Xinwei Hong, and Parthasarathy Krishnaswamy, Open DMIX: High Performance Web Services for Distributed Data Mining, 7th International Workshop on High Performance and Distributed Mining, in association with the Fourth International SIAM Conference on Data Mining, 2004.

[35]   Nguyen, D., et al. *Real-Time Feature Extraction for High Speed Networks.* in *15th International Conference on Field Programmable Logic and Applications.* 2005. Tampere, Finland.

[36]   Zaki, M.J., *Parallel and Distributed Association Mining: A Survey.* IEEE Concurrency, Special Issue on Parallel Mechanisms for Data Mining, Dec. 1999. 7(4): p. 14-25.

[37]   Han, J. and M. Kamber, *Data Mining: Concepts and Techniques.* 2001: Morgan Kaufmann.

[38]   Vretanos, P (ed.) (2002), Web Feature Service Implementation Specification, OpenGIS project document: OGC 02-058, version 1.0.0.

[39]   de La Beaujardiere, Jeff, Web Map Service, OGC project document reference number OGC 04-024.

[40]   Cox, S., Daisey, P., Lake, R., Portele, C., and Whiteside, A. (eds) (2003), OpenGIS Geography Markup Language (GML) Implementation Specification. OpenGIS project document reference number OGC 02-023r4, Version 3.0.

[41]   Sensor   Model   Language   (SensorML)   Project   Web   Site: http://vast.nsstc.uah.edu/SensorML/.

Grid Computing: The New Frontier of High Performance Computing
Lucio Grandinetti (Editor)
© 2005 Elsevier B.V. All rights reserved.

NewsGrid

Stefan Geisler, Gerhard R. Joubert

Clausthal, University of Technology
Department of Computer Science,
Julius-Albert-Straße 4, 38678 Clausthal-Zellerfeld, Germany
E-mail: {geisler, joubert}@informatik.tu-clausthal.de

Film archives—particularly those storing video material on all kinds of news items—are important information sources for TV stations. Each TV station creates and maintains its own archive by storing video material received via satellite and/or internet on tapes in analogue and/or digital form. It cannot be predicted in advance which of this archived material will actually be used. Thus all material received must be catalogued and stored. On average only a small percentage of the material stored is actually used. Due to the increase in data volumes the cost of maintaining such repositories and retrieving particular stored items has become prohibitive. To-day digital videos are increasingly replacing analogue material. Digital videos offer the advantage that they can be stored in distributed databases and then be transferred without loss of quality to the transmitting station. Such digital archives can be made accessible to many TV stations, thus spreading the maintenance cost. Individual stations can retrieve only the material they actually need for particular news casts. In this paper a grid architecture for distributed video archives for news broadcasts is proposed. A crucial aspect of such a grid approach is that advanced methods for retrieving data must be available.

1. Introduction

TV stations compile news casts from video material supplied by various news agencies. The video material is distributed on a twenty-four hour basis to subscribing TV stations.

In order to maintain the high quality needed for news casts the video material was until now recorded and stored in high quality analogue form on tapes. A fundamental problem with analogue based repositories is that content based searches can only be executed by humans. This results in a slow and expensive process. Indexing mechanisms can be used to support video retrieval, but the indexing also has to be done by humans, making it inaccurate and costly. It was shown already [1, 2] that the simultaneous archiving in high quality analogue and lower quality digitised form offers great advantages to editors for compiling news casts. These low quality digitised repositories already allow for more advanced information retrieval mechanisms than those available for analogue libraries.

To-day digital video broadcasts (DVB) via satellite, terrestrial transmitters or internet have reached quality levels approaching and even surpassing those of analogue video broadcasts (AVB). Digital video repositories furthermore open up the possibility of applying advanced content based information retrieval methods to search for particular video material needed for a broadcast.

An important aspect, which has not been addressed as yet, is that modern grid technologies enable the retrieval of news videos from geographically distributed databases. This potentially allows TV stations—that is the users—to discontinue or at least substantially reduce the effort and cost of maintaining their private repositories. An additional advantage is that only the material they actually require needs to be retrieved at the time the actually need it. The real savings are achieved through the sharing of archives amongst many TV stations and a substantially reduced demand on communication networks.

The NewsGrid proposed in this paper requires fundamentally new marketing and distribution strategies by news suppliers. Instead of distributing news content only, information about available news material will have to be distributed or made available on the Internet. Users, i.e. TV stations, can then retrieve the desired material on a subscription or pay per item basis directly from the news agencies' databases. Users will need fast and effective search mechanisms to retrieve specific news material. The major potential advantages for news agencies are a huge reduction in information broadcast costs and improved statistics on which news items are actually used by clients.

Essential requirements for the implementation of the proposed grid approach are:
- Reliable and easy to use grids comprising powerful database servers
- User friendly, effective, efficient and interactive methods for retrieving video material
- Compact information being made available on news—or for that matter other—content contained in supplier databases.

It is not the purpose of this paper to discuss all these problems, but rather to consider the required grid and information retrieval, as well as result presentation, technologies. Note also that the NewsGrid concept may be applied as a worldwide grid (WWG) or an intragrid (IG) for particular organisational clusters, such as the public TV stations in the EU.

Grid [3] technologies were investigated during the past decade with the aim to develop powerful parallel computing systems using the Internet as a communication platform. Often local high speed communication networks are integrated into the grid. Grid nodes can themselves be high-speed computing platforms such as clusters, vector machines, etc. A fundamental aim with grid technologies is to make distributed high-speed resources easily accessible to users. A number of such systems have already been developed by various groups. Most of these are, however, tailored to meet the particular requirements of a targeted user community.

Standard grid services enable access to distributed databases, including video repositories. The particular tools needed by users to retrieve video data using content based techniques must still be developed and implemented.

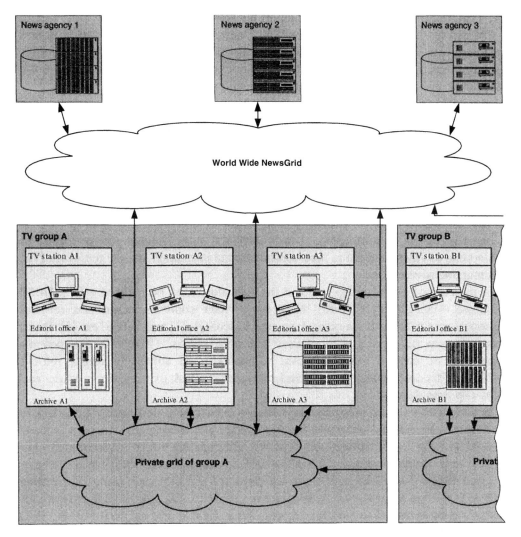

Figure 1. Structure of the NewsGrid. Several private grids (intragrids) of TV station groups are connected to the world wide NewsGrid.

2. NewsGrid

The NewsGrid approach discussed in this paper focuses on the processing of videos used for news broadcasts. The structure of the NewsGrid is depicted in figure 1. Extensions of the NewsGrid concepts to the storage and retrieval of general videos can easily be realised.

2.1. Traditional versus Grid Technologies for News Video Processing

TV newscasts are compiled by combining new video material received from news agencies, own correspondents or correspondents of other TV stations, with historic or reference material retrieved form archives. The text read by the news presenter is then added to tie everything together and create transitions from one theme to the next.

In order to use historic or reference material this must be stored in and retrieved from an appropriate repository. If the material is recorded in analogue form on magnetic tapes each tape is catalogued with content descriptions and placed in a local library. The subsequent retrieval of video material is achieved by using this catalogue and a final visual screening of selected items. This is a highly inefficient, cost intensive and often ineffective process, as all these actions require human interactions. This holds for both the cataloguing and retrieving of data.

The disadvantages of the presently used broadcast distribution method are obvious. A demand for high transmission bandwidths and huge storage spaces exists, the cataloguing of video material is time consuming and inaccurate and the retrieval of data is labour intensive.

In the case of digital video material the repository may be realised with a DBMS (Database Management System) adapted to video content storage and retrieval. Examples are OVID with the query language VideoSQL [4] and VideoText [5]. Digital techniques can be employed to process and store videos. These offer the potential advantages of content based retrieval technologies to solve the media retrieval problems. This could make the time and cost intensive task of manually indexing each video clip superfluous.

In this paper a system using dynamic feature extraction is described. This offers the possibility to execute powerful and flexible queries to retrieve particular video content. To cope with the high computational demands, efficient and effective search algorithms are required. Parallel processing is indispensable to achieve acceptable response times.

Three different levels of parallelism are discussed and compared using experimental results. A suitable SMP-cluster architecture is described. The results obtained with this cluster can be extended to the requirements for a suitable grid implementation, which may also be considered to be a wide-area heterogeneous cluster.

The use of digital and grid technologies drastically reduce the demands for high communication bandwidths between suppliers (news agencies) and consumers (TV stations). It is a well known fact that each TV station uses only a small percentage of all material presently received from news agencies. Using distributed databases and grid technologies the size of video archives and the costs to maintain these at individual TV stations can be significantly reduced. These factors offer a significant reduction in costs to individual TV stations.

A major disadvantage of the proposed NewsGrid concept is that it changes the standard work flow of editorial staff compiling news casts. Editors will not only view material stored in their private archive(s), but will have to learn how to search for, retrieve and select material from a wide range of news sources. They must have available and learn how to employ advanced content based retrieval methods using interactive grid technologies. In order to achieve acceptance of the new technologies it is essential that these must be easy to use, fast and offer sufficient functionality.

Due to the complex and compute intensive retrieval methods this also requires that a significant parallel compute power be available across the grid.

2.2. Archiving of News Videos

Access to a comprehensive archive is essential for the compilation of high quality news casts. Such video material is obtained from many different sources.

As was indicated already this material is presently replicated in a multitude of repositories and, if it is indexed, these can greatly differ. Thus, for example, the use of key words varies greatly amongst different specialists. The result is that searches on separate archives containing basically the same material often produce very different results. It is also possible that a particular item that is needed cannot be traced, although it is available in the archive.

The proposed NewsGrid changes the whole concept of archiving news videos. According to this concept data is stored in a relatively small number of distributed archives, thus reducing redundancy. This greatly reduces the overall cost of indexing archived material. In addition the indexing process can be better formalised resulting in more consistent results. An additional advantage is that by storing data in digital form content based search methods can be used to improve data retrieval results.

A requirement for the successful implementation and use of a NewsGrid is that a set of standard methods and protocols must be agreed and adhered to. Present grid standards as well as MPEG-7 [6] and MPEG-21 [7] form a good starting point for defining such standards.

MPEG-7 is an ISO-standard that enables the combination of content descriptions with video clips. The language used is an extension of XML that allows the description of multimedia data types and structures. Thus, for example, it is possible to add descriptions of the melody and sound effects in the case of music clips and information on colour, lighting, texture, lay-out, time, place of recording, etc. to visual material. Additional data types may be defined.

Table 1 gives a summary of an MPEG-7 description of a news video. In [8] a scheme was proposed that allows the management of news feeds stored in a cluster based database. This scheme can also be used as a basis for defining schemes that can be used in NewsGrid. MPEG-7 thus allows for the specification of a basic set of static data with respect to a video.

The fundamental approach taken is that a news header, containing static and dynamic information, is supplied. MPEG-7 can be used to achieve this. It is also possible to supply such descriptions as separate descriptions added to any stored videos.

In general the static information supplied includes, for example:

- Date, Time
- Title
- Keywords/Summary
- Source

Table 1. Data Types of the MPEG-7-Schema for news archives

Item	Field	Data type / Values
Telestation		String (ARD, BBC, CNN, …)
ContributionType		String (Speaker, Photo, FixedCamera, FreeCamera)
Frame	TimeCode	mp7:MediaRelTimePoint
	Description (mult.)	String
	ColourHistogram	mp7:Histogram
	…	
	Picture (mult.)	mp7:MediaInformation
Scene	StartTime	mp7:Time
	SkriptText	String
	Description (mult.)	String
Contribution	Type (attribute)	ContributionType
	StartTime	mp7:Time
	Title	String
	Description (mult.)	String
	KeyFrame (mult.)	Frame
	RelatedMaterialInt (mult.)	mp7:MediaURL
	RelatedMaterialExt (mult.)	mp7:MediaURL
	Scenes (mult.)	Scene
Newscast	SourceTelestation	Telestation
	Name	String
	BroadcastTime	mp7:Time
	Description (mult.)	String
	VideoPreviewQuality	mp7:MediaInformation
	VideoBroadcastQuality	mp7:MediaInformation
	Contrib (mult.)	Contribution

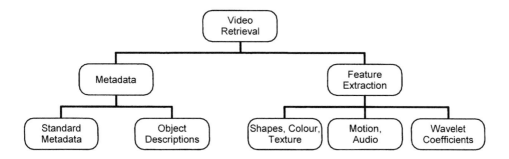

Figure 2. Object Description Vectors (ODV): classification and examples.

- Copyright/Price
- Characteristics for content based retrieval, e.g. colour moments of key frames
- etc.

Additionally dynamic information can be added, such as:

- Sample sketches
- Sample images
- Definition of regions of interest (ROI)
- etc.

Such descriptions can be used to define a search vector (see also section 3) that is defined for each video clip stored in the database. The search vector can be enhanced by adding key words and textual descriptions. These must be manually added when the video clip is stored in the database.

3. Video Storage and Retrieval

As was mentioned already the number of available news video files increased enormously during the last decade. The available methods using static data to define ODV's are becoming increasingly inadequate for information retrieval tasks. The addition of textual descriptions and/or key words is becoming too costly.

The storage and efficient and effective retrieval of video files were and are thus investigated in a number of research projects, for example VideoQ [9], the Virage video engine [10] and CueVideo [11]. The goal with all of these is a content-based search on the video data in order to avoid the expensive and inaccurate compilation of static and textual descriptions.

The media content of a video clip can be described by an object description vector (ODV) containing data describing various features of the clip. In the ODV metadata, for example title or date, and extracted features, such as colour, textures, shapes or motion can be stored. In figure 2 examples are given.

The presently available systems have in common that the ODV's are calculated when the video is stored in the database. As the provider cannot know what the interests of the later users will be, it is likely that significant information for the users will not be extracted and stored.

An alternate approach is to store video clips with a limited ODV containing only static data (SODV). The dynamic components of the ODV (DODV) are then calculated when the user submits his query to the video database. Thus the ODV, comprising the SODV and DODV, can only be calculated when the query of the user is known. This is an extension of a proposal by Kao for image databases [12].

Objects or persons can be found in video clips by a template matching algorithm that is performed on each image in each video clip in the database. Obviously such systems need a huge amount of computational power. This can only be achieved with parallel systems. In the case of the proposed NewsGrid this implies that the individual nodes accessing the video databases must have sufficient compute power available.

3.1. The retrieval process

Instead of key words and logical operators a query can consist of a sketch or an example image supplied by the user when he defines his search. Additionally the user can mark a region of interest (ROI), which is in most cases a figure or an object in an image. The objective is not to find exact matches, but rather to locate a set of video clips or shots that contain a frame or frames corresponding as closely as possible to the sample sketch, image or the specified region. The comparison between the query image and a video frame results in the same process as in the case of searches in image databases. In the case of an object search, template matching is used. This means the query template is compared to every equally sized region of the video frame with the same size.

The approach described here considers only static objects in each video clip frame [12]. Although the analysis of moving objects is an important aspect of video clips, these are not considered in this paper. The reason is that it is questionable whether motion analysis adds to the effectiveness of the video retrieval process.

3.2. Efficient non-parallel search

Before considering the use of parallelism to support the video retrieval process, it is important to consider in how far the computational workload can be reduced by other means. In [13] two techniques are described, which are presented in the following sections.

3.2.1. Reducing the number of frames to analyse

Videos normally contain 25 (PAL) or 30 (NTSC) frames per second, thus a one hour movie contains 90.000 or 108.000 frames respectively. The contents of all of these frames cannot be analysed in acceptable time even with very powerful high-speed processors. In practice it is, however, not necessary to analyse every frame in a sequence as many of them are the same or very similar. The problem is thus to identify which frames can be ignored.

The first notion is to search only one key frame, for example the first, of each scene. This is, however, not a good strategy as the relevant details that one is looking for may not be contained in that particular frame. Thus, for example, the salient details may be hidden by another object or appear before or after the key frame considered.

A better approach is to consider one frame in a fixed search interval. The length of the interval can be arbitrarily chosen. The interval length should be such that salient details are unlikely to be missed, but not too short as this unnecessarily increases the number of frames to be considered. In tests half second intervals gave good results. The reason for this is that single shots are usually three seconds or more.

In the case of MPEG-1 [14] and MPEG-2 [15] videos the structure of these can be used as the basis of a search strategy. In practice most of these are coded such that every 12th or 15th frame is an I-frame, which contains all information of the particular video frame. The video analysis can thus be implemented efficiently by performing the search on the I-frames only.

3.2.2. Processing MPEG-1/2-videos

In order to compress (code) videos using MPEG-1/2 the individual frames are partitioned into 8×8 pixel blocks. To each block the Discrete Cosine Transformation (DCT) is applied. In the compressed file only the coefficients of the transformation are stored. When decompressing (decode) an MPEG-1/2 video the inverse DCT must be applied, which constitutes the most time consuming step in the decoding process. In order to avoid decompressing the single I-Frames the content search is not performed on the pixel data but rather on the coefficients of the DCT. This implies that the same transformation is first performed on the query image or sketch. Falkemeier et al. [16] as well as Shen et al. [17] use similar approaches to work in the compressed domain for video parsing and indexing.

Another speed improvement is achieved by comparing only the first coefficient of each block, i.e. the so-called DC-coefficient, which represents the average value of the luminescence or chroma value of the block. The AC-components, representing the higher frequency values, are thus ignored. This can be compared to a search on the frame with reduced resolution. As objects in most cases will not be placed at the edges of the blocks, a search including subpixels of the DC-image leads to better results, but on the other hand increases the compute load.

3.3. Parallelising the search

With the methods described in section 3.2 the search in a video of 13.5 minutes length can be performed in 79 seconds on a 2.2 GHz Xeon system. In this example a query template with three different sizes, three rotation steps and four subpixel positions of the DC-image was used. If, however, the task is to analyse hundreds of videos stored in video databases, parallel computing techniques are required to achieve acceptable response times.

In [18] Bretschneider et al. showed that cluster architectures are a good choice for processing images stored in large image databases. Each node in the cluster has its own data store for saving a portion of the overall database. It can easily be seen that the number of access conflicts while using hard disks and other resources is lower than in the case of SMP computers using shared memory architectures. Extensive tests showed

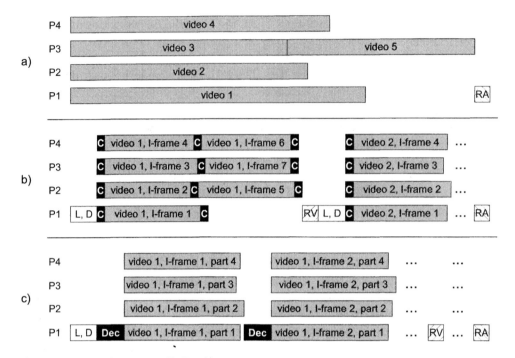

Figure 3a-c: Different parallelisation strategies

that for smaller databases and using systems with up to four processing elements (PE's) both architectures produce similar performance results. These results can be directly extended to the case of video databases where video clips are considered as image sequences.

In order to implement an optimal task scheduling strategy in the case of cluster architectures it is essential that videos be transferred between nodes. The reason for this is that a query usually consists of several steps, e. g. search for objects in videos with a particular author or videos produced on a specific date. The subsequent dynamic search for objects is then executed on a small part of the overall database. In general the video clips searched for are not distributed symmetrically over the cluster nodes. In order to have a balanced search, these files should be redistributed over the available processing elements. The transfer of hundreds of megabytes of video files would, however, slow down the overall processing speed significantly and thus wipe out the advantages offered by the optimal search strategy. Note that in the case of SMP-architectures the PE's all have the same access time to the (shared) video database.

A second aspect to be considered is that in the case of clusters the probability of a good distribution of videos increases with a smaller number of nodes.

These factors must be kept in mind when trying to achieve a good balance between SMP- and cluster architectures. Three levels of parallelism can be considered:

Coarse-grained parallelisation on video file level: The simplest way is to start one task for each PE (Figure 3a). Each task searches one video clip or file. The advantage is minimal communication efforts. On the other hand, idle times occur due to different video lengths and if the number of files to be analysed is not a multiple of P, with P the number of PE's in the SMP-computer.

Parallelisation on frame level: The second approach is to create P threads to analyse one video file (Figure 3b). Once the video is loaded and demultiplexed all threads start searching through the file from the beginning. A thread analyses a frame only if no other thread has processed it or is busy doing so. Hence communication is necessary before the search can be performed. Idle times are reduced to the time for the analyses of one frame per video and the demultiplexing needed at the beginning.

Fine-grained parallelisation by partitioning each frame: Each frame is divided into P sections. For each section a thread is generated, which searches the part of the frame for the query image (Figure 3c). The load of the PE's is nearly symmetric, but there is more communication overhead than in the other cases. Another drawback is that only the analysis is executed in parallel, not the decoding of the frames.

4. Performance and speedup

In this section the performance and speedup of the different parallelisation approaches are compared and a combination to improve the performance is discussed.

Two architectures are compared, viz. a dual Xeon 2.2 GHz system and an Alpha workstation with four 600 MHz PE's. The Xeon system is tested with and without hyperthreading. The hyperthreading technology allows using some functional units in parallel by pretending an additional PE. Results are taken from [13].

4.1. Parallel Speedup

4.1.1. Search in one video file
The results of the performance measurements for searching in one video file are shown in Figure 4a. The first interesting fact is that the parallelism on frame level works more efficiently than the finer grained algorithm. For this reason an even finer grained algorithm like parallelisation of the DCT, is not attractive. This applies to all tested architectures.

Secondly, the maximum speedup is 3.4. Not surprisingly it was achieved with the four processor Alpha workstation. A speedup of 2.2 can be achieved with two real PE's due to hyperthreading. It may even be increased, if special characteristics of the architecture are exploited.

4.1.2. Search in many video files
The next test scenario is to analyse more than one video file in parallel. The parallel search in separate files is compared to the parallelism at frame level. The test set contained more than 100 video files. The data in Figure 4b show that the coarse-grained algorithm is slightly more efficient on dual processor architectures. The advantage increases with an increase in the number of PE's. The parallel search in videos on the Alpha workstation with four PE's reaches a speedup of 3.9 whereas with the parallel

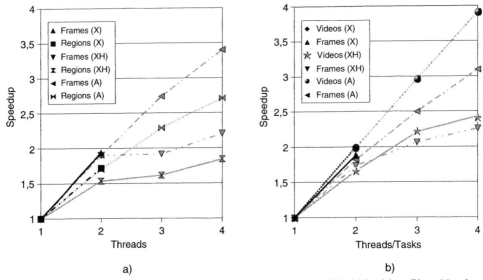

Figure 4. Parallelisation to accelerate the search in a) 1 and b) 100 video files. Used architectures are a dual Xeon with (XH) and without (X) hyperthreading and an Alpha workstation with 4 PE's (A).

search in separate frames of one video only a speedup of 3.1 is achieved on the same machine.

In this test it was assumed that the data set can be divided into equal sized subsets. A more realistic scenario is discussed in the next section, where a fixed number of videos of different lengths are analysed.

4.2. Execution times

The previous two sections gave an overview of the performance of the different algorithms. In the following the execution times of the individual steps are considered in more detail. For this a video file of 13.5 minutes, containing 1568 I-Frames and resulting in a MPEG-1 file size of 219 MByte is analysed. The test system used is a Dual Xeon, 2.2 GHz without Hyperthreading and equipped with 1 GByte RAM.

The initialisation of the program takes 0.03 sec. The first step is to load the video file. This normally takes 5.5 sec. If the video file is cached by the operating system, e.g. if it was previously loaded by another task, this value decreases to 0.6 sec. This value might also be relevant if the video is not stored on hard disk, but transferred by high performance networks. Demultiplexing the video, which means separating the video data from audio and other data, requires 0.31 sec.

These three steps are performed sequentially in all tested algorithms as the search cannot start without first loading the video file. When several video clips are to be analysed the next video file may of course be pre-loaded by a separate thread. This is similar to the situation mentioned above where the video is already available in the system cache.

Another solution might be to load the whole file in the background and start the search on the partially loaded bit stream. The drawback of this approach is the necessary validity checks required before accessing the data. This slows down the decoding process enormously and leads to longer execution times in the case of fast search algorithms. Thus it is only meaningful in the case of slower algorithms. In such a case the loading time becomes negligible compared to the overall processing time.

The execution times of the different algorithms are:

Single Thread: The mean time to analyse one frame is 0.043 sec, varying from 0.043 sec to 0.045 sec. The time between searching two frames, which is the time needed to seek the next frame start code, is 0.002 sec. The overall video analysis takes 78.8 sec.

Parallelisation on video level: The analysis of two videos in parallel has only little effect on the execution time. Overall it increases by nearly 1% per thread. This is also true for the required time per frame, which is 0.045 sec on average. Thus the speedup of 1.9 is close to the optimum achievable.

Parallelisation on frame level: Searching in two frames simultaneously increases the time required per frame. The execution time of thread one is 0.051, while thread two requires 0.048 sec on average. The standard deviation is comparable to the sequential search in the frames. The reason for this is presumably the concurrent memory access.

The time between the start of searching two frames increases by 50% compared to the single threaded method. This is also caused by the concurrent memory access and additional communication time between the threads to find the next unprocessed frame.

Putting the results together, 0.053 sec is required per frame, with two frames being analysed simultaneously. The speedup regarding only this value is 1.72. Thus the efficiency is 0.86.

The time for gathering the individual results is negligible. The maximum idle time per PE at the end of the search is the time needed to analyse one frame, thus 0.053 sec. Overall 47.4 sec are required.

Parallelisation by partitioning each frame: Searching in one frame with two threads leads to smaller execution times per frame. The measured values range from 0.028 sec to 0.035 sec with a mean value of 0.030 sec. The time to switch from one frame to the next is the same as in the non-parallel case. The speedup in this case is 1.66 and the efficiency is 0.83.

A closer look at the execution times of the threads reveals that they spend only 70% of their total compute time on searching the frame. The remaining 30% is spent on the sequential decoding of the frame. The overall processing time is 60.4 sec.

4.3. A cluster architecture with SMP-nodes

The results from the last sections form a basis for designing a cluster of SMP-computers that is suitable for handling the processing demands in the case of larger video databases. It is assumed that the stored video files are randomly distributed over the nodes. In practice this is the case as it is not known a priori which content based searches will be requested by users. It is furthermore assumed that a subset of all stored videos, e. g. all videos created on a specific date or by a particular author, must be inspected to find the query image or objects similar to it.

The query is processed as follows: First of all every node searches the locally stored videos. If a node runs idle, it requests a video, which was not yet analysed, from another node. The search is then continued on this video. The (temporary) video clip is deleted after the search has been completed. (It of course remains available at its original location in the distributed database.)

Speedup values were computed by simulation and extrapolating the experimental results. Three hardware configurations with altogether 32 PE's in each case are considered: eight nodes with four PE's each (8/4), 16 dual processor nodes (16/2) and 32 single processor nodes (32/1). The cluster nodes are interconnected with a Myrinet network. The results lead to the realisation that the best suited architecture and algorithm depends on the size of the video subset considered. For the small set of 50 frames the parallelisation on frame level gives better speedup values (up to 27.1 on the 16/2 cluster) than parallelisation on video level. The reason is not the algorithm itself, but rather that with smaller execution times a better schedule can be built and the load of the PE's can be more evenly distributed.

Furthermore, the best choice for the number of PE's per node is two for the small subset of videos considered here. The algorithm does not perform well with four nodes, as shown in section 4.1. Using 32 nodes with one PE each leads to a disadvantageous distribution of the video files.

For larger datasets the negative influence of the unbalanced schedule is lower than the positive influence of the better scalable parallelisation on video level. The speed up reaches a value of 31.8 for 500 video clips on the 16/2 cluster. The time for communication between the nodes is relatively small, as it takes less than a second to transfer a 100 megabyte video file with a high performance cluster.

For a more detailed discussion and a table with all simulation results see [13].

5. Retrieval Results

5.1. Quality

Two aspects are of particular importance to users when retrieving information from a repository, viz. the quality of the results and their presentation. As the acceleration of the search process is achieved by neglecting certain information, it is necessary to consider the quality of the retrieval results. As stated in [13] a precision of 0.9 can be reached for searching with a whole query frame. If the query object contains 100 000 pixels, on average 60% of the videos in the result set are relevant. Figure 5 gives an example.

Figure 5. A query image showing a scene from the flood of 2002 in East Germany and some selected frames from the corresponding result set. Rank 14 is a false detection.

5.2. Presentation

The result of the search process is a set of videos, which must be presented in a suitable way to the user. The simplest way for presenting images to users is to display a list of thumbnails. However, a similar approach for time-variant media such as videos would overburden the user as he cannot simultaneously focus on the interesting points in a number of concurrent video presentations.

The alternative of playing the videos successively would again cost too much time. (Note: This is the case with the currently used analogue archives.) For this reason, several techniques for result presentation in video databases were developed. The most important of these are discussed in the following section. Subsequently a new approach to present search results is proposed.

5.2.1. Existing presentation techniques

The simplest way to present a set of video clips is to select one key frame, e.g. the first frame or a frame from the middle of the scene, for each clip and present these in a thumbnail list. User selection of a thumbnail starts playback of the clip with a video player. A serious disadvantage of this approach is the limited information about a video clip of several minutes' length, even if three or five key frames are chosen. A larger number of key frames can be presented in a storyboard. This idea was implemented in CueVideo [11].

To reduce the number of frames displayed simultaneously the set of key frames can be ordered hierarchically. To view more frames of a scene one has to select the corresponding key frame. Examples of such systems are described in [19, 20].

Uchihashi developed VideoManga [21], where more than 20 frames are extracted, scaled to different sizes and reordered to fit in one rectangle, similar to a page of a comic strip. The size of the frame indicates the duration or importance of the corresponding shot. A specialised system for news videos was developed by Christel et al [22]. Collages are built containing not only video frames but also additional information about the content of the news cast.

The result viewer of Blobworld [23] has an additional feature for searching objects. In the displayed key frames the detected object is marked by a surrounding line.

Smith et al. suggested an approach to visualize object motion by adding motion vectors to the key frame [24]. This works well, if there are only a few objects, but becomes very complex with an increasing number of movements in the scene.

Additionally, camera motion can be visualized by concatenating several frames to one big panorama image. Object motion can be depicted through motion vectors or displaying several objects at different positions [25, 26].

While all techniques mentioned so far give a static view of the video content, CueVideo provides an alternative way by playing an animated video abstract. In motion-intensive scenes the speed is lowered to give the user the possibility for a more detailed view, while the speed increases in case of shots with restricted motion intensity.

5.2.2. Result presentation by region of interest video coding

As described above static result presentation is associated with the loss of information about motion or leads to very complex image compositions. To overcome these drawbacks an approach for animated result presentations was devised [27]. This technique was developed with the aim to allow the user to focus directly on the interesting parts of simultaneously playing videos.

This region of interest coding (ROIC) technique can be used to decrease file sizes, storage requirements and transmission times. It is applicable in all those cases where one or more sections of a frame or a video are of particular importance [28, 29]. In this approach ROIC is used to assist users in detecting interesting parts in several parallel running videos on a screen.

In the general case it is not easy to define a region of interest (ROI) in an arbitrary video automatically, but in the case of the video database the user defines the interesting object with a query template. An approximate position of the object is delivered by the search process. To find a more exact position a fuzzy search in the surrounding region with an eight pixel radius and a step size of four pixels is performed on the frame that most closely matches the query template. A circle around the bounding box of the best template match is defined as a ROI.

The detection of the ROI in the adjacent frames requires an increase of the search radius to compensate possible camera and object(s) motions. The test value applied in the case of an MPEG-1 video clip is 20 pixels starting from the location of the best position in the former processed frame.

The video abstract is created from the I-frames of the original video after some post processing. The pixels outside the ROI are modified such that their colour value is similar to the background value of the result viewer. For every colour channel the new value is the mean of the original value and the background colour. At the boundaries of

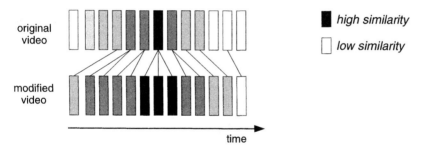

Figure 7. Temporal modification of the video abstract. The darkness of the rectangle indicates the similarity of the frame to the query image.

the ROI a smooth transition between the interesting and the uninteresting area is generated in order to give the user an overall impression of the frame contents.

To reduce the size of the compressed files areas outside the ROI are coded with lower resolution and a higher quantization of the colour values. An example result is shown in Figure 6.

This post processing allows a user to quickly find the interesting regions in retrieved videos at a glance. In addition to this support of the recognition process in the spatial domain, the recognition support can also be extended to the temporal domain. This is achieved by coding frames with a higher correspondence with a lower frame rate, while frames with a lower correspondence and a greater distance from the best matching frame are coded with a higher frame rate. Figure 7 gives a schematic description.

6. Grid Services

Access to the video files made available on the repositories of NewsGrid is realised by a number of grid services. In addition to the standard NewsGrid services each user must be able to start his own programs for processing data available in repositories to which he has access. By defining different user groups and domains particular services can be made available to a user group(s).

A number of sample services needed in the case of NewsGrid are listed here. The functionality of each service is merely exemplary and can be adapted to meet the needs of particular users:

File-Transfer (Download): This service enables the downloading of a video file in combination with the specification of start and end positions. This allows for only part of a video file to be selected for download. If a video file is available in different quality formats (MPEG-1, MPEG-2, MPEG-4, H.264, etc.) or transmission standards (PAL, NTSC, HDTV, etc.) the user must be able to specify which specific version he needs.

File-Transfer (Upload): With the aid of this service a new video can be uploaded and stored in the database. At the same time an indexing task is defined. Depending on the indexing mechanisms available the indexing can be executed manually by humans or an automatic indexing service can be initiated. The automatic indexing can be executed as soon as free compute capacity is available. The execution of manual indexing depends on the availability of a human operator. In both cases it must be possible to set the priority of the indexing task. This can be done by the person who submits the video or the database manager.

Video streaming (Video-on-Demand service): A video is transferred to a user not with the purpose of downloading the file, but rather to view and inspect the contents. The user must thus be able to start, pause, and spool forwards and backwards, etc. as is the case with a normal video player. The complete video file must thus not be transferred, but only the parts to be viewed. As the purpose is to give the user a quick insight into the video contents, the quality level can be comparatively low, which can be achieved through a stronger compression. This also reduces the amount of data to be transferred.

Addition of a Description: A manually generated textual description, additional metadata and references to similar material are stored in the database together with the video. Key words and metadata are used together with automatically generated descriptive data to generate an ODV for the particular video.

Data retrieval using static features (SODV): This service enables the *classic* data retrieval tasks using the static features from the ODV, These features can be defined manually or generated automatically. It must be possible to limit the search to a subset of the database.

Data retrieval using dynamic features (DODV): A dynamic content based search is enabled by this service. In order to execute the actual search an appropriate program supplied by the information supplier, e.g. a news agency, or a user's program may be used. As in the case of static data the search can be limited to a subset of the database.

Monitoring the search progress: This service supplies information about the progress of a search in the case of compute intensive content based searches. It must be possible for the user to ask for the display of intermediate results using the video streaming service.

Addition of a new static feature: This service allows for a new static feature to be added to all videos in the database. In the case of MPEG-7 this implies that an additional field is added. If the new feature is calculated from video content a routine to do this must be added and stored in the database for processing new videos entered. In the case of manual generation of the new feature the tasks to be executed must be defined, initiated and controlled by the database manager.

Video cutting: This service enables users to extract various cuts from different videos and join these to form a single new video. This is especially then the case when topical videos are to be combined with archived material. The video cutting process can thus be executed directly on the data in the repository. The advantages of this service are twofold. In the first instance the amount of data to be downloaded can be substantially reduced. Secondly, news editors who only have a moderately powerful computer, such as a notebook, available can more easily execute cutting tasks on a more powerful grid node.

7. NewsGrid workflows

In this section the two main workflows in NewsGrid are outlined in order to give a brief overview of the interaction between the techniques and services described in the previous sections. Some additional aspects will also be mentioned to complete the video database framework.

7.1. Storing new video files

If a new video file is to be stored in the database, some pre-processing is done in order to accelerate subsequent search processes. Firstly scene change detection is performed to get some knowledge about the structure of the video. For performance reasons this is also done in the compressed video domain. Appropriate algorithms were published by Falkemeier et al. [16], Meng et al. [30], and Yeo et al. [31].

To allow a very fast and rough search for whole frames one key frame is extracted every three seconds. The colour moments for these images are calculated and stored in the database. The scene cut list and the static colour moment feature vectors can be stored using for example the MPEG-7 [6] file format in combination with a XML database. In the database only a link to the video file is stored. The storage of the video files is distributed over the cluster nodes. Every node stores a subset of the complete data relative to its compute power.

7.2. Retrieving video files

Queries to search for particular video clips, i.e. news items, may be submitted to the NewsGrid repository via a web interface from anywhere. The user can submit an example image or use a simple drawing tool to prepare a sample sketch. Then it must be specified whether the image or sketch describes the whole frame or should be used as a template for an object to be searched for in frames. In the last instance the features to be used in the comparison of the images and some additional parameters, if necessary, must be defined. The image/sketch is sent via the internet connection to the grid database server, which may itself be a cluster.

The master node of the database server cluster checks whether the data supplied by the user are consistent and complete such that a content based search can be executed. If the check is positive the query image/sketch and the additional parameters are sent to the grid nodes. These can be nodes of the server cluster, but may of course also be other nodes of the NewsGrid. Note that these other nodes may themselves again be clusters. The grid scheduler thus triggers the various node-schedulers to each start the parallel search on video level as long as there are unsearched local files. Within each cluster, if only one file is left, the parallel search is started on frame level. If one cluster node runs idle it requests files from other (local) cluster nodes. Files from overloaded nodes are transferred via the high-bandwidth cluster network and stored temporarily on an idle node, which immediately starts the search process.

Finally, when all files have been processed, the results of the different frames from one shot are combined into a single result value per scene. To perform this task information from the scene cut list must be acquired from the database. Once this task has been completed every node sends its result file to the master node, which generates an overall result file. This is done for each grid node, i.e. each cluster in the NewsGrid. Subsequently the result videos are generated, which task is also executed in parallel by the cluster nodes. The final results are then dispatched to the master node of the database server cluster—or another designated grid node—in order to present the results to the user.

The result viewer presents the result page with the modified videos. If the user selects a video, a copy of the corresponding original video is transferred to him.

8. Conclusions

In this paper an infrastructure for a world wide NewsGrid was presented. The distributed digital archive, supplying versatile services for storing, searching and retrieving, downloading, and post-processing of news videos, change the workflow for news editors. The users of NewsGrid obtain access to videos from all over the world, from any TV station or news agency connected to the grid. The data is transmitted only on demand, which saves bandwidth and storage capacity compared to current procedures.

An efficient and reasonably effective method for content based searching in video repositories was presented. Working directly on the compressed video data allows for fast searches. The best strategy and computer architecture to parallelise the content based search for large video databases depends on the concrete use case, but in many instances a cluster consisting of SMP-nodes with 2 PE's and a coarse-grained algorithm will be the best choice. The precision of retrieved results is high, but always dependent on the search parameters supplied by users. A novel result presentation technique using region of interest coding allows the user to get an impression of the dynamic aspects of the scenes without being overextended by too much information presented at the same time.

Future work includes the development of parallel search algorithms in the compressed domain of the MPEG-4 video format. Specialised user clients, e.g. for mobile devices, will be developed. The design of the services will be more detailed and more services will be added to the system. The transferability to other use cases will be improved. Furthermore concepts for digital rights managements and user roles must be defined.

A further aspect to be investigated is the extension of the NewsGrid concepts to other application areas. Possible areas include e-Learning (for example finding particular videos for demonstration purposes), medical (for example searching for sample videos to compare patient data), geographic information systems, environmental systems, etc. In all these cases the presently available concepts can be applied. End user groups of a particular repository will normally be limited in size.

This may not be the case with repositories storing videos on more popular themes such as sporting events or general video-on-demand (VOD) systems. In such cases two performance aspects can become limiting factors, viz. the bandwidth of the network and the retrieval performance of the archiving systems.

Present developments in broadband communication networks for the internet already make the distribution of video material feasible, even to very large user groups. The distribution of sporting events to millions of viewers over the internet is presently planned in Europe. The required communication bandwidths of 4-5 MBit/sec are becoming readily available through cable and ADSL networks.

Making available the dynamic search methods employed in the NewsGrid to very large numbers of users could, however, result in bottle necks both in accessing the data stored in the archive as well as in the processing of complex search algorithms. In such cases response times may increase unduly. This can be solved by creating mirrors of the databases as well as duplicating or extending the parallel systems executing the search algorithms. The development of more efficient and effective search algorithms to reduce retrieval times is also of prime importance.

REFERENCES

1. G. Falkemeier, G. Joubert, and O. Kao. A system for analysis and presentation of MPEG compressed newsfeeds. *In Business and Work in the Information Society: New Technologies and Applications*, 454–460. IOS Press, 1999.
2. G. Falkemeier, G. Joubert, and O. Kao. Internet Supported Analysis and Presentation of MPEG Compressed Newsfeeds. *International Journal of Computers and Applications*, Volume 23(2), 129–136. 2001.
3. I. Foster, C. Kesselman (eds.). *The Grid: Blueprint for a New Computing Infrastructure*. Elsevier and Morgan Kaufmann, 2nd edition, 2004.
4. E. Oomoto and K. Tanaka. OVID: Design and implementation of a video object database system. *IEEE Trans. on Knowledge and Data Engineering*, 5:629–643, 1993.
5. H. Jiang, D. Montesi, and A.K. Elmagarmid. VideoText database systems. In *Proc. Of IEEE Multimedia Computing and Systems*, 344–351, 1997.
6. ISO/IEC 15938. Information technology – Multimedia content description interface, 2002.
7. ISO/IEC TR 21000. Information technology – Multimedia framework (MPEG-21), 2004.
8. S. Geisler, O. Kao. Cluster-Based Organisation and Retrieval of Newsfeed Archives. *Proc. of the 2nd International Workshop on Intelligent Multimedia Computing and Networking (IMMCN'2002)*, 1033–1036, 2002.
9. S.-F. Chang, W. Chen, H. Meng, H. Sundaram, and D. Zhong. VideoQ: An Automated Content Based Video Search System Using Visual Cues. *Proc. of ACM Multimedia*, 313–324, 1997.
10. A. Hampapur, A. Gupta, B. Horowitz, C.F. Shu, C. Fuller, J. Bach, M. Gorkani, and R. Jain. Virage video engine. Proc. *SPIE: Storage and Retrieval for Image and Video Databases*, 188–197, 1997.
11. D. Ponceleon, S. Srinivasan, A. Amir, and D. Petkovic. Key to Effective Video Retrieval: Effective Cataloging and Browsing. *Proc. of ACM Multimedia*, 99–107, 1998.
12. O. Kao, S. Stapel. Case study: Cairo – a distributed image retrieval system for cluster architectures. In T.K. Shih (edt.), *Distributed Multimedia Databases: Techniques and Applications*, 291–303. Idea Group Publishing, 2001.

13. S. Geisler. Efficient Parallel Search in Video Databases with Dynamic Feature Extraction, In *Parallel Computing: Software Technology, Algorithms, Architecture And Applications: Proc. of the Intern. Conference Parco2003*, 431–438, 2004.
14. ISO/IEC 11172-2:1993. Coding of Moving Pictures and Associated Audio for Digital Storage Media at up to About 1.5 Mbit/s – Part 2: Video, 1993.
15. ISO/IEC 13818-2:2000. Generic Coding of Moving Pictures and Associated Audio Information – Part 2: Video, 2000.
16. G. Falkemeier, G.R. Joubert, and O. Kao. A system for Analysis and Presentation of MPEG Compressed Newsfeeds. *In Business and Work in the Information Society: New Technologies and Applications*, IOS Press, 454–460, 1999.
17. K. Shen and E. Delp. A fast Algorithm for Video parsing using MPEG compressed Sequences, *Proc. of the IEEE International Conference on Image Processing*, 252–255, 1995.
18. T. Bretschneider, S. Geisler, and O. Kao. Simulation-based Assessment of Parallel Architectures for Image Databases, *Proc. of the Intern. Conference on Parallel Computingg (ParCo 2001)*, Imperial College Press, 401–408, 2001.
19. M. Mills, J. Cohen, and Y. Y. Wong. A magnifier tool for video data. In *Proc. of the SIGCHI conference on Human factors in computing systems*, 93–98. ACM Press, 1992.
20. H. Zhang, C. Y. Low, S. W. Smolier, and J. Wu. Video parsing, retrieval and browsing: an integrated and content-based solution. MIT Press, 1997.
21. S. Uchihashi, J. Foote, A. Girgensohn, and J. Boreczky. Video manga: generating semantically meaningful video summaries. In *Proc. of the seventh ACM international conference on Multimedia (Part 1)*, 383–392. ACM Press, 1999.
22. M. G. Christel, A. G. Hauptmann, H. D. Wactlar, and T. D. Ng. Collages as dynamic summaries for news video. In *Proceedings of the tenth ACM international conference on Multimedia*, 561–569. ACM Press, 2002.
23. C. Carson, M. Thomas, S. Belongie, J. M. Hellerstein, and J. Malik. Blobworld: A system for region-based image indexing and retrieval. In *Third International Conference on Visual Information Systems*, Springer, 1999.
24. S. M. Smith and J. M. Brady. Asset-2: Real-time motion segmentation and shape tracking. *IEEE Transactions Pattern Analysis and Machine Intelligence*, 17(8):814–820, 1995.
25. L. Teodosio and W. Bender. Salient video stills: content and context preserved. In *Proc. of the first ACM international conference on Multimedia*, 39–46, ACM Press, 1993.
26. Y. Taniguchi, A. Akutsu, and Y. Tonomura. Panoramaexcerpts: extracting and packing panoramas for video browsing. In *Proc. of the fifth ACM international conference on Multimedia*, 427–436. ACM Press, 1997.
27. S. Geisler and O.Kao. Region of Interest Video Coding for Result Presentation in Distributed Video Databases, *International Conference on Imaging Science, Systems, and Technology (CISST 2004)*, 427–433, 2004.
28. A. P. Bradley and F. W. M. Stentiford. Visual attention for region of interest coding in JPEG 2000. *Journal of Visual Communication and Image Representation*, 14(13):232–250, 2003.
29. J. Benoit-Pineau, N. Sarris, D. Barba, and M. G. Strintzis. Video coding for wireless varying bit rate communication based on areas of interest and region

representation. In *4th International Conference on Image Processing (ICIP 97)*, Santa Barbara, 1997.

30. J. Meng, Y. Juan, and S.-F. Chang. Scene change detection in a MPEG compressed video sequence. In *IS&T/SPIE Symposium Proceedings, volume SPIE2419*, 14–25, 1995.
31. B. Yeo and B. Liu. Rapid scene analysis on compressed video. *IEEE Trans. on Circuits and Systems for Video Technology*, 5(6):533–544, 1997.

Grid Computing: The New Frontier of High Performance Computing
Lucio Grandinetti (Editor)

357

© 2005 Elsevier B.V. All rights reserved.

UNICORE - From Project Results to Production Grids

A. Streit, D. Erwin, Th. Lippert, D. Mallmann, R. Menday, M. Rambadt, M. Riedel, M. Romberg, B. Schuller, and Ph. Wieder

John von Neumann-Institute for Computing (NIC)
Forschungszentrum Jülich (FZJ)
52425 Jülich, Germany
E-mail: {a.streit, d.erwin, th.lippert, d.mallmann, r.menday, m.riedel, m.rambadt, m.romberg, b.schuller,ph.wieder}@fz-juelich.de

The UNICORE Grid-technology provides a seamless, secure and intuitive access to distributed Grid resources. In this paper we present the recent evolution from project results to production Grids. At the beginning UNICORE was developed as a prototype software in two projects funded by the German research ministry (BMBF). Over the following years, in various European-funded projects, UNICORE evolved to a full-grown and well-tested Grid middleware system, which today is used in daily production at many supercomputing centers worldwide. Beyond this production usage, the UNICORE technology serves as a solid basis in many European and International research projects, which use existing UNICORE components to implement advanced features, high level services, and support for applications from a growing range of domains. In order to foster these ongoing developments, UNICORE is available as open source under BSD licence at SourceForge, where new releases are published on a regular basis. This paper is a review of the UNICORE achievements so far and gives a glimpse on the UNICORE roadmap.

1. Introduction

End of 1998 the concept of "Grid computing" was introduced in the monograph "The Grid: Blueprint for a New Computing Infrastructure" by I. Foster and C. Kesselman [1]. Two years earlier, in 1997, the development of the UNICORE - Uniform Interface to Computing Resources - system was initiated to enable German supercomputer centers to provide their users with a *seamless, secure, and intuitive access* to their heterogeneous computing resources. Like in the case of the Globus Toolkit® [2] UNICORE was started before "Grid Computing" became the accepted new paradigm for distributed computing.

The UNICORE vision was proposed to the German Ministry for Education and Research (BMBF) and received funding. A first prototype was developed in the UNICORE[1] project [3]. The foundations for the current production version were laid in the follow-up project UNICORE Plus[2] [4], which was successfully completed in 2002. Since then UNICORE was used in operation at German supercomputing centers and became a solid

---

[1]funded by BMBF grant 01 IR 703, duration: August 1997 - December 1999
[2]funded by BMBF grant 01 IR 001 A-D, duration: January 2000 - December 2002

basis for numerous European projects. In this paper we will describe the evolution of UNI-CORE from a prototype software developed in research projects to a Grid middleware used today in the daily operation of production Grids.

Although already set out in the initial UNICORE project proposal in 1997, the goals and objectives of the UNICORE technology are still valid:

- Foremost, the aim of UNICORE is to hide the rough edges resulting from different hardware architectures, vendor specific operating systems, incompatible batch systems, different application environments, historically grown computer center practices, naming conventions, file system structures, and security policies – just to name the most obvious.

- Equally, security is a constituent part of UNICORE's design relying on X.509 certificates for the authentication of users, servers, and software, and the encryption of the communication over the internet.

- Finally, UNICORE is usable by scientists and engineers without having to study vendor or site-specific documentation. A Graphical User Interface (GUI) is available to assist the user in creating and managing jobs.

Additionally, several basic conditions are met by UNICORE: the Grid middleware supports operating systems and batch systems of all vendors present at the partner sites. In 1997 these were for instance large Cray T3E systems, NEC and Hitachi vector machines, IBM SP2s, and smaller Linux clusters. Nowadays the spectrum is even broader, of course with modern hardware, such as IBM p690 systems. The deployed software has to be non-intrusive, so that it does not require changes in the computing centers hard- and/or software infrastructure. Maintaining site autonomy is still a major issue in Grid computing, when aspects of acceptability and usability in particular from the system administrator's point of view are addressed. In addition to UNICORE's own security model, site-specific security requirements (e. g. firewalls) are supported.

Near the end of the initial funding period of the UNICORE Plus project, a working prototype was available, which showed that the initial concept works. By combining innovative ideas and proven components over the years, this first prototype evolved to a *vertically integrated* Grid middleware solution.

The remainder of this paper is structured as follows. In Section 2 the usage of UNI-CORE in production is presented to give potential users a high-level glimpse on the UNICORE technology and architecture. In section 3 UNICORE's architecture and core features are described in more detail. European funded projects, which use UNICORE as a basis for their work are described in Section 4. Section 5 gives an outlook on the future development of UNICORE. The paper closes with conclusions and acknowledgements.

2. UNICORE in Production

From its birth in two German BMBF-funded projects to its extensive use and further development in a variety of EU and BMBF research projects (cf. Section 4 for details), the UNICORE technology ran through an evolutionary process transforming from an initial prototype software to a powerful production Grid middleware.

2.1. UNICORE@SourceForge

Since May 2004, the UNICORE technology with all its components is available as open source software under the BSD license. It can be downloaded from the SourceForge repository. Besides the core developers of UNICORE (namely Fujitsu Laboratories of Europe, Intel Germany and the Research Center Jülich), there are numerous contributors from all over the world, e. g. Norway, Poland, China and Russia. The Web site [5] offers a convenient entry point for interested users and developers. In the download section the UNICORE software is bundled in different packages, e. g. the client package and individual packages for the different server components Gateway, NJS, TSI/IDB, UUDB (cf. Section 3 for details), and plug-ins. Until January 2005 more than 2800 downloads of UNICORE are counted.

A tracker section linked on the Web site establishes a communication link to the core developer community. The corresponding mailing lists allow users to report bugs, to request new features, and to get informed about bug fixes or patches. For the announcement of new software releases a separate mailing list was created. The Grid team at the Research Center Jülich is responsible for UNICORE@SourceForge. Its work includes coordinating and driving the development effort, and producing consolidated, stable, and tested releases of the UNICORE software.

2.2. Production System on Jump

Since July 2004 UNICORE is established as production software to access the supercomputer resources of the John von Neumann-Institute for Computing (NIC) at the Research Center Jülich. These are the 1312-processor IBM p690 cluster (Jump) [6], the Cray SV1 vector machine, and a new Cray XD1 cluster system. As an alternative to the standard SSH login, UNICORE provides an intuitive and easy way for submitting batch jobs to the systems. The academic and industrial users come from all over Germany and from parts of Europe. The applications come from a broad field of domains, e. g. astrophysics, quantumphysics, medicine, biology, chemistry, and climate research, just to name the largest user communities. A dedicated, pre-configured UNICORE client with all required certificates and accessible Vsites is available for download. This alleviates the installation and configuration process significantly. Furthermore, an online installation guide including a certificate assistant, an user manual, and example jobs help users getting started.

To provide the NIC-users with adequate certificates and to ease the process of requesting and receiving a certificate, a certificate authority (CA) was established. User certificate requests are generated in the client and have to be send to the CA. Since introduction of UNICORE at NIC, more than 120 active users requested a UNICORE user certificate.

A mailing list serves as a direct link of the users to UNICORE developers in the Research Center Jülich. The list allows to post problems, bug reports, and feature requests. This input is helpful in enhancing UNICORE with new features and services, in solving problems, identifying and correcting bugs, and influences new releases of UNICORE available at SourceForge.

2.3. DEISA – Distributed European Infrastructure for Scientific Applications

Traditionally, the provision of high performance computing resources to researchers has traditionally been the objective and mission of national HPC centers. On the one hand, there is an increasing global competition between Europe, USA, and Japan with growing demands for compute resources at the highest performance level, and on the other hand stagnant or even shrinking budgets. To stay competitive major investments are needed every two years – an innovation cycle that even the most prosperous countries have difficulties to fund.

To advance science in Europe, eight leading European HPC centers devised an innovative strategy to build a Distributed European Infrastructure for Scientific Applications (DEISA)[3] [7]. The centers join in building and operating a tera-scale supercomputing facility. This becomes possible through deep integration of existing national high-end platforms, tightly coupled by a dedicated network and supported by innovative system and grid software. The resulting virtual distributed supercomputer has the capability for natural growth in all dimensions without singular procurements at the European level. Advances in network technology and the resulting increase in bandwidth and lower latency virtually shrink the distance between the nodes in the distributed super-cluster. Furthermore, DEISA can expand horizontally by adding new systems, new architectures, and new partners thus increasing the capabilities and attractiveness of the infrastructure in a non-disruptive way.

By using the UNICORE technology, the four core partners of the projects have coupled their systems using virtually dedicated 1 Gbit/s connections. The DEISA super-cluster currently consists of over 4000 IBM Power 4 processors and 416 SGI processors with an aggregated peak performance of about 22 teraflops. UNICORE provides the seamless, secure and intuitive access to the super-cluster.

The Research Center Jülich is one of the DEISA core partners and is responsible for introducing UNICORE as Grid middleware at all partner sites and for providing support to local UNICORE administrators.

In the following we describe the DEISA architecture. Note, a detailed description of UNICORE's architecture and server components can be found in Section 3 and in particular in Figure 2. All DEISA partners have installed the UNICORE server components Gateway, NJS, TSI, and UUDB to access the local supercomputer resources of each site via UNICORE. Figure 1 shows the DEISA UNICORE configuration. For clarity only four sites are shown. At each site, a Gateway exists as an access to the DEISA infrastructure. The NJSs are not only registered to their local Gateway, but to all other Gateways at the partner sites as well. Local security measures like firewall configurations need to consider this, by permitting access to all DEISA users and NJSs. This fully connected architecture has several advantages. If one Gateway has a high load, access to the high performance supercomputers through DEISA is not limited. Due to the fully connected architecture, no single point of failure exists and the flexibility is increased.

The DEISA partners operate different supercomputer architectures, which are all accessible through UNICORE. Initially all partners with IBM p690 clusters are connected to one large virtual supercomputer. In a second step other supercomputers of different variety are connected to DEISA, making the virtual supercomputer heterogeneous. UNICORE can handle this, as it is designed to serve such heterogeneous architectures in a seamless, secure, and intuitive way.

In December 2004 a first successful UNICORE demonstration between the four DEISA

---

[3]funded by EC grant FP6-508803, duration: May 2004 - April 2009

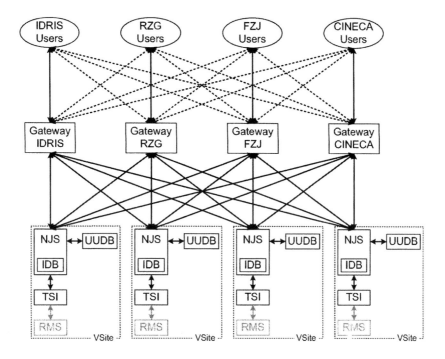

Figure 1. The DEISA architecture.

core sites FZJ (Research Center Jülich, Germany), RZG (Computing Center Garching, Germany), CINECA (Italian Interuniversity Consortium, Italy) and IDRIS (Institute for Development and Resources in Intensive Scientific Computing, France) was given. Different parts of a distributed astrophysical application were generated and submitted with UNICORE to all four sites.

The experience and knowledge of the researchers, developers, users, and administrators in working with UNICORE in the DEISA project on a large production platform will be used as useful input for future developments of the UNICORE technology. A close synchronization with the UniGrids project (cf. Section 5.1) is foreseen.

3. The Architecture of UNICORE

Figure 2 shows the layered Grid architecture of UNICORE consisting of user, server and target system tier [8]. The implementation of all components shown is realized in Java. UNICORE meets the Open Grid Services Architecture (OGSA) [9] concept following the paradigm of 'Everything being a Service'. Indeed, an analysis has shown that the basic ideas behind UNICORE already realizes this paradigm [10,11].

3.1. User Tier

The UNICORE Client provides a graphical user interface to exploit the entire set of services offered by the underlying servers. The client communicates with the server tier by sending and receiving Abstract Job Objects (AJO) and file data via the UNICORE Protocol Layer (UPL) which is placed on top of the SSL protocol. The AJO is the realization of UNICORE's job model and central to UNICORE's philosophy of abstraction and seamlessness. It contains platform and site independent descriptions of computational and data related tasks, resource information and workflow specifications along with user and security information. AJOs are sent to the UNICORE Gateway in form of serialized and signed Java objects, followed by an optional stream of bytes if file data is to be transferred.

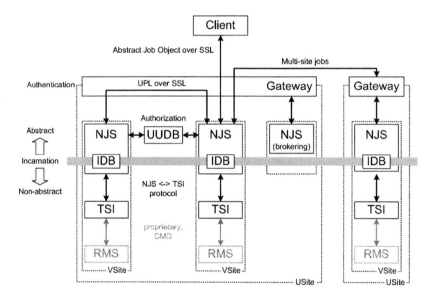

Figure 2. The UNICORE architecture.

The UNICORE client assists the user in creating complex, interdependent jobs that can be executed on any UNICORE site (Usite) without requiring any modifications. A UNICORE job, more precisely a job group, may recursively contain other job groups and/or tasks and may also contain dependencies between job groups to generate job workflows. Besides the description of a job as a set of one or more directed a-cyclic graphs, conditional and repetitive execution of job groups or tasks are also included. For the monitoring of jobs, their status is available at each level of recursion down to the individual task. Detailed log information is available to analyze potential error conditions. At the end of the execution of the job it is possible to retrieve the stdout and stderr output of the job. Data management functions like import, export, and transfer are available through the GUI as explicit tasks. This allows the user to specify data transfer from one target system to another (e. g. for workflows), from or to the local workstation before or after the execution of a job, or to store data permanently in archives.

The previously described features already provide an effective tool to use resources of different computing centers both for capacity or capability computing, but many scientists and engineers use application packages. For applications without a graphical user interface, a tool kit simplifies the development of a custom built UNICORE plug-in. Over the years many plug-ins were developed, so that plug-ins already exist for many standard scientific applications, as e. g. for CPMD (Car-Parrinello Molecular Dynamics) [12], Fluent or MSC Nastran.

3.2. Server Tier

The server tier contains the Gateway and the Network Job Supervisor (NJS). The Gateway controls the access to a Usite and acts as the secure entry point accepting and authenticating UPL requests. A Usite identifies the participating organization (e. g. a supercomputing center) to the Grid with a symbolic name that resolves into the URL of the Gateway. An organization may be part of multiple Grids offering the same or different resources to different communities. The Gateway forwards incoming requests to the underlying Network Job Supervisor (NJS) of a virtual site (Vsite) for further processing. The NJS represents resources with a uniform user mapping scheme and no boundaries like firewalls between them.

A Vsite identifies a particular set of resources at a Usite and is controlled by a NJS. A Vsite may consist of a single supercomputer, e. g. a IBM p690 System with LoadLeveler, or a Linux cluster with PBS as resource management system. The flexibility of this concept supports different system architectures and gives the organization full control over its resources. Note that, there can be more than one Vsite inside each USite as depicted in Figure 2.

The NJS is responsible for the virtualization of the underlying resources by mapping the abstract job on a specific target system. This process is called "incarnation" and makes use of the Incarnation Database (IDB). System-specific data are stored in the IDB describing the software and hardware infrastructure of the system. Among others, the available resources like software, incarnation of abstract commands (standard UNIX command like rm, cp, ...) and site-specific administrative information are stored. In addition to the incarnation the NJS processes workflow descriptions included in an AJO, performs pre- and post-staging of files and authorizes the user via the UNICORE User Database (UUDB). Typically the Gateway and NJS are running on dedicated secure systems behind a firewall, although the Gateway could be placed outside a firewall or in a demilitarized zone.

3.3. Target System Tier

The Target System Interface (TSI) implements the interface to the underlying supercomputer with its resource management system. It is a stateless daemon running on the target system and interfacing with the local resource manager realized either by a batch system like PBS [13] or CCS [14], a batch system emulation on top of e. g. Linux, or a Grid resource manager like Globus' GRAM [15,16].

3.4. Single Sign-On

The UNICORE security model relies on the usage of permanent X.509 certificates issued by a trusted Certification Authority (CA) and SSL based communication across 'insecure' networks. Certificates are used to provide a single sign-on in the client. The client unlocks the user's keystore when it is first started, so that no further password requests are handed to the user. All authentication and authorization is done on the basis of the user certificate. At each UNICORE site user certificates are mapped to local accounts (standard UNIX uid/gid), which may be different at each site, due to existing naming conventions. The sites retain full control over the acceptance of users based on the identity of the individual – the distinguished name – or other information that might be contained in the certificate. UNICORE can handle multiple user certificates, i.e. it permits a client to be part of multiple, disjoint Grids. It is also possible to specify project accounts in the client allowing users to select different accounts for different projects on one execution system or to assume different roles with different privileges.

The private key in the certificate is used to sign each job and all included sub-jobs during the transit from the client to sites and between sites. This protects against tampering while the job is transmitted over insecure internet connections and it allows to verify the identity of the owner at the receiving end, without having to trust the intermediate sites which forwarded the job.

4. UNICORE Based Projects

During the evolutionary development of the UNICORE technology, many European and international projects have decided to base their Grid software implementations on UNICORE or to extend the growing set of core UNICORE functions with new features specific to their project focus. The goals and objectives of projects using UNICORE are not limited to the computer science community alone. Several other scientific domains such as bio-molecular engineering or computational chemistry are using the UNICORE technology as the basis of their work. In the following we present short overviews of goals and objectives of UNICORE-based projects and describe additional functions and services contributed to the UNICORE development.

4.1. EUROGRID – Application Testbed for European Grid Computing

In the EUROGRID[4] project [17] a Grid network of leading European High Performance Supercomputing centers was established. Based on the UNICORE technology application-specific Grids were integrated, operated and demonstrated:

- Bio-Grid for biomolecular science

- Meteo-Grid for localized weather prediction

- CAE-Grid for coupling applications

- HPC-Grid for general HPC end-users

[4]funded by EC grant IST-1999-20247, duration: November 2000 - January 2004

As part of the project, the UNICORE software was extended by an efficient data transfer mechanism, resource brokerage mechanisms, tools and services for Application Service Providers (ASP), application coupling methods, and an interactive access feature [18]. Efficient data transfer is a important issue, as Grids typically rely on public parts of Internet connections. The available limited bandwidth has to be used efficiently to reduce the transfer time and the integrity of the transferred data has to be maintained, even if the transfer is interrupted. Depending on the application domain, additional security and confidentiality concerns need to be considered. This UNICORE high performance data transfer also uses X.509 certificates for authentication and encryption. To achieve not only a fast and secure transfer of data, but also high-performance capabilities, network Quality of Service (QoS) aspects, overlapping of streamed data transfers, and packet assembling and compression techniques are included.

In order to optimize the selection of resources – either done by the users manually or by a metascheduler automatically – resource brokerage mechanisms and detailed resource description abilities are important. Within the EUROGRID project, mechanisms were added to UNICORE, which allow users to specify their jobs in an abstract way improving the overall resource selection and accounting. In particular for the benefit of the industrial user aspects of security, convenience, and cost efficiency were addressed. To this end, the already existing security concepts of UNICORE were thoroughly evaluated and assessed as being adequate, hence no additional development had to be done. The task of the developed resource broker is to match the abstract specification of the users jobs and their requirements with the available resources in the Grid. The resource broker reports the best match back to the user including an estimate of the costs, which than allows the user to assign the appropriate resources to the job. For the suppliers of Grid resources (e. g. supercomputing centers) the resource broker allows to specify information about computational resources, architectures, processing power, storage and archiving facilities, post-processing facilities like visualization equipment, available software packages, and security guarantees. All this data is enhanced by billing information.

Supercomputing centers converge from pure providers of raw supercomputing power to Application Service Providers (ASP) running relevant scientific applications. For accounting and billing purposes the ASP needs to know the exact resources consumed by each customer in each run. For measuring the usage of supercomputers standard mechanisms provided by the resource management and operating system can be used, but measuring the usage of licenses requires a sophisticated approach. For some applications, e. g. from the Computer Aided Engineering (CAE) domain, this includes a connection to the applications licence manager. Establishing a link to the above mentioned resource broker is required to influence their decisions.

For solving complex problems applications from different domains, e. g. fluid-structure or electromagnetism-structure, need to be coupled. This is established by using the EU-ROGRID resource broker functionality and combining it with the available Metacomputing functionality developed in the UNICORE Plus project (cf. Section 1), which allows different schedulers of compute and application resources to cooperate. Finally, an interactive access to control and steer running application is needed for many scientific applications. The interactive use includes an interactive shell to actually login to computing resources using the UNICORE technology and security infrastructure.

EUROGRID used the UNICORE technology to provide the above described services and functionalities by developing new components. After the project ended, the developed components were revised and useful additions to the core UNICORE functions are now part of the available UNICORE software.

4.2. GRIP – Grid Interoperability Project

Grid computing empowers users and organizations to work effectively in an information-rich environment. Different communities and application domains have developed distinct Grid implementations some based on published open standards or on domain and community specific features. GRIP[5] [19] had the objective to demonstrate that the different approaches of two distinct grids can successfully complement each other and that different implementations can interoperate. Two prominent Grid systems were selected for this purpose: UNICORE and Globus[TM][20], a toolkit developed in the United States. In contrast to UNICORE, Globus provides a set of APIs and services which requires more in-depth knowledge from the user. Globus is widely used in numerous international projects and many centers have Globus installed as Grid middleware.

The objectives of GRIP were:

- Develop software to enable the interoperation of independently developed Grid solutions

- Build and demonstrate prototype inter-Grid applications

- Contribute to and influence international Grid standards

During the runtime of the GRIP project the Open Grid Service Architecture was proposed by the Global Grid Forum (GGF) [21]. The arrival of OGSA also was an opportunity to influence the standards directly which were to be created and to start developments that allow UNICORE to interoperate not only with Globus but with services on the Grid in general, once the definition of the services and their interfaces became mature. OGSA did not change the overall objectives of GRIP, however, it influenced directly some of the technical results.

A basic requirement of GRIP was that the Grid interoperability layer should not change the well-known UNICORE user environment. As developers from both communities cooperated in the GRIP project, this goal was reached with only little changes of the UNICORE server components and no changes of the Globus Toolkit. This was achieved by the development of the so called Globus Target System Interface (Globus TSI), which provides UNICORE-access to computational resources managed by Globus. The Globus TSI was integrated into a heterogeneous UNICORE and Globus testbed.

To achieve the main objective of GRIP, the interoperability between UNICORE and Globus and initial OGSA services, the following elements had to be implemented:

- The interoperability layer between UNICORE and Globus Version 2

- The interoperability layer between UNICORE and Globus Version 3

[5]funded by EC grant IST-2001-32257, duration: January 2002 - February 2004

- The Access from UNICORE to simple Web services as a first step towards full integration of Web services

- The Interoperability of the certificate infrastructures of UNICORE and Globus

- A resource broker capable of brokering between UNICORE and Globus resources

- The Ontology of the resource description on an abstract level

In GRIP, two important application areas were selected to prove that the interoperability layers work as specified:

- Bio-molecular applications were instrumented in such a way that they are Grid-aware in any Grid environment and capable to seamlessly use UNICORE and Globus managed resources. The techniques developed in GRIP were designed and implemented in a generalized way to ensure that they can be used in other application domains as well.

- A meteorological application, the Relocatable Local Model (RLM), was decomposed in such a way that the components could execute on the most suitable resources in a Grid, independent of the middleware.

The results of the GRIP project are important for understanding general interoperability processes between Grid middleware systems. The experience and knowledge of the GRIP partners allowed to work in many relevant areas within GGF, like security, architecture, protocols, workflow, production management, and applications, and to influence the work in GGF.

4.3. OpenMolGRID – Open Computing Grid for Molecular Science and Engineering

The OpenMolGRID[6] project [22] was focused on the development of Grid enabled molecular design and engineering applications. *In silico* testing [23] has become a crucial part in the molecular design process of new drugs, pesticides, biopolymers, and biomaterials. In a typical design process $O(10^5)$ to $O(10^6)$ candidate molecules are generated and their feasibility has to be tested. It is not economical to carry out experimental testing on all possible candidates. Therefore, computational screening methods provide a cheap and cost effective alternative to reduce the number of candidates. Over the years Quantitative Structure Activity/Property Relationship (QSAR/QSPR) methods have been shown to be reliable for the prediction of various physical, chemical, and biological activities [24].

QSPR/QSAR relies on the observation that molecular compounds with similar structure have similar properties. For each specific application a set of molecules is needed for which the target property is known. This requires searching globally distributed information resources for appropriate data. For the purpose of exploring molecular similarity, descriptors are calculated from the molecular structure. Thousands of molecular descriptors have been proposed and are used to characterize molecular structures with respect to different properties. Their calculation puts high demands on computer resources and requires high-performance computing.

[6]funded by EC grant IST-2001-37238, duration: September 2002 - February 2005

Based on this complex application the objectives of the OpenMolGRID project were defined as:

- Development of tools for secure and seamless access to distributed information and computational methods relevant to molecular engineering within the UNICORE frame

- Provision of a realistic testbed and reference application in life science

- Development of a toxicity prediction model validated with a large experimental set

- Provision of design principles for next generation molecular engineering systems.

In particular this included to use UNICORE to automatize, integrate, and speed-up the drug discovery pipeline.

The OpenMolGRID project addressed the objectives above by defining abstraction layers for data sources (databases) and methods (application software), and integrating all necessary data sources (e. g. ECOTOX [25]) and methods (e. g. 2D/3D Molecular Structure Conversion and Optimization, Descriptor Calculation, Structure Enumeration) into UNICORE. The project developed application specific user interfaces (plug-ins) and a mechanism to generate a complete UNICORE Job from an XML workflow specification. This so called Meta-Plug-in takes care of including all auxiliary steps like data format transformation and data transfers into the job, distributing data parallel tasks over available computational resources, and allocating resources to the tasks. Thereby the molecular design process was significantly improved as the time to build QSAR/QSPR models, the probability for mistakes, and the variability of results was reduced. In addition a command line client (CLC) for UNICORE was developed to enable the data warehouse to use Grid resources for its data transformation processes. The CLC offers the generation of UNICORE jobs from XML workflow description as well as the job submission, output retrieval, status query, and job abortion. The CLC consists of commands, an API, and a queuing component.

Besides the technical achievements of OpenMolGRID and the added value for pharmaceutical companies its results will contribute to the standardization of QSAR models.

4.4. VIOLA – Vertically Integrated Optical Testbed for Large Applications

The aim of the VIOLA[7] project [26] is to build up a testbed with the latest optical network technology (multi 10 Gigabit Ethernet links). The goals and objectives of VIOLA are:

- Testing of new network components and network architectures

- Development and testing of software for dynamic bandwidth management

- Interworking of network technology from different manufacturers

- Development and testing of new applications from the Grid and Virtual Reality (VR) domain

---

[7]funded by BMBF grant 01AK605F, duration: May 2004 - April 2007

The performance of the new network technology is evaluated with different scientific applications that need a very high network performance and network flexibility. UNICORE is used to build up the Grid on top of the hardware without taking fundamental software modifications. Only an interface to the meta-computer software library MetaMPICH [27] needs to be integrated into UNICORE. Grid applications from the High Performance Supercomputing and Virtual Reality domain are enhanced for an optimized usage of the available bandwidth and the provided Quality of Service classes. In this context a Meta-Scheduler framework is developed, which is able to handle complex workflows and multi-site jobs by coordinating supercomputers and the network connecting them.

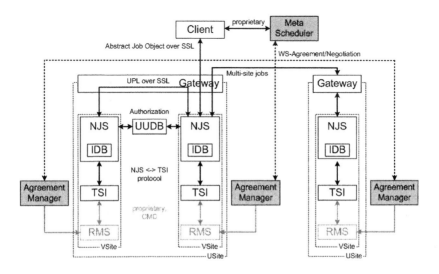

Figure 3. The VIOLA Meta-Scheduler architecture.

VIOLA's first generation Meta-Scheduler architecture focuses on the scheduling functionality requiring only minimal changes to the UNICORE system. As depicted in Figure 3, the system comprises the Agreement Manager, the Meta-Scheduler itself [28], and a Meta-Scheduling plug-in (which is part of the client and not pictured separately). Before submitting a job to a Usite (cf. Section 3.2), the Meta-Scheduling plug-in and the Meta-Scheduler exchange the data necessary to schedule the resources needed. The Meta-Scheduler is then (acting as an Agreement Consumer in WS–Agreement terms [29]) contacting the Agreement Manager to request a certain level of service, a request which is translated by the Manager into the appropriate resource management system commands. In case of VIOLA's computing resources the targeted resource management system is the EASY scheduler. Once all resources are reserved at the requested time the Meta-Scheduler notifies the UNICORE Client via the Meta-Scheduling plug-in to submit the job. This framework will also be used to schedule the interconnecting network, but potentially any resource can be scheduled if a respective Agreement Manager is implemented and the Meta-Scheduling plug-in generates the necessary scheduling information. The follow-on generation of the Meta-Scheduling framework will then be tightly integrated within UNICORE/GS (cf. Section 5.1.1).

4.5. NaReGI – National Research Grid Initiative

The Japanese NaReGI project [30] includes the UNICORE technology as the basic middleware for research and development. NaReGI is a collaboration project between industry, academia, and government. The goals and objectives are:

- Establishment of a national Japanese research Grid infrastructure

- Revitalization of the IT industry through commercialization of Grid middleware and strengthened international competitiveness

- Dissemination of Grid environments throughout industry

- Trailblazing the standardization of Grid technology

- Cultivation of human resources specializing in IT technology for Grids

Similar to the GRIP project (cf. Section 4) where an interoperability layer between UNICORE and Globus Toolkit 2 and 3 was developed, the NaReGI project plans to implement such a layer between UNICORE and Condor [31], called UNICONDORE. This interoperability layer will allow to submit jobs from the UNICORE client to Condor pools and to use Condor commands to submit jobs to UNICORE managed resources.

In the first phase of the NaReGI testbed UNICORE provides access to about 3000 CPUs in total with approximately 17 TFlops of peak performance. It is expected to increase the integrated peak performance to 100+ TFlops by the end of the project in 2007.

5. Future of UNICORE

The current UNICORE software implements a vertically integrated Grid architecture providing seamless access to various resources. Every resource is statically integrated into the UNICORE Grid by providing an interface to the appropriate resource manager.

One of the benefits Web services will bring to Grid computing is the concept of loosely coupled distributed services. Merging the idea of "everything being a service" with the achievements of the Grid community led to Grid services, enabling a new approach to the design of Grid architectures. The adoption of XML and the drive for standardization of the Open Grid Service Architecture provide the tools to move closer to the promise of interoperable Grids. A demonstrator validated the correspondence of UNICORE's architectural model with the OGSA/OGSI (Open Grid Service Infrastructure [32]) approach, which encouraged the development of an OGSA/OGSI compliant UNICORE Grid architecture in the GRIP project (cf. Section 4.2).

In [16] UNICORE is examined for the evolution of a Grid system towards a service oriented Grid, primarily focussing on architectural concepts and models. Based on the current architecture and the enhancements provided by GRIP, first steps already integrate Web services into UNICORE. This included the provision of OGSI compliant port types parallel to the proprietary ones as well as the design of XML based protocols. This work was continued in the UniGrids project.

As mentioned above the development of a Grid middleware is an continuous process of integrating new features, services, and adapting to emerging standards, and UNICORE is no exception. In the following we present new developments, some technical details, and report on projects, which enhance the UNICORE technology to serve the demands of the Grid in the future [33].

5.1. UniGrids – Uniform Interface to Grid Services

The strength of the UNICORE architecture is well-proven as described above. The rapid definition and adoption of OGSA allow the UNICORE development community to re-cast and extend the concepts of UNICORE through the use of Web services technologies. The goal of the UniGrids[8] project [34] is to lift UNICORE on an architecture of loosely-coupled components while keeping its 'end-to-end' nature.

Thus, the integration of Web services techniques and UNICORE, which already started in the GRIP project (cf. Section 4.2), will continue in the UniGrids project. Interoperability, through adopting and influencing standards, form the philosophical foundation for UniGrids. The project aims to transform UNICORE into a system with interfaces that are compliant with the Web Services Resource Framework (WS-RF) [35] and that interoperate with other WS-RF compliant software components.

Such an approach offers great advantages both for the ease of development of new components by aggregation of services and through the integration of non-UNICORE components into the standards-based infrastructure.

In this sense, work is continuing in the following areas:

- Development of a compliant WS-RF hosting environment used for publishing UNICORE job and file services as Web services.

- Support of dynamic virtual organizations by enhancing the UNICORE security infrastructure to allow different usage models such as delegation and collective authorization.

- Development of translation mechanisms, such as resource ontologies, to interoperate with other OGSA compliant systems. Support for Grid economics by developing a Service Level Agreement (SLA) framework and cross-Grid brokering services.

- Development and integration of generic software components for visualization and steering of simulations (VISIT [36]), device monitoring and control, and tools for accessing distributed data and databases.

Applications from the scientific and industrial domain, like biomolecular and computational biology, geophysical depth imaging by oil companies, automotive, risk-management, energy, and aerospace are used to prove the developments in UniGrids.

The development in the UniGrids project will lead to UNICORE/GS, which follows the architecture of OGSA through the standardization of WS-RF and related work like e. g. the Web Services Notification technology [37]. The results will be made available under an open source BSD license.

---

[8]funded by EC grant IST-2002-004279, duration: July 2004 - June 2006

5.1.1. UNICORE/GS

Web service technology, and in particular the WS-RF, forms the basis for the UNI-CORE/GS software. WS-RF is the follow-on to OGSI, but more in line with mainstream Web services architecture [38]. Based on this new technology, UNICORE/GS will retain its key characteristics of seamlessness, security, and intuitiveness from both the user and administrative perspective, but will be built on a service oriented framework. This means that there is a loosening of the coupling between the components of the system. UNICORE/GS keeps the classical UNICORE topology of Usites, each containing a number of Vsites, but provides a new framework for integrating other services and providing common infrastructure functionality as services. This has the implication that new services will be easily integrated into the UNICORE/GS environment. Conversely, UNICORE/GS will be well-prepared to make use of external services.

The WS-RF technology is used to model core functionalities such as job submissions and file transfers as WS–Resources. These services are accessible via web service interfaces and thus establishing the UniGrids atomic services layer. This layer will be realized making extensive use of existing UNICORE server components.

All services in a Usite are accessible through the UniGrids Gateway that provides a secure entrance into the UNICORE/GS infrastructure. The principal is exactly the same as for classic UNICORE, however, the Gateway now routes messages according to Web Services Addressing (WS–Addressing) [39]. Authentication is based on transport level HTTPS security, although the intention is to move to Web Services Security (WS–Security) [40]. Regarding authorized access to resources, the UNICORE User Database (UUDB) will be available as a service to other services in the Usite, and will form the basis for future work concerning virtual organizations and fine-grained authorization schemes.

The underlying UniGrids atomic services layer will provide an excellent framework to deploy higher-level services such as co-allocation schedulers, workflow engines, and services for provision and easy access to data-intensive, remotely-steerable simulations.

5.2. NextGrid – Architecture for Next Generation Grids

In comparison to the UniGrids project which evolves the existing UNICORE Grid system to a service-oriented one, the NextGRID[9] [41] project aims for the future: The goal is to provide the foundations for the next generation of Grids. NextGRID is not a project based on the UNICORE architecture or Grid system as-is, but institutions and people involved in the UNICORE development from the beginning on contribute expertise and experience to NextGRID.

Since it is obvious that there is no such thing as the one and only next generation Grid, and experts envisage the co-existence of multiple Grids with well-defined boundaries and access points, NextGRID is going to define a Grid architecture which can be seen as building blocks for Grids. It does not only provide interoperability by-design between entities which exist within one instantiation of such an architecture, but it also facilitates the interoperability between different Grids developed according to the NextGRID architecture.

Although developing a Grid one generation ahead, NextGRID is not starting from scratch. Properties to incarnate and functions to realize future Grids are expertly de-

---

[9]funded by EC grant IST-2002-511563, duration: September 2004 - August 2007

scribed in [42] and [33]. These reports frame NextGRID's architectural development while the Open Grid Services Architecture is going to define Grid services and their inter-actions and does therefore make up a staring point for the conceptualization and design of NextGRID. In addition, regarding the underlying technology and architectural model, NextGRID propagates the usage of Web Services and the adoption of Service-Oriented Achitecture (SOA) [43] concepts and models.

NextGRID focuses on security, economic sustainability, privacy/legacy, scalability and usability. The following properties have the highest priorities when carrying out the following work:

- Developing an architecture for next generation Grids

- Implementing and testing prototypes aligned with the concepts and design of the NextGRID architecture

- Creating reference applications which make use of the NextGRID prototypes

- Facilitating the transition from scientific- to business-oriented Grids by integrating the means to negotiate a certain Quality of Service (QoS) level

- Specifying the methods, processes, and services necessary to dynamically operate Grids across multiple organizations which comprise heterogeneous resources

Since the ongoing UNICORE development in projects like UniGrids shares resources as well as the technological foundation with NextGRID there is a high chance that the outcome of NextGRID will also represent the next step of UNICORE's evolution.

6. Conclusion

In this paper we presented the evolution of the UNICORE technology from a Grid software with prototype character developed in two German projects to a full-grown, well-tested, widely used and accepted Grid middleware. UNICORE – Uniform Interface to Computing Resources – provides a *seamless, secure and intuitive* access to distributed Grid resources. Although the UNICORE vision was already coined in 1997, the then stated goals and objectives of hiding the seams of resource usage, incorporating a strong security model, and providing an easy to use graphical user interface for scientists and engineers are still valid today: to achieve these goals and objectives, UNICORE is designed as a vertically integrated Grid middleware providing components at all layers of a Grid infrastructure, from a graphical user interface down to the interfaces to target machines.

Initially developed in the German projects UNICORE and UNICORE Plus, UNICORE was soon established as a promising Grid middleware in several European projects. In the GRIP project an interoperability layer between UNICORE and the Globus Toolkit 2 and 3 was developed to demonstrate the interoperability of independently developed Grid solutions, allowing to build and to demonstrate inter-Grid applications from the bio-molecular and meteorological domain. In the EUROGRID project, European high performance supercomputing centers joined to extend UNICORE with an efficient data transfer, resource brokerage mechanisms, ASP services, application coupling methods, and an interactive access. In addition, a Bio-Grid, Meteo-Grid, CAE-Grid, and HPC-Grid were established to integrate a variety of application domains. The main objective of the OpenMolGRID project is to provide a unified and extensible information-rich environment based on UNICORE for solving problems from molecular science and engineering. In the VIOLA project a vertically integrated testbed with the latest optical network technology is built up. UNICORE is used as the Grid middleware for enabling the development and testing of new applications in the optical networked testbed, which provides advanced bandwidth management and QoS features.

With these developments UNICORE grew to a software system usable in production Grids. In this context UNICORE is deployed in the large German supercomputing centers to provide access to their resources. At the John von Neumann-Institute for Computing, Research Center Jülich, many users submit their batch jobs through UNICORE to the 1312-processor 8.9 TFlop/s IBM p690 cluster and the Cray SV1 vector machine. Leading European HPC centers joined in the project DEISA to build a distributed European infrastructure for scientific applications based on UNICORE to build and operate a distributed multi tera-scale supercomputing facility.

The future of UNICORE is promising and follows the trend of "Everything being a Service" by adapting to Open Grid Service Architecture (OGSA) standards. In this context, the UniGrids project continues the effort of the GRIP project in integrating the Web Services and UNICORE technology to enhance UNICORE to an architecture of loosely-coupled components while keeping its "end-to-end" nature. To this end UNICORE/GS will be developed, which makes UNICORE compliant with the Web Services Resource Framework (WS-RF).

Today the UNICORE software is available as open source under a BSD licence from SourceForge for download. This enables the community of core UNICORE developers to grow and makes future development efforts open to the public.

7. Acknowledgments

The work summarized in this paper was done by many people. We gratefully thank them for their past, present, and future contributions in developing the UNICORE technology. Most of the work described here was supported and funded by BMBF and different programmes of the European Commission under the respective contract numbers mentioned above.

REFERENCES

1. I. Foster, C. Kesselman (Eds.). *The Grid: Blueprint for a New Computing Infrastructure*. Morgan Kaufmann Publishers Inc. San Fransisco, 1999.
2. I. Foster and C. Kesselman. Globus: A Metacomputing Infrastructure Toolkit. *International Journal on Supercomputer Applications*, 11(2):115–128, 1997.
3. D. Erwin (Ed.). *UNICORE - Uniformes Interface für Computing Ressourcen, final project report (in German)*. 2000.
4. D. Erwin (Ed.). *UNICORE Plus Final Report - Uniform Interface to Computing Resources*. Forschungszentrum Jülich, 2003.
5. UNICORE at SourceForge. http://unicore.sourceforge.net.

6. Jump - Juelich Multi Processor, 8,9 TFlop/s IBM p690 eServer Cluster. `http://jumpdoc.fz-juelich.de`.

7. DEISA - Distributed European Infrastructure for Supercomputing Applications. `http://www.deisa.org`.

8. M. Romberg. The UNICORE Grid Infrastructure. *Scientific Programming*, 10(2):149–157, 2002.

9. I. Foster, C. Kesselmann, J. M. Nick, and S. Tuecke. The Physiology of the Grid. In F. Berman, G. C. Fox, and A. J. G. Hey, editors, *Grid Computing*, pages 217–249. John Wiley & Sons Ltd, 2003.

10. D. Snelling, S. van den Berghe, G. von Laszweski, Ph. Wieder, D. Breuer, J. MacLaren, D. Nicole, and H.-Ch. Hoppe. A UNICORE Globus Interoperability Layer. *Computing and Informatics*, 21:399–411, 2002.

11. D. Snelling. UNICORE and the Open Grid Services Architecture. In F. Berman, G. Fox, and T. Hey, editor, *Grid Computing: Making The Global Infrastructure a Reality*, pages 701–712. John Wiley & Sons, 2003.

12. V. Huber. Supporting Car-Parrinello Molecular Dynamics Application with UNICORE. In *Proc. of the International Conference on Computational Science (ICCS 2001)*, pages 560–566, 2001.

13. PBS - Portable Batch System. `http://www.openpbs.org/`.

14. M. Hovestadt, O. Kao, A. Keller, and A. Streit. Scheduling in HPC Resource Management Systems: Queuing vs. Planning. In D. G. Feitelson and L. Rudolph, editor, *Proc. of the 9th Workshop on Job Scheduling Strategies for Parallel Processing*, volume 2862 of *Lecture Notes in Computer Science*, pages 1–20. Springer, 2003.

15. Globus: Research in Resource Management. `http://www.globus.org/research/resource-management.html`.

16. R. Menday and Ph. Wieder. GRIP: The Evolution of UNICORE towards a Service-Oriented Grid. In *Proc. of the 3rd Cracow Grid Workshop (CGW'03)*, pages 142–150, 2003.

17. EUROGRID - Application Testbed for European Grid Computing. `http://www.eurogrid.org`.

18. D. Mallmann. EUROGRID - Application Testbed for European Grid Computing. In *Proc. of Industrial GRID Conference 2001*, 2001.

19. GRIP - Grid Interoperability Project. `http://www.grid-interoperability.org`.

20. The Globus Project. `http://www.globus.org/`.

21. Global Grid Forum. `www.globalgridforum.org`.

22. OpenMolGRID - Open computing Grid for Molecular Science and Engineering. `http://www.openmolgrid.org`.

23. S. Sild, U. Maran, M. Romberg, B. Schuller, and E. Benfenati. OpenMolGRID: Using Automated Workflows in GRID Computing Environment. In *Proceedings of the European Grid Conference 2005*, 2005.

24. M. Karelson. *Molecular Descriptors in QSAR/QSPR*. John Wiley & Sons, New York, 2000.

25. U.S. Environmental Protection Agency ECOTOXicology database. `http://www.epa.gov/ecotox/`.

26. VIOLA - Vertically Integrated Optical Testbed for Large Applications in DFN. `http:`

376

//www.viola-testbed.de.

27. MetaMPICH - Flexible Coupling of Heterogeneous MPI Systems. http://www.lfbs.rwth-aachen.de/~martin/MetaMPICH/.

28. G. Quecke and W. Ziegler. MeSch - An Approach to Resource Management in a Distributed Environment. In R. Buyya, editor, *Proc. of 1st IEEE/ACM International Workshop on Grid Computing (Grid 2000)*, volume 1971 of *Lecture Notes in Computer Science*, pages 47–54. Springer, 2000.

29. Global Grid Forum GRAAP (Grid Resource Allocation Agreement Protocol) Working Group. https://forge.gridforum.org/projects/graap-wg/.

30. NaReGI - National Research Grid Initiative. http://www.naregi.org/index_e.html.

31. The Condor Project. http://www.cs.wisc.edu/condor/.

32. S. Tuecke, K. Czajkowski, I. Foster, J. Frey, S. Graham, C. Kesselman, T. Maquire, T. Sandholm, D. Snelling, and P. Vanderbilt (eds.). The Open Grid Services Infrastructure (OGSI) Version 1.0, 2003.

33. Next Generation Grids 2 – Requirements and Options for European Grids Research 2005-2010 and Beyond. ftp://ftp.cordis.lu/pub/ist/docs/ngg2_eg_final.pdf, 2004.

34. UniGrids - Uniform Access to Grid Services. http://www.unigrids.org.

35. OASIS Web Services Resource Framework (WSRF). http://www.oasis-open.org/committees/wsrf.

36. VISIT – A Visualization Toolkit. http://www.fz-juelich.de/zam/visit/.

37. OASIS Web Services Notification (WSN). http://www.oasis-open.org/committees/wsn.

38. W3C Web Services Architecture. http://www.w3.org/TR/ws-arch/.

39. Web Services Addressing. http://www.w3.org/Submission/2004/SUBM-ws-addressing-20040810/.

40. OASIS Web Services Security (WSS). http://www.oasis-open.org/committees/wss/.

41. NextGRID - Architecture for Next Generation Grids. http://www.nextgrid.org.

42. Next Generation Grids – European Grid Research 2005 - 2010. ftp://ftp.cordis.lu/pub/ist/docs/ngg_eg_final.pdf, 2003.

43. T. Erl. *Service-Oriented Architecture: A Field Guide to Integrating XML and Web Services*. Prentice Hall PTR, 2004.

Grid Computing: The New Frontier of High Performance Computing
Lucio Grandinetti (Editor)
© 2005 Elsevier B.V. All rights reserved.

Developing Innovative Technologies for Commercial Grids

J.-P. Prost[a], L. Berman[b], R. Chang[c], M. Devarakonda[c], M. Haynos[d],
W.-S. Li[e], Y.Li[f], I. Narang[e], J. Unger[g], D. Verma[c]

[a] IBM EMEA Products and Solutions Support Center,
Rue de la Vieille Poste, 34000 Montpellier, France

[b] IBM T.J. Watson Research Center,
1101 Kitchawan Road, Yorktown Heights, NY 10598, USA

[c] IBM T.J. Watson Research Center,
19 Skyline Drive, Hawthorne, NY 10532, USA

[d] IBM Systems and Technology Group,
Route 100, Somers, NY 10589, USA

[e] IBM Almaden Research Center,
650 Harry Road, San Jose, CA 95120, USA

[f] IBM China Research Laboratory,
Haohai Building, #7, 5th Street, Shangdi, Beijing 100085, PRC

[g] IBM Systems and Technology Group,
13108 Scarlet Oak Drive, Darnestown, MD 20878, USA

Grid computing, in the commercial space, builds upon a set of management disciplines, which aims at mapping available resource capabilities to application workloads, according to requirements these workloads depend upon and to business goals they must fulfill. This paper illustrates innovative technologies, developed at IBM Research, that address key issues found in commercial grid environments. These technologies fall into four main areas, workload virtualization, information virtualization, provisioning and orchestration, and application development.

1. INTRODUCTION

Grid computing allows for flexible, secure, and coordinated resource sharing among a dynamic collection of individuals, institutions, and resources [1]. Companies today use grid computing for better and faster decision making, for improved productivity and collaboration, and for an optimized use of their IT infrastructure.

In order to make this sharing as flexible as possible, commercial grids build upon a set of virtualization technologies, which aims at mapping available resource capabilities to application workloads, according to requirements these workloads depend upon and to business goals they must fulfill.

Key to allow universal sharing is for these virtualization technologies to expose common and open interfaces across all hardware and middleware platforms. To compose these technologies and make them interoperable, standards are essential.

A service oriented approach has been proposed by the Open Grid Service Architecture (OGSA) framework [2], building upon web services standards.

The management disciplines, required to create, manage, operate and exploit commercial grids, are enabled through a set of layered components, depicted in Figure 1.

At the core are the web services foundation, based on emerging standards, which specify how services are described (WSDL [3]), discovered (UDDI [4], WSIL[5]), accessed (SOAP [6], WS-Addressing [7]) securely (WS-Security [8], WS-SecureConversation [9], WS-Federation [10], WS-Trust[11], WS-SecurityPolicy [12]), managed (WS-RF[13], WS-Notification [14], WSDM[15]), and choreographed (WS-BPEL [16]), and the common resource model, based on the Common Information Model (CIM) [17, 18] specifications, which define the attributes and the basic manageability operations for all types of IT resources.

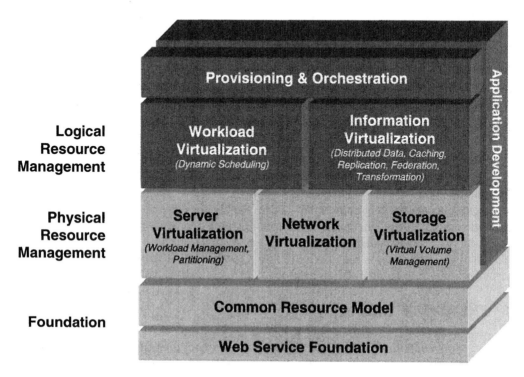

Figure 1. Commercial grid layered components.

The next level up is the management layer of physical IT resources (servers, network, storage devices), providing common services to expose and manage the capabilities of these resources. At this level, we find services to define and configure virtual server partitions, virtual volumes of storage, virtual networks.

The logical resource management layer contains the workload virtualization and the information virtualization components. Workload virtualization enables the dynamic scheduling of workloads onto a set of resources whose capabilities are exposed by the physical resource virtualization components, taking into account business goals associated with these workloads.

Information virtualization allows applications to access data wherever and in whatever format it is stored, with an expected quality of service, which may be expressed in terms of performance, security, or freshness. Typical information virtualization services are data federation, caching, replication, data placement, and transformation.

Provisioning is another important grid component, allowing to add and to configure new resources with appropriate capabilities, as required by specific workloads. Provisioning decisions are often orchestrated by a service, which constantly monitors the grid environment and triggers provisioning actions when specific conditions are raised, taking into account business goals and local administrative policies.

Application development builds upon the web services and common resource model foundation and a service oriented programming model can best leverage the virtualization services described above. Tooling is important to facilitate the deployment of applications as a set of choreographed services which can exploit with flexibility the virtual resources composing the grid.

Security is certainly an area, which is essential to grid computing. However, commercial grids today are mostly deployed at the enterprise level (i.e. within the intranet). Therefore, security issues are not nowadays the most critical in commercial grid settings. Security concerns are definitely more present in extranet and internet grid environments.

For the last two years, IBM Research has been focusing its efforts in the development of innovative technologies in the workload virtualization, information virtualization, provisioning and orchestration, and application development areas (depicted by the darker boxes in Figure 1). IBM researchers have been developing technologies aimed at providing solutions to key issues in commercial grid environments.

In the workload virtualization area, two key research technologies are being developed.

- Third party software vendor licenses are key resources for most commercial enterprises, and deploying applications in a grid environment tend to increase the complexity of managing such assets. Therefore, optimizing their allocation in scheduling decisions according to the business priorities associated with the applications requiring them is essential to maximize software license return on investment. The proactive license use management environment (PLUME) project [19] aims at optimizing the allocation of software licenses in scheduling decisions.

- Many companies, through mergers and acquisitions, end up having fragmented data centers with their own resources and administration. Providing the capability of a better sharing of resources across data centers, yet respecting each data center's own resource allocation policy, is a challenging objective. The policy-based multi-datacenter resource management project [20] aims at optimizing resource allocation to workloads across multiple data centers.

Many companies, in particular in the life sciences, automotive, and aerospace sectors, have the need for federating data across distributed data sources. However, guaranteeing performance objectives for such federated data accesses, transparently to the application, is a very difficult task.

In the information virtualization area, the TESLA project [21] is developing technologies aimed at providing to applications transparent access to dynamic, heterogeneous, and distributed data sources, satisfying specific quality of service goals. The data query advisor [22] monitors application execution patterns globally and derives a data placement strategy that yields desired throughput and response time for a query workload. An autonomic replication manager enables quality of service policy driven data replication.

Commercial enterprises have more and more the need for business resilience. In no circumstances can they afford to have their operations interrupted or their performance degraded. Therefore, having the capability to clone or to migrate grid services transparently to the applications accessing them and providing techniques to provision network resources according to workload needs are key components to achieving business resilience.

In the provisioning and orchestration area, the resilient grid service provisioning project [23] aims at providing an infrastructure for resilient and dynamic grid service provisioning that can guarantee quality of service requirements in terms of performance, reliability, or availability, even when service hosting resources and demand change. The network resource manager project [24] aims at orchestrating network connectivity provisioning to satisfy application quality of service requirements.

Most companies cannot afford to reengineer all of their existing applications so that they map well to a grid environment. Tooling needs to be provided to help the adaptation and the deployment of legacy applications onto a grid environment. In the application development area, the ApplicationWeb project [25] aims at developing a framework for deploying legacy applications onto a grid environment and at providing tooling for simplifying the development of service oriented grid applications.

This paper is organized as follows. Sections two through five present the various projects within each focus area. For each project, we describe its main objectives and we detail the key components that are being developed. We conclude the paper with the ongoing and planned IBM Research activities in the commercial grid computing space.

2. WORKLOAD VIRTUALIZATION

Workload virtualization enables the dynamic scheduling of workloads onto a set of resources whose capabilities are exposed by the physical resource virtualization components, taking into account business goals associated with these workloads. In this area, the PLUME project optimizes, according to business objectives, the allocation of software licenses to process workflows, and the policy-based multi-datacenter resource management project optimizes resource allocation to workloads across multiple data centers.

2.1. Proactive License Use Management Environment (PLUME)

While hardware cost keeps dropping, the cost of software licenses is increasing at a faster pace. A large e-business enterprise is likely spending millions of dollars in software licenses annually in support of its demand for computing services. Its software license cost could be more than ten times its annual IT hardware expenses already. Several leading market research firms have started advocating the importance of improved license use management capability in the marketplace with suggestions on the needed processes and tools. For example, Meta Group thinks *"best-practice asset management groups will shave 5% off competitive software costs by focusing on enterprise usage analysis and audits, coupled with negotiations, to identify key pricing opportunities."* Gartner suggests *"enterprises should begin with a baseline understanding of their existing software rights, requirements, and risks and develop a formal software asset management program"* to better manage their software investments.

An appealing approach to proactively manage the cost of software licenses is to manage the acquired licenses as shared IT resources, similar to the way shared server machines are managed in a grid computing environment. However, using this approach to develop a generic license use management solution is a challenging task. The solution must address license compliance management issues (given the extreme cost of noncompliance with software usage rights) and accommodate the heterogeneity of license use monitoring and control mechanisms implemented by the software vendors (given the current lack of standards on license use monitoring and control mechanisms).

The PLUME project aims at enabling a license-aware approach to proactively manage application workflow execution requests in a grid computing environment, based upon the requests' resource requirements and business value functions (which can change over time).

Figure 2 shows PLUME is architected as a three-layer system.

At the bottom layer, application instances consume physical licenses (i.e. licenses acquired from application vendors). Monitoring and control of the use of physical licenses can be done using vendor's license management solutions. User-oriented virtualization of physical licenses is realized and managed at the top layer. The realization includes the use of a vendor-neutral license type data model so that vendor-defined physical licenses can be managed and provisioned in the grid environment as sets of pooled virtual resources with standard interfaces.

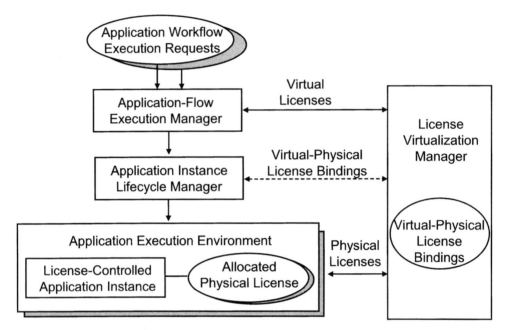

Figure 2. PLUME architecture.

The middle layer manages the bindings between virtual licenses and physical licenses. The middle layer can change the bindings dynamically, when appropriate, by exploiting late-binding based resource reservation schemes and the one-to-many relation between the functional requirements of a specific application workflow execution request and the needed set of computing resources to fulfill the request. The License Virtualization Manager, for example, can let an application instance use a node-locked physical license to finish its execution, though the physical license could not be allocated when the Application-Flow Execution Manager dispatches the execution request to the Application Instance Lifecycle Manager.

PLUME's business value driven approach to optimizing the execution of application workflow execution requests is mainly implemented by the Application-Flow Execution Manager [19].

Figure 3 illustrates the key components of our current PLUME prototype.

A demo scenario has been implemented to validate and evaluate PLUME's license-aware approach. In this scenario, the execution of each license-controlled application instance requires a node-floating license and a server on which the application instance executes. Each type of resource is managed by a specific resource manager which tracks resource status, availability, and constraints. Submitted requests are allocated resources by a Request Fulfillment Scheduler that continually optimizes the allocation based on the requests' business value functions, which may vary over time. Normally the business value is either non-decreasing (e.g. the penalty for delaying the processing of the request) or non-increasing (e.g. the revenue of fulfilling the request) over time. The business value functions are managed as request metadata. The demo scenario does not require that the end user defines the business value function of each submitted request.

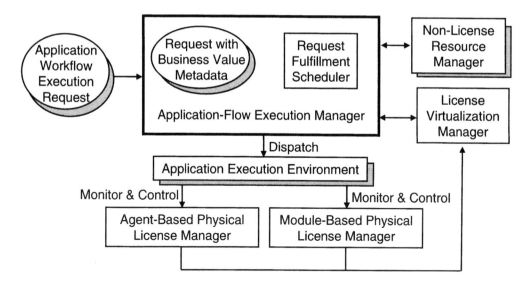

Figure 3. PLUME prototype components.

The Application-Flow Execution Manager is configured to automatically generate one business value function for each request with the assumption that a prior agreement with the user on the subject has been reached, for example, the agreed SLA management objectives and related business impact evaluation metrics. Once a request has been associated with an expected business value, the Request Fulfillment Scheduler contacts the appropriate Resource Managers to determine the availability of all of the resources required to satisfy the request. For software licenses, the Request Fulfillment Scheduler contacts the License Virtualization Manager, which is implemented as a set of cooperating virtual license servers using a peer-to-peer computing model [26].

The License Virtualization Manager obtains information from a Physical License Manager and supports an abstraction of the physical licenses. In the demo, there are two types of Physical License Managers. One of them is agent based and is implemented by the IBM Tivoli License Manager product [27]. It uses an agent which runs on the application execution server to check out and check in license instances or tokens based upon the application's state. The other is module-based and is implemented by an in-house prototype. The licensed applications that use this kind of licenses include a module which checks out and checks in license instances.

We have done some preliminary evaluations of PLUME's license-aware and business value driven approach to managing the execution of application workflows in a grid environment. When compared with a first-come-first-served with backfilling based approach to scheduling execution requests, our event-driven based simulation results show that PLUME can reduce the total penalty (loss of business value) by 90%. Our experiments with the PLUME prototype show that, when compared with a commercial workflow product, the PLUME can reduce the penalty of a set of process execution requests by 67% on average [28].

We are currently focusing on advancing the application-flow execution management technology in support of both scientific workflow execution management and business process performance management needs in grid environments.

2.2. Policy-Driven Multi-Datacenter Resource Management

In this section, we describe the role of policies in sharing resources in a multi-domain grid, formed of multiple datacenters [20]. The autonomy requirements of the model, the necessary simplicity, and the distributed nature of the system challenge us to define simple yet effective policies. It is necessary that these policies use a resource management paradigm that is in use today for a single datacenter, in order to leverage existing infrastructure. There is also a need for an analysis methodology that can help administrators understand the impact of the policies and tune them appropriately.

These requirements of the multi-datacenter resource sharing model led us to consider policy controls at the following four decision points:
1. when to request remote resources,
2. when to accept remote resource requests,
3. how to use remote resources,
4. and how to provision remote resources.

The policies at these decision points are in the form of thresholds above or below which appropriate actions are taken. The policies help the prioritization of workloads, determine how resources are to be utilized, decide the desired configuration for using remote resources, and so on. These policies are determined according to overall business goals.

Single Datacenter Architecture

The datacenter, as shown in Figure 4, consists of workloads, resources, resource managers, and service level objectives that the datacenter attempts to meet with the resources. Typical workloads are compute intensive long running jobs with multiple parallel threads or a collection of web requests involving content browsing and a variety of transactions such as buy, update, and query. The workloads can be categorized so that different workload classes and subclasses may be identified. Service level objectives (e.g. average response time and priority) are defined for each workload class.

A datacenter includes two levels of resource managers: workload managers, and a datacenter resource manager. A workload manager categorizes the workload into classes and subclasses, and then distributes the workload among a collection of resources that are assigned to the workload manager. Hence the role of a workload manager is to meet as well as possible service level objectives for the workload it is responsible for and with the resources assigned to it. In a datacenter, there may be one or more workload managers. The workload managers may be instances of the same workload manager product or they may be instances of different products.

The datacenter resource manager arbitrates resources among the workload managers and a pool (i.e. a set) of idle resources (referred to as free pool). The role of the resource manager is to achieve the best global resource utilization across workload managers by appropriately allocating datacenter resources among the workload managers. The datacenter resource manager takes decisions at a pace different from the workload managers – workload managers have a smaller decision cycle, request by request in the case of a transactional workload, whereas the datacenter resource manager operates in relative longer decision cycle, only intervening when there is a resource imbalance among the workload managers.

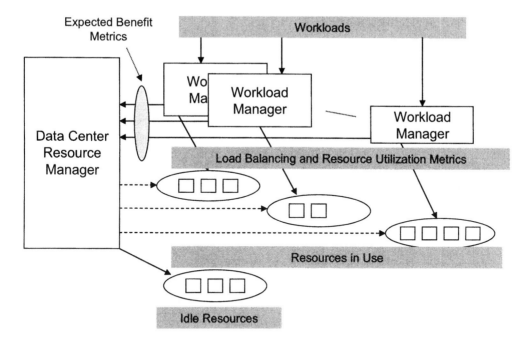

Figure 4. Single datacenter architecture.

The resource manager attempts to achieve an optimal allocation while maintaining resource usage policies set by the administrator of the datacenter (e.g. minimum CPU utilization or minimum number of resources in the free pool). To facilitate this arbitration, on an ongoing basis, workload managers make available to the resource manager metrics that reflect their ability to meet service level objectives at the present and potential benefit that they could achieve (also from the service level objectives point of view) if additional resources were available to them.

Multi-Datacenter Architecture
The multi-datacenter architecture is an extension of the single datacenter model for global resource sharing. The global resource sharing is enabled by new functional components that include the remote resource manager, the policy infrastructure, the resource negotiator, the remote deployment manager, and the protocol for establishing agreements between resource negotiators.

The remote resource manager has the responsibility for acquiring remote resources and for donating local resources for remote usage. The policy infrastructure supports specification of policies and helps the remote resource manager in making policy decisions. The resource negotiator finds a remote site with suitable resources for borrowing when the remote resource manager decides to acquire remote resources. The remote deployment manager oversees the provisioning of acquired resources with required software stack. The WS-Agreement protocol [29] is an evolving standard for establishing agreements.

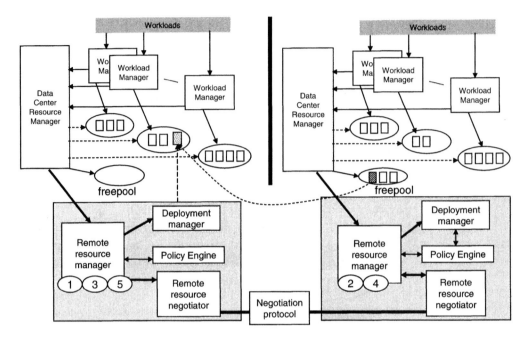

Figure 5. Multi-datacenter architecture.

Figure 5 shows this architecture for two datacenters, with one datacenter acting as a requestor and the second one acting as a donor. Note that in this peer-to-peer model every datacenter can be both a requester and a donor. In the service-provider model the second datacenter has only resources to donate but no workload managers of its own. The use of the architectural components and the overall flow will become clear in the following paragraphs as we discuss policies in this system.

Policies

For the purpose of our discussion, policies are of the form condition and action, where the action is to be carried out if the condition evaluates to True. The policy infrastructure helps users specify the condition and action parts of a policy, modify, store them in a repository, and activate them. The infrastructure also includes a policy evaluation engine, which, when presented with a set of variables and their values, returns the policy action whose condition evaluates to True because of the variables and values presented. We assume without the loss of generality that only one policy action is returned.

Policy#1: Remote resource request

The remote resource request policy controls conditions under which a datacenter is allowed to acquire remote resources. The conditional part specifies boolean conditions using workload identification, workload priority, resource type, and expected benefit. The action part specifies preferred datacenters (if any) from which resources may be borrowed.

A datacenter may request additional resources based on a predicted short fall or only when there is a clear and present need for additional resources. The choice depends on whether the workload is predictable or not. Monthly payroll processing is an example of a predictable workload, whereas a sudden spike in the web traffic as a result of a news event is unpredictable.

To enable the predictive approach, support for advance reservation is needed at the lending site. Advance reservation may be firm or soft with a range of choices in between. A firm reservation is a commitment, whereas a soft reservation is only an intention to use resources. The requesting datacenter may specify whether the reservation is soft or firm in its request.

Policy#2: Resource lending

This is the complementary policy to the remote resource request policy. The conditional part of this policy allows boolean conditions on the remote workloads, priority, resource type, expected benefit threshold, and the requesting remote site. The action part allows specification of limits on resources that may be given.

As a complementary policy to the previous policy, this policy gives a datacenter administrator the ability to decide datacenter preference and resource donation conditions. Note that there is a need to normalize workload identity, priority, resource type, and expected benefit so that all datacenters can make consistent policy decisions. A global optimization method such as auctioning would obviate the need for normalizing these factors across sites. However, the use of such techniques in resource management are still evolving.

In the case of predictive resource acquisition, the lending datacenter may use over commitment to deal with soft reservations. This is a part of the lending policy.

Policy#3: Workload distribution versus resource borrowing

Resource sharing may be accomplished through a redistribution of the workload to datacenters or by virtually borrowing resources from a lending data center. The DNS-based workload distribution of web traffic is a well known technique, and this technique can be used to offload workload from one datacenter to another.

In contrast, it is also possible to share remote resources by making them a virtual part of the local infrastructure. The advent of high-speed networking, secure VPNs (virtual private networks), and advanced network management technology allows one or more servers in a remote datacenter, for example, to be reconfigured as a part of the local cluster of a datacenter. The datacenter can then manage the remote servers as if they were local servers from a resource usage point of view.

The policy decisions datacenter administrators may make here is on how to use remote resources. The policy condition includes such criteria as the workload identification, resource types needed, and donating datacenters. The action would include whether to use workload distribution or resource borrowing.

Policy #4: Releasing or taking back resources

Having acquired remote resources, there are several choices for how long a datacenter can use them. One possibility is a finite, fixed length non-preemptive lease. Before the lease expires, the lessee may seek renewal. If the lease is not renewed, the lessee is required to give up the resource (or will be forced to do so). An alternative scheme is using a resource until preempted by the lending datacenter, i.e. an infinite preemptive lease time. The leasing schedule is a policy each datacenter administrator can set for lending resources, based on the resource type and requesting datacenters.

Policy #5: Resource provisioning

Once remote resources have been identified for a datacenter's use, the resources need to be "provisioned" for the use of the requesting data center. This process may involve reconfiguring the VLAN (virtual LAN) for appropriate access, installing or reconfiguring the necessary software stack. The software stack may include the operating system, language run time support (e.g. JVM), web server, database management system, web application server software, and finally the specific application code.

The choices are whether the provisioning is done under the control of the remote (lending) datacenter resource manager or under the local (requesting) datacenter resource manager. There are optimization considerations such as the time for transferring the necessary software stack from the local datacenter to the remote one. There are software distribution and maintenance issues such as which datacenter manager has the appropriate maintenance level code. There are trust and security issues when the remote data center is a service provider rather than a data center belonging to the same enterprise. Administrators of the requesting and donating datacenters may exercise control over this aspect, and the policies must match. The criteria for these policies may include requesting and lending datacenters, resource type, and application.

End-to-end Operation

As shown in Figure 5, first the need for remote resources is established through the metrics gathered by the datacenter resource manager from the workload managers. These metrics are passed on to the remote resource manager, which applies remote request threshold policies. As stated above these policies determine under what conditions and for what purposes remote resources will be requested. The requesting remote resource manager also decides how these resources will be used, i.e. whether to use the workload distribution approach or the resource borrowing approach. It also determines the software stack to be provisioned, and which datacenter will provision it. Once this determination is made, the next step is to use the resource negotiator to find datacenters that can provide the required resources.

Through an evolving standard protocol such as WS-Agreement, the resource negotiator presents its requirements to prospective donor datacenters. A simple technique is a round-robin scheme for contacting the known datacenters; remote request policy (i.e. policy #1) may require using a preferred list and order as well. The prospective donor sites use resource lending policies to decide whether they are willing to donate requested resource type. They also decide if they can support the way the requesting site is planning to provision and use the resources. If they do decide to donate resources an offer with terms of lease will be made, which include lease period specification, and a matched offer of a way of provisioning the resource. If the lease terms are acceptable the requesting datacenter will provision the resources jointly with the remote datacenter, and then start using them appropriately. Table 1 shows these steps with policies that come into play at the requesting and lending datacenters.

Table 1. Sequence of steps in acquiring remote resources and policies that apply at different datacenters.

Steps in the process of acquiring and using remote resources	Applicable policies by datacenter	
	Requesting datacenter	Lending datacenter
Recognize the need for resource acquisition	(1) remote resource request policy	
Find needed resources		(2) resource lending policy
Determine planned use of resources	(3) workload distribution vs. resource borrowing	
Accept lease terms		(4) leasing schedule policy
Provision and use the resources	(5) resource provisioning policy	

3. INFORMATION VIRTUALIZATION

A wide variety of applications require access to multiple heterogeneous, distributed data sources. By transparently integrating such diverse data sources, underlying differences in Data Base Management Systems (DBMSs), languages, and data models can be hidden and users can use a single data model and a single high-level query language to access the unified data through a global schema.

To address the needs of such federated information systems, IBM has developed the WebSphere Information Integrator (II) [30] (formerly DB2 Information Integrator) to provide relational access to both relational DBMSs and non-relational data sources, such as file systems and web services. These data sources are registered at the II as nicknames and thereafter can be accessed via wrappers. Statistics about the remote data sources are collected and maintained at the II for later use by the optimizer for costing query plans.

In such heterogeneous and distributed systems the administrative cost of manually placing data for performance and availability can be very high. In order to prevent users from explicitly specifying the remote data sources to be accessed and administrators from modifying their information infrastructure to meet desired Quality of Service (QoS) goals for performance and availability, we transparently enhance the WebSphere II-based federated system with three complementary components: (1) a meta-wrapper (MW), (2) a query cost calibrator (QCC), and (3) a data placement advisor (DPA). Figure 6 represents the system architecture of our prototype.

The meta-wrapper serves as a bridge between the II and the wrappers. At compile time, the MW receives queries from the II and records (a) the incoming federated queries, (b) the outgoing query fragments, (c) the estimated cost of the federated queries and query fragments, and (d) their mappings to the remote data sources. The overhead of logging in the meta-wrapper is inexpensive compared with the federated query processing cost. The log is periodically collected by QCC for analysis. At run time, the MW records (e) the actual response time of each query fragment.

This information, (a)-(e), is forwarded to the QCC [22] for further processing and analysis. Based on the estimated cost at compile time and the actual execution time monitored at runtime, the QCC derives an up-to-date query fragment processing cost calibration factor. Using this factor, the QCC can dynamically calibrate the future query estimation cost so that various system characteristics, such as remote system loads and network latency, are implicitly taken into consideration in global query costing. In addition to such transparent statistics collection, the QCC uses daemon programs that periodically access the remote data sources, through the MW, to ensure their availability. The daemon programs are also used to derive initial query cost calibration factors by exploring the processing and network latencies at the remote data sources.

When the wrappers are not able to provide cost estimation or it is not feasible to access the remote data sources to get the necessary database statistics for estimating the query processing cost, QCC features a simulated federated system, which has the same II, meta-wrapper, and wrappers as the original run time system, as well as a simulated catalog and virtual tables, to capture database statistics and data source characteristics without accessing the actual data. The simulated federated system allows QCC to derive alternative query plans.

Since data placement decisions have a significant system cost for creating replicas and keeping them in synchronization, the DPA performs "what-if" analysis for query routing and data placement, evaluates the performance benefits of replica creation on the overall query workload (rather than on an individual query), monitors the effectiveness of its recommendation, and iterates. The availability requirement must be factored in data placement as well.

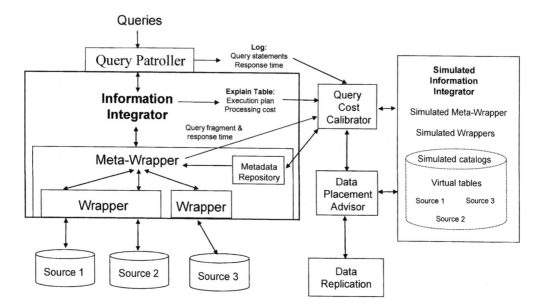

Figure 6. System architecture for information virtualization through WebSphere Information Integrator.

We have prototyped a data placement advisor for II [31] on top of the MQT (Materialized Query Table) advisor which fits within the framework of the existing DB2 Advisor [32]. WebSphere II is able to utilize the matched MQTs at the front-end database (i.e. the II node), rewrite the query, forward the rewritten query to the backend databases at the remote data sources, and merge the results from the backend databases and the MQTs. The DPA recommends MQTs to reduce computation latency and places MQTs and replicas close to the application to reduce network latency as well as offload the traffic to the backend databases.

4. PROVISIONING AND ORCHESTRATION

Provisioning allows for the addition and the configuration of new resources with appropriate capabilities, as required by specific workloads [33]. Provisioning decisions are often orchestrated by a service, which constantly monitors the grid environment and triggers provisioning actions when specific conditions are raised, taking into account business goals and local administrative policies. In this area, the resilient grid service provisioning project provides an infrastructure for resilient and dynamic grid service provisioning and the network resource manager project aims at orchestrating network connectivity provisioning to satisfy application QoS requirements.

4.1. Resilient Grid Service Provisioning

In a grid computing environment, resources from different organizations may constantly join and leave the grid infrastructure. This leads to frequent changes in the grid topology and in the grid resource capabilities. A major aspect of a grid infrastructure is to provide grid services with appropriate resources in order to satisfy user QoS requirements. Given the scale and complexity of most grid environments, manually mapping services to available resources would be difficult, error-prone, and time-consuming. The resilient grid service provisioning project attempts to automate this mapping.

In our proposed resilient grid service provisioning system [23], depicted in Figure 7, OGSA-based grid services can be dynamically migrated in response to changing demand on resources to satisfy the service level objective (SLO) of each service and optimize resource utilization. Components for run time monitoring and migration, as well as tools for defining the migration policy (time-based vs. SLO-based) have been developed. The main components include the Migration MAPE (Monitor-Analyze-Plan-Execute) Service and on each resource the Migrating Agent, Monitoring Agent, and Distilling Agent.

The Migration MAPE Service acts as an autonomic manager [34] by planning and executing migration actions based on the analysis of monitored data, e.g. the SLO of each service and the resource consumption of each end-point, collected by the Monitoring Agent on that end-point. The Distilling Agent mainly focuses on capturing the service metadata such as the (un)deployment description of each service. The Migrating Agent is responsible for moving or cloning services across the grid infrastructure. Users can define migration policies using the Policy Editor.

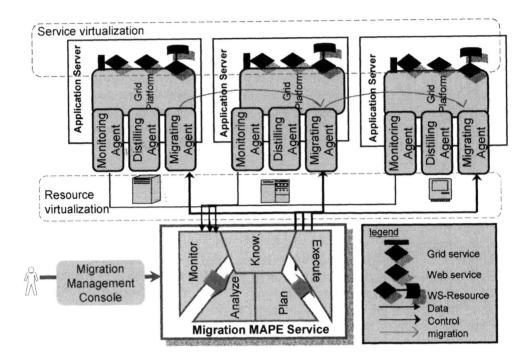

Figure 7. Resilient grid service provisioning architecture.

The Monitoring Agent, located at each end-point, is responsible for collecting the performance metrics such as the response time and throughput, the workload induced by the grid services hosted locally, as well as the resource utilizations, such as CPU and memory. It also provides an assessment on whether the response time of the service is satisfied or on whether the resource consumption of the end-point is within a migration policy-based interval. If the response time is not satisfied or if the resource consumption is outside the interval, the corresponding service is reported to the Migration MAPE Service for migration. In case the resource hosting the service is overloaded, the Monitoring Agent determines which service hosted locally causes the resource overload. The resource consumption by each service is calculated using a built-in statistical model expressing the relation between the request rate to the service and the resource utilizations (i.e. CPU and memory) of the end-point.

The Distilling Agent is in charge of capturing the metadata of the service. The metadata contains a description of the constituents of the service, e.g. EJBs, WS-Resources, so that the service can be migrated as a whole among the Grid resources. For example, if the service is implemented by EJBs in WAS, the information related to the EJBs involved will be captured.

The Migrating Agent is responsible for stopping, packing, forwarding, unpacking, and resuming the services among different Grid resources.

The Migration Management Console is an add-on component, and can be used for a variety of purposes, such as inputting the Migration Policy into the Migration MAPE Service, visualizing the current performance metrics, the current resource utilizations (CPU and memory), the policy violation records, and the status of any ongoing migration process.

A typical use case scenario of our service ecosystem is the following. Consider a Chinese mobile telecommunication company, which deploys and configures the Short Messaging Service (SMS) to meet the routine request rates. During the Chinese Spring Festival, millions of people send short messages to each other, causing the request rates for the SMS to increase to a very high peak quickly. After the three days of the Festival, the request rate to the SMS will drop back.

In this scenario, the telecommunication company can choose to buy additional SMS servers and deploy additional SMS instances on these servers during the Festival to handle the peak, or it can choose to dynamically deploy additional SMS instances on the available resources of its intranet, which may be a better cost-wise solution.

For this scenario, we developed a demo, entitled Grid service capacity on demand, in which a Grid service can be cloned dynamically on additional servers in our intranet environment when its request rate becomes high and the QoS (e.g., throughput) of the Grid service becomes degraded. These service replicas work together with the original Grid service as a cluster. When the request rate becomes low, these additional replicas are removed from the servers. The number and locations of the replicated Grid services are determined dynamically to satisfy the QoS requirement for the original Grid service according to the Grid service migration policy and the available resources.

4.2. Network Resource Manager

Network connectivity is a key element of current distributed applications such as web-applications as well as evolving paradigms such as Grid and on-demand computing. Continuous operation of distributed applications requires a dynamic and efficient network management infrastructure which demonstrates self-configuring, self-optimizing, and self-healing properties.

The traditional approach in network management is to view the network as a collection of devices connected in an ad-hoc manner. Each device is managed independently, and network management consists primarily of reading and changing device-specific information from each of the individual devices. For monitoring of the devices in the system, SNMP [35] is the primary mechanism, but the approach to configuration typically consists of command-line interfaces. The device-oriented view of network management provides the abstract virtualized network layer shown at the IT layer of the infrastructure.

As shown in Figure 8, the Network Resource Manager (NRM) provides the higher level provisioning and orchestration model for managing network connectivity. It provides an end-to-end view of network connectivity between different tiers of distributed/Grid applications, thereby abstracting away the myriad collections of devices that are needed to implement this connectivity. Network connectivity in our approach is modeled as an abstract resource that defines how servers and network elements are connected together in an on demand environment. The resource exposes attributes which provide the logical semantics of the network connectivity. End-to-end connectivity is explicitly established using network patterns and mapped by the NRM to virtualized device configurations. Since end-to-end connectivity among a set of devices is now explicit in a concrete software layer, collecting the connectivity-related state becomes feasible. Thus, redeploying a pattern-based configuration after some minor hardware changes or application end-point redeployment becomes possible and almost "hassle-free."

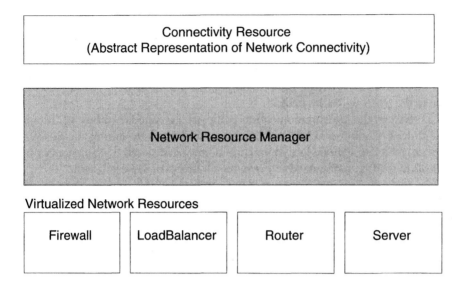

Figure 8. Network Resource Manager layering.

Connectivity Resource Model of NRM

As depicted in Figure 9, each network connectivity overlay is modeled as providing several common operational parameters. These parameters can be sub-classed to provide parameters specialized for a specific function within a Grid environment, e.g. for the support of business resiliency, or for the support of resource optimization. The common operational parameters associated with network connectivity include parameters such as current status, available bandwidth and monitored end-to-end delay. Specialized parameters for different functions differ. For example, business resiliency parameters would include aspects such as the time it takes for a network connectivity resource to be restored in case of failure, or the degree of redundancy available on a network path. Resource optimization parameters would include the QoS parameters associated with the network connectivity, e.g. the priority level of packets on the connection, any classification policies, etc.

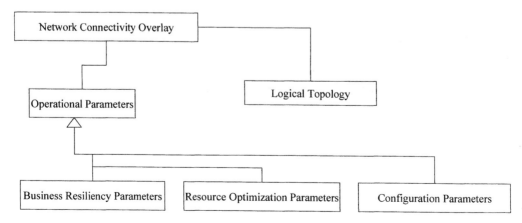

Figure 9. Network connectivity model.

Each network connectivity overlay is associated with a logical topology. The logical topology ties together different features of the server end-points that are connected. The logical topology is defined by describing the end-points that are involved in creating the connectivity resource. Such end-points include the definition of any entry-points into a Grid data center, and any associated network filters associated with communication on the connectivity overlay. Multiple end-points may be multiplexed onto a single end of the connectivity overlay. The filters, multiplexers, end-points, and entry-points of the connectivity overlay define its logical topology, which can be mapped onto the configuration of the devices that are used to implement the actual connection.

The next level of simplification offered by the NRM is the notion of the simplified-connectivity resource, which is a connectivity resource that has no logical topology but only a set of operational parameters. Each simplified-connectivity resource is mapped to a connectivity resource by means of templates. Each template provides the logical topology, and optionally additional parameters that are needed to determine the characteristics of the connectivity resource.

Usage Scenarios for the NRM

The notion of simplified connectivity resource allows a simplification in the development and management of several aspects of distributed Grid applications. In this section, we discuss some of the scenarios where the NRM model has been used to simplify the task of network management.

The first usage scenario consists of automating the task of network connectivity provisioning in the interconnection of the IBM Design Centers for ON DEMAND business [36]. By defining a simplified-connectivity resource and a set of templates that are customized for the various Design Centers, the task of provisioning network connectivity in a Design Center is automated. An operator only needs to provide the operational parameters required for network connectivity. The NRM software associates those parameters with the simplified connectivity resource, maps them to a logical topology, and then drives scripts and workflows that physically provision the network system.

Another important usage scenario of the connectivity model lies in the monitoring of the network infrastructure. The performance and QoS attributes of the network are modeled at the end-to-end level, which may spans the performance measurements across telecommunication networks and multiple Internet Service Providers. The monitoring of the end-to-end performance metrics and their composition from individual performance metrics lead to more efficient monitoring schemes. By virtualizing the ISP connection as a simplified overlay, and monitoring the performance of different segments, we have been able to monitor and isolate network performance problems in some multi-ISP environments.

Another useful usage scenario for the network resource manager is in the context of disaster recovery. By defining a simplified model of network connectivity, the network connectivity can be mapped easily to different datacenters, using a different template for each of the datacenters. This has allowed us to provide disaster recovery solutions in an automated manner for some of our customers.

We envision several possible future usages for the network resource manager, including the ability to provide a self-managing network connectivity overlay driven by policies, and the ability of cloning a network connectivity from one environment to another, varying only a few operational parameters between the two environments.

4. APPLICATION DEVELOPMENT

OGSA-based grid services form a natural infrastructure for on demand applications because they can track and manage available resources and their event driven computational model is an excellent choice for applications that need to respond to external changes. However, grid services can be difficult to develop and deploy, and, since the relevant standards and implementations are still evolving, they can be difficult to maintain as well.

As part of the ApplicationWeb project [25], we are developing and prototyping techniques that address both development and maintenance problems. Our experimental platform is an Eclipse [37] plug-in focused on helping developers convert their non-grid aware Java applications to a retargetable grid service, where by retargetable we mean that the development process should be as independent of the target grid infrastructure as possible. We expect this work to yield insight into problems relating to initial development and maintenance of applications in service oriented computing environments.

As anyone who has developed an OGSA-based grid service knows, deploying even the simplest application on the grid is a formidable task which requires a Java developer to master new, inscrutable technologies (such as WSDL and XSD), to create and package an assortment of artifacts, to deploy them into a grid infrastructure, and to debug the resulting installation. As time passes and the underlying infrastructure evolves, the developer (or maintainer) must modify old infrastructure code.

For example, the suggested methodology for Globus Toolkit [38] grid service developers requires that before beginning the debugging process they must:

- Create a WSDL document and an XSD schema to describe the data types which occur in the service specification,
- Generate Java code from these XML files,
- Modify the generated Java code using both infrastructure specific methods and application specific business logic,
- Package and deploy the resulting artifacts, and
- Develop unit test code that accesses the resulting service.

This complex process may be needed to utilize all of the intricacies of the standards defining grid computing; however, for the task of converting a legacy application for use as a grid service, this process is unnecessarily complex.

Our Eclipse plug-in minimizes the complexity by supporting specification at a conceptual level, automating the generation of infrastructure specific code and artifacts, and providing a uniform environment for development, packaging, deployment, and debugging.

The plug-in allows a grid service developer to:

- Specify the service interface/implementation by selecting Java classes,
- Define WS-Resources [13] associated with the service,
- Select properties that the WS-Resources will expose,
- Associate 'getter' and 'modifier' methods with the WS-Resources,
- Select libraries which are required in the service runtime,

- Separate application logic from grid related code, and
- Issue programmatic notifications and write life cycle code without writing infrastructure specific code.

The plug-in supports debugging by providing controls that:
- Select a target infrastructure,
- Build, package, and deploy the service for the target infrastructure,
- Start/stop a local grid container,
- Generate a unit test driver (and Eclipse launch configuration) which locates the service in the specified container, subscribes to the notifications associated with its defined resources, and calls each method defined in the original base interface.

The plug-in works by collecting the specification of the desired service, saving it in an XML file, and processing it using a combination of ANT scripts provided with the infrastructure and custom code written to augment the provided infrastructure tooling.

Using this approach, without writing any code, a developer can construct a grid service that:
- Exposes a Java interface involving complex Bean-like classes,
- Defines WS-Resources of these Bean-like types, and
- Issues notifications regarding these WS-Resources when selected interface methods return.

Using helper interfaces provided by the plug-in, the developer can easily add infrastructure neutral programmatic notification and lifecycle methods to her original application. These helper interfaces use infrastructure specific implementation classes to eliminate the need to write infrastructure specific code.

The sample code in Figure 10 shows a snippet which uses a resource of type **String[]** and helper interfaces to return messages to a client. Since the containing class, which is the service implementation class, has been declared to implement the **PublisherHelper** interface, the infrastructure insures that a non-null **Publisher** object is available to the service. The code works on any target infrastructure.

```
private void addMessages(String[] sa) {
  com.ibm.mathsci.ibmgrid.helper.Publisher pub = getPublisher();
  QName[] q = pub.getTopics();
  for (int i = 0; i < q.length; i++) {
    if (q[i].getLocalPart().indexOf("msg") >= 0) {
      try {
        pub.notify(q[i], sa);
      }
      catch (GridServiceException e) {
        // TODO Auto-generated catch block
        e.printStackTrace();
      }
    }
  }
}
```

Figure 10. Sample code snippet.

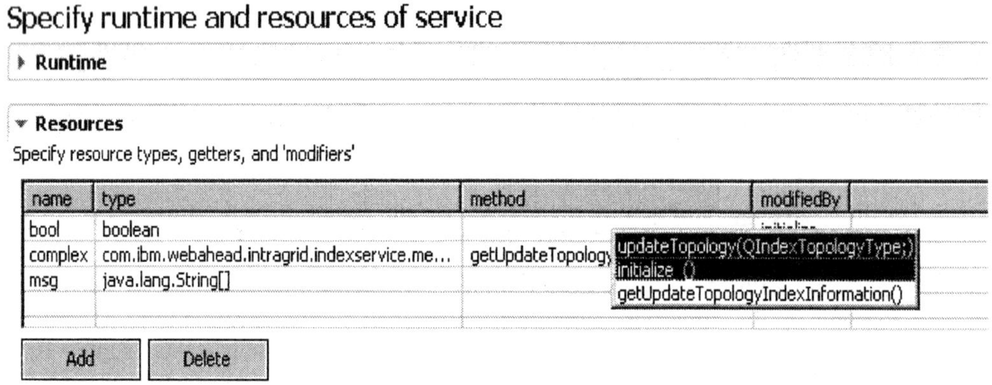

Specify runtime and resources of service

▸ **Runtime**

▾ **Resources**

Specify resource types, getters, and 'modifiers'

name	type	method	modifiedBy
bool	boolean		initialize
complex	com.ibm.webahead.intragrid.indexservice.me...	getUpdateTopology	updateTopology(QIndexTopologyType;)
msg	java.lang.String[]		initialize ()
			getUpdateTopologyIndexInformation()

    Add   Delete

Figure 11. Specification of a user-defined WS-Resource.

Figure 11 shows a GUI panel being used to define a WS-Resource, named **complex**, which has a user defined type. As shown, the GUI would result in the creation of a WS-Resource, whose value is fetched by the method **getUpdateTopology**. When either of the methods, **updateTopology** or **initialize**, returns, a notification will be sent to all registered listeners.

The goal of the ApplicationWeb project is to simplify the development, debugging, and maintenance of service oriented applications by:
- Automating the steps which are mechanical, thereby eliminating the opportunity to introduce bugs, and
- Eliminating the need for infrastructure specific code.

Our future work includes extending our techniques to interfaces which throw exceptions, integrating the plug-in more closely with the Rational Application Developer for Websphere Software [39], and investigating problems associated with the deployment of applications involving native libraries.

5. CONCLUSION

The management disciplines, required to create, manage, operate, and exploit commercial grids, are enabled through a set of layered components, such as workload virtualization, information virtualization, provisioning and orchestration, and application development. In this paper, we detailed various technologies IBM Research has been working on to build up innovative capabilities for these components. Prototype implementations of these technologies are under development and will be able to demonstrate the benefits they bring to commercial grid environments.

In the workload virtualization area, we showed how proactive license management can optimize the allocation of licenses to workflows according to business objectives, and how policies can play an essential role in sharing resources in a multi-domain grid, formed of multiple datacenters.

In the information virtualization area, we described how access to federated data sources can be tailored to satisfy user specified quality of service objectives by creating data set replicas and optimizing their placement according to run time conditions.

In the provisioning and orchestration area, we detailed how a grid service can be provisioned autonomously to achieve user specified performance or availability objectives, and how network connectivity can be configured to deliver a desired network performance to the application, thus enabling business resilience.

In the application development area, we explained how a Java legacy application could be converted, using an Eclipse plug-in, into a grid service, as independently of the target grid infrastructure as possible.

These technologies are complementary and attest of the importance of business objective driven resource management in commercial Grids. They could be combined together to provide user applications with end to end service level guarantees.

REFERENCES

1. I. Foster, C. Kesselman, S. Tuecke, "The Anatomy of the Grid: Enabling Scalable Virtual Organizations," International Journal on Supercomputer Applications, 15(3), 2001.
2. Global Grid Forum, "The Open Grid Services Architecture, Version 1.0," https://forge.gridforum.org/projects/ogsa-wg/document/draft-ggf-ogsa-spec/en/23.
3. W3C, "Web Services Description Language (WSDL)," http://www.w3.org/TR/wsdl.
4. OASIS, "Universal Description, Discovery and Integration," http://www.uddi.org/.
5. Microsoft and IBM, "Web Services Inspection Language (WS-Inspection)," http://www-106.ibm.com/developerworks/webservices/library/ws-wsilspec.html.
6. W3C, "Simple Object Access Protocol (SOAP)," http://www.w3.org/TR/soap/.
7. W3C, "Web Services Addressing (WS-Addressing)," http://www.w3.org/Submission/ws-addressing/.
8. OASIS, "Web Services Security (WSS)," http://www.oasis-open.org/committees/tc_home.php?wg_abbrev=wss.
9. Actional, BEA, CA, IBM, Layer 7 Technologies, Microsoft, Oblix, OpenNetwork Technologies, Ping Identity, Reactivity, RSA Security, and VeriSign, "Web Services Secure Conversation Language (WS-SecureConversation)," http://www-106.ibm.com/developerworks/library/specification/ws-secon/.
10. Verisign, Microsoft, IBM, BEA, RSA Security, "Web Services Federation Language (WS-Federation)", http://www-106.ibm.com/developerworks/webservices/library/ws-fed/.
11. Actional, BEA, CA, IBM, Layer 7 Technologies, Microsoft, Oblix, OpenNetwork Technologies, Ping Identity, Reactivity, RSA Security, and VeriSign, "Web Services Trust Language (WS-Trust)," http://www-106.ibm.com/developerworks/library/specification/ws-trust/.
12. Microsoft, Verisign, IBM, RSA Security, "Web Services Security Policy (WS-SecurityPolicy)," http://www-106.ibm.com/developerworks/library/ws-secpol/.
13. OASIS, "Web Services Resource Framework (WSRF)," http://www.oasis-open.org/committees/tc_home.php?wg_abbrev=wsrf.
14. OASIS, "Web Services Notification (WSN)," http://www.oasis-open.org/committees/tc_home.php?wg_abbrev=wsn.

15. OASIS, "Web Services Distributed Management (WSDM)," http://www.oasis-open.org/committees/tc_home.php?wg_abbrev=wsdm.

16. OASIS, "Web Services Business Process Execution Language," http://www.oasis-open.org/committees/tc_home.php?wg_abbrev=wsbpel.

17. DMTF, "Common Information Model (CIM)," http://www.dmtf.org/standards/cim/.

18. CA, Cisco, HP, IBM, "Proposal for a CIM Mapping to WSDM," http://www-128.ibm.com/developerworks/webservices/library/specification/ws-wsdm/.

19. M. J. Buco, R. N. Chang, L. Z. Luan, C. Ward, J. L. Wolf, and P. S. Yu, "Utility Computing SLA Management Based Upon Business Objectives," IBM Systems Journal, 43(1), 2004, pp. 159-178.

20. M. Srivatsa, N. Rajamani, and M. Devarakonda, "Multi-Site Resource Management: Policy and Performance Analysis," IBM Research Report #RC23497, Yorktown Heights, NY.

21. S. Bourbonnais, V. M. Gogate, L. M. Haas, R. W. Horman, S. Malaika, I. Narang, and V. Raman, "Towards an Information Infrastructure for the Grid," IBM Systems Journal, 43(4), 2004, pp. 665-688.

22. W.-S. Li, V. S. Batra, V. Raman, W. Han, K. Selçuk Candan, and I. Narang, "Load and Network Aware Query Routing for Information Integration," Proceedings 2005 IEEE International Conference on Data Engineering, Tokyo, Japan, April 2005.

23. Y. Li, F. Rao, Y. Chen, D. Liu, and T. Li, "Services Ecosystem: Towards a Resilient Infrastructure for On Demand Services Provisioning in Grid," Proceedings International Conference on Web Services 2004. San Diego, CA, July 2004.

24. P. Pradhan, M. Singh, D. Saha, and S. Sahu, "A Generalized Framework for Network Performance Management using End-to-end Mechanisms," New York Metro Area Networking Workshop 2004, New York, NY, September 2004.

25. L. Berman and D. Jensen, "A method for enabling cross platform function calls," Submitted to 2005 International Symposium on Parallel and Distributed Computing, Lille, France, July 2005.

26. C. Tang, R. N. Chang, and C. Ward, "GoCast: Gossip-enhanced Overlay Multicast for Fast and Dependable Group Communication," To appear in Proceedings of 2005 IEEE International Conference on Dependable Systems and Networks (DSN), June 2005.

27. "IBM Tivoli License Manager," http://www-306.ibm.com/software/tivoli/products/license-mgr/.

28. M. Buco, R. N. Chang, L. Z. Luan, E. So, C. Tang, and C. Ward, "PEM: A Framework Enabling Continual Optimization of Workflow Process Executions Based upon Business Value Metrics," To appear in Proceedings of 2005 IEEE International Conference on Services Computing (SCC), July 2005.

29. Global Grid Forum, "Web Services Agreement Specification (WS-Agreement)," http://www.gridforum.org/Meetings/GGF11/Documents/draft-ggf-graap-agreement.pdf.

30. V. Josifovski, P. Schwarz, L. Haas, and E. Lin, "Garlic: A New Flavor of Federated Query Processing for DB2," in Proceedings of ACM SIGMOD Conference, Madison, WI, May 2002.

31. W.-S. Li, D. C. Zilio, V. S. Batra, M. Subramanian, C. Zuzarte, and I. Narang, "Load Balancing for Multi-tiered Database Systems through Automatic Placement of Materialized Views," Submitted to the 31st International Conference on Very Large Databases, Trondheim, Norway, September 2005.

32. D. C. Zilio, J. Rao, S. Lightstone, G. M. Lohman, A. Storm, C. Garcia-Arellano, and S. Fadden, "DB2 Design Advisor: Integrated Automatic Physical Database Design," Proceedings of 30th International Conference on Very Large Databases, Toronto, Canada, September 2004.

33. H. Xu, P. Seltsikas, "Evolving the ASP Business Model: Web Service Provisioning in the Grid Era," Proceedings of 2nd IEEE P2P Computing International Conference, Sweden, 2002.

34. J. O. Kephart, and D. M. Chess, "The Vision of Autonomic Computing," IEEE Computer, January 2003, pp. 41-50.

35. W. Stallings, SNMP, SNMPv1, SNMPv3, and RMON 1 and 2, Addison-Wesley, 1998.

36. IBM Design Centers for ON DEMAND business, http://www-1.ibm.com/servers/eserver/design_center/.

37. Eclipse, http://www.eclipse.org/.

38. The Globus Alliance, "The Globus Toolkit," http://www-unix.globus.org/toolkit/.

39. IBM, "Rational Application Developer for WebSphere Software," http://www-306.ibm.com/software/awdtools/developer/application/support/.

Grid Computing: The New Frontier of High Performance Computing
Lucio Grandinetti (Editor)
© 2005 Elsevier B.V. All rights reserved.

Tools for Efficient Subsetting and Pipelined Processing of Large Scale, Distributed Biomedical Image Data[*]

Matheus Ribeiro[‡], Tahsin Kurc[†], Tony Pan[†], Kun Huang[†], Umit Catalyurek[†], Xi Zhang[†], Steve Langella[†], Shannon Hastings[†], Scott Oster[†], Renato Ferreira[‡], Joel Saltz[†]

[‡] Departamento de Ciência da
Computação
Universidade Federal de Minas Gerais
Belo Horizonte, MG - Brazil

[†] Dept. of Biomedical Informatics
The Ohio State University
Columbus, OH, 43210

This paper presents a suite of tools and techniques for efficient storage, retrieval, and processing of multi-dimensional, multi-resolution biomedical image datasets on parallel and distributed storage systems. We present the implementation of various services using these tools. We demonstrate the coordinated use of the services to support biomedical image analysis applications that access subsets of terabyte scale multi-resolution datasets and that make use of a variety of image processing algorithms on large-scale digitized microscopy slides.

1. Introduction

Large scale, multi-dimensional, multi-resolution datasets arise in a wide range of applications in biomedical research. The volume of data generated or collected in a typical research project has been increasing at a staggering rate, with the help of higher resolution instruments and high-end computing systems. As a result, data-driven applications have become an important application class that can benefit from distributed storage and computing.

Input datasets to these applications can be stored in databases or files. Examples of these datasets include images obtained through magnetic resonance imaging scans, digitized microscopy images, and datasets generated by simulation studies. The data elements in these datasets are oftentimes defined on 2-dimensional or 3-dimensional grids over multiple time steps. A single resolution dataset uniformly samples the multi-dimensional space, whereas a multi-resolution dataset consists of multiple subregions (potentially intersecting or overlapping each other) sampled at different rates. In biomedical research, for example, different imaging modalities (e.g., digital microscopes, MRI, CT) produce 2- and 3-dimensional images of the same subject region at different resolutions. Analysis of

[*]This research was supported in part by the National Science Foundation under Grants #ACI-9619020 (UC Subcontract #10152408), #EIA-0121177, #ACI-0203846, #ACI-0130437, #ANI-0330612, #ACI-9982087, #CCF-0342615, #CNS-0406386, #CNS-0426241, Lawrence Livermore National Laboratory under Grant #B517095 (UC Subcontract #10184497), NIH NIBIB BISTI #P20EB000591, Ohio Board of Regents BRTTC #BRTT02-0003.

data involves selecting a subset of the dataset via a user-defined predicate and processing it through a set of simple and complex operations (e.g., filtering, feature detection, visualization). The output of analysis operations can be stored as new datasets, which can further be processed by other applications.

In this paper, we describe a compendium of techniques and tools for navigation and analysis of very large biomedical image datasets. These tools provide support for (1) storage and subsetting of terabyte-scale multi-resolution volumetric image data and (2) support for distributed execution of image analysis workflows for large image datasets.

2. DataCutter and Mobius Frameworks

In this section we present two runtime middleware frameworks to support storage, retrieval, and pipelined data processing in a distributed environment. The first framework, DataCutter, enables the development of applications from a network of pipelined operations. The design and implementation of this framework is based on the observation that a wide range of data analysis applications can easily be represented as composed of data processing components. The second framework, Mobius, provides support for distributed management of metadata definitions and data instances as XML databases.

2.1. Distributed Processing: DataCutter

The DataCutter [1,2] framework supports a filter-stream programming model for developing data-intensive applications that execute in a distributed, heterogeneous environment. In this model, the application processing structure is implemented as a set of components, referred to as *filters*. Data exchange between filters is performed through a *stream* abstraction. A *filter* is a user-defined object that performs application-specific processing on data. A *stream* is an abstraction used for all filter communication, and specifies how filters are logically connected. A stream provides the means of data flow between two filters. All transfers to and from streams are through a provided buffer abstraction. A buffer represents a contiguous memory region containing useful data.

Once the application processing structure has been decomposed into a set of filters, it is possible to use multiple filters for implementing pipelined processing of data as it progresses from data sources to clients. The DataCutter runtime supports *transparent filter copies*, in which the filter is unaware of the concurrent filter replication. This abstraction aims at balancing the stages in the pipeline by allowing multiple copies of a bottleneck filter to be created. The filter runtime system maintains the illusion of a single logical point-to-point stream for communication between a logical producer filter and a logical consumer filter. When the logical producer or logical consumer is transparently copied, the system must decide for each producer which copy to send a stream buffer to. For distribution of buffers between copies, a Demand Driven (DD) mechanism based on buffer consumption rate sends buffers to the filter that will process them fastest. When a consumer filter starts processing of a buffer received from a producer filter, it sends a acknowledgement message to the producer filter to indicate that the buffer is being processed. A producer filter chooses the consumer filter with the minimum number of unacknowledged buffers to send a data buffer.

Besides the demand-driven mechanism, DataCutter implements a variation of streams called *Labeled Streams*. In this variation, for each Labeled Stream there is a user-defined hash function associated with it, which is called during the message transfer to determine, based on the message buffer, which transparent copy of the receiver should receive that particular buffer. This mechanism provides a user-controlled, but still transparent way of delivering messages to the appropriate copies of a filter. Generalized reduction operations can benefit from such abstraction. In addition, this hash function is not required to return just one recipient for any given buffer. A buffer can be delivered to a subset of copies of a filter.

2.1.1. Distributed Metadata and Data Management: Mobius

The Mobius framework [3–5] provides common tools and services for building service-oriented Data Grid applications. Mobius services employ XML schemas to represent metadata definitions or data models and XML documents to represent and exchange metadata instances or data instances.

The *Global Model Exchange* (GME) service of Mobius is responsible for storing and linking data models as defined inside namespaces in the distributed environment. The GME enables other services to publish, retrieve, discover, deprecate, and version metadata definitions. GME services are composed together in a domain name server-like architecture representing a parent-child namespace hierarchy wherein parents act as authorities for children and provide them with a sub-namespace. When a schema is registered in GME, it is stored under the name and namespace specified by the application and is given a version number. We refer to the tuple consisting of the schema's name, its namespace, and its version number as the global name id (GNI) of the schema. The GME protocol provides a mechanism for stating the exact version of the model that is requested. A model can also contain types defined by other models or references to types contained in other models, and can be assured that the referenced entities exist. This reference integrity might be considered the largest requirement for a GME that the current use of a URL does not provide. The role of the GME in the greater picture is to ensure distributed model evolution and integrity while providing the ability for storage, retrieval, versioning, and discovery of models of all shape, complexity, and interconnectedness in a distributed environment.

Mobius Mako is a service that exposes data resources as XML data services through a set of well-defined interfaces based on the Mako protocol. Data resource operations are exposed through a set of well-defined interfaces as XML operations. Clients interact with Mako over a network; the Mako architecture contains a set of listeners, each using an implementation of the Mako communication interface. Each Mako can be configured with a set of listeners, where each listener communicates using a specified communication interface. Our current Mako implementation provides support to expose XML databases that support the XMLDB API and contains an implementation of MakoDB. MakoDB is an XML database built on top of MySQL [6], and it is optimized for interacting in the Mako framework.

The Mako protocol defines methods for submitting, updating, removing, and retrieving XML documents. Upon submission, Mako assigns each entity a unique identifier. Documents, or subsets of XML documents, can be retrieved by specifying their unique identifier. Each element in an XML document is given an identifier, making any subset of a document uniquely addressable. XML documents can be removed by specifying their unique identifier or by specifying an element identifying XPath [7] expression. XML documents that reside in a Mako can be updated using XUpdate[2]. Mako currently provides query support through the use of XPath.

Alternate protocol handlers can be installed in a Mako server to enable it to utilize remote Mako instances. The *Virtual Mako* is a collection of protocol handler implementations that extend the operation of the data services to operate on an administrator defined set of remote Makos. It maps a number of Virtual Collections to a set of remote collections. This simplifies the client-side complexity of interfacing with multiple Makos by presenting a single virtualized interface to a collection of federated Makos.

3. Supporting Data Subsetting Operations on Multi-resolution Datasets

In this section, we describe the design and implementation of a data server using DataCutter for efficient storage and subsetting of multi-resolution datasets on parallel and distributed disk-based storage clusters [8]. The data server provides support for navigation and visualization of Terabyte scale 3-dimensional biomedical image datasets.

3.1. Server Implementation

The data server is implemented as a set of services (see Figure 1). These services are realized as multiple groups of DataCutter filters that perform functions required for efficient storage and retrieval of datasets and execution of queries. The metadata service is responsible from maintaining information about datasets stored in the server. Clients interact with the query service to submit queries. When a query is received, the query service calls the metadata and execution services to execute the query. The execution service coordinates the execution of data source, indexing, aggregation, and data mover services.

A set of filter groups implement the data source service functionality and are responsible from data distribution and retrieval on a cluster of storage nodes. One filter group implements the operations for partitioning a multi-resolution dataset into chunks, computing a placement for the chunks, and moving the chunks to their host nodes for storage on disk. A multi-resolution dataset is assumed to be made up of multiple subgrids (also called *subregions*) at different sizes and resolutions. A subgrid is defined by a bounding box in the multi-dimensional space of the dataset and a resolution in each dimension. The dataset is stored in the system in files as a set of data chunks. Each subgrid of the dataset is partitioned into data chunks (which corresponds to a subvolume of a subgrid) and declustered across the system independent of other subgrids. The meta-data associated with a data chunk consists of the minimum bounding box of the data chunk, its resolution, and $(filename, offset, size)$ tuple. The tuple denotes the location and extent of the data chunk in the file. The hilbert-space filling curve algorithm is employed for distribution of chunks [9]. The mid-points of the bounding boxes of data chunks are used to sort the data chunks in hilbert-curve order. The data chunks are then distributed across disks in this order.

A filter implements the indexing service functionality. Multiple copies of this filter can be instantiated and executed in the computing environment. Each copy handles a subset

---

[2]http://www.xmldb.org

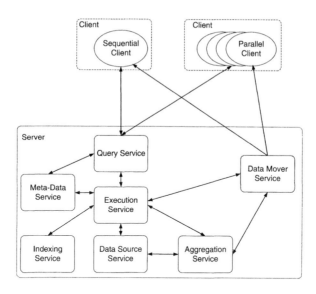

Figure 1. The architecture of the server framework.

of the index files associated with a dataset. The current indexing service employs two indexing methods based on R-trees [10]. The first indexing method employs a single level R-tree. An index is created for all the data chunks assigned to a storage node. When a query is received, an index lookup is performed using all index files. The second method is based on a two-level index. On each storage node, an R-tree index is created for each subgrid on the local chunks assigned to that storage node. These indices are the second level of the index. A single R-tree index is created on the bounding boxes of subgrids in the dataset. This index forms the first level. This indexing scheme is implemented with a filter group, in which one filter is the first level index filter and another filter is the second level index filter. The first level index filter runs on the node where the first level index is stored, while multiple copies of the second level index filter are instantiated on all the storage nodes. With this indexing scheme, upon receiving a query, the indexing service performs a lookup on the first level index. This lookup returns the subgrids that intersect the query bounding box. The query box along with the list of the subgrids is sent to the second level indexing filters. These filters search the local indices for data chunks that can be used to answer the query. However, only the second level indexes for the subgrids in the list are accessed.

The aggregation service functionality is deployed as a set of filters. They are responsible for executing application-specific aggregation and transformation operations specified in the query. Multiple transparent and/or explicit copies of the filters can be executed in the system. Note that when multiple copies of the filters are executed across the nodes, partial results or subregions of the final query product will be computed on different nodes. Another set of filters, referred to as *Assembling Filters*, merge or assemble the partial results and subregions into the final result and transfer it to the client. In the case the client is a parallel program, each copy of the filters is responsible for transferring data to a subset of the client machines based on the partitioning specified in the query. For example, a filter copy can be created for each client machine. A subregion of the final result is assembled in the corresponding filter copy and transferred to the corresponding client node by that filter.

3.2. Client Query

A client query specifies the following: 1) a bounding box in the underlying multi-dimensional space and its resolution in each dimension, 2) an aggregation function, and 3) additional selection criteria. The bounding box defines the region of interest within the dataset and it may overlap or intersect multiple subgrids. The aggregation function is an application-specific operation and is used to generate the data product to be transferred to the client. For instance, a client program may require that the result be a single resolution grid and may specify a function that will interpolate the multi-resolution subgrids to the resolution of the result grid. The selection criteria defines additional predicates for generating the elements of the result grid based on the resolutions of the subgrids that intersect the query: a) use only the highest or lowest resolution data, b) use only the data at resolution less than, or greater than, or equal to the resolution of the result grid, c) use the data that best matches the resolution of the result grid, and d) use the data at all resolutions (e.g., the value of a result element is computed as the average of the corresponding input data element values at all resolutions).

3.3. Query Execution Algorithm

A query is executed by splitting the original query box into a set of non-intersecting boxes based on the intersection of the query box with the bounding boxes of the data chunks. The data chunks that intersect the query box are inserted into a priority queue. The current implementation clusters data chunks into three groups: those that are at the same resolution as the requested resolution, those that are at higher resolution, and those that are at lower resolution. The second and third groups are sorted in increasing order of the absolute difference between the resolution of the subvolume and the requested resolution. The subvolumes in the first group are inserted into the priority queue first. Then, the subvolumes in the second group are inserted in the sorted order. Finally, the subvolumes in the last group are inserted in the sorted order.

Once the data chunks have been inserted into the priority queue, the algorithm proceeds as follows. It dequeues the first data chunk in the priority queue and intersects the query bounding box with the bounding box of the data chunk. Based on the intersection, the query bounding box is partitioned into a set of sub-bounding boxes. One sub-bounding box is the intersection of the query box and the bounding box of the data chunk. This sub-bounding box is called the result sub-box and inserted into the list of result bounding boxes along with the metadata information about the data chunk. The remaining list of rectangular bounding boxes are intersected with the second data chunk in the priority queue. Each sub-bounding box is further divided into smaller bounding boxes. The result sub-box for each sub-bounding box is inserted into the list of result bounding boxes. The algorithm proceeds in this way until either all the data chunks in the priority queue are visited or the original query box is fully partitioned into result sub-boxes. After the list of all result sub-boxes has been created, the list is distributed to the storage nodes based

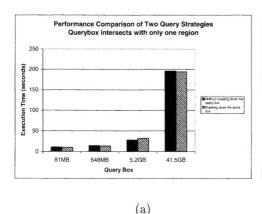
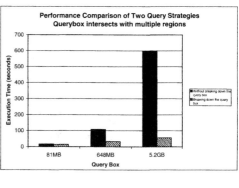

(a)   (b)

Figure 2. Execution time with two query strategies when the query box intersects with (a) a single region and (b) multiple regions.

on the distribution of the data chunks. The read filters of the data source service retrieve the local data chunks, clip them to the boundaries of the corresponding result sub-boxes, and forward the clipped data chunks to the aggregation service filters for processing.

3.4. Experimental Results

As a case study, we created an application that facilitates the navigation within a scaled-up version of Visible Woman cryosection dataset[3]. The original visible woman dataset consists of 5189 axial slices, each with 2048x1216 pixels. The total size for the dataset is roughly 38.8GB, which presents difficulties in visualizing the entire or an arbitrary portion of the dataset even at this coarse resolution. To further simulate the situation where higher resolution, spatially related datasets are present, the entire visible woman was supersampled at 2X magnification. Various regions within the dataset are supersampled at even higher magnifications: the left lung at 4X, and the head and heart at 8X. Such scenarios are not uncommon in CT or MR, where focused scans and reconstructions are done for targeted fields of view. The total size of the final dataset is about 1TB.

The hardware configuration used for the experiments consists of a Linux PC cluster, namely OSUMED. OSUMED is made up of 24 Linux PCs. Each node has a PIII 933MHz CPU, 512MB main memory, and three 100GB IDE disks. The nodes are inter-connected via Switched Fast Ethernet. The visible woman dataset is declustered across the disks of 16 nodes of the OSUMED cluster.

A client query specifies a three-dimensional bounding box, its location in the 3-dimensional space of the volume, and a desired magnification (e.g., 1x, 2x, 4x). The result of the query is a 3-dimensional volume at a single resolution. The application-specific aggregation function performs subsampling and supersampling of the data. If the query box intersects an input sub-volume at a higher resolution than the requested resolution, multiple input voxels will map to the same output voxel. The subsampling algorithm chooses one of

---

[3]http://www.nlm.nih.gov/research/visible/getting_data.html

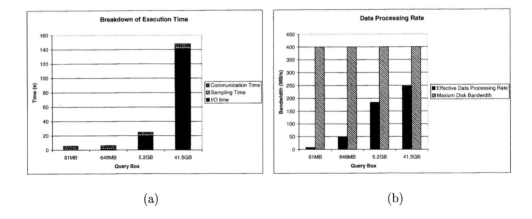

Figure 3. (a) Breakdown of execution time.(b) Effective data processing rate.

the input voxels and sets the value of the output voxel to that of the chosen input voxel. If the query bounding box intersects a lower resolution sub-volume, a single input voxel will cover multiple output voxels. The supersampling algorithm sets the values of all the output voxels covered by the same input voxel to the value of that input voxel. The additional selection criteria for this case study is "use the data that best matches the resolution of the result grid." That is, if there are multiple input voxels that map to the same output voxel, the value of the output voxel is computed using the input voxels in the sub-volume, the resolution of which is closest to that of the output volume. A data chunk retrieved from disk by a read filter is forwarded to the supersampling or subsampling filter based on the resolution of the data chunk. The Assembling filters stitch the results from different aggregation filters into the final result volume and send it to the client.

In the first set of experiments, we compare the query execution algorithm described earlier with an algorithm that does not split the query bounding box. The second algorithm reads all the data that intersects the query bounding box regardless of the resolution level. The main difference between the two algorithms is that the first one reduces the amount of data retrieved from disk, but spends more time on partitioning the query bounding box into smaller boxes. The other algorithm avoids this overhead, but introduces overhead due to extra data retrieval. In these experiments, we vary the size of the query box (i.e., the amount of data returned as query result) from 81MB to 41.5GB. Figure 2(a) shows that both algorithms achieve nearly identical performance when the original query box only intersects a single region. This is expected because both algorithm essentially become identical in that case. Figure 2(b)shows that when the query box intersects multiple multi-resolution regions, the first algorithm clearly outperforms the simple algorithm. The reason of this performance difference is that with the second algorithm, the system will have to read redundant data chunks in the areas that many region are overlapping, resulting in wasted I/O time. Breaking up the original query box will prevent reading any redundant data chunks.

The second set of experiments evaluates the overall system performance using four query boxes with different sizes. The output size is fixed at 512^3 in this experiment. There are 16 data source (read) filters, 16 subsampling filters and 8 Assembling filters. Assembling filters were colocated with 8 of the reader filters and subsampling filters were colocated with data source filters. Figure 3(a) displays the breakdown of the execution time into I/O, processing and communication times. Since the subsampling filters are colocated with the read filters, the volume of communication is proportional to output size ($\approx$400MB), hence it is constant across different queries. Although subsampling time increases with the increasing query size, it is overlapped with I/O and communication. We observe that for queries that process large amount of data (larger than 1GB) substantial time of the execution (80-95%) is spent in I/O. Figure 3(b) displays the effective data processing rate of the system compared against expected aggregate disk I/O bandwidth. Our measurements of disk bandwidth shows that the disks in our system achieves roughly 25MB/s for large (10MB or bigger) disk reads. Since the dataset has been declustered into 16 nodes, expected aggregate I/O bandwidth is around 400MB/s. Note that since the output size is 512^3 ($\approx$400MB), the performance of small queries will be bounded by the communication bandwidth. In other words, in the best case, about 4 seconds of query execution time will be spent for communication (Our configuration consists of 8 Assembler nodes and 100Mbps Fast Ethernet connection between the server and the client, so $\frac{400MB}{8} \times \frac{1}{100Mbps} = 4$ seconds). If the communication can be overlapped totally with I/O for queries that request 400MB data, effective data processing rate will be 100MB/s in the best case. The figure illustrates this behavior; effective data processing rate is below 50MB/s for small queries. However, we achieve up to $\approx$250MB/s processing rate for queries that request processing of larger amounts of data.

4. Support for Execution of Data Analysis Workflows

In this section, we describe a system that consists of two integrated components to support image analysis workflows: a *data management service* that enables on-demand creation of databases, which can be used to implement a persistent communication channel between two stages in a workflow, to check-point intermediate results exchanged between two consecutive steps of a workflow, and to store final analysis results, and a *distributed execution service* that supports execution of the workflow in a parallel and distributed environment. In this system, the distributed execution service is built on DataCutter and the data management service on the Mobius framework. We present the implementation of an application using this system for analysis of large digitized microscopy images. This application consists of a network of DataCutter filters that exchange data through streams and an external filter that interacts with the system through data stored in the data management service.

4.1. Data Management

The data management service [5] provides support for 1) distributed management using Mobius GME of XML schemas which describe the input data models used by the data analysis application or the stages of the analysis workflow and 2) on-demand creation and management using Mobius Mako of XML databases that conform to these data models. The system is *distributed* in that service components can run on a networked group of machines. It provides a shareable storage environment; multiple instances of an application or multiple applications with different input and output schemas can concurrently store and retrieve data in the system.

An application using this service reads input data conforming to some schema and generates output data, again conforming to a schema. The input and output data sets of an application are defined by XML schemas and instance data is stored as XML databases. For an input dataset, one or more selection criteria can be specified. The selection criteria defines the subset of data to be processed from input datasets and should be executed as a query into the corresponding input datasets. The application can be a parallel or sequential program, or a component in a data processing workflow. In a cluster environment, multiple Makos can be instantiated on each node, and one or more GMEs can be instantiated to manage schemas.

When the application (or an instance of the application) outputs a data instance, it can send the instance to any Mako server to which the application is authorized to write. The data instance identifies the GNI of the schema to which the data adheres. When a Mako server receives a data instance, it firsts checks if the schema is locally stored and a database has already been created from this schema. If the schema does not exist locally the Mako contacts a Mobius GME to retrieve the corresponding schema definition associated with the particular GNI. After the schema definition is retrieved, it is cached locally and a database conforming to the schema definition is created. Note that a Mako server can control multiple databases distributed across multiple machines. Hence, a schema can be instantiated on a distributed database. Once the database has been created, data instances can be inserted into, retrieved from, updated, and queried from the database.

An application programming interface allows for an application to partition a large byte array into smaller pieces (chunks), associate meta-data description with each piece (represented by a schema), and distribute these pieces across multiple Mako servers. For example, for a large 2D image, each chunk can be defined as a rectangular subsection of the image. The meta-data associated with a chunk can be any application-specific, user-defined set of attributes, including the bounding box of the chunk, its location within the image, the image modality, etc. The data can be distributed across an application-specified set of Mako servers.

4.2. Application: Study of Genotype-Phenotype Relationships

We now describe the implementation of a biomedical image analysis application, which involves analysis of digital mouse placenta slides to carry out quantitative examination of phenotypes and measurements of tissue structure within the placenta. In this paper, we focus on the segmentation of each image into regions of tissue layers. Specifically, we describe an approach to segment the labyrinth layer in the placenta from the rest of the image. This algorithm is based on the observation that the labyrinth layer (1) has a higher red blood cell (RBC) density compared to the spongiotropoblast and glycogen layers and (2) is elongated in shape, forming a confined strip in the image.

We have developed the algorithm for segmenting digitized placenta images as a chain of data processing operations. Our implementation consists of two main stages. The first stage is made up of three filters that operate in a filter-stream fashion and pipelines the processing of data across filters. The second stage is implemented as a separate external

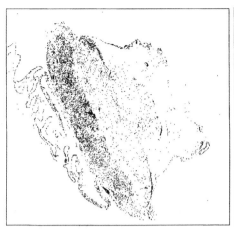

Figure 4. Left: Pixels identified as "Red" pixels by thresholding the red, green, and blue channels of a mouse placenta image. Right: Largest connected component after morphological manipulation.

filter. Data exchange between the two stages is done through the data management system presented in Section 4.1. The overall implementation could consist of one stage with all the processing pipelined using the filter-stream model of DataCutter. However, in some cases, a component of the application might have been already implemented as a program or a shell script. In our case, the PCA filter (described below), which constitute the second stage of the application, was an external component that received data from the other filters making up the application using the data management system.

1. **RedFinder:** This is the first filter in our pipeline. It detects red pixels that belong to red blood cell (RBC). We choose a set of thresholds for red, green, and blue channels to detect "red" pixels in the image. The result is a bit map with red pixels marked (Figure 4 Left; pixels identified as "red" pixels are shown as black dots in the figure). The RedFinder filter reads image chunks, each of which represents a rectangular subregion of the image, from disk. For each image chunk, it applies the thresholds to colors of each pixel in the image chunk. If the pixel values are above the threshold, the pixel is considered a red pixel. In our implementation, a pixel with a high value on the red component and a low value on the blue component is marked as a red pixel. Every pixel identified as red is propagated down the pipeline to the next filter. In order to reduce the high latency cost, we use buffers: the coordinates of each red pixel is put into the buffer; when the buffer is full, it is sent to the next filter. Multiple transparent copies of the RedFinder filter can be instantiated at runtime.

2. **Counter:** This filter along with the Histogram Aggregation filter is used to identify red pixels in the regions with high RBC density. The Counter filter computes the

number of red pixel neighbours each red pixel has. For each red pixel, the number of red neighbours is computed within a circle with a radius of K pixels around the pixel. In our implementation, we use a k-d tree for these computations. Every new red pixel the filter receives from the RedFinder filter is inserted into the k-d tree data structure. When all red pixels are inserted into the tree, the count of neighbor red pixels for each red pixel is computed. Multiple copies of this filter are created during runtime to achieve parallelism. We employ an image space partitioning approach, in which each filter copy is assigned a subregion of the image and is responsible for computing the portion of the k-d tree for pixels within that region.

To exclude blood sinuses, we use density histogram to determine the appropriate threshold for density. After calculating the local neighborhood red pixel density for every red pixel, a histogram of the red pixel density is generated. After processing all of the input red pixels, the Counter filter computes a histogram on its local data. This local histogram is then forwarded to the next filter for further processing.

3. **Histogram Aggregation:** The third filter down the pipeline collects all local histograms and aggregates them into the global histogram. Once the global histogram has been generated, red pixels in the region with high density are determined using user-defined thresholds. This region is sent back from the Histogram Aggregation filter to the *Counter* filter. This is done because that filter already has all the red pixels conveniently stored in a spatial data structure.

Once the Counter filter receives this data, it collects the red pixels within that region, groups them into chunks, associates metadata with each chunk, and sends them to the data management system for storage.

4. **PCA:** This external component retrieves the data stored in the data management system by the Counter filter and processes it to: (1) *Compute the principal direction of the high RBC density regions.* The high RBC density regions consist primarily of labyrinth layer, along with random distribution of RBC outside of the labyrinth layer. As the labyrinth layer is confined in a strip, we apply principal component analysis (PCA) to the high RBC density regions to determine the orientation of this strip. (2) *Determine the bounding box for the labyrinth layer.* The red pixels in the high RBC density regions are projected along the principle direction via Radon transform. From the resulting projection profile, we determine the line segment with high projection values. Two bounding lines are derived from the endpoints of the line segment to delineate the labyrinth layer in the image. This removes random occurrences of RBCs outside of the labyrinth layer (Figure 4 Right).

This algorithm can be used as a good initialization step for refinement and segmentation of other tissues. The algorithm may generate higher segmentation errors when image datasets with high color variations between images are encountered. In such situations, an optional pre-processing "normalization" step can be included. This is achieved by performing histogram equalization to match the image's color histogram to that of a pre-selected image.

The main processing structure and implementation of the application is shown in Figure 5. The RedFinder, Counter, and Histogram Aggregation filters are connected to form

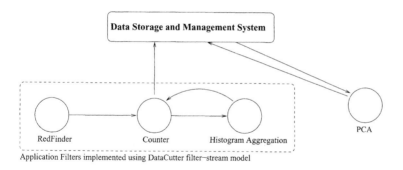

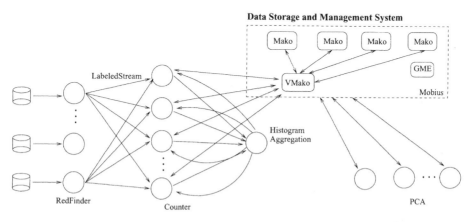

Figure 5. Top: The network of filters which form the processing skeleton of the application. Bottom: An instance of the application with multiple copies of RedFinder, Counter, and PCA filters and the Data Management system instantiated as Mobius GME, Mako, and Virtual Mako (VMako) instances). The Counter filter interacts with Mobius to store the image regions with high red pixel density to the data management service for storage.

the first processing stage of the application. The Counter filter interacts with the data management system to store regions of red pixels. The regions for a given image are then retrieved using the PCA filter in the second processing stage of the application. Each copy of the PCA filter processes data for a different image. This two stage implementation allows a user to first process a set of images using a filter-stream model in a distributed environment. The results are then stored in the data management system so that copies of another data processing program (in our case PCA) can access them in a distributed environment. Through storage and sharing of data via the data management system, an application consisting of components processing data in a pipelined fashion and external programs can be composed and executed.

4.3. Experimental Evaluation

We carried out an experimental evaluation of the application implementation on a PC cluster, referred to here as *OSUMED*. Each node has a Pentium III 900MHz CPU,

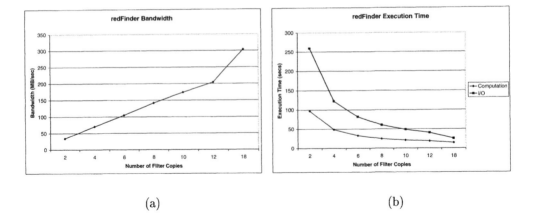

(a)   (b)

Figure 6. (a) I/O Bandwidth achieved by the redFinder filter. (b) The breakdown of redFinder execution time into I/O cost and the cost of finding red pixels.

512MB main memory, and three local disks (300GB local storage space). The nodes in the cluster are inter-connected through a 100Mbit/sec Ethernet Switch. We used 20 images digitized from mouse placenta slides. Each image was 600MB in size. Every image in the dataset was partitioned into 1MB chunks, and the set of chunks was randomly and evenly distributed across all the nodes used in the experiments. Chunks from the same image which were mapped to the same node were stored in a file.

Figure 6 shows the disk I/O bandwidth and the breakdown of execution time in the redFinder filter, which reads in chunks and finds the red pixels in a chunk. In this experiment, we varied the number of nodes from 2 to 18. A redFinder filter was assigned to each node. As is seen from the figure, the data read and processing bandwidth of the redFinder filter increases almost linearly as we increase the number of nodes, since the image chunks are distributed across all of the N nodes in each configuration. We also observe that the redFinder filter is I/O-intensive because the operations to determine if a pixel is red or not are very simple.

Figure 7 shows the overall execution time to process 20 images when the number of copies of the RedFinder and Counter filters is varied. Only one copy of the Histogram Aggregation filter was executed. In this experiment we used upto 18 nodes. When the number of filter copies exceeded the number of nodes, two copies of the same filter were co-located on the same node. As is seen from the results, the execution time decreases almost linearly upto 18 filter copies. Beyond that number, we do not observe any discernible performance improvement. This can be attributed to the fact that adding more filter copies increases parallelism. However, at the same time, it introduces overhead due to multiplexing of CPU of a node among too many filter copies. In our configuration, this overhead eliminated any gain from more parallelism when too many filter copies are assigned to a node.

In Figure 8, the execution time of the Counter filter is broken down into the various operations performed by that filter; inserting pixels into the k-d tree, doing neighborhood

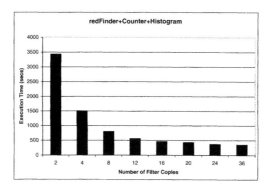

Figure 7. Execution time when the number of copies of redFinder and Counter is varied.

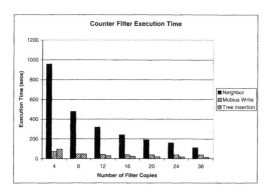

Figure 8. The breakdown of execution of the Counter filter.

computations, and writing data to the data management system (i.e., Mobius). In these experiments, we executed four Mako instances controlled by a single Virtual Mako. The Virtual Mako used the round-robin distribution strategy when inserting data to backend Mako instances. As is seen from the figure, most of the time is spent performing the operations for neighborhood computations. The overhead of storing data in Mobius is very small compared to the neighborhood computations and comparable to tree insertion. The overhead of tree insertion and neighborhood computations decreases as the number of filter copies is increased as expected. The cost of storage in Mobius remains almost constant as the number of backend Makos does not change. Our results show that interaction with the XML-based storage services do not become a bottleneck in this configuration as the number of filters writing data is increased. The last set of experiments shows the execution time of the second stage of the image analysis application (the PCA computations). In our implementation, the second stage is executed after the first stage is completed, i.e.,

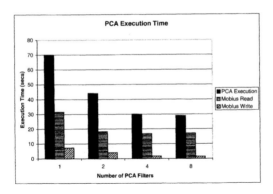

Figure 9. The execution time of the PCA filter as the number of filter copies is varied. The figure also shows the time spent reading data from Mobius and writing to Mobius.

after the redFinder-Counter-Histogram Aggregation filter group has finished its execution. As is seen from Figure 9, the execution time decreases as the number of PCA filters is increased. Since the number of Mobius Mako servers is fixed, the cost of I/O (Mobius Read+Write) remains constant. Hence, the decrease in the total execution time is not linear.

5. Related Work

Chiang and Silva [11] propose methods for iso-surface extraction for datasets that cannot fit in memory. They introduce several techniques and indexing structures to efficiently search for cells through which the iso-surface passes, and to reduce I/O costs and disk space requirements. Cox and Ellsworth [12] show that relying on operating system virtual memory results in poor performance. They propose a paged system and algorithms for memory management and paging for out-of-core visualization. Their results show that *application controlled paging* can substantially improve application performance. Arge et. al. [13] present efficient external memory algorithms for applications that make use of grid-based terrains in Geographic Information Systems. Bajaj et. al. [14] present a parallel algorithm for out-of-core isocontouring of scientific datasets for visualization. SCIRun [15] is a problem solving environment that enables implementation and execution of visualization and image processing applications from connected modules. Dv [16] is a framework for developing applications for distributed visualization of large scientific datasets. It is based on the notion of active frames, which are application level mobile objects. An active frame contains application data, called frame data, and a frame program that processes the data. Active frames are executed by active frame servers running on the machines at the client and remote sites.

Several types of middleware systems have been developed for implementing and executing applications in distributed environments. The *Everyware* toolkit developed by Wolski et. al. [17] enables applications to transparently use computational resources in the Grid.

While Everyware targets compute-intensive applications, our middleware is focused on data intensive applications. The Storage Resource Broker (SRB) [18] provides unified file system-like interfaces to distributed and heterogeneous storage systems. The Chimera system [19] implements support for establishing virtual catalogs that can be used to describe how a data product in an application has been derived from other data. The system allows storing and management of information about the data transformations that have generated the data product.

Parallel file systems and I/O libraries have been a widely studied research topic, and many systems and libraries have been developed [20–23]. These systems mainly focus on supporting regular strided access to uniformly distributed datasets. Distributed data storage, discovery, and retrieval are also supported by distributed file systems and peer-to-peer content delivery networks [24–27]. The Distributed Parallel Storage Server (DPSS) [28,29] project developed tools to use distributed storage servers to supply data to multi-user applications in an Internet environment.

The IBP [30] framework is a common framework for storing and retrieving large amounts of data. IBP does have some similarities to our infrastructure from the storage and retrieval of possibly large data quantities with a uniform protocol. IBP could be used as the storage and delivery protocol for large data objects which travel through our framework.

Several research projects have targeted systems for databases of multi-dimensional datasets. Some of these systems are designed to optimize performance of one application and are not customizable for different data types and operations on data. Most of the database systems (DBMS) treat multidimensional data as data cubes [31–33]. RasDaMan [34,35] is a commercially available domain-independent DBMS for multi-dimensional arrays of arbitrary size and structure. It employs a Client-Server architecture, where the server is responsible for carrying out predefined operations on data. The system offers the flexibility that some basic data transformations can be done on the client side, thus reducing the server load.

6. Conclusions

Analysis of large volumes of scientific data remains to be a challenging issue in biomedical and engineering research. In biomedical imaging, with the help of high-resolution digitizing microscopes, the size of an individual image can be very large. The datasets can be multi-resolution, consisting of multiple 2D or 3D grids sampling the space at different resolutions. In this paper, we presented a suite of tools that are designed to support metadata and data management, efficient execution of queries against terabyte-scale multi-resolution datasets, and efficient execution of complex image analysis workflows, which may consist of multiple stages of data processing. These tools target distributed compute and storage platforms for data storage and management and data processing. We presented the use of these tools in different application scenarios; querying of terabyte-scale multi-resolution 3D volumes and analysis of digitized mouse placenta slides. Our work demonstrates that distributed component-based models along with support for distributed XML databases form viable frameworks to address the storage, management, and processing requirements of large image datasets.

420

REFERENCES

1. M. Beynon, T. Kurc, A. Sussman, J. Saltz, Design of a framework for data-intensive wide-area applications, in: Proceedings of the 9th Heterogeneous Computing Workshop (HCW2000), IEEE Computer Society Press, 2000, pp. 116–130.
2. M. D. Beynon, T. Kurc, U. Catalyurek, C. Chang, A. Sussman, J. Saltz, Distributed processing of very large datasets with DataCutter, Parallel Computing 27 (11) (2001) 1457–1478.
3. The Mobius Project, http://www.projectmobius.org.
4. S. Hastings, S. Langella, S. Oster, J. Saltz, Distributed data management and integration: The mobius project, in: GGF Semantic Grid Workshop 2004, GGF, 2004, pp. 20–38.
5. S. Langella, S. Hastings, S. Oster, T. Kurc, U. Catalyurek, J. Saltz, A distributed data management middleware for data-driven application systems, in: Proceedings of 2004 IEEE International Conference on Cluster Computing, 2004.
6. MySql Database, *http://www.mysql.com/*.
7. A. Berglund, S. B. X. WG), D. Chamberlin, M. F. Fernndez, M. Kay, J. Robie, J. Simon, XML Path Language (XPath), World Wide Web Consortium (W3C), 1st Edition (August 2003).
8. X. Zhang, T. Pan, U. Catalyurek, T. Kurc, J. Saltz, Serving queries to multi-resolution datasets on disk-based storage clusters, in: Proceedings of 4th IEEE/ACM International Symposium on Cluster Computing and the Grid (CCGrid2004), Chicago, IL, 2004.
9. C. Faloutsos, P. Bhagwat, Declustering using fractals, in: Proceedings of the 2nd International Conference on Parallel and Distributed Information Systems, 1993, pp. 18–25.
10. A. Guttman, R-trees: A dynamic index structure for spatial searching, in: Proceedings of SIGMOD'84, ACM Press, 1984, pp. 47–57.
11. Y.-J. Chiang, C. Silva, External memory techniques for isosurface extraction in scientific visualization, in: J. Abello, J. Vitter (Eds.), External Memory Algorithms and Visualization, Vol. 50, DIMACS Book Series, American Mathematical Society, 1999, pp. 247–277.
12. M. Cox, D. Ellsworth, Application-controlled demand paging for out-of-core visualization, in: Proceedings of the 8th IEEE Visualization'97 Conference, 1997.
13. L. Arge, L. Toma, J. S. Vitter, I/o-efficient algorithms for problems on grid-based terrains, in: Proceedings of 2nd Workshop on Algorithm Engineering and Experimentation (ALENEX '00), 2000.
14. C. L. Bajaj, V. Pascucci, D. Thompson, X. Y. Zhang, Parallel accelerated isocontouring for out-of-core visualization, in: Proceedings of the 1999 IEEE Symposium on Parallel Visualization and Graphics, San Francisco, CA, USA, 1999, pp. 97–104.
15. SCIRun:A Scientific Computing Problem Solving Environment., Scientific Computing and Imaging Institute (SCI), http://software.sci.utah.edu/scirun.html.
16. M. Aeschlimann, P. Dinda, J. Lopez, B. Lowekamp, L. Kallivokas, D. O'Hallaron, Preliminary report on the design of a framework for distributed visualization, in: Proceedings of the International Conference on Parallel and Distributed Processing

Techniques and Applications (PDPTA'99), Las Vegas, NV, 1999, pp. 1833–1839.

17. R. Wolski, J. Brevik, C. Krintz, G. Obertelli, N. Spring, A. Su, Running Everyware on the computational grid, in: Proceedings of the 1999 ACM/IEEE Supercomputing Conference, ACM Press, Portland, OR, 1999.

18. SRB: The Storage Resource Broker, *http:// www.npaci.edu/ DICE/ SRB/ index.html.*

19. I. Foster, J. Voeckler, M. Wilde, Y. Zhao, Chimera: A virtual data system for representing, querying, and automating data derivation, in: Proceedings of the 14th Conference on Scientific and Statistical Database Management, 2002.

20. P. H. Carns, W. B. Ligon, R. B. Ross, R. Thakur, PVFS: A parallel file system for Linux clusters, in: Proceedings of the 4th Annual Linux Showcase and Conference, 2000, pp. 317–327.

21. N. Nieuwejaar, D. Kotz, The Galley parallel file system, in: Proceedings of the 1996 International Conference on Supercomputing, ACM Press, 1996, pp. 374–381.

22. R. Thakur, A. Choudhary, R. Bordawekar, S. More, S. Kuditipudi, Passion: Optimized I/O for parallel applications, IEEE Computer 29 (6) (1996) 70–78.

23. X. Shen, A. Choudhary, A distributed multi-storage i/o system for high performance data intensive computing, in: International Symposium on Cluster Computing and the Grid (CCGrid 2002), 2002.

24. J. Kubiatowicz, D. Bindel, Y. Chen, S. Czerwinski, P. Eaton, D. Geels, R. Gummadi, S. Rhea, H. Weatherspoon, W. Weimer, C. Wells, B. Zhao, OceanStore: An architecture for global-scale persistent storage, in: Proceedings of the Ninth International Conference on Architectural Support for Programming Languages and Operating Systems (ASPLOS IX), ACM Press, 2000, pp. 190–201, aCM SIGPLAN Notices, Vol. 35, No. 11.

25. X. Shen, A. Choudhary, DPFS: A distributed parallel file system, in: IEEE 30th International Conference on Parallel Processing (ICPP), 2001.

26. I. Stoica, R. Morris, D. Karger, M. F. Kaashoek, H. Balakrishnan, Chord: A scalable peer-to-peer lookup service for internet applications, in: Proceedings of the 2001 conference on Applications, technologies, architectures, and protocols for computer communications, ACM Press, 2001, pp. 149–160.

27. S. Ratnasamy, P. Francis, M. Handley, R. Karp, S. Schenker, A scalable content-addressable network, in: Proceedings of the 2001 conference on Applications, technologies, architectures, and protocols for computer communications, ACM Press, 2001, pp. 161–172.

28. W. Johnston, J. Guojun, G. Hoo, C. Larsen, J. Lee, B. Tierney, M. Thompson, Distributed environments for large data-objects: Broadband networks and a new view of high performance, large scale storage-based applications, in: Proceedings of Internetworking'96, Nara, Japan, 1996.

29. B. Tierney, W. Johnston, J. Lee, G. Hoo, M. Thompson, An overview of the distributed parallel storage server (DPSS), available at http:// www-didc.lbl.gov/ DPSS/ Overview/ DPSS.handout.fm.html.

30. J. S. Plank, M. Beck, W. Elwasif, T. Moore, M. Swany, R. Wolski., The internet backplane protocol: Storage in the network., in: 99: Network Storage Symposium., 1999.

31. J. Gray, A. Bosworth, A. Layman, H. Pirahesh, Data cube: A relational aggregation

operator generalizing group-by, cross-tab, and sub-totals, in: Proceedings of the 1996 International Conference on Data Engineering, IEEE Computer Society Press, 1996, pp. 152–159.

32. T. B. Pedersen, C. S. Jensen, Multidimensional database technology, IEEE Computer 34 (12) (2001) 40–47.

33. C. Stolte, D. Tang, P. Hanrahan, Polaris: a system for query, analysis, and visualization of multidimensional relational databases, IEEE Transactions on Visualization and Computer Graphics 8 (1) (2002) 52–65.

34. P. Baumann, P. Furtado, R. Ritsch, Geo/environmental and medical data management in the RasDaMan system, in: Proceedings of the 23rd International Conference on Very Large Data Bases (VLDB97), 1997, pp. 548–552.

35. P. Baumann, A. Dehmel, P. Furtado, R. Ritsch, N. Widmann, The multidimensional database system rasdaman, in: Proceedings of the 1998 ACM SIGMOD international conference on Management of data, ACM Press, 1998, pp. 575–577.

AUTHOR INDEX

SUBJECT INDEX